The Emergency Department Technician

by Marianne McBrien, RN, MS

Clinical Allied Healthcare Series

Kay Cox, RN, MA
Series Editor

Career Publishing, Inc.
Orange, CA

Series Editor: Kay Cox
Senior Editor and Project Coordinator: Valerie L. Harris
Assistant Editor: Joani C. Saari
Illustrators: Alan J. Borie
             Valerie L. Harris
             Additional Graphics obtained from
             the LifeART™ Collections from
             Techpool Studios, Inc., Cleveland, OH.
Cover Design: Harris Graphics

Apple is a trademark of Apple Computers, Inc.
Macintosh is a trademark of Apple Computers, Inc.
PageMaker is a trademark of Aldus, Inc.
FreeHand is a trademark of Aldus, Inc.
Word is a trademark of Microsoft Corp.
PhotoShop is a trademark of Adobe Systems Inc.

This guide was produced by Desktop Publishing techniques using Microsoft Word, Aldus PageMaker, Aldus FreeHand and Adobe PhotoShop on Macintosh computers and output to a LaserMaster 1200 printer.

This publication is designed to provide accurate and authoritative information in regard to the subject matter covered. It is sold with the understanding that the publisher is not engaged in rendering legal, medical or other professional service. If legal advice or other expert assistance is required, the service of a competent professional person should be sought.

Disclaimer: Information has been obtained by Career Publishing Inc., from sources believed to be reliable. However, because of the possibility of human or mechanical error by our sources, Career Publishing Inc., does not guarantee the accuracy, adequacy, or completeness of any information and is not responsible for any errors or omissions or the results obtained from the use of such information. The publisher and editors shall not be held liable in any degree for any loss or injury by any such omission, error, misprinting or ambiguity. If you have questions regarding the content of this publication, the editorial staff is available to provide information and assistance.

ISBN 0-89262-432-9
Library of Congress Catalog Card Number 94-71971

Text, graphics and illustrations copyright © 1995 by Career Publishing Inc. All rights reserved. Printed in the United States of America. Except as permitted under the Copyright Act of 1976, no part of this publication may be reproduced or distributed in any form or by any means—graphic, electronic, or mechanical, including photocopying, recording, taping, or information and retrieval systems—without the prior written permission of the publisher.

The blue Star of Life symbol is a registered certification mark owned by the National Highway Traffic Safety Administration (NHTSA) and is used with their permission.

PRINTED AND BOUND IN THE UNITED STATES OF AMERICA

Career
PUBLISHING INCORPORATED
VOCATIONAL & APPLIED TECHNOLOGY
910 N. Main St.,
P.O. Box 5486
Orange, CA 92667

National/Canada
1 (800) 854-4014
**Includes Canada, Alaska,
and Hawaii**

FAX 1-714-532-0180

10 9 8 7 6 5 4 3 2 1

Contents

Acknowledgments xi

Introduction xii

Contributors xiii

Editor's Note xiv

Chapter One: Health Careers in Emergency Care
    Objectives 1-1
    Key Terms 1-2
    Introduction to Careers in Emergency Care 1-2
    Characteristics of Emergency Healthcare Professionals 1-4
    Chapter Summary 1-6
    Student Enrichment Activities 1-7

Chapter Two: Introduction to Emergency Medical Services
    Objectives 2-1
    Key Terms 2-2
    The History of Emergency Medical Services 2-2
    Emergency Medical Services 2-5
    The Components of EMS 2-5
    911 and the EMS System 2-10
    The Emergency Healthcare Team 2-12
    Emergency Physicians 2-12
    Emergency Nurses 2-13
    Licensed Vocational Nurses 2-13
    EMTs 2-13
    Paramedics 2-14
    Emergency Department Technicians 2-14
    Clerical Staff 2-14
    Chapter Summary 2-15
    Student Enrichment Activities 2-17

Chapter Three: The Working Environment
    Objectives 3-1
    Key Terms 3-2
    The Location of the Emergency Department 3-2
    Admission and Triage 3-3
    The Physical Layout 3-4

Chapter Summary 3-8
Student Enrichment Activities 3-9

Chapter Four: Asepsis
Objectives 4-1
Key Terms 4-2
Disease-Causing Agents 4-2
The Chain of Infection 4-7
Medical Asepsis 4-9
Surgical Asepsis 4-10
Using Sterile Gloves 4-11
Care of Equipment and Supplies 4-15
Controlling Communicable Diseases 4-26
Chapter Summary 4-29
Student Enrichment Activities 4-31

Chapter Five: Admitting Procedures
Objectives 5-1
Key Terms 5-2
Emergency Department Documentation 5-2
The Importance of Medical Records 5-2
Computers 5-3
Triage 5-4
Admitting Patients 5-6
The ER Record 5-7
Obtaining Accurate Information 5-9
Data Collection 5-10
Patient Confidentiality 5-17
Patients Who Refuse Treatment 5-18
Chapter Summary 5-19
Student Enrichment Activities 5-21

Chapter Six: Patient Evaluation
Objectives 6-1
Key Terms 6-2
The Importance of Accurate Evaluations 6-2
Observational Skills 6-3
The Primary Survey 6-4
The Secondary Survey 6-6
Vital Signs 6-17
The Pulse 6-18
The Respiration 6-26
The Temperature 6-31

Contents

    The Blood Pressure 6-46
    Performing a Neuro Check 6-55
    Height and Weight 6-58
    Documentation 6-62
    Chapter Summary 6-62
    Student Enrichment Activities 6-63

Chapter Seven: Safety In the Emergency Department
    Objectives 7-1
    Key Terms 7-2
    Safety Responsibilities 7-2
    Fire 7-2
    Points to Remember if a Fire Occurs 7-4
    Disasters 7-5
    Emergency Signals 7-6
    Personal Safety 7-7
    Transporting Patients 7-9
    Safety and Defibrillation 7-10
    Chapter Summary 7-11
    Student Enrichment Activities 7-13

Chapter Eight: Basic Life Support
    Objectives 8-1
    Key Terms 8-2
    Cardiopulmonary Resuscitation 8-2
    Sudden Death 8-3
    Clinical and Biological Death 8-5
    How the Heart Works 8-6
    Emergency Resuscitation 8-8
    Basic Life Support (BLS) 8-9
    Foreign Body Airway Obstructions 8-16
    Pediatric Basic Life Support 8-17
    CPR for Children and Infants 8-18
    Airway Obstruction in Infants and Children 8-21
    Rescue Breathing for Adults, Children, and Infants 8-23
    CPR in Transport 8-24
    The Crash Cart 8-25
    Chapter Summary 8-26
    Basic Life Support for the Adult Victim 8-27
    Basic Life Support for the Child Victim 8-29
    Basic Life Support for the Infant Victim 8-31
    Student Enrichment Activities 8-33

Chapter Nine: Emergencies of the Eye, Ear, Nose, and Throat
    Objectives 9-1
    Key Terms 9-2
    EENT Disorders 9-2
    Eye Emergencies 9-3
    Eye Examinations 9-4
    Foreign Bodies in the Eye 9-6
    Burns to the Eye 9-8
    Eye Trauma 9-9
    Eye Infections 9-9
    Other Eye Emergencies 9-12
    Emergencies Involving the Ear 9-12
    Nasal Emergencies 9-14
    Dental Emergencies 9-16
    Throat Emergencies 9-16
    Chapter Summary 9-18
    Student Enrichment Activities 9-19

Chapter Ten: Medical Emergencies
    Objectives 10-1
    Key Terms 10-2
    Emergency Medical Situations 10-2
    Seizures 10-3
    Providing Care to an Unconscious Patient 10-5
    Diabetic Emergencies 10-6
    Respiratory Emergencies 10-8
    Cardiac Emergencies 10-14
    Chapter Summary 10-17
    Student Enrichment Activities 10-19

Chapter Eleven: Abdominal Emergencies
    Objectives 11-1
    Key Terms 11-2
    Acute Abdomen 11-2
    Abdominal Trauma 11-9
    Completing a Laboratory Requisition Form 11-10
    Urine Specimens and Catheterization 11-10
    Preparing a Patient for Surgery 11-18
    Chapter Summary 11-20
    Student Enrichment Activities 11-21

Contents

Chapter Twelve: Emergencies of the Reproductive System
- Objectives 12-1
- Key Terms 12-2
- The Patient's Right to Privacy 12-2
- Disorders of the Female Reproductive System 12-3
- Pelvic Examination 12-3
- Vaginal Bleeding 12-5
- Infections 12-6
- Care of Sexual Assault Victims 12-6
- Emergency Childbirth 12-7
- Emergencies of the Male Reproductive System 12-11
- Foreign Bodies Affecting the Reproductive System 12-12
- Chapter Summary 12-12
- Student Enrichment Activities 12-13

Chapter Thirteen: Wound Care
- Objectives 13-1
- Key Terms 13-2
- Types of Wounds 13-2
- Controlling Bleeding 13-7
- Foreign Bodies 13-11
- Bites 13-12
- General Principles of Wound Care 13-14
- Preparing a Wound for Suturing 13-14
- Dressings and Bandages 13-18
- Suture Removal 13-26
- Staple Removal 13-29
- Chapter Summary 13-30
- Student Enrichment Activities 13-31

Chapter Fourteen: Traumatic Emergencies
- Objectives 14-1
- Key Terms 14-2
- Injuries Resulting From Trauma 14-2
- Trauma Centers 14-5
- Airways and Breathing 14-6
- Controlling Arterial Bleeding 14-10
- Shock 14-10
- Head Injuries 14-12
- Increased Intracranial Pressure 14-15
- Spinal Injuries 14-16
- Chest Trauma 14-18
- Chapter Summary 14-19
- Student Enrichment Activities 14-21

Chapter Fifteen: Bone and Joint Injuries
Objectives 15-1
Key Terms 15-2
Injuries to the Bones and Joints 15-2
Fractures 15-3
The Signs and Symptoms of a Fracture 15-5
Splints 15-7
Cervical Collars 15-8
Treating a Fracture 15-8
Other Orthopedic Injuries 15-10
Compression Bandages 15-11
Immobilizers 15-12
Applying a Sling 15-14
Assisting With a Cast Application 15-14
Patient Instructions for Cast Care 15-15
Crutches 15-16
Gait Training 15-17
Using Crutches on Stairs 15-19
Canes 15-20
Chapter Summary 15-20
Student Enrichment Activities 15-21

Chapter Sixteen: Moving and Positioning Patients
Objectives 16-1
Key Terms 16-2
Body Mechanisms 16-2
Helping a Patient Get Out of a Car 16-4
Unloading Patients Who Arrive in Ambulances 16-7
Using a Gurney 16-8
Assisting Patients From a Gurney to a Bed 16-10
Patient Positioning 16-12
Chapter Summary 16-13
Student Enrichment Activities 16-15

Chapter Seventeen: Environmental Emergencies
Objectives 17-1
Key Terms 17-2
How Environmental Emergencies Occur 17-2
Types of Burns 17-2
Causes and Treatment of Burns 17-5
Emergencies Resulting From Excessive Exposure to Heat 17-8
Emergencies Resulting From Excessively Cold Temperatures 17-9
Chapter Summary 17-10
Student Enrichment Activities 17-11

Contents

Chapter Eighteen: Poisoning and Overdose
- Objectives 18-1
- Key Terms 18-2
- How Poisonings and Overdoses Occur 18-2
- Caring for a Poisoning or Overdose Victim 18-3
- Getting a History of the Incident 18-4
- Caring for an Unconscious Patient 18-6
- Chapter Summary 18-8
- Student Enrichment Activities 18-9

Chapter Nineteen: Emotional and Behavioral Emergencies
- Objectives 19-1
- Key Terms 19-2
- Stress 19-2
- Confusion and Emotional Shock 19-2
- Fear 19-3
- Denial 19-3
- Regression 19-4
- Depression 19-4
- Anger 19-4
- Dealing With Behavioral Problems 19-5
- Psychiatric Emergencies 19-6
- Abnormal Behavior 19-7
- Approaches to Therapeutic Communication 19-8
- Disposition of Psychiatric Patients 19-10
- Suicidal Patients 19-10
- Personal Stress Management 19-10
- Chapter Summary 19-11
- Student Enrichment Activities 19-13

Chapter Twenty: Caring for Children
- Objectives 20-1
- Key Terms 20-2
- Emergencies Involving Children 20-2
- The Patient History 20-3
- Safety Measures 20-4
- Restraints 20-6
- Vital Signs 20-7
- Measuring Height and Weight 20-8
- Collecting Specimens 20-9
- Infection 20-9
- Injuries 20-9
- Illness 20-10
- Congenital Conditions 20-11

    Child Abuse 20-11
    Sudden Infant Death Syndrome 20-12
    Chapter Summary 20-12
    Student Enrichment Activities 20-13

Chapter Twenty-One: Care of the Elderly
    Objectives 21-1
    Key Terms 21-2
    How Age Affects the Human Body 21-2
    Caring for Elderly Patients 21-4
    Chapter Summary 21-5
    Student Enrichment Activities 21-7

Appendix A: Glossary A-1

Appendix B: Community Resources B-1

Appendix C: The Manual Alphabet C-1

Appendix D: Bibliography D-1

Appendix E: Index E-1

Acknowledgments

Although my interest in emergency care has been continuous since my first experience as a student nurse in the emergency room, I never dreamed that someday I would be writing a textbook for students to follow. I would like to thank everyone involved in the formation of this text. The contributions of the following are particularly appreciated.

Kay Cox, RN, MA, Series Editor, for conceiving this series, and in particular, for her encouragement and dedication to detail in the review and technical editing of the manuscript.

Valerie Harris, Project Coordinator and Senior Editor for this series, for her mechanical and substantive editing of the manuscript, as well as coordinating the production of the book.

Harold Haase, Publisher, and the rest of the staff at Career Publishing, Inc. for recognizing the need for proper entry-level training in the rapidly changing field of healthcare, and for responding to the need in such an enthusiastic manner.

Pat Wilson and Elaine Dethlefsen for reviewing the text with provocative thought.

Nancy Cushing for her contribution of time and expertise in several areas.

Pamela Turner, a very special person, for steadfastly and diligently reviewing and critiquing each chapter, and for her guidance and direction.

Ruth and William Anderson, my loving parents, who continued to show support and encouragement by correcting my written work, and making sure the t's were crossed and the i's were dotted.

I would like to thank the many students over the years who provided me with inspiration to teach. You are the reason for this textbook.

Thanks to the Health Occupations students of the North Orange County Regional Occupation Program for their participation in this textbook.

Of course, no acknowledgment would be complete without recognizing the efforts and continuous support of my husband, Ben, and daughters, Debbie and Julie. Without their continuous love and encouragement this book would never have been completed.

Introduction

To work in the medical field is to make a real contribution to your fellow man. This is a career that will ask much of your mind and heart and give much in return. The satisfaction gained from calming a frightened child or brightening the day of a lonely patient will enrich you. The pride felt will be lasting when your observations and skills someday help to save a patient's life. This is a career where you can really make a difference!

Some of you have already made a decision to seek a career in some area of healthcare. Some of you are just exploring your options. Everything you learn will build a foundation of skills and knowledge, so learn well. Become competent in everything you are taught along the way and be your own task master. We all must be responsible for our own education. If at some point you discover you didn't learn a skill well enough, go back and practice until you do. Remember, some day a patient's life may depend on you and your mastery of what you are taught.

Today's healthcare industry places many demands on care givers. We must keep costs down, document everything we do, and have more knowledge and skills than ever before because of new technology. This textbook series was designed to help you build a sound foundation of knowledge and provide many opportunities for cross-training. The core textbook, *Introduction to Clinical Allied Healthcare*, contains the skills and information we feel is common to all students. Each of the other textbooks provide training for a specific job title. The more you can learn, the better. Always remember, however, to practice the art, the science, and the SPIRIT of your new career. Good luck!

Kay Cox
Series Editor

Contributors

About the Author

Marianne McBrien, RN, MS, is currently employed at the North Orange County Regional Occupational Program in Anaheim, California as Program Coordinator for the Emergency Medical Technician Program. Her nursing background includes both critical care and emergency nursing. She has taught prehospital and emergency nursing for the past ten years.

Actively involved in curriculum development, Marianne participated in the development of the California State Model Curriculum for Emergency Medical technicians and has developed model curriculum standards for allied health occupations. She has also been instrumental in the development of a secondary health career academy, and several continuing education courses for health-care providers.

About the Series Editor

Kay Cox, RN, MA, conceived this textbook series, and recruited and coordinated the authors in the development of each of their texts. She is the author of *Being a Health Unit Coordinator,* and the editor of a Medical-Clerical Textbook Series for Brady. Before entering education, she worked in medical/surgical and critical care nursing and in the inservice department as a clinical instructor.

Formerly a professional development contract consultant for special projects and curriculum development for the California Department of Education, Kay has also served as chairperson of the California Health Careers Statewide Advisory Committee, and been a Master Trainer for Health Careers Teacher Training through California Polytechnic University of Pomona. She also is a founding member of the national association of Health Unit Coordinators. Kay is currently Program Coordinator of the Medical Assistant Program at Saddleback College in Mission Viejo, California, and operates her consulting business, Achiever's Development Enterprises.

Editor's Note

I would like to take this opportunity to thank the authors of this series. Their dedication and sense of mission made it a joy to work on this challenging project.

I would also like to express my sincere gratitude to the staff of Career Publishing and most particularly to Valerie Harris, Senior Editor, for her professional and talented assistance throughout. I also would like to express my appreciation to Harold Haase, Publisher, for his enthusiasm for this project and for his humanistic approach to education.

Kay Cox
Series Editor

Chapter One
Health Careers in Emergency Care

Objectives

After completing this chapter you should be able to do the following:

1. Define and correctly spell all key terms.
2. Identify areas of employment in emergency care.
3. Determine whether you are well-suited for a career in emergency care.
4. List five characteristics of a good emergency department technician.

Key Terms

- cardiopulmonary resuscitation
- empathy
- gurney
- manual dexterity
- paramedic
- suturing
- tolerance
- trauma
- vital signs

Introduction to Careers in Emergency Care

Emergency care is an exciting area of healthcare. This field offers many job opportunities in hospital emergency departments and free standing **urgent care** centers. (Figure 1-1) Other opportunities exist in the student health centers of large universities and in the health centers of large companies. These employee health centers are located right on the company's site to handle various emergencies that may occur on the job. Some large companies have thousands of people at their facilities and provide these health services as a benefit to employees.

Figure 1-1: Hospital emergency departments and urgent care centers offer many job opportunities in emergency care.

Chapter One • Health Careers in Emergency Care

As an emergency department technician in a hospital, you will assist the physician and nurse with emergency procedures by admitting the patient and obtaining **vital signs** and documenting them on the patient's record. You will apply dressings, assist the physician with applying casts and **suturing**, and assist the nurse in collecting specimens. You also might transport patients by **gurney** to radiology or the patient's room. Other aspects of your job description will include restocking supplies, cleaning equipment, and making sure that all supplies and equipment are readily available.

If you work in an urgent care center you will be an assistant to both the physician and the nurse. It will be your responsibility to fit patients for crutches and teach the patients how to use them. You also will be responsible for talking with the patient's family members to find out what happened and obtain vital information for the medical record.

As an emergency department technician working in a health center for a large company or university you will assist with routine physical examinations. The employees or students will need to have their blood pressure, pulse, and respirations measured and recorded. You will assist the patients by obtaining and recording their weight, or you may be asked to perform other health tests or measurements. The health center also provides emergency first aid. If you work in a student health center you will be involved with caring for students with athletic injuries and providing other types of first aid for minor injuries and illnesses. Emergency department technicians who are employed in industrial clinics are available to respond to first aid calls for accidental injuries. For instance, an employee might accidentally splash a chemical in his eye, cut himself, or even have a heart attack. As an emergency department technician, you must be ready to handle all of these situations swiftly, skillfully, and calmly.

Working in emergency healthcare is never boring. In fact, no two days are ever the same. Each day brings the challenges of new patients with unique problems and different situations; and each day can end with the feeling of satisfaction that comes from helping others.

You have made an excellent choice by selecting a career in healthcare. The medical field offers numerous opportunities for jobs and advancement. The healthcare industry needs qualified workers! In fact, many companies are willing to help employees who want to return to school and study to become **paramedics**, nurses, doctors, or further their education in related health occupations.

---

vital signs: assesments of blood pressure, pulse, temperature, and respirations; body functions essential to life

suturing: the process of making one or more stitches to close a wound

gurney: a stretcher with wheels used for transporting patients

paramedic: a certified or licensed prehospital care worker trained in advanced life support procedures

Characteristics of Emergency Healthcare Professionals

What type of person is best suited for work in emergency care? It takes a special person to be an emergency department technician. Emergency care units are stressful work environments that demand responsible and mature individuals who are able to cope with the ever-changing patient population. Emergency departments are very busy; they provide care to about seventy million patients a year. These individuals come from all walks of life and range in age from newborn to elderly. Some of these people seek treatment for medical emergencies and many are there as a result of **trauma**. Nowhere else in healthcare do you see such diversity.

trauma: physical or psychological injury caused by an accident, violence, or a poisonous substance

Patients expect healthcare personnel to be knowledgeable and attentive to their special needs. Therefore, an emergency department technician must have the following characteristics:

manual dexterity: physical coordination; the ability to perform specialized tasks requiring fine motor movements

- good physical health
- motor coordination and **manual dexterity**
- communication skills (verbal and written)
- dependability
- **empathy**
- **tolerance**
- a neat appearance
- emotional stability
- the ability to set priorities
- an interest in helping others
- courtesy
- common sense
- flexibility
- a calm manner
- the ability to respond to orders
- consideration for others

empathy: to understand and relate to the emotional state of another; to show concern

tolerance: a fair and objective attitude toward others of different race, creed, color, or opinion

Chapter One • Health Careers in Emergency Care

Some of these qualities can be developed through training, education, and experience, and some of these characteristics must be part of your unique personality. Do you have the traits that are necessary to become an emergency department technician? Take a few minutes to answer the following questions.

Self-Assessment Test

	Yes	No
Do I like to help other people?	___	___
Do I want to work where I can make a difference in people's lives?	___	___
Do I like new and exciting things?	___	___
Do I like to work with my hands?	___	___
Do I enjoy doing something different every day?	___	___
Do I like a fast-paced environment?	___	___
Do I wonder what has happened when I hear a siren?	___	___
Do I want to learn how to perform **cardiopulmonary resuscitation** (CPR)?	___	___
Am I a leader?	___	___
Do I like to make decisions?	___	___
Do I want to learn first aid procedures?	___	___
Am I a team player?	___	___

cardiopulmonary resuscitation: (CPR) a basic life saving procedure of artificial ventilation and chest compressions that is done for cardiac arrest

If you answered *yes* to at least eight of the questions, then emergency care is for you. Emergencies can happen anytime and anywhere. The skills you learn in this class may help you save the life of a friend or family member. These are **life skills;** and they can help you both on and off the job. This is a chance to change your life and learn skills that will help you every day.

Chapter Summary

The role of today's healthcare worker has expanded greatly over the last few years. This is due to a tremendous need for qualified healthcare workers combined with a shortage of nurses and all healthcare providers. The need for emergency department technicians is greater now than ever before. The skills you learn in this course will make you a very valuable employee with many job opportunities.

Chapter One • Health Careers in Emergency Care 1-7

Name _____

Date _____

Student Enrichment Activities

Unscramble the following characteristics of an emergency department technician.

1. THYEMPA _____
2. UANALM ERDETIXYT _____ _____
3. CEOTEALNR _____
4. TIONMEOAL IILTYBTSA _____ _____
5. EYSTRCOU _____
6. MOCNOM SSEEN _____ _____
7. ERSIDONCONIAT _____

Circle the correct answer for the following two questions.

8. A facility that is not a hospital, but that provides emergency care is called a(n):

    A. emergency department   C. urgent care center

    B. medical clinic   D. medical office

9. Emergency department technicians are able to:

    A. assist the physician with procedures.

    B. obtain vital signs.

    C. transport patients on gurneys.

    D. all of the above.

10. Look in the local newspaper for jobs in emergency care, clip the advertisements from the newspaper, and turn them in with these pages.

1-8 The Emergency Department Technician

Answer the following questions.

11. List six personal characteristics that describe you best and that relate in some way to providing good emergency care:

   A. _____

   B. _____   C. _____

   D. _____   E. _____

   F. _____

12. Write a paragraph below about each characteristic (six paragraphs) and explain why these characteristics are necessary for emergency care.

   A. _____
   _____
   _____
   _____
   _____
   _____
   _____
   _____
   _____
   _____

Chapter One • Health Careers in Emergency Care

Name_____

Date_____

B. _____

C. _____

D. _____

E. _____

F. _____

13. Interview an EMT, paramedic, nurse, or doctor and complete the form on the next page.

Chapter One • Health Careers in Emergency Care

Name_____

Date_____

Name of Person Interviewed _____

Title _____

A. How long have you been working at your current job?

_____
_____
_____
_____
_____
_____
_____
_____
_____

B. What type of education and training prepared you for this career?

_____
_____
_____
_____
_____
_____
_____

C. Do you enjoy your work? Why or why not?

_____
_____
_____
_____
_____
_____
_____
_____

D. What is the best thing about your occupation?

_____
_____
_____
_____
_____
_____
_____
_____

E. How did you get this job?

_____
_____
_____
_____
_____
_____
_____
_____

F. Do you have any advice for someone who is just starting a career in emergency medical care?

_____
_____
_____
_____
_____
_____
_____
_____

Chapter Two
Introduction to Emergency Medical Services

Objectives

After completing this chapter you should be able to do the following:

1. Define and correctly spell all key terms.

2. Identify three areas of responsibility for the emergency department technician.

3. Discuss the concept of the healthcare team.

4. Discuss the role of the Emergency Medical Services (EMS).

5. List thirteen essential components of an EMS system.

Key Terms

- Critical Care Unit (CCU)
- Emergency Care Unit (ECU)
- Emergency Medical Service (EMS)
- intravenous (IV)
- licensed vocational nurse (LVN)
- registered nurse (RN)
- trauma center
- triage

The History of Emergency Medical Services

Emergency care can be traced back to biblical times. During that time, injured patients were carried by **litter** to healing centers. In the days of Napoleon, horse drawn carts were used to transport injured soldiers to treatment stations. Until 1906 when the first ambulance was designed and built, all patients had to be carried or taken there by horse and cart.

Historically, the Red Cross has been known for its care of injured soldiers and disaster victims. In 1859 a Swiss philanthropist named Jean Henri Dunant was traveling in northern Italy when he encountered the tragedy of 50,000 dead and wounded soldiers left by the Battle of Solferino, a French victory over the Austrians. Inspired by the work of Florence Nightingale in the Crimean War, he helped the wounded soldiers by providing emergency first aid and sending his coach to Switzerland for supplies. Dunant, greatly moved by the lack of care for wounded soldiers, later wrote a book that formed the basis of an international organization to provide trained volunteers and supplies for the sake of humanity. In 1864, a diplomatic conference on the matter held in Geneva, Switzerland established the terms of the Geneva Convention. This convention laid down the rules for the treatment of the wounded and for the protection of medical personnel and hospitals. It led to the beginning of the International Committee of the Red Cross. The red cross on a white background was adopted as the symbol of the organization.

The American Red Cross was founded by Clara Barton in 1881. During the Civil War, Barton was instrumental in providing supplies and volunteers to the wounded soldiers. She started a movement to search for soldiers who were missing in action. Through the years, many Americans have turned to the Red Cross for help in times of emergency and disaster. There are currently 1.2 million Red Cross volunteers helping their neighbors. Workers assist the military in emergencies and respond to human needs in more than 40,000 disasters a year. The disasters this agency responds to range from house fires to major life-threatening hurricanes and floods. The American Red Cross conducts blood drives and provides training in first aid, CPR, and disaster preparedness. The fundamental principle of the Red Cross is to help all people, and to prevent and alleviate human suffering.

In the beginning emergency rooms consisted of one room, usually located on the basement level of a hospital. When a patient arrived for care, he or she either rang a bell or spoke to a clerk. The clerk would call for the nurse, who then would evaluate the patient and call for the doctor. Often, the physician was not in the hospital, and valuable time was lost waiting for the doctor to arrive. Even when the doctor was present, the quality of care in life-threatening situations often was inadequate.

Figure 2-1: Early Emergency Vehicles

Emergency Care Unit (ECU): a specific area of an acute care facility staffed and equipped to handle patients with life threatening illnesses or injuries. Also known as the Emergency Department or the ER

trauma center: a medical facility or department in a medical facility that is capable of providing care to critically injured patients 24 hours a day

Today the situation is different. Systems are designed for the rapid stabilization and transportation of the sick or injured to the nearest appropriate receiving center. Emergency rooms are now complex departments that are staffed with highly trained physicians, nurses, and support personnel. This department is known as the **Emergency Care Unit (ECU)** or **Emergency Department**. Some hospitals still call it the **ER**. The initials *ER* stand for emergency room, but the term now refers to the entire emergency department. The Emergency Care Unit occupies a large area of the hospital; it includes patient treatment rooms (Figure 2-2), a lobby, an admission area, a nurses' station, and other facilities. Some hospitals have expanded their emergency departments and have set up **trauma centers**, burn centers, or other specialty treatment centers.

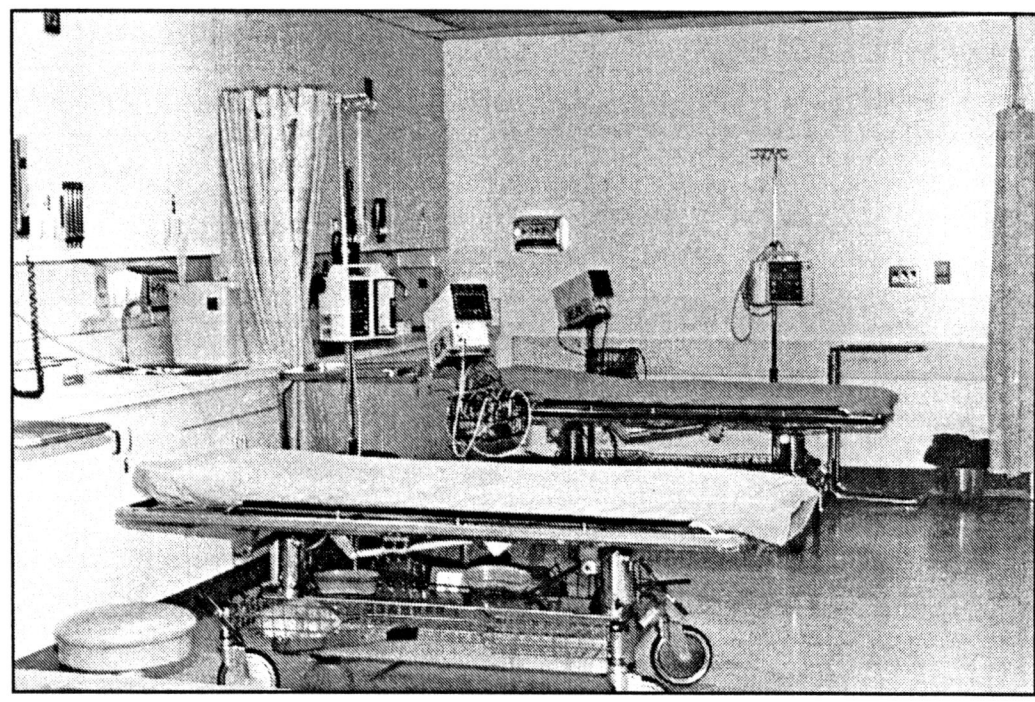

Figure 2-2: A Patient Treatment Room

Some emergency departments have added facilities for **urgent care**. This is because many people use the emergency room for all their healthcare needs. Some find it more convenient, while others may not have a physician or are visiting from out of town. These patients use the Emergency Department as a clinic. The urgent care clinic handles these patients with non life-threatening problems. The staff members in these departments must deal with a wide range of illnesses and/or injuries on a day to day basis. They must also be prepared to handle critical incidents.

Chapter Two • Introduction to Emergency Medical Services

Emergency Medical Services

The **Emergency Medical Service (EMS)** was established to provide comprehensive emergency healthcare to the community. It began in 1966 when the National Highway Safety Act charged the Department of Transportation with developing an Emergency Medical Services System. However, the concept of EMS remained only a theory without proper funding. A national strategy was needed to ensure everyone's access to emergency care. Thus, in 1973 the Emergency Medical Services Systems (EMSS) Act was established in an effort to reduce the percentage of illness and accidents resulting in disability and death. This Act encouraged each state to plan to meet the needs of accident victims by providing money for emergency medical services. Some states established communication networks, some began training programs for paramedics, and others used the funding to improve transportation of the sick and injured.

> **Emergency Medical Service (EMS):** a national network of emergency care providers, from the first responder to basic life support and advanced life support procedures coordinated by a central communication system

The Components of EMS

The EMSS Act led to the creation of the Division of Emergency Medical Services (DEMS). This federal agency oversees local EMS and has outlined the elements of a comprehensive emergency plan. (Figure 2-3) Each element or link in the system includes critical issues that affect the quality of care the emergency medical services in your community are able to provide.

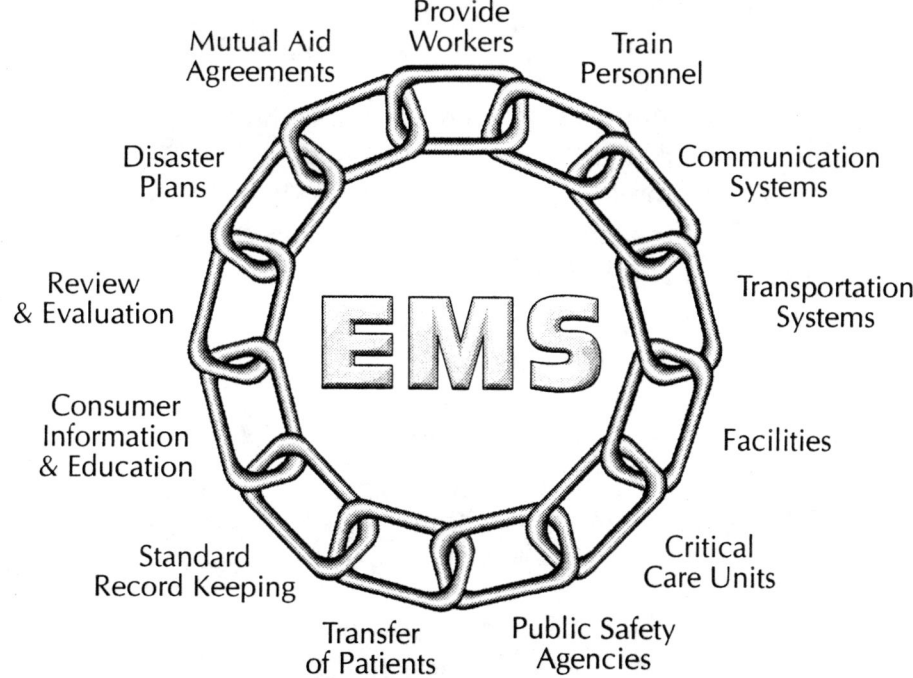

Figure 2-3: The Emergency Medical Service System

1. **Provide Workers:** The availability of qualified workers is a problem currently faced by EMS. A shortage of healthcare workers is making it necessary for new personnel to be trained. Furthermore, changes in healthcare make it necessary to continually retrain existing personnel.

2. **Training of Personnel:** Technology is changing. As new equipment becomes available, it is necessary to retrain all employees. New equipment alone is not enough; healthcare workers must be trained in the proper use of all new equipment if they are going to be effective in their duties. Proper training cannot be stressed enough. Emergency healthcare technology in untrained hands can be deadly.

3. **Communications:** Communication systems also are constantly being upgraded to include new technology and improve the system. Using a radio, paramedics are able to communicate with the mobile intensive care nurse at the base station hospital. The nurse can relay information to the physician and the physician can prescribe medication as needed. The radio is capable of transmitting a patient's ECG (electrocardiogram), or heart tracing, for the physician to analyze. Due to technological advances, cellular phones are now being used for communication in areas where satellite communication is better than radio frequency. Some emergency crews are using computers in the field that instantly tie in with the base station hospital, the local EMS agency, and other emergency personnel to transmit lifesaving data immediately.

4. **Transportation:** Transportation of the sick and injured is very important to the EMS system. Decisions must be made on a patient-by-patient basis as to whether air or ground transportation is the most advantageous.

Chapter Two • Introduction to Emergency Medical Services

5. **Facilities:** Prior to transport, a decision is made as to the most appropriate receiving center for the patient. Depending on the community, there may be a university or teaching hospital, cancer center, burn center, transplant center, or trauma center available to emergency patients. Furthermore, some services that may be offered at one hospital may not be available at others, such as an intensive care unit, cardiac care unit, or neonatal unit. It is best to transport the stable patient to the nearest appropriate receiving center. If the patient requires lifesaving treatment, he or she is taken to the nearest receiving center; but a burn patient is best be treated at a burn unit if the transport time is not excessive. The decision of how and where to transport a patient is made at the scene by the paramedics, the base station, and the physician. Consideration is given to the patient's status, type of care required, time of transport, and facilities available. A child who has nearly drowned may be transported by helicopter to a major university pediatric center, whereas an expectant mother may be transported by ambulance to the community hospital. Each situation is unique; how and where to transport depends on the circumstances of each specific incident.

6. **Critical Care Units: Intensive Care Units**, or **Critical Care Units (CCU)**, are available in acute care hospitals and are essential in the overall care of emergency patients. If a **CCU** is not available, it may be necessary to transfer the patient to a facility that has this specialty service.

   Critical Care Unit (CCU): a specialized nursing unit that is staffed and equipped to care for the most seriously ill patients

7. **Use of Public Safety Agencies:** Public safety agencies are very much involved with emergency care. Sometimes, the police, fire fighters, forestry service, coast guard, military, and highway patrol are needed at the scene to assist with a particular incident. These agencies work together as a team in disaster situations and whenever mutual aid is required. It is essential that consumers participate in the planning and delivery of healthcare in their community. Everyone must know how to use the 911 system, because unless people know how to use it, the system is no good. People who are trained in first aid procedures and CPR can make a big difference in the survival rates of injured citizens.

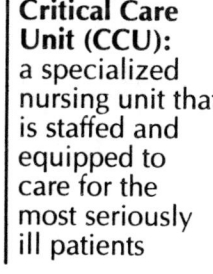

8. **Transfer of Patients:** Emergency care must be accessible to all members of the community. So the EMS system includes a system for patient transfers to specialty centers. If a patient is burned and can best be treated in a burn center, transportation must be available as soon as possible. Patients requiring a transfer to a critical care unit will need an advanced life support (ALS) unit for transfer. An ALS unit is a specially equipped ambulance that is staffed with a paramedic or registered nurse. There is specialized monitoring equipment and lifesaving medication available inside every ALS unit.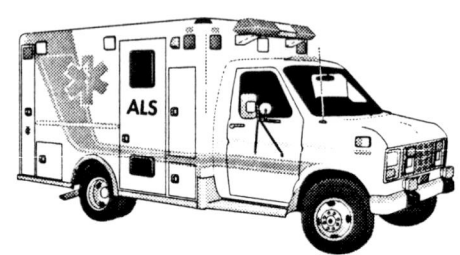

9. **Standard Medical Record Keeping:** Medical record keeping is necessary for proper patient care as well as for legal documentation. The condition of the patient and his or her plan of care is best communicated by a medical chart. An account of everything that occurs to the patient is written down on the patient's chart. The procedures that are performed, the treatments that are given, the times they took place, and the results are all documented for future reference. The patient's chart allows healthcare workers to see, at a glance, how the patient is progressing, and what care he or she has received.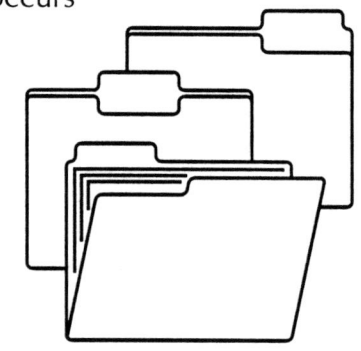

10. **Consumer Information and Education:** It is essential that all members of the community be informed and educated about emergency care and the 911 system. Communities that promote awareness of pool safety, bicycle safety, and offer first aid, CPR, and disaster preparedness classes will have citizens who know how to prevent accidents and care for themselves in an emergency. Many communities have provided public education programs about the use of child and infant car seats and the dangers of drinking and driving, thus, lowering the statistics that reflect death and injury in these communities.

Chapter Two • Introduction to Emergency Medical Services

11. **Review and Evaluation:** Emergency cases are reviewed and the care evaluated. The emergency record is part of the patient's medical record or chart. The hospital has a quality assurance committee that reviews these records monthly. The completeness of the records is evaluated along with the quality of care administered. If it is found that changes are needed in healthcare delivery, then steps are taken to improve the system.

12. **Disaster Plans:** An EMS system should have plans for dealing with disasters such as earthquakes, floods, hurricanes, fires, etc. Periodic drills are conducted to test this system, and the system is revised as needed.

    FIRE FLOOD EARTHQUAKE

13. **Mutual Aid Agreements:** A community that has a sound EMS program has established mutual aid agreements. For example, if a fire starts and the community resources of personnel and equipment are not enough to get the fire under control, then assistance is available from a neighboring fire department. All emergency departments, police, fire, and ambulance personnel work together for the total benefit of the community.

Each part of the EMS is vital and all parts must work together in a team effort. If a patient is to receive the best care that is possible, then that care must be started as quickly as possible. Emergency care is started at the scene and continues during transport to an emergency care unit where the patient is re-evaluated and emergency care is continued. The patients medical problems are diagnosed with laboratory tests, x-rays, and a physical examination by the doctor. If emergency surgery is necessary, the patient will be prepared for surgery. If closer observation is needed, the patient will be admitted to the hospital. Sometimes the injury can be treated in the Emergency Department and the patient is discharged the same day.

911 and the EMS System

The 911 system, though not available in all communities, was designed to provide people with rapid access to EMS. The electronic switching equipment allows the **dispatcher** to obtain as much information as possible by automatic telephone number identification, automatic call location identification, and automatic ring back. If a caller dials 911, his or her phone number and address appear on a screen. If the caller accidentally hangs up, the system prevents the call from being disconnected by automatically calling back the number. Let's look at a potential emergency in which a caller has dialed 911:

"911 this is an emergency—I'm having a heart attack, I'm dizzy and think I'm going to pass out..."

If this were a real emergency call and the victim lost consciousness, the 911 system would already have the address on the screen and emergency help could be dispatched to the victim's house.

The dispatcher obtains as much information as possible about the emergency and gives immediate instructions to the caller. (Figure 2-4) The dispatcher also sends the appropriate personnel and vehicles to the scene. Some emergencies need fire, police, paramedics and/or ambulance services, while some emergencies only require the ambulance.

Some communities have dispatchers who are trained to provide pre-arrival instructions to the caller. It takes a very calm and reassuring person to control an emergency situation quickly. Dispatchers have saved lives by telling panicked callers exactly how to

Figure 2-4: Emergency dispatchers can save lives.

Chapter Two • Introduction to Emergency Medical Services

make an airway and provide rescue breathing to a drowning victim; how to apply pressure to control severe bleeding; and in some cases, how to do CPR on a person in cardiac arrest.

The first responder on the scene should be trained in basic life support. These individuals should be able to do CPR and provide first aid. Emergency medical technicians (EMTs) are trained emergency care givers. They can assess the scene and note the cause of injury, examine the patient, obtain a medical history, administer oxygen, stabilize the patient and prepare him or her for transport. When the paramedics arrive they are able to provide advanced life support, administer medications, start an **intravenous (IV)** line, place the patient on a **cardiac monitor**, and interpret the heart rhythm. (Figure 2-5) Paramedics establish radio contact with the base station hospital and prepare patients for transportation to the nearest appropriate facility. Some communities have special facilities that are designated **trauma centers**, burn centers, **pediatric** centers, spinal cord injury centers, acute cardiac care centers, **neonatal** intensive care units and **psychiatric** receiving centers.

intravenous: directly into the vein

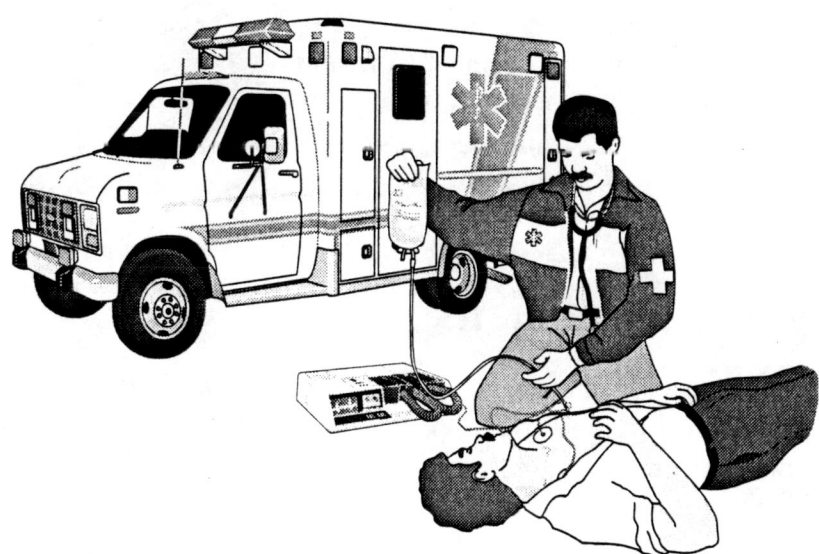

Figure 2-5: Paramedics can provide advanced life support to critically injured or ill patients.

Patients are transported by ground in an ambulance, or by air in a helicopter or fixed wing aircraft. When he or she arrives in the Emergency Department the physician evaluates the patient and prescribes the appropriate emergency treatment. The patient is then admitted for further evaluation and treatment, or transferred to another facility, or discharged.

The Emergency Healthcare Team

The healthcare team includes all the staff members who work together to provide the most efficient care to the patient in the least amount of time. It is essential that a spirit of cooperation, communication and commitment exists among all members of this team.

Together, the members of the healthcare team have a goal of maximizing health and wellness, and preventing complications and **disease**. Paramedics and EMTs provide pre-hospital care in both basic and advanced life support. The physician (MD) directs and monitors the emergency care that is delivered. The registered nurse (RN) plans the nursing care, carries out the physician's orders and administers medications and treatments. The licensed vocational or practical nurse (LVN, LPN) provides nursing care as directed by the physician or RN, and the emergency department technician helps all team members as needed. The clerical staff provides support for these healthcare givers. All members have an equally important role to play and are dependent upon one another. A healthcare team can accomplish many tasks simultaneously; thereby giving the patient emergency care in a timely manner.

Emergency Physicians

An emergency room physician is an MD (medical doctor) with special training in emergency care and pre-hospital **protocols**. Such a doctor is available at all times to provide care to patients in the emergency room. An emergency physician in a base station hospital also provides medical direction to the paramedics in the field. Communication from the base station to the paramedic in the field is done through radio contact on a specially designated frequency. The physician determines how and where a patient should be transported according to the severity of the situation. The physician makes all the decisions about the emergency care of the patient and directs the emergency care team. He or she must decide if a specialist is needed and be aware of all the community resources available for patient referral. The emergency room physician may be an employee of the hospital, or he or she may work independently under contract to the hospital to provide emergency services.

Emergency Nurses

A **registered nurse** (**RN**) gives care to patients. RNs assigned to the emergency room have acute care nursing experience and a critical care background. A mobile intensive care nurse (MICN), sometimes called an authorized radio nurse (ARN), has been certified to provide emergency care and issue emergency instructions to paramedics via radio communication. MICNs (ARNs) have had special training in emergency care. These nurses must learn radio communication skills and understand the paramedic treatment guidelines. They are certified in advanced cardiac life support and participate in continuing education programs and case reviews. A certified emergency nurse (CEN) has passed a national certification exam in the speciality of emergency nursing and also has clinical experience working in the emergency room. Some nurses care for patients during transport. These nurses provide advanced life support in an ambulance or in the air. If these nurses work in helicopters or fixed wing aircraft they are called flight nurses. There are special physical, mental, and emotional requirements for this type of nursing. These nurses must be physically fit, emotionally stable and able to work under stress. They also must like to fly.

> **registered nurse (RN):** a nurse who has completed a course of study at a state-approved nursing school and who has passed the state licensing exam for nursing. This nurse is granted the right to practice nursing for hire

Licensed Vocational Nurses

The **licensed vocational nurse (LVN)** or licensed practical nurse (LPN) is another member of the healthcare team. Working under the direction of the physician and the registered nurse, the LVN provides nursing care to patients. LVNs assess the condition of patients and administer medication and treatments. They also assist with medical procedures.

> **licensed vocational nurse (LVN):** a licensed nurse trained in patient care procedures, treatments and medication administration who must practice under the supervision of a registered nurse

Emergency Medical Technicians

Emergency medical technicians (EMTs) are trained in basic life support procedures. EMT-As may be ambulance attendants or fire service personnel, or they may be employed by private companies. Emergency medical technicians-Intermediates (EMT-Is) may have additional training in specific procedures, depending on the local protocol. In certain areas of the country the local EMS authority may authorize the education and training of EMTs to start IVs, intubate (insert an airway) patients, or treat for shock by placing the patient in the pneumatic anti-shock garment (PASG).

Paramedics

Emergency medical technician-paramedics (EMT-Ps) have been trained and certified in pre-hospital care treatments and procedures. They provide advanced life support at the scene and during transport. Paramedics may be fire service personnel, or they may work for private companies. Paramedic training includes classroom instruction, clinical experience, and field training. Paramedic training programs often are available at hospitals, fire academies, and local colleges.

Emergency Department Technicians

Emergency department technicians have many responsibilities. As an assistant to the doctor and nurse, the technician sets up instruments and equipment for patient examinations and treatments; checks the vital signs of patients; safely transports patients in wheelchairs or on **gurneys** (stretchers); and performs **triage**. The technician also must be familiar with admission procedures and be able to document information. Other duties include maintaining equipment and supplies, taking inventory, and performing other duties as instructed by the registered nurse.

> **triage:** to sort and prioritize care for a group of patients

Clerical Staff

The clerical staff varies in size according to the size of the Emergency Department. It is vital for the smooth operation of a busy ER. Some clerical staff members handle admissions, and others do billing, medical records, and statistics. A **unit secretary** answers the phone and orders lab work, x-rays, and other tests. The secretary also makes arrangements for admission, transfers, and discharges of patients and controls the flow of the paperwork that moves through the department. The unit secretary is responsible for maintaining inventory of supplies and equipment.

Chapter Two • Introduction to Emergency Medical Services 2-15

Figure 2-6: Quality emergency medical care requires teamwork.

Chapter Summary

The Emergency Medical Service is a relatively new government agency established to give access to quality emergency care. Each community determines the extent of the services available. Private industry works with public safety agencies to provide these services. A comprehensive plan includes: providing workers, training personnel, communication, transportation, facilities, critical care units, use of public safety agencies, transfer of patients, standardized medical record keeping, consumer information and education, review and evaluation, disaster plans, and mutual aid agreements.

The emergency healthcare team is made up of highly trained, specialized care givers who work together to provide the best quality of emergency care that is possible in the least amount of time.

Chapter Two • Introduction to Emergency Medical Services 2-17

Name_____

Date_____

Student Enrichment Activities

Answer the following questions.

1. To activate the EMS system dial_____on the telephone.

2. The emergency department technician is responsible for: **(Circle the best choice.)**
   a. Assisting the physician.
   b. Checking the patient's blood pressure.
   c. Stocking supplies.
   d. Cleaning equipment.
   e. All of the above.

3. What do the following abbreviations mean?
   LVN _____
   RN _____
   MICN _____
   MD _____
   EMT-1 _____
   EMT-P _____

4. Explain what happens when a person calls 911.
   _____
   _____
   _____
   _____
   _____
   _____
   _____

5. Write a paragraph about the goal of the healthcare team.

_____
_____
_____
_____
_____
_____
_____
_____
_____
_____
_____
_____

Unscramble the following elements of a successful EMS system.

6. SEROWKR   _____
7. IINNGRAT   _____
8. TMOICICUNONSMA _____
9. AITTPNORSNRATO _____
10. LITIFIACES   _____
11. LITACLRIC EARC _____ _____
12. LIPUBC TEFYAS _____ _____
13. SNATRREF   _____
14. ORDERCS   _____
15. ATIONMROFNI   _____
16. WEEIRV   _____
17. SSIDTERA SANLP _____ _____
18. UUAMTL DIA   _____ _____

Chapter Two • Introduction to Emergency Medical Services 2-19

Name_____

Date_____

19. Describe how the EMS system works in your community.

_____
_____
_____
_____
_____
_____
_____
_____
_____
_____
_____
_____

20. Cut out an article or picture from the newspaper about a recent emergency and the EMS in your community. (Paste here.)

Chapter Three
The Working Environment

Objectives

After completing this chapter you should be able to do the following:

1. Define and correctly spell all key terms.

2. Describe the physical layout of an emergency department.

3. Identify equipment commonly found in the emergency care unit.

Key Terms

- chart
- contaminated
- crash cart
- isolation
- patient history
- patient log

The Location of the Emergency Department

An emergency department is an area within an acute care hospital that is set aside for the treatment of patients with sudden illness and injury. Part of the hospital complex, it is located close to the hospital's main entrance with easy access from the street. Signs posted on the hospital grounds clearly mark the emergency entrance.

Emergency workers are allowed direct access to the ER through an ambulance entrance with a double door. (Figure 3-1) Ambulances back up to the *AMBULANCE ONLY* area and the patients are unloaded on a **gurney**.

gurney: a stretcher with wheels used for transporting patients

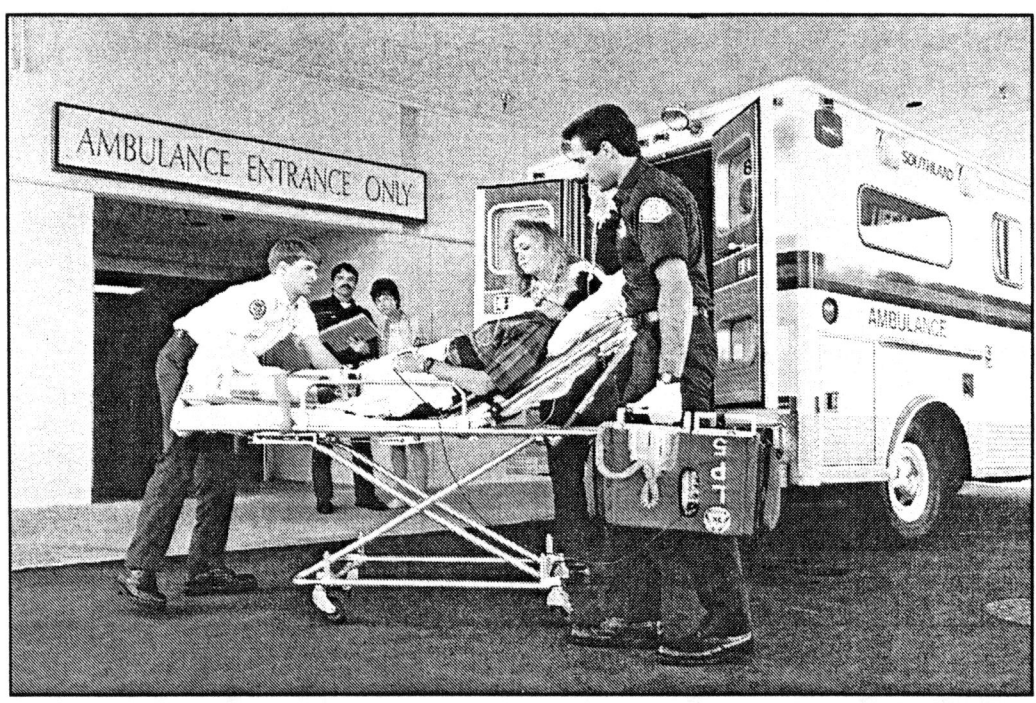

Figure 3-1: The Ambulance Entrance

Chapter Three • The Working Environment

Patients who are driven to the hospital in private automobiles and are unable to walk are met in the parking lot by a hospital staff member with a **wheelchair**. Patients who are able may walk directly into the ER.

Admission and Triage

A staff member greets the patients and begins the admission procedures. If the patient is in **critical** condition, essential information can be obtained from relatives at the admitting desk. If the patient is in stable condition, a **patient history** is done to determine the chief complaint (the reason they have come to the ER). In a patient history, patients are asked questions about their past and current health problems. This form is then added to the patient's **chart** and is used by the doctor to help decide the best method of treatment for each patient. Some questions that are asked in the patient history follow.

- What problem are you having today?
- When did it happen?
- Do you have any pain?
- Can you describe it?
- Do you see a doctor for any medical problems?
- Are you **allergic** to anything?
- When was your last **tetanus** shot?

The patient's name, address, phone number, social security number, insurance company and policy number, next of kin, responsible party, place of employment, date of birth, religious preference, and method of arrival (ambulance or private auto) are also required information on the patient history. Complete admission procedures will be discussed in detail in the following chapters.

Once the necessary patient information is obtained, an evaluation of the patient is done. In life-threatening cases, they may be done simultaneously. Vital signs (blood pressure, pulse, respiration, and temperature) are taken and the patient is **triaged** for treatment. If life-threatening emergencies exist, the patient is seen immediately by the doctor. If the patient is in mild status, requiring basic first aid or medical evaluation, he or she is seen as time permits. If there are no patients in more serious condition currently in the emergency room the patient in mild status is seen right away.

patient history: a form that is filled out by the patient or close family member that describes the patient's medical history and chief medical complaint

chart: a form used by the hospital staff to record the progression of a patient's illness or injury; it becomes a part of the patient's medical record (includes vital signs, treatments, output, and physicians and nurses notes)

The Physical Layout

The physical design of the Emergency Department varies from hospital to hospital; but there are some common areas found in all ERs. A central nurses' station is the communication and coordination center of the department. (Figure 3-2) This station is the center for all phone messages and doctor's orders. The unit secretary or charge nurse will order laboratory tests and x-rays, coordinate the physician's orders with the nursing care, and make arrangements for the patients' admission to the hospital or discharge home. The nurses' station also maintains a **patient log** or **roster**. This roster documents the admission, **diagnosis** and discharge of each patient. A status sheet, or board, is maintained to indicate what patient should be seen by the doctor next, who has had x-ray or lab work done, and who is waiting for a procedure. The status sheet allows the staff to see the progress of each patient at a glance.

patient log: a roster kept by the nurses that documents the status of every patient in that department, including information on admissions, diagnoses, and discharges

Figure 3-2: Central Nurses' Station

Most emergency departments have an area set aside for **pediatric** cases. This area has specific pediatric equipment, such as a crib, a baby scale, and a pediatric exam tray. Chairs are usually available for parents to sit in while their child is examined and treated.

Chapter Three • The Working Environment 3-5

Emergency departments usually include an **isolation** room used for patients with suspected **contagious** diseases, a procedure room for examining female patients, and a quiet area for psychiatric cases. Another area is designated for eye, ear, nose and throat emergencies.

The Critical Care Unit takes up a large area in the ER and has a **crash cart**, oxygen, and equipment for monitoring the vital signs of patients. Patients who arrive in acute distress with life-threatening problems are treated here. Victims of automobile accidents, heart attacks, drug overdoses, or gunshot wounds will be taken directly to the critical care room.

Another area is designated for minor trauma. It is used for **suturing** and for applying casts, dressings, and bandages.

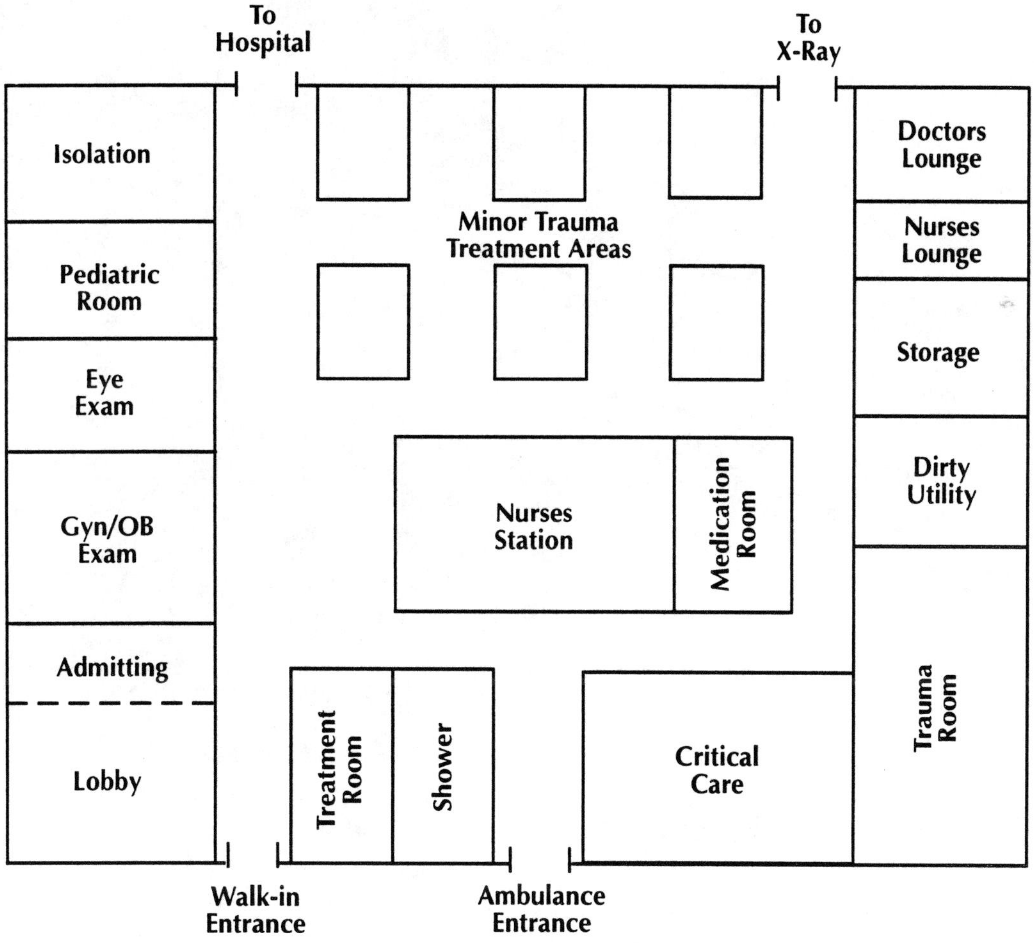

isolation: an area that is able to be closed off to contain contaminated patient and equipment

crash cart: a portable supply cabinet that contains all of the necessary emergency equipment needed in a full arrest or code blue

Figure 3-3: A Sample Layout of an Emergency Department

When patients are admitted for treatment they are placed in the appropriate areas so that the necessary equipment and supplies will be readily available. Sometimes, two patients with the same type of emergency conditions arrive at the same time. If there is not enough room to accommodate both patients in the designated area, a decision must be made as to where to place the additional patient.

Sterile supplies, which come from Central Supply, are located on carts in a central storage area. These carts are stocked daily, or more often if necessary. A closet or cupboard area, generally in the center of the emergency department, contains stock supplies, wheelchairs, **gurneys**, crutches, splints, and slings. (Figure 3-4)

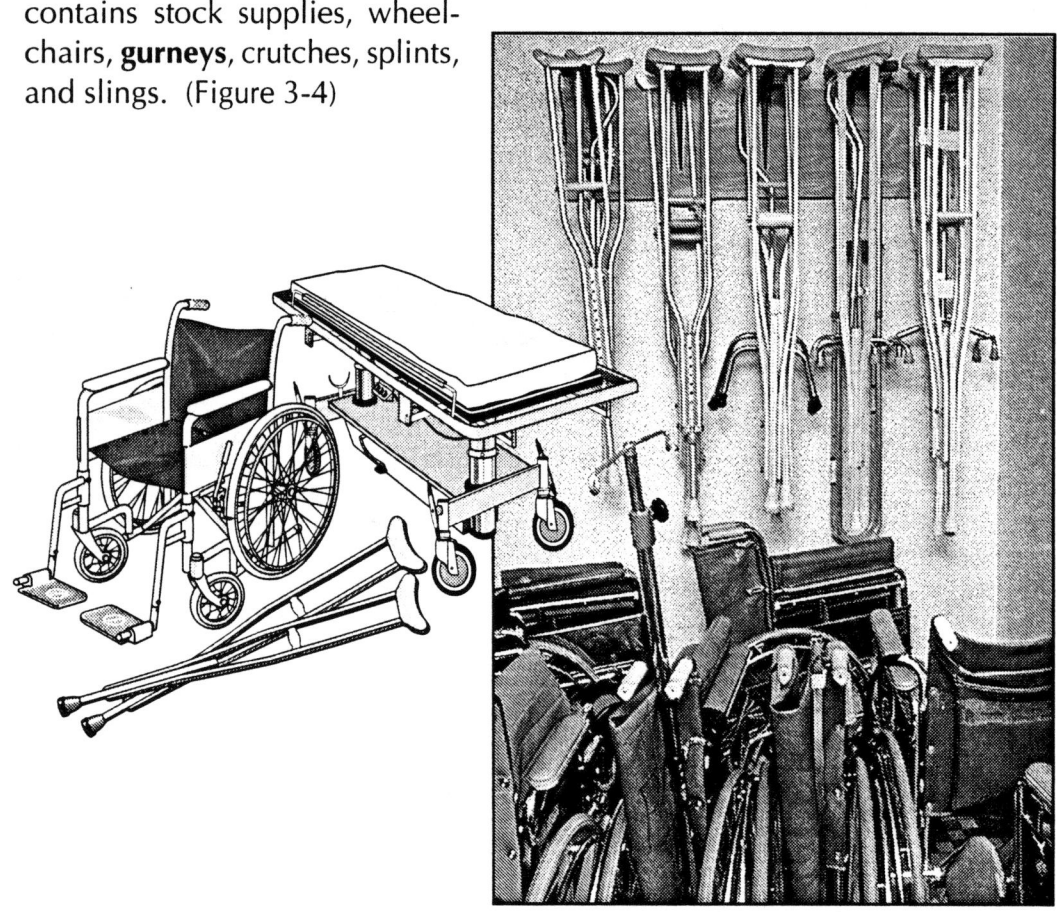

Figure 3-4: These items can be found in the central storage area.

Chapter Three • The Working Environment

The dirty utility room is where used supplies and equipment are taken for cleaning or disposal. All used disposable supplies are bagged and considered to be **contaminated** waste. After being used, major equipment items are either cleaned and stored in the Emergency Department or returned to Central Supply. All sharps (needles, syringes, knife blades, scalpels, etc.) are disposed of in special sharps containers to prevent injuries and contamination from needle sticks. These rigid, plastic containers are usually red, and are labeled with the "biohazardous waste" symbol. (Figure 3-6) Contaminated linen and trash are disposed of by the Environmental Services Department.

contaminated: not sterile; unclean; exposed to harmful bacteria or radiation

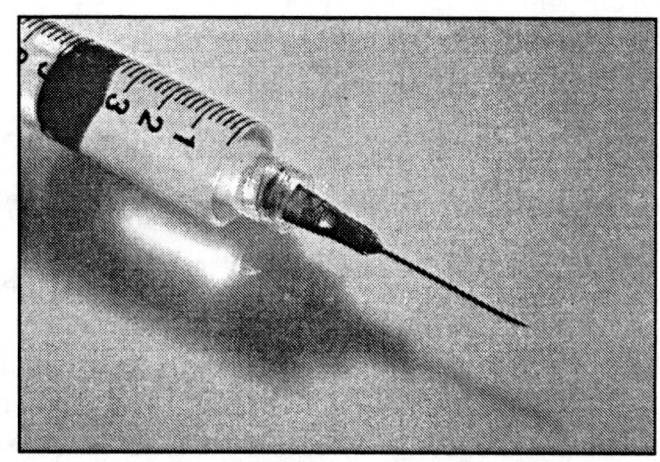

Figure 3-5: Sharps must be handled carefully.

Nurses have access to a medication room or medication and intravenous solution preparation area. This area includes a small refrigerator to store medications that require refrigeration. Other supplies that are needed to administer medications (syringes, medication cups, etc.) are stored here.

Some emergency departments have a nutritional area. Patients, especially diabetics, may need juice or food. Snacks and juice are stored in the refrigerator. There is a sink, ice machine, and coffee for family and visitors. Generally, there also is an area set aside as a staff lounge and another room set aside for the physicians.

The radiology and laboratory departments are located very close to the ER. When patients are returned from x-ray, the films are brought with them so that the ER physician can immediately read and interpret the x-ray using the x-ray view box.

Figure 3-6: Sharps Container With Biohazardous Waste Symbol

Emergency care units are designed to accommodate many patients at any given time. They are arranged in a way that allows traffic to flow smoothly and effectively. The department must be laid out so that all patients are visible by the nursing staff at all times. This is necessary for the continuous monitoring of each patient's condition. Security must be available to limit unauthorized access to patient treatment areas by people who are not patients, family members, or healthcare workers.

Chapter Summary

Although the bed capacity of each emergency department will vary, there are some general treatment areas that are common to all emergency care units. As you work in different environments you will become familiar with these treatment areas and the various supplies and equipment that are common to all facilities.

Chapter Three • The Working Environment

Name _____

Date _____

Student Enrichment Activities

Complete the crossword puzzle.

ACROSS
3. a vehicle used for the transportation of the ill or injured
4. a wheeled cot (stretcher)
6. free from bacteria
7. a very serious condition
8. an area for contagious patients to keep germs from spreading
10. a device used to transport a sitting patient
11. a wheeled container with emergency medications and supplies
12. to sort and prioritize
13. exposed to harmful bacteria

DOWN
1. an area in a hospital set aside for the care of patients with sudden illness or injury
2. unable to tolerate a food or medication
5. pertaining to children
9. needles, scalpels, knife blades, etc.

Chapter Four
Asepsis

Objectives

After completing this chapter you should be able to do the following:

1. Define and correctly spell all key terms.
2. Identify conditions that promote the growth of microorganisms.
3. Describe the chain of infection.
4. List three things healthcare workers can do to prevent infections.
5. Demonstrate proper handwashing technique.

Key Terms

- acquired immune deficiency syndrome (AIDS)
- asepsis
- autoclave
- bacteria
- biopsy
- contaminated
- cross infection
- direct transmission
- disinfection
- host
- immunization
- indirect transmission
- lockjaw
- medical asepsis
- pathogen
- pertussis
- purulent
- septic shock
- sterile
- sterile field
- sterilization
- surgical asepsis
- tetanus
- universal precautions

pathogen: a disease-causing microorganism

acquired immune deficiency syndrome (AIDS): a viral disease caused by the human immuno-deficiency virus (HIV), which destroys the immune system and renders the patient susceptible to other infections. It is contracted through blood and other body fluids and is incurable.

indirect transmission: the transfer of an infection by the touching of a contaminated object

contaminated: not sterile; unclean; exposed to harmful bacteria or radiation

Disease-Causing Agents

Microorganisms that cause diseases are called **pathogens**. Much can be done to prevent the growth and spread of these microorganisms. Diseases are transmitted by different routes. Some diseases, such as **acquired immune deficiency syndrome** (**AIDS**), are transmitted through blood or other body fluids, meaning that direct contact with the contaminated body fluid must occur to acquire the disease.

However, diseases are more frequently spread by **indirect transmission**. For example, some diseases are airborne; we can become ill by breathing the **contaminated** air from an infected person or inhaling as an ill person coughs. Colds and flu viruses are very common diseases that are spread by indirect transmission. The bite from a rodent or mosquito can spread diseases like rabies or malaria.

Still other diseases are present in the **gastrointestinal** tract and are spread through the **oral-fecal** route. Using the restroom without washing your hands and then preparing food is a good example of how these infections are spread.

Chapter Four • Asepsis

This is the reason most restaurants and public places have signs in the bathroom that read, "Wash Your Hands." We also can become sick from eating contaminated food or drinking contaminated water. Using contaminated silverware that has not been **disinfected** could give us the same illness.

Methods of Direct Transmission	Methods of Indirect Transmission
Contact with an infected person	Contact with a droplet of mucous from an infected person
Contact with infected body fluids	Contact with contaminated objects, instruments, or equipment
Sexual transmission	Bites from bugs or animals
Contact with infected blood through a break in the skin	Ingestion of contaminated food or drink

direct transmission: the transfer of an infection by immediate contact with infected body fluid or tissue

The best defense you have as a healthcare worker is to wash your hands before and after patient contact, and to wear gloves when handling blood or other body fluids. **Bacteria** normally are present on your hands, but washing your hands will reduce the number of bacteria that are present.

bacteria: more than one of any of the small, one-celled microorganisms in the class Schizomycetes

The following procedure is the accepted method for handwashing to protect healthcare workers and patients from the spread of disease.

Figure 4-1: Wash your hands before and after patient contact to prevent the transmission of diseases.

Handwashing Technique

Materials needed:
- ✓ liquid soap
- ✓ dry paper towels

1. **Procedural Step:** Turn on the faucet. Adjust the temperature of the water to warm—don't let it get too hot!
   Reason: To avoid burning yourself.

2. **Procedural Step:** Always wet your hands with the fingertips pointing down into, but not touching, the sink.
   Reason: Keeping your hands down keeps your forearms dry and prevents contaminated water from your forearms from running over your clean hands. (In most cases, your hands will be dirtier than your arms anyway, so concentrate on getting your hands clean.)

3. **Procedural Step:** Use a liberal amount of soap and rub the palms of your hands together several times.
   Reason: This friction will create a lather and help remove any unwanted viruses or bacteria from the skin surface.

4. **Procedural Step:** Put the palm of one hand over the back of the other hand and briskly rub them together.
   Reason: All parts of the hands are capable of carrying germs.

5. **Procedural Step:** Repeat step #4 using the opposite hands.
   Reason: To clean the other hand.

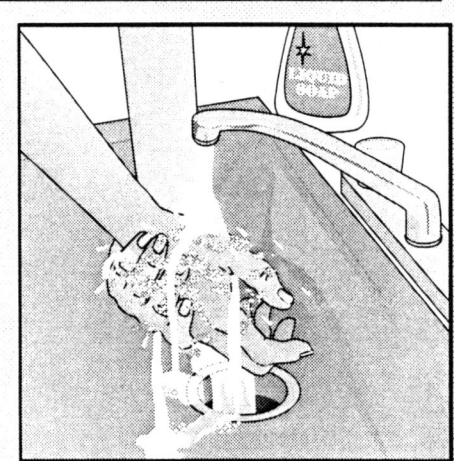

6. **Procedural Step:** Interlock the fingers of both hands and vigorously rub them together. You should scrub your hands for a total of two minutes.
   Reason: To remove harmful germs.

7. **Procedural Step:** Use an orange (cuticle) stick to clean under each nail. If a cuticle stick is not available, use a sterile brush.
   Reason: To remove germs from under the nails.

8. **Procedural Step:** Rinse all soapy lather from the wrists and hands, continuing to point the hands downward.
   Reason: To prevent contaminated water from your forearms from running over your clean hands.

Chapter Four • Asepsis

Handwashing Technique (Cont.)

9. **Procedural Step:** Leave the water running and dry all areas of the hands using a paper towel.
   Reason: *Paper towels are disposable and prevent the spread of germs.*

10. **Procedural Step:** Dispose of the wet paper towel. Obtain another paper towel and, placing the paper towel on the faucet handles, turn off the water. Make sure the towel is dry.
    Reason: *A wet paper towel allows microorganisms to pass through the towel and back onto your clean hands. The dry paper towel will shield your hands from germs on the faucet. THE FAUCET AND SINK ARE ALWAYS CONSIDERED TO BE CONTAMINATED.*

11. **Procedural Step:** Discard all debris and leave the sink and surrounding area clean, taking care not to recontaminate your hands.
    Reason: *The area must be ready for the next person who wants to wash.*

Proper handwashing will minimize the risk of spreading infection from one patient to another, from the clinical healthcare worker to patients, and from patients to the clinical healthcare worker. Handwashing must be done at the following times.

- WHEN FIRST ARRIVING TO WORK
- BEFORE PERFORMING EACH PROCEDURE ON A PATIENT
- DURING A PROCEDURE IF YOUR HANDS BECOME CONTAMINATED
- BETWEEN EACH PATIENT FOR WHOM YOU PROVIDE CARE
- AFTER USING THE RESTROOM
- AFTER REMOVING GLOVES FROM YOUR HANDS
- BEFORE EATING

Remember, handwashing is the key to successful medical asepsis.

Infections occur when a pathogen enters the cell. Infections are caused by **viruses, bacterium, fungi,** and **rickettsia.** Viruses are tiny microscopic organisms that are known to cause disease and cancer. Larger organisms called bacteria are present in the human body. It has been estimated that each of us carries 100,000,000,000,000 (10^{14}) bacterial organisms in and on our bodies. Many of these bacteria are harmless and some are beneficial. However some forms of bacteria are responsible for diseases like strep throat, pneumonia, and tuberculosis. Fungi are yeasts and molds that can cause allergies, athletes foot, and ring worm, and rickettsia are organisms that are responsible for many tropical diseases. Infections cause harmful alterations to the body's cells and structure. A person with an infection will have all or some of the following symptoms.

- pain
- redness
- swelling
- fever
- limited mobility
- foul smelling drainage
- **purulent** drainage

purulent: pus-like

At first, the symptoms are **localized** (limited to the area of infection). As the infectious disease spreads, the person will show signs and symptoms of generalized infection. When the infection spreads throughout the body, **septic shock** occurs, causing a rapid pulse, low blood pressure, and increased temperature. This patient will be very ill and require hospitalization and IV medications. Sometimes, however, a person carries the pathogens in his or her body and transmits the disease to others without being affected by the disease. This person is known as a **carrier** of the disease.

septic shock: a form of shock that occurs when pathogenic bacteria are present in the blood

Most microorganisms prefer to live in a moist, warm, and dark environment. These organisms multiply rapidly in decaying material. Many microorganisms need oxygen for survival, but the one that causes **tetanus** prefers an environment without oxygen. This pathogen is found in dirt and usually enters the body through a puncture wound. Stepping on a nail is an example of how a tetanus infection can be spread. Once the pathogen is inside the human body, the wound closes over and blocks out the oxygen. Without oxygen the bacteria multiply rapidly. This deadly disease can be prevented with a tetanus immunization. Therefore, anyone who comes to the ER must be asked about the date of his or her last tetanus shot. If the patient has an open wound, cut, or burn,

tetanus: a deadly bacterial infection of the central nervous system that results from a contaminated wound

and it has been longer than five years since his or her last tetanus shot, the person is given a booster shot to promote immunity from tetanus infection or **lockjaw**. Always make sure that the tetanus immunization is current before discharging a patient from the Emergency Room. If there is any doubt about current immunization, check with the doctor before allowing the patient to leave the ER.

lockjaw: a contraction or spasm of the muscles of the jaw

The Chain of Infection

The spread of pathogens can be thought of as a cycle or chain of events. (Figure 4-2) All links must be present for the disease process to continue.

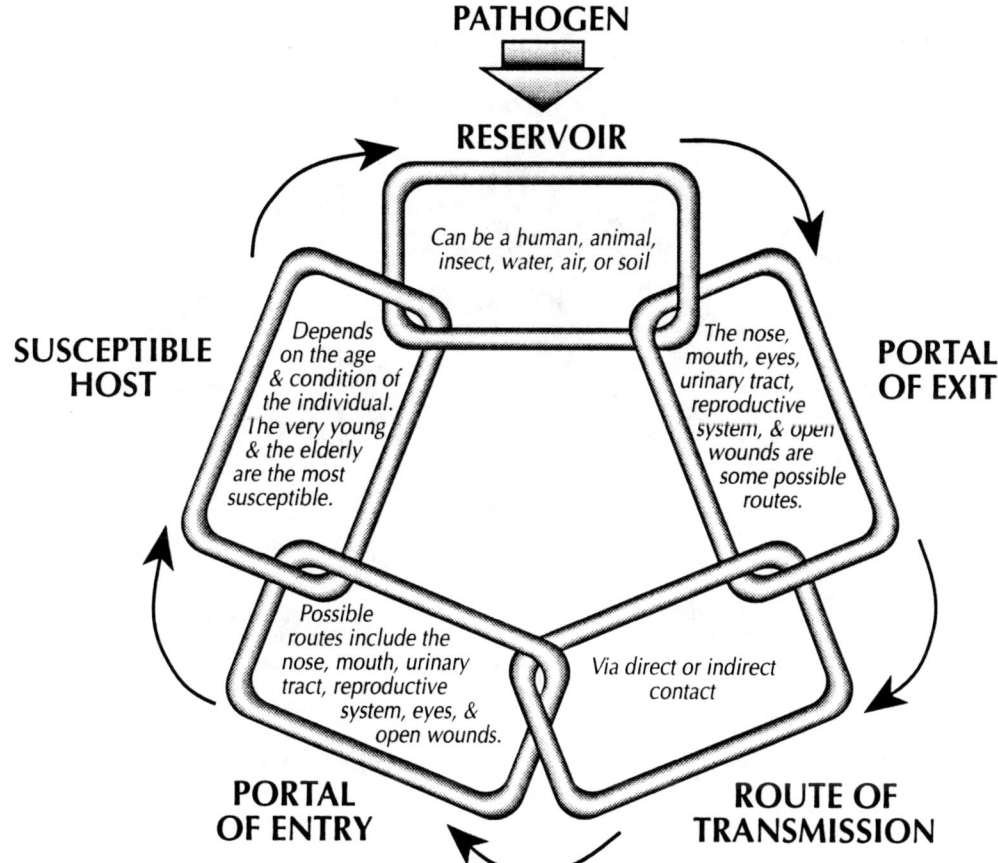

Figure 4-2: The Chain of Infection

The spread of disease can be stopped by removing any link in the chain of infection. (Figure 4-3) One way of doing this is to kill the bacteria before it enters a susceptible **host**. This can be done by changing the environment in which it lives. If the bacteria need moisture to survive, the environment should be clean and dry. If the bacteria require a temperature of 98.6 degrees, raise the temperature of the item to kill the bacteria. This is the principle of **sterilization**.

host: an organism that is invaded by a parasite and from which the parasite obtains its nutrition

sterilization: the complete destruction of all forms of microbial life

The following steps can help you prevent infection.

- Wash your hands frequently.
- Wear gloves.
- Use correct procedures.
- Keep yourself healthy and rested.
- Keep your **immunizations** up to date.
- Wash raw fruits and vegetables before eating them.
- Drink **pasteurized** milk.
- Use individually wrapped drinking straws in public restaurants.
- Maintain **asepsis** in the work environment.

immunization: a vaccination against disease

asepsis: a condition in which no pathogens are present

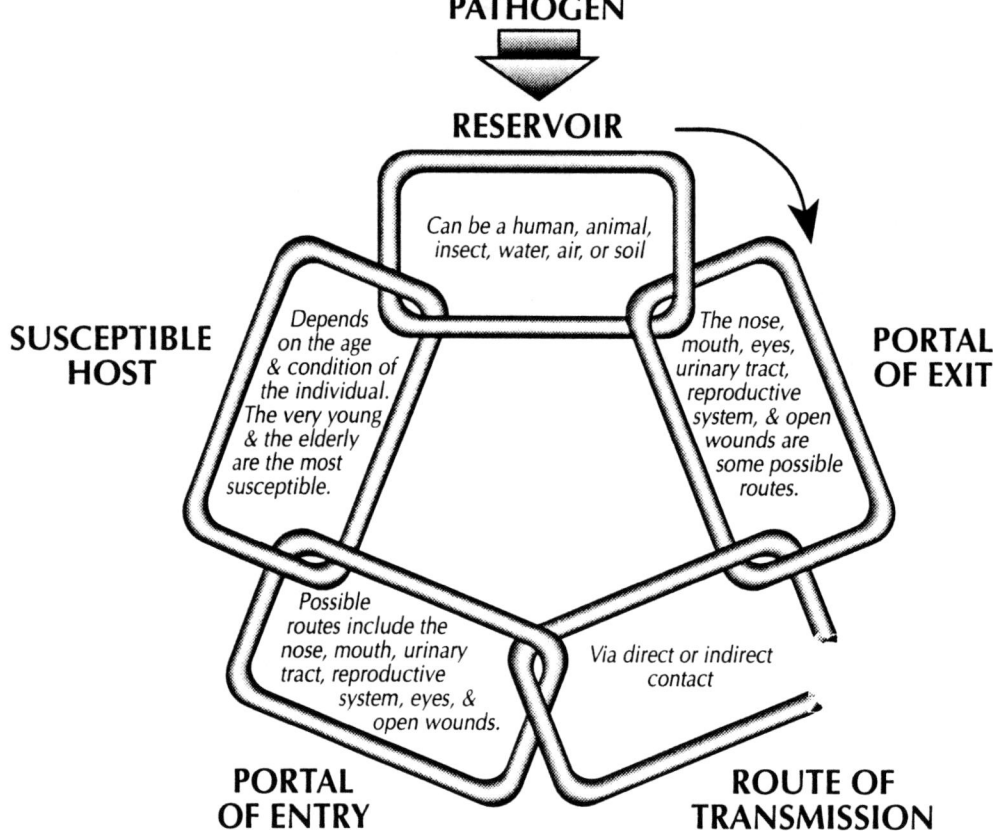

Figure 4-3: Breaking the Chain of Infection

Medical Asepsis

When **asepsis** is maintained, the transfer of disease is prevented. **Medical asepsis** is the destruction of organisms after they leave the body. Healthcare workers must continually take steps to reduce the number of **pathogens** in the environment. The goal is to prevent reinfection of the patient and **cross infection**. If contaminated instruments are used from one patient to the next, an infection is likely to occur. The following procedures and concepts are designed to promote the principles of medical asepsis.

medical asepsis: the removal or destruction of infected material or organisms

cross infection: the spread of contagious disease from one person in a hospital to another

- Use paper towels in public restrooms.
- Wash your hands prior to food preparation.
- Maintain a proper temperature for prepared food. (Proper temperatures are under 40° F for cold food, and above 140° F for hot foods).
- Wash your hands after using the bathroom.
- Use individual personal care items, lipstick, toothbrush, comb, etc.
- Wash your hands before and after patient contact.
- Wash your hands between patients.
- Wear disposable gloves when handling blood and other body fluids.
- Keep soiled and wet items from touching your uniform.
- Do not use supplies that have fallen on the floor for patient care.
- Avoid letting a patient cough or sneeze directly into your face. (Have the patient cough into disposable tissues.)
- Use disposable equipment whenever possible.
- Sterilize non-disposable items immediately after use.
- Avoid raising dust by not shaking linens.
- Keep soiled items in the dirty areas and clean items in the clean area.
- Shampoo your hair and keep it neat and off the collar.
- Bathe or shower daily.
- Keep your fingernails short and clean.
- Avoid wearing rings and bracelets that can harbor bacteria.

You can do a great number of things both on and off the job to decrease the chances of obtaining an infectious disease. The two most important things to remember are to WASH YOUR HANDS and WEAR GLOVES.

Surgical Asepsis

surgical asepsis: the prevention of infection before, during, and after surgery through the use of sterile technique

Surgical asepsis involves the use of **sterile technique** to ensure that supplies and equipment used for the care of patients are free from microorganisms. The use of sterile technique requires that you do the following:

- Wash your hands prior to touching instruments or the patient.
- Assemble all equipment prior to donning gloves.
- Don gloves using the correct procedure to avoid **contaminating** them.
- Maintain an awareness of the **sterile field**.
- Pour all liquids into sterile containers without splashing the liquid and without touching the container of liquid with the sterile container. To reduce the risk of pathogens falling from your hands or arms, do not extend the containers over the sterile field.

sterile field: the area considered to be free from contamination during a surgical procedure

sterile: aseptic; free from all contamination

To maintain surgical asepsis, instruments, dressings, **catheters**, and other items will come wrapped in a **sterile** package. These packages are opened carefully with clean hands, touching only the corners of the wrapper to prevent contamination of the contents, or the sterile field. The edge of the wrapper is considered to be contaminated, so do not touch it once you have donned gloves, and do not touch the sterile package itself with your clothing or your body. Since moisture promotes the growth of bacteria, avoid spilling any solution onto the sterile field. Never reach, cough, or sneeze over the sterile field, and never turn your back on it. Always hold sterile objects above the waist, and keep them in sight at all times so that an accidental contamination will be prevented. If an item used in a sterile area is accidentally contaminated, it must be replaced before use.

When is it necessary to use sterile technique?

- When an item is in contact with broken skin (i.e., cut, burn, surgery).
- When an item is used to penetrate the skin (i.e., sutures, injections, IVs, blood withdrawal, surgery).
- When a sterile body cavity is entered (i.e., catheterization, examination, **biopsy**, surgery).

biopsy: the removal of a small piece of living tissue for examination under a microscope

If you are ever in doubt as to whether or not to use sterile procedures, it is better to be safe than sorry. Use sterile technique rather than risk the possibility of the patient getting an infection. Patients can become infected when medical or surgical procedures are done and the sterile technique is broken. These hospital-acquired infections are called **nosocomial infections.**

Chapter Four • Asepsis

Using Sterile Gloves

Sterile gloves must be worn when using sterile technique. Touch only the inside of the gloves as you put them on.

Donning Sterile Gloves

Materials needed:
✓ 1 pair sterile gloves

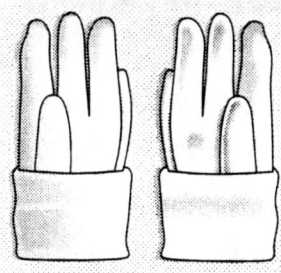

1. Procedural Step: Obtain a pair of sterile gloves in your hand size.
   Reason: For proper fit.

2. Procedural Step: Inspect the glove package for signs of contamination: water spots, moisture, tears, rips.
   Reason: The gloves must be sterile.

3. Procedural Step: Remove all jewelry and scrub your hands.
   Reason: Universal precaution. This reduces the number of normal bacteria on the skin.

4. Procedural Step: Dry your hands well.
   Reason: Moisture increases bacterial growth.

5. Procedural Step: Peel open the sterile package and lay the inner package on a flat, clean, dry surface so the end nearest you shows the word "cuff."
   Reason: This will allow you to don them properly.

6. Procedural Step: Open the inner wrapper like a book with the right glove on the right, touching only the folded edge of the wrapper.
   Reason: A 1-inch border around the wrapper of the inner package is considered to be contaminated. The inside of the package is sterile.

7. Procedural Step: With the non-dominant hand pick up the glove touching only the inside of the cuff. (You will glove your dominant hand first.)
   Reason: The inside of the glove will be next to the skin. This area is not sterile.

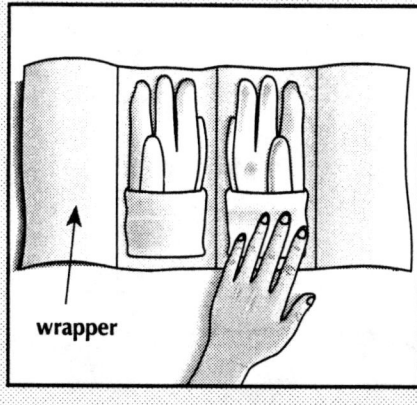
wrapper

Donning Sterile Gloves (Cont.)

8. **Procedural Step:** Keeping your hands above your waist, step back from the table or tray. Hold your hands away from your body and slide your dominant hand into the sterile glove. Leave the cuff folded for now.
Reason: To avoid contamination.

9. **Procedural Step:** Pick up the second glove with the gloved hand by slipping the fingers of the gloved hand under the cuff.
Reason: Sterile surfaces can only touch other sterile areas.

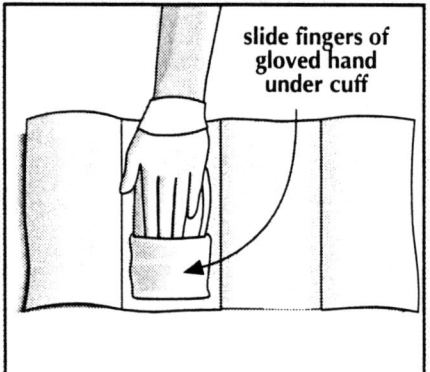

slide fingers of gloved hand under cuff

10. **Procedural Step:** Slide your second hand into the glove, keeping the gloved thumb extended (like a hitchhiker) to avoid touching your skin. Avoid touching anything else while you do this.
Reason: To avoid contamination.

11. **Procedural Step:** Move the glove up the hand and slide the fingers into position.
Reason: To secure the glove properly.

12. **Procedural Step:** Unroll the cuff of the first glove, touching only the outside of the glove. Do not touch your bare arm with the sterile fingers of the glove.
Reason: To avoid contamination.

touch only the outside of the glove

13. **Procedural Step:** Unroll the cuff of the second glove, touching only the outside of the glove. Do not touch your bare arm with the sterile fingers of the glove.
Reason: To avoid contamination.

14. **Procedural Step:** Interlock your fingers to adjust the gloves, but do not adjust the gloves below the heels of your hands.
Reason: To obtain a snug fit and to avoid contamination.

15. **Procedural Step:** Keep your hands above your waist and do not touch anything outside the sterile field. Ask for assistance if needed.
Reason: To avoid contamination.

Once the sterile gloves are in place, only sterile objects can be touched. When not directly performing a procedure, the hands are held above the waist away from any objects. It is important to obtain all supplies and equipment before putting on gloves to prevent touching the areas that are not sterile. If you need additional supplies and equipment you will need to call for assistance. If your glove should accidentally become contaminated, you must obtain a new sterile pair and follow the correct procedure for putting them on. If your glove rips or gets a hole in it you must replace it immediately.

To remove your gloves, use the procedure on the next page.

Removing Contaminated Gloves

Materials needed:
✓ a trash can lined with a red biohazard bag

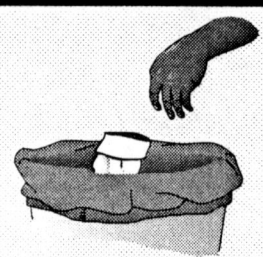

1. **Procedural Step:** Hold your gloved hands over a trash can.
   Reason: You will throw away your used gloves.

2. **Procedural Step:** Without touching the bare skin of your forearm, grasp the contaminated (or outside) area of the dominant glove cuff (approximately 1-2 inches from the top) with your gloved nondominant hand.
   Reason: To avoid contamination.

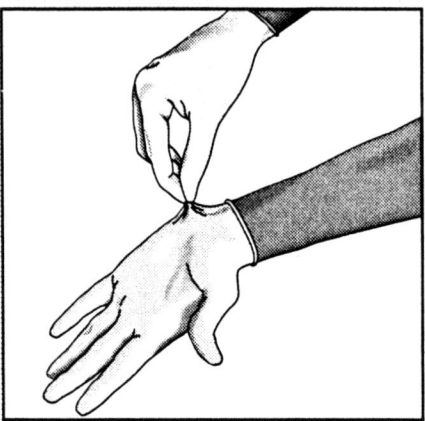

3. **Procedural Step:** Pull the glove off. It will now be inside out. Do not snap gloves when removing them.
   Reason: Microorganisms on the gloves could become airborne.

4. **Procedural Step:** Discard the glove directly into the trash container.
   Reason: Gloves cannot be reused.

5. **Procedural Step:** Place the bare fingertips of the dominant hand inside the other glove and grasp it near the top. Don't let your bare hand touch the contaminated part of the glove.
   Reason: To avoid contamination.

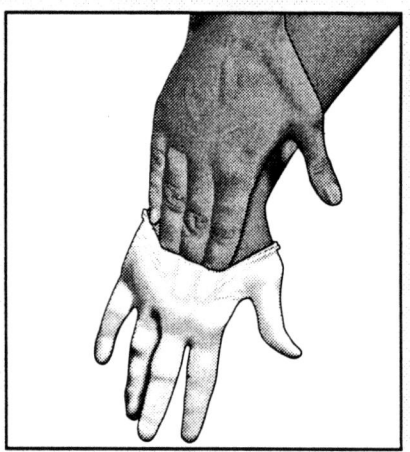

6. **Procedural Step:** Pull the second glove off. It also will be inside out. Discard it in the trash can lined with a red biohazard bag.
   Reason: Gloves cannot be reused. They are considered hazardous waste, and therefore must be disposed of in the proper manner.

7. **Procedural Step:** Wash your hands thoroughly before touching anything.
   Reason: Universal precaution.

Chapter Four • Asepsis

Care of Equipment and Supplies

All nondisposable instruments and equipment must be cleaned carefully before use by **disinfection** and **sterilization**. Disinfection can be done with chemicals or moist heat (boiling). All non-disposable patient care items must be disinfected and sterilized before they are used again. It is far better to use disposable equipment, but some precision instruments are not available as disposable items and, therefore, must be cleaned after use. (Figure 4-4)

disinfection: the removal of infectious material from an item

Instruments and equipment are prepared for sterilization with a thorough cleaning known as sanitization. **Sanitization** is the careful scrubbing of all used instruments and equipment with a brush and special detergent. The instruments are washed and rinsed in hot water and towel or air dried. Instruments should be cleaned as quickly as possible after use. Blood should not be allowed to dry on an instrument. If you cannot immediately sanitize instruments, let them soak in a solution of detergent and water.

Always pay close attention to sharp objects. Sharp instruments should be soaked by themselves to avoid accidental puncture wounds. Keep sharp objects together and take care not to injure yourself. As you clean the instruments make sure that they are in good working order. Any broken, dull, or bent supplies should be sent for repairs or replaced. If an instrument needs a lubricant, use a silicone-based product and follow the manufacturer's directions. Sanitization, disinfection, and sterilization are procedures that are done to guarantee a bacteria-free environment for the patient. Instruments are sanitized, then disinfected, then sterilized. For example, it doesn't do any good to put a bloody hemostat in soaking solution unless it has been scrubbed (sanitized) first, because the dried blood won't come off without scrubbing.

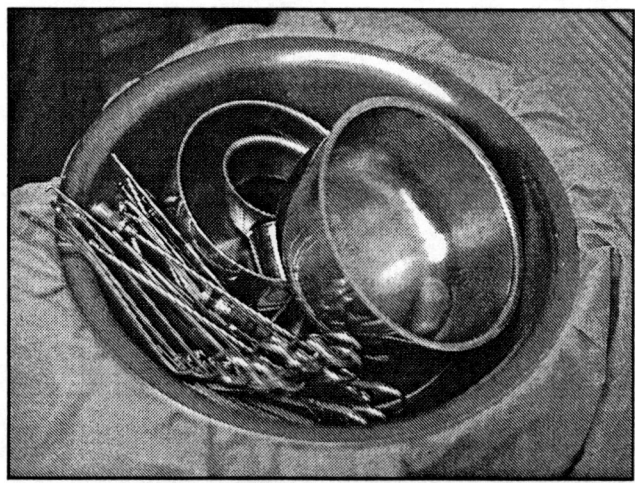

Figure 4-4: Nondisposable instruments must be disinfected and sterilized after use.

autoclave:
a device that is used to sterilize items by steam under pressure

If sterilization is done in **Central Supply**, the clean items are sent to that department and replaced. If you have an **autoclave** in the ER you may be responsible for sterilizing the department's instruments. (Figure 4-5) Items are wrapped and packaged for sterilization. All instruments that have been sterilized will have a tape on the outside of the package and a marker tag on the inside of the package. During sterilization this tape and tag will turn a different color. The package is dated, and if the equipment inside it is unused for more than one month it will require resterilization. Some items are sealed in plastic wrappers and may not expire until six months after sterilization. They will expire much later than those that are unsealed.

Figure 4-5: Autoclave

Do not use a sterile package that has become wet, torn, or punctured. It is considered to be contaminated. Always look at the package before opening it; check for signs of contamination, tears, holes, and the expiration date.

Due to the variety of clinical procedures that are performed in the Emergency Department, many different types of instruments are used in the ER. Most of the instruments are disposable, such as suture sets, but some specialized instruments and trays may come from Central Supply and are cleaned after use, sterilized, and repackaged.

Make the following checks when cleaning the instruments.

1. Check for any signs of rust or deterioration.

2. Check for sharp fragments that could tear the surgeon's gloves.

3. Check scissors for sharpness.

4. Check teeth and serrations for exact fit.

5. Check the tension in spring handled instruments.

6. Check to make sure the instruments are not closed.

7. Check to make sure instruments are not bunched together.

Chapter Four • Asepsis

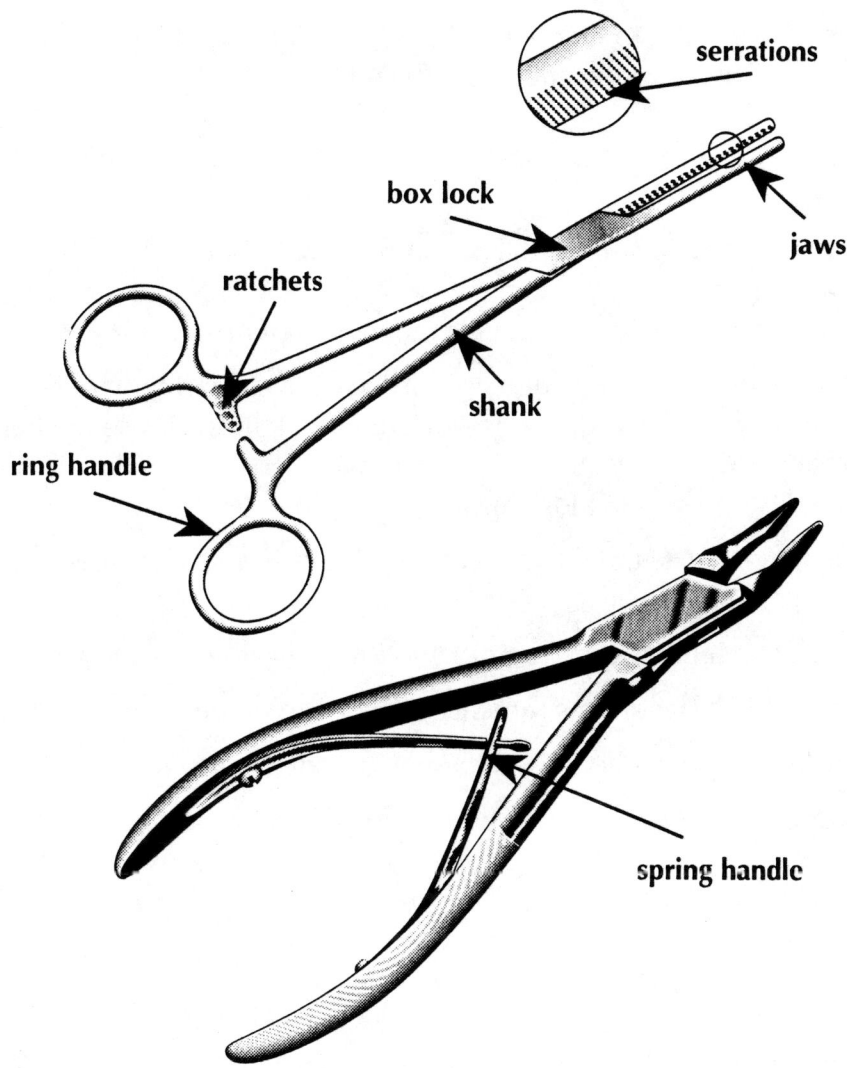

Figure 4-6: Parts of Instruments

All sharp disposable instruments are disposed of in the rigid, red, plastic sharps containers. Nondisposable instruments are soaked in disinfecting solution, scrubbed, and then sent to Central Supply for sterilization.

Many minor surgical procedures are done in day surgical centers, urgent care centers, and in emergency care units. The doctor or nurse may ask you to get a special instrument, so it is essential to know the names of the instruments commonly used in this department. Furthermore, you will need to know these names when you stock the supply carts, take inventory, and document reports.

You will need to be able to recognize the following types of instruments if you are going to work in an emergency department.

- **scalpel**: a small, straight surgical knife that has a handle and a detachable blade
- **scissors**: cutting instruments that can be straight or curved. They usually are named for the procedure for which they are used (i.e., bandage scissors, suture scissors). The tips may be blunt or sharp.
- **forceps**: tweezer-like instruments that may have a spring handle. Some have tooth-like clasps on the handle called ratchets. These ratchets are used to close the instrument at three or more positions. The tips can be serrated (saw-like teeth for grasping) or smooth.
- **hemostats**: clamps that have a handle. These instruments are curved or straight.
- **clamps**: instruments used to hold two items together (i.e., towel clamps)
- **probe**: a long, slender instrument used for exploration
- **speculum**: an instrument used to open a body cavity
- **curette**: a spoon-like instrument used for scraping

There are numerous instruments, and as you become more experienced you will learn the names of more of them. As you assist the physician you will notice that there is a special instrument for each job that is done. A physician needs specialized instruments for much the same reason a mechanic needs specialized tools for automotive repairs. Just as a mechanic needs certain tools for brake jobs, transmission work, etc., a physician needs certain tools for eye examinations, ear examinations, surgeries, etc.

The following pages illustrate some of the instruments you are likely to encounter in an emergency department.

INSTRUMENTS TO LEARN

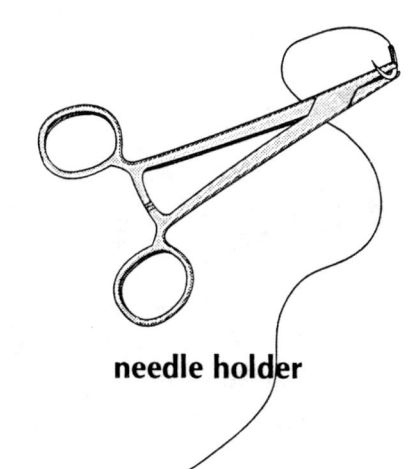
needle holder

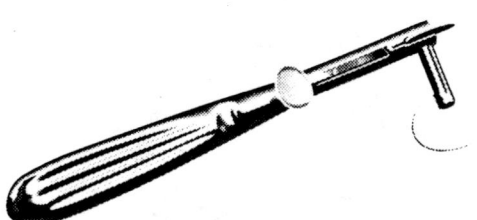
ring cutter

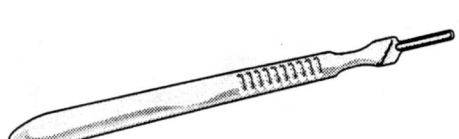
knife handle

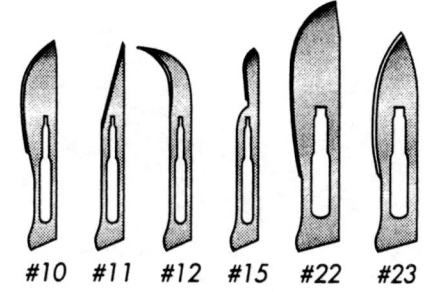
#10 #11 #12 #15 #22 #23
scalpel blades

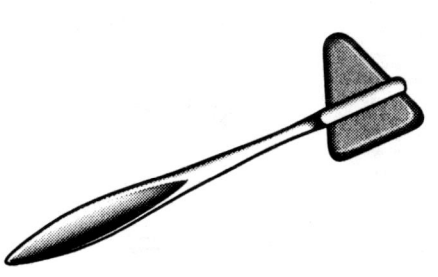
percussion hammer

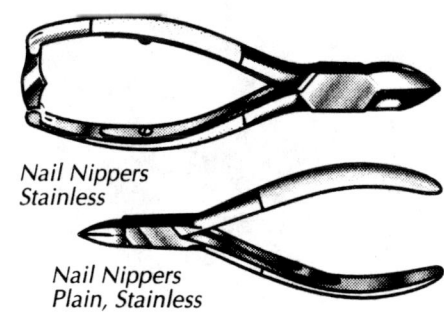
Nail Nippers Stainless

Nail Nippers Plain, Stainless

nail clippers

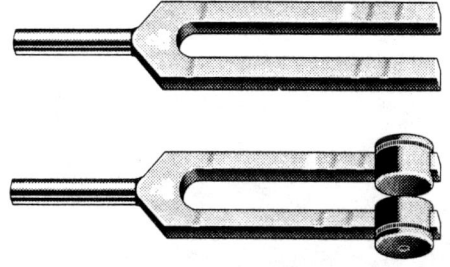
tuning fork

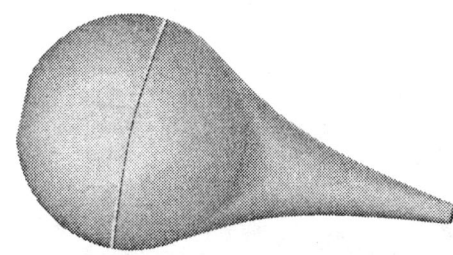
ear syringe

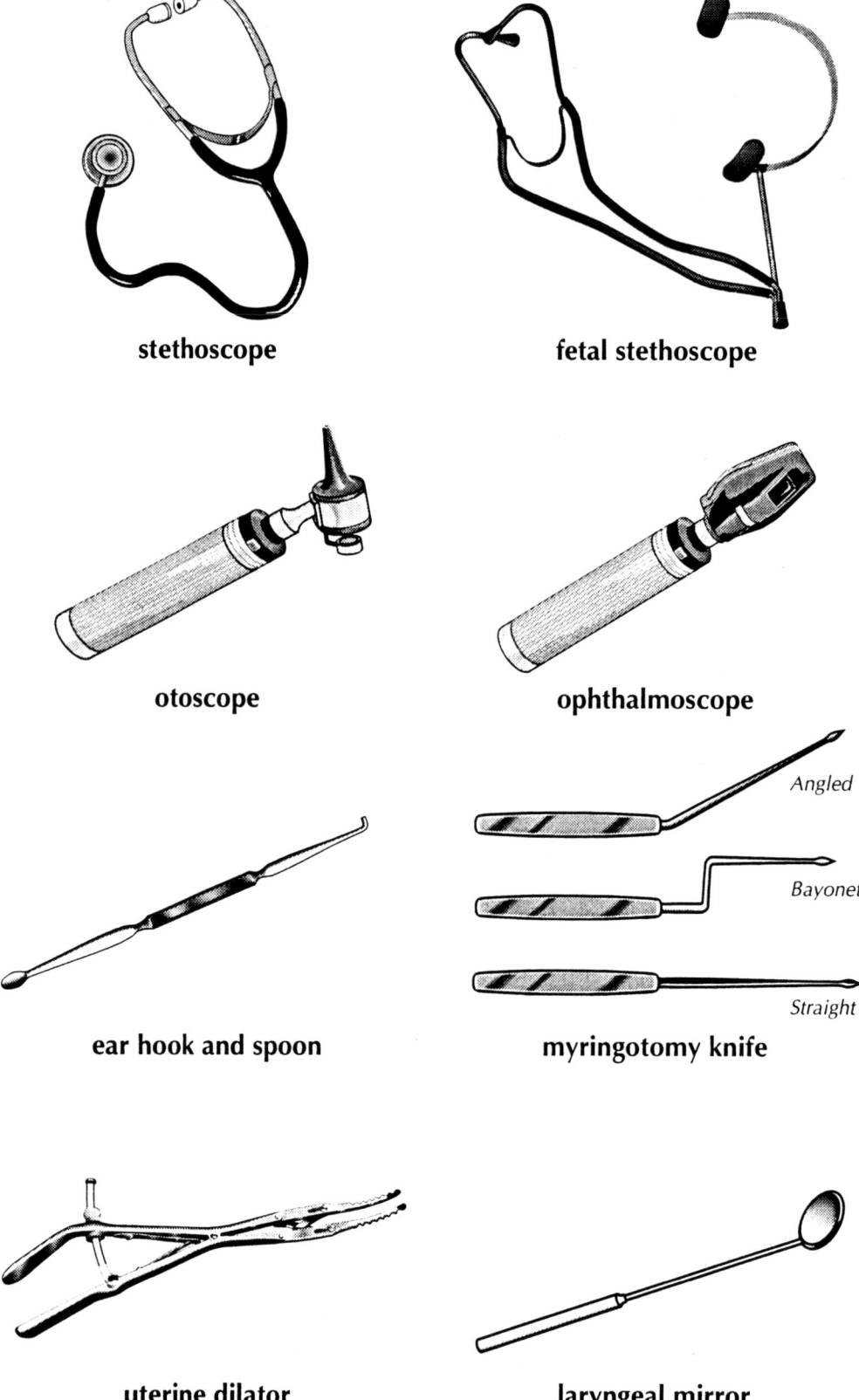

Chapter Four • Asepsis

PROBES

grooved probe

metal tongue depressor

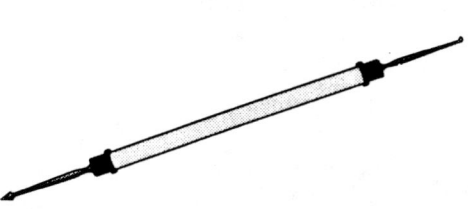

eye spud

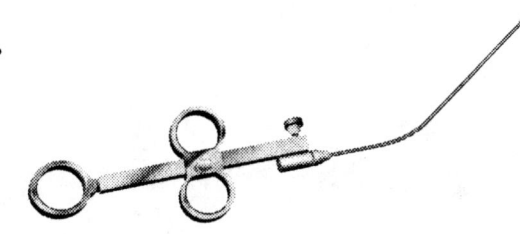

nasal snare

RETRACTORS

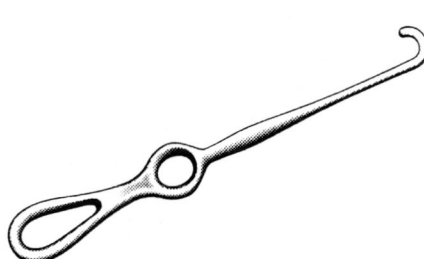

finger retractor

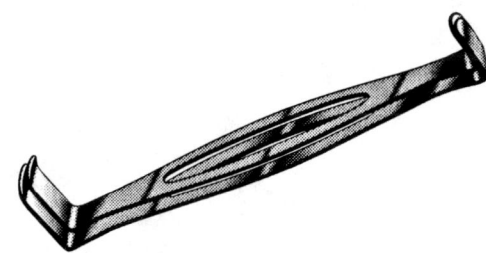

army/navy retractor

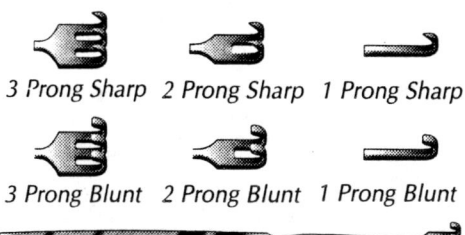

skin hook

SPECULUMS

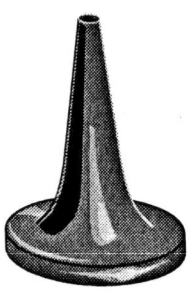
ear speculum

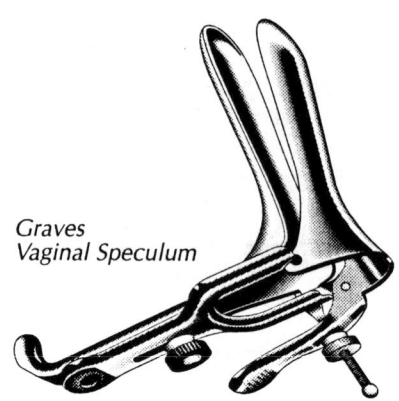
Graves Vaginal Speculum
vaginal speculum

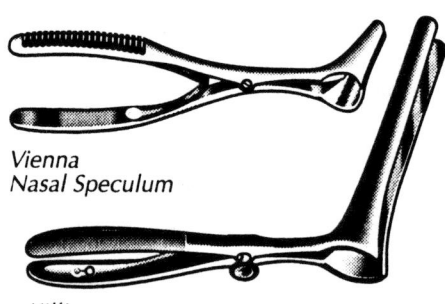
Vienna Nasal Speculum
Killian Nasal Speculum
nasal speculum

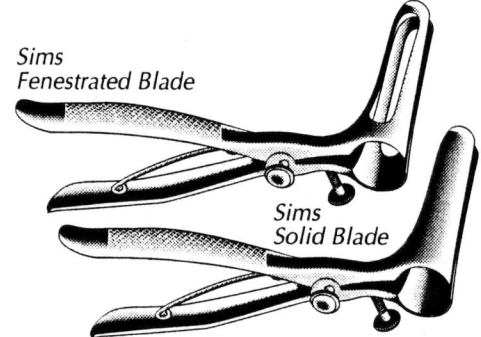
Sims Fenestrated Blade
Sims Solid Blade
rectal speculum

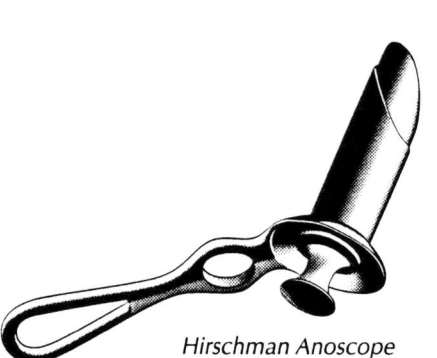
Hirschman Anoscope
anoscope

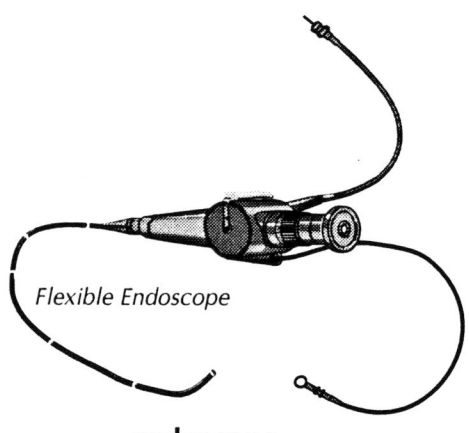
Flexible Endoscope
endoscope

Chapter Four • Asepsis

SCISSORS

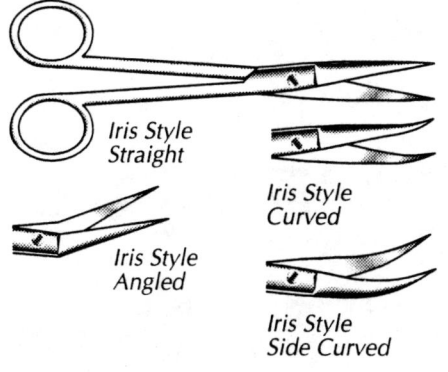

fine scissors

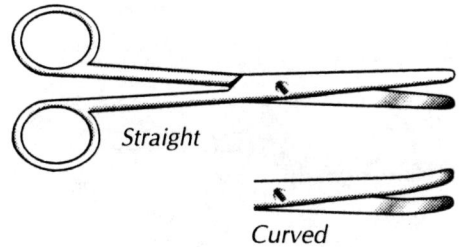

Metzenbaum scissors

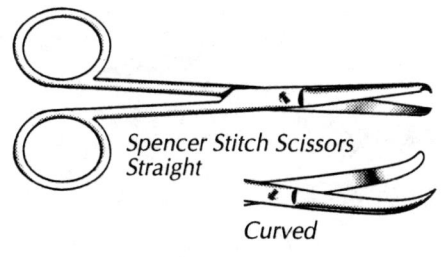

suture scissors

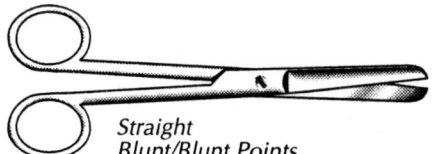

operating scissors

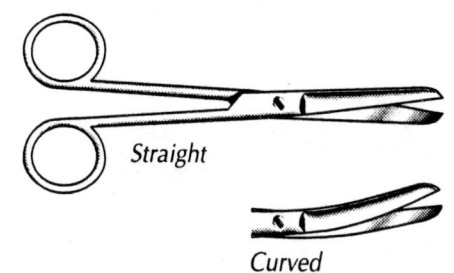

bandage scissors

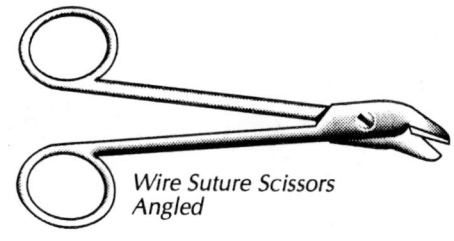

Mayo dissecting scissors

FORCEPS

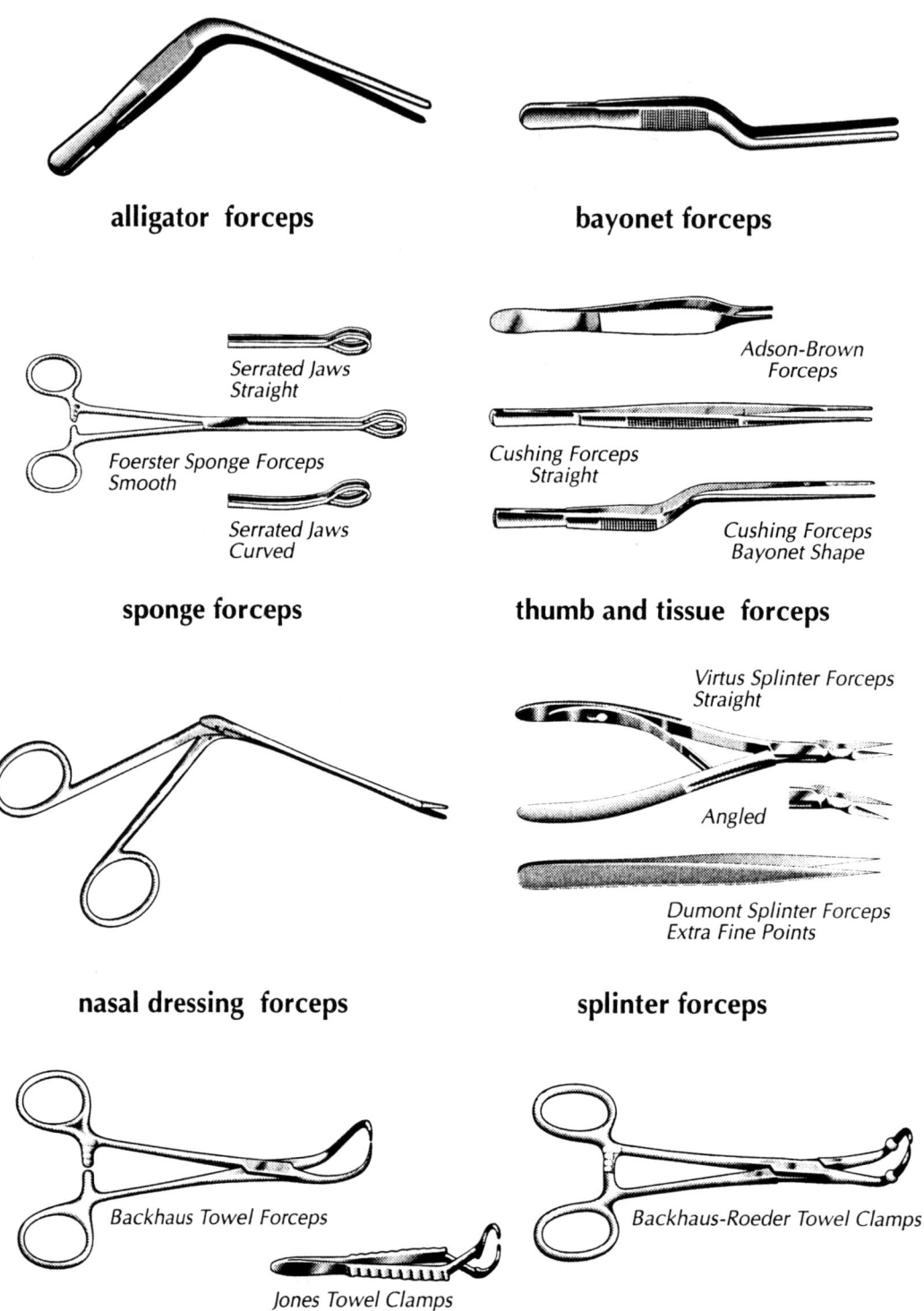

Chapter Four • Asepsis

FORCEPS CONTINUED

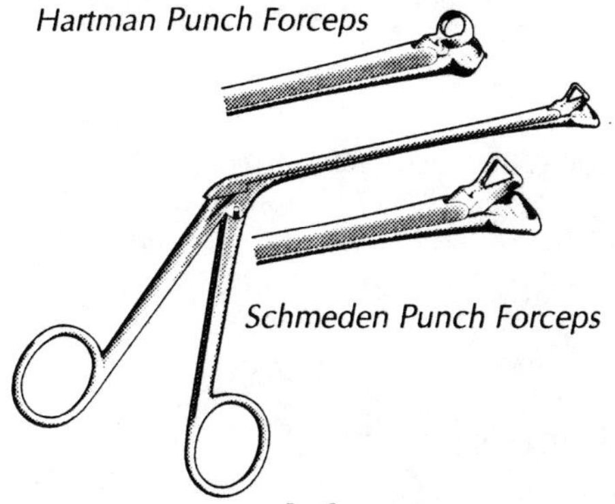

punch forceps

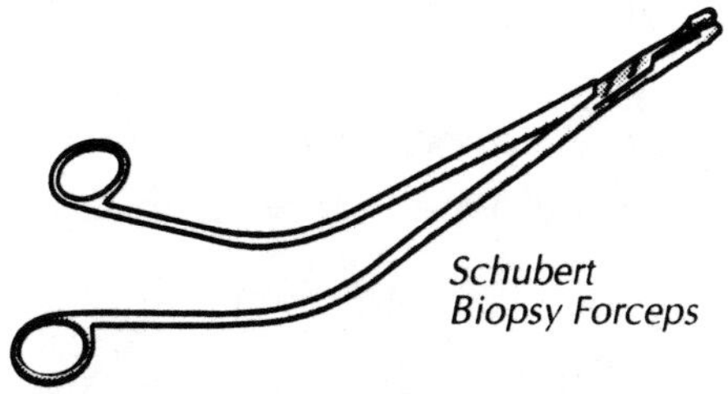

- Hartman Punch Forceps
- Schmeden Punch Forceps

biopsy forceps

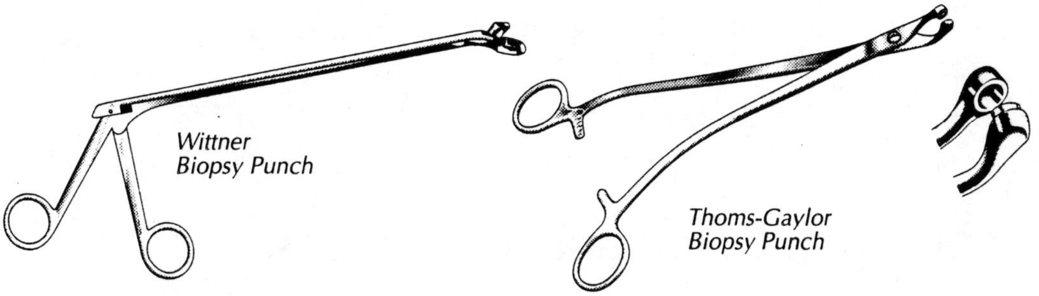

- Schubert Biopsy Forceps

biopsy punch forceps

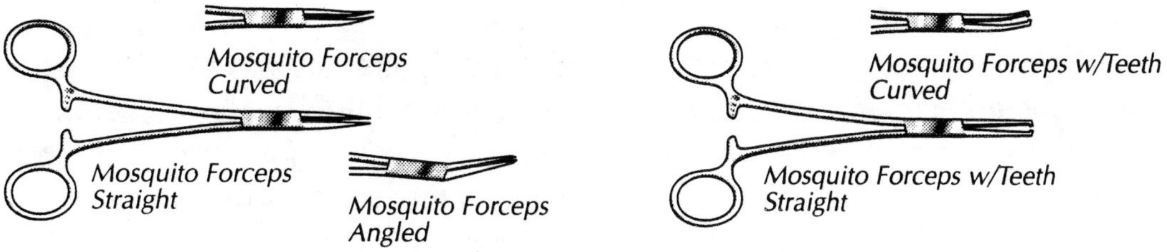

- Wittner Biopsy Punch
- Thoms-Gaylor Biopsy Punch

mosquito forceps

- Mosquito Forceps Curved
- Mosquito Forceps Straight
- Mosquito Forceps Angled
- Mosquito Forceps w/Teeth Curved
- Mosquito Forceps w/Teeth Straight

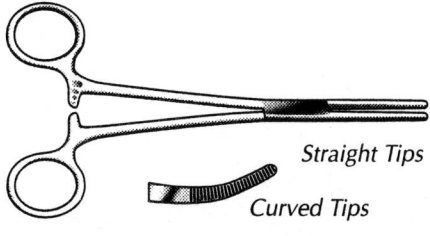

kelly forceps

- Straight Tips
- Curved Tips

Medical instruments are expensive precision tools. Remember the following key points when handling instruments to keep them in the best working condition.

- Always handle instruments carefully; they are delicate and can be damaged by rough handling.
- Keep instruments separated to prevent damage to delicate structures.
- Be careful with sharp instruments.
- Use care when handling lens-type instruments.
- Store instruments with ratchets in the open position.
- Clean nondisposable instruments immediately after use.
- Check instruments before use and make sure they are not bent, they close properly, work effectively, and are not bent.

Controlling Communicable Diseases

Every effort must be made to control the spread of infection. Many patients pass through the Emergency Department in a day's time. Patients who come to the ER are not yet diagnosed, so it is not certain what disease they may have. Furthermore, visitors, family members, and staff members all carry germs and the degree of activity and traffic in the department increases the potential for the rapid spread of infection. It is best to think in terms of **universal precautions** as you perform your daily duties. Developed by the Centers for Disease Control, universal precautions are guidelines for preventing the transmission of infections from all patients to other patients, visitors, and personnel.

universal precautions: a concept that stresses that all patients should "be assumed to be infectious for HIV, Hepatitis B, and other blood-borne pathogens." Guidelines to prevent infection include washing hands and wearing gloves, masks, gowns, and protective eyewear whenever exposure to body secretions exists.

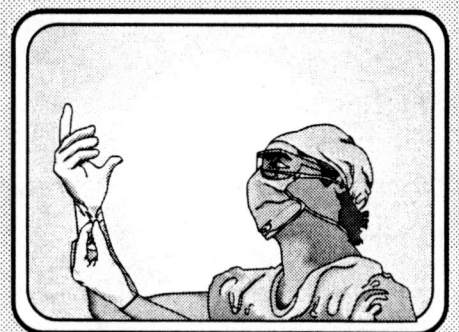

Universal Precautions

1. Wash your hands before and after patient contact.

2. Wash your hands before and after gloving.

3. Wash your hands after leaving the patient's room.

4. Wear gloves when your hands will be in contact with body fluids (i.e., blood, urine, feces, wound drainage, oral secretions, **sputum**, **vomitus**, and **amniotic fluid**).

5. Wear gloves when touching **mucous membranes**.

6. Wear gloves when touching skin that is not intact.

7. Change gloves after each patient contact.

8. Wear a mask and/or goggles when eyes or mucous membranes may be splashed with substances.

9. Wear a gown when soiling your clothing is likely.

10. Avoid needle-stick injuries.

11. DO NOT RECAP OR BEND NEEDLES.

12. Use a rigid, plastic, puncture-resistant container for all disposable needles and other sharps.

13. Use disposable pocket masks for rescue breathing.

pertussis: whooping cough; an acute, infectious disease characterized by inflammation of the mucous membranes and sudden bouts of coughing that end in a whooping inspiration

Universal precautions are required when caring for patients who have an airborne infection such as **chickenpox**, **diphtheria**, **Haemophilus influenza**, **measles**, **meningitis**, **pneumonia**, **mumps**, **pertussis**, **rubella**, or **tuberculosis**. Furthermore, the following additional steps should be taken for these patients:

- Place the patient in a private area.
- Keep the door closed.
- Wear a mask when in direct contact with the patient.

Only personnel who are immune from chickenpox, measles, and rubella should care for patients with these diseases. Pregnant staff members should not care for these patients if there is someone else who can do it.

A patient with a communicable disease will be admitted to an **isolation** room. Care must be taken in the transport of this patient to his or her room. If the patient has an airborne disease, place a mask over his or her nose and mouth. A clean sheet can drape the gurney. Take the closest route to the new room and avoid delays in the hallways.

Upon returning to the ER, the gurney must be disinfected and all items double bagged. One person waits outside the contaminated room and holds the laundry bag or plastic trash bag with his or her hands protected by a wide cuff. The person inside the room places the bag of laundry or bag of trash into the one outside the room. The bag is closed so that only the inner surface is contaminated. (Figure 4-7)

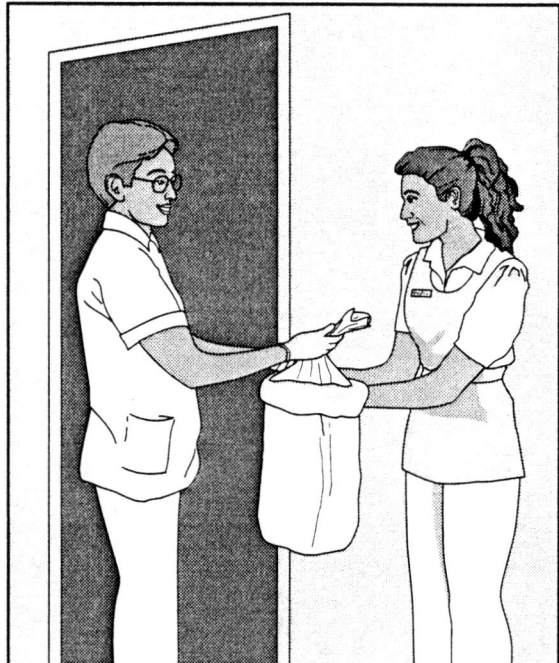

Figure 4-7

Chapter Four • Asepsis

The room in the Emergency Department where the patient stayed also will need to be thoroughly cleaned. The Housekeeping Department should be notified that this is not a routine cleaning, but an isolation room. Dispose of all disposable equipment and supplies in double red bags, or in bags marked *isolation*. Clean all contaminated equipment, double bag it, and sterilize it.

Chapter Summary

As an emergency department technician, you always must be aware of the possibility of infection. Whenever you are in doubt about the potential for transmission of disease take universal precautions! The prevention of the spread of disease is everyone's responsibility—INCLUDING YOURS! This involves using **sterile technique** for minor surgical procedures done in the Emergency Department, and taking proper steps in the care and cleaning of instruments. Disinfection, sterilization, and equipment and instrument checks will do much to prolong the life of the instruments as well as prevent the spread of infection.

Chapter Four • Asepsis   4-31

Name _____
Date _____

Student Enrichment Activities

1. Label the links of the chain of infection.

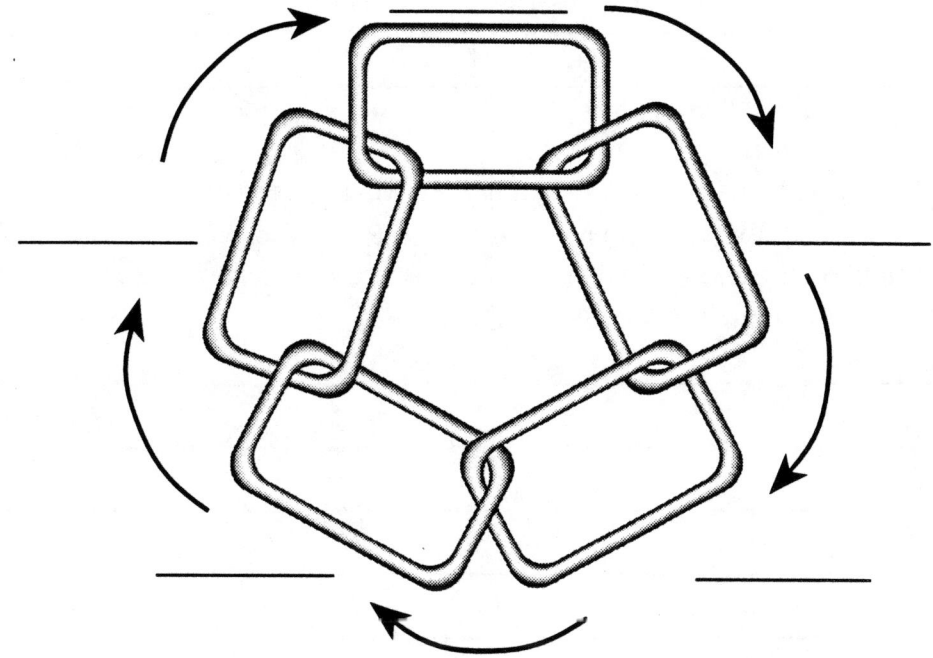

2. Select a patient in the clinical setting who has an infection and answer the following questions. How did the patient acquire the infection? How was it transmitted? How did it enter the patient's body? Why was this patient susceptible to an infection?

_____
_____
_____
_____
_____
_____
_____
_____
_____
_____

3. You are requested to assist Dr. Michaels with a sterile procedure. What part of the package and wrapper are you permitted to touch when preparing the sterile tray for use?
   _____

4. List three conditions that promote the growth of microorganisms.
   A. _____
   B. _____
   C. _____

5. Mr. Johnson injured his hand while gardening last week. At the time he thought it was a minor injury, so he only put a bandage on it. He is in the ER today with an open wound on the hand that has purulent drainage. Describe how you will use universal precautions to obtain a wound culture and apply a sterile dressing and bandage.
   _____
   _____
   _____
   _____
   _____
   _____

6. List three things an ER technician can do to prevent the spread of infections.
   A. _____
   B. _____
   C. _____

7. Using a clock to time yourself, wash your hands. Use the correct procedure by scrubbing between the fingers. How long did it take? _____ minutes.

Chapter Four • Asepsis

Name _____

Date _____

Match the following words with their definitions.

_____ 8. medical asepsis   A. cleaning by scrubbing with soap

_____ 9. surgical asepsis   B. free from all living microorganisms

_____ 10. sanitization   C. soap

_____ 11. sterilization   D. an agent that destroys infectious organisms

_____ 12. disinfection   E. the destruction of all living organisms

_____ 13. detergent   F. the destruction of organisms after they leave the body

Chapter Five
Admitting Procedures

Objectives

After completing this chapter you should be able to do the following:

1. Define and correctly spell all key terms.
2. Interview a patient and prepare a patient chart.
3. List three reasons for maintaining accurate medical records.
4. Explain the principle of patient confidentiality.
5. Triage a group of patients.

Key Terms

- acute
- ashen
- confidentiality
- DOA
- disposition
- emergent
- expired
- intoxicated
- non-urgent
- urgent

Emergency Department Documentation

When a patient is admitted to the Emergency Department, information must be gathered and documented on a medical record. This chapter will describe the type of data that is needed, various ways to obtain this information, and how to fill out an admission record. Although each hospital has its own forms, the information on them is essentially the same from institution to institution. As an emergency department technician, you will need to understand the importance of accurate data collection and proper documentation on the medical record.

The Importance of Medical Records

Medical records, also known as patient charts, are necessary for both medical and legal reasons. Every patient has an individual medical chart on which all the information needed to plan the total care of the patient is recorded. The chart is used to communicate with all members of the healthcare team. If the patient is transferred to another facility, portions of the medical record will accompany the patient to maintain continuity of care. If the patient is admitted to the hospital, the emergency care record becomes a part of the total patient chart. Pre-hospital care that is administered by paramedics or an emergency medical technician is documented on a field report form and also becomes a part of the patient's chart. Medical records provide vital statistics. Statistics are used for medical research and help document how often a facility is used. This information is useful to government agencies, and becomes increasingly

Chapter Five • Admitting Procedures

important for financial reimbursement of Medicare and other government sponsored healthcare programs. Documentation on the medical record is important so that the hospital will be paid for services rendered. A patient's medical record is a legal document and is recognized by a court of law.

Computers

Emergency records must contain factual and accurate information. Many facilities have computers at the admission desk to aid with the collection of information. If your facility uses computers for admission procedures, you will be responsible for knowing how to operate that equipment.

The information on a patient's medical record is confidential. To ensure that patient confidentiality is maintained, a form of computer security must be available. In some situations, there may be limited access to the computer itself, or the user may have to enter a special code before gaining access to the information it contains. Computers can save valuable time in emergency admissions. For example, if the patient has visited the facility before, all the information is stored in the computer and may be accessed immediately. All that is required to admit this patient again is to verify the information, and update it if necessary.

Figure 5-1: Vital patient information can be stored on computers.

Triage

Patients are treated according to the severity of their condition. **Triage** is the prioritizing of patients for treatment. Patients who are brought by ambulance are generally admitted directly to the hospital, or are placed on a gurney in the ER for immediate evaluation. Some patients who are brought by ambulance are able to wait for treatment if their condition is not life-threatening. Patients who are escorted by paramedics and who have received advanced life support (ALS) treatments in the field are considered more **critical** and will be seen first. As an emergency department technician you may be assigned to the admission desk. It is important for you to be able to determine which emergencies can wait until information is obtained, and which patients need to be seen immediately by the physician. Terms used to describe the severity of illness or injury may vary among hospitals. The following is a list of some of the more common terms.

non-urgent: able to wait for care

| GREEN | mild / non-urgent | able to wait for care |

urgent: to be seen as soon as possible

| YELLOW | moderate / urgent / delayed | should be seen soon; medication or treatment is needed |

acute: sudden onset

emergent: life-threatening; urgent; sudden or unforeseen

| RED | acute / critical / emergent / immediate | the condition is life-threatening and the patient must be seen now |

Chapter Five • Admitting Procedures

A patient who arrives by private automobile, or who walks in to the ER may be more difficult to triage. Pay attention to the **ABCs:**

- **A**irway
- **B**reathing
- **C**irculation

Sometimes a patient may have a life-threatening condition that may not appear serious at first. However, any of the following symptoms should alert you to a possible serious injury:

- difficulty speaking
- difficulty breathing
- noisy, labored breathing
- skin color is pale, **ashen**, gray, or blue
- skin rash
- sweating
- dizziness, faintness, or mental confusion
- chest pain
- jaw pain
- head pain
- pain that radiates down the patient's arm
- complaint of indigestion
- bleeding
- shock
- high fever

ashen:
a gray skin color seen in shock patients

All of the above may be indications of a serious condition. Do not waste time gathering information. The patient should be taken by wheelchair to the treatment area promptly and the nurse notified immediately.

Admitting Patients

The person at the admissions desk is usually the patient's first contact with the hospital. When you work at the admissions desk, it is important for you to be calm, understanding, and professional. Patients can tell if you are genuinely interested in them; your attitude will project an image of the entire hospital. First impressions are lasting ones, and your professional assurance in a difficult situation can mean a great deal to the patient, his or her family, and the hospital. The patient may be in pain, frightened, **hostile**, angry, or **intoxicated**. Emergency patients usually are anxious. They are eager to know who will be taking care of them, how soon they will be treated, and what is going to happen to them. The patient's family members are also anxious and can become impatient or demanding. It is up to you to try to keep the patients and their families calm and informed.

intoxicated: in a drunken state

The length of a patient's stay in the emergency department can be very short or very long. It depends on what types of tests are ordered, how many other patients are ahead of the patient, and what is going on in the rest of the hospital. It also depends on whether there is a bed ready for admission or transfer, how busy the doctor is, and whether the on-call specialist is available.

The on-call specialist is a physician who is specially trained in **orthopedics**, **pediatrics**, **trauma** surgery, or any other specialty. He or she is available for a 24 hour period to see patients requiring that specialized care. These physicians must be called in from home or the office, so their travel time must always be considered when estimating waiting periods for patients and their families.

Admitting patients can be very stressful. You must concentrate on establishing a **rapport** with the patient and family. You need to communicate effectively and understand the apprehension that is felt by the patient and his or her family members. A positive attitude is necessary when dealing with both the condition and the behavior of patients. You cannot be judgmental or show disapproval about the way a patient looks, smells, dresses, speaks, or chooses to live. Your job is to help all those who need emergency care regardless of their way of life. If the patient is not mentally competent, is a danger to themselves or others, or is gravely disabled, the law allows the hospital to temporarily detain patients for a psychiatric evaluation. If a crime is involved, the patient will be placed in protective custody, and a police officer will guard the patient. Consider your personal safety when dealing with hostile patients. Hostility often is associated with alcohol or substance abuse. If a patient or anyone else acts in a threatening manner, disrupts the operation of the Emergency Department, or interferes with patient care, call security for assistance. If additional assistance is needed call the local police department.

The ER Record

The ER record, or chart, is a written document that contains the following patient information:

- time of arrival
- method of arrival
- physician's evaluation of the patient
- tests and procedures performed on the patient
- medical treatment given to the patient
- nursing care received by the patient
- status of the patient (i.e., admitted to the hospital, discharged home, transferred to another facility, **expired**)

expired: died

Figure 5-2 shows an example of an emergency record. Each hospital has its own form, but the information on the forms is standard on all patient records. It is important to become familiar with the forms used by your hospital. By becoming familiar with the forms you will be able to complete them more efficiently, saving valuable time in the treatment of patients.

Figure 5-2: An Emergency Record

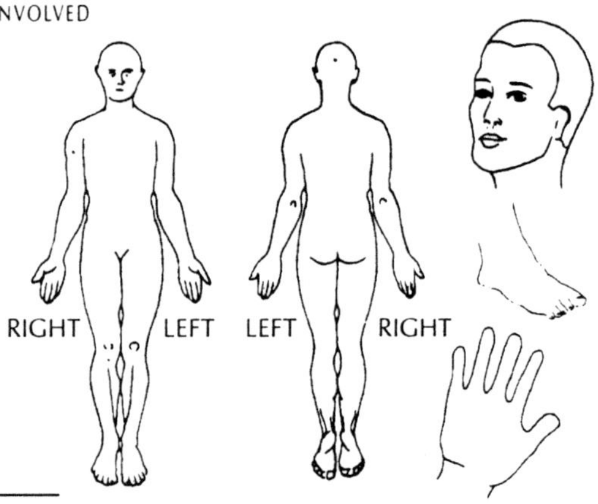

Obtaining Accurate Information

Emergency care is very important. Often many things must be done at once. When a patient is admitted to the ER, the first thing you must do is find out why the patient is there, and obtain as much medical information about the patient as you can. The best source of information is the patient. However, if the situation is life-threatening, or if the patient is not fully conscious, it may be difficult to obtain any information at all. A family member is the next best source of information, but if the patient is unable to talk and there is no family present, information can be obtained from a bystander, neighbor, police, or the paramedic who was at the scene. Sometimes a person will be brought to the ER who is unable to communicate and who has no identification or history available. These patients are given the name John or Jane Doe. Emergency care is started immediately, and additional information is obtained as soon as possible.

The patient is usually the most accurate source of information, so obtain all the information you can from him or her. Use your best judgement at all times. If the patient is in a serious state, you may have to wait to obtain the information. However, accurate information can greatly assist the physician and nurses who are caring for that patient. Do your best to get a clear and correct account of what happened. Record it and all other necessary information as accurately as you can on the patient's chart.

Figure 5-3: Accurate patient information is vital to the patient's treatment.

Data Collection

Collecting data means gathering information. Patient information can be obtained by using your five senses and making observations. This type of data is called **objective data**. Information also can be obtained from the patient. This is called **subjective data**. Both objective and subjective data are used to make an assessment or evaluation of the medical condition.

The first thing to do when collecting objective information is to note the patient's general appearance.

- Is the patient of average age and weight?
- Does he or she complain of pain?
- Does the patient's facial expression indicate discomfort?
- Is there a body position, (i.e., holding an arm, clutching of the chest, etc.) that indicates the location of the pain?
- Does the patient appear to be in good health?
- What about personal hygiene? Is the person dirty? Does he or she have matted hair or body odor?
- Is the patient's behavior and dress consistent with the type of injury or illness?
- Is the patient conscious?
- Is the patient alert and well-oriented?
- Is the patient confused?
- Can the patient communicate?

By questioning the patient, an emergency department technician can obtain the following subjective data about the patient:

- name
- address
- age
- place of employment

Chapter Five • Admitting Procedures

- chief medical complaint
- description of the pain
- history of previous hospitalization
- physician's name
- known allergies
- current medications

The registered nurse obtains objective data such as: a physical assessment, breath sounds, neurological exam, bowel sounds, a cardiovascular assessment, and a skin assessment. Next, you must establish the patient's chief complaint. This is subjective information. Ask the patient the following questions.

- What problem brings you to the Emergency Department today?
- When did the pain start? (How long ago?)
- Where does it hurt the most?
- Does the pain move around or does it **radiate**?
- Can you describe the type of pain? (sharp, ache, stabbing, crushing, heavy, or throbbing)
- Can you describe the intensity of the pain? (mild, moderate, or extreme)
- Is the pain continuous or does it come and go?
- Does anything relieve the pain? (medication, position change, rest, heat, cold, elevation, etc.)

When asking about the problem, find out the time of **onset**. You can get this information by asking a few questions.

- When did you first have this pain?
- What were you doing?
- How did it happen?

The next thing to determine is the **duration** of the pain.

- How long does the pain last?

It also is important to find out the particular characteristics of the **symptoms.**

- Did you ever experience anything like this before?
- What makes it better?
- What makes it worse?
- Can you describe it in your own words?

It is helpful to get the patient's own words to describe the severity of symptoms. Many times the patient can describe the symptoms so accurately that the physician can immediately diagnose the problem...

> "I was working in the garden and saw a bee land on my left arm. I felt a stinging sensation, my arm started to swell. It became red and hot, and my hand began to tingle."

From this information the doctor would be able to conclude that this person had a bee sting that probably caused an allergic reaction.

When taking a patient history, information is gathered about the current problem. The patient may have a long history of health problems and it is important to obtain information that is important to the current admission quickly. If the patient has a history of diabetes, or heart or breathing problems, these factors could greatly affect the care of the patient. For example, if a 56 year old male entered the ER saying, "I have chest pains and feel dizzy," the fact that he had chicken pox at the age of two or stitches in his arm when he was ten is not relevant to the treatment of his chest pains. The fact that he had open heart surgery last year and is a diabetic who took **insulin** this morning, but didn't eat breakfast is VERY important. This information will help the physician prescribe the proper treatment for this patient.

Usually, you can determine if the patient is under the care of a physician for a current medical problem by asking him or her. However, some patients may have a condition that they are unaware of and, therefore, are not currently receiving treatment or medication. A previous illness should be documented on the patient's medical history or recorded as *unknown* if that information cannot be determined.

Chapter Five • Admitting Procedures

Ask the patient if he or she takes medications regularly. If so, record the name of the medication, the amount, and when the medication was last taken. Some patients may arrive with pill bottles full of medication they are currently taking. A list of these medications should be made and the medications placed with the patient's belongings and given to the relatives to take home. If the patient has been poisoned, or is the victim of an **overdose** (**OD**), he or she may have been instructed to bring in the container of poison. In this case the physician will want to see the container and the name of the chemicals. If someone has been poisoned make sure you get the following information:

1. When was the poison taken?

2. How was it taken? (i.e., swallowed, injected, inhaled, absorbed)

3. How much was taken?

4. Do you know how much was in the container before the poison was ingested? Was any spilled?

5. What kind of symptoms is the patient having now? Is the patient vomiting or confused, or have **diarrhea**, blisters, rashes, or burns?

Ask the patient if he or she has any allergies. People can be allergic to medication, foods, or substances. If there was an allergic reaction, what were the symptoms? Did the patient have a rash? Did the patient become nauseated? Did the patient stop breathing? Document the allergy, the reaction that followed, and when the reaction occurred.

Ask the patient if he or she has had a **tetanus** injection (shot) and when the last one was received. Document this in the space provided. If the patient has an open wound, this information is very important. If it has been more than five years since the last tetanus injection, the patient will need to receive another one. If they are unsure, the tetanus injection will be given as a precaution.

There is a place on the emergency chart for the time of admission. The time of admission should be the time the patient first entered the ER. As procedures are done, they are documented on the chart and the time is noted as well. Some hospitals use military time. If this is the case, 1:00 pm becomes 1300 hours. See Figure 5-4 for military times.

a.m.		p.m.	
Standard Time	Military Time	Standard Time	Military Time
12:00 (midnight)	00:00	12:00 (noon)	12:00
1:00	01:00	1:00	13:00
2:00	02:00	2:00	14:00
3:00	03:00	3:00	15:00
4:00	04:00	4:00	16:00
5:00	05:00	5:00	17:00
6:00	06:00	6:00	18:00
7:00	07:00	7:00	19:00
8:00	08:00	8:00	20:00
9:00	09:00	9:00	21:00
10:00	10:00	10:00	22:00
11:00	11:00	11:00	23:00

Figure 5-4

Whichever procedure your hospital follows, remember that proper documentation is essential, and that patient charts contain a special place to indicate the time of admission, procedures, treatments, and discharge. Time is valuable information in legal matters. Because time is so important, some facilities have time clocks that stamp the time of laboratory and x-ray procedures as they are ordered. A computer also may be programmed to indicate the time certain tests are requested, when they are completed, and when the results are reported to the physician.

There is a place on the chart to indicate how the patient arrived, such as by private automobile, ambulance, walk-in, or wheelchair. Another space is used to indicate the **disposition** of the patient. Was he or she admitted, discharged (released home), **DOA**, or transferred to another facility?

All of this data is collected and added to the emergency record. It then becomes a permanent part of the total patient chart. This valuable information can assist both the nurse and the physician in providing emergency care to the patient in a timely manner.

disposition: the outcome of a patient's visit (i.e., admitted, discharged, or expired)

DOA: abbreviation for *dead on arrival*

In addition to the emergency record, a patient admission form is filled out by an admitting clerk or an emergency department technician. Information that is needed for this form is vital information. Vital statistics include the following patient information:

- legal name
- marital status
- street address
- telephone number
- place of employment
- spouse's place of employment
- insurance company and policy number
- workers compensation information
- responsible party
- social security number
- next of kin
- previous hospital admission history
- religious preference

Vital statistical information is needed to bill the patient for services rendered. There is also a consent for treatment form that must be signed by the patient prior to treatment. If the patient is a minor, this form must be signed by the parent or guardian. The consent for treatment form may be a separate form, or it may be attached to the admission form.

Collecting information for the medical record is a very important responsibility delegated to the ER technician. Every effort should be made to communicate effectively, listen to the patient, and document the information accurately on the patient chart. The following is a sample of proper documentation of a patient admission on the chart. (Figure 5-5)

Figure 5-5: Patient Chart

EMERGENCY DEPARTMENT NURSING ASSESSMENT/DOCUMENTATION RECORD

- BED #: 7
- PMD: B. Wallace
- NAME: John Doe
- AGE: 67
- WEIGHT: 190
- MEDICAL RECORD NO.: 000-000-002
- DATE: 3-28-93
- HOW ARRIVED: ☒ AMBULANCE; CARRIED FROM ☒ SNF

CHIEF COMPLAINT: Fall from w/c c/o pain Ⓛ hip

- ARRIVED WITH: ☒ SPOUSE
- VISUAL ACUITY: OD 20/20 C ☒ GLASSES
- BP: Ⓛ 160/90, T 98, R 16, P 82 AP, R 16
- INITIAL RHYTHM: NSR

LEVEL OF CONSCIOUSNESS: ☒ AWAKE ALERT

MENTAL ASSESSMENT:
- PHYSICAL APPEARANCE
- GAIT: Unstable
- HYGIENE: ☒ Normal
- OVERALL PE: ☒ Normal
- MOOD/AFFECT: ☒ Appropriate, ☒ Cooperative
- MEMORY-RECENT: ☒ Intact
- THOUGHTS: ☒ Clear
- SPEECH: ☒ Normal

MEDICAL HISTORY: ☒ HYPERTENSION, ☒ CARDIAC
- OTHER: Surg 1990 Ⓡ hip
- ALLERGIES: ☒ NKA
- MEDS: ☒ NONE
- LAST TETANUS: unk
- LNMP: N/A

TIME	BP	PULSE	RESP	TEMP
0930	164/90	88	16	
0100	170/88	84	14	
1030	168/80	82	16	

RESPIRATORY: CHEST SYMMETRICAL Y
- BREATH SOUNDS R/L: CLEAR

BLEEDING: ☒ NONE

SKIN: COLOR: ☒ NORMAL; MOISTURE: ☒ DRY; SKIN TEMP: ☒ WARM

GU: (none checked)
GI: (none checked)
FONTANELLES: (none checked)

INJURY/SKIN INTEGRITY: LABEL AND SHADE AREAS INVOLVED
- A - ABRASIONS
- B - BRUISE
- C - BURNS
- D - SWOLLEN
- E - LACERATION
- F - PUNCTURE
- G - POSSIBLE FX
- H - C/O PAIN
- I - REDDENED
- J - DECUBITUS
- K - RASH
- + PULSE PRESENT
- - - PULSE ABSENT

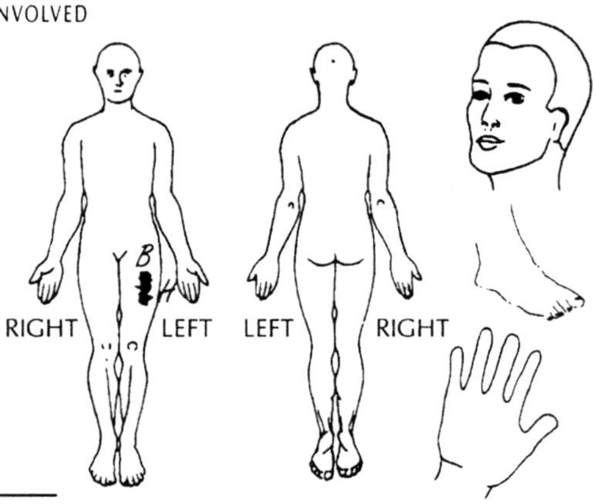

SPINAL PRECAUTIONS: (none checked)

ALL WOUNDS CLEANSED WITH _____

PUPIL SIZE AND REACTION: 9 8 7 6 5 4 3 2
- N = NORMAL S = SLUGGISH F = FIXED

PULSES EXTREMITY MOVEMENT:
- S = STRONG
- W = WEAK
- A = ABSENT
- D = NOT PALPABLE BUT PRESENT WITH DOPPLER

ADULT GLASGOW COMA SCALE
- EYE OPENING: Spontaneous 4, To Voice 3, To Pain 2, None 1
- VERBAL RESPONSE: Oriented 5, Confused 4, Inappropriate Words 3, Incomprehensible Words 2, None 1
- MOTOR RESPONSE: Obeys Command 6, Localizes Pain 5, Withdraw (Pain) 4, Flexion (Pain) 3, Extension (Pain) 2, None 1

CHILD GLASGOW COMA SCALE UP TO 3 YEARS OLD
- EYE OPENING: Spontaneous 4, Reaction to Speech 3, Reaction to Pain 2, None 1
- MOTOR RESPONSE: Obeys Command 6, Localizes Pain 5, Withdraw (Pain) 4, Flexion (Pain) 3, Extension (Pain) 2, None 1
- CRYING: Consolable 4, Inconsistently Consolable 3, Inconsolable 2, None 1
- INTERACTS VERBAL RESPONSE: Inappropriate 4, Moaning 3, Irritable, Restless 2, None 1

PATIENT CHART

Chapter Five • Admitting Procedures 5-17

> Mr. John Doe was transferred from the skilled nursing facility to the emergency room via ambulance. Mr. Doe fell from the wheelchair and is complaining of pain in his left hip. There is a 6 cm bruise on his left thigh. Mr. Doe arrived with his wife. He is alert and awake and in no acute distress. His blood pressure taken while sitting up is 160/90, oral temperature 98.4, respirations 16, and apical pulse 82 and regular. He has a history of a previous hip surgery on the right hip done in 1990.

Patient Confidentiality

Patients have a legal right to **confidentiality**. This means that hospitals, physicians' offices and other healthcare facilities are legally bound to keep all patient information private. Information that is needed in order to provide proper medical care is very personal. All patient information is confidential and cannot be discussed outside the healthcare environment. Healthcare workers never should discuss hospital cases using the patient's name or other identifying information outside the hospital. Nor should they discuss patient problems in the hospital with anyone not directly involved with the patient's care. Written permission must be obtained from the patient to release his or her medical records to another facility or information to a third party (such as an insurance company). Patients trust healthcare workers to keep their confidence. This trust cannot be broken.

confidentiality: privacy; refers to the limiting of access to information to authorized personnel only

Sometimes a friend, relative, or employer of the patient may ask about the patient's condition. Every effort should be made to reassure anxious family members and friends that the appropriate care is being provided; but specific information about a patient's condition is best related by the physician or nurse. There are few exceptions to the confidentiality rule. These exceptions are cases in which a birth, death, or crime is involved. Healthcare workers are required to report and provide information about all births, deaths, communicable disease, suspected child abuse, elder abuse, poisoning, animal bites, sexual assaults, gunshot wounds, stabbings or physical assaults to the proper authorities. If you suspect any of the above situations, report the information to the physician immediately. Failure to report it can result in legal action and fines.

Patients Who Refuse Treatment

Patients who are mentally competent and who do not wish to be treated cannot be forced into receiving care. Forcing a patient to stay against his or her will could be considered **false imprisonment**. The physician will advise the patient of the serious nature of the illness or injury and describe the medical treatment needed. If the patient does not want to be treated, the hospital has an *AMA* (Against Medical Advice) form that should be signed before releasing the patient. (Figure 5-6)

**RELEASE FROM RESPONSIBILITY FOR
LEAVING MEDICAL CENTER AGAINST MEDICAL ADVICE**

Date _____ Time _____

This is to certify that _____, a patient at (facility name), is leaving the medical center against the advice of the attending physician and the medical center administration. I acknowledge that I have been informed of the risk involved and hereby release the attending physician, and the medical center, from all responsibility and any ill effects which may result from this action.

Witness_____ Patient or Responsible Party_____

Figure 5-6

This form includes a place for the date, time, patient name, patient signature, and witness signature. If the patient is refusing treatment, he or she should be encouraged to sign this form. However, if he or she refuses, document on the medical record that the patient was advised to seek medical attention, refused care, and refused to sign the AMA form. You should also record the time the patient left the facility, and the method he or she used (i.e., driven home by husband, walked out, left by taxi, etc.).

Chapter Summary

The medical record is a very important document. Information recorded on it must be accurate and thorough. This information is a legal record of patient care. It is essential that the person filling out the ER admission form accurately record the time and method of admission. The chart must be filled in as completely as possible. Information that is documented as described by the patient should be in quotation marks, for example, "I was hit in the leg with a baseball." Patient information is confidential. Although chart forms will differ in format for each facility, there is universal information that is necessary in every emergency room. As you practice filling out the forms in the student enrichment activities you will become familiar with the medical record.

Chapter Five • Admitting Procedures 5-21

Name_____
Date_____

Student Enrichment Activities

1. List three reasons for maintaining a patient chart.

   A. _____
   _____

   B. _____
   _____

   C. _____
   _____

2. What is patient confidentiality? Why is it important?

   _____
   _____
   _____
   _____
   _____
   _____

3. Triage the following patients using the terms; emergent (e), urgent (u), or non-urgent (n).

   _____ A 3-year-old who took ten aspirin tablets and is crying.

   _____ A firefighter with smoke inhalation and a cough.

   _____ A college student with cold and flu symptoms for five days.

   _____ A pregnant lady with abdominal pain and pressure.

   _____ A tree trimmer with something in his right eye and blurred vision.

   _____ An adult male with a sore throat.

   _____ An 8-year-old who fell off monkey bars and has pain in the wrist.

   _____ A mechanic with second and third degree burns on his chest and face.

   _____ A 55-year-old **asthmatic** with shortness of breath and wheezing.

4. Using the forms on the following pages, admit these patients to the ER.

   A. John Smith, a 34-year-old plumber for AJAX Plumbing Company, 12568 West Elm Street, Forest Falls, Idaho, 93124, injured himself at work. His construction supervisor brought him to the ER in the company truck. John has a bloody towel covering his right hand and says that he got his hand caught in a pipe bender. This accident just happened and it took about ten minutes to drive from the job site. John is allergic to Penicillin and breaks out in a rash when he takes it. He appears to be in pain and says that his "hand is killing him." He can't remember when he last had a tetanus shot and hates needles. He doesn't take any medication and has been "pretty healthy." He is married, has two children and lives at 408 Maple Street in Forest Falls. His company has Green Diamond Insurance and the supervisor has the information. John wants you to call his wife, Carolyn, at work. She works full-time at Northern State Bank on Main Street in Forest Falls.

   B. Joey Smith, 18 months old, and 20 lbs. has been carried into the emergency room crying and hot. His mother says he has been ill for 24 hours, and seems to have an earache and a fever. His mother carried him into the emergency room and says that he has been a healthy baby until now and is current with all his immunizations. The baby has a rectal temperature of 103, a pulse rate of 120, and respirations are 22.

   C. Jane Johnson, a 33-year-old, 125 pound female is admitted to the emergency room following an MVA (motor vehicle accident). She was treated by paramedics at the scene and brought in by ambulance. She is complaining of neck pain, right arm pain, facial lacerations, and leg pain. She is disoriented and confused. She responds to pain and is able to move all extremities. There is a 4 cm laceration on her forehead, a bruise on the right arm and left leg. Her skin is dry and vital signs are blood pressure 110/60, pulse 88 and irregular, respirations 16 and temperature 98.6. She arrived with a cervical collar and backboard in place. There is no medical history but she is allergic to Iodine.

Chapter Five • Admitting Procedures

EMERGENCY DEPARTMENT
NURSING ASSESSMENT/DOCUMENTATION RECORD

BED #	PMD		
NAME	AGE	WEIGHT	MEDICAL RECORD NO.	DATE

HOW ARRIVED ☐ WALKED ☐ WHEELCHAIR ☐ AMBULANCE ☐ CRUTCHES ☐ CARRIED FROM ☐ HOME ☐ SNF ☐ OTHER:

CHIEF COMPLAINT TIME _____ INFORMANT ☐ SELF ☐ PARENT ☐ OTHER:

ARRIVED WITH: ☐ SELF ☐ PARENT ☐ SPOUSE ☐ FRIEND ☐ POLICE ☐ PARAMEDIC ☐ OTHER:

VISUAL ACUITY: OD ___ C ___ ☐ GLASSES ☐ CONTACT LENS

F0912-43-1		11166PC		LOSS OF CONSCIOUSNESS	
ALERTED	FILED	ALERTED	FILED	ALERTED	FILED

BP L○— R___ T___ O___ P___ AP___ R___ INITIAL RHYTHM

LEVEL OF CONSCIOUSNESS:
☐ AWAKE ALERT
☐ ORIENTED
☐ PURPOSEFUL RESPONSE TO PAIN
☐ NON-PURPOSEFUL RESPONSE TO PAIN
☐ UNRESPONSIVE TO PAIN
☐ ODOR OF ALCOHOL ON BREATH
☐ LETHARGIC
☐ DISORIENTED
☐ COMBATIVE

RESPIRATORY: ☐ N/A
CHEST SYMMETRICAL Y/N
R L BREATH SOUNDS
☐ ☐ CLEAR
☐ ☐ RALES
☐ ☐ WHEEZES
☐ ☐ DIMINISHED
☐ ☐ ABSENT
☐ ☐ DYSPNEA
☐ ☐ RETRACTION
☐ ☐ NASAL FLARING
☐ ☐ COUGH
   ☐ PRODUCTIVE
   ☐ NON-PRODUCTIVE

MENTAL ASSESSMENT:
PHYSICAL APPEARANCE
GAIT ☐ Normal ☐ Unstable
HYGIENE ☐ Normal ☐ Other _____
OVERALL PE ☐ Normal ☐ Frail ☐ Robust

MOOD/AFFECT
☐ Appropriate ☐ Cooperative
☐ Inappropriate ☐ Fearful
☐ Blunted/flat ☐ Hopelessness
☐ Defensive

MEMORY-RECENT ☐ Intact ☐ Impaired

THOUGHTS
☐ Clear ☐ Spontaneous
☐ Vague/disconnected ☐ Slow to answer questions

SPEECH
☐ Normal ☐ Clear
☐ Silent ☐ Mumbling/Garbled
☐ Talkative ☐ Monotone
☐ Loud ☐ Slurred
☐ Deliberate

MEDICAL HISTORY: ☐ BLIND ☐ DEAF/HARD OF HEARING
☐ ASTHMA COPD ☐ HYPERTENSION ☐ NO PREVIOUS MED
☐ CARDIAC ☐ SEIZURES ☐ NONE AVAILABLE
☐ DIABETES ☐ GASTRITIS/ULCER DISEASE

☐ OTHER _____

ALLERGIES: ☐ NKA _____

MEDS: ☐ NONE _____

LAST TETANUS: _____ LNMP: _____

TIME	BP	PULSE	RESP	TEMP

BLEEDING:
☐ NONE ☐ CONTROLLED
☐ UNCONTROLLED ☐ UNOBSERVABLE
SITE: _____

SKIN:
COLOR: ☐ NORMAL   MOISTURE:
☐ PALE/ASHEN   ☐ DRY ☐ MOIST ☐ PROFUSE
SKIN TEMP:
☐ HOT ☐ WARM
☐ COOL ☐ COLD

GU:
☐ INCONTINENT
☐ FREQUENCY
☐ URGENCY
☐ DYSURIA
☐ RETENTION
☐ FOLEY

GI:
☐ DIARRHEA
☐ CONSTIPATION
☐ NAUSEA
☐ VOMITING
☐ OTHER

FONTANELLES:
☐ NORMAL
☐ BULGING
☐ SUNKEN

INJURY/SKIN INTEGRITY:
LABEL AND SHADE AREAS INVOLVED
A - ABRASIONS
B - BRUISE
C - BURNS
D - SWOLLEN
E - LACERATION
F - PUNCTURE
G - POSSIBLE FX
H - C/O PAIN
I - REDDENED
J - DECUBITUS
K - RASH
+ - PULSE PRESENT
- - PULSE ABSENT

RIGHT LEFT   LEFT RIGHT

SPINAL PRECAUTIONS:
☐ C-COLLAR
☐ TAPE/SANDBAGS
☐ BACKBOARD
☐ OTHER
_____

ALL WOUNDS CLEANSED WITH _____

NEURO SIGNS

TIME	INITIAL	VERBAL RESPONSE	MOTOR RESPONSE	EYE OPENING	GRIP R L	UPPER EXTREMITY MOVEMENT R L	LOWER EXTREMITY MOVEMENT R L	PUPILS SIZE R L	PUPILS REACTION R L

ADULT GLASGOW COMA SCALE

EYE OPENING:
- Spontaneous — 4
- To Voice — 3
- To Pain — 2
- None — 1

VERBAL RESPONSE:
- Oriented — 5
- Confused — 4
- Inappropriate Words — 3
- Incomprehensible Words — 2
- None — 1

MOTOR RESPONSE:
- Obeys Command — 6
- Localizes Pain — 5
- Withdraw (Pain) — 4
- Flexion (Pain) — 3
- Extension (Pain) — 2
- None — 1

CHILD GLASGOW COMA SCALE UP TO 3 YEARS OLD

EYE OPENING:
- Spontaneous — 4
- Reaction to Speech — 3
- Reaction to Pain — 2
- None — 1

MOTOR RESPONSE:
- Obeys Command — 6
- Localizes Pain — 5
- Withdraw (Pain) — 4
- Flexion (Pain) — 3
- Extension (Pain) — 2
- None — 1

CRYING VERBAL RESPONSE:
- Consolable — 4
- Inconsistently Consolable — 3
- Inconsolable — 2
- None — 1

INTERACTS VERBAL RESPONSE:
- Inappropriate — 4
- Moaning — 3
- Irritable, Restless — 2
- None — 1

PUPIL SIZE AND REACTION

● ● ● ● ● • •
9 8 7 6 5 4 3 2

N = NORMAL   S = SLUGGISH
F = FIXED

PULSES EXTREMITY MOVEMENT
S = STRONG
W = WEAK
A = ABSENT
D = NOT PALPABLE BUT PRESENT WITH DOPPLER

PATIENT CHART

EMERGENCY DEPARTMENT
NURSING ASSESSMENT/DOCUMENTATION RECORD

BED #	PMD

NAME	AGE	WEIGHT	MEDICAL RECORD NO.	DATE

HOW ARRIVED ☐ WALKED ☐ WHEELCHAIR ☐ AMBULANCE ☐ CRUTCHES ☐ CARRIED FROM ☐ HOME ☐ SNF ☐ OTHER:

CHIEF COMPLAINT	TIME	INFORMANT ☐ SELF ☐ PARENT ☐ OTHER:	ARRIVED WITH: ☐ SELF ☐ PARENT ☐ SPOUSE ☐ FRIEND ☐ POLICE ☐ PARAMEDIC ☐ OTHER:

VISUAL ACUITY: OD ___ C ___ ☐ GLASSES CONTACT ☐ LENS

F0912-43-1	11166PC	LOSS OF CONSCIOUSNESS
ALERTED	FILED	ALERTED	FILED	ALERTED	FILED

BP ℞ R___ T___ O___ P___ AP___ R___ INITIAL RHYTHM
   L

LEVEL OF CONSCIOUSNESS:
☐ AWAKE ALERT
☐ ORIENTED
☐ PURPOSEFUL RESPONSE TO PAIN
☐ NON-PURPOSEFUL RESPONSE TO PAIN
☐ UNRESPONSIVE TO PAIN
☐ ODOR OF ALCOHOL ON BREATH
☐ LETHARGIC
☐ DISORIENTED
☐ COMBATIVE

RESPIRATORY: ☐ N/A
CHEST SYMMETRICAL Y/N
R L BREATH SOUNDS
☐ ☐ CLEAR
☐ ☐ RALES
☐ ☐ WHEEZES
☐ ☐ DIMINISHED
☐ ☐ ABSENT
☐   DYSPNEA
☐   RETRACTION
☐   NASAL FLARING
☐   COUGH
     ☐ PRODUCTIVE
     ☐ NON-PRODUCTIVE

MENTAL ASSESSMENT:
PHYSICAL APPEARANCE
GAIT ☐ Normal ☐ Unstable
HYGIENE ☐ Normal ☐ Other ___
OVERALL PE ☐ Normal ☐ Frail ☐ Robust

MOOD/AFFECT
☐ Appropriate   ☐ Cooperative
☐ Inappropriate   ☐ Fearful
☐ Blunted/flat   ☐ Hopelessness
☐ Defensive

MEMORY-RECENT ☐ Intact ☐ Impaired

THOUGHTS
☐ Clear   ☐ Spontaneous
☐ Vague/disconnected ☐ Slow to answer questions

SPEECH
☐ Normal   ☐ Clear
☐ Silent   ☐ Mumbling/Garbled
☐ Talkative ☐ Monotone
☐ Loud   ☐ Slurred
☐ Deliberate

BLEEDING:
☐ NONE   ☐ CONTROLLED
☐ UNCONTROLLED ☐ UNOBSERVABLE
SITE: ___

SKIN:
COLOR: ☐ NORMAL   MOISTURE:
       ☐ PALE/ASHEN ☐ DRY ☐ MOIST ☐ PROFUSE
       ☐   SKIN TEMP:
                    ☐ HOT   ☐ WARM
                    ☐ COOL   ☐ COLD

MEDICAL HISTORY: ☐ BLIND ☐ DEAF/HARD OF HEARING
☐ ASTHMA COPD ☐ HYPERTENSION ☐ NO PREVIOUS MED
☐ CARDIAC   ☐ SEIZURES   ☐ NONE AVAILABLE
☐ DIABETES   ☐ GASTRITIS/ULCER DISEASE

☐ OTHER ___

ALLERGIES: ☐ NKA ___

MEDS: ☐ NONE ___

LAST TETANUS: ___ LNMP: ___

TIME	BP	PULSE	RESP	TEMP

GU:
☐ INCONTINENT
☐ FREQUENCY
☐ URGENCY
☐ DYSURIA
☐ RETENTION
☐ FOLEY

GI:
☐ DIARRHEA
☐ CONSTIPATION
☐ NAUSEA
☐ VOMITING
☐ OTHER

FONTANELLES:
☐ NORMAL
☐ BULGING
☐ SUNKEN

INJURY/SKIN INTEGRITY:
LABEL AND SHADE AREAS INVOLVED
A – ABRASIONS
B – BRUISE
C – BURNS
D – SWOLLEN
E – LACERATION
F – PUNCTURE
G – POSSIBLE FX
H – C/O PAIN
I – REDDENED
J – DECUBITUS
K – RASH
+ – PULSE PRESENT
– – PULSE ABSENT

RIGHT LEFT   LEFT RIGHT

SPINAL PRECAUTIONS:
☐ C-COLLAR
☐ TAPE/SANDBAGS
☐ BACKBOARD
☐ OTHER ___

ALL WOUNDS CLEANSED WITH ___

NEURO SIGNS

TIME	INITIAL	VERBAL RESPONSE	MOTOR RESPONSE	EYE OPENING	GRIP R L	UPPER EXTREMITY MOVEMENT R L	LOWER EXTREMITY MOVEMENT R L	PUPILS SIZE R	PUPILS REACTION R	PUPILS SIZE L	PUPILS REACTION L

ADULT GLASGOW COMA SCALE

EYE OPENING:
Spontaneous – 4
To Voice – 3
To Pain – 2
None – 1

VERBAL RESPONSE:
Oriented – 5
Confused – 4
Inappropriate Words – 3
Incomprehensible Words – 2
None – 1

MOTOR RESPONSE:
Obeys Command – 6
Localizes Pain – 5
Withdraw (Pain) – 4
Flexion (Pain) – 3
Extension (Pain) – 2
None – 1

CHILD GLASGOW COMA SCALE UP TO 3 YEARS OLD

EYE OPENING:
Spontaneous – 4
Reaction to Speech – 3
Reaction to Pain – 2
None – 1

VERBAL RESPONSE:
Obeys Command – 6
Localizes Pain – 5
Withdraw (Pain) – 4
Flexion (Pain) – 3
Extension (Pain) – 2
None – 1

CRYING / INTERACTS VERBAL RESPONSE:
Consolable – 4 / Inappropriate – 4
Inconsistently Consolable – 3 / Moaning – 3
Inconsolable – 2 / Irritable, Restless – 2
None – 1 / None – 1

PUPIL SIZE AND REACTION
9 8 7 6 5 4 3 2
N = NORMAL   S = SLUGGISH
F = FIXED

PULSES EXTREMITY MOVEMENT
S = STRONG
W = WEAK
A = ABSENT
D = NOT PALPABLE BUT PRESENT WITH DOPPLER

PATIENT CHART

Chapter Five • Admitting Procedures

EMERGENCY DEPARTMENT
NURSING ASSESSMENT/DOCUMENTATION RECORD

NAME		AGE	WEIGHT	MEDICAL RECORD NO.	DATE
BED #				PMD	

HOW ARRIVED ☐ WALKED ☐ WHEELCHAIR ☐ AMBULANCE ☐ CRUTCHES ☐ CARRIED FROM ☐ HOME ☐ SNF ☐ OTHER:

CHIEF COMPLAINT TIME | INFORMANT ☐ SELF ☐ PARENT ☐ OTHER:

ARRIVED WITH: ☐ SELF ☐ PARENT ☐ SPOUSE ☐ FRIEND ☐ POLICE ☐ PARAMEDIC ☐ OTHER:

VISUAL ACUITY: OD C ☐ GLASSES ☐ CONTACT LENS

F0912-43-1		11166PC		LOSS OF CONSCIOUSNESS	
ALERTED	FILED	ALERTED	FILED	ALERTED	FILED

BP ♡ ⊶ R L   T   O R   P   AP R   R   INITIAL RHYTHM

LEVEL OF CONSCIOUSNESS:
☐ AWAKE ALERT
☐ ORIENTED
☐ PURPOSEFUL RESPONSE TO PAIN
☐ NON-PURPOSEFUL RESPONSE TO PAIN
☐ UNRESPONSIVE TO PAIN
☐ ODOR OF ALCOHOL ON BREATH
☐ LETHARGIC
☐ DISORIENTED
☐ COMBATIVE

MENTAL ASSESSMENT:
PHYSICAL APPEARANCE
GAIT ☐ Normal ☐ Unstable
HYGIENE ☐ Normal ☐ Other _____
OVERALL PE ☐ Normal ☐ Frail ☐ Robust

MOOD/AFFECT
☐ Appropriate ☐ Cooperative
☐ Inappropriate ☐ Fearful
☐ Blunted/flat ☐ Hopelessness
☐ Defensive

MEMORY-RECENT ☐ Intact ☐ Impaired

THOUGHTS
☐ Clear ☐ Spontaneous
☐ Vague/disconnected ☐ Slow to answer questions

SPEECH
☐ Normal ☐ Clear
☐ Silent ☐ Mumbling/Garbled
☐ Talkative ☐ Monotone
☐ Loud ☐ Slurred
☐ Deliberate

MEDICAL HISTORY: ☐ BLIND ☐ DEAF/HARD OF HEARING
☐ ASTHMA COPD ☐ HYPERTENSION ☐ NO PREVIOUS MED
☐ CARDIAC ☐ SEIZURES ☐ NONE AVAILABLE
☐ DIABETES ☐ GASTRITIS/ULCER DISEASE

☐ OTHER _____

ALLERGIES: ☐ NKA _____

MEDS: ☐ NONE _____

LAST TETANUS: _____ LNMP: _____

TIME	BP	PULSE	RESP	TEMP

RESPIRATORY: ☐ N/A
CHEST SYMMETRICAL Y/N
R L BREATH SOUNDS
☐ ☐ CLEAR
☐ ☐ RALES
☐ ☐ WHEEZES
☐ ☐ DIMINISHED
☐ ☐ ABSENT
☐ ☐ DYSPNEA
☐ ☐ RETRACTION
☐ ☐ NASAL FLARING
☐ ☐ COUGH
  ☐ PRODUCTIVE
  ☐ NON-PRODUCTIVE

BLEEDING:
☐ NONE ☐ CONTROLLED
☐ UNCONTROLLED ☐ UNOBSERVABLE
SITE: _____

SKIN:
COLOR: ☐ NORMAL
☐ PALE/ASHEN

MOISTURE:
☐ DRY ☐ MOIST ☐ PROFUSE
SKIN TEMP:
☐ HOT ☐ WARM
☐ COOL ☐ COLD

GU:
☐ INCONTINENT
☐ FREQUENCY
☐ URGENCY
☐ DYSURIA
☐ RETENTION
☐ FOLEY

GI:
☐ DIARRHEA
☐ CONSTIPATION
☐ NAUSEA
☐ VOMITING
☐ OTHER

FONTANELLES:
☐ NORMAL
☐ BULGING
☐ SUNKEN

INJURY/SKIN INTEGRITY:
LABEL AND SHADE AREAS INVOLVED
A - ABRASIONS
B - BRUISE
C - BURNS
D - SWOLLEN
E - LACERATION
F - PUNCTURE
G - POSSIBLE FX
H - C/O PAIN
I - REDDENED
J - DECUBITUS
K - RASH
+ - PULSE PRESENT
− - PULSE ABSENT

SPINAL PRECAUTIONS:
☐ C-COLLAR
☐ TAPE/SANDBAGS
☐ BACKBOARD
☐ OTHER

RIGHT   LEFT   LEFT   RIGHT

ALL WOUNDS CLEANSED WITH _____

NEURO SIGNS

TIME	INITIAL	VERBAL RESPONSE	MOTOR RESPONSE	EYE OPENING	GRIP R L	UPPER EXTREMITY MOVEMENT R L	LOWER EXTREMITY MOVEMENT R L	PUPILS SIZE R	PUPILS REACTION R	PUPILS SIZE L	PUPILS REACTION L

ADULT GLASGOW COMA SCALE

EYE OPENING:
Spontaneous 4
To Voice 3
To Pain 2
None 1

VERBAL RESPONSE:
Oriented 5
Confused 4
Inappropriate Words 3
Incomprehensible Words 2
None 1

MOTOR RESPONSE:
Obeys Command 6
Localizes Pain 5
Withdraw (Pain) 4
Flexion (Pain) 3
Extension (Pain) 2
None 1

CHILD GLASGOW COMA SCALE UP TO 3 YEARS OLD

EYE OPENING:
Spontaneous 4
Reaction to Speech 3
Reaction to Pain 2
None 1

MOTOR RESPONSE:
Obeys Command 6
Localizes Pain 5
Withdraw (Pain) 4
Flexion (Pain) 3
Extension (Pain) 2
None 1

CRYING RESPONSE:
Consolable 4
Inconsistently Consolable 3
Inconsolable 2
None 1

INTERACTS VERBAL RESPONSE:
Inappropriate 4
Moaning 3
Irritable, Restless 2
None 1

PUPIL SIZE AND REACTION
● ● ● ● • • •
9 8 7 6 5 4 3 2

N = NORMAL S = SLUGGISH
F = FIXED

PULSES
EXTREMITY MOVEMENT

S = STRONG
W = WEAK
A = ABSENT
D = NOT PALPABLE BUT PRESENT WITH DOPPLER

PATIENT CHART

Chapter Six
Patient Evaluation

Objectives

After completing this chapter you should be able to do the following:

1. Define and correctly spell all key terms.
2. Perform a primary survey.
3. Perform a secondary survey.
4. Perform a pupil check.
5. Measure height and weight on an adult and infant.
6. Obtain blood pressure, pulse, respiration, and temperature readings, and document this information on the medical record.

Key Terms

- alveoli
- apical pulse
- arterial
- ashen
- assessment
- auscultate
- bradycardia
- carotid pulse
- circulatory
- clammy
- crackles
- cyanosis
- dehydration
- diaphragm
- diastolic
- distended
- dyspnea
- edema
- expiration
- hypothermia
- inspiration
- Medic-Alert
- orientation
- PERL
- popliteal artery
- priapism
- radial pulse
- respiratory
- systolic
- tachycardia

The Importance of Accurate Evaluations

In the previous chapters we discussed the importance of gathering information for patient admission. Although the patient often can tell you much of this information, you can gather information in other ways as well. By observing facial expressions you can tell if someone is in pain or upset; by looking at an injured hand you can tell if it is bleeding, swollen, or bruised; and by taking multiple readings of the patient's **vital signs** you can detect changes in the patient's condition. Accurate measurement of vital signs and observation of the patient are the keys to providing rapid and appropriate emergency care. Therefore, this chapter focuses on the specific observational skills that are needed to perform a head-to-toe check, or **secondary survey**, on patients who arrive at the Emergency Department for admission, and describes the procedures that must be followed to measure and record a patient's vital signs.

Chapter Six • Patient Evaluation

Note: It is recognized that gloves will not always be worn in all procedures. However, universal precautions require the use of gloves whenever blood or other body fluids are present. Because this is a book for the emergency department technician, and because there is a greater chance of exposure to blood in an ER, gloves are included in all procedures.

Observational Skills

ER technicians use observational skills to perform an **assessment** on emergency patients. These skills include listening, looking, touching, and smelling. For example, the patient's appearance can tell you a great deal about the urgency of his or her condition and perhaps what caused it. Listening to the patient can alert you to abnormal breathing sounds and provide a description of the patient's pain. By touching the patient you can determine swelling, skin temperature, and moisture. Feeling with the hands is called **palpation**. Using the sense of smell, you can detect certain odors of alcohol, chemicals, and poisons. All of these senses can be helpful in assessing the patient. Talking to the patient and making observations will help you gather information.

LOOK LISTEN TOUCH SMELL

assessment: evaluation of a patient's physical condition

For example, a 45-year-old, unconscious female was brought by ambulance to the ER. She was found by a bus driver in the back of his bus and had no identification. Using observation skills alone, the ER technician noted the following:

- a 1-inch laceration to the left arm
- a **Medic-Alert** bracelet with *diabetic* written on it
- a deformity and swelling on the right ankle
- the right foot was cooler to touch than the left foot
- irregular and noisy breathing
- an odor of alcohol on her breath

Medic-Alert: a symbol that indicates important medical information

The patient was immediately placed on the ER gurney. The doctor examined the unconscious patient while the ER technician set up the oxygen, obtained vital signs, and gathered supplies to cleanse the wound and prepare for suturing. Meanwhile, the nurse started an intravenous line and placed the patient on a monitor. Precious moments are saved when working together as a team.

The Primary Survey

A fast and efficient method for detecting life-threatening emergencies is essential in the ER. Therefore, a systematic approach is used to evaluate the patient. A rapid check is done to determine if the patient has any life-threatening conditions. This is called the **primary survey**. As you approach the patient lying on the gurney, the first thing to determine is his or her level of consciousness. You want to know immediately if the patient is awake and alert, or unconscious. By introducing yourself and telling the patient why you are there, you are able to see if the patient can respond to you. Ask the patient how he or she is feeling.

"Hello, I'm Mary Smith, Emergency Department Technician. How are you feeling?"

Does the patient respond? If so, are the answers appropriate to the question? Is the patient **alert** and **oriented**? If the patient is non-responsive, perform the primary survey. Remembering the primary survey is as easy as A-B-C.

A = AIRWAY
B = BREATHING
C = CIRCULATION

Airway. Is the airway open? If not, and the patient was a trauma victim or arrived with a **cervical collar** in place, make an airway using the **jaw-thrust** (Figure 6-1a) or **modified jaw-thrust maneuver**. If the patient is not a trauma victim, open the airway using the **head-tilt/chin-lift maneuver.** (Figure 6-1b) Is the airway clear? Note: If blood or other body fluids are present, put on gloves before touching the patient.

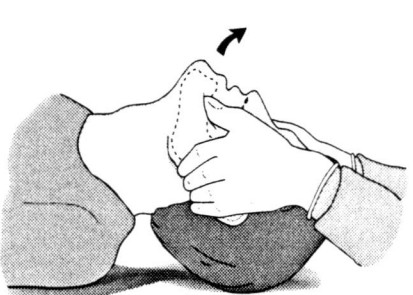
Jaw-Thrust Maneuver

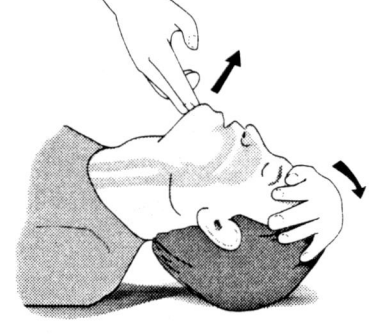
Head-Tilt/Chin-Lift Maneuver

Figure 6-1a   *Figure 6-1b*

Chapter Six • Patient Evaluation

IF THE AIRWAY IS NOT CLEAR:

1. WEAR GLOVES.

2. GRASP THE MOUTH AND OPEN THE JAW WITH YOUR THUMB AND INDEX FINGER.

3. DO A FINGER SWEEP TO REMOVE ANY OBJECTS. DO NOT perform a blind finger sweep on a child or infant. This is only done on a child or infant if you can see the object! (Figure 6-2)

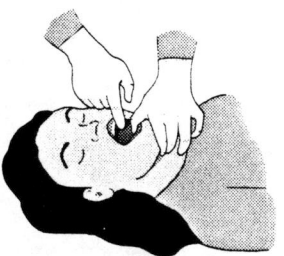

Finger Sweep

Figure 6-2

4. PERFORM HEAD-TILT/CHIN-LIFT MANEUVER. (Figure 6-1b)

Breathing. Is the patient breathing? What is the rate of breathing? Look at the chest, is it moving? (Figure 6-3a) Listen to the mouth for air movement. (Figure 6-3b) Feel for the presence of air. Again, is the patient breathing? Is it adequate? Are the respirations noisy, labored or gurgling? Gurgling respirations indicate fluid in the lungs.

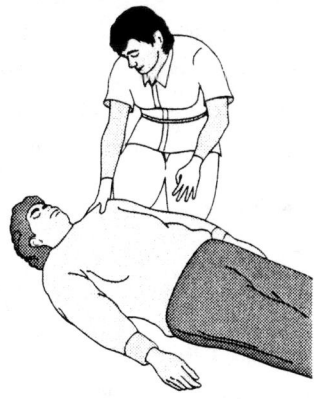

Look for Breathing

Figure 6-3a

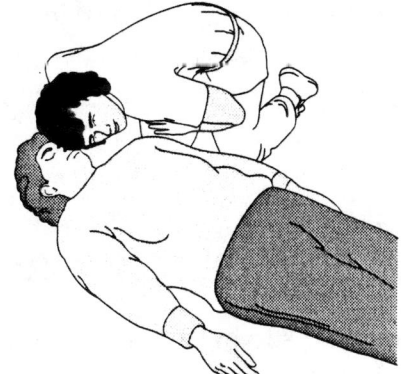

Listen for Breathing

Figure 6-3b

IF THE PATIENT IS NOT BREATHING:

1. CALL FOR HELP.

2. BEGIN RESCUE BREATHING. (See Chapter Eight.)

3. IMMEDIATELY CORRECT ANY SEVERE BREATHING PROBLEMS.

radial pulse: the pulse located in the wrist near the radial bone

Circulation. Does the patient have a pulse? Check the **carotid** artery located in the neck. (Figure 6-4a) If there is a carotid pulse, check the **radial pulse** for rate and regularity. (Figure 6-4b)

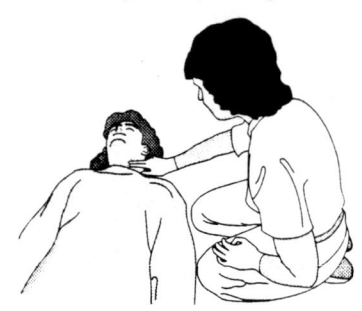

Check Carotid Pulse

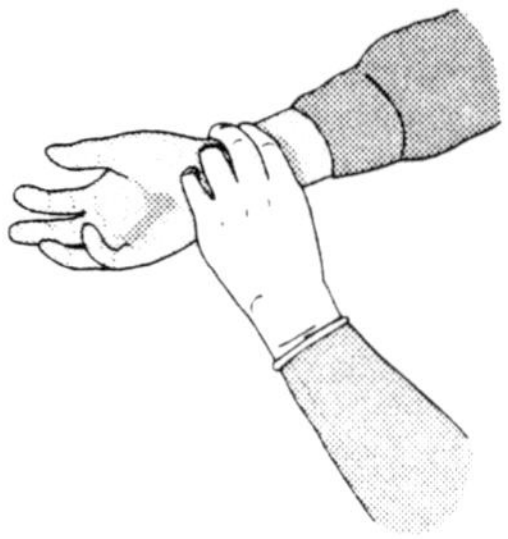

Check Radial Pulse For Rate and Regularity

Figure 6-4a

Figure 6-4b

IF THERE IS NO PULSE BEGIN CPR. (See Chapter Eight.)

Assessment of the ABCs is known as the primary survey. It is done on all patients. If the patient is talking, it's obvious the patient is both breathing and has a pulse. If the patient is non-responsive or in a **coma**, it is essential to do a primary survey immediately. Reassessment of the patient also is necessary at frequent intervals. A patient can be awake and responding one moment and unconscious the next. Always begin with the primary survey when approaching an unconscious patient.

The Secondary Survey

The **secondary survey** is a head-to-toe physical assessment that is done on all patients to determine the extent of illness or injury. To do this, the areas to be observed must be exposed and examined. Clothing is carefully removed and the patient is given a hospital gown prior to further examination by the doctor.

When caring for an emergency patient, pay attention to the chief complaint. Why is he or she here? Some injuries and illnesses are obvious, but some are not so obvious. Always do a head-to-toe assessment, or secondary survey, to locate all major injuries. This should take about 2 minutes. While you are examining the patient, ask them questions about the injury or illness. By talking to the patient, you can relieve some of his or her anxiety and check the patient's orientation level at the same time. Orientation levels will be described later in the chapter when you learn how to do a **neurological check**.

Performing a Secondary Survey

Materials needed:
- ✓ gloves (If blood or other body fluids are present.)

1. Procedural Step: Wash your hands.
   Reason: Universal precaution.

2. Procedural Step: Wear gloves if any blood or any other body fluid is present.
   Reason: Universal precaution.

3. Procedural Step: Identify the patient by his or her identification bracelet.
   Reason: To make sure you are working with the correct patient.

   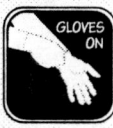

4. Procedural Step: Explain the procedure to the patient using terms he or she will understand.
   Reason: This keeps the patient calm and provides the information necessary for the patient to give informed consent.

5. Procedural Step: Begin at the neck, handling the patient gently.
   Reason: To avoid injuries to the patient's spine.

6. Procedural Step: Look for bleeding, swelling, or deformities.
   Reason: Presence indicates trauma.

7. Procedural Step: Determine the **mechanism of injury**. The mechanism of injury refers to how the injury occurred. Was there a fall, auto accident, shooting, overdose, etc.?
   Reason: This helps you determine if there may be injury to the cervical spine.

8. Procedural Step: Does the patient have any pain in the neck?
   Reason: Pain may indicate injury.

9. Procedural Step: Look at the veins in the neck. Are they flat, **distended**, or bulging?
   Reason: When a person is lying down, the neck veins are normally slightly distended, stretched out, or inflated. A patient who is having problems with circulation may have neck veins that bulge.

10. Procedural Step: Is there any swelling in the neck?
    Reason: Swelling can interfere with the airway.

11. Procedural Step: Look for a **stoma** in the throat.
    Reason: A stoma is a permanent opening in the throat. The patient may have had a **tracheostomy** or **laryngectomy**. If so, he or she now breathes from this opening in the neck rather than through the nose or mouth.

distended: expanded or swollen

Performing a Secondary Survey (Cont.)

12. Procedural Step: Palpate (feel) the back of the neck for any deformity or tenderness.
    Reason: Deformity or tenderness may indicate injury.

13. Procedural Step: Check the neck for a **Medic-Alert** tag.
    Reason: These tags provide useful medical information when treating children, confused adults, or unconscious patients.

14. Procedural Step: Gently palpate the entire scalp with both hands.
    Reason: To gently search the entire scalp for bleeding, swelling, or deformity.

15. Procedural Step: Feel for swelling by touching lightly all around the back of the head.
    Reason: **Lacerations** may not be obvious on people with a lot of hair until the scalp is palpated.

16. Procedural Step: Palpate the face for tenderness or fractures.
    Reason: A response to pain may indicate an injury.

17. Procedural Step: Look at the patient's face for signs of **symmetry** (the equality of body parts). The parts should be equal in size, shape, and location.
    Reason: Asymmetry may indicate an injury. For example, the eyes are symmetrical except when there is an injury. In this case, the injured eye may be swollen, or the pupil may appear to be a different size or shape than the other.

18. Procedural Step: Check the ears for any drainage.
    Reason: Bloody drainage can indicate trauma. Clear drainage may be **cerebrospinal fluid** from a fractured skull.

19. Procedural Step: Look at the shape of the nose.
    Reason: Deformity could indicate a fracture.

20. Procedural Step: Check the nose for any fluid, drainage or bleeding.
    Reason: Clear drainage may be **mucous** or cerebrospinal fluid.

21. Procedural Step: Look in the mouth and check for any loose or missing teeth.
    Reason: Teeth can block an airway if they get caught in the trachea. It may be possible to re-implant lost teeth if they were brought in with the patient.

Chapter Six • Patient Evaluation

Performing a Secondary Survey (Cont.)

22. Procedural Step: Check to see if the patient is wearing dentures. If so, remove the dentures and place them in a container labeled with the patient's name and admission number. Place the dentures in a bag with the patient's other belongings.
    Reason: Dentures are personal property and must be accounted for. They also may obstruct the airway.

23. Procedural Step: Look at the color of the lips and the inside of the mouth.
    Reason: A blue tinge to the lips (**cyanosis**) can indicate a lack of oxygen. This may indicate shock.

24. Procedural Step: Check to see if the mouth is dry or if **saliva** is present.
    Reason: Dry, cracked lips may indicate a fever, diabetic problem, or **dehydration**.

25. Procedural Step: Look at the eyes. Is the patient wearing contact lenses? If so, and if it is necessary to remove the lenses, place them in labelled containers with the patient's name and admission number. Label one container *right eye lens* and one container *left eye lens*.
    Reason: Contact lenses are personal property and must be accounted for. They can cause eye injury and can interfere with treatment.

26. Procedural Step: Look at the pupils by shining a penlight into each one.

    Reason: Pupils that are **constricted** (small) can indicate a drug overdose or other medical problem. Normal pupils will react to light by becoming smaller (constricting). Pupils that do not react to light, or pupils that are dilated (large) can indicate a serious problem such as a head injury, drug abuse, etc. Unequal pupils can be a sign of head injury.

27. Procedural Step: When checking the pupils for reaction to light, make sure that an overhead light is not shining in the patient's face.
    Reason: This may alter the results.

    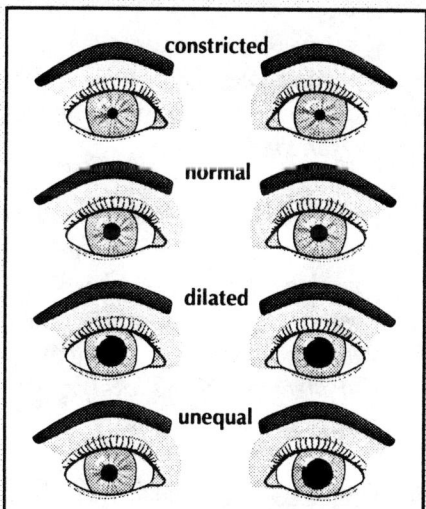

28. Procedural Step: Take the penlight from the side of the patient's face and shine directly into one eye and watch for a reaction. When done, repeat this procedure with the other eye.
    Reason: Pupils that are equal and react to light are normal. It is documented on the chart as pupils **PERL**.

cyanosis: a bluish tint to the skin and mucous membranes caused by a decrease in oxygen

dehydration: the loss of water from a body or substance

PERL: the abbreviation for pupils equal and react to light

Performing a Secondary Survey (Cont.)

clammy: moist

ashen: a gray skin color seen in shock patients

hypothermia: an unusually low body temperature capable of causing problems with the central nervous system and cardiac arrest

29. Procedural Step: While inspecting the head and face, check the skin. Is the skin warm and dry, cold and **clammy**, **ashen**, or pale?
    Reason: Warm and dry is the normal skin condition. Hot skin can indicate fever or heat stroke. Cold skin can indicate shock or **hypothermia**.

30. Procedural Step: Is the skin **diaphoretic** (moist)?
    Reason: Wet skin can occur with fever, shock, heart attack, stroke, and **diabetes**.

31. Procedural Step: What is the color of the skin? Is it red, pale, or cyanotic (blue)?
    Reason: Color changes in the skin are indications of how well the blood is circulating and carrying oxygen to the tissues.

32. Procedural Step: While talking to the patient, determine the **level of consciousness**.
    Reason: Head injuries and problems with the central nervous system can alter the patient's level of consciousness.

33. Procedural Step: Check the patient's level of consciousness by asking him or her these questions:

    "Tell me what time of day it is."
    Reason: Checks **orientation** regarding time.

    "Tell me where you are."
    Reason: Checks orientation regarding place.

"What's your name?"
Reason: Checks orientation regarding person.

"What were you doing when this happened?"
Reason: Checks orientation regarding purpose.

34. Procedural Step: If the patient can answer all of the above questions appropriately, he or she is oriented times four. Record this as *Ox4*. If the patient only can answer three out of the four questions, he or she is *Ox3*.
    Reason: To track the patient's level of consciousness.

If the patient can answer...

4 out of 4 questions = *Ox4*

3 out of 4 questions = *Ox3*

2 out of 4 questions = *Ox2*

1 out of 4 questions = *Ox1*

0 out of 4 questions = *Ox0*

Chapter Six • Patient Evaluation

Performing a Secondary Survey (Cont.)

35. <u>Procedural Step:</u> Check the chest for **symmetry**. Are both sides moving up and down with respirations?
    <u>Reason:</u> *Normal breathing is quiet and effortless. Both sides of the chest should move with each breath. If only one side of the chest is moving, there may be a serious respiratory problem.*

36. <u>Procedural Step:</u> Look at the chest for scars.
    <u>Reason:</u> *Scars could indicate a previous surgical procedure or injury.*

37. <u>Procedural Step:</u> Look for any deformities, bruises, or **contusions.**
    <u>Reason:</u> *Bruises and deformities can be caused by a fractured rib.*

38. <u>Procedural Step:</u> Palpate the chest by feeling both sides of the chest. Watch the patient for signs of discomfort.
    <u>Reason:</u> *Pain may indicate an injury.*

39. <u>Procedural Step:</u> Feel the clavicles and ribs for tenderness, pain, or instability.
    <u>Reason:</u> *Pain may indicate an injury.*

40. <u>Procedural Step:</u> Listen to the breathing pattern. Is it regular or noisy? Is there a wheeze, rattle, or cough?
    <u>Reason:</u> *There may be fluid in the lungs.*

41. <u>Procedural Step:</u> If respirations are noisy or difficult, **auscultate** the chest with a **stethoscope**.
    <u>Reason:</u> *To hear the chest sounds better.*

42. <u>Procedural Step:</u> Listen to the front, back, left, and right sides of the chest, and compare the sounds heard during both **inspiration** and **expiration**. (See illustration.) Listen in at least four places.
    <u>Reason:</u> *To get an accurate assessment. If breath sounds are absent (or mostly absent) in one or both lobes, report this to the nurse and start artificial respiration immediately. (See Chapter Seven.)*

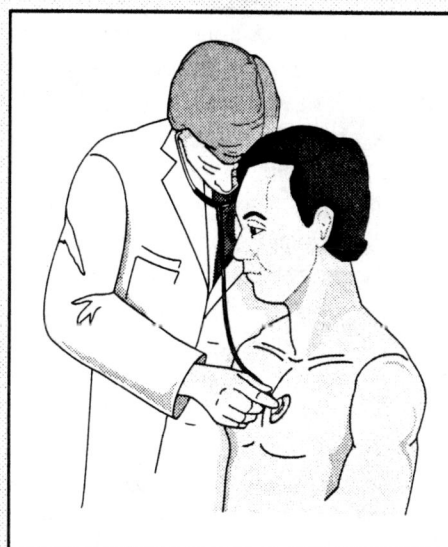

43. <u>Procedural Step:</u> Check the abdomen for scars, bruises, and distention.
    <u>Reason:</u> *Scars will alert you to any previous surgeries.*

44. <u>Procedural Step:</u> Palpate the abdomen in all four quadrants (see illustration) for any tenderness, **guarding**, pain, or **rigidity**.
    <u>Reason:</u> *A rigid or tender abdomen could be a sign of internal bleeding.*

inspiration: inhalation; the act of breathing something into the lungs

expiration: to exhale; the act of breathing out

auscultate: to listen

Performing a Secondary Survey (Cont.)

45. **Procedural Step:** Start at the right upper quadrant and carefully palpate the entire abdomen in a clockwise direction.
    Reason: To cover the whole abdomen.

46. **Procedural Step:** Feel the skin. Is it warm, cold, dry, moist?
    Reason: Remember, moist, cold skin can indicate fever or shock.

47. **Procedural Step:** Look at how the patient is positioned. Is the patient **guarding** (lying on his or her side with knees flexed)?
    Reason: Guarding is a nonverbal sign of pain.

48. **Procedural Step:** Check to see if the patient appears to be in pain?
    Reason: Facial grimace, abdomen clutching, and drawn up lower legs are all signs of pain.

49. **Procedural Step:** Check for **nausea** or **vomiting**. What color is the **vomitus** and how much is there?
    Reason: Bright red **vomitus** indicates bleeding. Yellow could be bile, and may mean the liver has been injured. Dark red may indicate old blood in the stomach.

50. **Procedural Step:** Check the pelvis and look for **incontinence**, or any vaginal or rectal bleeding.
    Reason: Incontinence (loss of bladder or bowel control) may indicate a problem with the nervous system.

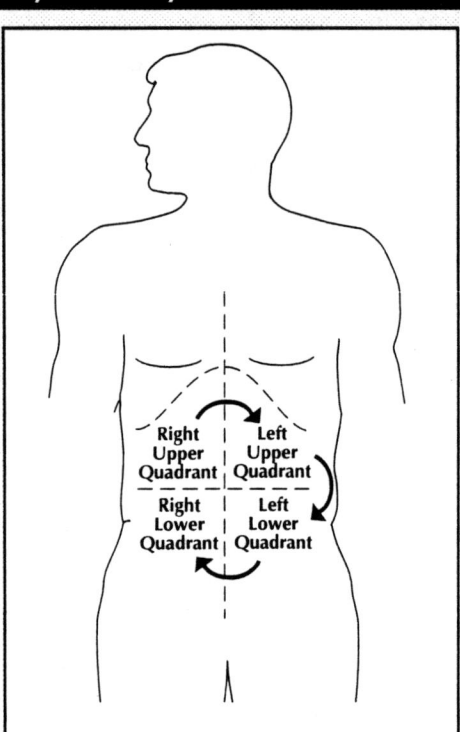

51. **Procedural Step:** Check for pain in the pelvic area. If the patient is male, is there a **priapism?**
    Reason: A priapism is often associated with **paralysis** (the loss of sensation or voluntary motion).

52. **Procedural Step:** Look at the lower extremities. Are there any deformities?
    Reason: Deformity is one of the first signs of a fracture.

priapism: a penile erection caused by a central nervous system disorder

Performing a Secondary Survey (Cont.)

53. Procedural Step: Check to see how the legs are positioned. Palpate for the **femoral** pulse.
Reason: The femoral pulse is located in the groin on the inner side of the femur. A strong pulse indicates adequate circulation.

54. Procedural Step: Evaluate one leg at a time. Start with the upper thigh and palpate for any tenderness, swelling or pain. Continue down the leg and feel the knee, lower leg and foot. What is the skin temperature? Is the skin wet or dry?
Reason: To check for injuries and evaluate circulation.

55. Procedural Step: Compare the legs to each other.
Reason: Deformities may indicate an injury.

56. Procedural Step: Check for movement and sensation in both legs.
Reason: This is an assessment for paralysis or other circulatory or neurologic problems.

57. Procedural Step: Check for pulses in the lower legs and feet. What color are the feet?
Reason: A strong pulse indicates adequate circulation. Skin color also indicates the quality of circulation.

58. Procedural Step: Look for **edema** in the ankles.
Reason: Swollen ankles are signs of trauma, heart disease, and/or increased fluid.

59. Procedural Step: Ask the patient to move his or her feet. Can the patient feel and move both lower extremities?
Reason: Indicates function of the nervous system.

60. Procedural Step: Check both arms as you did the legs. Look at the color of the skin and check for cuts or bruises.
Reason: To check for injuries and evaluate circulation.

61. Procedural Step: Look for **track marks** (red marks over veins) or **abscesses** (localized collections of pus).
Reason: May indicate IV substance abuse.

62. Procedural Step: Look for a **Medic-Alert** bracelet.
Reason: This is a tag that provides information about known medical conditions or allergies.

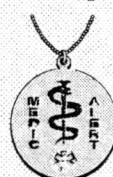

63. Procedural Step: Feel for pulses at the **brachial** and **radial** arteries. The **brachial pulse** is located on the inside of the arm at the bend of the elbow. The **radial pulse** is located in the wrist on the thumb side.
Reason: The strength of a pulse indicates the quality of circulation.

64. Procedural Step: Ask the patient to move his hand, make a fist, or squeeze your hands.
Reason: To assess the central nervous system.

edema: swelling due to fluid in the tissues

Performing a Secondary Survey (Cont.)

65. **Procedural Step:** Check the strength of hand grips. They should be equal.
    Reason: Weakness occurs in stroke victims and with head injuries.

66. **Procedural Step:** Depending on his or her condition, you may need to **log roll** the patient to see the back. ALWAYS get help to turn a trauma victim.
    Reason: To prevent injury to yourself and further injury to the patient.

67. **Procedural Step:** Look for bruises, scars, or wounds.
    Reason: To check for injuries.

68. **Procedural Step:** Palpate the **thoracic**, **lumbar**, and **sacral** areas for pain and tenderness.
    Reason: Pain or tenderness may indicate an injury.

69. **Procedural Step:** Remove your gloves if it was necessary to put them on.
    Reason: Universal precaution.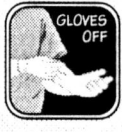

70. **Procedural Step:** Wash your hands.
    Reason: Universal precaution.

71. **Procedural Step:** Record your findings on the patient's chart.
    Reason: To provide documentation.

The Log Roll

Carefully position a draw sheet under the patient, and place a pillow lengthwise between his or her legs. Use the draw sheet to move the patient near one side of the bed, making sure that both side rails are up before you leave the patient's side. Place another pillow against the other side rail to protect the patient, and cross the patient's arms over the chest.

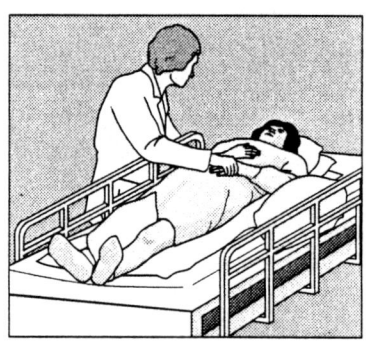

Go to the other side of the bed. Using the draw sheet, you and a helper will turn the patient toward you (and the pillow) as one unit, keeping the head and spine straight, and rolling the patient like a log.

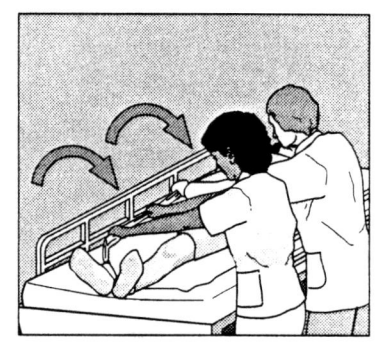

Always perform a secondary survey on ER patients. Remember, ER patients may have more than one problem, one of which might be overlooked unless the secondary survey is performed. An example of how to chart your findings from a secondary survey is on the following pages.

Chapter Six • Patient Evaluation

Case History

A 56-year-old male was brought to the ER by ambulance following an **MVA** (motor vehicle accident). He had pain in the left lower leg, and there was a deformity and a large three-inch **laceration** at that location. The patient said his foot got caught under the brake pedal as he attempted to stop at a red light.

The emergency department technician performed a complete secondary survey and found the following:

- The patient was oriented x 3 (person, place, and purpose, but not time).
- The pupils could be recorded as PERL.
- Bleeding from a one-inch laceration of the scalp hidden by the hair.
- A scar over the left upper chest indicating the patient had a **pacemaker.**
- A Medic-Alert bracelet that said the patient was **diabetic** and allergic to penicillin.
- A three-inch laceration to the lower left leg with **arterial** bleeding.
- A deformity in the lower left leg and inability to move it.
- No pulse could be felt in the left foot below the **fracture.**

By performing a secondary survey, the aide was able to alert the nurse and doctor to the head injury and the altered level of consciousness. The fact that the patient had a history of heart problems (indicated by the pacemaker), and was a diabetic will alert the healthcare providers to observe him carefully and frequently for complications. Because there was no pulse below the fracture, immediate steps had to be taken to restore circulation. The doctor was promptly notified to examine this patient, and the operating room was alerted about the impending surgery.

arterial: pertaining to the large vessels that carry oxygenated blood

Figure 6-5: The results of a secondary survey are recorded on the patient's emergency record.

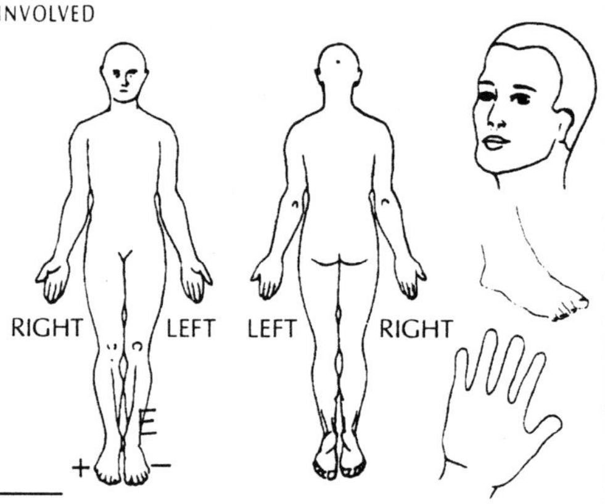

Chapter Six • Patient Evaluation

By performing a secondary survey, important information was gathered on this patient. Had the patient not had a secondary survey, perhaps only the leg injury would have been treated and the other problems overlooked. Many emergencies are not what they appear to be when analysis is based solely upon the chief complaint. Some symptoms and signs are obvious, as in the case of a large laceration with **arterial** bleeding. However, a person may be just as seriously injured with an **internal** wound that you cannot see. Great care must be taken when assessing emergency victims. It is essential that nothing is overlooked.

Vital Signs

The blood pressure, pulse, respiration, and temperature fall under the heading **vital signs**. Vital signs are used to determine how the **circulatory** and **respiratory** systems are working. They are measured frequently because changes can indicate a serious problem. One set of vital signs may not be very meaningful, but a series of blood pressure readings can establish the patient's normal ranges and then alert you to sudden changes. The more **critical** the patient's condition, the more frequently vital signs should be taken. In the ER vital signs are taken immediately upon admission and then repeated as necessary. Sometimes vitals are taken every 5 minutes and sometimes every 30 minutes. Vitals are always taken before and after medication and treatments are given. It is better to take vital signs more often than needed rather than not often enough. Changes in one sign, such as blood pressure, may affect the other signs, such as pulse and respiration. For this reason, all of the vital signs should be observed at the same time.

circulatory: refers to the system responsible for transporting blood throughout the body

respiratory: of or relating to breathing

> **Note:** Good technique dictates that the gloves should be removed and the hands washed before charting the results of any procedure. You should then wash your hands again after handling the patient or equipment and before caring for the next patient.

The Pulse

Each time the heart beats the blood vessels expand and contract. The blood flows through the vessels and waves of blood cause pulsations in the arteries. You can feel these pulsations by placing your fingertips directly over one of the large arteries that lie close to the skin. Pulses are easily felt over areas where an artery lies close to a bone. The **radial pulse** (in the wrist) is the most convenient pulse to monitor.

Taking a patient's pulse requires accurate counting and sensitivity to irregular rhythms and quality. Pulse rates vary with the size of the patient, physical condition, and age. General guidelines for determining normal rates follow.

1. Infants (under 1 year of age): 90 to 140 beats per minute.

2. Children (1 to 7 years old): 80 to 120 beats per minute.

3. Children (over 7 years old): 72 to 90 beats per minute.

4. Adults: 60 to 100 beats per minute, with average heart rate being 70 to 80. Rates higher than 100 are known as **tachycardia**; rates below 60 are called **bradycardia**.

tachycardia: a rapid heartbeat, more than 100 beats a minute

bradycardia: a pulse rate below 60 beats a minute

Pulse rates can vary with many conditions. Fast pulse rates occur with exercise, fear, fever, shock, drugs, or heart conditions. Slow pulse rates can be caused by various drugs, alcohol, and heart conditions, or may be normal in athletes with healthy **cardiovascular** systems.

The rhythm of the pulse is described as *regular* or *irregular*. Quality refers to the strength of the pulse, and is noted as *weak, strong,* ***thready*** (weak and rapid), or ***bounding*** (unusually full and strong). When noting the pulse on the medical record or designated form, be sure to indicate the rate, the regularity of the rhythm, and the strength or quality. Follow the procedural requirements for your healthcare facility.

Chapter Six • Patient Evaluation

Measuring a Radial Pulse

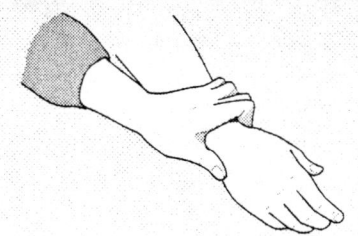

Materials needed:
- ✓ a watch with a second hand
- ✓ gloves (If blood or other body fluids are present.)

1. Procedural Step: Wash your hands.
   Reason: Universal precaution.

2. Procedural Step: Put on gloves if there is any blood or other body fluid present.
   Reason: Universal precaution.
   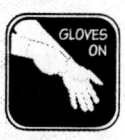

3. Procedural Step: Identify the patient by his or her identification bracelet.
   Reason: To make sure you are working with the correct patient.

4. Procedural Step: Have the patient sit, stand, or lie down, according to his or her medical condition. If he or she has recently changed position, wait a few minutes before taking the pulse.
   Reason: This allows the heart rate to adjust to the patient's shift in position.

5. Procedural Step: Tell the patient what you are going to do using terms he or she will understand.
   Reason: This keeps the patient calm and provides the patient with necessary information to give informed consent.

6. Procedural Step: Place the palm of the hand downward. If the patient is lying down, rest his or her forearm across the chest.
   Reason: This position will help you count the patient's respirations.

7. Procedural Step: Place the pads of your first two fingers directly over the **radial artery**. Apply slight pressure.
   Reason: The fingertips are sensitive and can feel the pulse, located on the inside of the wrist on the thumb side.

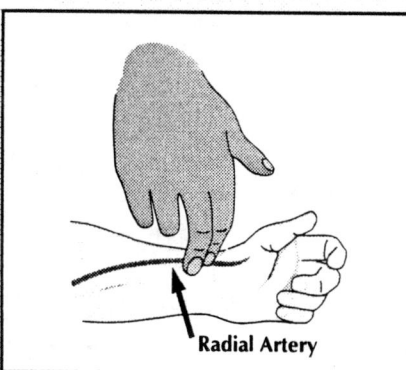
Radial Artery

8. Procedural Step: Feel for the pulsations as the heart beats. Don't push too hard.
   Reason: You could stop the blood flow and stop the pulse.

Measuring a Radial Pulse (Cont.)

9. <u>Procedural Step:</u> Look at the second hand on your watch and begin counting. Ideally, the pulse should be counted for one full minute; however, if the pulse is regular it is acceptable to count for 30 seconds and multiply the number by 2.
<u>Reason:</u> *This will give you the rate per minute quickly. The pulse rate is charted as the rate per minute.*

10. <u>Procedural Step:</u> If the rhythm is irregular, then count it for a full minute.
<u>Reason:</u> *It is possible to miss some heartbeats by not counting an irregular pulse for a full minute.*

11. <u>Procedural Step:</u> When measuring a pulse rate, note the RHYTHM and QUALITY of the beat as well.
<u>Reason:</u> *Rhythm refers to whether the pulse is regular (doesn't change) or irregular (speeds up and/or slows down). Quality refers to the strength of the pulse. A weak, thready pulse may indicate* **shock***, while a full bounding (strong) pulse could indicate high blood pressure.*

12. <u>Procedural Step:</u> Remove and discard your gloves.
<u>Reason:</u> *Universal precaution.*

13. <u>Procedural Step:</u> Wash your hands before providing care to another patient.
<u>Reason:</u> *Universal precaution.*

14. <u>Procedural Step:</u> Record the rate, rhythm, and quality of the pulse in the designated place on the proper form.
<u>Reason:</u> *To provide documentation.*

15. <u>Procedural Step:</u> Before leaving the patient, be sure the side rails have been pulled up.
<u>Reason:</u> *To protect the patient.*

16. <u>Procedural Step:</u> Immediately report any abnormalities to your supervisor.
<u>Reason:</u> *An abnormality may indicate a health problem.*

The pulse rate is recorded in the vital signs section of the patient's chart. Chart it like this:

BP ?—R/L   T   O/R   P 80 AP(R)   R   INITIAL RHYTHM regular strong

Or, on a less detailed chart you can simply record it as P=80, R/S (regular & strong)

or P=116, irreg/thready (irregular, thready)

Note: Although the radial artery is the most common place for measuring the pulse rate, a pulse can be measured anywhere the pulsations of an artery can be felt.

Measuring an Apical Pulse

Materials needed:
- ✓ a stethoscope
- ✓ a watch with a second hand
- ✓ gloves (If blood or other body fluids are present.)

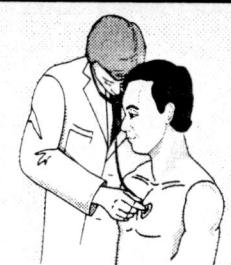

1. Procedural Step: Wash your hands.
   Reason: Universal precaution.

2. Procedural Step: Clean the earpieces of the stethoscope with alcohol before using it.
   Reason: Protects against possible infection.

3. Procedural Step: Put on gloves if there is any blood or other body fluid present.
   Reason: Universal precaution.

4. Procedural Step: Identify the patient by his or her identification bracelet.
   Reason: To ensure you are working with the correct patient.

5. Procedural Step: Tell the patient what you are going to do using terms he or she will understand. (ie, "I am going to listen to your heart," tells the patient exactly what is going to happen.)
   Reason: This keeps the patient calm and provides the information necessary for the patient to give informed consent.

6. Procedural Step: Close the curtains around the bed or close the door to the patient unit.
   Reason: To protect the patient's privacy.

7. Procedural Step: Carefully expose the left breast of the patient. Be careful not to expose more of the patient's chest than necessary.
   Reason: To protect the patient's privacy.

8. Procedural Step: The **apical pulse** can be heard with a stethoscope placed over the **apex** of the heart. It is located at the left fifth intercostal space, mid-clavicular line.
   Reason: The radial pulse may be too faint to feel if the patient is in shock.

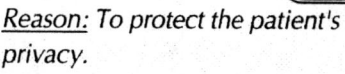

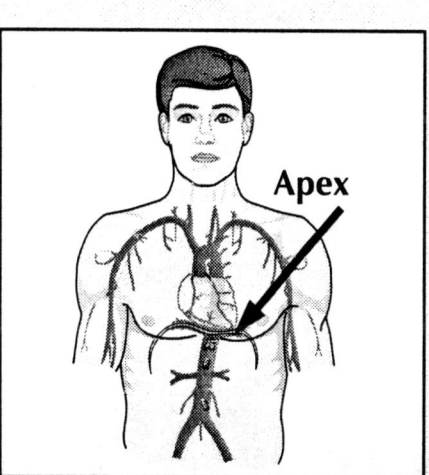

apical pulse: the pulse at the apex of the heart, located at the left fifth intercostal space, mid-clavicular line

Measuring an Apical Pulse (Cont.)

diaphragm: the portion of the stethoscope that is used for picking up sound

9. **Procedural Step:** Place the tips of the stethoscope in your ears and place the **diaphragm** of the stethoscope directly below the left nipple or, if the patient is a woman, under the left breast (apex of the heart).
   Reason: This is where the apical pulse is located.

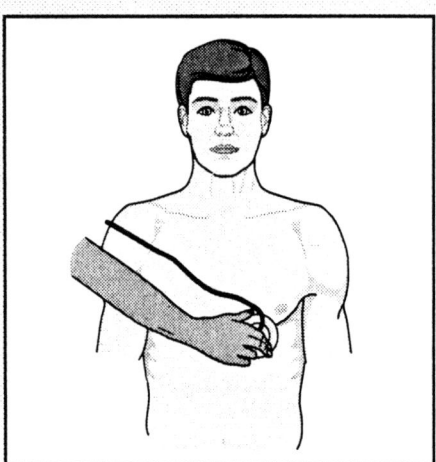

10. **Procedural Step:** Move the diaphragm until you hear the loudest heart sounds or **PMI** (point of maximal impulse). Listen for the sound of the heartbeat, *lubb-dubb*. Count each lubb-dubb as one beat. Count the apical pulse for a full minute.
    Reason: The apical pulse is measured when it is difficult to feel a pulse, when there is an irregular pulse, or when the patient has a heart condition.

11. **Procedural Step:** After covering your patient, open the patient unit.
    Reason: You have obtained the pulse rate.

12. **Procedural Step:** Remove and discard your gloves.
    Reason: Universal precaution.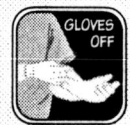

13. **Procedural Step:** Wash your hands before providing care to another patient.
    Reason: Universal precaution.

14. **Procedural Step:** Record the rate, rhythm, and quality of the pulse in the designated place on the proper form.
    Reason: To provide documentation.

15. **Procedural Step:** Before leaving the patient, be sure the side rails have been pulled up.
    Reason: To protect the patient.

16. **Procedural Step:** Immediately report any abnormalities to your supervisor.
    Reason: An abnormality may indicate a health problem.

Chart it like this:

| BP ℒ o— | R
L | T | O
R | P 88 ⒶⓅ
R | R | INITIAL
RHYTHM | regular
strong |

Or, on a less detailed chart you can simply record it as P=88 ⒶⓅ R/S.

Chapter Six • Patient Evaluation

Measuring a Carotid Pulse

Materials needed:
- ✓ a watch with a second hand
- ✓ gloves (If blood or other body fluids are present.)

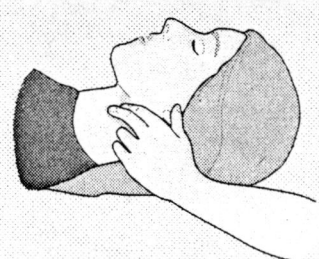

1. <u>Procedural Step:</u> Wash your hands.
   <u>Reason:</u> Universal precaution.

2. <u>Procedural Step:</u> Put on gloves if there is any blood or other body fluid present.
   <u>Reason:</u> Universal precaution.

3. <u>Procedural Step:</u> Identify the patient by his or her identification bracelet.
   <u>Reason:</u> To make sure you are working with the correct patient.

4. <u>Procedural Step:</u> Tell the patient what you are doing in terms he or she will understand.
   <u>Reason:</u> This keeps the patient calm.

5. <u>Procedural Step:</u> The **carotid** arteries on each side of the front of the neck are used to check for a pulse when **cardiac arrest** is suspected.
   <u>Reason:</u> The **carotid pulse** is the closest point to the heart and can still be felt when a patient may only have fainted. There will be no pulse on a patient in cardiac arrest.

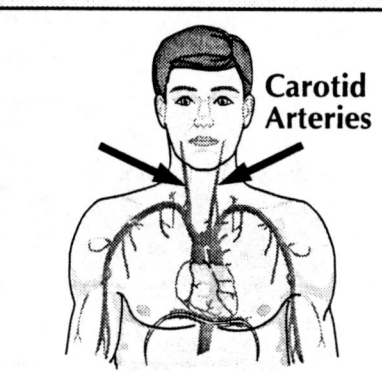

6. <u>Procedural Step:</u> Use the pads of your first two fingers and place them directly over one side of the front of the patient's neck. Check either the right or the left pulse for five to ten seconds. If no pulse is felt, then **cardiac compressions** are begun.
   <u>Reason:</u> This is how the carotid pulse is measured.

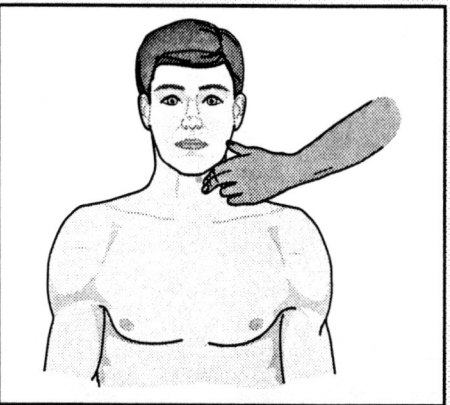

carotid pulse: the pulse that can be heard or felt at the carotid artery

Measuring a Carotid Pulse (Cont.)

7. **Procedural Step:** Only feel one side of the carotid pulse at a time.
   Reason: *Pressing on both carotid arteries could decrease the blood supply to the brain.*

8. **Procedural Step:** Remove and discard your gloves.
   Reason: *Universal precaution.*
   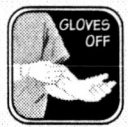

9. **Procedural Step:** Wash your hands before providing care to another patient.
   Reason: *Universal precaution.*

10. **Procedural Step:** Record your findings on the patient's chart.
    Reason: *To provide documentation.*

11. **Procedural Step:** Before leaving the patient, be sure the side rails have been pulled up.
    Reason: *To protect the patient.*

12. **Procedural Step:** Immediately report any abnormalities to your supervisor.
    Reason: *An abnormality may indicate a health problem.*

Chart it like this:

BP ℒo— R/L	T	O/R	P 62 AP/R	R	INITIAL RHYTHM

Or, on a less detailed chart you can simply record it as P=62.

Note: This pulse is not used routinely to monitor vital signs. It is saved for emergencies only. Therefore, rhythm and quality are not usually noted.

Other places where the pulse may be felt include the following:

- The **temporal** artery, located on the face in front of the ear. This is generally not used for a pulse rate as it may be difficult to locate.

- The **brachial** artery, found on the inside of the arm at the crease near the elbow. This pulse is used primarily for a blood pressure check.

- The **femoral** artery, found in the right and left **groin**; the **popliteal artery**, located behind the knee; and the **dorsalis pedis**, located on top of the foot. These are used primarily to check for circulation in the legs and feet.

popliteal artery: the large blood vessel located behind the knee

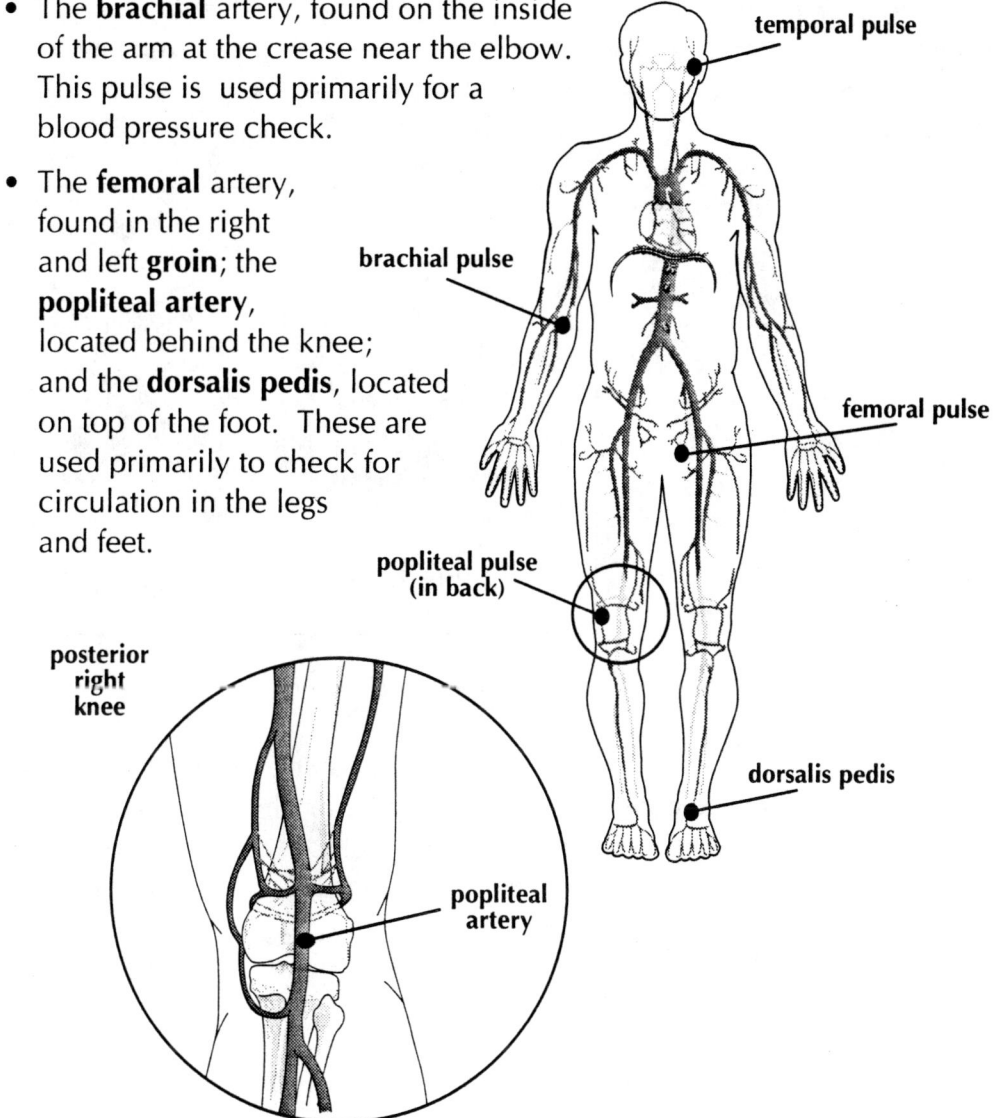

There are many other pulse sites in the human body, but these are the most common and must be learned. All of these pulses are measured by palpation.

Remember!

The Respiration

Respiration (breathing) is the process of bringing oxygen into the lungs and removing carbon dioxide waste. A single respiration consists of one **inspiration** and one **expiration**. On average, an adult breathes twelve to twenty times a minute. The normal rate of breathing can be altered by excitement, pain, exercise, fever, pneumonia, trauma, heart disease, or drugs. Breathing is controlled by the brain and regulated by carbon dioxide changes in the blood stream. The ribs, chest muscles, and **diaphragm** move to allow air to enter and exit the body. (Figure 6-5) If there is an injury or illness to the brain, central nervous system, chest, or ribs, breathing can be affected. If breathing patterns are altered and the body is deprived of oxygen, serious damage can occur to the heart, brain, and kidneys.

diaphragm: the partition that separates the chest and abdominal cavities

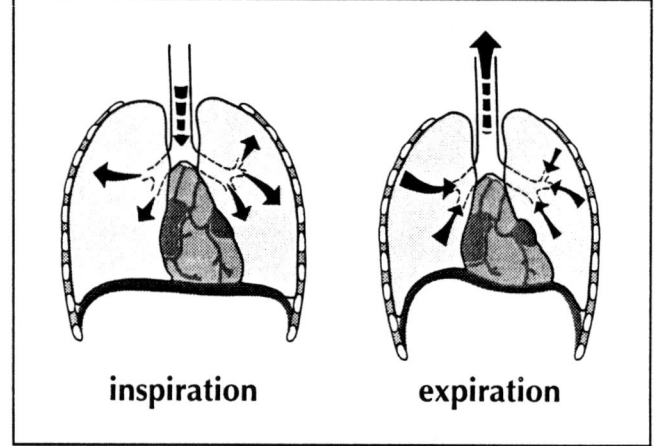

Figure 6-5: Respiration

The volume of air exchanged with each breath can be determined by placing your hand on the patient's chest and feeling the chest rise and fall. The respirations can be deep or **shallow**. When respirations are deep, the patient has **air hunger** and takes long, deep breaths. There may be a prolonged inspiration which could indicate an upper airway obstruction, or a prolonged expiration which could indicate chronic obstructive pulmonary disease (COPD), like asthma, bronchitis, or emphysema.

The patient should not know you are counting his or her respiratory rate. If the patient is aware that it is being determined, he or she may become self-conscious and inadvertently alter the true rate. You can do this procedure without the patient's knowledge by observing and counting the patient's respirations after you have completed taking the pulse.

Measuring Respiration

Materials needed:
- ✓ a watch with a second hand
- ✓ a stethoscope (if done following measurement of the apical pulse)
- ✓ gloves (If blood or other body fluids are present.)

1. **Procedural Step:** Measure the respiration after obtaining the patient's pulse.
   Reason: To prevent the patient from knowing when his or her breathing is being counted.

2. **Procedural Step:** Wash your hands.
   Reason: Universal precaution.

3. **Procedural Step:** Wear gloves if any blood or other body fluid is present.
   Reason: Universal precaution.

4. **Procedural Step:** Identify the patient by his or her identification bracelet.
   Reason: To make sure you are working with the correct patient.

5. **Procedural Step:** Do not tell the patient when you will be monitoring the respiratory rate.
   Reason: This could alter the results.

6. **Procedural Step:** If you measured the radial pulse, keep the patient's arm across the chest and count one inspiration and one expiration as one breath.
   Reason: Having the patient's arm in this position will make it easier to detect the rise and fall of the patient's chest.

7. **Procedural Step:** Count the rate for 30 seconds and multiply that number by two. This final value will be the number of breaths per minute. (ie, if you count eight full respirations in 30 seconds, multiply 8 x 2 = 16 breaths per minute.
   Reason: Respiration is documented as the rate per minute.

8. **Procedural Step:** Remove your gloves.
   Reason: Universal precaution.

   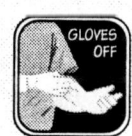

9. **Procedural Step:** Wash your hands.
   Reason: Universal precaution.

10. **Procedural Step:** Record the results on the patient's chart.
    Reason: To provide documentation.

11. **Procedural Step:** If you detect any difficulty in breathing, note it on the patient's chart after the rate.
    Reason: Difficulty in breathing indicates a health problem.

> ### Measuring Respiration (Cont.)
>
> Chart it like this:
>
> | BP ᛝ | R/L | T | O/R | P | AP/R | R 16 labored | INITIAL RHYTHM |
>
> Or, on a less detailed chart, you can simply record it as R=16, labored
>
> **Note:** If you are taking an apical pulse, keep the stethoscope in place on the chest and observe the rise and fall of the chest. Count the respirations in the manner described above.

Use the following general guidelines for the normal rates of respirations:

- premature infants (babies born before being carried in the uterus for 40 weeks): 40 to 90 breaths per minute
- newborn infants (babies less than 6 weeks old): 30 to 50 breaths per minute
- 6 weeks to 12 months old: 20 to 40 breaths per minute
- 2 to 5 years old: 20 to 30 breaths per minute
- 5 to 15 years old: 20 to 25 breaths per minute
- 15 years and older: 15 to 20 breaths per minute

dyspnea: difficulty breathing

A patient whose breathing is labored usually will sit up and lean forward in an effort to breathe easier. The first signs of oxygen deprivation are mental confusion and restlessness. A person who is experiencing **dyspnea** must be seen immediately by the physician.

crackles: fine noises caused by moisture in the lungs

Normal breathing should be quiet and effortless. Noisy respirations indicate an obstruction in the air passages. Snoring sounds signal an airway obstruction and the position of the airway should be checked. If the patient has a lot of secretions, immediate suctioning may be needed. **Crackles** or **gurgling** may indicate fluid in the air passages. **Stridor** is a high-pitched noise, like a squeak, and is caused by a narrowing of the airway from **laryngeal edema** or swelling in the air passages. Narrowing of the airways also can produce a **wheeze** such as that heard in patients with asthma. To listen for sounds within the lungs, use the following procedure.

Chapter Six • Patient Evaluation

Listening for Lung Sounds

Materials needed:
- ✓ a stethoscope
- ✓ gloves (If blood or other body fluids are present.)

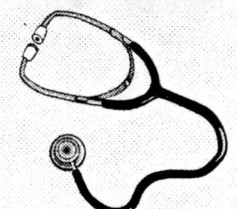

1. Procedural Step: Wash your hands.
   Reason: Universal precaution.

2. Procedural Step: Put on gloves if any blood or other body fluid is present.
   Reason: Universal precaution.

3. Procedural Step: Identify the patient by his or her identification bracelet.
   Reason: To make sure you are working with the correct patient.

4. Procedural Step: Tell the patient what to expect using terms he or she can understand.
   Reason: This keeps the patient calm and provides information necessary for the patient to give consent.

5. Procedural Step: Place the stethoscope over the patient's chest. (See illustration for positions.) Move from points 1 through 5 on the anterior chest and then repeat on the posterior chest.
   Reason: To listen for lung sounds.

6. Procedural Step: Listen for air entering the lungs and for abnormal sounds.
   Reason: Normal breathing is quiet.

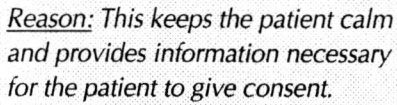

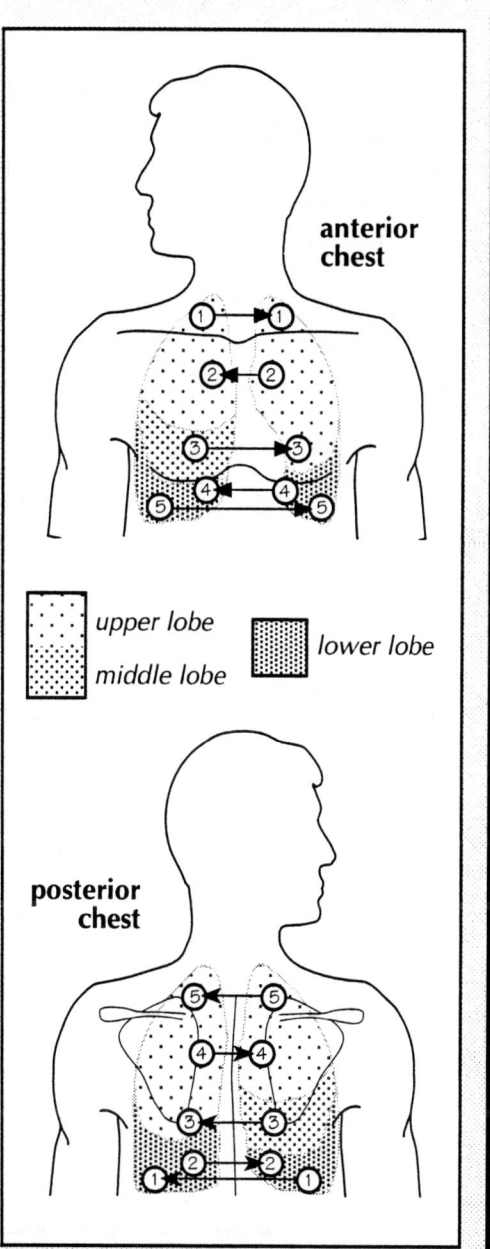

Listening for Lung Sounds (Cont.)

alveoli: microscopic air sacs in the lungs responsible for the exchange of oxygen and carbon dioxide

7. Procedural Step: Ask the patient to breathe deeply through the mouth while you listen to the chest.
   Reason: It amplifies the chest sounds.

8. Procedural Step: Listen for abnormal sounds. Crackles sound similar to the sounds made by rolling a few strands of hair next to your ear.
   Reason: Crackles indicate fluid in the **alveoli** of the lungs. If the lungs are full of fluid, as in **pulmonary edema**, the sounds can be heard without a stethoscope.

9. Procedural Step: Always compare the right and left sides of the chest as well as the front and back sounds.
   Reason: To detect differences in the sounds that are being made.

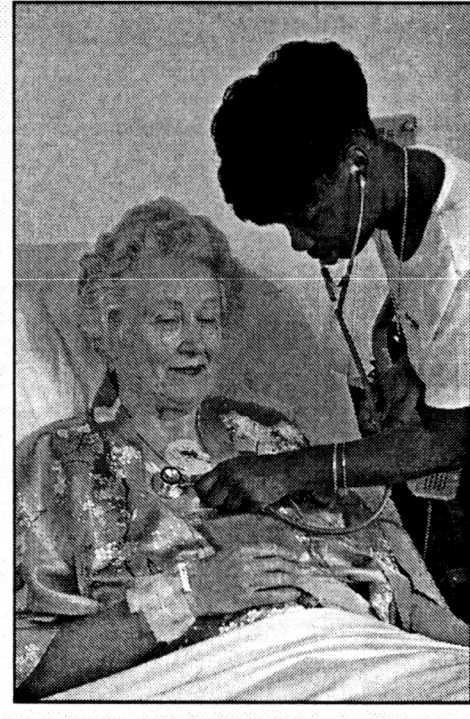

10. Procedural Step: Identify the area from which the sounds are coming.
    Reason: To help locate the problem.

11. Procedural Step: Count the number of breaths for one full minute.
    Reason: Respirations are recorded by the number of breaths per minute.

12. Procedural Step: Remove your gloves.
    Reason: Universal precaution.

13. Procedural Step: Wash your hands.
    Reason: Universal precaution.

14. Procedural Step: Record your findings on the patient's chart.
    Reason: To provide documentation.

Chart it like this:

Lungs clear, bilateral

or, Wheezes, left anterior lower lobe

Both lungs are always checked after any tubes or airway devices are placed in the patient. Continually watch the chest to make sure both sides of the chest are moving equally. If a **pneumothorax** (a lung collapse) occurs, breath sounds will be heard only on the side of the chest where the lung is expanding with each respiration; the side of the chest with the collapsed lung will not move.

The Temperature

Because of our ability to produce and lose heat, body temperature normally remains in the constant range of 98.6° Fahrenheit. Our temperature changes to meet the body's needs. Heat is produced in the body by burning calories as we **metabolize** (use) food for energy. Heat is lost through the skin by **perspiration**, and through the lungs as we exhale. Temperature imbalances occur because of illness and fever, or exposure to extremes in the environment.

Temperature is measured with a glass, digital, or electronic thermometer. The temperature can be taken **orally** (via the mouth), **rectally** (via the rectum), **aurally** (via the ear), or **axillarily** (via the skin). The type of thermometer that is used depends on the way the temperature is to be taken.

Measuring an Oral Temperature Using an Electronic Thermometer

Materials needed:
- ✓ an electronic oral thermometer
- ✓ a disposable thermometer cover
- ✓ gloves (If blood or other body fluids are present.)

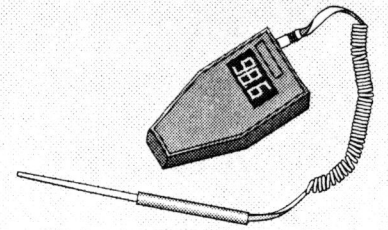

1. Procedural Step: Wash your hands.
   Reason: Universal precaution.

2. Procedural Step: Put on gloves if blood or other body fluids are present.
   Reason: Universal precaution.

3. Procedural Step: Identify the patient by his or her identification bracelet.
   Reason: To make sure you are working with the correct patient.

4. Procedural Step: Explain the procedure to the patient using terms he or she can understand.
   Reason: This keeps the patient calm and provides information the patient needs to give informed consent.

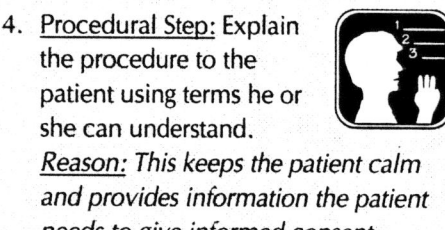

5. Procedural Step: Remove the thermometer from the charging unit or unplug the machine.
   Reason: The unit is charged when not in use.

6. Procedural Step: Remove the temperature probe from the storage compartment and place a disposable cover over the probe.
   Reason: To avoid contamination.

7. Procedural Step: Have the patient discard any chewing tobacco or gum.
   Reason: It may affect the temperature reading.

8. Procedural Step: Ask the patient if he or she has had anything by mouth within the last 15 minutes. Wait 15 minutes if he or she has had anything to eat, drink, chew, or smoke.
   Reason: It may affect the temperature reading.

9. Procedural Step: Wait for the *ready* signal to be displayed.
   Reason: This means the thermometer is ready for use.

10. Procedural Step: Place the probe in the patient's mouth under the tongue. Have the patient close his or her lips.
    Reason: This area is close to a rich blood supply.

Chapter Six • Patient Evaluation

Measuring an Oral Temperature Using an Electronic Thermometer (Cont.)

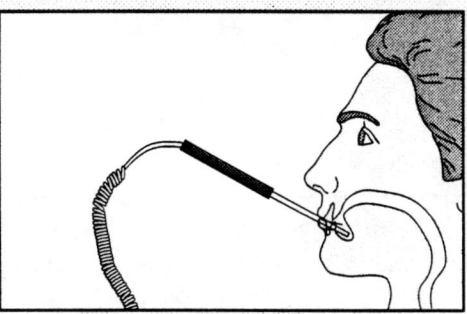

11. **Procedural Step:** At the sound or flashing light, remove the probe from the patient's mouth.
Reason: The signal indicates the thermometer is ready to read.

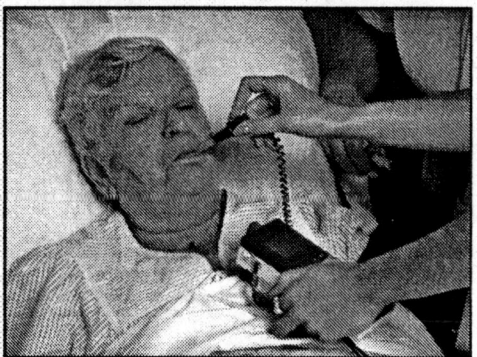

12. **Procedural Step:** Press the probe cover release and dispose of the cover. Do not insert the probe into the body of the thermometer until you have recorded the temperature.
Reason: This allows removal of the probe cover without touching it and prevents alteration of the thermometer reading.

13. **Procedural Step:** Remove your gloves if it was necessary to put them on.
Reason: The gloves are now contaminated and must be removed before touching anything or another patient.

14. **Procedural Step:** Wash your hands.
Reason: Universal precaution.

15. **Procedural Step:** Read the display. Record the temperature on the patient's chart.
Reason: To provide documentation.

16. **Procedural Step:** Return the thermometer to the charging unit.
Reason: The equipment will be ready for the next patient.

17. **Procedural Step:** Report any abnormal readings to the primary health-care provider immediately.
Reason: This may indicate a health problem. A normal oral temperature is 98.6°F.

Chart it like this:

BP ℓ∘— R/L	T 99⁶ Ⓞ/R	P	AP R	R	INITIAL RHYTHM

Or, on a less detailed chart, you would simply write it as T=99⁶.

Measuring an Oral Temperature Using a Glass Thermometer

Materials needed:
- ✓ a glass oral thermometer
- ✓ a thermometer cover (optional)
- ✓ a clock or watch
- ✓ gloves (If blood or other body fluids are present.)

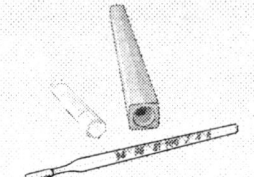

1. Procedural Step: Wash your hands.
   Reason: Universal precaution.

2. Procedural Step: Put on gloves if blood or other body fluids are present.
   Reason: Universal precaution.

3. Procedural Step: Identify the patient by his or her identification bracelet.
   Reason: To make sure you are working with the correct patient.

4. Procedural Step: Explain the procedure to the patient using terms he or she can understand.
   Reason: This keeps the patient calm and provides information the patient needs to give informed consent.
   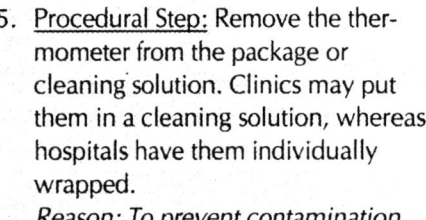

5. Procedural Step: Remove the thermometer from the package or cleaning solution. Clinics may put them in a cleaning solution, whereas hospitals have them individually wrapped.
   Reason: To prevent contamination.

6. Procedural Step: Hold the thermometer at eye level and rotate it until the column of silver-colored mercury can be seen. Check for cracks, breaks, or chips in the glass.
   Reason: A cracked or chipped thermometer can injure the patient.

7. Procedural Step: Grasp the thermometer with your thumb and forefinger. With a sharp, snapping motion of the wrist, shake it until the mercury line falls below 96°F. DO NOT DROP THE THERMOMETER OR HIT IT AGAINST ANY OBJECT! Read it by holding it horizontally at eye level and rotating it between your fingers until the mercury line can be seen easily. Each long line designates 1 degree and each short line indicates 0.2 of a degree (2 tenths, 4 tenths, etc.). A longer line usually indicates 98.6° F (ideal body temperature).
   Reason: For accurate interpretation of the temperature reading, the thermometer must be below 96°F at the time the procedure is begun.

Measuring an Oral Temperature Using a Glass Thermometer (Cont.)

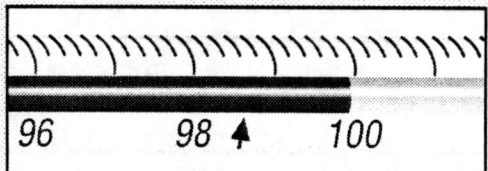

8. **Procedural Step:** Place a disposable cover over the thermometer if one is to be used.
   Reason: Universal precautions.

9. **Procedural Step:** Warn the patient about the hazards of biting the glass.
   Reason: If the glass is broken, the patient may cut his or her mouth and swallow the mercury.

10. **Procedural Step:** Place the probe in the patient's mouth under the tongue. Have the patient close his or her lips.
    Reason: This area is close to a rich blood supply.

11. **Procedural Step:** Wait at least 3 minutes before removing the thermometer.
    Reason: Non-electronic oral temperatures take at least 3 minutes to register.

12. **Procedural Step:** Remove the thermometer and read it to the nearest tenth degree.
    Reason: The temperature is recorded to the nearest tenth degree.

13. **Procedural Step:** If the thermometer has been used with a protective cover, discard the cover and replace the thermometer in the package.
    Reason: To prevent contamination of other objects.

14. **Procedural Step:** Shake the mercury below 96° F, wash it in cold water, and dry it with a paper towel.
    Reason: Washing in cold water removes secretions so the disinfectant will be effective (See step #15), and prevents the mercury from rising. Items must be dried before being disinfected to prevent the solution from becoming diluted by the water.

15. **Procedural Step:** Place the thermometer in disinfecting solution for at least 15 minutes. Continue to wear your gloves until the thermometer is submerged in the solution.
    Reason: Aseptic technique and universal precaution.

16. **Procedural Step:** Remove and discard your gloves if it was necessary to put them on.
    Reason: Universal precaution.

Measuring an Oral Temperature Using a Glass Thermometer (Cont.)

17. **Procedural Step:** Wash your hands before caring for another patient.
    Reason: Universal precaution.

18. **Procedural Step:** Record your findings on the patient's chart.
    Reason: To provide documentation.

19. **Procedural Step:** Report any abnormalities to your supervisor or the primary healthcare provider.
    Reason: An abnormality may indicate a health problem.

Chart it like this:

| BP ⇃o— R/L | T 98⁶ Ⓡ | P | AP/R | R | INITIAL RHYTHM |

Or, on a less detailed chart, you would simply write it as T=98⁶.

Measuring an Aural Temperature Using a Tympanic Thermometer

Materials needed:
- ✓ a tympanic thermometer (electronic)
- ✓ a disposable thermometer cover
- ✓ gloves (If blood or other body fluids are present.)

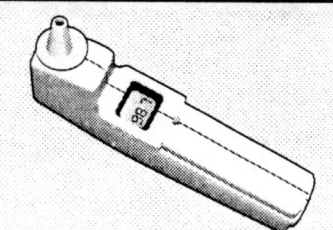

1. Procedural Step: Wash your hands.
   Reason: Universal precaution.

2. Procedural Step: Put on gloves if any blood or other body fluid is present.
   Reason: Universal precaution.

3. Procedural Step: Identify the patient by his or her identification bracelet.
   Reason: To make sure you are working with the correct patient.

4. Procedural Step: Explain the procedure using terms the patient can understand.

   Reason: This reassures the patient and provides information necessary for the patient to give informed consent.

5. Procedural Step: Remove the electronic device from the charging unit.
   Reason: The device is portable.

6. Procedural Step: Place the disposable ear cover over the ear speculum.
   Reason: Aseptic technique.

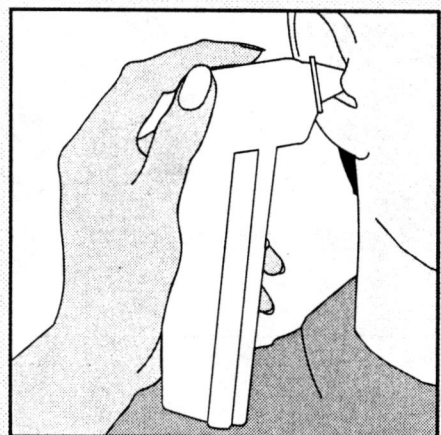

7. Procedural Step: Have the patient turn his or her head to one side. If the patient is a child, gently turn his or her head to one side and hold it in place.
   Reason: This makes the ear easily accessible.

8. Procedural Step: Place the speculum in either ear canal for five seconds. It only has to cover the opening!
   Reason: This measures the temperature of the tympanic membrane.

9. Procedural Step: Press the scan button, and release it when the temperature is flashing on the display screen.
   Reason: The signal indicates the thermometer is ready to be read. It usually takes about 2 seconds.

Measuring an Aural Temperature Using a Tympanic Thermometer (Cont.)

10. **Procedural Step:** Remove the thermometer from the patient's ear.
    Reason: The temperature has been obtained.

11. **Procedural Step:** Read the thermometer and discard the disposable cover.
    Reason: 98.6 F is normal.

12. **Procedural Step:** Remove and discard your gloves if it was necessary to wear them.
    Reason: Universal precaution.

13. **Procedural Step:** Wash your hands.
    Reason: Universal precaution.

14. **Procedural Step:** Return the device to the charging unit.
    Reason: It will be ready for use the next time.

15. **Procedural Step:** Chart the temperature using a T to show that it was a tympanic reading.
    Reason: To provide documentation.

Chart it like this:

BP ℓ₀— R/L	T 98⁴ ᵀ/R	P	AP/R	R	INITIAL RHYTHM

Or, on a less detailed chart, you would simply write it as T=98⁴ Ⓣ.

Chapter Six • Patient Evaluation

Measuring a Rectal Temperature Using a Glass Rectal Thermometer

Materials needed:
- ✓ a glass rectal thermometer (red-tipped)
- ✓ a prelubricated disposable thermometer cover
- ✓ gloves

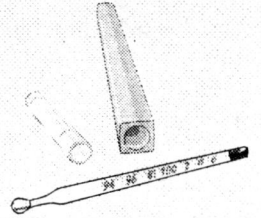

1. Procedural Step: Rectal temperatures are taken on children under age five, unconscious patients, and patients who cannot tolerate an oral thermometer.
   Reason: To provide more accurate measurement on a patient who is unable to follow safety directions regarding glass thermometers.

2. Procedural Step: Wash your hands.
   Reason: Universal procedure.

3. Procedural Step: Wear gloves.
   Reason: Universal procedure.

4. Procedural Step: Identify the patient by his or her identification bracelet.
   Reason: To ensure you are working with the correct patient.

5. Procedural Step: Explain the procedure to the patient using terms he or she can understand.
   Reason: Keeps the patient calm and provides information necessary for the patient to give informed consent.

6. Procedural Step: Make sure the thermometer has a red-tipped end and a short bulb.
   Reason: This means it is a rectal thermometer.

7. Procedural Step: Read the thermometer.
   Reason: To make sure it is below 96° F for an accurate reading.

8. Procedural Step: If it is not there already, shake down the mercury column in thermometer below 96° F.
   Reason: To make the mercury level drop.

9. Procedural Step: Place a prelubricated disposable cover over the thermometer.
   Reason: Disposable covers prevent contamination.

10. Procedural Step: Provide privacy for the patient and position the patient on his or her side. Turn back the sheets to expose the **anus.**
    Reason: It may be more comfortable for the patient to lie on his side with one knee bent.

Measuring a Rectal Temperature Using a Glass Rectal Thermometer (Cont.)

11. **Procedural Step:** Insert the thermometer into the anus 1 to 1-1/2 inches in an adult, 1-inch in a child, and 1/2 inch in an infant.
Reason: This is the proper position for an accurate reading.

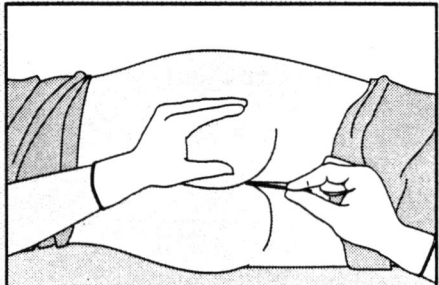

12. **Procedural Step:** Hold the thermometer in place for 3 to 5 minutes.
Reason: To prevent injury.

13. **Procedural Step:** Carefully remove the thermometer.
Reason: It is ready to read.

14. **Procedural Step:** Remove the protective cover and discard. Wipe the thermometer from stem toward bulb end and discard the tissue.
Reason: The sheath and tissue are contaminated.

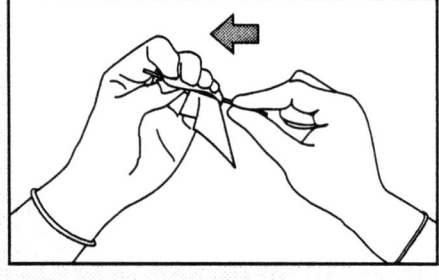

15. **Procedural Step:** Remove your gloves.
Reason: Universal precaution.

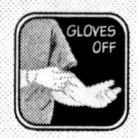

16. **Procedural Step:** Wash your hands.
Reason: Universal precaution.

17. **Procedural Step:** Read the thermometer and record the temperature on the patient's chart using the abbreviation, R, to indicate *rectal*.
Reason: The normal rectal temperature is 99.8° F.

18. **Procedural Step:** Cover and reposition your patient comfortably.

19. **Procedural Step:** Disinfect the thermometer according to facility policy. Open the curtain and return equipment to its proper place.
Reason: Aseptic technique. The equipment will be ready for the next patient. Universal precaution.

20. **Procedural Step:** Report any abnormal findings immediately, and wash your hands again before providing care to another patient.
Reason: Abnormal findings may indicate a health problem. Universal precaution.

Chart it like this:

BP ♀ o— R/L	T 101⁴ ○/Ⓡ	P	AP/R	R	INITIAL RHYTHM

Or, on a less detailed chart, you would simply write it as T=101⁴Ⓡ

Measuring a Rectal Temperature Using an Electronic Rectal Thermometer

Materials needed:
- ✓ an electronic rectal thermometer (red-tipped probe)
- ✓ a disposable probe cover
- ✓ lubricating jelly
- ✓ gloves

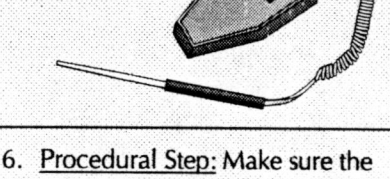

1. Procedural Step: Rectal temperatures are taken on children under age five, unconscious patients, and patients who cannot tolerate an oral thermometer.
   Reason: Provides more accurate measurement on a patient who is unable to follow safety directions regarding oral thermometers.

2. Procedural Step: Wash your hands.
   Reason: Universal precaution.

3. Procedural Step: Wear gloves.
   Reason: Universal precaution.

4. Procedural Step: Identify the patient by his or her identification bracelet.
   Reason: To ensure you are working with the correct patient.

5. Procedural Step: Explain the procedure to the patient using terms he or she can understand.
   Reason: This keeps the patient calm and provides the information the patient needs to give informed consent.

6. Procedural Step: Make sure the thermometer has a red-tipped end.
   Reason: This means it is a rectal thermometer.

7. Procedural Step: Place a protective probe cover over the thermometer.
   Reason: The disposable cover prevents contamination.

8. Procedural Step: Lubricate the probe cover with **KY Jelly** or **Lubifax**.
   Reason: For ease of insertion.

9. Procedural Step: Provide privacy for the patient by drawing the curtain completely around the patient's bed or closing the door to the patient's unit.
   Reason: This makes the procedure less embarrassing for the patient.

10. Procedural Step: Position the patient on his or her side with the top thigh and knee pulled toward the chest. Have the patient lean forward slightly. Turn back the sheets to expose the anus.
    Reason: This allows easy access to the rectum.

Measuring a Rectal Temperature Using an Electronic Rectal Thermometer (Cont.)

11. Procedural Step: Insert the thermometer into the anus 1 to 1-1/2 inches in an adult, 1-inch in a child, and 1/2 inch in an infant. If the thermometer does not advance easily, remove the probe and report this to the primary care provider. NEVER FORCE THE RECTAL PROBE!
    Reason: This is the proper position for an accurate reading. Forcing the probe could injure the patient.

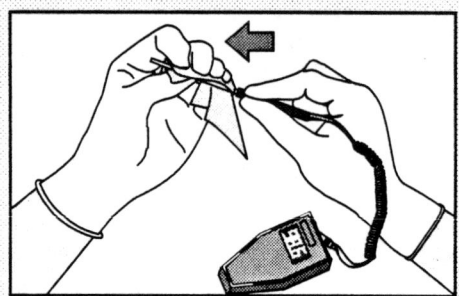

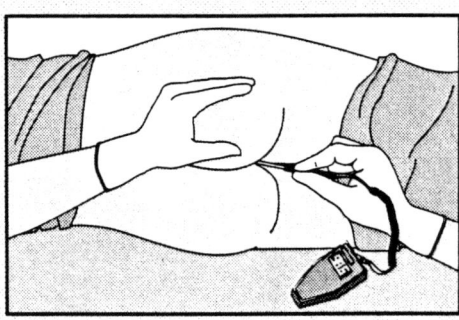

12. Procedural Step: Hold the thermometer in place until you hear the sound or see a flashing light.
    Reason: Prevents injury in case the patient moves and ensures an accurate reading.

13. Procedural Step: Carefully remove the thermometer.
    Reason: The thermometer is ready to read.

14. Procedural Step: Remove the protective probe cover and discard. Wipe the thermometer from stem toward bulb end and discard tissue.
    Reason: The probe cover and tissue are contaminated.

15. Procedural Step: Remove your gloves.
    Reason: Universal precaution.

16. Procedural Step: Wash your hands.
    Reason: Universal precaution.

17. Procedural Step: Read the thermometer and record the temperature on the patient's chart using the proper abbreviation, R, to indicate that it is a rectal temperature.
    Reason: Normal rectal temperature is 99.8° F.

18. Procedural Step: Cover your patient and reposition him or her comfortably.
    Reason: To make the patient as comfortable as possible.

Measuring a Rectal Temperature Using an Electronic Rectal Thermometer (Cont.)

19. **Procedural Step:** Clean and disinfect the thermometer according to facility policy. Open the curtain surrounding the patient and return the equipment to its proper place.
    Reason: Aseptic technique. The equipment will be ready for the next patient. Universal precaution.

20. **Procedural Step:** Report any abnormal findings to the appropriate healthcare provider and your supervisor immediately.
    Reason: Abnormal findings may indicate a health problem.

21. **Procedural Step:** Wash your hands again before providing care to another patient.
    Reason: Universal precaution.

Chart it like this:

| BP ℓ o— R/L | T 102⁴ O/R | P | AP/R | R | INITIAL RHYTHM |

Or, on a less detailed chart, you would simply write it as T=102⁴ ®

Measuring an Axillary Temperature

Materials needed:
- ✓ an oral (glass or electronic) thermometer
- ✓ gloves (If blood or other body fluids are present.)

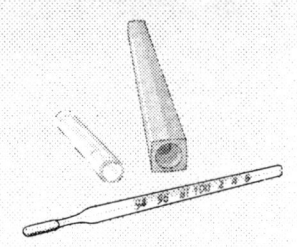

1. <u>Procedural Step:</u> Wash your hands.
   <u>Reason:</u> Universal precaution.

2. <u>Procedural Step:</u> Put on gloves if there is any blood or other body fluid present.
   <u>Reason:</u> Universal precaution.

3. <u>Procedural Step:</u> Identify the patient by his or her identification bracelet.
   <u>Reason:</u> To ensure you are working with the correct patient.

4. <u>Procedural Step:</u> Explain the procedure to the patient using terms he or she will understand.
   <u>Reason:</u> This keeps the patient calm and provides the information necessary for the patient to give informed consent.

5. <u>Procedural Step:</u> Remove the patient's top piece of clothing.
   <u>Reason:</u> To gain access to the axilla.

6. <u>Procedural Step:</u> If there is moisture in the axilla, gently pat the area dry.
   <u>Reason:</u> Both moisture and intense rubbing can affect the temperature reading.

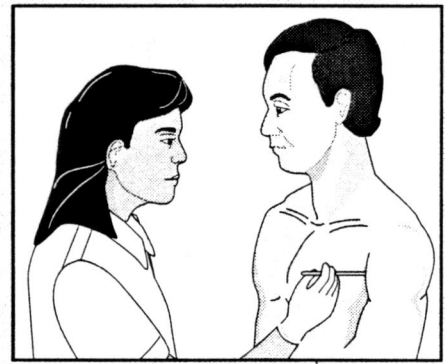

7. <u>Procedural Step:</u> Place the thermometer in the armpit, and bring the patient's arm close to the chest.
   <u>Reason:</u> To get an accurate reading.

8. <u>Procedural Step:</u> If using an electronic thermometer, wait for the signal indicating the reading is complete. If using a glass thermometer, hold it in place for at least 10 minutes.
   <u>Reason:</u> This is necessary for an accurate reading.

9. <u>Procedural Step:</u> Remove and discard your gloves.
   <u>Reason:</u> Universal precaution.

10. <u>Procedural Step:</u> Wash your hands.
    <u>Reason:</u> Universal precaution.

Chapter Six • Patient Evaluation

Measuring an Axillary Temperature (Cont.)

11. <u>Procedural Step:</u> Read the thermometer and record the temperature on the patient's chart. Be sure to use the abbreviation *Ax* to indicate axillary temperature.
    <u>Reason:</u> A normal axillary temperature is 97.8° F. (About 1 lower than an oral temperature.)

12. <u>Procedural Step:</u> Help the patient dress again if necessary.
    <u>Reason:</u> To assist the patient.

13. <u>Procedural Step:</u> Report any abnormalities to your supervisor and the primary healthcare provider immediately.
    <u>Reason:</u> An abnormality may indicate a health problem.

Chart it like this:

| BP ℒ⟋ R/L | T 102⁴ ⒶⓍ/R | P | AP/R | R | INITIAL RHYTHM |

Or, on a less detailed chart, you would simply write it as T=102⁴ ⒶⓍ.

Note: On a child, a thermometer patch can be placed on the forehead to obtain the skin temperature. The temperature is determined by color changes on the paper patch.

The Blood Pressure

Blood pressure is a measure of the force of blood against the walls of the arteries. Many factors can affect the blood pressure. Some of these factors follow:

- the amount of blood in the circulatory system
- the amount of fluid in the body
- the force of the heartbeat
- the condition of the arteries (whether they have elasticity, or whether they have lost this resistance)
- the distance from the heart (blood pressure is normally lower in the legs than in the arms)

Exercise, age, eating, pain, stress, **stimulants** (substances that speed up the body), **obesity**, and hereditary factors can cause the blood pressure to increase. Other factors can lower blood pressure, such as fasting (not eating), weight loss, grief, depression, shock, or blood loss. A patient's blood pressure can also be influenced by his or her gender. For example, pre-menopausal women tend to have lower blood pressure than men.

> **systolic:** the top number in a blood pressure reading; refers to the time between the first and second heartbeat

Blood pressure is measured using a sphygmomanometer applied to the upper arm over the **brachial artery**. The brachial artery is found on the inside of the arm at the bend of the elbow. The normal blood pressure is 120 mm of mercury **systolic** and 80 mm of mercury **diastolic**. The blood pressure reading is recorded as a fraction (ie, 120/80). To get a proper reading, the width of the blood pressure cuff should cover approximately 3/4 the size of the patient's upper arm. A false high reading can be obtained if the cuff is too narrow, and a false low reading can be obtained if the cuff is too wide. Pediatric cuffs are available for children.

> **diastolic:** the bottom number in a blood pressure reading; refers to the period of time between heart contractions

There are two methods of obtaining a blood pressure reading: by palpation and by auscultation. The palpated blood pressure is obtained for two primary reasons: (1) As a prelude to obtaining an auscultated blood pressure (one heard with a stethoscope) in order to determine the approximate systolic blood pressure, and (2) When the blood pressure is difficult or impossible to hear and a blood pressure determination is needed.

Only the approximate systolic blood pressure can be obtained by the palpation method. The diastolic blood pressure cannot be felt. The palpated systolic blood pressure and the auscultated systolic blood pressure will not be exactly the same in most cases because the palpated blood pressure is not as accurate a method as auscultation, in which you hear both the systolic and the diastolic blood pressure.

Taking a Palpated Systolic Blood Pressure

Materials needed:
- ✓ a sphygmomanometer (In the proper size for the patient.)
- ✓ gloves (If blood or other body fluids are present.)

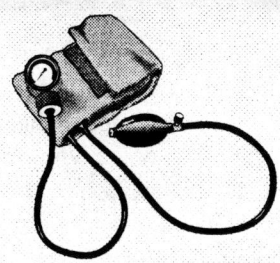

1. Procedural Step: Wash your hands and assemble the equipment.
   Reason: Universal precaution.

2. Procedural Step: Put on gloves if there is any blood or other body fluid present.
   Reason: Universal precaution.
   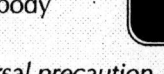

3. Procedural Step: Identify the patient.
   Reason: This confirms that you are assessing the correct patient.

4. Procedural Step: Explain the procedure to the patient using terms he or she will understand.
   Reason: This keeps the patient calm and provides the information necessary for the patient to give informed consent.

5. Procedural Step: Have the patient sit or lie down. Roll the patient's sleeve about 6 inches above the elbow. If the sleeve is too tight, remove the arm from the sleeve. Extend the arm, palm up, at heart level.
   Reason: A sleeve that is too tight may compress the brachial artery and distort the results. If the arm is above heart level the reading may be incorrectly low.

6. Procedural Step: Palpate the brachial artery, located on the inner aspect of the elbow on the patient's little finger side. Then place the blood pressure cuff smoothly and securely around the patient's arm about 2 inches above the bend in the elbow. Be sure the middle of the cloth-enclosed cuff is directly over the brachial artery. If the cuff has an arrow to indicate right or left arm, the arrow should be placed over the brachial artery.
   Reason: The cuff should be tight enough to stay on, but not so tight as to be constricting. It should be high enough so that you can easily palpate the brachial artery, and if you will be auscultating the blood pressure after palpating it, the stethoscope will not touch the cuff and cause extraneous sounds. By placing the center of the bladder of the cuff over the brachial artery you assure that the pressure is applied equally over the artery.

Taking a Palpated Systolic Blood Pressure (Cont.)

7. Procedural Step: Place two fingers of your nondominant hand over the patient's radial artery, which is located on the inside of the wrist on the thumb side. Do not use your own thumb to feel for the pulse.
   Reason: The thumb has a pulse of its own that could be mistaken for the patient's pulse.

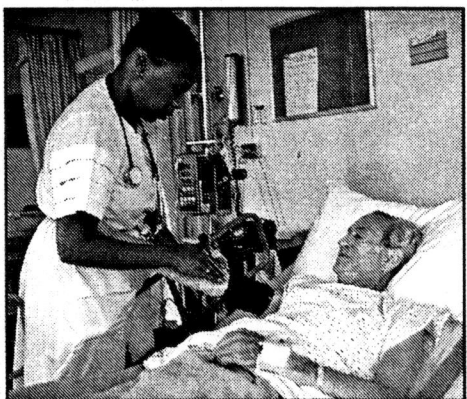

8. Procedural Step: Hold the rubber bulb of the blood pressure cuff in your dominant hand with your palm upward and the knob of the control valve pointing toward your thumb. Continue to palpate the radial pulse while you turn the control valve away from you using your thumb.
   Reason: This will close the valve.

9. Procedural Step: Rapidly squeeze the bulb to pump air into the blood pressure cuff. Note on the calibrated scale of the sphygmomanometer the point at which the radial pulse cannot be felt.

10. Procedural Step: Do not pause. Continue to pump air into the blood pressure cuff to a level of 20 to 30 mmHg above the point where the radial pulse disappeared.

11. Procedural Step: Immediately begin to release the air in the cuff by slowly and steadily turning the knob of the control valve toward you with your thumb.

12. Procedural Step: Note the point on the calibrated scale when you once again feel the pulse.
    Reason: This is the palpated systolic pressure.

13. Procedural Step: Now you may rapidly deflate the cuff. Remember, you cannot obtain a diastolic blood pressure using the palpation method.
    Reason: The diastolic blood pressure cannot be felt.

14. Procedural Step: If you are now going to take an auscultated blood pressure, wait at least 1 minute before inflating the cuff again.
    Reason: To reduce the congestion of the blood vessels which can result in incorrect results.

15. Procedural Step: If you are not going to take an auscultated blood pressure, remove the cuff and proceed to steps 16, 17, and 18.

Chapter Six • Patient Evaluation

Taking a Palpated Systolic Blood Pressure (Cont.)

16. <u>Procedural Step:</u> Remove your gloves if it was necessary to put them on.
<u>Reason:</u> Universal precaution.

17. <u>Procedural Step:</u> Wash your hands before providing care to another patient.
<u>Reason:</u> Universal precaution.

18. <u>Procedural Step:</u> Record the results on the patient's chart.
<u>Reason:</u> To provide documentation.

Chart it like this, indicating which arm was used and whether the patient was sitting or lying down:

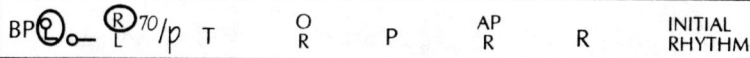

Or, on a less detailed chart you can simply record it as *BP=70/ palpated RA, sitting* meaning the blood pressure was taken on the right arm, and a systolic blood pressure of 70 was palpated.

After palpating the systolic pressure, you are ready to take an auscultated blood pressure. Both a systolic blood pressure reading and a diastolic blood pressure reading can be obtained by the auscultation method. To do this, use the procedure on the next page.

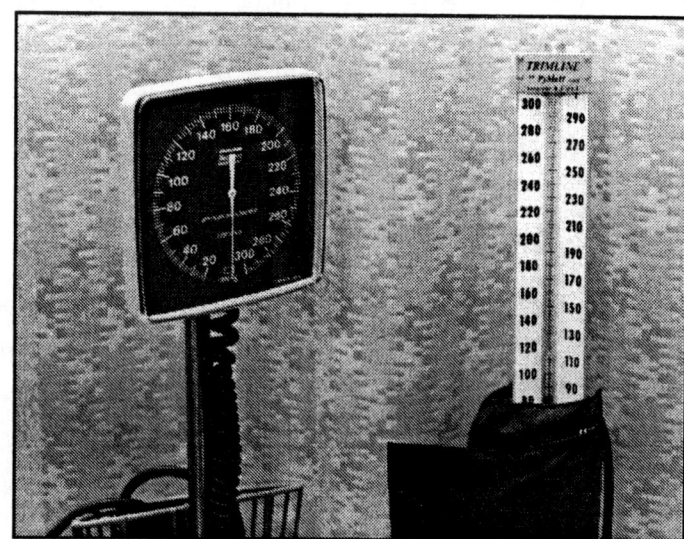

Figure 6-6: Types of Sphygmomanometers

Auscultating a Blood Pressure

Materials needed:
- ✓ a stethoscope
- ✓ a sphygmomanometer
- ✓ an alcohol sponge
- ✓ gloves (If blood or other body fluids are present.)

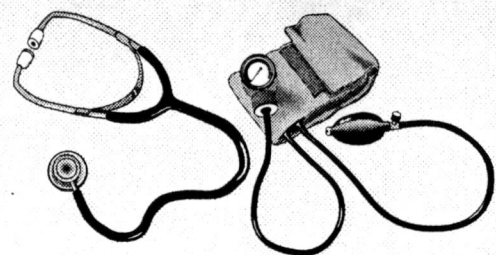

1. **Procedural Step:** Wait 1 minute after taking a palpated blood pressure before inflating the cuff again.
   Reason: To reduce the congestion of the blood vessels which can result in incorrect results.

2. **Procedural Step:** Place the earpieces of the stethoscope in your ears with the tips pointing slightly forward. Avoid letting the tubes of the stethoscope rub together.
   Reason: The forward position of the earpieces will make it easier to hear because they will be following the direction of the ear canal. The tubes should be hanging freely so extraneous sounds won't be heard.

3. **Procedural Step:** Palpate the pulse at the brachial artery. Place the diaphragm of the stethoscope firmly over the point of maximal impulse (PMI).
   Reason: Proper placement of the diaphragm of the stethoscope will help you hear the sounds of the blood pressure.

4. **Procedural Step:** Hold the diaphragm in place with your nondominant hand, close the control valve and quickly squeeze the bulb with your dominant hand to a level of 20 or 30 mmHg above the point at which you palpated the systolic blood pressure.
   Reason: The range of 20 to 30 mmHg is sufficient to be sure you have pumped the cuff high enough to accurately hear the systolic pressure. Inflating the rubber bladder in the cuff stops the flow of blood in the artery. The cuff is inflated quickly and smoothly to avoid congestion in the blood vessels.

5. **Procedural Step:** Slowly and steadily open the control valve at a rate of approximately 2 to 3 mmHg per heartbeat. This will release the air in the cuff. Listen for the first clear, tapping sound. This is the systolic pressure. Notice the reading on the calibrated scale.
   Reason: The systolic blood pressure represents the pressure against the walls of the arteries when the ventricles of the heart contract and blood surges through the aorta and pulmonary arteries.

Auscultating a Blood Pressure (Cont.)

6. **Procedural Step:** Continue to steadily deflate the cuff until the last sound is heard. This is the diastolic pressure.
   Reason: The disatolic pressure refers to the point at which there is the least pressure in the arteries and occurs when the heart relaxes (diastole) before the next contraction (systole).

7. **Procedural Step:** Quickly release the rest of the air from the cuff and remove the cuff from the patient's arm. (Or leave the deflated cuff in place if frequent blood pressure readings are to be done.)
   Reason: If left inflated, it will prevent circulation to the hand and arm.

8. **Procedural Step:** Immediately record the measurements obtained as a fraction, noting the time, arm used (right or left), and the patient's position (lying, sitting, or standing).
   Reason: Charting immediately will ensure accuracy.

9. **Procedural Step:** Clean the earpieces and the diaphragm of the stethoscope with an alcohol sponge.
   Reason: The equipment will be ready for use the next time.

10. **Procedural Step:** Remove your gloves if it was necessary to put them on.
    Reason: Universal precaution.

11. **Procedural Step:** Wash your hands before providing care to another patient.
    Reason: Universal precaution.

Chart it like this, indicating which arm was used and whether the patient was sitting or lying down:

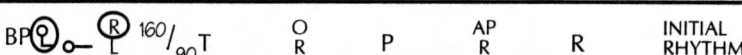

Or, on a less detailed chart you can simply record it as BP=160/90 RA, sitting meaning the blood pressure was 160 mmHg systolic and 90 mmHg diastolic, and the reading was taken on the right arm with the patient in a sitting position.

Note: When listening for the diastolic pressure, you will notice a change in the quality of the sounds before they completely disappear. Some physicians consider this first diastolic sound to be the diastolic blood pressure. If you are asked to record this sound, chart it as follows: B/P 180/100/90. This would mean that the first sound you heard was 180 (systolic blood pressure), a change or muffled sound was noted at 100 (first diastolic sound), and the last sound you heard was at 90 (final diastolic pressure).

Continuous Monitoring of Blood Pressure Automatically

Automatic continuous blood pressure monitoring is common practice in an emergency department. There are less errors using the automated method than with the traditional method because it is done by a machine. This method also is convenient and is easily used by all medical staff. One type of monitor has the capability of monitoring not only the blood pressure, but also of continuous monitoring of an electrocardiograph tracing, heart rate, and the pulse oximetry, or oxygen level of the blood. Always observe the equipment carefully and alert the nursing staff to changes in the system or any alarms you hear.

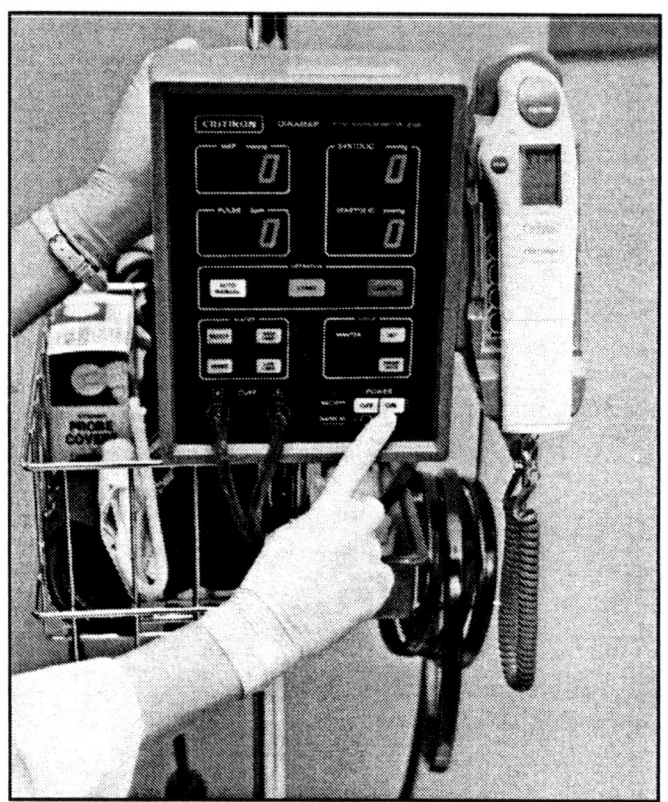

Figure 6-7: Automatic monitoring of the blood pressure is possible with an automatic sphygmomanometer.

Continuous Monitoring of Blood Pressure Automatically

Materials needed:
- ✓ an automated blood pressure monitoring device
- ✓ an automatic blood pressure cuff
- ✓ an electrical outlet
- ✓ gloves (If blood or other body fluids are present.)

1. <u>Procedural Step:</u> Wash your hands.
   <u>Reason:</u> Universal precaution.

2. <u>Procedural Step:</u> Put on gloves if there is any blood or other body fluid present.
   <u>Reason:</u> Universal precaution.

3. <u>Procedural Step:</u> Identify the patient.
   <u>Reason:</u> This confirms that you are assessing the correct patient.

4. <u>Procedural Step:</u> Explain the procedure to the patient using terms he or she will understand.
   <u>Reason:</u> This keeps the patient calm and provides the information necessary for the patient to give informed consent.

5. <u>Procedural Step:</u> Connect the tubing to the monitor and the cuff.
   <u>Reason:</u> Air tubing must be connected to the monitor to obtain a blood pressure reading.

6. <u>Procedural Step:</u> Make sure the cuff is deflated.
   <u>Reason:</u> This will ensure an accurate reading.

7. <u>Procedural Step:</u> Apply the automatic blood pressure cuff to the patient. Make sure it is the correct size and that it fits the patient properly.
   <u>Reason:</u> *Proper fit and placement of the cuff is essential for correct measurement.*

8. <u>Procedural Step:</u> Press the power "ON" button located on the front of the monitor.
   <u>Reason:</u> The machine must be turned on in order for it to work. The digital display will light up when it is receiving power.

9. <u>Procedural Step:</u> Select the "AUTO" or "MANUAL" mode.
   <u>Reason:</u> For a one-time reading, use the manual setting. For frequent readings at specified intervals (from 1 to 60 minutes) select the automatic setting.

Continuous Monitoring of Blood Pressure Automatically (Cont.)

10. <u>Procedural Step:</u> To change the time interval between readings, press the appropriate button (according to the manufacturer's instructions) and enter the desired amount of time between readings.
    <u>Reason:</u> *The physician may decide that less frequent readings are appropriate. Machines vary from model to model, so you will need to study the manufacturer's manual to learn which button to use for setting the time interval.*

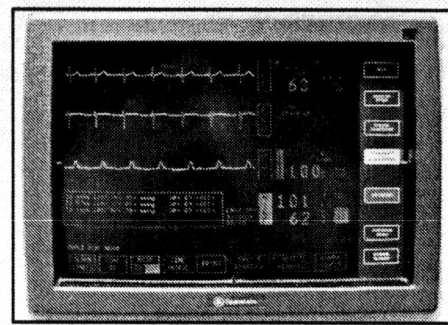

11. <u>Procedural Step:</u> Set the alarms for the high and low limits of blood pressure according to the manufacturer's instructions.
    <u>Reason:</u> *The alarms will alert the medical staff to a sudden, critical change in the blood pressure.*

12. <u>Procedural Step:</u> To read the blood pressure look at the display.
    <u>Reason:</u> *The display will indicate the blood pressure and the time it was obtained.*

13. <u>Procedural Step:</u> Remove your gloves if it was necessary to put them on.
    <u>Reason:</u> *Universal precaution.*
    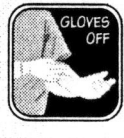

14. <u>Procedural Step:</u> Wash your hands.
    <u>Reason:</u> *Universal precaution.*

15. <u>Procedural Step:</u> Record the results of each reading on the patient's chart according to the physician's orders.
    <u>Reason:</u> *For documentation.*

Chart it like this, indicating which arm was used and whether the patient was sitting or lying down:

8:00 a.m. BP=160/90 RA, lying down
8:30 a.m. BP=160/90 RA, lying down
9:00 a.m. BP=160/90 RA, lying down

Performing a Neuro Check

A neuro check is an evaluation of a patient's **neurological** status, and is used to detect subtle changes in a patient's condition. Patients with head injuries, trauma, seizures, or who are unconscious or in a coma should have a neuro check done as a routine part of the vital signs. A neuro check includes the following checks:

- ✓ a pupil check
- ✓ an **orientation** check
- ✓ response to pain check
- ✓ a movement check
- ✓ a sensation check

orientation: the ability to comprehend one's environment regarding time, situation, place, and identity of persons

Performing a Neuro Check

Materials needed:
- ✓ A penlight
- ✓ gloves (If blood or other body fluids are present.)

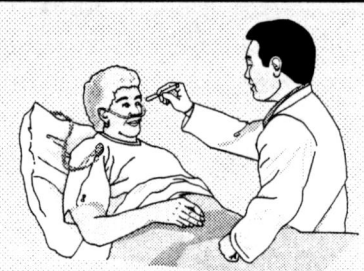

1. <u>Procedural Step:</u> Wash your hands.
   <u>Reason:</u> Universal precaution.

2. <u>Procedural Step:</u> Put on gloves if there is any blood or other body fluid present.
   <u>Reason:</u> Universal precaution.

3. <u>Procedural Step:</u> Identify the patient.
   <u>Reason:</u> This confirms that you are assessing the correct patient.

4. <u>Procedural Step:</u> Explain the procedure to the patient using terms he or she can understand.
   <u>Reason:</u> This keeps the patient calm and provides the information necessary for the patient to give informed consent.

5. <u>Procedural Step:</u> A pupil check is done by opening the eyes and shining a penlight into each pupil.
   <u>Reason:</u> A normal pupil will react to a light by constricting.

6. <u>Procedural Step:</u> Ask the patient his or her name.
   <u>Reason:</u> Oriented times one (a person will know his or her name).

   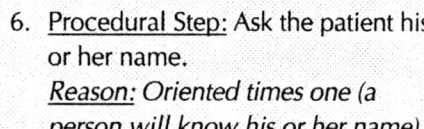

7. <u>Procedural Step:</u> Ask the patient where he or she is.
   <u>Reason:</u> Oriented times two (a person will know where he or she is).

8. <u>Procedural Step:</u> Ask the patient what happened.
   <u>Reason:</u> Oriented times three (a person will know what happened).

9. <u>Procedural Step:</u> Ask the patient what time it is.
   <u>Reason:</u> Oriented times four (a person will know the approximate time).

10. <u>Procedural Step:</u> Check for a response to pain by observing the reaction to an injection or a procedure.
    <u>Reason:</u> A normal patient will respond to pain with purposeful movement. A person in a coma will have no response to pain.

Chapter Six • Patient Evaluation

Performing a Neuro Check (Cont.)

11. <u>Procedural Step:</u> Check for movement and sensation in all extremities by asking the patient to grip your hands or move his feet.
<u>Reason:</u> *If the central nervous system is intact, the patient can move the arms and legs equally. Weakness on one side or both sides indicates a problem and must be documented on the chart.*

12. <u>Procedural Step:</u> Remove your gloves if it was necessary to put them on.
<u>Reason:</u> *Universal precaution.*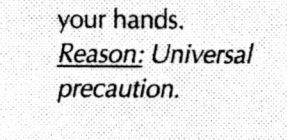

13. <u>Procedural Step:</u> Wash your hands.
<u>Reason:</u> *Universal precaution.*

14. <u>Procedural Step:</u> Record the results of the neuro check on the patient's chart.
<u>Reason:</u> *To provide documentation.*

Chart it like this:

TIME	INITIAL	VERBAL RESPONSE	MOTOR RESPONSE	EYE OPENING	GRIP		UPPER EXTREMITY MOVEMENT		LOWER EXTREMITY MOVEMENT		PUPILS			
											SIZE	REACTION	SIZE	REACTION
					R	L	R	L	R	L	R		L	
14:00	MM	Ox3	S	S	S	W	S	W	S	S	5	N	5	N
14:20	MM	Ox4	S	S	S	W	S	W	S	S	5	N	5	N

Key

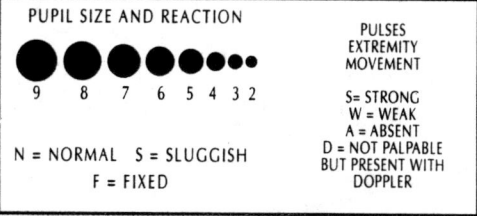

PUPIL SIZE AND REACTION
9 8 7 6 5 4 3 2
N = NORMAL S = SLUGGISH
F = FIXED

PULSES
EXTREMITY
MOVEMENT
S = STRONG
W = WEAK
A = ABSENT
D = NOT PALPABLE BUT PRESENT WITH DOPPLER

On a less detailed chart you can simply record the pupils as PERL if they are normal.

Weight and Height

Height and weight measurements are used to determine a patient's overall health status. They also are used to determine the amount of medication to be administered. Weight loss can indicate dehydration, poor nutrition, diabetes, cancer, and other diseases. Weight gain can indicate tumors, pregnancy, congestive heart failure, and other conditions. Most patients can tell you their height or weight, but it may not be accurate. If it is critical to the patient's treatment, the doctor will order the patient weighed. If it is necessary to determine a patient's weight, use the stand-up scale located in the Emergency Department.

It is preferable to convert the patient's weight from pounds (lbs) to kilograms (kg). Kilograms are part of the metric system that is universally used in the medical field. To do this, divide the weight by 2.2; for example:

$$150 \text{ lbs} \div 2.2 = 68.18 \text{ kg}$$

Children 2 years and older can also be weighed on the adult scale. Infants and children younger than 2 years old must be weighed using a baby scale that has pounds and ounces. If the child is uncooperative, have one of the parents hold the child and step on the scale. Record this weight. Have the parent put the child down and step back up on the scale. Record this weight. Subtract the second weight from the first weight and this will give you the approximate weight of the child. Infants should be undressed, including the diaper, and placed on their back on the scale. Be sure to record the weight on the patient's chart.

A baby's height can be measured by laying the child down on examination paper and marking a line on the paper above the infant's head and straightening the leg and marking a line at the end of the foot. Lift the baby up and measure between the two marks. Always keep one hand on the baby for safety and NEVER LEAVE AN INFANT UNATTENDED!

An adult's height can be determined using the measuring scale that is usually located on the hospital's weight scale. Record the measurement in inches on the patient's chart.

Chapter Six • Patient Evaluation

Measuring the Weight of an Adult

Materials needed:
✓ a scale with a measuring device

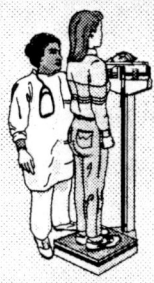

1. <u>Procedural Step:</u> Identify the patient.
   <u>Reason:</u> To confirm that you are assessing the correct patient.

2. <u>Procedural Step:</u> Ask the patient if he or she knows his or her correct weight.
   <u>Reason:</u> *This will assist you in setting the weight on the scale in the general area; it also avoids embarrassment if you judge the patient to weigh more than he or she actually does.*

3. <u>Procedural Step:</u> Ask the patient to remove any heavy outer wear such as coats and sweaters. If the patient wishes, shoes may be removed too.
   <u>Reason:</u> *Clothing and footwear can add 3-6 lbs.*

4. <u>Procedural Step:</u> Make sure both the weights on the scale are pushed completely to the left. They should be at the "zero" position.
   <u>Reason:</u> *To prevent an inaccurate reading.*

5. <u>Procedural Step:</u> If the patient is barefoot, place a paper on the scale for him or her to stand on.
   <u>Reason:</u> *Aseptic technique.*

6. <u>Procedural Step:</u> Inform the patient the scale may move and assist him or her onto the scale by gently taking an arm for extra support.
   <u>Reason:</u> *To prevent the patient from falling.*

7. <u>Procedural Step:</u> Always be ready to physically assist the patient. Constantly watch for any unsteadiness.
   <u>Reason:</u> *To prevent a fall if the patient loses his or her balance.*

8. <u>Procedural Step:</u> Instruct the patient to stand still, with arms at sides. The patient should not hold on to any part of the scale or on to you.
   <u>Reason:</u> *If the patient touches you, the scale, or anything else, some of his or her weight will be displaced, causing an inaccurate reading.*

9. <u>Procedural Step:</u> The bottom weight on the scale marks increments of 50 lbs. Slide this weight to the mark (50, 100, 150, or 200) that is closest to, but not over, the patient's stated weight. Make sure the weight rests securely in the incremental groove on the register.
   <u>Reason:</u> *Unless this bottom weight is properly set, your measurement may be off by several pounds.*

Measuring the Weight of an Adult

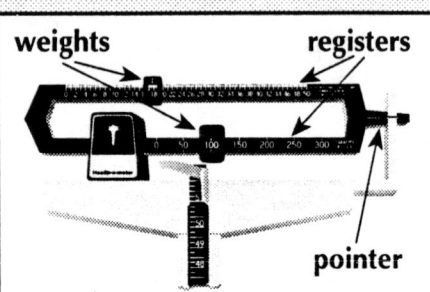

10. **Procedural Step:** Gradually move the upper weight, which indicates individual pounds, across the upper register until the pointer on the right end of the set of registers rests in the center of the metal frame. The registers should not touch the sides of the frame.
Reason: When the set of registers balances in the center of the metal frame, the scale is set to the patient's correct weight.

11. **Procedural Step:** Assist the patient from the scale.
Reason: To prevent the patient from falling.

12. **Procedural Step:** Return the weights to the "zero" setting.
Reason: To prepare the scale for the next patient.

13. **Procedural Step:** Record the patient's weight in kilograms to the nearest fraction of a pound and indicate whether the patient was weighed in a hospital gown or while wearing street clothes.
Reason: To provide documentation. Street clothes are usually heavier than a hospital gown and may affect the physician's interpretation of the patient's weight.

14. **Procedural Step:** Remove and discard the paper you placed on the scale.
Reason: Aseptic technique.

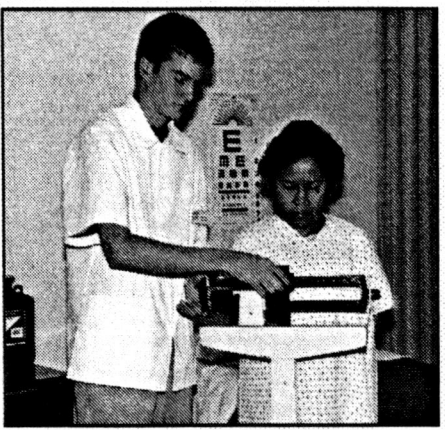

Chart it like this:

9:00 a.m. 45 kg, wearing hospital gown

Chapter Six • Patient Evaluation

Measuring the Height of an Adult

Materials needed:

✓ a scale with a measuring device

1. **Procedural Step:** Identify the patient.
   Reason: To confirm that you are assessing the correct patient.

2. **Procedural Step:** Have the patient step on the scale and face away from it.
   Reason: To obtain the most accurate measurement.

3. **Procedural Step:** With the hinged arm in the lowered position, raise the height bar above the patient's head.
   Reason: To prevent the arm from injuring the patient.

4. **Procedural Step:** Instruct the patient to look straight ahead.
   Reason: This will keep the top of the head level.

5. **Procedural Step:** Extend the hinged arm and gently slide the measuring bar down until it rests lightly on the patient's head.
   Reason: If done too quickly, the patient may be injured.

6. **Procedural Step:** Read the last digit or fraction of a digit that is visible on the moveable portion of the bar, just above the stationary portion.
   Reason: This is the patient's height.

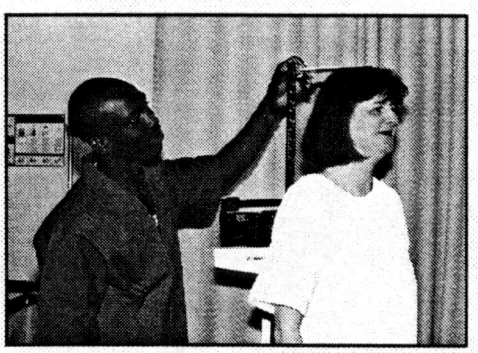

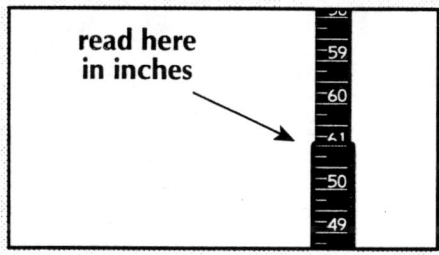

7. **Procedural Step:** Record the patient's height in inches.
   Reason: To provide documentation.

Chart it like this:

9:00 a.m. 60 ¾ ins.

Documentation

The vital signs, neuro check, height, and weight are recorded on the patient chart. One set of vital signs may give you important information, but a series of blood pressure readings taken every five minutes can show a trend of impending shock. It is important to obtain vital signs immediately upon admission of the patient. Recheck them as often as necessary. Vital signs are always taken before and after any procedure or when medication is administered. Patients are generally held in the ER for at least fifteen minutes after medication is given and their vital signs are monitored for any changes prior to discharge from the hospital.

Chapter Summary

Evaluation of patients is a very important part of the emergency department technician's job responsibilities. Knowing how and when to perform a primary and secondary survey is crucial to the care of the patient. You may discover important information about a patient during the admission procedure. During the evaluation of the patient you may detect subtle changes and report them to the nurse or doctor. You must work hard to improve your observational skills. Learning to make detailed observations and take accurate vital signs are skills every emergency department technician will need.

Name_____

Date_____

Student Enrichment Activities

1. Complete the following on at least twenty classmates.

NAME	BP	P	R	T	PUPILS
1.					
2.					
3.					
4.					
5.					
6.					
7.					
8.					
9.					
10.					
11.					
12.					
13.					
14.					
15.					
16.					
17.					
18.					
19.					
20.					

Determine the pupil findings:

2. _____

3. _____

4. _____

5. _____

6. A head to toe survey of patient condition is called a _____.
   - A. primary survey
   - B. triage
   - C. secondary survey
   - D. head to toe check

7. To feel an area of the body is to _____ it.
   - A. palpate
   - B. observe
   - C. auscultate
   - D. percuss

8. The primary survey includes checking for _____.
   - A. airway
   - B. breathing
   - C. circulation
   - D. all of the above

9. When you look, listen, and feel, you are checking for _____.
   - A. pulse
   - B. breathing
   - C. circulation
   - D. orientation

10. Pupils normally react to light by _____.
    - A. dilating
    - B. constricting

Chapter Six • Patient Evaluation

Name_____

Date_____

11. Identify the name of the arterial pulse by its location:
    A. _____ neck
    B. _____ wrist
    C. _____ arm near elbow
    D. _____ thigh
    E. _____ knee
    F. _____ foot

12. Define *mechanism of injury*.
    _____
    _____

13. _____ is the term for equality of body parts and also refers to when both sides of the chest rise and fall with respiration.
    A. Assessment   C. Symmetry
    B. Constrict   D. Rigidity

14. What are the four questions to ask a patient in order to check for level of orientation?
    A. _____
    B. _____
    C. _____
    D. _____

15. When a patient takes a deep breath it is known as _____.
    A. expiration   C. inspiration
    B. wheezing   D. rales

16. Vital signs include:

    A. _____   C. _____

    B. _____   D. _____

17. The pulse occurs because:

    A. blood vessels constrict with each heartbeat.

    B. blood flowing through vessels causes pulsations in the arteries.

    C. blood vessels dilate with each heartbeat.

    D. pressure changes in the walls of the veins.

18. A 36-year-old female complaining of chest pain and with a pulse rate of 130 is experiencing _____.

    A. systole   C. bradycardia
    B. tachycardia   D. normal rhythm

19. When listening to the heart with a stethoscope and counting the pulse rate you are taking the _____ pulse.

    A. radial   C. carotid
    B. popliteal   D. apical

20. As you listen to a patient's chest, you listen to one side and then the other, as well as the front and back of the chest. Why is this important?

    _____
    _____
    _____
    _____

21. A person with shortness of breath and difficulty breathing is experiencing _____.

    A. apnea   C. dyspnea
    B. tachypnea   D. all of the above

Chapter Six • Patient Evaluation 6-67

Name_____

Date_____

22. Look at the following thermometers and read the temperature.

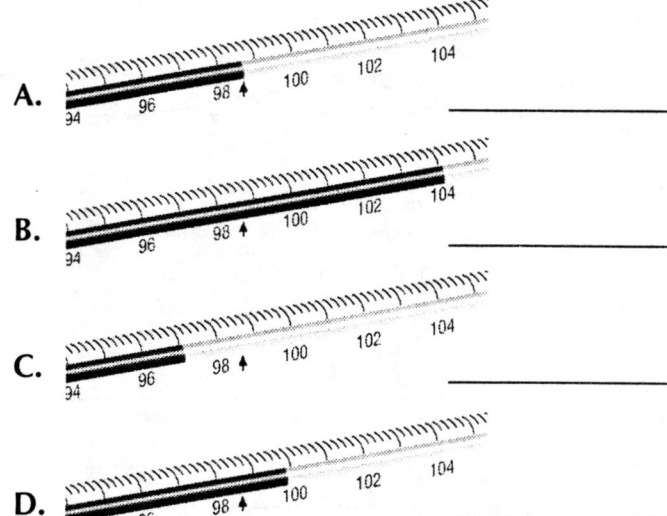

A. _____

B. _____

C. _____

D. _____

23. The oral glass thermometer or electronic probe is placed in the patient's mouth _____.

    A. in the cheek   C. between the teeth

    B. under the tongue   D. inside the lip

24. The blood pressure is:

    A. a measure of the electrical activity of the heart.

    B. a measure of the force of blood against the arterial wall.

    C. an indication of the patient's health.

    D. a measure of the total body fluid.

25. In a blood pressure reading of 140/80, 140 represents the _____ pressure.

    A. diastolic   C. inspiration

    B. pulse   D. systolic

26. Perform a primary and secondary survey on a fellow classmate. Imagine an emergency situation and role play the symptoms to your partner. Use the medical record form on the next page to record your findings.

EMERGENCY DEPARTMENT
NURSING ASSESSMENT/DOCUMENTATION RECORD

NAME		AGE	WEIGHT	MEDICAL RECORD NO.	DATE
				BED #	PMD

HOW ARRIVED ☐ WALKED ☐ WHEELCHAIR ☐ AMBULANCE ☐ CRUTCHES ☐ CARRIED FROM ☐ HOME ☐ SNF ☐ OTHER:

CHIEF COMPLAINT TIME ___ INFORMANT ☐ SELF ☐ PARENT ☐ OTHER:

ARRIVED WITH: ☐ SELF ☐ PARENT ☐ SPOUSE ☐ FRIEND ☐ POLICE ☐ PARAMEDIC ☐ OTHER:

VISUAL ACUITY: OD ___ C ___ ☐ GLASSES ☐ CONTACT LENS

	ALERTED	FILED	ALERTED	FILED	ALERTED	FILED
	F0912-43-1		11166PC		LOSS OF CONSCIOUSNESS	

BP ___ R ___ L ___ T ___ O ___ R ___ P ___ AP ___ R ___ INITIAL RHYTHM ___

LEVEL OF CONSCIOUSNESS:
☐ AWAKE ALERT
☐ ORIENTED
☐ PURPOSEFUL RESPONSE TO PAIN
☐ NON-PURPOSEFUL RESPONSE TO PAIN
☐ UNRESPONSIVE TO PAIN
☐ ODOR OF ALCOHOL ON BREATH
☐ LETHARGIC
☐ DISORIENTED
☐ COMBATIVE

RESPIRATORY: ☐ N/A
CHEST SYMMETRICAL Y/N
R L BREATH SOUNDS
☐ ☐ CLEAR
☐ ☐ RALES
☐ ☐ WHEEZES
☐ ☐ DIMINISHED
☐ ☐ ABSENT
☐ ☐ DYSPNEA
☐ ☐ RETRACTION
☐ ☐ NASAL FLARING
☐ ☐ COUGH
☐ PRODUCTIVE
☐ NON-PRODUCTIVE

MENTAL ASSESSMENT:
PHYSICAL APPEARANCE
GAIT ☐ Normal ☐ Unstable
HYGIENE ☐ Normal ☐ Other ___
OVERALL PE ☐ Normal ☐ Frail ☐ Robust

MOOD/AFFECT
☐ Appropriate ☐ Cooperative
☐ Inappropriate ☐ Fearful
☐ Blunted/flat ☐ Hopelessness
☐ Defensive

MEMORY-RECENT ☐ Intact ☐ Impaired

THOUGHTS
☐ Clear ☐ Spontaneous
☐ Vague/disconnected ☐ Slow to answer questions

SPEECH
☐ Normal ☐ Clear
☐ Silent ☐ Mumbling/Garbled
☐ Talkative ☐ Monotone
☐ Loud ☐ Slurred
☐ Deliberate

MEDICAL HISTORY: ☐ BLIND ☐ DEAF/HARD OF HEARING
☐ ASTHMA COPD ☐ HYPERTENSION ☐ NO PREVIOUS MED
☐ CARDIAC ☐ SEIZURES ☐ NONE AVAILABLE
☐ DIABETES ☐ GASTRITIS/ULCER DISEASE
☐ OTHER ___

ALLERGIES: ☐ NKA ___

MEDS: ☐ NONE ___

LAST TETANUS: ___ LNMP: ___

TIME	BP	PULSE	RESP	TEMP

BLEEDING:
☐ NONE ☐ CONTROLLED
☐ UNCONTROLLED ☐ UNOBSERVABLE
SITE: ___

SKIN:
COLOR: ☐ NORMAL ☐ PALE/ASHEN
SKIN TEMP:
☐ HOT ☐ WARM
☐ COOL ☐ COLD

MOISTURE:
☐ DRY ☐ MOIST ☐ PROFUSE

GU:
☐ INCONTINENT
☐ FREQUENCY
☐ URGENCY
☐ DYSURIA
☐ RETENTION
☐ FOLEY

GI:
☐ DIARRHEA
☐ CONSTIPATION
☐ NAUSEA
☐ VOMITING
☐ OTHER

FONTANELLES:
☐ NORMAL
☐ BULGING
☐ SUNKEN

INJURY/SKIN INTEGRITY:
LABEL AND SHADE AREAS INVOLVED
A - ABRASIONS
B - BRUISE
C - BURNS
D - SWOLLEN
E - LACERATION
F - PUNCTURE
G - POSSIBLE FX
H - C/O PAIN
I - REDDENED
J - DECUBITUS
K - RASH
+ - PULSE PRESENT
− - PULSE ABSENT

RIGHT LEFT   LEFT RIGHT

SPINAL PRECAUTIONS:
☐ C-COLLAR
☐ TAPE/SANDBAGS
☐ BACKBOARD
☐ OTHER ___

ALL WOUNDS CLEANSED WITH ___

NEURO SIGNS

TIME	INITIAL	VERBAL RESPONSE	MOTOR RESPONSE	EYE OPENING	GRIP R/L	UPPER EXTREMITY MOVEMENT R/L	LOWER EXTREMITY MOVEMENT R/L	PUPILS SIZE R/L	PUPILS REACTION R/L

ADULT GLASGOW COMA SCALE
EYE OPENING: Spontaneous 4, To Voice 3, To Pain 2, None 1
VERBAL RESPONSE: Oriented 5, Confused 4, Inappropriate Words 3, Incomprehensible Words 2, None 1
MOTOR RESPONSE: Obeys Command 6, Localizes Pain 5, Withdraw (Pain) 4, Flexion (Pain) 3, Extension (Pain) 2, None 1

CHILD GLASGOW COMA SCALE UP TO 3 YEARS OLD
EYE OPENING: Spontaneous 4, Reaction to Speech 3, Reaction to Pain 2, None 1
MOTOR RESPONSE: Obeys Command 6, Localizes Pain 5, Withdraw (Pain) 4, Flexion (Pain) 3, Extension (Pain) 2, None 1
CRYING VERBAL RESPONSE: Consolable 4, Inconsistently Consolable 3, Inconsolable 2, None 1
INTERACTS VERBAL RESPONSE: Inappropriate 4, Moaning 3, Irritable, Restless 2, None 1

PUPIL SIZE AND REACTION
9 8 7 6 5 4 3 2
N = NORMAL S = SLUGGISH
F = FIXED

PULSES EXTREMITY MOVEMENT
S = STRONG
W = WEAK
A = ABSENT
D = NOT PALPABLE BUT PRESENT WITH DOPPLER

PATIENT CHART

Chapter Seven
Safety in the Emergency Department

Objectives

After completing this chapter you should be able to do the following:

1. Define and correctly spell all key terms.

2. List the duties to perform if there is a fire in the Emergency Department.

3. List the signs and symptoms of infectious disease in an emergency patient.

4. Outline a disaster plan for the Emergency Department.

Key Terms

- code blue
- code red
- defibrillator
- exposure
- flammable
- hazardous
- hospital disaster plan
- purulent
- ulceration
- ventilate
- ventricular fibrillations

Safety Responsibilities

Once a patient arrives in the Emergency Department it becomes your responsibility to provide a safe environment. Unconscious, confused, and severely injured individuals are not able to care for themselves. As an ER technician, you must make sure that further injuries do not occur. Any hazards must be removed so that all patients and visitors are safe.

hazardous: dangerous

Safety is everyone's responsibility. A lot can be done to prevent accidents and injuries on the job. A team effort is needed to recognize, report, and correct situations that are **hazardous**. Figure 7-1. lists some MUSTS for accident prevention in and around the Emergency Department.

Fire

flammable: capable of producing fire

Fire is an ever present danger in the hospital. Oxygen and other gases are extremely **flammable**. Fires can be caused by faulty equipment, frayed wires, careless smokers, and improper use of flammable materials or gases. If a fire starts, early intervention is needed to put it out and prevent injury to the patients.

code red: the verbal alarm for a fire

If a fire starts, immediately rescue the patient and then sound the alarm. Pull the fire alarm on the wall if there is one, or use the telephone to dial the emergency fire number. Know the procedure for reporting a fire in your hospital. For example, in some facilities you would dial the operator and say, "**code red**." Then you would give your location.

Chapter Seven • Safety In The Emergency Department

Safety Procedures in the ER

1. Keep floors clean and dry to prevent falls.
2. Adequate lighting must be available.
3. Obey *no smoking* signs.
4. Seek assistance when moving heavy objects.
5. Use good body mechanics at all times.
6. Entrances and exits should be clearly marked.
7. Keep hallways, entrances, and exits free of clutter and obstacles.
8. Make sure the brakes are on when transferring a patient from a bed to a wheelchair, or from a car to a wheelchair.
9. Keep medication and instruments out of the patient's reach.
10. Always check the temperature of any solution that touches a patient.
11. Use side rails for all patients.
12. Do not leave children or disoriented, confused, or sedated patients in an area where they cannot be continuously observed.
13. Make sure that machines with alarms are turned on and operational.
14. Do not perform procedures that are unfamiliar to you.
15. Check equipment prior to use to make sure it is in working order.
16. Report broken or faulty equipment immediately and remove the damaged equipment from the area so that it will not be used.
17. Check sterile packages for tears, openings, and expiration dates.
18. Continually check patients to make sure they are not in distress.
19. Know and follow the safety policies and procedures where you work.
20. Know the location of the fire extinguishers and how to use them.
21. Wear gloves when handling blood and other body fluids.
22. Always check the patient's identification band before giving any treatments.

Figure 7-1: Safety Procedures in the ER

Once the fire has been reported, make sure the patients are safe. If patients are in immediate danger, remove them from the scene using any available means. You may drag a patient out on a blanket if necessary. If patients are not in immediate danger, close all doors to prevent smoke inhalation and turn off the oxygen to prevent an explosion. Put out the fire using a fire extinguisher.

Points to Remember if a Fire Occurs

- STAY CALM.
- Sound the alarm.
- Rescue any patients that are in danger.
- Close the doors.
- Turn off oxygen.
- Fight the fire with a fire extinguisher.
- No elevators should be used in a fire.
- Do not use telephones unnecessarily.
- Turn off or unplug electrical equipment.
- Report to the charge nurse for instructions.

The fire department must be notified even if the fire is extinguished. Many items, like mattresses, can smolder and rekindle a fire. If a fire occurs in another area of the hospital, the Emergency Department must be prepared to handle an increased number of injured patients and staff. The Emergency Department is affected any time there is an accident in the hospital.

Remember — RACE!

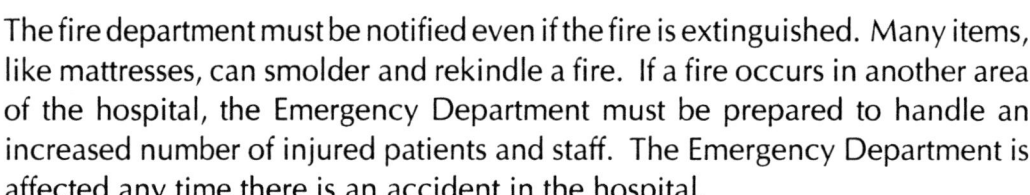

1. **R**ESCUE THE PATIENT.

2. **A**CTIVATE (SOUND) THE ALARM.

3. **C**ONTAIN THE FIRE. (CLOSE DOORS)

4. **E**XTINGUISH THE FIRE.

Disasters

Complications can occur if there are several injured people and not enough trained personnel, supplies, or equipment to handle the emergency. If the community has a natural disaster like a flood, fire, tornado, or earthquake, many people may require immediate medical assistance. Provisions must be made for triage and treatment, and back up supplies and staff must be available. When a disaster occurs, all patient care units in the hospital are immediately evaluated. Patients who can be are discharged quickly. Extra staff members are sent to the Emergency Department to assist with the increase in admissions. The Housekeeping Department may bring extra beds to the ER, and Central Supply brings extra supplies and equipment to meet the increased demand.

The emergency rooms of all area hospitals are part of county-wide disaster plans. The hospitals participate in frequent drills to test disaster preparedness. These simulations are designed to coordinate efforts among fire, police, ambulance companies, communications systems, and area hospitals for rapid treatment and transportation of the injured. As a student, you may have an opportunity to participate in one of these drills and see how the system works. Participation will prevent you from being flustered in a real emergency because you will know exactly what to do. YOU are responsible for knowing the **hospital disaster plan** and for carrying it out calmly and effectively in an emergency.

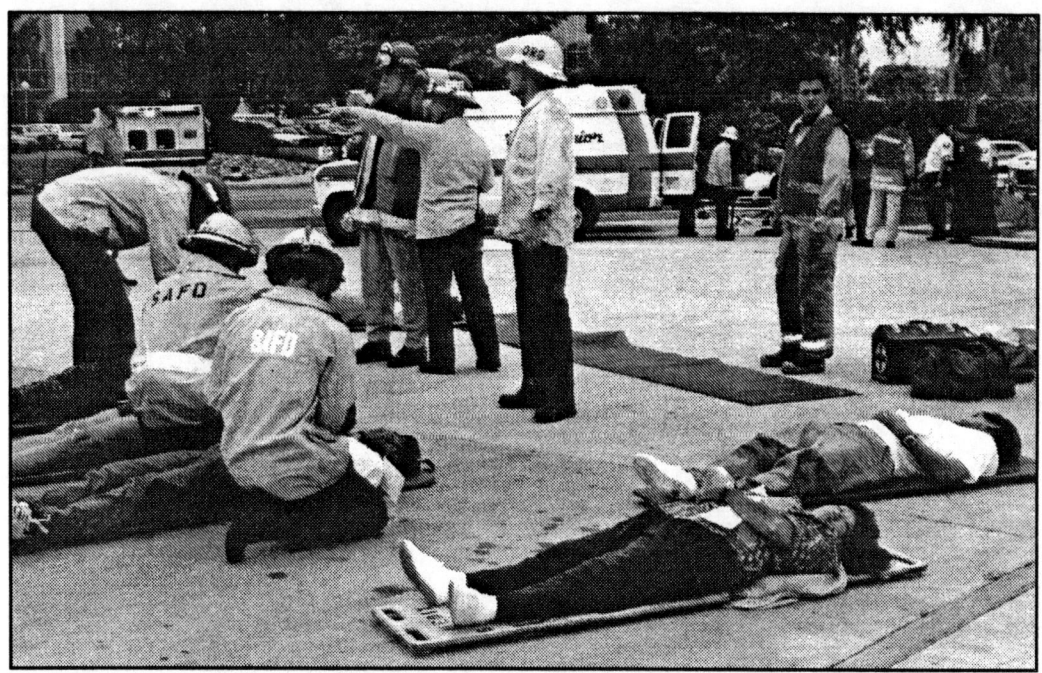

hospital disaster plan: a pre-defined set of procedures for the care and evacuation of hospital patients and personnel during and after a natural disaster

Figure 7-2: A Disaster Drill

Disasters that occur in the community may affect the hospital as well. If a tornado or earthquake threatens the hospital, the patients and staff are endangered. It is the staff's responsibility to keep the patients as safe as possible. Immediately remove patients from areas close to glass windows. Protect patients from large pieces of furniture, equipment, and falling debris. If there is time, all patients should be moved to a safer area. If a bomb threat occurs, all staff and patients must be evacuated immediately. The area must then be searched by local law enforcement and fire personnel.

Emergency Signals

Emergency signals are in hospital bathrooms and at the bedside. When a patient in distress presses the emergency button, a light flashes or a buzzer sounds indicating that assistance is needed. (Figure 7-3) For example, if you walk by a patient's bed and notice that he is not breathing, press the emergency button. You can start **CPR** immediately, knowing that help will arrive quickly. More advanced life-saving measures can be started when additional staff and equipment arrive.

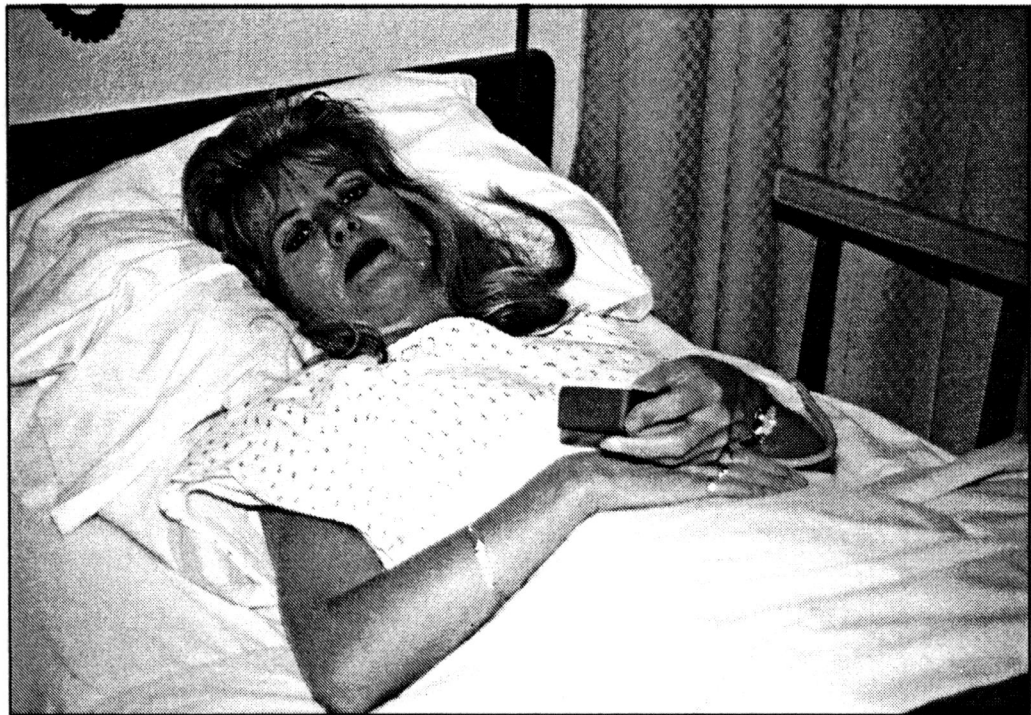

Figure 7-3: When a patient presses the emergency call button, a signal tells the nurse that assistance is needed.

Personal Safety

Many procedures that are done in the Emergency Department can be a risk to your personal health. By taking certain precautions, the risk to the caregiver can be minimized while still providing quality care to the patient. Portable x-ray equipment is often used for trauma victims or patients who are in acute distress and cannot be moved to the Radiology Department. If you are assisting with these procedures, lead aprons and lead gloves are available to shield you from the x-rays. Women who may be pregnant should avoid direct **exposure** to x-rays. Some state laws dictate age limits. Often, no one under the age of 18 may be in the room when the x-ray is taken.

Blood and other body fluids always are considered to be contaminated infectious waste. GLOVES MUST ALWAYS BE WORN when cleaning wounds, controlling hemorrhages, handling wound drainage, vomitus, urine, or feces. **Universal precautions** state that one must always wear gloves when handling blood and other body fluids. Gowns are worn to protect clothes during procedures that are messy, and when there is a lot of blood exposure, protective eye goggles should be worn. Whenever possible, use disposable supplies and equipment. Dispose of contaminated waste in specifically marked bags (usually red or yellow).

All sharps (needles, syringes, scalpels, etc.) are disposed of in rigid plastic containers specifically designed for this use. Never put sharps in the trash can or leave them lying around. The containers prevent others from being pricked or cut by contaminated sharps. Use the utmost care when cleaning an area after a procedure has been performed. NEVER assume all sharps have been removed, and NEVER use your hands or feet to push trash into a trash container.

> **exposure:** the state of being subject to the effects or influence of something, such as radiation, heat, cold, etc.

Infectious diseases can be transmitted in blood and other body fluids, or by way of the respiratory system. If a patient has a productive cough (is coughing up phlegm) or a possible respiratory disease, protect yourself by teaching the patient to cough into a tissue and disposing of it in the container provided. If possible, avoid handling these secretions. If handling the secretions is unavoidable, such as when collecting **sputum** specimens, wear gloves and a surgical face mask. You also should turn your head away when the patient coughs. Masks can be put on infectious patients who are in a common area (elevator, hallway) to prevent the spread of disease. Many patients admitted to the ER are not yet diagnosed, and may unknowingly have an infectious disease.

If the symptoms are such that you suspect a contagious disease, place the patient in the isolation room. Symptoms of infectious disease include the following:

- a rash
- a fever
- **purulent** drainage
- a productive cough
- sores or **ulcerations**
- red, swollen, hot, and/or painful area
- painful urination
- a vaginal discharge
- foul smelling drainage

purulent: pus-like

ulceration: a skin lesion

To protect yourself, you should keep your **immunizations** current and avoid unnecessary exposure to infectious agents. It is recommended that healthcare workers have an annual tuberculin skin test for detection of exposure to tuberculosis. Also, make sure you have been immunized for measles, mumps, rubella, tetanus, and hepatitis.

An unsafe situation may result from a person's aggressive or hostile behavior. If a person enters the facility with a weapon, IMMEDIATELY notify hospital security and the local police department. DO NOT PROVOKE AN ANGRY INDIVIDUAL! Instead, attempt to diffuse the person's anger by saying that you understand how he or she feels and offering to help in any way you can.

If a person is irrational or mentally ill you will need to obtain additional help from staff members. Don't work alone in these situations, and don't turn your back on the patient. Some facilities have a special code that is used in these cases, such as, "Dr. Strong to the E.R." When this call is made security and additional personnel are dispatched for control.

Transporting Patients

Patients may be transported to the hospital by land or air. Ambulances transport patients Code 3 (lights and siren) to save valuable time. Helicopters also may be used for transport. When receiving a Code III patient from the ambulance, do not approach the vehicle until it has completely stopped and the engine is off. Steps must always be taken to ensure the safety of the patient and staff. Use proper body mechanics when moving the stretcher from the ambulance and have someone go ahead of you to open the doors. Body mechanics means using the muscles and bones properly to prevent injury. It is important to use proper body mechanics in all daily activities and to understand the principles so you can teach patients the proper way to move and turn to prevent illness and injury. The principles of body mechanics are detailed in Chapter Sixteen.

Time is an important factor when transporting critical patients from the ER, the OR, or ICU. Organize the move by checking to see that all portable equipment is ready for transport as follows:

- The portable suction machine is charged.
- The oxygen tank is full and secured to the gurney.
- The portable **defibrillator**/monitor is connected.
- All **IV** lines and tubes are secure for transport.
- The transport pack is on the gurney, including emergency airways, medications, and IV supplies.
- If the patient is being **ventilated**, the **Ambu bag** (bag valve mask) is ready.

defibrillator: an electronic device used to shock the heart into a normal rhythm

ventilate: to assist a patient's breathing

If the patient arrives by helicopter it is very important to take the following precautions.

- Remove sheets and loose material from the stretcher so it won't be blown into the helicopter rotor.
- Remove hats and loose clothing from the staff members receiving the patient.
- Approach the helicopter only after it has landed and the pilot has given the OK sign.
- Stay clear of the propeller and the rotor.

Safety and Defibrillation

code blue:
the emergency call signal in the hospital for a full arrest situation, which alerts all emergency resuscitation team members to respond to a specific location

ventricular fibrillation:
a rapid, irregular or chaotic, deadly heart rhythm

During a cardiac arrest, or **code blue**, **defibrillation** may be necessary. The heart can beat erratically, or **fibrillate**. This is a life-threatening condition called **ventricular fibrillation.** The doctor treats this heart problem by defibrillating (shocking) the heart. Two paddles that are connected to an electrical defibrillator (Figure 7-4) are coated with conductive jelly. This jelly helps the defibrillator deliver a controlled electrical shock to the heart. If successful, the heart will return to a normal rhythm. Before discharging the electrical current, the nurse or the doctor says, "Stand clear." At that moment it is essential that nothing touches the patient or bed. If you are touching the bed or the patient, or if your stethoscope is hanging down and touching the side rail you could receive a shock. When you hear the words, "Stand clear," move away from the patient and the bed. This means you must stop CPR for the moment. At the command, "All clear," CPR is resumed and other lifesaving procedures are continued.

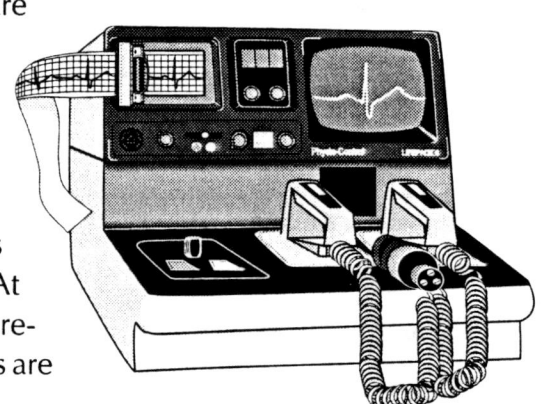

Figure 7-4: A Defibrillator

Sometimes, a series of defibrillation attempts may be necessary before the patient's heart returns to normal rhythm, so stay alert to the commands to "Stand clear." Anticipate the needs of the physician and nurse and be prepared to assist as needed. You may be needed to perform CPR, assist with starting the IV, or hook up the patient to the monitor. You also may be needed to deliver specimens to the lab, obtain specialized equipment from the operating room or Central Supply, open sterile packages, take vital signs, or even mop up the floor. Remember, each job is important and must be done quickly and correctly.

Chapter Summary

Safety in the Emergency Department is everyone's responsibility. If you see an unsafe situation such as water spilled on the floor, cluttered hallways, broken or faulty equipment, side rails down, or smoking in a nonsmoking area, report it so it can be corrected immediately. Prevention is the key word with safe medical practice. Recognizing unsafe situations and correcting them is imperative. Periodic review of emergency procedures is essential so that all healthcare workers are prepared to act in case of a fire or disaster. Knowing what to do and staying calm while carrying out the emergency plan is the only way to save lives and prevent further destruction.

Chapter Seven • Safety In The Emergency Department

Name _____

Date _____

Student Enrichment Activities

1. Smoke is coming out of the doorway to the emergency department nurses' lounge, and five patients are in the department. List in order of importance (1 being the most important) what you should do:

    _____ sound the alarm
    _____ fight fire
    _____ turn off oxygen
    _____ evacuate the patients
    _____ close the door

2. List six symptoms of infectious disease.
    A. _____
    B. _____
    C. _____
    D. _____
    E. _____
    F. _____

3. Define *universal precautions*.
    _____
    _____
    _____
    _____

4. Describe a safety measure to follow during a cardiac arrest or code blue.

   _____
   _____
   _____
   _____
   _____
   _____

5. Conduct a safety inspection of your living area.

YES	NO	
___	___	Are floors clean and dry?
___	___	Are hallways free of clutter?
___	___	Are doorways free from obstruction?
___	___	Is there adequate lighting?
___	___	Is there a smoke alarm?
___	___	Is there a fire extinguisher?
___	___	Do you know how to use a fire extinguisher?
___	___	Are there heavy objects or mirrors over sleeping areas?
___	___	Is the water heater secure?
___	___	Are tall cabinets fastened to wall?
___	___	Are medications and poisons out of reach of children?
___	___	Are weapons unloaded and out of reach of children?
___	___	Is there any broken equipment or faulty wiring?
___	___	Are the electrical outlets overloaded?
___	___	Do you know how to turn off the gas and water?
___	___	Do you have emergency first aid supplies?
___	___	Do you have emergency food and water supplies?
___	___	Do you have a flashlight and portable radio?

Chapter Seven • Safety In The Emergency Department

Name _____

Date _____

6. As an emergency department technician you will assist the emergency staff with several procedures. Using the following symbols, identify which supplies you will use for each of the following procedures:

    G = gown
    E = goggles (protective eyewear)
  GL = gloves
    M = mask

Symbol or Symbols	Procedure
A. _____	cleansing a wound
B. _____	obtaining a sputum specimen
C. _____	applying a sterile dressing
D. _____	taking an oral temperature
E. _____	obtaining a throat culture
F. _____	assisting a patient with chest pain to a stretcher
G. _____	assisting a physician with a suture procedure
H. _____	cleaning up the trauma room after a case
I. _____	helping the nurse clean an incontinent patient

Chapter Eight
Basic Life Support

Objectives

After completing this chapter you should be able to do the following:

1. Define and correctly spell all key terms.
2. Recognize the signs of cardiac or respiratory arrest.
3. Define CPR.
4. Perform CPR on an infant manikin.
5. Perform CPR on a child manikin.
6. Perform one-rescuer and two-rescuer CPR on an adult manikin.
7. Perform the obstructed airway procedure on infant, child, and adult manikins.
8. List the items that can be found on a crash cart.

Key Terms

- Ambu bag
- anaphylactic shock
- biological death
- cardiac arrest
- cardiac compressions
- cardiopulmonary resuscitation (CPR)
- clinical death
- code blue
- crash cart
- defibrillator
- endotracheal tube
- epiglottis
- esophageal airway
- full arrest
- head-tilt/chin-lift maneuver
- Heimlich maneuver
- intubate
- jaw-thrust maneuver
- obstructed airway maneuver
- prone
- reoxygenate
- respiratory arrest
- supine
- trachea
- xiphoid process

Cardiopulmonary Resuscitation

cardio-pulmonary resuscitation (CPR): a lifesaving procedure of artificial ventilation and chest compressions that is done for cardiac arrest

There are many essential skills that you must learn to become an emergency department technician. However, the most important skill of all is to be able to provide lifesaving **cardiopulmonary resuscitation (CPR)**. CPR, when performed correctly, can maintain life in the victim of a sudden or unexpected death while all available emergency personnel gather to provide both basic and advanced life support. Saving a life is what the emergency room is all about. When you master this skill you will find that the satisfaction you feel by being a part of this lifesaving team is the most valuable reward of all.

Cardiopulmonary resuscitation (CPR) is a procedure that combines rescue breathing, which supplies oxygen to the lungs, and chest compressions, which circulate blood throughout the body. Because CPR has proven to be effective in restoring a pulse and respirations, it is done whenever the heart and lungs stop working.

Chapter Eight • Basic Life Support

Sudden Death

Sudden death is the immediate cessation of breathing and pulse. The causes of sudden death are numerous. It can occur to an individual in any age group at any time.

Faulty wiring or the inadequate grounding of an electrical source can produce an electrical shock that can cause the heart to beat in a type of irregularity known as **ventricular fibrillation**. Victims of electrical shock can range from the week-end handyman working on the household wiring, to a 3-year-old playing with an electrical outlet, or an employee in an industrial accident.

Water-related accidents can also result in sudden death. Often these accidents involve small children who accidentally fall into the pool and drown.

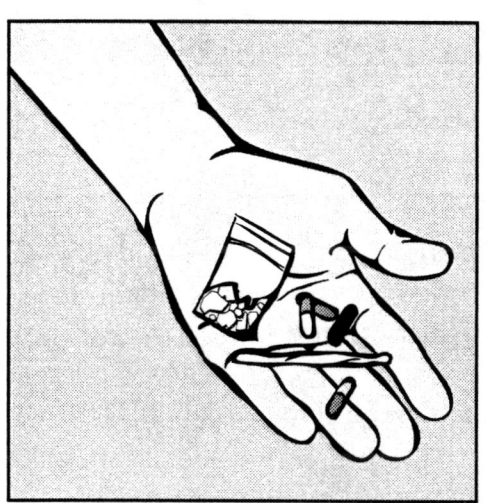

Drug **overdoses**, whether they are accidental or intentional, can cause both respiratory and cardiac arrest.

Trauma can lead to significant blood loss that causes shock and cardiac arrest. Automobile accidents can cause multisystem injuries that, left untreated, will eventually lead to death.

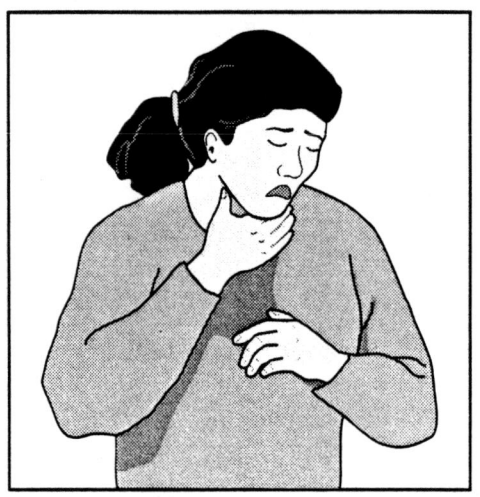

Choking, or blockage of the air passage by a foreign object, food, or vomitus, can result in a respiratory arrest.

Heart attacks and ventricular fibrillation can cause immediate death. Not everyone who has a heart attack will suffer a cardiac arrest, but injuries to the heart muscle often can cause irregularities in the heart rhythm that can be very serious.

Suffocation deprives the body of its oxygen supply and results in death to all the tissues. Unfortunately, many suffocation victims are children. Children like to hide in small airtight places that may have very little oxygen supply. Children also can suffocate by chewing or sucking on plastic bags or by placing them over their heads.

Chapter Eight • Basic Life Support

Allergic reactions can be severe enough to result in respiratory arrest. People can be allergic to any substance, including medication, a bee sting, and certain foods. When an allergic reaction occurs it is an immediate response; and if left untreated, the respiratory arrest will progress to a cardiac arrest.

Poisoning or inhaling poisonous gases from household or industrial accidents or fires can cause a respiratory emergency. The breathing can become labored and lead to a respiratory arrest.

There are numerous causes of sudden death. As an emergency department technician, you must be ready to deal with these situations by knowing when and how to perform CPR.

Clinical and Biological Death

When respirations stop, the oxygen supply to the body is cut off. This condition is known as **respiratory arrest**. The heart will continue to beat for a few minutes, but if oxygen is not available to the heart muscle, it also will stop beating. This is called **cardiac arrest**. When both respirations and pulse cease, the patient is classified as **clinically dead**. However, the body cells have a **residual** oxygen supply and can survive a short time without new oxygen. If CPR is started immediately upon clinical death, the victim's chances of survival are greatly increased.

respiratory arrest: the absence of breathing

cardiac arrest: asystole; the absence of a heartbeat

clinical death: lack of a pulse, respiration, and blood pressure

biological death: brain and other cell death caused by a lack of oxygen to the tissues; occurs within 4 to 6 minutes of respiratory arrest

Clinical death is determined by checking for both the pulse and respirations and finding there is no pulse or breathing present. After 4 to 6 minutes without a pulse or respirations the brain does not receive the oxygen that is so vital to all the body organs. The brain cells begin to die and the brain is damaged. When the brain cells die it is called **biological death**. The period between clinical and biological death is very short. If you recognize the **full arrest** and immediately begin CPR and rescue breathing, getting oxygen to the brain by cardiac compressions, you can save the patient from biological death. The key is IMMEDIATE RECOGNITION of cardiac arrest and IMMEDIATE RESPONSE with CPR.

full arrest: respiratory and cardiac arrest

How the Heart Works

The heart, like all other organs, requires energy and oxygen to perform its work. The heart muscle is nourished by a system of arteries which originate from the aorta: the right and left coronary arteries. (Figure 8-1) These two main arteries lie on the surface of the heart and divide into smaller branches that supply every portion of the heart with nutrients.

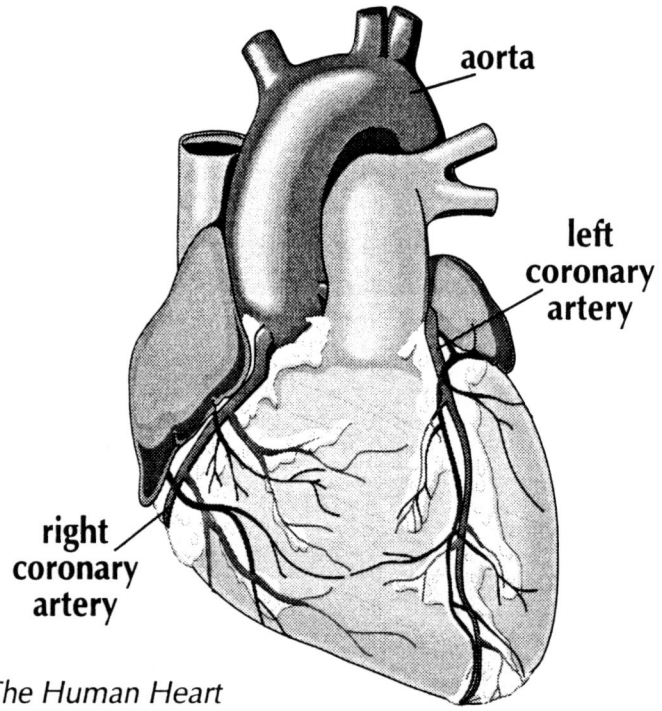

Figure 8-1: The Human Heart

The left coronary artery has a short beginning portion called the *left main*. It divides into the left anterior descending branch, which nourishes the front of the heart muscle, and the **circumflex artery**, which carries blood to the back of the heart. The right coronary artery nourishes the right side of the heart and has branches that extend to the back.

Normally, the inner wall of an artery is smooth and firm. This allows the blood to flow with a minimum of interference.

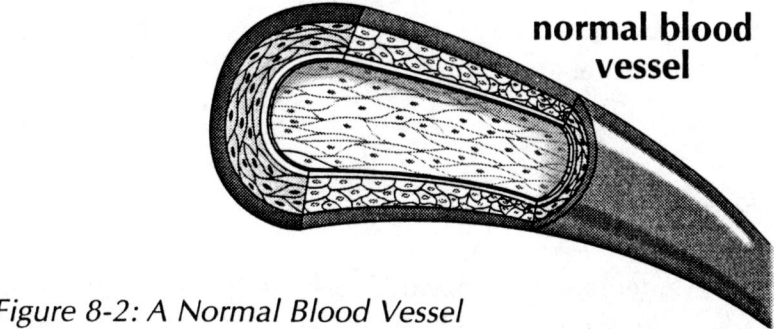

Figure 8-2: A Normal Blood Vessel

As a person gets older, however, the coronary arteries may be affected by arteriosclerosis, commonly called "hardening of the arteries." In arteriosclerosis the inner lining of an artery is thickened and made rough by fatty deposits of cholesterol. The passageway is narrowed like a pipe with rusty buildup, and blood flow beyond the blockage is decreased. Because there is a decrease in blood flow through the narrowed blood vessels, there also is a decrease in the amount of oxygen that is delivered to the heart muscle. Since oxygen is crucial to the health of the muscle, part of the heart muscle dies when it is deprived of oxygen. The patient experiences chest pain, difficulty breathing, and the heart rhythm often becomes irregular. This is a life-threatening situation known as a **myocardial infarction** or a **heart attack**. Immediate medical care is essential to the survival of heart attack victims!

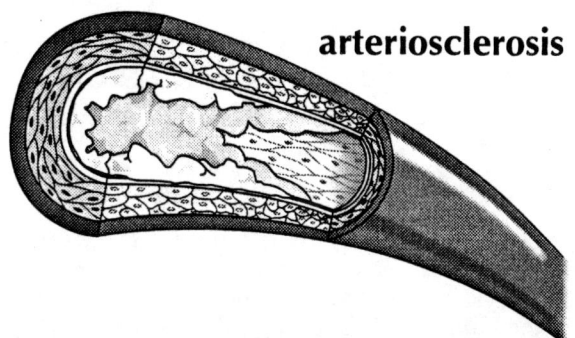

Figure 8-3: A Blood Vessel Affected by Arteriosclerosis

We do not yet understand why arteriosclerosis develops in the coronary arteries, but following the guidelines below may reduce the risk of heart attack.

- Avoid foods that are high in cholesterol and fat such as eggs, red meat, and dairy products.
- Maintain a normal weight.
- Exercise regularly.
- Stop smoking.
- Control high blood pressure.

Emergency Resuscitation

Some patients arrive in the emergency room with CPR in progress. Paramedics at the scene may already have started lifesaving techniques. CPR is continued in the ambulance, as the patient is brought into the ER, and as the patient is brought to the critical care room or major trauma room. This basic life support also must continue while the physician evaluates the patient and begins more advanced treatment. For instance, the physician may need to start another **IV** and administer various medications, or the doctor may want to **intubate** the patient. It also may be necessary to **defibrillate** the patient and continually monitor the heart rhythm. In addition to all this, laboratory work or x-rays may be ordered.

intubate: to insert a tube, such as placing an airway into the trachea of a patient

Many things need to be done at once, so teamwork is essential. This is a very stressful situation for everyone involved, and each person must be able to do several tasks at once. CPR is continued until the patient has spontaneous respirations or a pulse, or the physician pronounces the patient **DOA** (dead on arrival). Another situation that might occur is that a patient who has been admitted to the ER for another problem might have a cardiac and/or respiratory arrest while in the Emergency Department. When a patient goes into full arrest it is called a **code blue**, and CPR is started immediately.

code blue: the emergency call signal in the hospital for a full arrest situation, which alerts all emergency resuscitation team members to respond to a specific location

Chapter Eight • Basic Life Support

Case History

A 32-year-old gardener received a large laceration to his foot from a lawn mower. He was cutting grass while wearing tennis shoes and somehow his foot got caught in the blade. The foreman at work applied a clean dressing to the wound and brought the worker to the emergency room where the wound was cleansed and sutured closed. The patient was given a tetanus injection and an **antibiotic** injection and told to wait in the department for twenty minutes before being discharged home.

Immediately after receiving the antibiotic injection the patient complained of numbness in the lips and tongue, tightness in the chest, and difficulty breathing. He also developed a rash over the chest and back and developed a rapid pulse. He became dizzy and confused, and within five minutes stopped breathing and had no pulse.

CPR was started immediately by the emergency department technician and a code blue was called. Medication for the allergic reaction (**anaphylactic shock**) was given by the emergency response team. After fifteen minutes of CPR, the patient's pulse and respirations returned and he was conscious, alert, and talking.

anaphylactic shock: a life-threatening allergic reaction causing the blood pressure to drop, the pulse to increase and respirations to become labored and difficult. Can lead to cardiac and respiratory arrest.

Without an immediate response from the ER technician with CPR, this man would probably have lost his life.

Basic Life Support (BLS)

Basic life support involves the prompt recognition of breathing difficulties or cardiac arrest, and emergency treatment using the obstructed airway maneuver, rescue breathing, and CPR. Rescue breathing may be all that is needed for respiratory arrest, but CPR is required for patients experiencing both respiratory and cardiac arrest.

Note: Remember, wear gloves and other protective devices (such as goggles, face masks, etc.) whenever there is potential for exposure to blood or other body fluids. If you are not wearing them at the time of the incident (sudden hemorrhage, vomiting, etc.), don them immediately.

In providing basic life support, it is essential first to determine unresponsiveness, then to determine breathlessness, and finally to determine pulselessness. An unresponsive victim must be continually assessed for the ABCs of CPR. According to the American Heart Association, the ABCs of CPR include airway, breathing, and circulation.

1. DETERMINE UNRESPONSIVENESS. To prevent further injury, quickly assess any injury and determine if the victim is unconscious. If there has been any trauma to the head and neck, the victim should be moved only if absolutely necessary. Tap or gently shake the victim and shout, "Are you OK?" (Figure 8-4) This step is important to prevent unnecessary CPR to a sleeping victim or one who is not truly unconscious.

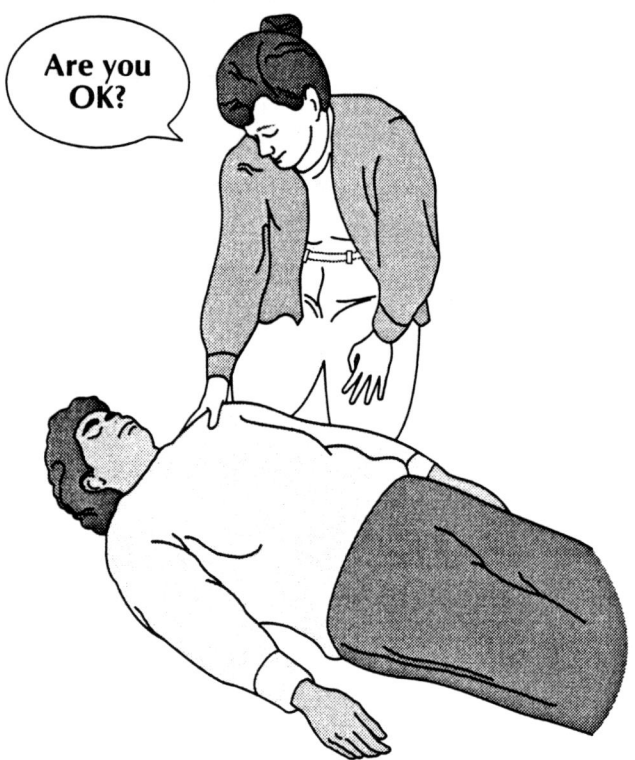

Figure 8-4: Determine unresponsiveness.

2. CALL FOR HELP. If the person does not respond to touch or voice, then additional help is needed. Call out for help. If the crisis has occurred somewhere in the community, yell, "Help." If someone responds, send them to phone 911 and activate the EMS. If the crisis has occurred in the ER, you should yell, "Code blue," and the location.

Chapter Eight • Basic Life Support

3. POSITION THE VICTIM. For CPR to be effective, the victim must be on a firm, flat surface. If the victim is **prone**, **log roll** the victim **supine** with the victim's arms alongside the body. When you roll the patient, make sure his or her head, shoulders, and torso move as a unit, without twisting. If the head of the bed is raised, lower it so the victim is flat. As soon as possible, place the cardiac board under the patient's back to provide a firm surface for CPR. (Figure 8-5) You will find the cardiac board on the **crash cart**.

prone: a position in which a patient is lying face down

supine: a position in which a patient is lying flat on the back

crash cart: a portable supply cabinet that contains all of the emergency equipment necessary to treat a full arrest or code blue

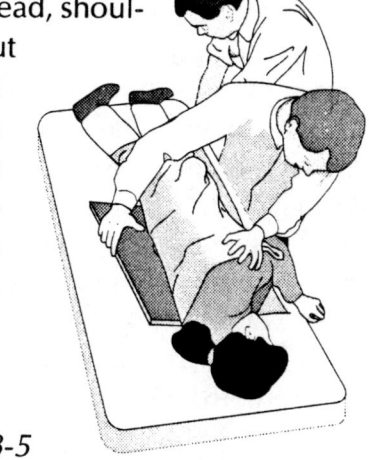

Figure 8-5

4. RESCUER POSITION. If the victim is on the floor, kneel close to the victim's shoulders in a position to perform both rescue breathing and chest compressions. (Figure 8-6a) If the victim is lying on the emergency room stretcher, begin one-rescuer CPR. You should be positioned close to the victim's shoulders for ventilation and management of the patient's airway. It will be necessary to stand on a foot stool to deliver chest compressions when the stretcher is in the high position. As soon as possible, two-rescuer CPR should be started. (Figure 8-6b) One rescuer will manage the airway, and the second rescuer will manage the chest compressions.

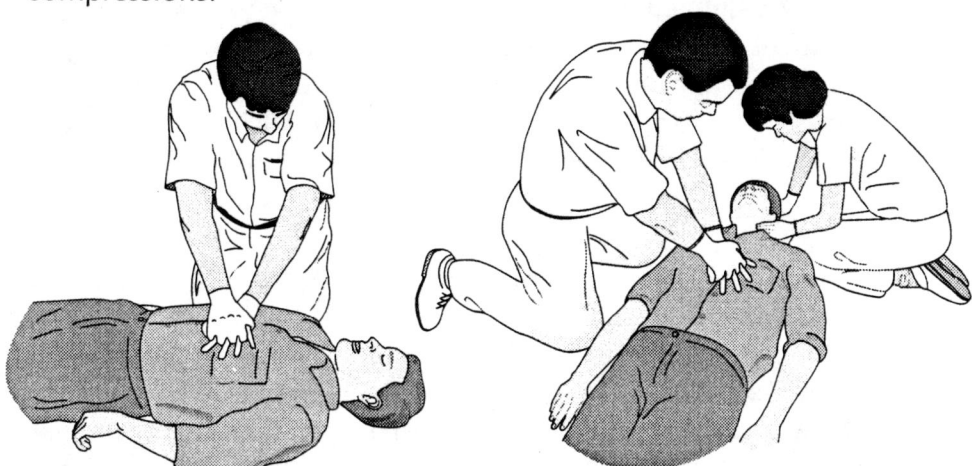

Figure 8-6a   Figure 8-6b

These first four steps must be completed within seconds. TIME IS CRITICAL!

epiglottis: tissue in the throat that allows air to enter the trachea and food to enter the esophagus

head-tilt/ chin-lift maneuver: a procedure for opening a blocked airway in which the head is tilted back and the chin is lifted; the most effective method for opening the airway of an unconscious person without a neck or back injury

jaw-thrust maneuver: a method used to open the airway in a neck injured patient in which the jaw is lifted up and the neck is not moved

5. OPEN AIRWAY. The most urgent action that must be taken is to open the airway. In an unconscious person, the tongue or **epiglottis** may obstruct the airway by blocking the pharynx and larynx. (Figure 8-7a) The tongue is attached to the lower jaw. By moving the lower jaw forward, the tongue will be lifted away from the back of the throat, opening the airway. The **head-tilt/chin-lift** maneuver is most effective, and is done by placing one hand on the victim's forehead and applying firm backward pressure to tilt the head back. Place the fingers of the other hand under the lower jaw and lift to bring the chin forward. (Figure 8-7b) Another method for opening the airway, and the method of choice for a possible neck and spine injury, is the **jaw-thrust maneuver**. Grasp the angle of the victim's lower jaw and lift with both hands, one on each side, and displace the mandible forward.

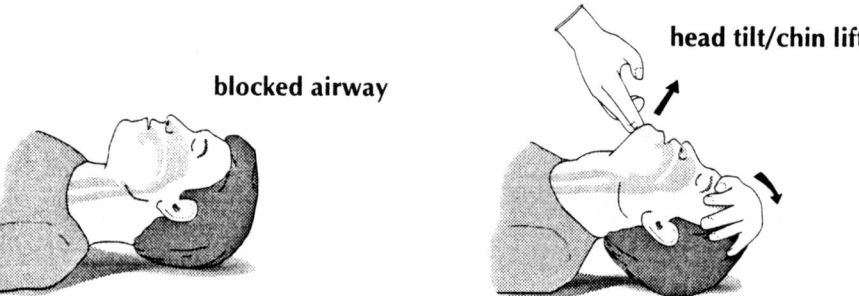

Figure 8-7a *Figure 8-7b*

6. DETERMINE BREATHLESSNESS. Place your ear over the victim's mouth and watch the chest for movement, listening for the escape of air from the victim's nose and mouth and feeling for the presence of air. Look, listen, and feel for breathing for 3 to 5 seconds. If the victim is breathing, maintain an open airway. If the victim is not breathing, rescue breathing must be started.

7. RESCUE BREATHING. Inflate the victim's lungs with your own oxygen supply using the mouth-to-mask, mouth-to-mouth, mouth-to-nose, or mouth-to-stoma method. When available, use a pocket mask or bag-valve mask connected to a source of oxygen. Oxygen outlets are found in the wall at each patient unit, and an oxygen tube can be connected to the oxygen inlet of the mask while mouth-to-mask ventilations are performed. This will protect you and provide additional oxygen to the patient.

Chapter Eight • Basic Life Support

The patient is always given two initial ventilations, followed by a pulse check. (See Step #8.) If a pulse is present, continue rescue breathing by giving one breath every 5 seconds for an adult victim, and one breath every 3 seconds for an infant or child. If no pulse is felt, cardiac compressions also must be started. (See Step #9.)

To perform mouth-to-mask ventilation, place the mask over the victim's mouth and nose. Press the heel and thumb of each hand along the border of the mask to prevent air from leaking out around the edges. Use your remaining fingers to lift the jaw while performing a head-tilt. (Figure 8-8) Ventilate twice, and watch for the rise and fall of the chest. This should take 1-1/2 to 2 seconds per breath for adult patients and 1 to 1-1/2 seconds per breath for a child or infant. If the victim cannot be ventilated, reposition the head and try again. If ventilation is still unsuccessful, perform the **obstructed airway maneuver**. To perform mouth-to-mouth ventilation, pinch the victim's nostrils, cover his or her mouth with your mouth, and ventilate twice. (Figure 8-8) Proceed with rescue breathing as you would for mouth-to-mask resuscitation.

obstructed airway maneuver: the procedure used to clear a foreign body from the trachea; the Heimlich maneuver

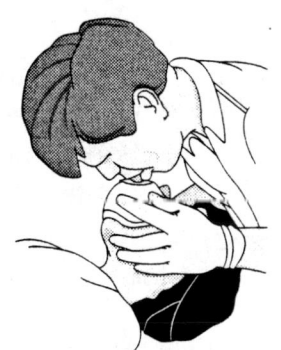
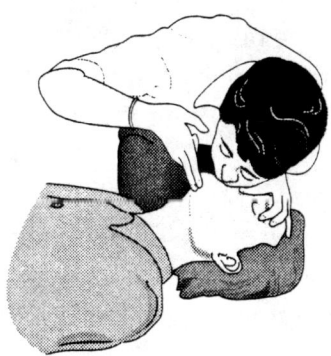

mouth-to-mask resuscitation   **mouth-to-mouth resuscitation**

Figure 8-8: The Most Common Methods of Emergency Resuscitation

Mouth-to-nose ventilation is used when the mouth cannot be opened. The head is tilted back and the mouth closed while air is blown into the victim's nose. Mouth-to-stoma ventilation is performed on patients who have undergone a **laryngectomy** or **tracheostomy**. These people have an opening in the front of the neck through which they breathe. To perform this procedure, seal the area around the stoma with your mouth and blow air into the opening. If you can feel air escaping from the nose and mouth, close the mouth and pinch the nostrils as you perform the ventilations.

Remember, if you must begin ventilating a patient without a mask, obtain a mask as soon as possible. Pocket masks are carried in the pockets of staff members and are found at the bedside near the disposable gloves.

Ambu bag: a type of bag-valve mask used for assisting respirations and increasing oxygenation

endotracheal tube: a large tube inserted in the trachea through the mouth or nose to assist in administering oxygen

esophageal airway: a special breathing tube inserted into the esophagus that allows the trachea to be ventilated

reoxygenate: to replace or replenish with oxygen

trachea: the windpipe; a tube of cartilage that extends from the larynx to the bronchial tubes and which leads air into the lungs

A bag-valve device (**Ambu bag**) can be used with a face mask. (Figure 8-9) Stay at the top of the victim's head and maintain the airway position and an airtight seal between the mask and the patient's face with one hand while squeezing the bag with the other hand. These devices are used for rescue breathing and in conjunction with two-person CPR. Bag-valve masks are found on the crash cart and in the critical care and major trauma rooms. As soon as the

Figure 8-9

physician, respiratory therapist, or paramedic has intubated the patient, the mask is removed and the bag-valve device is used with a **universal adapter** to ventilate the patient through the **endotracheal tube** or the **esophageal airway**.

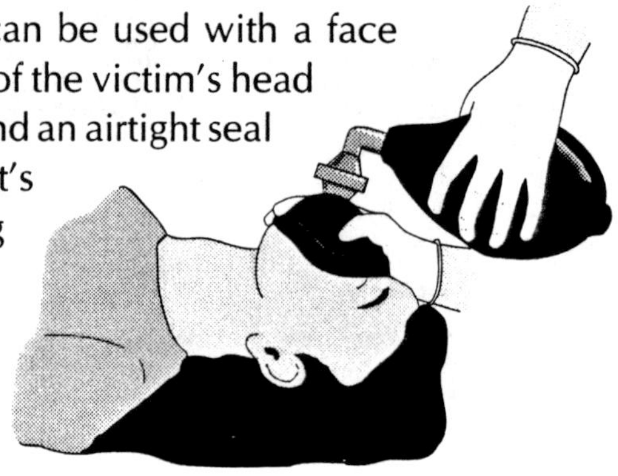

In the hospital, respiratory therapists respond to all code situations. They are specially trained in the use of equipment and ventilators (breathing machines) that can be used to **reoxygenate** the patient. They will do special blood tests to measure oxygen levels and take blood from an artery. This test is called an **arterial blood gas (ABG)**. After the blood is drawn, a gloved hand and a cotton ball are used to apply pressure to the puncture site for at least 6 to 10 minutes. When the bleeding stops, a pressure bandage is applied.

8. DETERMINE PULSELESSNESS. The two initial ventilations must be followed by a pulse check. This check should take about 5 to 10 seconds as the pulse may be slow, irregular, or weak. The **carotid** artery is used for this check. (See Chapter Six.) It is found in the groove created by the **trachea** and muscles of the neck. (Figure 8-10) If the pulse is present and respirations are absent, continue rescue breathing. If there is no pulse, begin cardiac compressions. (Note: If the patient is an infant, the brachial pulse is used for this check. See Pediatric Basic Life Support later in this chapter.)

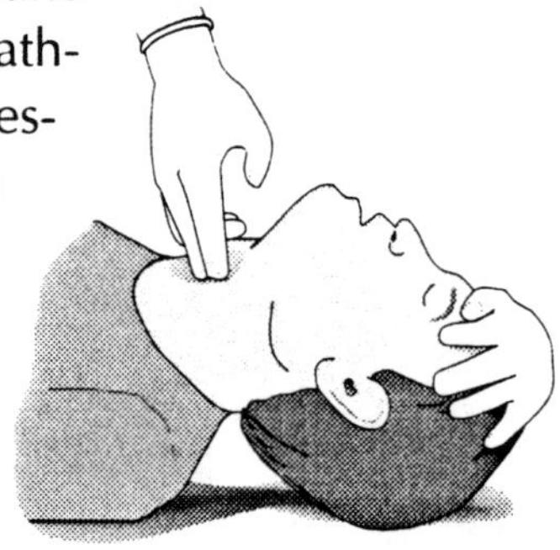

Figure 8-10

Chapter Eight • Basic Life Support

9. **EXTERNAL CHEST COMPRESSIONS. Cardiac compressions** provide circulation to the heart, lungs, brain, and other organs. When accompanied by rescue breathing, chest compressions can circulate sufficient oxygen to these vital organs to sustain life. The victim must be supine, and a board is placed under the back for effective compressions. You can assure proper hand placement by placing your middle and index fingers over the lower margin of the victim's rib cage and moving them up the rib cage to the **sternum** in the center of the lower part of the chest. With the middle finger in this notch, place the index finger next to it on the lower end of the sternum. The heel of the hand is placed on the lower half of the sternum. The long axis of your hand should be placed on the long axis of the sternum. (Figure 8-11a)

    The first hand is removed from the notch and placed on top of the hand on the sternum so that both hands are parallel to each other. Keeping the fingers off of the chest, and the elbows locked in position, straighten the arms and thrust the hands straight down, depressing the sternum 1-1/2 to 2 inches. Release the pressure, keeping the hands in position on the chest. The compression rate should be 80-100 per minute. For one-rescuer CPR, the ratio of compressions to ventilations is 15:2. This means that for every 15 compressions there should be two ventilations. For two-rescuer CPR, the ratio of compressions to ventilations is 5:1. (Figure 8-11b)

cardiac compressions: controlled and repeated application of pressure to the sternum of a cardiac arrest victim to keep the oxygen supply moving throughout the body

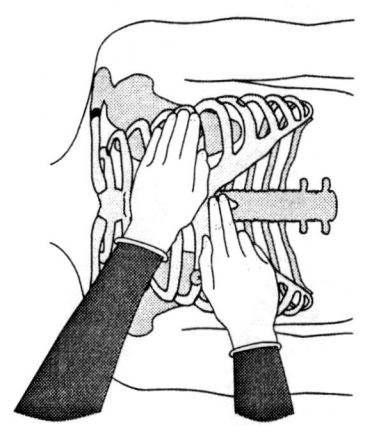

Figure 8-11a

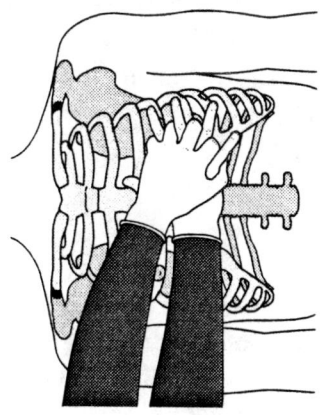

Figure 8-11b

10. **REASSESSMENT.** After four cycles (four sets of fifteen compressions and two ventilations) of compressions and ventilations or 1 minute of CPR, the pulse and breathing are reevaluated. If there still is no pulse or ventilations, continue CPR and reevaluate the patient every few minutes.

Foreign Body Airway Obstructions

An unconscious person can have an obstructed airway due to the position of the airway. For example, the tongue or **epiglottis** can block the air passage in certain positions. Making an airway using the head-tilt/chin-lift maneuver can correct this problem.

A foreign body obstruction or choking emergency can occur in a conscious or unconscious person. Choking results in a partial or complete airway obstruction. If there only is a partial obstruction the victim will be able to cough and exchange some air. In this case, encourage the victim to cough and do not interfere. If the airway is completely obstructed, the victim won't be able to cough, speak, or breathe. Usually the victim's hands grasp his or her neck. This is the universal sign for choking.

Heimlich maneuver: an obstructed airway maneuver in which sudden, upward pressure is applied to the abdomen with a fist to remove a foreign body in the trachea

Ask the victim if he or she is choking, and then perform the **Heimlich maneuver**. (Figure 8-12) This maneuver is performed with you, the rescuer, standing behind the conscious victim. Wrap your hands around the victim's waist and make a fist with one hand. Place the thumb side of the fist against the victim's abdomen directly above the navel, but below the **xiphoid process**. Grasp the fist with your other hand, and with a quick upward thrust, attempt to knock the wind out of the person to remove the obstruction. This is done five times until the obstruction is removed or the victim becomes unconscious.

xiphoid process: the bone tip of the sternum

Repeat five times until the object is removed or the victim becomes unconscious.

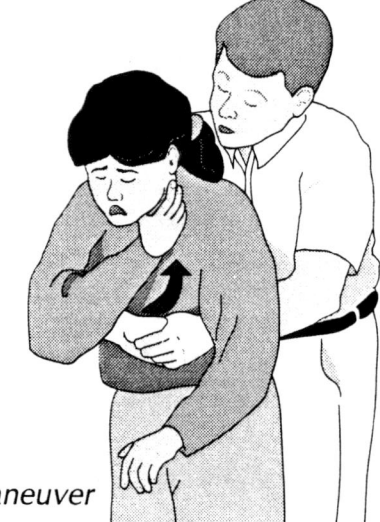

Figure 8-12: The Heimlich Maneuver

Chapter Eight • Basic Life Support

If the victim becomes unconscious, lay him or her in a supine position and kneel **astride** the victim's thighs. Place the heel of one hand against the victim's abdomen above the navel, but below the xiphoid process. Place your other hand on top of the first hand and deliver upward abdominal thrusts five times. Open the victim's mouth using the **tongue-jaw lift** and do a **finger sweep**. To do a **tongue-jaw lift**, lift the victim's jaw up and forward by placing your thumb inside the victim's mouth just behind the front teeth, and grasp the victim's chin with your fingers. While you are doing this, do a **finger sweep** using your index finger to search for a foreign object. (Figure 8-13) Remove the object if you can find it, using a suction machine if one is available.

If the victim is pregnant or obese, an alternate chest thrust can be used. (Figure 8-14) Stand behind the victim, place your arms under the victim's armpits, and encircle his or her chest. Place the thumb side of your fist in the middle of the victim's chest, grab your other hand, and with a quick upward thrust, attempt to knock the wind out of the person to remove the obstruction. Do this five times until the obstruction is removed or the victim becomes unconscious.

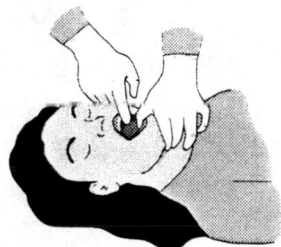

Figure 8-13: Finger Sweep

Figure 8-14: Alternate Chest Thrust

Pediatric Basic Life Support

Emergencies involving children are due more often to breathing problems than to cardiac problems. Children are more likely to choke, drown, suffocate, poison themselves, or have an accident than to have a heart attack. If the respiratory arrest is dealt with immediately, a cardiac arrest can be prevented.

The procedure for CPR in infants and children is the same as with adults except for a few modifications due to the size of the individual. For the purpose of CPR, the word *child* is used to describe an individual 1 to 8 years of age, or the physical size of an average 1- year-old to 8-year-old. The term *infant* is used for babies up to 1 year of age.

CPR for Children and Infants

1. **DETERMINE UNRESPONSIVENESS.** Gently shake the child or tap the infant's feet and shout, "Are you OK?"

2. **CALL FOR HELP.**

3. **POSITION THE VICTIM.** The infant or child must be supine on a firm surface. If an injury is suspected, log roll the victim onto his or her back.

4. **OPEN THE AIRWAY.** Use the **head-tilt/chin-lift** method. Avoid overextending the neck in infants. For traumatic injuries, use the **jaw-thrust maneuver**.

5. **DETERMINE BREATHLESSNESS.** Look, listen, and feel for ventilations.

6. **BEGIN RESCUE BREATHING.** If the victim is not breathing, and the patient is a child, pinch the nose and give two mouth-to-mask or mouth-to-mouth ventilations that are 1 to 1-1/2 seconds each in duration. (See the procedure for mouth-to-mask ventilation on page 8-13.) Pocket masks can be used for children, but they are too large for infants. Bag-valve masks can be used for both infants and children, but they must be the pediatric type. Follow the two initial ventilations with a pulse check.

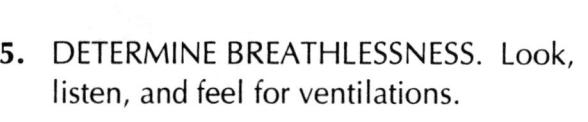

If the patient is an infant, cover the baby's nose and mouth with your mouth, or use a pediatric bag-valve mask, and deliver enough air to make the infant's chest rise and fall. Give two initial ventilations that are 1 to 1-1/2 seconds each in duration, followed by a pulse check.

Figure 8-15: If a pediatric bag-valve mask is unavailable, mouth-to-nose ventilations must be performed on infants.

7. **CHECK THE PULSE.** In an older child, the carotid pulse is monitored, but the best pulse to monitor on an infant is the brachial pulse. This pulse is found on the inside of the upper arm, between the elbow and the shoulder. If a pulse is present, continue rescue breathing by giving a breath every 3 seconds.

Chapter Eight • Basic Life Support

8. **BEGIN CHEST COMPRESSIONS:** If no pulse is found, perform chest compressions. Chest compressions are done with rescue breathing. Place the infant or child supine on a firm surface. If necessary, you can transport the infant while doing CPR using the football position. Lay the infant supine on the palm of your hand and cradle the baby's head with your fingers to maintain the airway position. (Figure 8-16b)

To begin chest compressions on an infant, locate an imaginary line between the nipples over the sternum. The index finger of your hand closest to the infant's feet is placed one finger's width below this imaginary line. Use two fingers and compress the sternum 1/2 to 1 inch at a rate of at least 100 times a minute. The compression to ventilation ratio is 5:1. (Figures 8-16a and 8-16b)

Chest Compressions for Infants

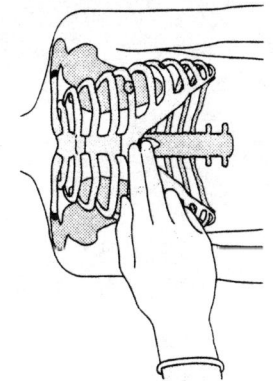
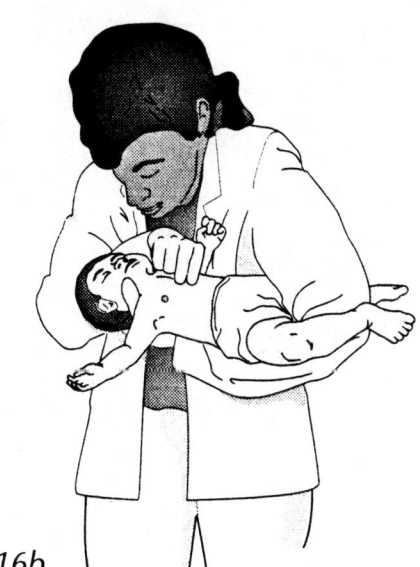

Figure 8-16a   Figure 8-16b

CPR	INFANT ONE PERSON	CHILD (1 - 8 yrs) ONE PERSON	CHILD (1 - 8 yrs) TWO PERSON	ADULT (over 8 yrs) ONE PERSON	ADULT (over 8 yrs) TWO PERSON
INITIAL BREATHS	2	2	2	2	2
COMPRESSIONS to BREATHS	5 to 1	5 to 1	5 to 1	15 to 2	5 to 1
COMPRESSIONS PER MINUTE	100	100	100	80	80
COMPRESS THE STERNUM	½ to 1 inches	1 to 1½ inches	1 to 1½ inches	1½ to 2 inches	1½ to 2 inches
APPLICATIONS	two fingers	one hand	one hand	two hands	two hands

To do chest compressions on a child, locate the lower margin of the victim's rib cage with your middle and index fingers. Follow this margin up the rib cage to the sternal notch. With the middle finger on the notch and the index finger placed next to the middle finger, note the location of your index finger. (Figure 8-17a) Now place the heel of the same hand in that spot. The long axis of the heel of your hand should align with the long axis of the sternum. (Figure 8-17b) The chest is compressed 1 inch with the heel of one hand at a rate of 80 to 100 times a minute. The compression to ventilation ratio is 5:1. Remember to keep your fingers off of the chest. (Figure 8-17c)

Chest Compressions for Children

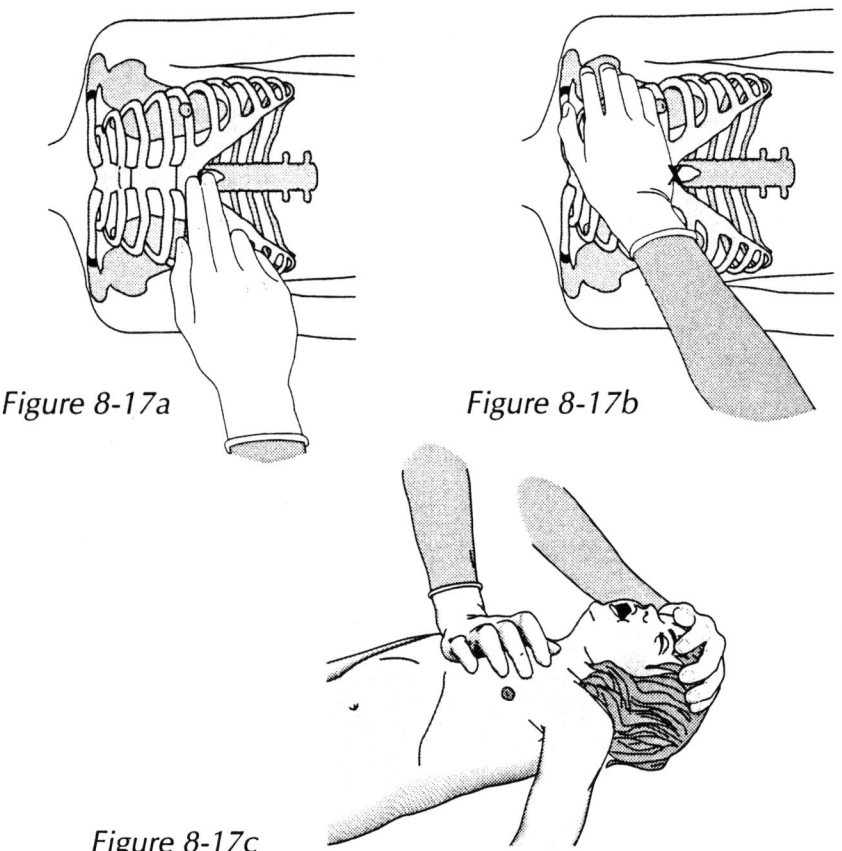

Figure 8-17a

Figure 8-17b

Figure 8-17c

Do the compressions with the hand nearest the victim's feet, and maintain the airway position with your other hand. MAINTAIN THE AIRWAY POSITION AT ALL TIMES! If you move your hand from the patient's head at any time, you will lose the airway position. If this happens, you must reposition the airway and recheck it.

Chapter Eight • Basic Life Support

Airway Obstruction in Children and Infants

The Heimlich maneuver is the same for children as it is for adults. However, the procedure for infants is quite different. The abdominal thrusts are not performed on infants; chest thrusts are done instead. If a child is choking and still conscious, stand behind the victim. (Figure 8-18a) Wrap your hands around the child's waist and make a fist with one hand. Place the thumb side of the fist against his or her abdomen directly above the navel, but below the **xiphoid process**. Grasp the fist with your other hand, and with a quick upward thrust, attempt to knock the wind out of the child to remove the obstruction. Repeat this five times until the obstruction is removed or the victim becomes unconscious.

If the child becomes unconscious, lay him or her in a supine position and kneel **astride** the victim's thighs. Place the heel of one hand against the child's abdomen above the navel, but below the xiphoid process. Place your other hand on top of the first hand and deliver upward abdominal thrusts five times. (Figure 8-18b) Open the child's mouth, visually examine for a foreign object, and, if present, do a finger sweep using your index finger or use a suction device to remove the object. Reassess the child's breathing and attempt to ventilate. Repeat the procedure if ventilation is unsuccessful.

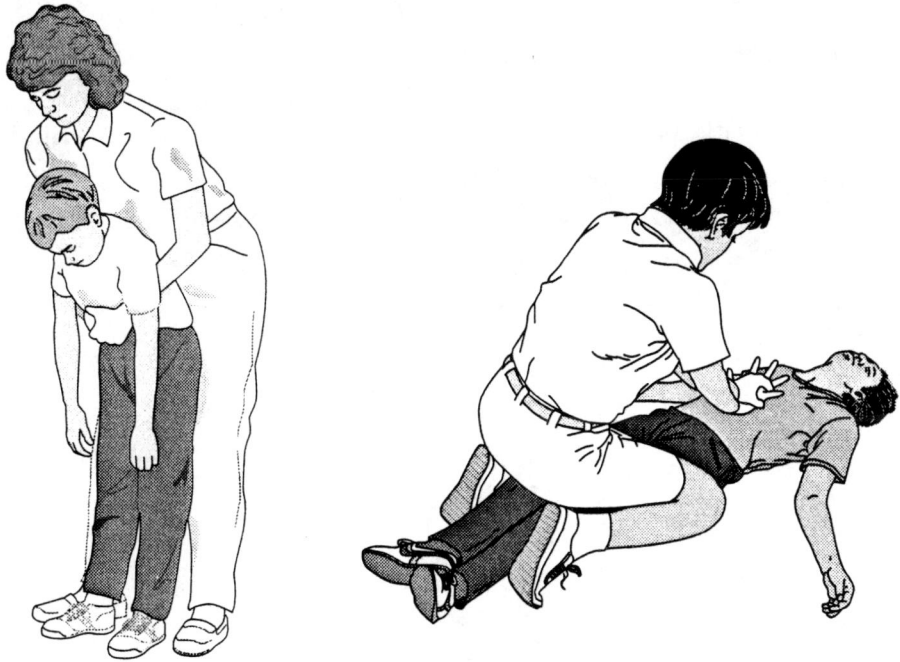

Figure 8-18a					Figure 8-18b

If the victim is an infant, you will need to use chest thrusts instead of abdominal thrusts. Straddle the infant over your arm, positioning the head lower than the trunk. Supporting the infant's head by firmly holding the jaw, deliver five back blows with the heel of one hand between the baby's shoulder blades.

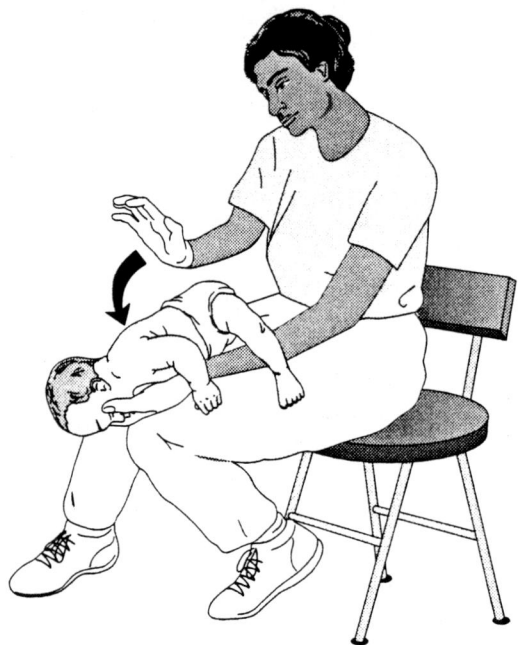

Figure 8-19: Deliver five back blows.

Next support the infant with one hand on the back and one hand on the chest. Turn the infant over, and perform five chest thrusts. Check the infant's mouth and remove any objects that you find. Reassess the infant's breathing and attempt to ventilate the baby. Repeat the procedure if ventilation is unsuccessful.

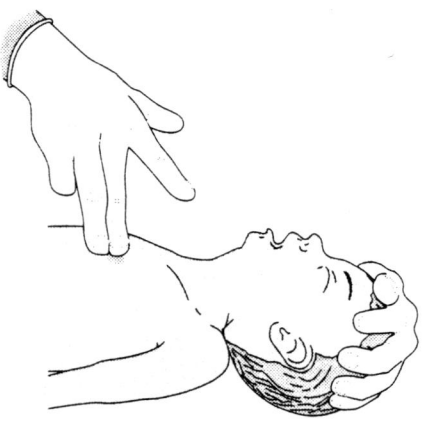

Figure 8-20: Perform five chest thrusts.

Extra caution must be used when dealing with airway obstructions in infants and children. The airway can become obstructed by a foreign body (a marble, hard candy, a button, food, etc.), or by an anatomical obstruction. Anatomical obstructions can occur with illnesses that cause swelling in the air passages. A history of a recent illness, fever, sore throat, or noisy breathing should alert you to the possibility of an anatomical obstruction. Many childhood diseases like **croup**, **epiglottitis**, and **tonsillitis** can cause the tissues in the airway to swell and obstruct the airway. The Heimlich maneuver will not be successful in treating anatomical obstructions, but it can be helpful if a foreign object is blocking the airway.

Rescue Breathing for Adults, Children, and Infants

If the pulse is present in a victim, but breathing is absent, give two ventilations followed by one breath every 5 seconds for an adult, or one breath every 3 seconds for a child or an infant.

Rescue Breathing	
Adult	1 breath every 5 seconds
Child	1 breath every 3 seconds
Infant	1 breath every 3 seconds

CPR in Transport

A critical patient may need CPR while being transported to the operating room or intensive care unit. A patient who is stable in the ER may go into full arrest during transport to the unit, requiring CPR in transit. Or, CPR may be in progress as the patient arrives via ambulance and is placed on the ER gurney. Proper planning is essential to keep IV lines and airways from being dislodged in the process of moving the patient.

The person at the head of the patient is in charge of the move. Before the patient is moved from one stretcher to another, all IV lines, tubes, and monitor wires must be checked. Pay attention to the location of safety straps and the position of the patient's arms and legs. On command, the person doing the ventilations will deliver two ventilations and disconnect the bag-valve mask, the compressor will stop compressions, and everyone will move the patient to the new gurney or bed. Each person must pay close attention to the patient and the many tubes, IV lines, and equipment. The rescuer in charge of ventilating will quickly reconnect the bag-valve mask, and the compressor will resume CPR.

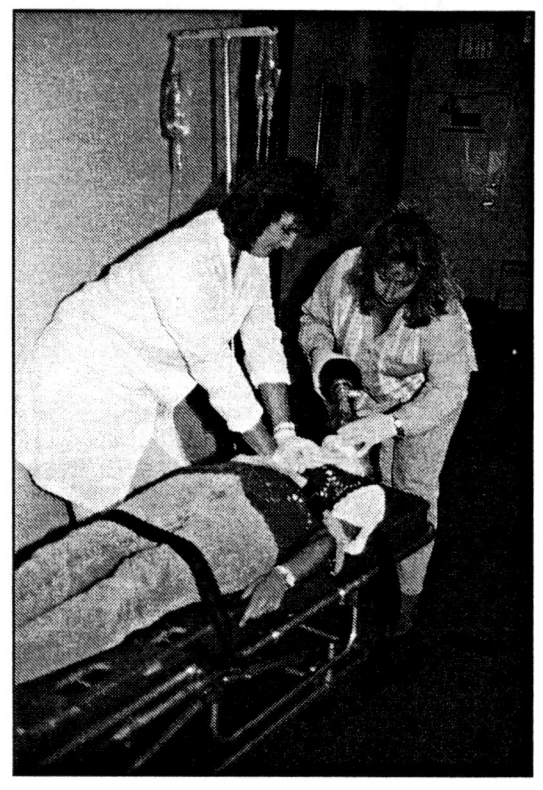

Figure 8-21: Sometimes CPR must be done during transport.

Provisions also must be made for additional equipment when moving critical patients. Patients being transported to critical care units will have several IVs, oxygen, a portable ventilator, a portable monitor with a **defibrillator**, an emergency drug box, and other equipment. Hallways must be cleared, and an elevator must be ready and waiting if necessary. If the patient is on a hospital gurney, a footstool sometimes is required for some people to do effective compressions. Although efforts should be made to avoid pauses during CPR, it may be necessary to pause while the patient is intubated, defibrillated, or the pulse or **EKG** is reassessed. Working in a **code blue** procedure requires teamwork and good communication.

defibrillator: an electronic device used to shock the heart into a normal rhythm

Chapter Eight • Basic Life Support

The Crash Cart

The **crash cart** is found in a central area of the ER. The critical care room has similar equipment and supplies. These carts are checked each shift and restocked immediately after use. Though the size and shape of these carts will vary, the equipment on all of them is basically the same. A crash cart usually will hold the following items.

- emergency medications in prefilled syringes to treat heart rhythm disturbances
- IV solutions in bags or bottles
- IV tubing and supplies to start an IV lifeline
- a **central venous pressure (CVP) tray** used by the physician to start an IV into a central vein. Using this, fluid and medication can be given as well as pressure measured.
- a **subclavian tray** to start a central IV line
- an EKG monitor/defibrillator to monitor heart rhythms
- leads and paddles to attach the patient to the EKG monitor
- a pacemaker to insert into the patient if his or her heart fails to beat on its own
- a suction machine and tubing to clear the patient's airway
- oxygen equipment to assist breathing
- assorted nasopharyngeal airways to provide an airway through the nose
- assorted oropharyngeal airways to provide an airway through the mouth

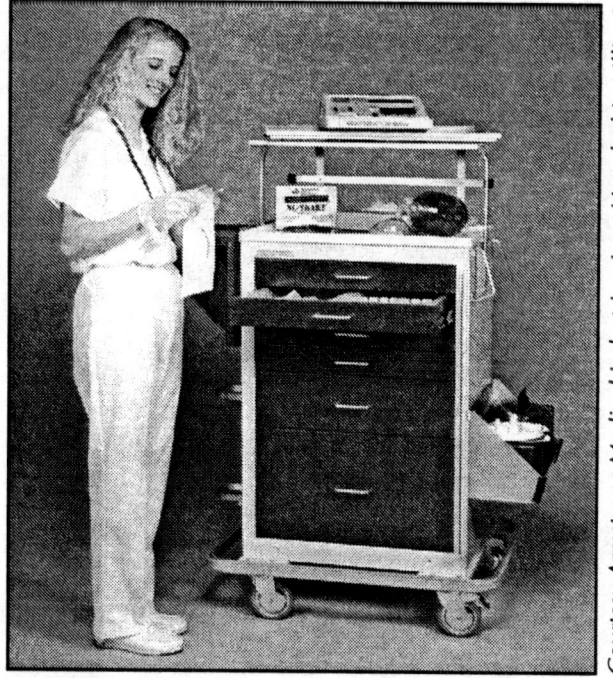

Figure 8-22: A Crash Cart

- endotracheal tubes and blades to provide an airway through the trachea
- a laryngoscope to view the back of the throat
- a tracheostomy tray to make a surgical opening in the neck for breathing
- a bag-valve mask to ventilate the patient
- pressure-cycled breathing equipment to assist non-breathing patients
- chest tubes to treat a collapsed lung
- catheters to insert or remove fluid
- Levin's tubes to keep the stomach clear of excess fluid and gas
- gloves to protect the healthcare workers and the patient

Chapter Summary

CPR is a lifesaving skill used in emergency situations. An emergency department technician must be proficient in this skill, so repeated practice on manikins is essential. It also is necessary to review CPR procedures often to maintain your proficiency in these skills. Remember—you never know when the next full arrest patient will come through the door. You must be ready to make the best effort possible to save a life.

Basic Life Support for the Adult Victim

Adult One-Rescuer CPR
- ❏ Establish unresponsiveness
- ❏ Activate the EMS system
- **A** ❏ Open airway
- **B** ❏ Check breathing (look, listen, feel)
  - ❏ Give two slow breaths (1-1/2 to 2 sec/breath)
    - watch chest rise
    - allow for exhalation between breaths
- **C** ❏ Check carotid pulse
  - ❏ If breathing is absent, but pulse is present, provide rescue breathing (one breath every 5 seconds, about twelve breaths a minute)
  - ❏ If no pulse, give fifteen chest compressions
  - ❏ Followed by two slow breaths
  - ❏ After four cycles of 15:2, check pulse
  - ❏ If no pulse, continue 15:2 cycle beginning with chest compressions

Adult Two-Rescuer CPR
- ❏ Establish unresponsiveness (EMS system has been activated)

RESCUER #1
- **A** ❏ Open airway
- **B** ❏ Check breathing (look, listen, feel)
  - ❏ Give two slow breaths (1-1/2 to 2 sec/breath)
    - watch chest rise
    - allow for exhalations between breaths
- **C** ❏ Check carotid pulse
  - ❏ If no pulse, say "No pulse, start CPR"

RESCUER #2
- ❏ If no pulse, give five chest compressions
- ❏ Rescuer #1 gives one slow breath
- ❏ Both rescuers continue 5:1 ratio of CPR
- ❏ After 1 minute, check pulse
- ❏ If no pulse, continue 5:1 cycles

Adult Foreign Body Airway Obstruction— Conscious
- ❏ Ask, "Are you choking?"
- ❏ Deliver abdominal thrusts (chest thrusts for pregnant/obese victim)
- ❏ Repeat thrusts until effective or the victim becomes unconscious

If Victim Becomes Unconscious:
- ❏ Activate the EMS system
- ❏ Perform a tongue-jaw lift, followed by a finger sweep to remove the object
- ❏ Open airway and try to ventilate; if still obstructed, reposition head and try to ventilate again
- ❏ Deliver five abdominal thrusts
- ❏ Repeat until effective

Adult Foreign Body Airway Obstruction — Unconscious
- ❏ Establish unresponsiveness
- ❏ Activate EMS system
- A ❏ Open airway
- B ❏ Check breathing (look, listen, feel)
- ❏ Attempt to ventilate
- ❏ If obstructed, reposition head
- ❏ Attempt to ventilate again
- ❏ Deliver five abdominal thrusts
- ❏ Perform a tongue-jaw lift/finger sweep
- ❏ Repeat until effective

Basic Life Support for the Child Victim

Child One-Rescuer CPR
- ☐ Establish unresponsiveness
- ☐ If second rescuer is present, activate the EMS system
- A ☐ Open airway
- B ☐ Check breathing (look, listen, feel)
- ☐ Give two slow breaths (1 to 1-1/2 sec/breath)
  - watch chest rise
  - allow for exhalation between breaths
- C ☐ Check carotid pulse
- ☐ If breathing is absent, but pulse is present, provide rescue breathing (one breath every 3 seconds, about twenty breaths/minute)
- ☐ If no pulse, give five chest compressions followed by 1 slow breath
- ☐ Repeat 5:1 cycle
- ☐ After about 1 minute, check pulse
- ☐ If rescuer is alone, activate EMS system
- ☐ If no pulse, continue 5:1 cycle

Child Foreign Body Airway Obstruction — Conscious
- ☐ Ask, "Are you choking?"
- ☐ Deliver abdominal thrusts
- ☐ Repeat thrusts until effective or victim becomes unconscious

If Victim Becomes Unconscious:
- ☐ If second rescuer is present, have them activate the EMS system
- ☐ Perform a tongue-jaw lift
- ☐ If object is seen, perform a finger sweep
- ☐ Open airway and try to ventilate; if still obstructed, reposition head and try to ventilate again
- ☐ Deliver five abdominal thrusts
- ☐ Repeat until effective
- ☐ If airway obstruction is not relieved after 1 minute, activate the EMS system

Child Foreign Body Airway Obstruction — Unconscious

- ❏ Establish unresponsiveness
- ❏ If second rescuer is present, have them activate the EMS system
- **A** ❏ Open airway
- **B** ❏ Check breathing (look, listen, feel)
- ❏ Attempt to ventilate
- ❏ If obstructed, reposition head
- ❏ Attempt to ventilate again
- ❏ Deliver five abdominal thrusts
- ❏ Perform a tongue-jaw lift
- ❏ If object is seen, perform a finger sweep
- ❏ Repeat until effective
- ❏ If airway obstruction is not relieved after 1 minute, activate the EMS system

Basic Life Support for the Infant Victim

Infant One-Rescuer CPR

- ❏ Establish unresponsiveness
- ❏ If second rescuer is present, activate the EMS system
- **A** ❏ Open airway ("sniffing position")
- **B** ❏ Check breathing (look, listen, feel)
- ❏ Give two breaths
  - watch chest rise
  - allow for exhalation between breaths
- **C** ❏ Check brachial pulse
- ❏ If breathing is absent, but pulse is present provide rescue breathing (one breath every 3 seconds, about twenty breaths/minute)
- ❏ If no pulse, give five chest compressions
- ❏ Followed by one breath
- ❏ Repeat 5:1 cycle
- ❏ After about 1 minute, check pulse
- ❏ If rescuer is alone, activate EMS system
- ❏ If no pulse, continue 5:1 cycle

Infant Foreign Body Airway Obstruction — Conscious

- ❏ Determine airway obstruction - observe breathing difficulties
- ❏ Deliver five back blows
- ❏ Deliver five chest thrusts
- ❏ Repeat back blows and chest thrusts until effective or victim becomes unconscious

If Victim Becomes Unconscious:

- ❏ If second rescuer is present, have them activate the EMS system
- ❏ Perform a tongue-jaw lift
- ❏ If object is seen, perform a finger sweep
- ❏ Open airway and try to ventilate; if still obstructed, reposition head and try to ventilate again
- ❏ Deliver five back blows
- ❏ Deliver five chest thrusts
- ❏ Repeat until effective
- ❏ If airway obstruction is not relieved after 1 minute, activate the EMS system

Infant Foreign Body Airway Obstruction — Unconscious
- ❑ Establish unresponsiveness
- ❑ If second rescuer is present, have them activate the EMS system
- **A** ❑ Open airway
- **B** ❑ Check breathing (look, listen, feel)
- ❑ Attempt to ventilate
- ❑ If airway is still obstructed, reposition head
- ❑ Attempt to ventilate again
- ❑ Deliver five back blows
- ❑ Deliver five chest thrusts
- ❑ Perform a tongue-jaw lift
- ❑ If object is seen, perform a finger sweep
- ❑ Repeat until effective
- ❑ If airway obstruction is not relieved after 1 minute, activate the EMS system

Chapter Eight • Basic Life Support   8-33

Name _____
Date _____

Student Enrichment Activities

1. Name six foods that are high in cholesterol.
   A. _____   D. _____
   B. _____   E. _____
   C. _____

2. List four major risk factors of heart disease and strokes that a person is able to control.
   A. _____   D. _____
   B. _____   E. _____
   C. _____

3. List four major risk factors of heart disease and stroke that a person is not able to control.
   A. _____   C. _____
   B. _____   D. _____

4. Most people having chest pain believe that they are having a heart attack. **(Circle the best choice.)**   TRUE or FALSE

5. Describe the pain associated with a heart attack.
   _____
   _____

6. The chances of surviving a cardiac arrest is greatest if CPR is begun: **(Circle the best choice.)**
   A. Within six minutes of the arrest
   B. After ten minutes of the arrest
   C. Between six and ten minutes after the arrest
   D. Time is not a factor

7. When you are alone with an adult victim in full arrest you should: **(Circle the best choice.)**
   A. Go for help.
   B. Do nothing.
   C. Do CPR for one minute and then activate the EMS.
   D. Activate EMS before opening the airway.

8. List six signs or symptoms of a heart attack.
   A. _____   D. _____
   B. _____   E. _____
   C. _____   F. _____

9. The first thing to do for a victim who is not responding is:
   _____

10. Describe how you would position an unconscious victim who is not breathing.
    _____

Choose a match from the list on the right.

11. _____ Before giving breath   A. Check the breathing

12. _____ Before chest compressions   B. Check the pulse

13. _____ Before calling for help   C. Check for brain damage

14. _____ After 1 minute of CPR   D. Check the pulse and breathing

                                            E. Check for non-response

Chapter Eight • Basic Life Support

Name _____
Date _____

15. How many manual thrusts are given to an adult choking victim? _____

16. List two reasons to check a victim for unresponsiveness.
    A. _____
    B. _____

17. Describe the technique used to determine if a person is breathing.
    _____
    _____

18. In two-person CPR when does the person ventilating give a breath?
    _____

19. When do you ventilate an unconscious victim with an obstructed airway?
    _____

20. List six signs of respiratory difficulty in an infant or child.
    A. _____
    B. _____
    C. _____
    D. _____
    E. _____
    F. _____

21. List five causes of sudden death in adults.
    A. _____
    B. _____
    C. _____
    D. _____
    E. _____

22. List five causes of sudden death in infants or children.
    A. _____
    B. _____
    C. _____
    D. _____
    E. _____

23. Cardiac arrest will occur as a result of _____ arrest.

Fill in the blanks.

24. Open the airway by _____ _____

25. For a neck injured patient, open the airway by _____ _____

26. Rescue breathing for an **adult** with a pulse is _____ breath(s) every _____ seconds.

27. Rescue breathing for a **child** with a pulse is _____ breath(s) every _____ seconds.

28. Rescue breathing for an **infant** with a pulse is _____ breath(s) every _____ seconds.

Chapter Eight • Basic Life Support

Name _____
Date _____

29. Compressions should be applied using hands or fingers as follows:

   Adult _____
   Child _____
   Infant _____

30. Chest compressions should be this deep:

   Adult _____
   Child _____
   Infant _____

31. There should be this many chest compressions in one minute:

   Adult _____ (one rescuer)
   Adult _____ (two rescuer)
   Child _____
   Infant _____

32. The compression/ventilation ratio should be:

   Adult _____ (one rescuer)
   Adult _____ (two rescuer)
   Child _____
   Infant _____

33. When performing CPR, the pulse is checked _____.

34. Each ventilation for an adult should take _____ seconds.

35. An infant with airway obstructions should receive five _____ _____ followed by five _____.

36. Check an **infant** pulse in the _____ artery.

37. Check an **child** pulse in the _____ artery.

38. Check an **adult** pulse in the _____ artery.

39. Identify three complications of CPR
    A. _____
    B. _____
    C. _____

40. An infant is defined as up to _____ years old.

41. A child is defined as up to _____ year old.

42. After successful CPR a person has a pulse and is breathing. How should you position the victim?
    _____

43. What do A, B, and C stand for in basic life support?
    A. _____   C. _____
    B. _____

Chapter Eight • Basic Life Support 8-39

Name _____
Date _____

Define the following terms.

44. EMS: _____
_____

45. ABCs: _____
_____

46. Arteriosclerosis: _____
_____

47. Myocardial infarction (MI): _____
_____

48. Compression: _____
_____

49. Sternum: _____
_____

50. Biological death: _____
_____

51. Clinical death: _____
_____

52. Ventilation: _____
_____

53. Cardiac arrest: _____
_____

54. Respiratory arrest: _____
_____

55. Unresponsive: _____
_____

56. Obstruction: _____
_____

57. Heimlich maneuver: _____
_____

58. Abdominal thrusts: _____
_____

59. BLS: _____
_____

60. Jaw-thrust meneuver: _____
_____

61. Resuscitation: _____
_____

Chapter Nine
Emergencies of the Eye, Ear, Nose, and Throat

Objectives

After completing this chapter you should be able to do the following:

1. Define and correctly spell all key terms.
2. Perform a visual acuity exam using the Snellen eye chart.
3. Apply an eye dressing to a simulated patient.
4. Assemble the equipment necessary for an ear lavage.
5. Set up the equipment needed to assist a physician with a nasal packing.
6. Demonstrate the procedure for obtaining a throat culture.

Key Terms

- cerumen
- conjunctiva
- conjunctivitis
- cornea
- electrocautery
- equilibrium
- fluorescein sodium
- glaucoma
- grounding pad
- lavage
- nasal speculum
- ophthalmoscope
- otoscope
- sclera
- speculum
- upper respiratory infection (URI)
- vertigo
- visual acuity

EENT Disorders

glaucoma: an eye disorder caused by an increase in intraocular pressure

conjunctivitis: inflammation of the white of the eye characterized by redness and a sticky discharge; pink eye

equilibrium: a person's sense of balance

Injuries and illnesses of the eyes, ears, nose, and throat need special treatment. These are known as **EENT** disorders. Eye emergencies can include trauma, acute **glaucoma**, infection, or **conjunctivitis**. Prompt and appropriate vision care can help reduce the pain and prevent permanent damage to the eyes. Injuries and illnesses that involve the nose and throat are potentially life-threatening. They must be evaluated quickly to detect any breathing problems, and immediate measures must be taken to ensure an adequate airway. Problems with the ear can lead to a loss of hearing and can disturb the patient's balance, or **equilibrium**.

Patients with these types of emergencies are taken to the examination room designated for EENT care. This room is smaller than the other treatment areas in the emergency room, and contains a patient examination chair instead of a gurney. Since this room is reserved for the examination of eye, ear, nose, and throat problems, it is stocked with special equipment to aid in the diagnosis and treatment of these types of complaints. As an emergency department technician you will be responsible for preparing these equipment items for use. EENT equipment includes the following items:

- a **Snellen eye chart**
- a **slit lamp**
- a **tonometer** (an instrument used in testing for glaucoma that measures the pressure in the eye)
- an **ophthalmoscope**
- an **otoscope**
- various eye medications
- a **tuning fork**
- an ear syringe
- a **cobalt lamp**

ophthalmoscope: a lighted instrument used to see inside the eye

otoscope: a lighted instrument used to see inside the ear

In this chapter you will learn methods that are used to test for normal vision and hearing, as well as procedures to follow in the treatment of eye, ear, nose, and throat emergencies. You will be responsible for assisting the physician with many of the examinations and procedures.

Eye Emergencies

Trauma to the eye can result from automobile accidents, industrial accidents, foreign bodies that invade the eye, and numerous other things. Eye trauma can be very painful; it also can lead to vision loss. Therefore it must be treated immediately. Infections of the eye are another type of eye emergency. Eye infections can cause pain, visual disturbances, swelling, redness, and **purulent** (pus-like) drainage. Other emergencies involving the eye can be caused by various diseases and medical disorders.

When a patient arrives in the ER, a history regarding the nature of the illness or injury is obtained and the patient is **triaged**. Except for life-threatening conditions, the following complaints are given top priority:

- sudden, painless loss of vision
- chemical burns to the eye
- a foreign body in the eye
- pain and signs of infection in the eye

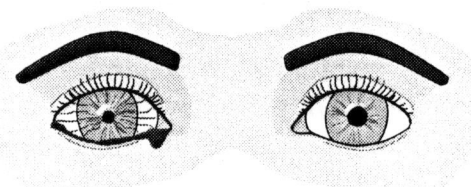

All patients who enter the emergency room with eye problems should have their **visual acuity** and pupils checked. Refer to the procedures for a neuro check and a secondary survey procedures in Chapter Six if you cannot remember how to do a pupil check.

visual acuity: the degree to which a person can see objects clearly

Eye Examinations

Eye examinations are done to evaluate a patient's visual acuity. The Snellen eye chart is used to determine the effect of distance on visual acuity. (Figure 9-1) Various letters of the alphabet are arranged on this chart and are read from a distance of twenty feet. The symbol on the top of the chart can be read by someone with normal vision at 200 feet. In each row of the chart, the size of the letters becomes smaller. A person with normal vision can read the second row of letters at 100 feet. This chart is not accurate if the person cannot read or is too young, so a child's version o the chart uses pictures rather than letters.

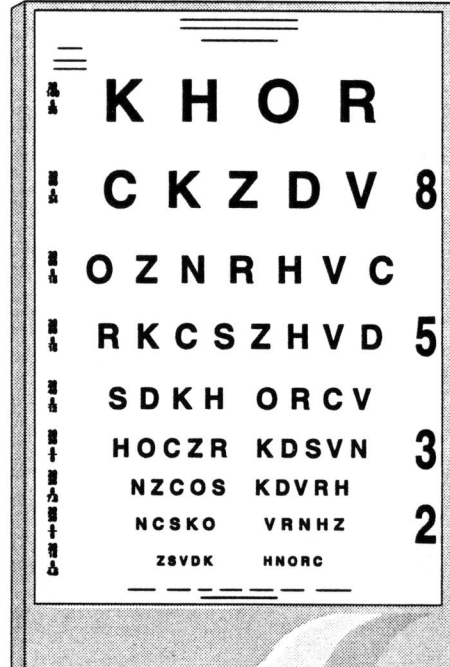

Figure 9-1: Snellen Eye Chart

Here are some guidelines to follow when testing visual acuity.

1. If the patient wears glasses, check the patient first while he or she is wearing the glasses and check the patient again with the glasses off. Record both findings.

2. Check each eye separately.

3. Cover the eye that is not being checked with a piece of cardboard. (Figure 9-2)

4. Check both eyes together.

5. The patient must stand twenty feet away from the Snellen chart.

6. The patient should not have time to study the chart before the test.

Figure 9-2

7. Identify clearly which line on the chart is to be read.

8. Record the smallest line the patient can read without any mistakes.

9. Record the results as a fraction (i.e., 20/20). The top number is the distance the patient is standing from the chart. The bottom number is the lowest line the patient read correctly. 20/20 vision means the person can read line number twenty at twenty feet.

10. Record any observations you make, such as squinting, tearing, or turning the head.

11. **OD** means right eye.

12. **OS** means left eye.

13. **OU** means both eyes.

If the patient cannot see as far as the Snellen chart, hold up your fingers and record the distance from which the patient can see your fingers. If the patient cannot see your fingers ask if he or she can see your hand in motion, or if light can be seen, or if there is any vision at all.

The **ophthalmoscope** is an instrument the doctor uses to examine the eye. Before using this device, the doctor may ask you to turn off the overhead lights.

The ophthalmoscope's light will then be used to view the internal structures of the patient's eyes. (Figure 9-3) During an eye examination the patient may be apprehensive; if the eyes are painful the patient will want to keep them closed. Therefore, the doctor may administer eye drops to **anesthetize** the patient's eyes before the exam. Anesthetic will reduce the pain and prevent excessive movement of the eye, which will allow the doctor to diagnose the problem. Since the patient must remain still during this procedure, his or her head should be supported in the chair's head rest, and the chair should be adjusted to fit the patient properly.

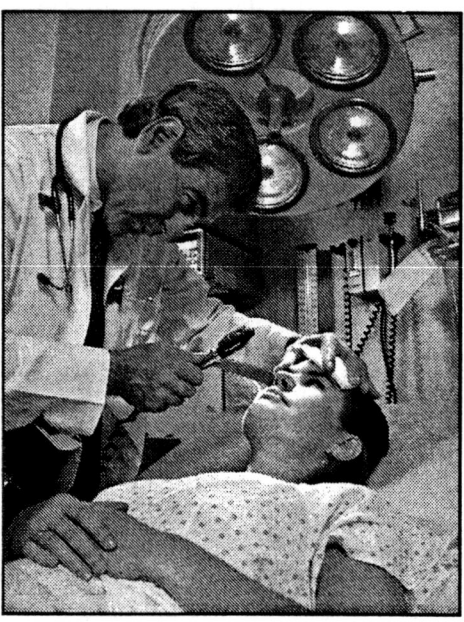

Figure 9-3: Physician's use an ophthalmoscope to view the internal structures of the eye.

If the patient is wearing contact lenses, the doctor may ask you to remove them. If the patient can remove the contacts, you should provide assistance. Make sure you wear gloves if you must touch the mucous membranes of the eye. Gloves MUST be worn when removing contact lenses, irrigating an eye, applying eye dressings, or examining the eyes. This is one of the universal precautions. Hard lenses are removed with a contact lens remover, which is similar to a tiny suction cup. Remove soft lenses by placing your index finger on the lens over the cornea, and gently sliding the lens to the **sclera** of the eye. Remove it from the eye with your thumb and index finger. Place the contact lenses in separate containers labelled with the patient's name, and mark each container as either the right lens or left lens. Make a notation on the patient's chart indicating what was done with his or her belongings. Remember, all patient property must be tracked.

sclera: the tough, fibrous membrane that covers the white of the eye, and to which the muscles of the eye are attached

Foreign Bodies in the Eye

The most common eye emergency is the presence of a foreign body or object. Foreign objects can become lodged under the eyelid, causing tearing and pain. If this occurs, the patient may be able to tell you exactly where it is located, or the physician may have to locate it before it can be removed. Have a sterile cotton tip applicator available. The doctor may wish to moisten the applicator with sterile saline to make it easier to remove the object. After the object is removed and the nurse treats the eye with antibiotic medication, you can apply an eye dressing. Ask the doctor if both eyes are to be covered. With eye injuries, both eyes often are covered to decrease eye movement and promote healing.

Applying an Eye Dressing

Materials needed:
- ✓ gloves
- ✓ oval pads
- ✓ paper tape

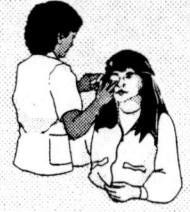

1. <u>Procedural Step:</u> Wash your hands.
   <u>Reason:</u> Universal precaution.

2. <u>Procedural Step:</u> Identify the patient.
   <u>Reason:</u> To ensure you are dealing with the correct patient.

3. <u>Procedural Step:</u> Put on gloves.
   <u>Reason:</u> Universal precaution.

4. <u>Procedural Step:</u> Explain the procedure to the patient using terms he or she can understand.
   <u>Reason:</u> To keep the patient calm and provide the information necessary for him or her to give informed consent.

5. <u>Procedural Step:</u> Instruct the patient to close the eye.
   <u>Reason:</u> The eyelid protects the eye.

6. <u>Procedural Step:</u> Place one or two oval eye pads over the eye.
   <u>Reason:</u> All facial structures are different. One pad may not be enough.

7. <u>Procedural Step:</u> Using paper tape, tape the eye pad in place, avoiding the hair and eyebrows.
   <u>Reason:</u> Removing tape from the hair and eyebrows is painful for the patient and could remove the hair.

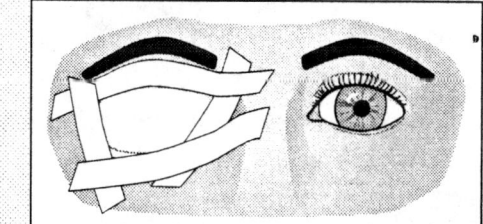

8. <u>Procedural Step:</u> Remove and discard your gloves.
   <u>Reason:</u> Universal precaution.

9. <u>Procedural Step:</u> Wash your hands.
   <u>Reason:</u> Universal precaution.

10. <u>Procedural Step:</u> Document the procedure as appropriate.
    <u>Reason:</u> To provide documentation.

Burns to the Eye

Burns to the eyes can occur from fire or flash burns. Standing too close to a flame can cause a flash burn. The ultraviolet light used by a welder can cause a very painful flash burn. Victims of flash burns will experience a sensitivity to light and pain in the eyes. Ultraviolet burns to the eyes can be caused by the sun's reflection on snow. Snow skiers who do not wear protective glasses can get **snow blindness** from this reflection. To relieve the patient's discomfort, dim the overhead lights while he or she is waiting for treatment. Treatment of these injuries includes a physical examination, the application of eye medication and eye dressings, and rest for 24 hours.

Gasoline, tear gas, pepper spray, mace, or other chemicals are irritating and can burn the eyes. This type of burn requires immediate attention. Any chemical that gets splashed in the eyes must be washed out immediately with tap water. First aid should be done at the scene of the emergency and the patient's eyes washed with tap water. (Figure 9-4) Any patient who is involved in a chemical spill should be showered with large amounts of water at the scene. The eyes are always **irrigated** (rinsed) with sterile **normal saline** upon arrival in the emergency room, using the irrigating tray in the EENT room. Eyes are irrigated for 10 to 20 minutes with 500 ccs of fluid. If only one eye is involved, it is important to wash that eye from the inner aspect (from the nose to the ear) to avoid contamination of the other eye. Continuous eye wash, or **lavage**, can be done using morgan lenses and saline. These lenses are placed in the eyes, like contact lenses, and then saline is flushed through them into the eyes. After all the chemical has been removed, the physician will examine the eyes, place antibiotic drops in them, and ask you to put a dressing on one or both eyes.

lavage: to wash or irrigate

Figure 9-4: Chemical burns to the eye must be treated immediately by flushing the immediately with tap water.

Eye Trauma

Whenever there has been an injury to the eye, the patient must be checked for other injuries too. A history of how the accident occurred can alert you to other possible problems. For example, if a patient is admitted with an eye injury that occurred in an automobile accident, and you know that the patient's head went through the windshield, you would suspect that head and neck injuries may have occurred as well as the eye trauma. If there are other injuries present, the patient may be taken to the trauma room instead of the EENT room. Always check patients with traumatic eye injuries for additional injuries.

Injuries to the eyelids, such as cuts or **lacerations**, can cause bleeding. These injuries will be repaired by an **ophthalmologist** or **cosmetic surgeon**. Any injuries to the **globe**, or eyeball, must be evaluated and treated by a specialist. Facial fractures that are near the **orbit**, or eye socket, may need repair in the operating room. If this is the case, time will be a very important factor. The doctor may order ice to reduce the swelling and prevent **ecchymosis**, or bruising. Fill a **latex** glove with crushed ice and place it on a washcloth over the swollen area.

A **corneal abrasion**, or scratch to the **cornea**, is another common emergency. Abrasions occur when an object, such as a contact lens or blowing sand, comes in contact with the eye and injures the cornea. The patient will complain of eye pain, experience tearing (watering) of the eye, and spasms of the eyelid. The doctor will examine the eye and look for damage to the cornea. You may be asked to help with this procedure, called *fluorescein staining,* which uses **fluorescein sodium**. The procedure for assisting with a fluorescein stain is on the following page.

cornea: the transparent front part of the eye; the lens of the eye

fluorescein sodium: a red powder used primarily for detecting injuries to the cornea of the eye

Eye Infections

Any area of the eye can become inflamed (red) and infected. Many organisms can cause eye infections, such as the organisms that live on the skin and hands. These are transferred to the eye easily by touching or wiping the eyes. An infection of a small gland on the lower lid can create a white, swollen, and painful **abscess** on the lower lid called a **sty**. Inflammation or redness of the **conjunctiva** (the white portion of the eyeball) is called **conjunctivitis**, or pink eye. This is a painful, contagious infection, and the eyelids may stick together with drainage.

conjunctiva: the membrane of the eye

Assisting With Fluorescein Staining

Materials needed:
- ✓ package of fluorescein stain
- ✓ cobalt lamp
- ✓ cotton tip applicator
- ✓ liquid tears
- ✓ tissue
- ✓ gloves for the physician

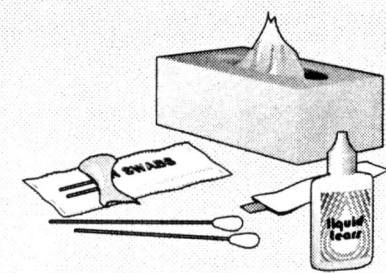

1. <u>Procedural Step:</u> Wash your hands.
   <u>Reason:</u> *Universal precaution.*

2. <u>Procedural Step:</u> Identify the patient.
   <u>Reason:</u> *To ensure you are dealing with the correct patient.*

3. <u>Procedural Step:</u> Explain the procedure to the patient using terms he or she can understand.
   <u>Reason:</u> *This keeps the patient calm and provides the information necessary for the patient to give informed consent.*

4. <u>Procedural Step:</u> Obtain a disposable individual fluorescein strip.
   <u>Reason:</u> *Material is sterile.*

5. <u>Procedural Step:</u> Assist the physician.
   <u>Reason:</u> *The physician will be looking in the patient's eyes and will need help obtaining supplies.*

6. <u>Procedural Step:</u> Open the sterile package by grasping the ends and tearing the paper downward.
   <u>Reason:</u> *To keep the strip sterile.*

7. <u>Procedural Step:</u> Moisten the end of the strip with sterile saline.
   <u>Reason:</u> *To start the chemical reaction.*

8. <u>Procedural Step:</u> The physician will touch the fluorescein strip to the lower eyelid.
   <u>Reason:</u> *To perform stain.*

9. <u>Procedural Step:</u> Turn on the cobalt lamp at the physician's request.
   <u>Reason:</u> *There will be a color change in the area of injury.*

10. <u>Procedural Step:</u> At the physician's request, dim the lamp or turn it off.
    <u>Reason:</u> *The procedure is completed.*

11. <u>Procedural Step:</u> Wash your hands.
    <u>Reason:</u> *Universal precaution.*

12. <u>Procedural Step:</u> Document the procedure as appropriate.
    <u>Reason:</u> *To provide documentation.*

The physician will examine the infected eye and order a **culture**, or test, to determine the cause of the infection. Always wear gloves when treating any type of eye infection. A culture is obtained by touching the sterile culture cotton tip applicator to the infected area. Without touching anything else, return the swab to the sterile culture container. If the container is a **Culturette**, squeeze the soft plastic end over the end of the applicator to moisten the culture with liquid. Label the specimen with the patient's name, room number, culture site, and time the culture was obtained. The specimen and the laboratory slip must then be taken to the **bacteriology** section of the laboratory. The laboratory slip is filled out with the time, the specimen collected (pus, urine, blood, etc.), the date, your name, the source of the culture, and whether it is a routine or STAT (at once) culture.

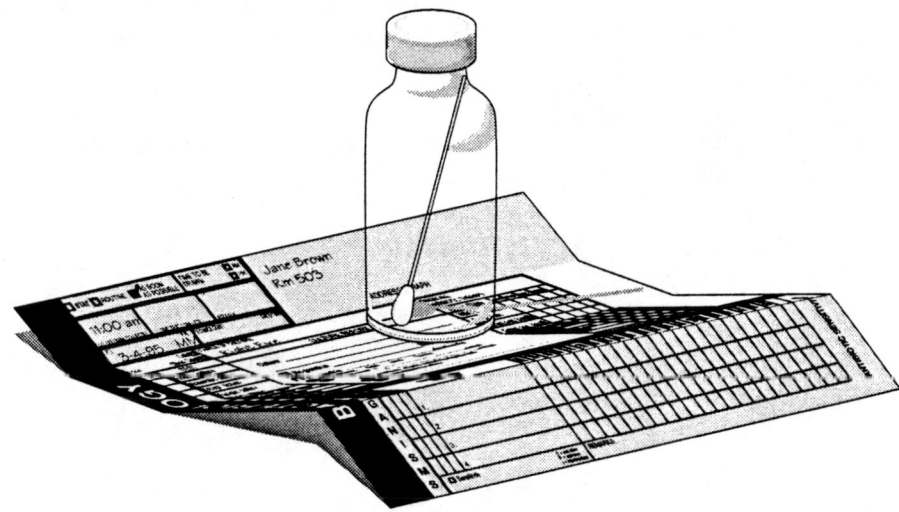

Figure 9-5: Specimens are taken with the laboratory slip to Bacteriology.

The physician may order medication for the patient's eyes. A nurse must administer these medications, but you may be asked to assist. A hot, moist compress also may be ordered to help reduce the swelling and help the infection drain. This is a small, disposable, soft towel that has been moistened with hot water and wrung out. The temperature of the water should NOT exceed 105° F. The patient must hold the hot compress over the eye as much as he or she can tolerate it.

All supplies and equipment used on any area of infection should be disposed of in the contaminated waste container. If non-disposable items are used, they should be cleaned, double bagged, marked *isolation*, and sent to Central Supply for terminal cleaning.

Other Eye Emergencies

A patient may come into the emergency room complaining of pain, vision loss, or visual disturbance unrelated to a trauma or an infection. Several causes of altered vision can be of an urgent nature. They include the following:

- **retinal artery occlusion:** a blockage of the blood vessel in the eye
- **retinal detachment:** a tear in the inner lining of the eyeball
- **glaucoma:** a rise in pressure in the eye due to increased fluid

These are all medical eye emergencies. The patient is evaluated by the emergency department physician, but he or she may find it necessary to call an eye specialist or ophthalmologist for a consultation. Some patients will require immediate eye surgery and hospital admission.

Emergencies Involving the Ear

upper respiratory infection (URI): a general term used to describe an infectious disease process involving the nasal passages, pharynx, and bronchi

speculum: an instrument, often disposable, used for inspecting canals

Ear infections often follow **upper respiratory infections** (URIs). Such infections can cause pain, a feeling of fullness, hearing loss, and drainage from the ear. When the patient lays down, the ear pain usually becomes worse. Children with ear infections may cry or tug at their ears. These symptoms usually indicate a middle ear infection (**otitis media**).

The doctor will need an **otoscope** to examine the ear. An otoscope allows the physician to shine a beam of light into the ear so that he or she can see inside the ear canal. Before it is inserted in the patient's ear, place a disposable ear **speculum** (cover) on the tip of the instrument. Since children must hold still for an ear examination, the doctor will need assistance for this procedure.

Swimmer's ear is a **bacterial** or **fungal** infection of the outer ear and the **ear canal**. It is most common during the swimming season and in patients with a history of frequent exposure to water in the ear. Ear infections are treated with medications. If the nurse places ear drops in the patient's ears, a small cotton ball usually is left in the external ear to keep the medication inside the ear.

Untreated ear infections can cause pressure to build up within the ear drum, or **tympanic membrane**. As the pressure increases, the ear drum may **rupture**. The patient will complain of pain and pressure in the ear, a recent upper respiratory infection, and bloody drainage from the ear. These patients must be seen by a specialist, or otolaryngologist, and may need ear surgery.

Hearing loss can result from a foreign object in the ear or the accumulation of **cerumen** in the ear. When an ear becomes clogged by an excessive buildup of cerumen, the ear must be irrigated by the physician or nurse to remove the wax. The doctor may administer a softening solution before cleaning the ear. To assist with this procedure, gather the following equipment:

cerumen: ear wax

- ✓ a bulb syringe or ear syringe
- ✓ irrigating solution
- ✓ a basin
- ✓ gauze squares
- ✓ an otoscope
- ✓ a towel
- ✓ gloves

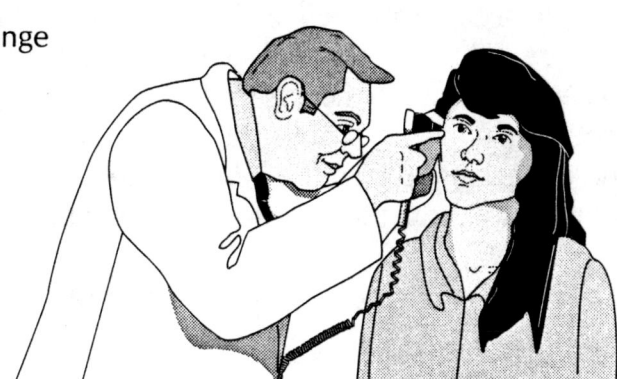

Injuries to the ears can include **lacerations** (cuts), **contusions** (bruises), or burns. These injuries are treated as soft tissue injuries and may require **sutures**, medication, and a dressing. Any head trauma that results in bleeding from the ear must be evaluated immediately using sterile technique. The best way to apply an ear dressing is to secure gauze fluffs over the wound with a bandage and tape. In doing so, avoid applying pressure on the neck or throat and taping the hair. Sometimes a little creativity is required in applying dressings to ensure that the dressing covers the wound securely and is tolerable to the patient.

Some patients may complain of **vertigo**. **Equilibrium** is maintained by the inner ear, but dizziness is not always related to ear disease. Heart disease, diabetes, high blood pressure, and other conditions also are associated with dizziness; therefore the doctor will examine the patient to determine the cause of the symptom. If a patient has an inner ear disease, he or she also may complain of **tinnitus** (ringing), hearing loss, nausea, and vomiting. These symptoms can be disabling and often are intensified by loud noise and bright lights. Keep the patient quiet and dim the lights to reduce some of these symptoms. Always assist these patients with walking to prevent them from falling.

vertigo: dizziness

Nasal Emergencies

The most common EENT problem seen in the emergency room is **epistaxis** (a nosebleed). There are numerous causes of nosebleeds, including dry weather, temperature changes, trauma, and high blood pressure. Bleeding can be controlled by pinching the nostrils. If possible, the patient should sit up. If not, try to keep the patient's head elevated to help stop the bleeding. Make sure you check the patient's blood pressure too. This should be done on all ER patients, but is especially important for patients with nosebleeds since high blood pressure may be the cause of the epistaxis. You also should provide a basin for the patient if there is any blood to be removed from the mouth. Since some people become alarmed by the sight of blood, attempts to reassure the patient will be helpful. Some patients may require **sedation** if other methods of bleeding control are necessary. If the nosebleed is from the back of the nose the doctor may need to **cauterize**, or burn, the area of excessive bleeding or use nasal packing to stop the **hemorrhage**. Remember to protect yourself from potentially contaminated blood by wearing gloves.

To assist with the examination of the nose gather the following equipment:

- ✓ gloves
- ✓ a **nasal speculum**
- ✓ suction equipment
- ✓ an electric headlight
- ✓ large cotton balls
- ✓ a **tongue blade**
- ✓ **electrocautery** equipment
- ✓ silver nitrate or chromic acid sticks
- ✓ a nasal balloon
- ✓ nasal packing

nasal speculum: a device used to spread the nostrils and look into them

electrocautery: a device used to burn or destroy tissue and which causes the blood to clot

The doctor will suction the nose for blood clots and apply a local anesthetic, then view the area of bleeding with the nasal speculum. He or she also may use the electrocautery to control the bleeding. Be sure you are familiar with this equipment, and follow the safety rule: THE **GROUNDING PAD** MUST BE APPLIED TO THE PATIENT BEFORE USE! There are many different types of grounding pads, so make sure you have been properly trained in their use before applying them to a patient.

grounding pad: a safety device used with an electrocautery to prevent electrical shock

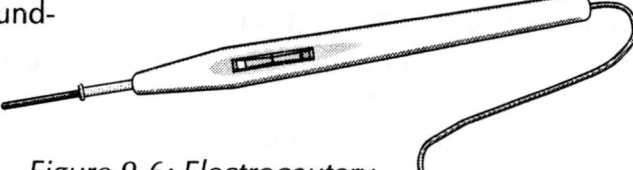

Figure 9-6: Electrocautery

The doctor may wish to pack the nasal cavity with gauze, or insert a nasal balloon or epistaxis tampon. Assemble the equipment requested by the physician and assist with suctioning the patient during the procedure. Observe the patient's breathing and monitor the blood pressure, pulse, and respirations throughout the procedure.

Nosebleeds can result from trauma to the face. If the trauma is severe enough, the nose may be broken. This would require surgery. Bleeding must be controlled, and an ice bag placed on the nose to reduce swelling. Patients with nasal problems may have trouble breathing, so it is very important to watch the breathing pattern and alert the nurse if breathing becomes labored.

Another common emergency involves a foreign object that has become lodged in the nose. Children sometimes place beans or other items in the nose, and then are unable to remove them. If a foreign body is involved in the injury to the nose, the doctor will use the nasal speculum and **forceps** and suction to remove it.

Dental Emergencies

Some patients come to the emergency room with pain or trauma to the teeth. The most common cause of dental pain is a cavity or an infection; but don't forget that patients having a heart attack can have **referred pain** to the jaw instead of the usual chest pain. Patients with dental pain are seen by the emergency room physician and referred to a dentist. On weekends and during the night when the dentist is unavailable, the emergency room physician may write a prescription for medication to be taken until the patient can be seen by a dentist. If the teeth have been avulsed (knocked out of the mouth), control the bleeding by placing a sterile 2" x 2" gauze pad over the socket and holding it in place with a gloved finger, or having the patient bite down to induce pressure. The tooth can be reimplanted, so place it in a saline solution until the oral surgeon arrives.

Throat Emergencies

A sore throat is another emergency that can force a patient to seek treatment in the local ER. Sore throats are caused by an infection, so the doctor must examine the throat. He or she may request a dental mirror and a tongue blade, or may require additional light to see the back of the throat or **nasopharynx**. Hold the mirror over a heated light bulb for a few seconds before giving it to the doctor to prevent fogging of the mirror when it is inserted in the patient's mouth. The doctor will check the tonsils, **larynx**, **pharynx**, and **glottis** for redness, drainage, and swelling. It is important to obtain an accurate temperature on patients with a suspected infection. If the doctor wants to obtain a throat culture, a sterile cotton tip applicator and culture tube or a **Culturette** will be needed.

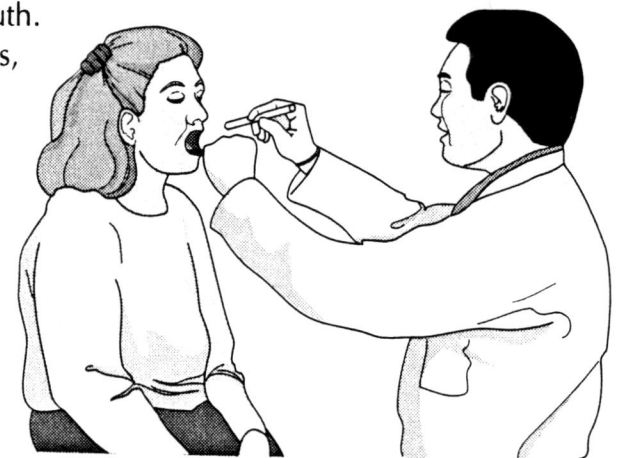

As an emergency department technician, you can take the culture once you have been properly instructed in the procedure. When a culture is taken, a swab of the infected area is taken, and the cotton-tip applicator is inserted into the test tube. If a culturette is used, squeeze the plastic tip end to moisten the culture after it has been obtained. Label the specimen and take it, with the laboratory slip, to the Bacteriology Department of the facility's laboratory.

People having allergic reactions may experience **edema** (swelling) of the larynx. This swelling makes breathing and swallowing difficult, and the patient may complain that his throat is closing off. Allergic reactions are serious emergencies. Immediate attention is required to prevent the airway from closing completely.

Sudden breathing problems can occur if something gets caught in the air passage and obstructs the airway. If a person has a foreign body in the trachea and cannot cough, speak, or breathe, the lifesaving measures are performed. If these procedures are not successful, the patient may arrive in the emergency room with attempts still being made to relieve the obstruction. The physician will attempt to remove the obstruction using suction and curved forceps. If it cannot be removed, the doctor will need to perform a **tracheostomy**. The tracheostomy tray is located in the major trauma room. You will need to open it and set it up immediately.

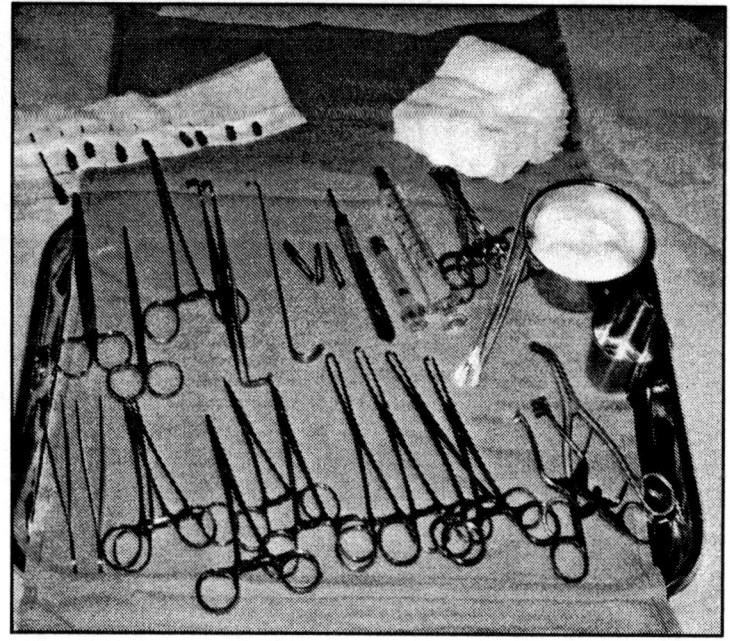

Figure 9-8: Tracheostomy Tray

Auto accidents and sports-related injuries are the causes of most neck injuries. Neck injuries present the potential for very serious airway problems due to swelling, as well as serious nerve damage to the spinal cord that can result in **paralysis** of the muscles used for breathing. Patients with suspected neck injuries arrive with the head immobilized and a rigid neck collar and backboard in place. Portable x-rays of the **cervical spine** are taken immediately, and efforts are made to stabilize the neck and spine. The patient's breathing pattern is monitored continually.

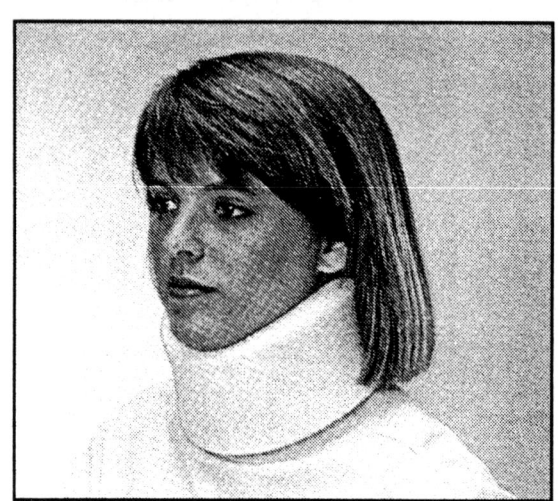

Stab wounds to the neck can result in serious blood loss and the patient may require immediate surgery. Lifesaving measures are begun as the operating room or trauma team is preparing the patient for surgery.

Figure 9-6: Neck Collar

Chapter Summary

All emergencies to the eyes, ears, nose, and throat require you, the emergency department technician to watch the patient carefully. Any changes in airway status must be reported immediately as these can be life-threatening situations. Since no two patients are alike, and no two physicians are the same either, you must remain flexible to be a valuable assistant during emergency procedures. Make sure you know where all equipment and supplies are located. This will enable you to set up for these examinations in a timely manner.

Chapter Nine • Emergencies of the Eye, Ear, Nose, and Throat 9-19

Name _____

Date _____

Student Enrichment Activities

Fill in the blanks to complete the following exercises.

1. The eye chart used to check visual acuity is called the _____.

2. Define the following:
   OD:_____   OS: _____
   OU:_____

3. Explain 20/20 vision.
   _____
   _____
   _____
   _____

4. Perform the Snellen eye chart test on five students in your class and record the results below.

	Student initials	Visual Acuity		
		OD	OS	OU
A.				
B.				
C.				
D.				
E.				

5. Describe how you would apply a dressing to the eye.

   _____
   _____
   _____
   _____
   _____
   _____
   _____
   _____
   _____

6. Explain how you would apply a dressing to the ear.

   _____
   _____
   _____
   _____
   _____
   _____
   _____
   _____
   _____

7. Explain how to obtain a throat culture.

   _____
   _____
   _____
   _____
   _____
   _____
   _____
   _____
   _____

Chapter Nine • Emergencies of the Eye, Ear, Nose, and Throat 9-21

Name _____

Date _____

8. Steven Jamison, a 19-year-old college student, is admitted with a sore throat, and general muscle aches. His temperature is 103° F. Complete the following bacteriology form by checking the appropriate boxes. The doctor has ordered a routine throat culture for strep screen, routine culture, and sensitivity. Add the patient's name, the time the specimen was obtained, the source of the culture, and the type of test to be done.

BACTERIOLOGY

☐ STAT ☐ ROUTINE ☐ AS SOON AS POSSIBLE	TIME TO BE DRAWN	☐ AM ☐ PM	
TIME SPECIMEN COLLECTED	TIME TEST COMPLETED	ACCESS#	
DATE	R.N.	TECHNOLOGIST	DATE/TIME

ADDRESSOGRAPH

If Urine	☐ Cath ☐ Clean Catch	SOURCE OF CULTURE:	DIAGNOSIS: ANTIBIOTIC THERAPY:

X	TEST	CULTURE REPORT	GRAM STAIN	RARE	FEW	MOD	MANY
	Routine culture	Culture: _____	WBC's				
	Anaerobic culture		Epith. cells				
	Strept. screen	☐ No growth in _____ hours	Gram neg. bacilli				
	Fungus culture	☐ No growth in _____ days/weeks	Gram pos. bacilli				
	AFB culture	☐ Normal flora: light mod. heavy	Gram neg. cocci				
	AFB conc. stain	☐ Colony count 1 _____ col/ml	Gram pos. cocci				
	AFB unconc. stain	2 _____ col/ml	RBC's				
	Gram stain	☐ Less than 10,000 col/ml (insignificant)	No org. seen				
	Wet mount	☐ I.D. + sensitivity to follow	Other:				
	Blood culture	☐ Other: _____					
	Blood Culture Anaerobic						

ORGANISMS — Light/Mod/Heavy — SENSITIVITY REPORT — Amikacin, Ampicillin, Carbenicillin, Cefamandole, Cefotaxime, Cefoxitin, Cephalothin, Chloramp, Clindamycin, Erythromycin, Gentamicin, Methicillin, Naladixic Acid, Nitrofurantoin, Penicillin, Pipercillin, Sulfisoxazole, Tetracycline, Tobramycin, Trimethoprim, Vancomycin — ANTIBIOTIC SENSITIVITIES

1.
2.
3.
4.

☐ Sensitivity   S = sensitive R = resistant I = intermediate   REMARKS:

9. 18-year-old George Watson is in the ER with an infection. Several tests are to be done to determine the source of the infection. Complete the laboratory requisition on the next page. The doctor orders: *Sputum — C & S*   *Urinalysis — midstream*
Sputum — acid fast culture   *Cerebral Spinal Fluid — cell count, glucose, & protein*
Beta Strep — screen

GENERAL HOSPITAL LABORATORY 2

STAT ☐ PRE OP ☐ ISOLATION	DATE	ISSUED BY	
	DATE/TIME OF COLLECTION		PATIENT STAMP

24 HR. SPECIMEN
COLLECTED FROM: _____ TO: _____

PATIENT LOCATION AT COLLECTION: ORDERING PHYSICIAN:

DIAGNOSIS: ANTIBIOTICS IN USE:

CLOCK IN SPECIMENS HERE

SOURCE OF SPECIMEN

☐ CSF	**CSF**	☐ BODY FLUIDS	**BODYFL**	☐ URINE	**URINE**
☐ GENITAL	**GENITL**	☐ ABDOMINAL	**ABDFLD**	☐ MIDSTREAM	**URINMS**
☐ URETHRAL		☐ ASCITES	**ASCFLD**	☐ CLEAN CATCH	**URINCC**
☐ VAGINAL		☐ CYST	**CYSTFL**	☐ CATHETERIZED	**URINCA**
☐ OTHER: _____		☐ DRAINAGE	**DRNAGE**	☐ FOLEY	**URINFO**
		☐ KNEE FLUID	**KNEEFL**	☐ OTHER: _____	
☐ NOSE	**NOSE**	☐ PARACENTESIS	**PARCNT**		
☐ THROAT	**THROAT**	☐ PERICARDIAL	**PERICA**	☐ STOOL	**STOOL**
☐ RESP		☐ PLEURAL	**PLEU**	☐ COLONOSCOPY	**COLO**
☐ BRONCH	**BRONCH**	☐ SUBDURAL	**SUBDFL**	☐ RANDOM SPECIMEN	**RANDOM**
☐ BRONCH BRUSHING	**BRNCBS**	☐ SYNOVIAL	**SYN**	☐ RECTAL SWAB	**RECTAL**
☐ BRONCH WASHING	**BRNCWS**	☐ THORACENTESIS	**THOR**	☐ SIGMOIDOSCOPY	**SIGM**
☐ SPUTUM	**SPUTUM**	☐ OTHER: _____		☐ WOUND (SPECIFY BELOW)	**WOUND**
☐ SPUTUM EXPECTORATED	**SPUTEX**			☐ TISSUE (SPECIFY BELOW)	**TISSUE**
☐ SPUTUM INDUCED	**SPUTIN**			☐ MISC. (SPECIFY BELOW)	**MISC**
☐ TRACH	**TRACH**				

REQUISITION

CEREBRAL SPINAL FLUID

☐ CELL COUNT TUBE: _____	**CSFH**
☐ GLUCOSE & PROTEIN TUBE: _____	**CSFCH**
☐ MULTIPLE SCLEROSIS PANEL	**MSP**
☐ OTHER: _____	

BODY FLUIDS (Remember to specify type of fluid in SOURCE OF SPECIMEN area)

☐ CELL COUNT	**FLCT**
☐ AMYLASE	**FLAMY**
☐ GLUCOSE	**FLGL**
☐ LDH	**FLLDH**
☐ PROTEIN	**FLTP**
☐ OTHER: _____	

URINE

☐ ROUTINE ANALYSIS	**UA**
☐ PREGNANCY TEST	**UPREG**
☐ OSMOLALITY	**UOSM**
☐ DIASTASE (2 hr specimen)	**DIAS**
☐ CREATININE CLEARANCE (24 hr)	**CRECLR**
☐ PROTEIN (24 hr)	**UPROT**
K ☐ 24 hr **UK** ☐ Random **KU**	
NA ☐ 24 hr **UNA** ☐ Random **NAU**	
CREATININE ☐ 24 hr **UCRET** ☐ Random **CRETU**	
☐ OTHER: _____	

☐ ROUTINE CULTURE (Includes Gram Stain & Sensitivity, if positive)	
☐ ANAEROBIC CULTURE	**ANAC**
☐ ACID FAST CULTURE (Includes Acid Fast Smear/Stain)	**AFC**
☐ ACID FAST SMEAR/STAIN ONLY	**AFS**
☐ BETA STREP SCREEN	**BETASS**
☐ CHLAMYDIA DFA	**CHL**
☐ CLOSTRIDIUM DIFFICILE TOXIN	**CLOTOX**
☐ CRYPTOCOCCUS ANTIGEN	**CAL**
☐ FUNGUS CULTURE	**FCUL**
☐ GRAM STAIN ONLY	**GMST**
☐ OCCULT BLOOD	**OB**
☐ OVA & PARASITES	**OP**
☐ PINWORM PREP	**PIN**
☐ SKIN SCREEN (DECUBITUS)	**SKINSC**
☐ WET MOUNT	**WET**
☐ OTHER: _____	

Chapter Nine • Emergencies of the Eye, Ear, Nose, and Throat 9-23

Name _____

Date _____

10. Aurelita Muldanado a 56-year-old female is being seen in the ER for abdominal pain. There is a possibility she will go to surgery and the doctor has ordered the following:

- Serum Analase
- Bilirubin
- T & C 4 units (type & cross match)
- Serum glucose
- Creatinine
- CBC
- BUN
- electrolytes

Please fill out the laboratory requisition on the following page.

GENERAL HOSPITAL

LABORATORY 1

REQUISITIONS

	STAT		PRE OP
	TIMED		ISOLATION
DATE		ISSUED BY	
	TODAY		FUTURE DATE
TIME TO BE DRAWN: _____			
ORDERING PHYSICIAN			

PATIENT STAMP

CLOCK IN SPECIMENS HERE

☐ ALCOHOL	ALC	
☐ ALKALINE PHOSPHATASE	ALK	
☐ AMYLASE	AMY	
☐ ANTI-NUCLEAR ANTIBODY	ANA	
☐ ANTIBODY SCREEN	ABS	
☐ BILIRUBIN	BILI	
☐ BLEEDING TIME	BT	
☐ BLOOD CULTURE	BLDC	
Diagnosis _____		
Antibiotic in use _____		
☐ BLOOD TYPE (includes ABO, RH)	TYP	
☐ BUN	BUN	
☐ CALCIUM	CA	
☐ CARBAMAZEPINE/TEGRETOL	CRBAM	
☐ CARDIAC ENZYME PANEL	CARD	
(includes LDH, CPK, & CPK isoenzymes, if indicated)		
☐ CBC (includes Hemogram, Diff and Platelet Count)	CBC	
☐ CEA	CEA	
☐ CHOLESTEROL (Fasting)	CHOL	
☐ COCCI COMP FIX	COCF	
☐ CPK	CPK	
☐ CPK ISOENZYMES	CPMB	
☐ CREATININE	CRET	
☐ DIC PANEL (includes PTT, PT, fibrinogen, D-Dimer, fibrin monomer, platelet, count)	DIC	
☐ DIGOXIN/LANOXIN	DIG	
Time of last dose: _____		
☐ DILANTIN/PHENYTOIN	PTN	
☐ DIRECT COOMBS	DC	
☐ DRUG ANALYSIS	YCOM	
(comprehensive, blood & urine)		
☐ ELECTROLYTES (includes NA, K, Chloride & CO_2)	LYTE	
☐ FERRITIN	FERR	
☐ FIBRINOGEN	FIBR	
☐ FOLATE	FOL	
GENTAMYCIN		
☐ TROUGH and PEAK	GENT/GENP	
Time of dose: _____		
☐ TIMED	GENR	
☐ GGTP	GGTP	
☐ GLUCOSE Fasting? _____	GLUC	
☐ GLUCOSE 2HR PP	TGLU	
☐ GLYCOHEMOGLOBIN	GHGB	

☐ HAPTOGLOBIN	HAP	
☐ HCG	HCG	
☐ HDL (Fasting)	HDL	
☐ HEMOGRAM (H & H)	HGRM	
☐ HEPATITIS B SURFACE ANATOMY	HAB	
☐ HIV SCREEN	HIV	
☐ IRON (includes iron & TIBC)	FEB	
☐ LDH	LDH	
☐ LEGIONNAIRES SCREEN	LEGSCR	
☐ LIPASE	LIPS	
☐ LIPID SCREEN (Fasting)	LIPW	
(includes CHOL, TRIG, HDL, LDL, VLDL, and risk factor)		
☐ LIVER FUNCTION STUDIES	LIVP	
(includes SGOT, SGPT, bilirubin, alk phos, GGTP, protime)		
☐ LUPUS PANEL	LUPUS	
☐ MAGNESIUM	MG	
☐ MEASLES (RUBEOLA)	MEAS	
☐ MYCOPLASMA COMP FIX	MTCF	
☐ MONOSPOT	MONOSP	
☐ OSMOLALITY, SERUM	SOSM	
☐ PANEL 7 (includes Glucose, BUN, Creatinine and Electrolytes)	P7	
☐ PANEL 20 (includes Panel 7 plus SGOT, LDH, SGPT, Alk Phos, Calcium, Magnesium, Phosphorus, Total Bili, Uric Acid, TP, Albumin, Cholesterol, Triglycerides)	P20	
☐ PHENOBARBITAL	PHNO	
☐ PHOSPHORUS	PHOS	
☐ PLATELET COUNT ONLY	PLTC	
☐ POTASSIUM	K	
☐ PREGNANCY TEST, SERUM	SPREG	
☐ PROTEIN, TOTAL	TP	
☐ PROTHROMBIN TIME	PT	
Coumadin? ☐ Yes ☐ No		
☐ PSA	PSAAM	
☐ PTT Heparin? ☐ Yes ☐ No	PTT	
☐ RA LATEX	RA	
☐ RETICULOCYTE COUNT	RETI	
☐ RUBELLA	RUBS	
☐ SED RATE	ESR	
☐ SGOT/AST	SGOT	
☐ SGPT/ALT	SGPT	
☐ SODIUM	NA	

☐ T3 UPTAKE	T3U	
☐ T4	T4	
☐ THEOPHYLLINE/AMINOPHYLLINE	THE	
☐ THYROID PANEL	THY	
(includes T3 uptake, T4 and FTI)		
TOBRAMYCIN		
☐ TROUGH and PEAK	TOBT/TOBP	
Time of dose: _____		
☐ TIMED	TOBR	

TRANSFUSION SERVICE:

☐ TYPE AND SCREEN	TS	
☐ TYPE AND CROSSMATCH	TXM	
(Check one of the above only)		

Packed Red Cells: _____ (qty)
Autologous Units: _____ (qty)
Directed Donor Units: _____ (qty)

Date needed: _____
☐ Surgery ☐ To be given
   (Do not select with T & S)

☐ Other (specify): _____
Special Instructions: _____

☐ SINGLE DONOR PLATELETS _____ (qty)	TPLT	
☐ FRESH FROZEN PLASMA _____ (qty)	TFFP	
☐ CRYOPRECIPITATE _____ (qty)	TCRYO	

☐ TRIGLYCERIDES (Fasting)	TRGL	
☐ TSH	TSH	
☐ URIC ACID	URIC	
VANCOMYCIN		
☐ TROUGH and PEAK	VANT/VANP	
Time of dose: _____		
☐ TIMED	VANR	
☐ VIRAL HEPATITIS PANEL	VHP	
(includes, HAA, ANtibody to Hepatitis B Core, Hepatitis A Total and IGM, if indicated, and Hepatitis C)		
☐ VIRAL RESPIRATORY PANEL	VIR	
(includes Adenovirus, Flu A, Flu B, Mycoplasma)		
☐ VITAMIN B12	B12	

ADDITIONAL TESTS
_____
_____
_____
_____
_____

Chapter Nine • Emergencies of the Eye, Ear, Nose, and Throat 9-25

Name _____
Date _____

Match the following numbers with the letter of the correct definition.

11. _____ cerumen   **a.** sac around eye

12. _____ conjunctiva   **b.** otoscope

13. _____ equilibrium   **c.** ophthalmoscope

14. _____ irrigate   **d.** vertigo

15. _____ dizzy   **f.** lavage

16. _____ instrument to look into ear   **g.** balance

                                          h. ear wax

17. List the equipment needed to assist the physician with a nasal packing.
    A. _____
    B. _____
    C. _____
    D. _____
    E. _____
    F. _____
    G. _____
    H. _____
    I. _____
    J. _____

9-26

Chapter Ten
Medical Emergencies

Objectives

After completing this chapter you should be able to do the following:

1. Define and correctly spell all key terms.
2. Assist with lead placement and monitoring of a cardiac patient.
3. Position an unconscious patient on the gurney.
4. List five signs or symptoms of hypoglycemia.
5. Obtain a sputum specimen.
6. Identify three safety measures for a victim having a seizure.

Key Terms

- aspirate
- aura
- blood sugar
- chronic obstructive pulmonary disease (COPD)
- cannula
- cerebrovascular accident (CVA)
- coma
- electrocardiogram (ECG)
- electrode
- heart block
- hyperglycemia
- hypertension
- hypoglycemia
- hypotension
- insulin
- palpitation
- premature ventricular contraction (PVC)
- seizure

Emergency Medical Situations

There are many kinds of medical emergencies. Emergency departments often are filled with people who are suffering from potentially life-threatening medical problems such as seizures, respiratory or cardiac problems, sudden illnesses, etc. Caring for someone with a medical emergency requires skillful evaluation. Knowing the signs and symptoms of serious medical problems can alert the emergency team to take the necessary action to prevent serious complications. Medical emergencies can affect all body systems, but be especially alert to the following symptoms:

- breathing problems
- irregular or noisy breathing
- chest pain
- irregular pulse
- abnormally low or high blood pressure
- any changes in the level of consciousness
- personality changes or confusion
- severe vomiting or diarrhea
- bleeding

Seizures

Seizures can be caused by a number of medical or neurological problems. Although the cause of a seizure cannot always be determined, the following are some known causes of seizures.

- drugs/alcohol
- **trauma**
- **cerebrovascular accident (CVA)**
- tumor
- infection
- **diabetes**
- **epilepsy**
- poison

seizure: a neurological dysfunction characterized by loss of consciousness and involuntary, spasmodic muscle twitching; a sudden attack of pain or symptoms

cerebrovascular accident (CVA): a stroke; a blockage, hemorrhage, or compression of a blood vessel in the brain

A seizure can be a frightening thing to witness. Symptoms can range from a tingling or twitching of a small area of the body to hallucinations, intense fear, violent muscular contractions, and loss of consciousness. Some patients with known seizure disorders can tell when a seizure is going to start, but often seizures occur without warning. Patients who receive a warning that a seizure is about to begin may have an **aura,** hear a loud noise, see a bright light, or scream prior to the seizure. These patients have time to seek a safe location before experiencing the seizure activity.

aura: a subjective sensation of warmth or light that may precede a seizure or a migraine

Case Study

A 58-year-old unconscious female arrives in the Emergency Care Unit. She is brought in by ambulance after being found sitting in her car in the parking lot of the local shopping mall. She does not respond to either verbal or painful stimuli. There is no available medical history. Her breathing is rapid and she is hot to the touch. The ambulance personnel, nurse, and emergency department technician prepare to transfer her to the ER gurney, and she begins to have a seizure. Her arms and legs become rigid and are moving violently, her jaw becomes tight and she bites down, there is an increase in saliva production, and her eyes are closed. The seizure activity lasts for 30 seconds.

What are your responsibilities when a patient is having a seizure? Care of the seizure victim requires that you provide a safe environment. DO NOT ATTEMPT TO RESTRAIN THE VICTIM! Follow these steps if you are caring for a patient who begins to have a seizure.

1. Call for help.

2. Remove harmful objects.

3. Place the patient in a safe location (i.e., on the floor or bed with the rails raised).

4. Protect the patient from injury (pad the side rails, prevent falls, and do not restrain him or her).

5. Observe the seizure (ie, note the time of **onset**, how long it lasted, the patient's behavior and response level).

6. Observe the parts of the body that are involved.

7. Do not place anything in the patient's mouth during the seizure.

8. MAKE SURE THE PATIENT IS BREATHING. (Check the ABCs.)

9. Suction the airway if necessary.

10. Provide oxygen for the patient.

11. Check the victim from head to toe for additional injuries. (See secondary survey in Chapter Six.)

12. Check the patient's vital signs and monitor breathing.

13. Check the patient's pupils and level of consciousness.

14. When the seizure has ended, position victim's head so the airway is open.

15. Note what the person was doing before the seizure.

Many tests and x-ray procedures will be ordered for the patient after a seizure. You may need to accompany this patient during these procedures. This is because patients who have just had a seizure usually are very sleepy and may have difficulty breathing or experience another seizure. If you go with this patient to a different department for tests, take his or her vital signs at least every ten minutes, and be in close attendance should the patient have any difficulty. Never leave a patient who has recently had a seizure alone or in a place where he or she cannot be observed constantly.

Providing Care to an Unconscious Patient

A patient who is unconscious must be continually observed. Maintaining an adequate airway is especially important. The patient should be positioned so that the airway is open and clear. If the victim was involved in an accident, a rigid collar will be in place and the patient will be on a backboard. A portable x-ray will be taken to check for spinal injuries. Position the patient on his or her side if the victim does not have a traumatic injury. This will allow any drainage from the mouth to flow out the side of the mouth, and will prevent any vomit from being **aspirated**. (Figure 10-1)

aspirate: to take foreign material or vomit into the lungs

Take frequent vital signs on an unconscious patient. The blood pressure, pulse, respirations, pupils, and level of consciousness should be checked at least every fifteen minutes, and sometimes every five minutes. Be sure to use side rails at all times and use safety straps on the gurney. Never leave an unconscious patient unattended.

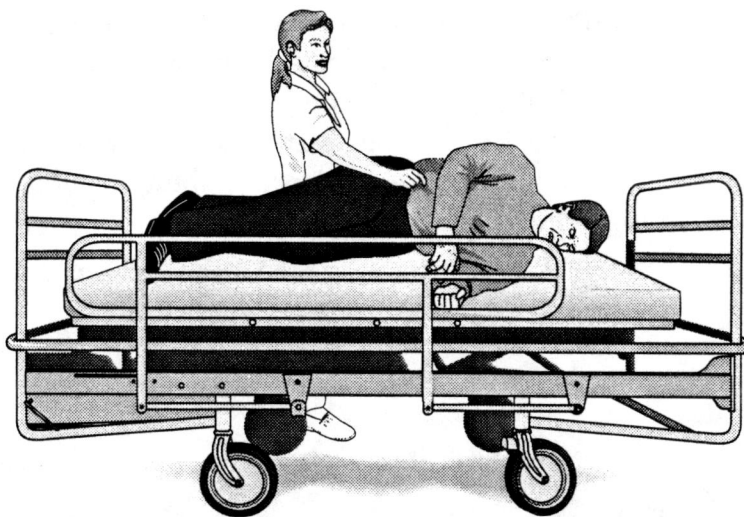

Figure 10-1: Position an unconscious patient on his side if he does not have a traumatic injury.

Diabetic Emergencies

Diabetes is a chronic (long term) disease caused by the body's inability to produce or use **insulin**. Insulin is a **hormone** that is manufactured in the body's pancreas. Insulin is needed by the body to break down food into sugar (**glucose**) and use it for energy or store it for later use. Carbohydrates, fats, and proteins all break down into glucose.

insulin: a hormone secreted by the pancreas that causes glucose, or sugar, to leave the bloodstream and enter the cell

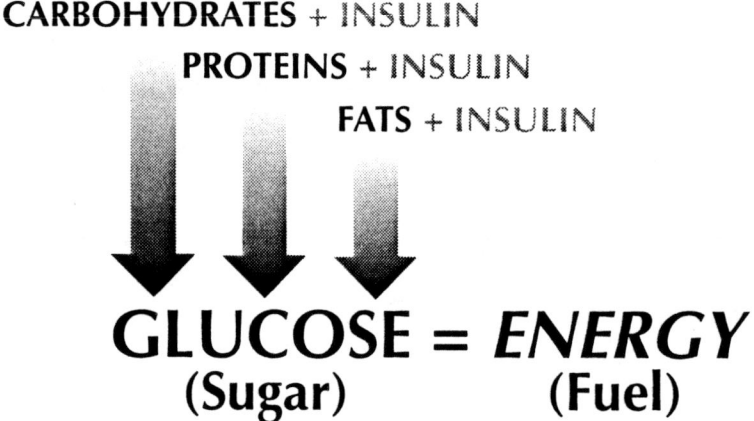

Cells need glucose to function properly. All the food we eat is eventually broken down into glucose or sugar. Without sugar, the cells will not work. If the brain and other organs do not have an adequate supply of glucose, the cells begin to die. According to the Diabetes Association, diabetes is the third leading cause of death in the United States, and currently affects eleven million Americans. Diabetic patients who are admitted to the emergency room may already know they have diabetes or, they may be admitted with several symptoms and be unaware that diabetes is the cause. If the level of sugar in the bloodstream becomes too high or too low, serious symptoms will develop. As an ER technician, it is important for you to understand the signs and symptoms of abnormal **blood sugar** levels.

blood sugar: sugar, in the form of glucose, that exists in the blood, and which is necessary to process food

Chapter Ten • Medical Emergencies

Too little sugar in the blood (**hypoglycemia**) is caused by taking too much insulin, not eating, or excessive physical exercise. It is diagnosed by drawing a specimen of blood for a blood sugar level test, and treated by administering sugar. If the patient is conscious and can swallow, a glass of orange juice with two teaspoons of sugar is given. If the patient is drowsy or unconscious, an IV is started and glucose is given directly into the vein by the registered nurse or doctor. Characteristic symptoms of hypoglycemia include:

hypoglycemia: a low blood sugar level

- mental confusion
- slurred speech
- double vision
- staggering
- sweating
- a fast pulse
- nervousness
- drowsiness
- **coma**

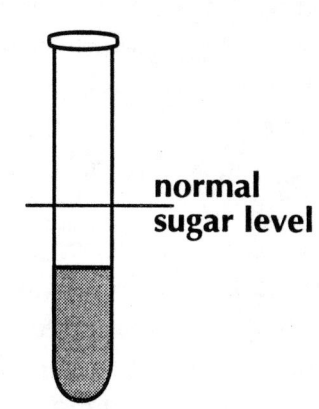

coma: a state of unconsciousness or deep stupor

Too much sugar in the blood, or **hyperglycemia**, is caused by not taking insulin, not taking enough insulin, or not producing enough insulin in the body. Characteristic symptoms include:

hyperglycemia: an elevated blood sugar level

- excessive urination
- excessive thirst
- fatigue
- blurred vision
- muscle aches
- weight loss
- a bounding pulse
- labored breathing
- a fruity smell to the breath
- drowsiness
- coma

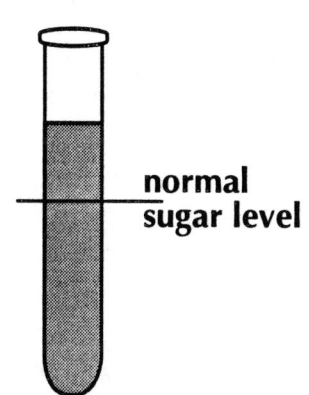

Hyperglycemia is diagnosed by drawing a specimen of blood for a blood sugar level test. Once it is diagnosed, the registered nurse will start an IV and monitor the patient's breathing. Appropriate medications, like insulin, will be given and the patient will be admitted to the hospital.

A diabetic patient can be put in a crisis by ingesting either too much or too little sugar. The symptoms are confusing; the patient may appear **intoxicated** or under the influence of a substance, like drugs or alcohol. Because the symptoms are so vague, evaluating these patients can be difficult. Diabetics must be seen by a physician and are a top priority for care. If the patient is confused, drowsy, or comatose, it is vital that the doctor see him or her immediately. Patients who know they are diabetic may be wearing a **Medic-Alert** tag for identification.

Diabetic patients who come to the emergency room for another problem must be given special consideration due to their medical history. If a person is taking medication for a medical condition or has a chronic illness, it can affect emergency treatment for other conditions. A diabetic patient who has been in an automobile accident, has been burned, has an infection, or is pregnant will need extra attention due to the fact that he or she is diabetic.

Respiratory Emergencies

Breath is essential to life. Breathing difficulties can be very frightening for the patient, family, and staff. Emergency measures for respiratory arrest and choking have already been discussed in Chapter Eight and should be reviewed at this time.

chronic obstructive pulmonary disease (COPD): an incurable condition in which the lungs' ability to provide ventilation is decreased over time

There are a number of **chronic obstructive pulmonary diseases (COPD)** that may require a visit to the emergency room. Asthma, chronic bronchitis, and emphysema are long-term diseases that affect the respiratory system. Asthma is a condition that affects the bronchial passages in the lungs. These passages become narrow and cause a wheezing sound with each breath. Emphysema damages the lungs so that they cannot function normally. Normal lungs allow the exchange of **oxygen** and **carbon dioxide** to take place at the cellular level.

A patient with emphysema is not able to make this exchange very well. Emphysema patients have very little energy, experience a loss of weight and appetite, and have difficulty breathing even at rest. Chronic bronchitis is characterized by a constant cough and numerous respiratory infections. These conditions can be made worse by stress, changes in climate, infections, air pollution, and smoke inhalation. Patients with these chronic conditions may be able to care for themselves at home with the aid of oxygen, breathing treatments, and medication, but a visit to the emergency room may be necessary if a crisis occurs and the patient can no longer get enough oxygen. In crisis, the patient will become anxious and short of breath, develop a rapid heart rate and a rapid respiratory rate. This patient will need to sit up to breathe, and may be **cyanotic** (have bluish skin from lack of oxygen). If immediate steps are not taken to improve the oxygen intake to the body, the patient will become unconscious and eventually will stop breathing entirely. The patient must be continually observed for acute respiratory failure.

Although bronchitis and asthma are listed as chronic diseases, it is possible to have acute asthma and acute bronchitis. A person can have a sudden attack of asthma from an allergic reaction, or a sudden bronchitis condition from a respiratory infection. Patients with acute problems will have no previous history of breathing difficulties, but will have signs and symptoms of acute respiratory failure.

Signs and symptoms of acute respiratory failure include the following:

- extreme shortness of breath
- **tachycardia**
- apprehension
- cyanosis
- labored breathing
- **orthopnea** (must sit up to breathe)
- confusion
- noisy breathing
- restlessness
- **coma**
- moist skin

Patients admitted to the ER with acute respiratory failure are seen immediately by the physician. The Respiratory Therapy Department is notified, and breathing treatments are started to open the air passages. Additional oxygen is given either by nasal **cannula** or by mask. (Figure 10-2) If breathing is severely difficult and blood tests indicate low oxygen levels, the physician may need to insert various airway devices and assist the patient's **ventilation** with a machine called a ventilator.

cannula: a tube that delivers oxygen through the nose

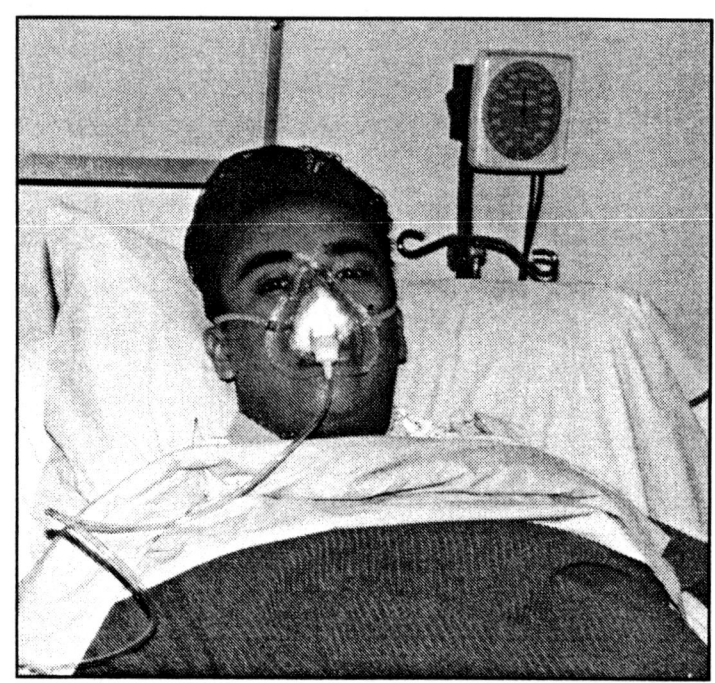

Figure 10-2: O₂ Mask

The following additional devices may be used to assist the patient's breathing.

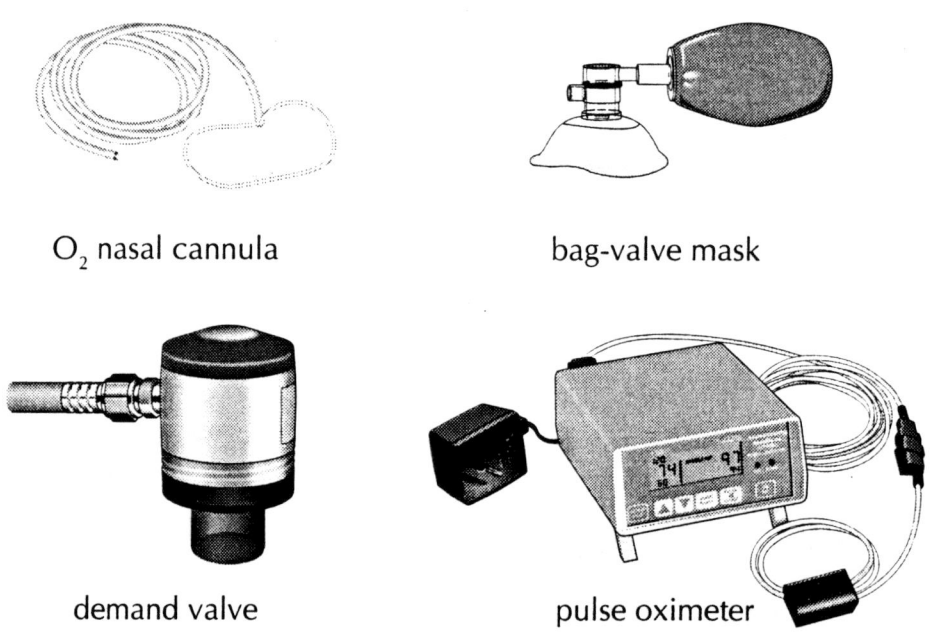

O₂ nasal cannula

bag-valve mask

demand valve

pulse oximeter

Chapter Ten • Medical Emergencies

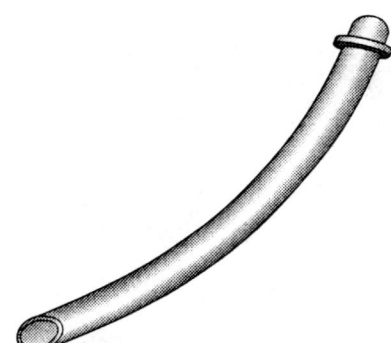
nasopharyngeal airway

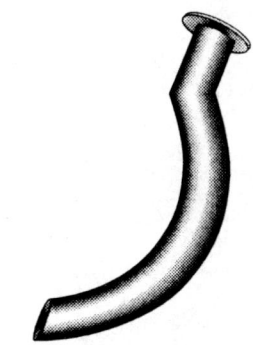
oropharyngeal airway

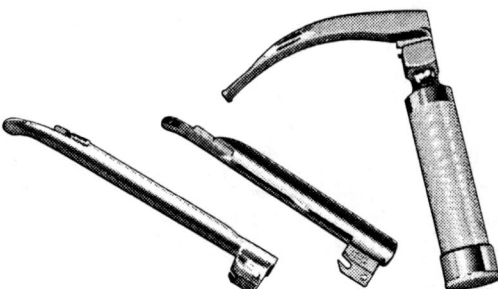
laryngoscope and blades

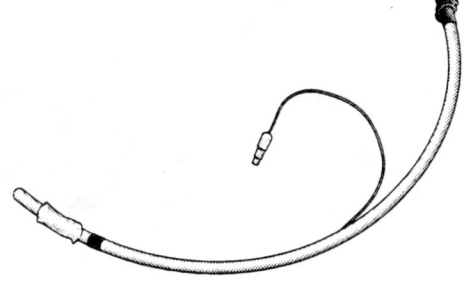
endotracheal tube

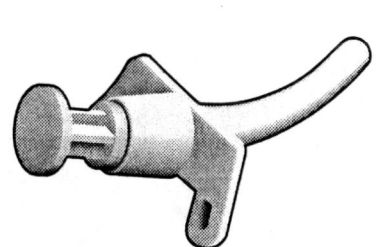
tracheostomy tube

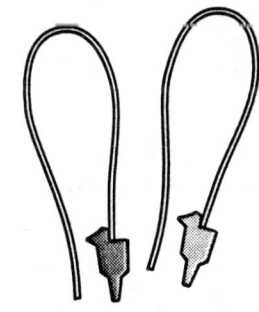
suction catheters

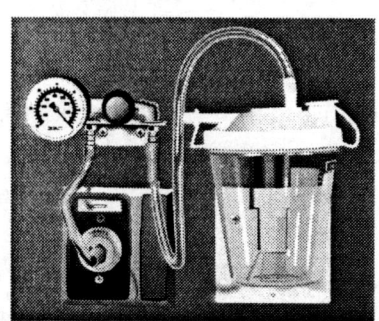
wall suction unit

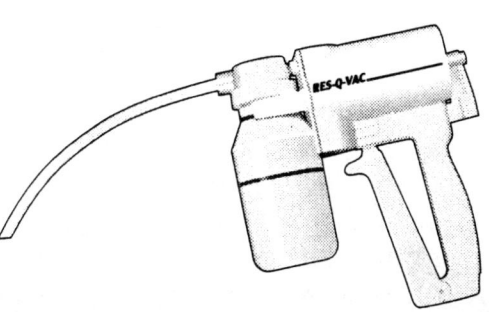
portable emergency suction unit

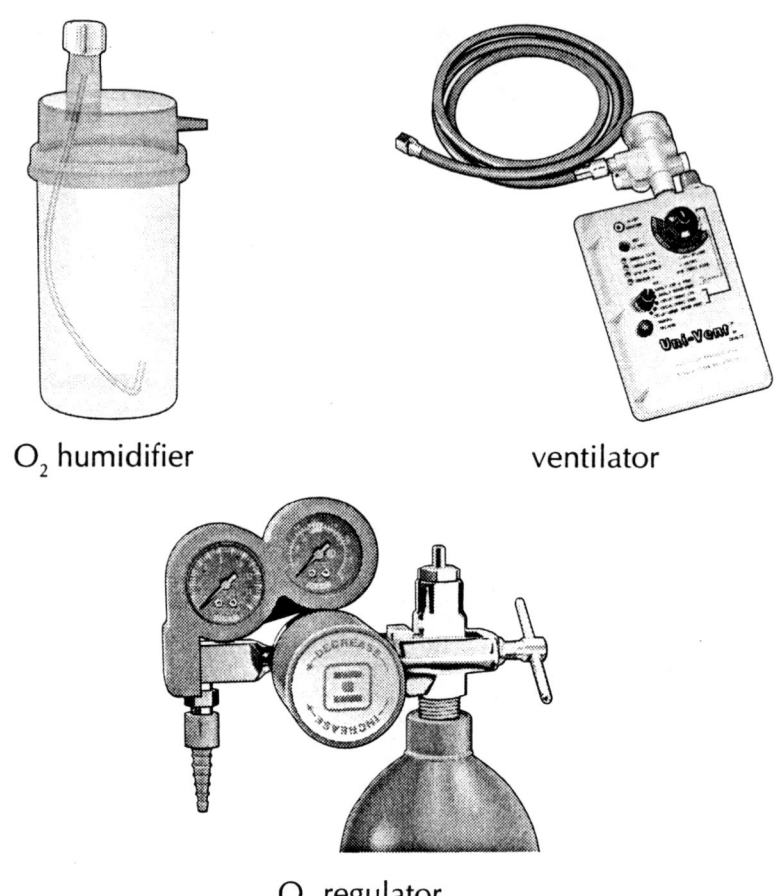

O_2 humidifier   ventilator

O_2 regulator

If the doctor orders a check of the **arterial blood gases**, a specimen of blood usually will be taken from the **radial artery**. Apply direct pressure with a gloved hand to this site for ten minutes following the blood withdrawal. Check the puncture site frequently to ensure that bleeding is controlled. The doctor also may order a chest x-ray to check for lung expansion. Help the x-ray technician position the film and patient for the best x-ray possible. Be sure to protect yourself by wearing a lead apron if you are present during the x-ray.

Breathing treatments, or inhalation of medication, may be ordered for the patient, and are given by the respiratory therapist. The therapist also may need help positioning the patient for the treatments. After a breathing treatment is given, the patient is encouraged to cough to clear the mucous and secretions that can block the air passages. Humidified breathing treatments can help loosen these secretions so the patient can cough. The doctor may want to obtain a sputum culture to determine the cause of infection after the treatment. To do this, use the following procedure.

Chapter Ten • Medical Emergencies

Obtaining a Sputum Specimen

Materials needed:
- ✓ gloves
- ✓ a culture cup

1. **Procedural Step:** Wash your hands.
   Reason: Universal precaution.
   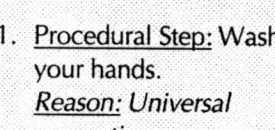

2. **Procedural Step:** Put on gloves.
   Reason: Universal precaution.

3. **Procedural Step:** Identify the patient.
   Reason: To ensure that you are dealing with the correct patient.

4. **Procedural Step:** Explain the procedure to the patient using terms he or she will understand.
   Reason: To provide the information necessary for the patient to give informed consent.

5. **Procedural Step:** Obtain a culture cup.
   Reason: The cup will hold the specimen.

6. **Procedural Step:** Open the cup carefully, and do not touch the outer rim or the inside of the container.
   Reason: To avoid contaminating the specimen.

7. **Procedural Step:** Instruct the patient to take a deep breath and cough into the cup.
   Reason: This will produce a sputum specimen.

8. **Procedural Step:** Replace the lid and label the container with the patient's name and room number.
   Reason: To avoid contaminating the specimen and to identify the source of the culture.

9. **Procedural Step:** Remove your gloves.
   Reason: The procedure is completed.
   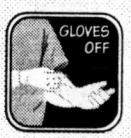

10. **Procedural Step:** Wash your hands.
    Reason: Universal precaution.

11. **Procedural Step:** Take the specimen and the completed laboratory slip to the bacteriology department.
    Reason: The specimen will be analyzed in the laboratory.

12. **Procedural Step:** Document the procedure as appropriate.
    Reason: To provide documentation.

If the patient is unconscious, a nurse can obtain a specimen through suction. If no specimen is needed, instruct the patient to breathe deeply and cough into a tissue and discard the tissue into the bedside trash bag.

Near-drowning victims may be brought to the emergency room in any condition. If the patient is awake, alert, and not in any respiratory distress, the physician will examine the patient, order x-rays, and may send the patient home with instructions to watch for certain symptoms. If the patient is having some respiratory problems, the doctor may want the patient admitted for observation. If the patient is in critical condition and has required **resuscitation**, the patient is treated as either a respiratory or **full arrest** (both cardiac and respiratory arrest). Procedures for assisting with a **code blue** were discussed in Chapter Eight.

Cardiac Emergencies

Cardiac (heart) emergencies compose a great percentage of the emergency 911 calls. Recognizing the early symptoms of heart disease can prevent serious complications later. A cardiac emergency is any condition that interferes with normal lung and heart function. The heart and lungs work interdependently; when one fails the other will be affected too. Patients with heart problems have difficulty breathing; patient's with respiratory problems will experience some heart problems. Patients who arrive in the ER with chest pain are top priority. If the patient arrives with paramedics, an IV will be in place, oxygen will be running, and the patient will be on a cardiac monitor. If the patient walks into the emergency room with any of the following complaints he or she must immediately be taken by wheelchair to the cardiac care room.

palpitation: fluttering, pounding, or racing of the heart

hypotension: an abnormally low blood pressure that impairs functioning

hypertension: high blood pressure that has been diagnosed on the basis of several random readings of 140/90 or higher; known as the silent killer

- chest pain
- arm pain
- jaw pain
- back pain
- indigestion
- shortness of breath
- **palpitations**
- anxiety
- perspiration
- **ashen** color
- **cyanosis**
- **hypotension**
- **hypertension**
- irregular pulse

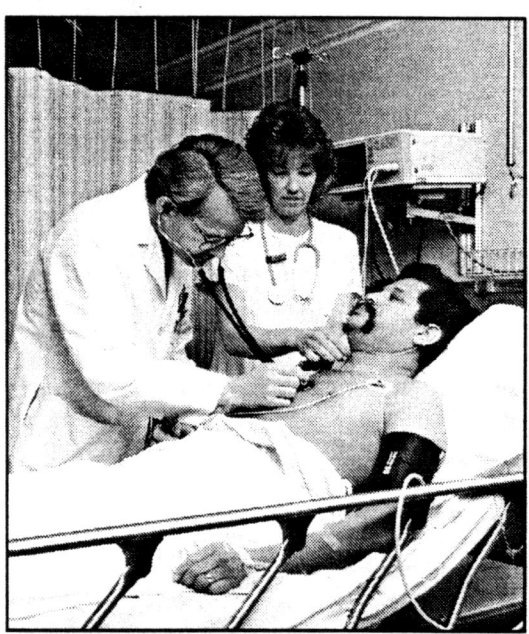

Figure 10-3: The heart rhythm of a cardiac patient must be monitored.

Chapter Ten • Medical Emergencies

The doctor and nurse must be notified immediately and the patient placed on a gurney while preparation is made to monitor the heart rhythm. The heart has an electrical rhythm that can be picked up by **electrodes** and watched closely on a monitor for changes that indicate an irregular or life-threatening heartbeat.

electrode: a conductor used to establish contact for recording electrical activity within the body

To place a patient on the monitor, open the foil package containing the electrodes by tearing off the top edge. Cleanse the patient's skin of dirt and body oil using a skin prep solution or dry gauze pad. It may be necessary to shave some of the patient's body hair if access to the skin is not possible. Next, you must remove the protective paper from the pad that covers the electrode. There will be some gel under this covering. Place the electrode firmly on the chest as indicated in Figure 10-4. Place one just below the right **clavicle**, the second below the left clavicle, and the third on the lower edge of the rib cage on the left side of the chest. If a fourth electrode is used, place it on the right side opposite the lower left one. Lead placement may vary depending on the condition of the patient and the heart rhythm.

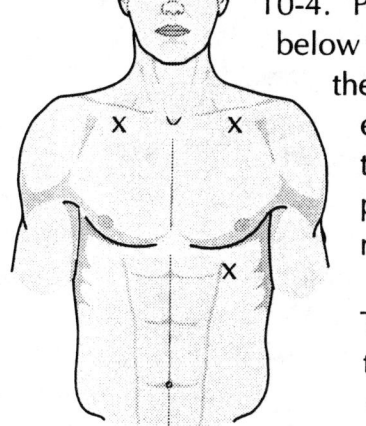

Figure 10-4: Proper Positions for Electrodes

The internal electricity of the body is picked up by the electrode and transferred through a hard wire, or cable, to a monitor. The electrical impulse is amplified and shown on the **oscilloscope** (monitor), where the patients heart rhythm can be watched or monitored in the patient's room and at the nurses' station. (Figure 10-5)

The monitor in the patient's room has alarm buttons that are set by the nurse. After the patient is placed on the monitor, the nurse will start an IV, place the patient on oxygen by mask or **cannula**, and request a set of vital signs. If the pulse is irregular, take it for a full minute and report to the nurse. The monitor provides a continuous digital readout of the pulse.

Figure 10-5: An Oscilloscope

electrocardiogram (ECG): a diagnostic test for heart disease that measures the electrical activity of the heart

The monitoring equipment is connected to a machine that can generate a printout of the **electrocardiogram** (**ECG**). You can receive a monitor **strip** of the patient's heart rhythm by pushing a button. Monitoring equipment is not the same in every hospital. You should know where the alarm buttons are located and how to run a rhythm strip. It is important to learn about your equipment and how it operates. The nurse can interpret this rhythm and notify the doctor of any serious irregularities or **dysrhythmias**. As you work in the emergency room and monitor heart rhythms, you will become more familiar with dysrhythmias. For advanced study, classes are available in ECG interpretation and identification.

The doctor will order lab work, x-rays, and a 12 lead ECG to be done. These tests help to confirm the possibility of a heart attack. When the results are read by the doctor the patient will either be admitted to the Cardiac Care Unit, medical floor or discharged home. All of these tests are necessary to determine if the patient has had a **myocardial infarction** (heart attack).

Cardiac patients are observed continually, and vital signs need to be taken every 5, 10, or 15 minutes. As you obtain vital signs, it is important to report any changes immediately to the nurse. If the blood pressure is higher or lower than your previous reading or if there are any changes in the heart rate, or in the patient's general condition, tell the nurse right away. Always look at the heart rhythm. Although it is not essential that you be able to interpret the rhythm, you MUST be able to detect changes in it and alert the nurse. Some dysrhythmias, like **heart block**, ventricular tachycardia, ventricular fibrillation, or frequent **premature ventricular contractions** (**PVCs**), are life-threatening and must be treated immediately with medication or **defibrillation.**

heart block: a condition in which the conductive tissue of the heart fails to send signals from the atrium to the ventricles, resulting in dysrhythmia

premature ventricular contractions (PVCs): an early electrical beat in the heart that can lead to serious cardiac disrhythmias

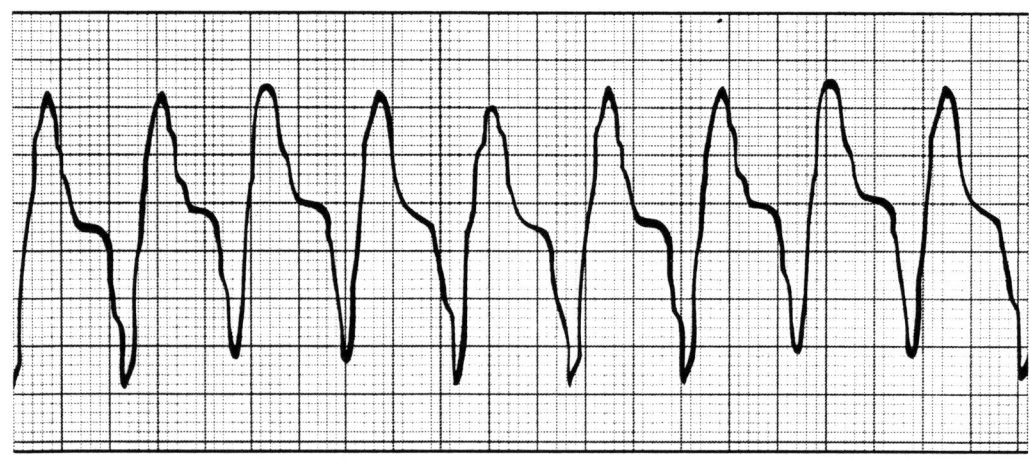

Figure 10-6: An ECG Strip Showing Ventricular Tachycardia

Chapter Ten • Medical Emergencies

If a patient has a cardiac problem, he or she will be admitted to the **Coronary Care Unit** or **Telemetry** Unit. You will need to help transport the patient and equipment to the specialty unit. Check to be sure that the portable oxygen tank is at least half full and make sure it is secured to the gurney. Obtain the emergency transport box, bag-valve mask, and portable monitor/defibrillator unit and move them with the patient for emergency use during transport.

Supplies and equipment that are used on any patients must be replaced as soon as possible. It is very important to keep all the necessary equipment ready for use. This includes keeping all batteries fully charged. As soon as you return to the emergency room with the empty gurney, be sure to return all equipment to the correct place and plug in the portable monitor and defibrillator unit so that it can be recharged. Remove the oxygen tank and return it to the storage area. Check the oxygen tank to make sure there is at least half a tank of oxygen left. If the tank is less than half full, replace it with a full tank. Check the oxygen level by turning the hand screw knob on the top of the tank. Watch the gauge as the oxygen comes through the valve.

Check all cupboards and shelves and restock all supplies. Critical Care rooms must always be ready for the next patient to arrive. Running out of lifesaving supplies is not acceptable.

Chapter Summary

Caring for patients with medical emergencies demands immediate attention from the healthcare worker. Listening to what the patient tells you about what he feels, observing the patient for signs of distress, and reporting these findings to the nurse or doctor are vital to delivering quality healthcare to the patients. As an emergency department technician, this aspect of emergency care will become your responsibility.

10-18

Chapter Ten • Medical Emergencies 10-19

Name _____

Date _____

Student Enrichment Activities

1. List five signs and symptoms of low blood sugar.
   A. _____
   B. _____
   C. _____
   D. _____
   E. _____

2. Another word for low blood sugar is _____.

3. List, in order, the steps to take in obtaining a sputum culture.
   _____
   _____
   _____
   _____
   _____

4. Place an X where you would attach electrodes for cardiac monitoring.

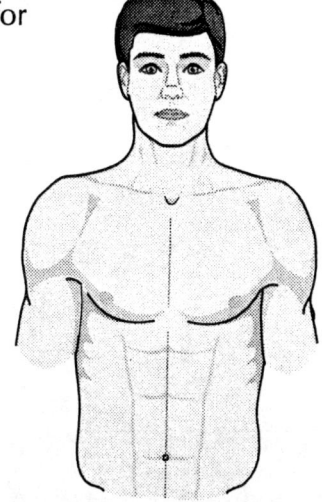

5. The unconscious patient with a spinal injury is positioned _____.

6. The unconscious diabetic is positioned _____.

7. Explain how to care for a patient having a seizure.

   _____
   _____
   _____
   _____
   _____

8. List eight signs and symptoms of a heart attack.

   A. _____
   B. _____
   C. _____
   D. _____
   E. _____
   F. _____
   G. _____
   H. _____

9. Identify the following oxygen equipment.

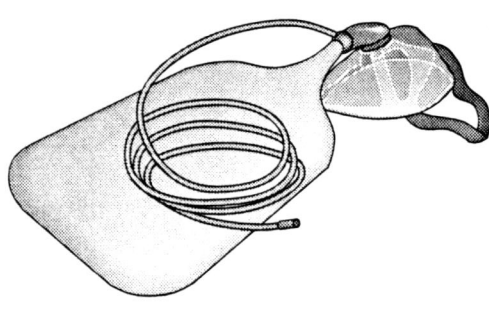

_____

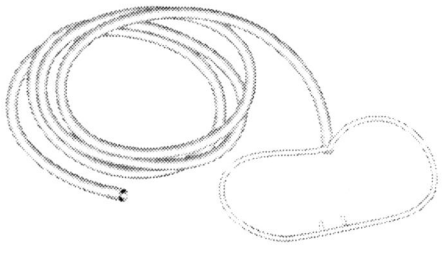

_____

Chapter Ten • Medical Emergencies

10-21

Name _____

Date _____

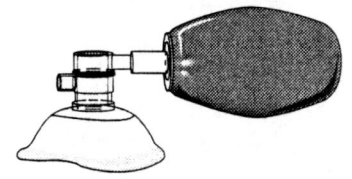

_____

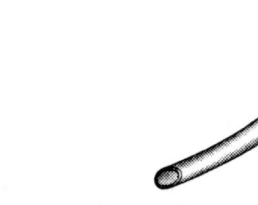

_____

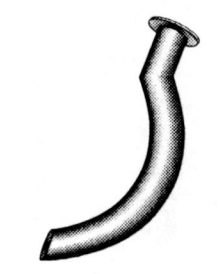

_____

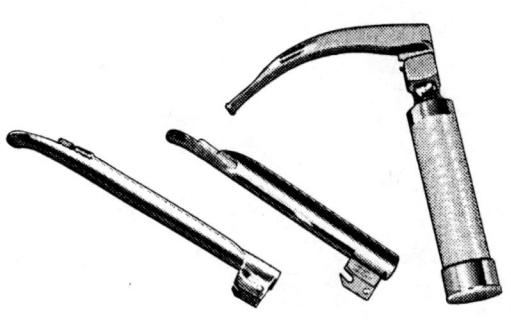

_____

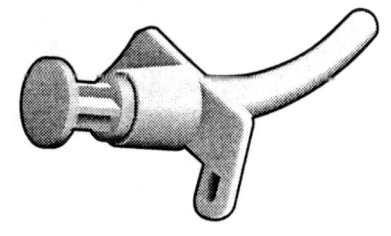

_____

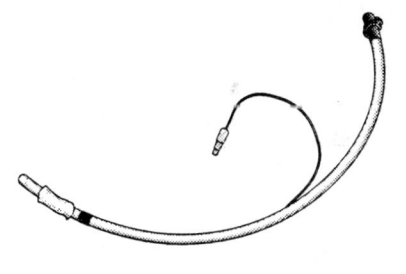

_____

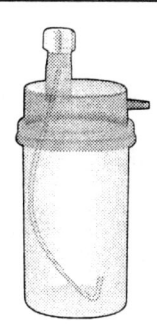

_____

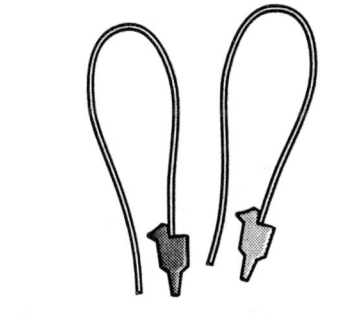

_____

10-22

Chapter Eleven
Abdominal Emergencies

Objectives

After completing this chapter you should be able to do the following:

1. Define and correctly spell all key terms.
2. Recognize the signs and symptoms of an acute abdomen.
3. Perform a urinary catheterization.
4. Obtain a urine specimen.
5. Assist with gastric tube placement.

Key Terms

- catheterization
- catheters
- comatose
- distention
- guarding
- labia
- localized
- meatus
- NPO
- nasogastric tube
- referred pain
- rigid
- urinary retention
- urine
- void

Acute Abdomen

Imagine that the following patients arrive in the emergency room within a period of an hour. What do they all have in common?

- A 12-year-old boy with fever, vomiting, and pain in the right lower abdominal **quadrant**.
- A 40-year-old executive vice president in shock and vomiting blood.
- A 33-year-old plumber with back pain and blood in his **urine**.
- A 45-year-old school teacher who ate fried shrimp, french fries, and cole slaw for lunch and now has pain in the right upper quadrant, and is vomiting a green-yellow liquid.

urine: the liquid waste produced by the body

distention: the enlargement of a body cavity caused by air or fluid

localized: occurring in one special area

referred pain: pain at a location other than the injured organ or site

All of these patients have different symptoms, but what they have in common is called an **acute abdomen**. Acute abdomen is a combination of symptoms characterized by abdominal pain, vomiting, and abdominal **distention** (air or fluid in the abdomen), which sometimes requires surgery. This pain can be described as dull, sharp, aching, cramping, heavy, or knife-like, and it may be continuous or intermittent (comes and goes). The pain can be **localized** (located in one spot), or it can be **referred pain** (radiating or traveling to various locations in the body).

Chapter Eleven • Abdominal Emergencies

A patient with an acute abdomen may experience a variety of signs and symptoms. The following is a list of potential symptoms of acute abdomen, but it is important to note that the patient may exhibit all of these, some of these, or even none of these.

- fever
- nausea
- vomiting
- **diarrhea**
- **constipation**
- **tachycardia**
- **hypotension**
- rectal bleeding
- vomiting blood
- dizziness
- perspiration
- **guarding**, or pulling the legs up to the chest
- blood in the urine
- **urinary retention** (unable to urinate)
- **apprehension**
- abdominal **distention**
- a rigid abdomen
- weakness
- surgical scars on the abdomen
- difficulty breathing

guarding: protecting a painful area; pulling up the knees in reaction to abdominal pain

urinary retention: the inability to void the bladder

Several diseases can cause an acute abdomen. Most of the diseases result in **inflammation** of an organ. This inflammation will produce redness, heat, swelling, and pain. If it is not treated it will lead to a loss of function of the organ involved. The following conditions can lead to an acute abdomen.

- **pancreatitis**: inflammation of the pancreas
- **hepatitis**: inflammation of the liver
- **appendicitis**: inflammation of the appendix
- **colitis**: inflammation of the colon
- **cholecystitis**: inflammation of the gall bladder
- **peritonitis**: inflammation of the intestinal lining
- **diverticulitis**: inflammation of one of the pouches in the lining of the intestinal wall
- **nephritis**: inflammation of the kidney

Notice that each of these terms ends in "*itis?*" This is a suffix that refers to inflammation, usually of a particular organ. There are other conditions that can result in an acute abdomen. They include the following:

- **abdominal trauma**: injury to the abdomen that can cause the internal organs to tear and bleed, or lose gastric fluid
- an **aneurysm**: a bulging of the wall of a blood vessel
- **kidney stones:** a mineral build up in the kidney that may block the passage of urine
- **gall stones**: a mineral build up in the gall bladder that can block the passage of bile
- **peptic ulcers**: areas of loss in the lining of the stomach that can cause bleeding
- a **ruptured spleen**: a tear in the spleen that leads to bleeding and shock
- **ruptured ectopic pregnancy**: a fertilized egg that implants in the fallopian tube and grows to a size that causes the tube to tear

Chapter Eleven • Abdominal Emergencies

When discussing the abdomen, medical personnel will refer to **quadrants**. The abdomen is divided into quadrants, or fourths. Using the **umbilicus** (belly button) as the center, draw an imaginary line vertically across the abdomen, and a second imaginary line horizontally through the umbilicus. The abdomen is now divided into four sections: the right upper quadrant (RUQ), the left upper quadrant (LUQ), the right lower quadrant (RLQ), and the left lower quadrant (LLQ). (Figure 11-1)

When a patient is admitted to the ER with abdominal pain, you must question the patient to determine which quadrant the pain is located in, or if the pain is in each of the four quadrants. When obtaining a history from the patient, it is important to determine if the abdominal pain is related to anything. You can ask the following questions:

1. Does the pain appear only after eating?

2. What types of food cause the pain?

3. Is the pain relieved by eating or drinking?

4. Does physical activity affect the level of pain?

5. Is there a position in which you feel more comfortable?

6. What relieves the pain?

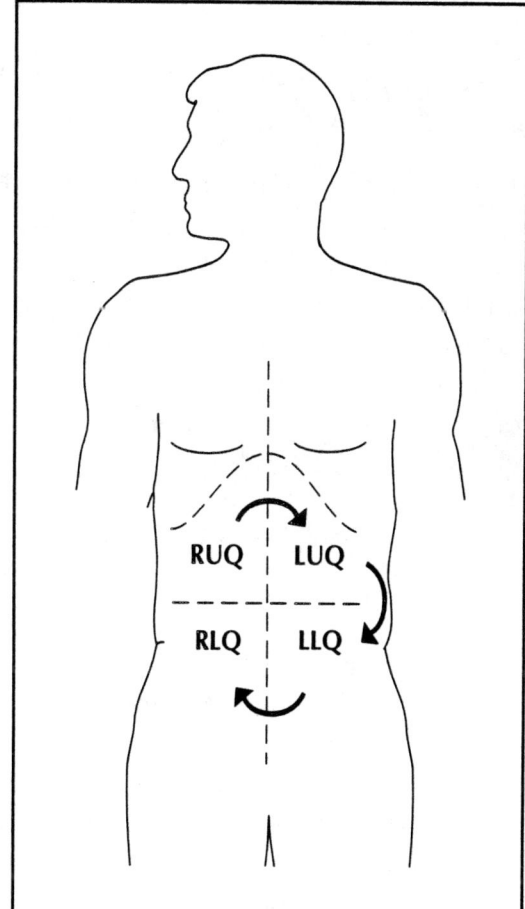

Figure 11-1:
The Abdominal Quadrants

NPO:
nothing by mouth (from the Latin, *non per os*)

Since these conditions can be very serious and may require immediate surgery, patients with any of the signs of acute abdomen must be examined by a physician. Suspected acute abdomen patients are not given anything by mouth (**NPO**) until after x-rays, lab work, and surgery have been done. Vital signs are taken frequently, and any signs of developing shock are reported to the nurse immediately. The following symptoms are signs of shock.

- bleeding
- a rapid pulse
- low or dropping blood pressure
- **abdominal distention** and **rigidity**
- patient complains of dizziness or light-headedness
- vomiting
- diarrhea

The doctor may wish to perform a rectal examination. If so, he or she will need an examination glove, lubricating jelly, and a specimen container for a **stool** sample. Explain the procedure to the patient and attempt to position him or her on the left side. If the doctor obtains a specimen and places it in the container, label the container and take the specimen and laboratory requisition form to the laboratory. The doctor also may ask you to check the specimen for the presence of blood. (See the procedure on the following page.)

The doctor will also need to perform a pelvic examination on female patients who show symptoms of acute abdomen. This procedure is described in Chapter Twelve.

Lab work and x-rays will be ordered for all acute abdomen patients, so the patient may need to go to Radiology for these tests. Depending on the patient's condition, you may be asked to go with him or her. If so, take an **emesis** basin with you to X-ray in case the patient needs to vomit. Before leaving the ER, always ask the nurse what you need to do for the patient while you are in X-ray. Find out how often the vital signs should be taken and what observations you are to make about the patient.

Chapter Eleven • Abdominal Emergencies

Checking a Stool Specimen for Blood

Materials needed:
- ✓ gloves
- ✓ bedpan or commode
- ✓ wooden stick
- ✓ hemocult packet
- ✓ reaction solution
- ✓ sterile specimen container

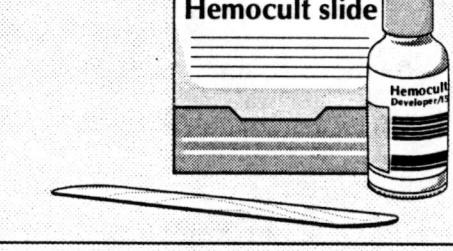

1. Procedural Step: Wash your hands.
   Reason: Universal precaution.
   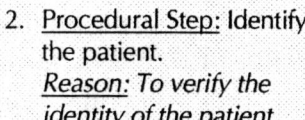

2. Procedural Step: Identify the patient.
   Reason: To verify the identity of the patient.

3. Procedural Step: Put on gloves.
   Reason: Universal precaution.

4. Procedural Step: Take the specimen in the bedpan to bathroom.
   Reason: To obtain specimen and dispose of waste.

5. Procedural Step: Using a wooden stick, smear a bit of stool on a filter paper or Hemocult slide packet.
   Reason: To test for blood.

6. Procedural Step: Place two drops of solution on the stool smear.
   Reason: To test for blood.

7. Procedural Step: After 30 seconds, look for a blue-green color change.
   Reason: The color will change if blood is present.

8. Procedural Step: Discard the filter paper.
   Reason: The test is completed.

9. Procedural Step: If a specimen is needed for further testing, place it in a sterile container, fill out the requisition form, and take it to the laboratory. If no other testing is necessary, flush the waste down the toilet.
   Reason: Other tests may be needed to determine the source of the bleeding.

10. Procedural Step: Remove your gloves.
    Reason: Universal precaution.
    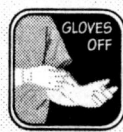

11. Procedural Step: Wash your hands.
    Reason: Universal precaution.

12. Procedural Step: Report the results to the physician or the nurse and chart the results.
    Reason: This is important information for patient care.

If the patient has **abdominal distention** the doctor may order a **nasogastric tube** to be inserted by the nurse. You can gather the equipment and assist with this procedure. The following equipment items will be needed.

- ✓ a disposable towel
- ✓ an **emesis** basin
- ✓ a **nasogastric tube**
- ✓ an irrigating set
- ✓ 1000 ml of irrigating normal saline
- ✓ a gastric tube suction setup
- ✓ gloves

nasogastric tube: a catheter placed in the stomach through the nose for removal or insertion of fluids

The nasogastric tube is inserted to relieve abdominal distention by draining air or fluid. If the fluid is bright red or the color of coffee grounds, there may be a bleeding problem. The nasogastric tube is connected to a suction unit that is set for low, intermittent suction. The tube must be secured in place with tape to the patient's nose or face. Don't pull on the tube or move the patient until you are sure that the tube is secured in place. It is your responsibility to make sure that all tubes stay in place and are not accidentally disconnected while moving the patient. Always check the position of the IV, nasogastric tube, catheters, monitor cables, airway tubes, and oxygen before moving a patient.

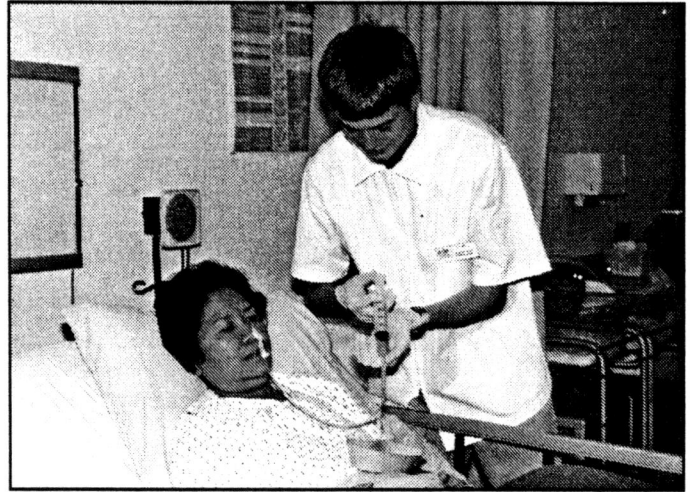

If the patient has internal bleeding, the pulse will become rapid, irregular, and weak. The blood pressure will drop, and there will be very little urine **output**. The patient will become confused, restless, and eventually **comatose**. The patient's abdomen can become **rigid** and distended. The nurse will start one or two IVs and the patient may receive blood **transfusions**. All of these procedures must be done very rapidly while preparations are made for surgery. Patients with internal bleeding need immediate surgical intervention.

Abdominal Trauma

Most injuries to the abdomen are a direct result of blunt trauma following a motor vehicle accident (**MVA**), but the abdomen also can be injured in falls from high places and from penetrating wounds like those received from a knife. These kinds of injuries can cause a massive amount of internal bleeding and often involve more than one organ. The patient will show signs and symptoms of shock, the blood pressure will be low, the pulse rate will be high, and the abdomen will become increasingly larger and firmer. These critical patients are generally brought in by the paramedics with one, two, or three IVs in place. Antishock trousers also may be in place when the patient arrives. This antishock garment, also known as a **MAST** suit (Military Anti-Shock Trousers) or **PASG** suit (Pneumatic Anti-Shock Garment), has three sections, one for each leg and one for the abdomen. This air suit is put on the patient and then inflated.

comatose: unconscious

rigid: firm and board-like

When the trousers are inflated, the blood that is normally in the legs is forced back into the rest of the body, promoting circulation. The suit works by squeezing the veins, which empties the blood from them and transfuses the patient with his own blood. The pressure in the suit causes the veins to constrict and send more blood back to the heart, brain, and lungs. It also compresses the arteries and veins in the lower extremities and controls bleeding.

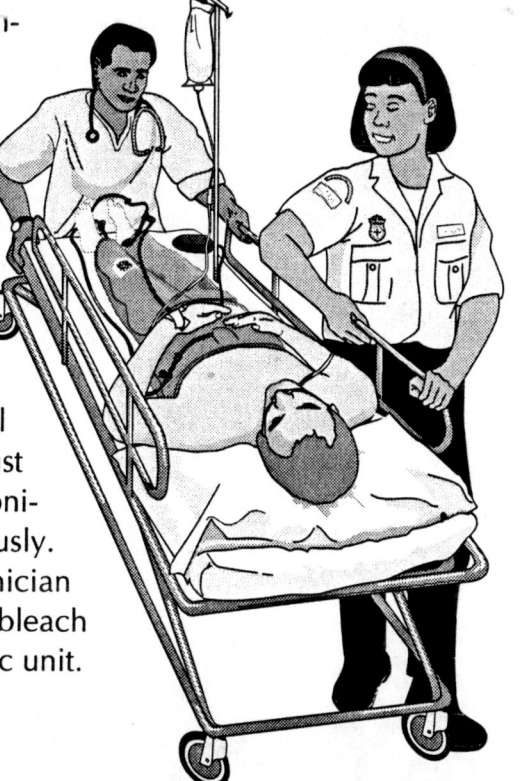

The MAST suit is used as a lifesaving measure to prevent shock. THIS SUIT SHOULD NEVER BE CUT OFF OF THE PATIENT. It is removed slowly after several IVs and blood transfusions have been given. If the suit is removed too rapidly the patient's blood pressure will immediately decrease. A physician must direct the removal of the MAST suit, monitoring the blood pressure continuously. After it has been removed, an ER technician will clean it with a 10% chlorine bleach solution and return it to the paramedic unit.

If the patient arrives with the MAST suit in place the paramedics will borrow a MAST suit from the ER until the one the patient is wearing is returned. The patient will be seen immediately by the physician, and arrangements will be made for exploratory surgery in the OR. Lab work and x-rays must be obtained rapidly, and the patient must be prepared for surgery. A nasogastric tube and urinary **catheter** will be inserted, and the patient will be placed on oxygen and a cardiac monitor. He or she also will be infused with one or two IVs.

catheter: a tube that is passed through the body to transport fluids in or out of a body cavity

Completing a Laboratory Requisition Form

Specimens sent to the laboratory for analysis are labeled with the patient's name, his or her hospital number, the date, and the time the specimen was collected. The appropriate requisition form is filled out and stamped with the patient information data. Fill in the time the specimen was collected, the source of the specimen, and the name of the test that is to be done. Then sign your name to the requisition form. Take the labeled specimen with the requisition form to the laboratory. If a time clock is available to check in the specimen at the laboratory, use it to time stamp the requisition form.

Urine Specimens and Catheterization

void: to urinate

Patients with abdominal emergencies will need to produce a urine specimen. If the patient can **void**, a clean catch (or midstream urine specimen) is obtained. The urine specimen should be taken to the laboratory within fifteen minutes. If the patient is not able to get up and go to the bathroom, a bedpan or urinal may be used. If, after the specimen is obtained, the patient wishes to urinate again it is essential that you measure the amount voided. This is documented as **output**. Make note of the amount, color, and consistency of the urine.

Chapter Eleven • Abdominal Emergencies

Obtaining a Mid-Stream Urine Specimen

Materials needed:
- ✓ gloves
- ✓ cleansing solution and/or wipes
- ✓ sterile specimen container
- ✓ bedpan or urinal (if needed)

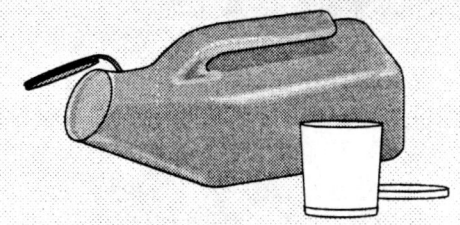

1. <u>Procedural Step:</u> Complete the laboratory requisition form.
   <u>Reason:</u> This is sent with the specimen to the laboratory.

2. <u>Procedural Step:</u> Wash your hands.
   <u>Reason:</u> Universal precaution.

3. <u>Procedural Step:</u> Put on gloves.
   <u>Reason:</u> Universal precaution.

4. <u>Procedural Step:</u> Identify the patient by his or her identification bracelet.
   <u>Reason:</u> To make sure you obtain the correct patient's specimen.

5. <u>Procedural Step:</u> Explain the procedure to the patient in terms he or she can understand.
   <u>Reason:</u> The patient will assist with the procedure.

6. <u>Procedural Step:</u> Instruct the patient to clean the urinary **meatus** with the antiseptic solution you provide.
   <u>Reason:</u> This ensures a clean specimen.

7. <u>Procedural Step:</u> Instruct the patient to clean from front to back.
   <u>Reason:</u> This avoids contamination.

8. <u>Procedural Step:</u> If the patient is an uncircumcised male, instruct him to retract his foreskin before cleansing.
   <u>Reason:</u> This allows a thorough cleaning.

9. <u>Procedural Step:</u> Instruct the patient to begin urinating, and capture only the midstream urine in the specimen container. Explain that the midstream urine is that which comes out between the time the patient begins to urinate and the time he or she stops.
   <u>Reason:</u> Only midstream urine is desired.

10. <u>Procedural Step:</u> If the patient cannot obtain the specimen unassisted, you will need to capture the midstream urine in a clean urinal or bedpan.
    <u>Reason:</u> The urine must not be contaminated.

11. <u>Procedural Step:</u> If a urinal or bedpan was used, cover it and take it and the specimen container to the bathroom, and pour the urine from the bedpan or urinal into the specimen container. Do not touch the inside of the container.
    <u>Reason:</u> To avoid contamination.

meatus: the anatomical opening where urine is expelled from the body

Obtaining a Mid-Stream Urine Specimen (Cont.)

12. <u>Procedural Step:</u> When the specimen has been collected, replace the cap on the container.
    <u>Reason:</u> *To secure the contents.*

13. <u>Procedural Step:</u> Label the specimen container with the patient's name, the date, and the time.
    <u>Reason:</u> *To ensure correct identification.*

14. <u>Procedural Step:</u> Remove your gloves.
    <u>Reason:</u> *Universal precaution.*

15. <u>Procedural Step:</u> Wash your hands.
    <u>Reason:</u> *Universal precaution.*

16. <u>Procedural Step:</u> Document the procedure as appropriate.
    <u>Reason:</u> *To provide documentation.*

catheterization: the process of inserting a catheter into a patient

The doctor may order a continuous indwelling **catheter** for the patient. This is inserted when the patient cannot **void** to relieve **urinary retention** or to monitor the urine output. This type of catheter also is inserted prior to any abdominal surgery. Catheters (tubes) are inserted into the bladder using **sterile technique** to prevent infections. Urinary tract infections are easily acquired. Because of this, sterile precautions must be taken with the **catheterization** procedure. Catheterizations should not be done without proper instruction in both the procedure and sterile technique.

Chapter Eleven • Abdominal Emergencies

Catheterizing a Female Patient

Materials needed:
- ✓ gloves
- ✓ sterile catheterization set

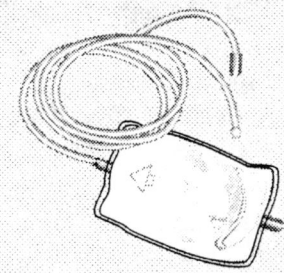

1. Procedural Step: Wash your hands.
   Reason: Universal precaution.

2. Procedural Step: Identify the patient by his or her identification bracelet.
   Reason: To ensure you obtain the correct patient's specimen.

3. Procedural Step: Explain the procedure to the patient using terms he or she can understand.
   Reason: This keeps the patient calm and provides the information necessary for the patient to give informed consent.

4. Procedural Step: Position the patient on her back with the knees bent.
   Reason: To give you access to the urinary system.

5. Procedural Step: Open the sterile package of the catheterization set by tearing off the plastic wrap.
   Reason: To prepare for the procedure.

6. Procedural Step: Place the cath tray on the bed between the patient's legs.
   Reason: This is a convenient location.

7. Procedural Step: Open the package using **sterile technique**. Touching only the corners, fold the top-most part of the covering away from you.
   Reason: This leaves the sterile tray covered so that it cannot be contaminated when you reach across it.

   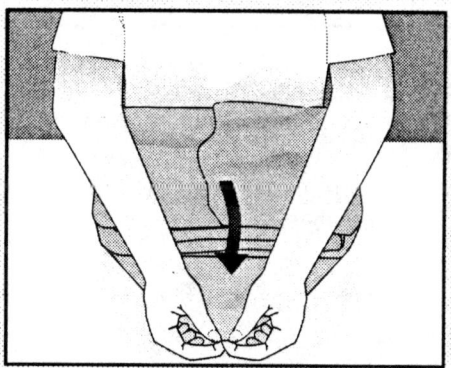

8. Procedural Step: Fold the side flaps away from the sides of the tray.
   Reason: The tray is still covered by the final layer of the wrapper.

   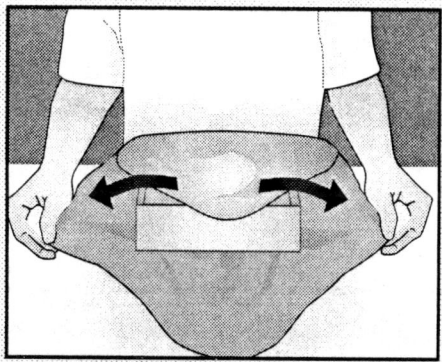

Catheterizing a Female Patient (Cont.)

9. **Procedural Step:** Open the final layer of the wrapper by unfolding it toward you.
   Reason: The wrapper becomes part of the sterile field surrounding the sterile tray.

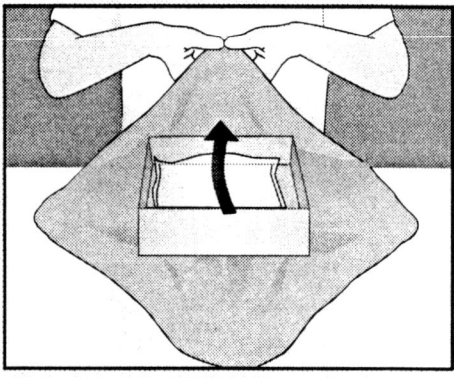

labia: the two folds of skin that lie on either side of the vaginal opening

10. **Procedural Step:** Place the plastic liner under the patient's buttocks using only the corners of plastic.
    Reason: To create and maintain a **sterile field**.

11. **Procedural Step:** Put on sterile gloves.
    Reason: Universal precaution.

12. **Procedural Step:** Place a container with cotton balls, antiseptic cleanser, and lubricant near the patient.
    Reason: These are used to clean the **meatus**.

13. **Procedural Step:** Place the container holding the catheter and bag on the sterile field.
    Reason: This will be used later.

14. **Procedural Step:** Open the package containing the catheterization set and pour antiseptic solution over the cotton balls.
    Reason: This will be used for cleansing the meatus.

15. **Procedural Step:** Lubricate the catheter with lubricant.
    Reason: This makes the catheter easier to insert.

16. **Procedural Step:** Position a drape over the patient that is cut out over the **genitalia**.
    Reason: To prevent contamination.

17. **Procedural Step:** Spread the **labia** so you can see the urinary meatus.
    Reason: You must be able to see clearly where the catheter is going to be inserted.

18. **Procedural Step:** Using the sterile cotton balls and antiseptic solution, cleanse the meatus and surrounding area in a circular motion.
    Reason: To decrease the number of microorganisms that are present.

19. **Procedural Step:** With your uncontaminated hand, take the catheter and gently insert it into the meatus $1/2$ to 2 inches, or until urine starts to flow.
    Reason: Urine will flow if the catheter is in the bladder.

Chapter Eleven • Abdominal Emergencies

Catheterizing a Female Patient (Cont.)

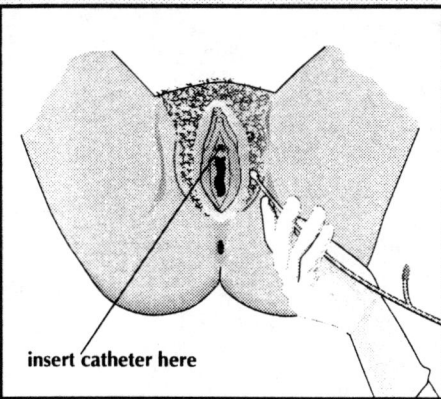
insert catheter here

20. **Procedural Step:** Inject the contents of the prefilled syringe (5-10 ml of sterile water) into the side arm of the catheter to inflate the balloon.
    Reason: The inflated balloon will keep the catheter in place.

21. **Procedural Step:** Gently pull back on the catheter until you feel resistance.
    Reason: This indicates the catheter is in place.

22. **Procedural Step:** Obtain the specimen.
    Reason: This will be sent to the laboratory for analysis.

23. **Procedural Step:** Check the doctor's orders.
    Reason: Specific laboratory tests may have been ordered.

24. **Procedural Step:** Tape the catheter to the patient's leg.
    Reason: To prevent movement of the tube.

25. **Procedural Step:** Attach the drainage bag to the bed frame.
    Reason: Urine drains by gravity.

26. **Procedural Step:** Remove any unnecessary equipment and dispose of the used supplies.
    Reason: To clean the area.

27. **Procedural Step:** Remove your gloves.
    Reason: Universal precaution.

28. **Procedural Step:** Wash your hands.
    Reason: Universal precaution.

29. **Procedural Step:** Record the procedure on the patient's chart, noting the size of the catheter that was used and the amount of sterile water instilled into the balloon.
    Reason: To provide documentation.

30. **Procedural Step:** Record the output on the patient's chart.
    Reason: To provide documentation.

Chart it like this:

#16 Foley catheter inserted. Balloon inflated w/ 10 ml sterile H_2O, 600 ml clear yellow urine, specimen to lab, Foley to gravity drainage.

Catheterizing a Male Patient

Materials needed:
- ✓ gloves
- ✓ sterile catheterization set

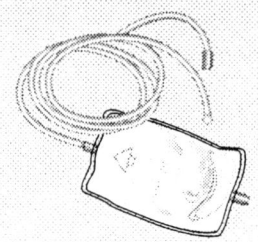

1. Procedural Step: Wash your hands.
   Reason: Universal precaution.

2. Procedural Step: Identify the patient by his or her identification bracelet.
   Reason: To make sure you obtain the correct patient's specimen.

3. Procedural Step: Explain the procedure to the patient using terms he or she can understand.
   Reason: This keeps the patient calm and provides the information necessary for the patient to give informed consent.
   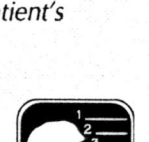

4. Procedural Step: Position the patient on his back with his legs together.
   Reason: The procedure is easier if patient's legs are together.

5. Procedural Step: Drape the patient so only the area around the penis is exposed.
   Reason: To prevent contamination.

6. Procedural Step: Place the catheter tray next to the patient's legs.
   Reason: It should be placed within reach.
   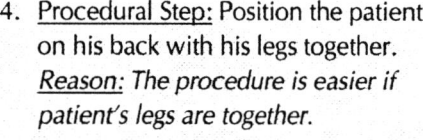

7. Procedural Step: Open the tray using **sterile technique** by lifting one corner at a time.
   Reason: Sterile procedure.
   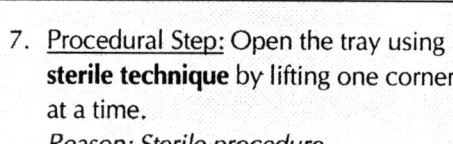

8. Procedural Step: Put on gloves.
   Reason: Universal precaution.

9. Procedural Step: Lubricate the tip of the catheter.
   Reason: This makes insertion easier.

10. Procedural Step: Lift the penis with one hand and cleanse the area at the meatus with cotton balls and cleansing solution. This is now the contaminated hand.
    Reason: To decrease the number of microorganisms that are present.

11. Procedural Step: If the patient is uncircumcised the foreskin should be retracted so you can cleanse the area.
    Reason: To eliminate microorganisms.

12. Procedural Step: Gently pull up the penis.
    Reason: This is the proper position for catheterization.

13. Procedural Step: Gently insert the catheter into the end of the penis 6 to 8 inches.
    Reason: This will ensure that the catheter reaches the bladder.

Chapter Eleven • Abdominal Emergencies

Catheterizing a Male Patient (Cont.)

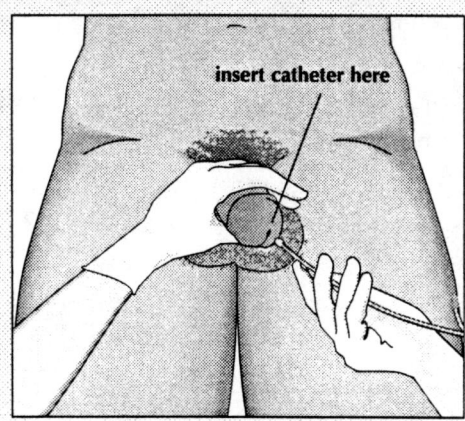

14. <u>Procedural Step:</u> Watch for the flow of urine.
    <u>Reason:</u> *This indicates that the tube is in the bladder.*

15. <u>Procedural Step:</u> Inject the contents of the prefilled syringe (5-10 ml) into the side arm of the catheter and inflate the balloon.
    <u>Reason:</u> *The inflated balloon will keep the catheter in place.*

16. <u>Procedural Step:</u> Gently pull back on the catheter until you feel resistance.
    <u>Reason:</u> *The catheter is in place.*

17. <u>Procedural Step:</u> Obtain specimen.
    <u>Reason:</u> *This will be sent to the laboratory for analysis.*

18. <u>Procedural Step:</u> Check the doctor's orders.
    <u>Reason:</u> *You will need to know which tests have been ordered.*

19. <u>Procedural Step:</u> Tape the catheter to the patient's leg.
    <u>Reason:</u> *To prevent movement of the tube.*

20. <u>Procedural Step:</u> Attach the drainage bag to the bed frame below the level of the patient's bladder.
    <u>Reason:</u> *Urine drains by gravity.*

21. <u>Procedural Step:</u> Remove and/or dispose of any used equipment and supplies.
    <u>Reason:</u> *To clean the area.*

22. <u>Procedural Step:</u> Remove your gloves.
    <u>Reason:</u> *Universal precaution.*

23. <u>Procedural Step:</u> Wash your hands.
    <u>Reason:</u> *Universal precaution.*

24. <u>Procedural Step:</u> Document the procedure on the patient's chart, noting the size of the catheter you used and the amount of sterile water instilled into the balloon.
    <u>Reason:</u> *To provide documentation.*

25. <u>Procedural Step:</u> Record the output.
    <u>Reason:</u> *To provide documentation.*

Chart it like this:

#16 Foley catheter inserted. Balloon inflated w/ 10 ml sterile H_2O, 600 ml clear yellow urine, specimen to lab, Foley to gravity drainage.

Preparing a Patient for Surgery

To prepare a patient for surgery, remove all of the patient's clothing and help him or her put on a patient gown. If the patient is wearing dentures, remove them and place them in a labeled container. Remove any jewelry the patient is wearing and either give it to a relative of the patient or label the jewelry and put it in the hospital safe. You will need to document a description of the patient's belongings and what was done with them on the pre-procedure (or pre-surgical) checklist. An example of a pre-surgical checklist appears in Figure 11-2. A checklist like this must be filled out before every surgical procedure.

PRE-SURGICAL CHECKLIST

	YES	NO	OR
Surgery Consent Signed			
Correct Surgical Site & Side Identified			
Sterilization Consent Signed			
Surgical Procedure Scheduled			
Safety Strap In Place On Gurney			
Special Equipment (oxygen, monitor)			
History & Physical On Chart			

	Date Done		
EKG			
Chest X-Ray			
CBC Within 72 Hours			
Type X-Match _____ Units			
Urinalysis Within 72 Hours			
Allergies			

Surgical Prep (State if None) _____
Prosthesis   Removed   None
Dentures   Partial   Bridge   Caps
Artificial Limbs ❑ Yes ❑ No   Artificial Eyes ❑ Yes ❑ No
Contacts   Glasses   Hearing Aid

NURSING	YES	NO	OR
Pre-Op Bath or Shower			
Voided Time			
Retention Catheter in Place			
Hair Pieces/Pins/Combs Removed			
Jewelry and/or Valuables:			
Other:			
Disposition of:			

T____ P____ R____ BP_____
Name Plate ❑ Yes ❑ No
Location of Family _____
Identaband No. _____
Pre-Op Medication & Time:
_____
_____

Unit Nurse Signature _____
Date _____
OR Nurses Signature _____
Date _____
Special Note _____
_____
_____
_____
_____

Stamp Name Here:

Patient Name Plate

Figure 11-2: A pre-surgical checklist must be completed before every surgical procedure.

Chapter Summary

Acute abdomen can be brought on by a number of illnesses and traumatic injuries. Patients with this condition will be very ill; they will complain of pain, nausea, vomiting, and diarrhea or constipation, all of which can lead to shock. Therefore, it is vital to evaluate these conditions quickly. Laboratory and x-ray procedures may need to be done rapidly to determine the extent of the illness or injury. The ER technician may be required to accompany the patients to various departments for these additional procedures. The patient's vital signs must be taken at least every fifteen minutes and any changes must be reported to the nurse or physician. Patients showing symptoms of acute abdomen are not allowed to have anything to eat or drink and preparations may need to be made for surgery.

Chapter Eleven • Abdominal Emergencies 11-21

Name _____
Date _____

Student Enrichment Activities

1. List six signs and symptoms of an acute abdomen.

   A. _____ D. _____
   B. _____ E. _____
   C. _____ F. _____

2. The suffix "itis" means inflammation. Name six inflammatory conditions that can lead to an acute abdomen.

   A. _____ D. _____
   B. _____ E. _____
   C. _____ F. _____

3. Outline the procedure for catheterizing a patient.

   _____
   _____
   _____
   _____
   _____
   _____
   _____
   _____
   _____
   _____
   _____
   _____
   _____
   _____

4. Write an explanation to a patient describing how to obtain a midstream urine specimen.

_____
_____
_____
_____
_____
_____

Match the following conditions with the definitions.

5. _____ pancreatitis   a. bulging blood vessel

6. _____ hepatitis   b. mineral deposit in the kidney

7. _____ appendicitis   c. fertilized egg in the fallopian tube

8. _____ colitis   d. inflammation of colon

9. _____ ruptured spleen   e. mineral deposit in the gall bladder

10. _____ cholecystitis   f. injury to internal abdominal organs

11. _____ peritonitis   g. tear in spleen

12. _____ diverticulitis   h. inflammation of kidney

13. _____ nephritis   i. bleeding caused by a tear in the lining of the stomach and intestines

Chapter Eleven • Abdominal Emergencies

14. _____ aneurysm

15. _____ kidney stones

16. _____ gall stones

17. _____ peptic ulcer

18. _____ abdominal trauma

19. _____ ruptured ectopic pregnancy

j. liver inflammation

k. inflamed appendix

l. gall bladder disease

m. inflamed pancreas

n. inflamed intestinal pouch

o. inflammation of the intestine

What do the following abbreviations mean?

20. RUQ _____

21. LUQ _____

22. RLQ _____

23. LLQ _____

24. NPO _____

25. MAST _____

26. List the equipment and supplies you will need to assist with gastric tube placement.

   A. _____
   B. _____
   C. _____
   D. _____
   E. _____
   F. _____
   G. _____

27. Prepare the following pre-op check list for this patient going to the operating room.

   Henry Miller is a 42-year-old teacher. He is allergic to Penicillin and wears contact lenses. He last ate at 8:00 am when he had toast, jelly, and coffee. He is scheduled for a cholecystectomy. His blood pressure is 140/82, his pulse is 88, his respiration is 16, and his temperature is 100.2° F.

PRE-SURGICAL CHECKLIST

	YES	NO	OR
Surgery Consent Signed			
Correct Surgical Site & Side Identified			
Sterilization Consent Signed			
Surgical Procedure Scheduled			
Safety Strap In Place On Gurney			
Special Equipment (oxygen, monitor)			
History & Physical On Chart			

	Date Done	YES	NO	OR
EKG				
Chest X-Ray				
CBC Within 72 Hours				
Type X-Match Units				
Urinalysis Within 72 Hours				
Allergies				

Surgical Prep   (State if None)

Prosthesis   Removed   None

Dentures   Partial   Bridge   Caps

Artificial Limbs ❏ Yes ❏ No   Artificial Eyes ❏ Yes ❏ No

Contacts   Glasses   Hearing Aid

NURSING	YES	NO	OR
Pre-Op Bath or Shower			
Voided Time			
Retention Catheter in Place			
Hair Pieces/Pins/Combs Removed			
Jewelry and/or Valuables:			
Other:			
Disposition of:			

T _____ P _____ R _____ BP _____
Name Plate ❏ Yes ❏ No
Location of Family _____
Identaband No. _____
Pre-Op Medication & Time:
_____
_____

Unit Nurse Signature _____
Date _____
OR Nurses Signature _____
Date _____
Special Note _____
_____
_____
_____

Stamp Name Here:

Patient Name Plate

11-26

Chapter Twelve
Emergencies of the Reproductive System

Objectives

After completing this chapter you should be able to do the following:

1. Define and correctly spell all key terms.
2. Assist with a pelvic examination.
3. Obtain specimens for culture.
4. Care for a victim of sexual assault.
5. Assist with an emergency childbirth.
6. Care for a newborn.

Key Terms

- abortion
- Apgar score
- crowning
- fallopian tube
- gonorrhea
- hemorrhage
- herpes
- incubator
- Isolette
- lithotomy position
- neonatal
- perineum
- peripad
- pelvic inflammatory disease (PID)
- placenta
- STD
- syphilis
- torsion

The Patient's Right to Privacy

Patient confidentiality is essential in all aspects of emergency care, but when dealing with emergencies involving the reproductive system, the patient's privacy must be protected. If the admitting area is located in the main lobby it may be advantageous to direct the patient to a private area prior to obtaining the history. Questions that must be asked in reproductive emergencies often are sensitive in nature and are best dealt with in an examination room away from the public. Furthermore, when a patient is examined by the physician, it is important for you to remain in the examination room. This reassures the patient and provides legal protection for the physician. If a female patient requests a female physician and/or assistant to care for her, the patient's request should be granted if at all possible.

Disorders of the Female Reproduction System

The chief complaint will be that of pain, vaginal discharge, or a history of vaginal bleeding. Ask the following questions when obtaining a patient history.

1. When did the symptoms begin?

2. Can you describe the type of bleeding?

3. Can you describe the amount of bleeding?

4. Does the blood clot?

5. Can you describe the color, consistency, and amount of vaginal discharge?

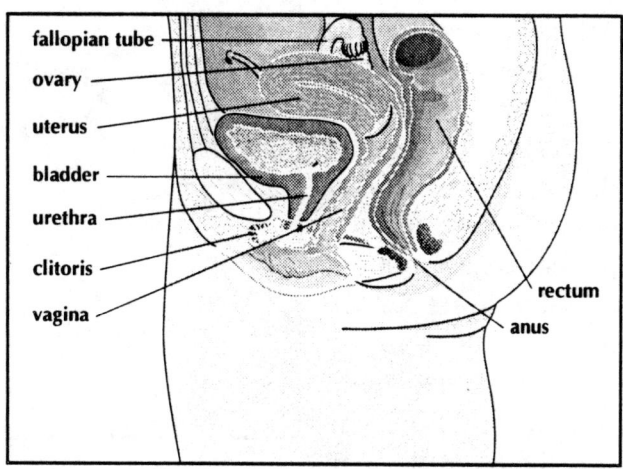

6. When was your last menstrual period?

7. Where does it hurt?

8. Is the problem a result of a traumatic injury? If so, what caused the injury?

9. Are there any special circumstances that relate to the problem?

Pelvic Examination

A pelvic examination must be done to diagnose and treat disorders of the female reproductive system. If possible, the patient should empty her bladder prior to a pelvic examination. If she is experiencing severe vaginal bleeding, do not allow her to get up to go to the bathroom because she might faint. Provide her with a bed pan instead. Since the patient must put on an examination gown for the examination, you should provide her with any assistance that is necessary in undressing and getting into the gown.

lithotomy position: a position in which the patient lies on the back with legs in stirrups; the position usually used for a pelvic exam

The exam table has **stirrups** so that the patient can assume the **lithotomy position**. (Figure12-1) In this position, the patient lies on her back and places both legs up in the stirrups with her legs spread apart. Provide her with a **drape** sheet to cover herself before and after the exam. Because this position is both awkward and embarrassing for the patient, it is important to offer reassurance to the patient as you assist the doctor with this examination. The physician will need the following items:

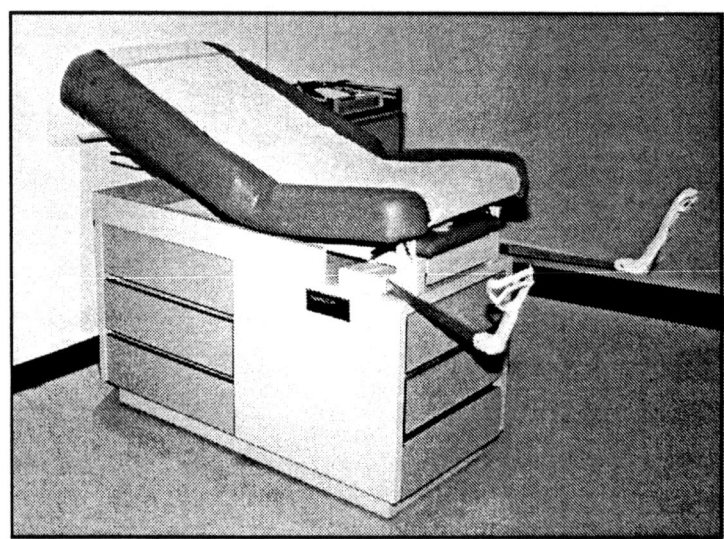

Figure12-1: Examination Table

- ✓ an exam light
- ✓ examination gloves
- ✓ a **vaginal speculum**
- ✓ lubricating jelly
- ✓ cotton applicators
- ✓ slides

perineum: the part of the body between the inner thighs from the anus in the rear to the vulva in the front of the female, and between the anus and scrotum in the male

To assist the physician, wash your hands and follow all universal blood and body fluid precautions, including wearing gloves. Explain the procedure to the patient and position her for examination. Position the exam light over the **perineum**, and assist the physician with gloving. Prepare the examination equipment. Open the package containing the vaginal speculum and provide the physician with lubricating jelly. The physician will do a visual inspection and then insert the vaginal speculum. Place the specimens in the proper container and label them with the patient's name, date, and room number. The physician will remove the speculum, and do a **bimanual pelvic exam**. This is done by placing one hand on the abdomen and one or two fingers in the **vagina**. With his or her hands in this position, the doctor can check the **uterus** for abnormalities. He or she also may perform a rectal exam at this time.

When the exam is completed the patient can be cleansed with tissue wipes or a wash cloth. If the patient is bleeding, a **peripad** should be secured in place. Pull the extension piece out of the end of the exam table, and remove the patient's legs from the stirrups, placing them on the end of the table.

peripad: an absorbent dressing to place on the perineum

The physician may order a urine specimen and other tests, such as x-rays or a pelvic **ultrasound**. For some ultrasound procedures it is necessary for the patient to drink 4 to 6 glasses of water. Check with the physician about which tests have been ordered. Many patients are to be given nothing by mouth (**NPO**), and others will be required to drink numerous glasses of water.

Vaginal Bleeding

Vaginal bleeding can be mild, or it can be severe enough to lead to shock. If the patient has a history of vaginal bleeding, the blood pressure, pulse, and respirations may be taken as often as every five minutes. If the patient is bleeding severely, the nurse will start an IV and preparations will be made for immediate surgery. The patient may experience vaginal bleeding, pass clots and tissue, have abdominal cramps, and exhibit signs and symptoms of shock. The bleeding may be associated with pregnancy. Any tissue that is passed must be saved, labeled *products of conception*, and sent to the laboratory. These patients are candidates for surgery. The physician will perform a pelvic exam and order other lab tests and x-rays. Sometimes bleeding is the result of **abortion** or **miscarriage**. A miscarriage, or spontaneous abortion, happens unexpectedly. When this happens the products of conception are expelled from the vagina and there can be considerable blood loss.

abortion: the ending of a pregnancy before the fetus is viable, before the twenty-fourth week; miscarriage

Excessive bleeding can occur after childbirth. Sometimes a patient is discharged from the hospital after delivering a baby and experiences a vaginal **hemorrhage** at home. This patient will need a pelvic exam by her doctor and may require immediate surgery to prevent further hemorrhaging. Vaginal bleeding can lead to shock; therefore you must continually check the vital signs of this patient. The skin is monitored for temperature, moisture, and color. Any changes in mental status, like confusion or diminished responsiveness must be reported to the nurse immediately.

hemorrhage: profuse bleeding that can lead to shock

Shock also can occur in a female from a **ruptured ectopic pregnancy**, in which the fertilized **ovum** is implanted in the **fallopian tube** rather than the uterus. As the pregnancy progresses and the fertilized ovum gets larger, it eventually causes the fallopian tube to rupture. The result is internal bleeding. The patient will have abdominal pain, vaginal bleeding, and signs and symptoms of shock. These patients are acutely ill and require surgery.

fallopian tube: the part of the female reproductive system through which the egg travels on the way to the uterus

STD: the abbreviation for sexually transmitted disease

Infections

A female with an infection of the reproductive system will complain of fever, pain, vaginal discharge, itching, and burning on urination. A pelvic examination is done and specimens are obtained for **culture**. Blood and urine tests also may be ordered. Sexually transmitted diseases (**STDs**), such as **hepatitis B**, **AIDS**, **herpes**, **syphilis**, **gonorrhea**, and **chlamydia** are treated with antibiotics. Severe **pelvic inflammatory disease** (**PID**) may require hospitalization and intravenous antibiotics.

herpes: a viral infection, a form of which can be a sexually transmitted disease

syphilis: a chronic, sexually transmitted disease characterized by lesions on an organ or on the skin; may be present without symptoms for years

Care of Sexual Assault Victims

Sexual assault is an emotionally and physically traumatic event. Documentation and preservation of the chain of evidence are extremely important in these cases. Unless they accompany the patient to the hospital, law enforcement officials must be notified by the charge nurse or ER physician. Sexual assault may result in a legal action. If so, the patient's chart will become part of the evidence. Sexual assault cases always should be referred to a registered nurse. The nurse and physician will complete a sexual assault form and obtain numerous specimens for laboratory analysis using a sexual assault kit or rape kit that contains all the appropriate forms and supplies for obtaining specimens. The entire experience is extremely frightening and humiliating to the patient. As an ER technician, you must approach the situation with compassion and empathy. These patients have a tremendous need for emotional support as well as referrals to community resources for follow-up care and counseling.

gonorrhea: a sexually transmitted disease characterized by a foul-smelling, thick, white discharge, burning on urination, and abdominal pain

pelvic inflammatory disease (PID): an infection that ascends from the vagina or cervix to the uterus

Emergency Childbirth

The hospital in which you work may have a complete labor, delivery, **postpartum**, and nursery facility, or it may not. A pregnant woman can walk into the hospital at any time, unaware of the **obstetrical** services that are available. Emergency care units must always be prepared to deal with an emergency childbirth. If the patient has been examined by the physician and there is time for her to be transferred to a more suitable facility, that would be in the patient's best interest. If delivery is imminent (rapidly approaching), then preparations are made to assist with the delivery in the ER. Sometimes the patient is not aware of the pregnancy. A teen age female may come to the ER with "stomach pain" and be nine months pregnant. Other women may be pregnant and unaware of it, or they may be in denial about their condition. Labor typically lasts for about 12 hours for a first pregnancy and about 8 hours for a second pregnancy, although some women have very short labor periods.

If it is necessary to deliver the baby in the Emergency Care Unit, **medical asepsis** must be ensured. The mother will deliver the baby and you will assist her. Look between the mother's legs for **crowning**. If crowning is occurring, delivery is imminent. Immediately notify both the doctor and the nurse, and prepare for the delivery. If you are alone, you will need to assist the mother with childbirth. Follow the procedure on the next page.

crowning: the presence of the baby's head in the birth canal, indicated by the bulging of the perineum; a signal that delivery is imminent

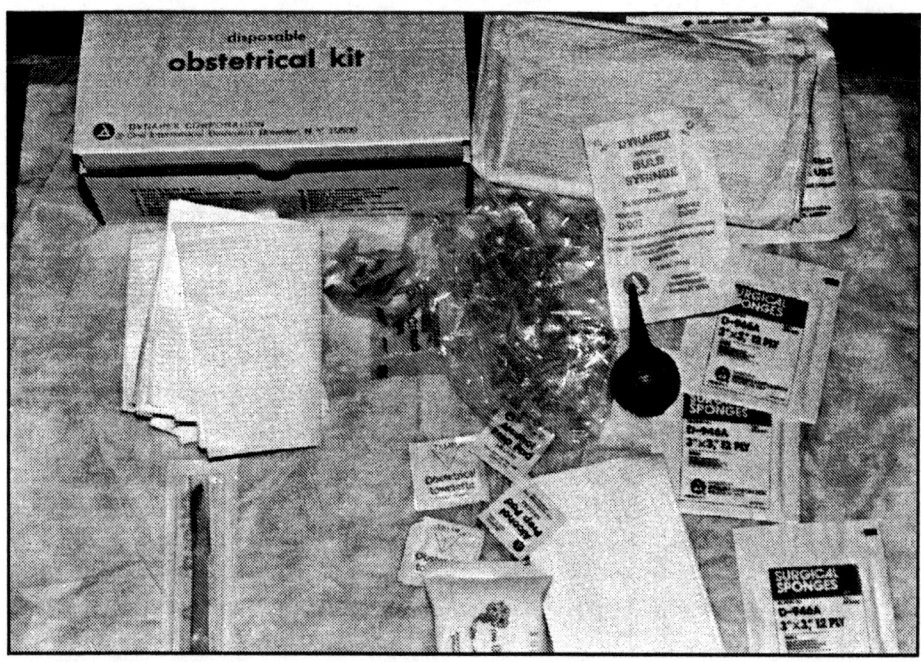

Figure 12-2: An OB kit

Assisting With an Emergency Childbirth

Materials needed:
- ✓ gloves
- ✓ OB kit
- ✓ bulb syringe
- ✓ incubator or isolette

Apgar score: a test used to measure the health of a newborn based on appearance, pulse, grimace, airway, and reflex

incubator: a temperature-controlled isolated baby bed

Isolette: a trademark name for an incubator that is used in the care of premature infants and low-weight newborns

1. **Procedural Step:** Wash your hands.
   Reason: Universal precaution.

2. **Procedural Step:** Put on sterile gloves.
   Reason: Universal precaution.

3. **Procedural Step:** Call for the **OB kit** and **incubator** or **Isolette**.
   Reason: The OB kit contains the supplies necessary to deliver the baby.

4. **Procedural Step:** Place sterile or clean sheets around the mother, and prepare to **suction** the infant's nose and mouth with a **bulb syringe**.
   Reason: The airway will be blocked with mucus.

5. **Procedural Step:** Create space for the infant on the bed.
   Reason: You will need a place to put the baby.

6. **Procedural Step:** After the infant has been delivered, check the baby's airway, suction the infant's nose and mouth, and keep the infant warm.
   Reason: To keep the airway clear and to regulate the baby's temperature.

7. **Procedural Step:** Evaluate the infant using the **Apgar Score**.
   Reason: This is a test for newborns that uses numbers to evaluate important functions. A ten is a perfect score, seven to nine is mild distress, four to six is moderate distress, and zero to three is acute distress in the infant that requires immediate resuscitation.

8. **Procedural Step:** Perform the Apgar test as soon as the baby is born, and repeat the test five minutes after birth.
   Reason: To assess the status of the infant to determine if additional medical care is needed.

9. **Procedural Step:** Check the umbilical cord for pulsations.
   Reason: If the cord is still pulsating, it is still the source of the infant's blood supply. Thus, the baby can start to hemorrhage if the cord is cut too soon.

10. **Procedural Step:** When pulsations stop, clamp the cord in two places with sterile clamps and cut the cord between the clamps with sterile scissors.
    Reason: To prevent hemorrhaging and infection.

Chapter Twelve • Emergencies of the Reproductive System

Assisting With an Emergency Childbirth (Cont.)

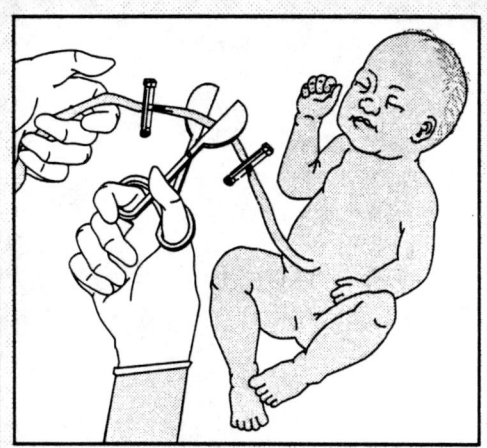

11. **Procedural Step:** Dry the infant immediately and wrap the baby in a blanket.
    Reason: To keep the baby warm.

12. **Procedural Step:** If the baby is in stable condition, place him or her on the mother's abdomen.
    Reason: Skin-to-skin contact provides additional heat for the baby. It also provides an opportunity for mother/infant bonding.

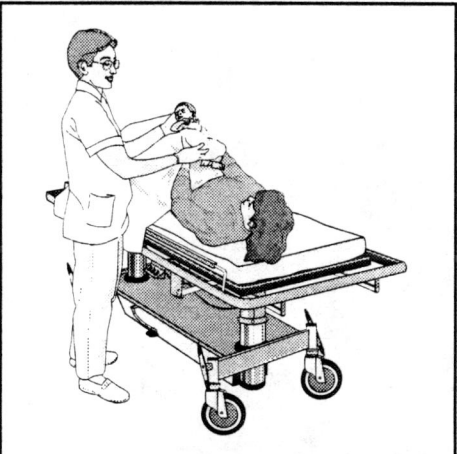

13. **Procedural Step:** Visually inspect the mother for external bleeding.
    Reason: To recognize and treat excessive vaginal bleeding.

14. **Procedural Step:** After about 20 minutes, the **placenta** should be delivered. If bleeding is severe after the placenta is delivered, massage the abdomen.
    Reason: Massaging causes the blood vessels in the uterus to constrict, which stops the hemorrhaging.

15. **Procedural Step:** Note the time of delivery on the mother's chart.
    Reason: To provide documentation.

16. **Procedural Step:** Check the baby's airway and temperature frequently. Babies must be kept warm at all times.
    Reason: To regulate the body temperature and maintain vital signs.

17. **Procedural Step:** Check the mother frequently for bleeding and signs of shock.
    Reason: Hemorrhaging sometimes occurs after the infant is delivered.

18. **Procedural Step:** The infant will receive an identification band, and a new chart will be started on the baby.
    Reason: The baby is a new patient.

19. **Procedural Step:** As soon as the delivery is completed, the patients will either be admitted to the hospital or transferred to a specialty center such as a **neonatal** intensive care unit.
    Reason: Neonatal intensive care units are areas in the hospital that are equipped and staffed to care for critical infants.

placenta: a structure in the uterus from which a fetus obtains its nourishment

neonatal: a term used to describe an infant from the moment of birth to one month in age

Assisting With an Emergency Childbirth (Cont.)

20. **Procedural Step:** Remove all soiled and contaminated equipment.
    Reason: To clean the room for the next patient.

21. **Procedural Step:** Remove your gloves.
    Reason: Universal precaution.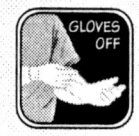

22. **Procedural Step:** Wash your hands.
    Reason: Universal precaution.

23. **Procedural Step:** Restock all equipment and supplies.
    Reason: The room must be ready for the next patient.

24. **Procedural Step:** Document the procedure as appropriate.
    Reason: To provide documentation.

Apgar Score

Sign	0	1	2
Skin Color	Blue/pale	Blue hands and feet	Pink all over
Pulse	None	Below 100	Above 100
Respiratory effort	Absent	Slow, irregular	Good, crying
Reflex irritability	No response	Grimace	Coughing, sneezing, or vigorous crying
Muscle tone	Limp	Some movement of extremities	Active motion

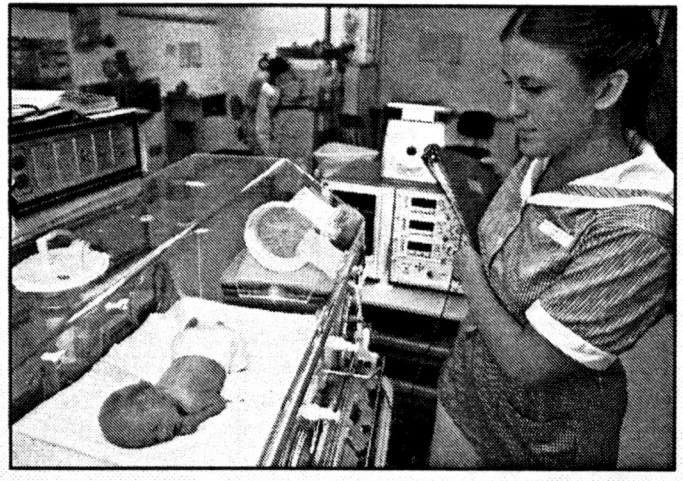

Emergencies of the Male Reproductive System

A male with a disorder of the reproductive system may enter the ER complaining of painful urination, penile discharge, **hematuria** (blood in the urine), and pain in the groin area. Venereal disease is the most common cause of penile discharge. If there is discharge, a culture or smear is taken. A culture is obtained with a sterile cotton-tip applicator, and a smear is obtained using a sterile slide. Blood tests also may be ordered. These specimens are sent to the laboratory.

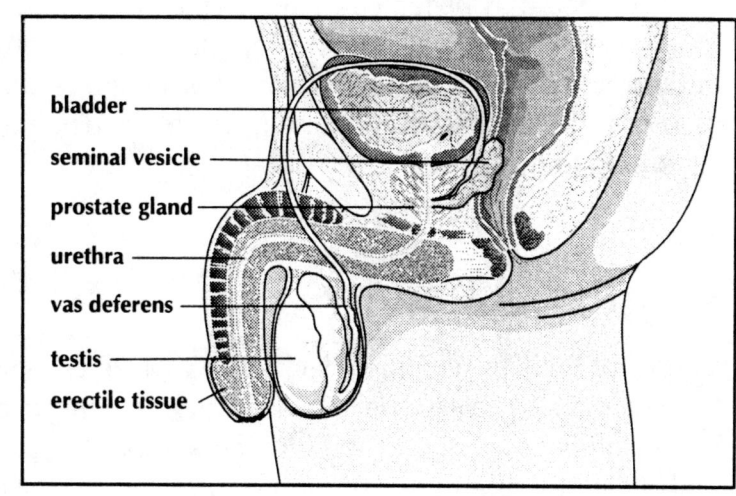

Traumatic injuries can occur to the external male **genitalia**. If this happens, bleeding must be controlled, the wounds must be cleansed, and sutures may be needed. Sometimes ice is applied to reduce swelling. To apply ice, fill a small plastic bag or glove with crushed ice and place the bag on a wash cloth or disposable towel next to the swollen area.

Torsion of the testicle can occur from an injury, or it can happen spontaneously. When this happens, the spermatic cord is twisted and the blood supply to the testicle is stopped. This is a very painful injury and requires immediate surgery.

torsion: twisting

Another injury that sometimes affects male patients occurs when a zipper becomes entangled in the foreskin of the penis. This is a very embarrassing and painful injury. The doctor will administer a local anesthetic and the zipper will be untangled. If the zipper has created a laceration or abrasion, the wound is cleansed and a dressing is applied.

Foreign Bodies Affecting the Reproductive System

Foreign bodies can invade the male and female reproductive systems, damaging the tissue and structure of the urethra, rectum, or vagina. Some objects can be seen on x-ray, while others must be located through exploratory surgery. These objects may be removed in the Emergency Care Unit or in the operating room. Prepare these patients for examination by the physician by helping them undress and obtaining the necessary information. During the examination you can assist the physician by obtaining supplies and helping to position the patient according to the physician's request.

Chapter Summary

Caring for patients with disorders of the reproductive system is a challenge for the healthcare professional. The patient's right to **confidentiality** must be maintained at all times. Therefore, efforts should be taken to provide privacy and prevent embarrassment while obtaining the history and caring for the patient. Childbirth is a natural event, and in normal deliveries the healthcare worker assists the mother. However, emergency personnel are prepared with the proper supplies and equipment to deal with both the mother and the infant if an abnormal situation arises.

Chapter Twelve • Emergencies of the Reproductive System   12-13

Name _____
Date _____

Student Enrichment Activities

1. Describe the procedure for assisting the physician with a pelvic examination.
   _____
   _____
   _____
   _____
   _____
   _____

2. What are the five components of the APGAR score?
   A. _____
   B. _____
   C. _____
   D. _____
   E. _____

3. Baby Charles has just been born. His color is pink, and his heart rate is 80 beats a minute. His breathing is good, he is very active, and has a vigorous cry. What is the APGAR score for baby Charles? _____

4. What two things are the most important in caring for a newborn?
   A. _____
   B. _____

5. The term that describes the presence of the baby's head in the perineum and which indicates that delivery is imminent is _____.

6. Describe the procedure used to obtain a specimen for culture, and fill out the laboratory slip below. The patient's name is Jane Doe. This is a STAT vaginal culture for gram stain, wet mount, culture and sensitivity.

____

____

____

____

____

____

____

____

____

BACTERIOLOGY

☐ STAT ☐ ROUTINE ☐ AS SOON AS POSSIBLE | TIME TO BE DRAWN ☐ AM ☐ PM

TIME SPECIMEN COLLECTED	TIME TEST COMPLETED	ACCESS#

DATE	R.N.	TECHNOLOGIST	DATE/TIME

ADDRESSOGRAPH

If Urine: Cath ☐ Clean Catch ☐ | SOURCE OF CULTURE: | DIAGNOSIS: ANTIBIOTIC THERAPY:

X	TEST
	Routine culture
	Anaerobic culture
	Strept. screen
	Fungus culture
	AFB culture
	AFB conc. stain
	AFB unconc. stain
	Gram stain
	Wet mount
	Blood culture
	Blood Culture Anaerobic

CULTURE REPORT

Culture: ______________________

☐ No growth in ______________ hours

☐ No growth in ______________ days/weeks

☐ Normal flora: light mod. heavy

☐ Colony count 1 ______________ col/ml

2 ______________ col/ml

☐ Less than 10,000 col/ml (insignificant)

☐ I.D. + sensitivity to follow

☐ Other: ______________________

GRAM STAIN	RARE	FEW	MOD.	MANY
WBC's				
Epith. cells				
Gram neg. bacilli				
Gram pos. bacilli				
Gram neg. cocci				
Gram pos. cocci				
RBC's				
No org. seen				
Other:				

ORGANISMS

Light	Mod.	Heavy	SENSITIVITY REPORT	Amikacin	Ampicillin	Carbenicillin	Cefamandole	Cefotaxime	Cefoxitin	Cephalothin	Chloramp	Clindamycin	Erythromycin	Gentamicin	Methicillin	Naladixic Acid	Nitrofurantoin	Penicillin	Pipercillin	Sulfisoxazole	Tetracycline	Tobramycin	Trimethoprim	Vancomycin
			1.																					
			2.																					
			3.																					
			4.																					

☐ Sensitivity S = sensitive R = resistant I = intermediate

REMARKS:

ANTIBIOTIC SENSITIVITIES

Chapter Thirteen • Wound Care 13-1

Chapter Thirteen
Wound Care

Objectives

After completing this chapter you should be able to do the following:

1. Define and correctly spell all key terms.
2. Identify five types of wounds.
3. Control bleeding.
4. Describe the treatment for a wound created by a foreign body.
5. Care for a patient with an animal bite.
6. Prepare a patient for suturing.
7. Assist the physician with wound care.
8. Remove sutures and staples.
9. Apply dressings and bandages to a wound.

Key Terms

- abrasion
- adaptic
- amputate
- avulsion
- blunt trauma
- butterfly bandage
- contusion
- hematoma
- hemophilia
- impaled
- incision
- laceration
- occlusive
- pressure point
- puncture
- rabies
- suture
- tourniquet
- vasoconstriction
- vasodilation
- venom
- xeroform

Types of Wounds

hematoma: a blood-filled swollen area; a *goose-egg* caused by bleeding under the tissues

contusion: a soft tissue injury caused by the seepage of blood into tissue; a bruise

vasodilation: widening of the blood vessels

Wounds are either *open* or *closed*. A closed wound does not break the skin. For example, a **hematoma** is a closed wound. There is usually considerable damage to the soft tissues surrounding the area, including the muscles, blood vessels, and skin. Bruising also may occur. The discoloration of the skin is caused by the ruptured capillaries bleeding into the tissues. A bruise is called a **contusion**. These injuries are quite common with sports-related activities; therefore, it is recommended that athletes wear protective gear to decrease the possibility of injury. To treat a contusion apply ice or cold compresses to constrict the blood vessels, and immobilize the affected area. If the possibility of a fracture does not exist, elevate the injured area by raising it above the level of the heart. This will reduce swelling and decrease the pain. If a fracture is suspected, the physician will order an x-ray of the affected area. Twenty-four hours following the injury, heat should be applied to the area. Heat causes **vasodilation** or the widening of the blood vessels, and will increase circulation to the injured area.

Chapter Thirteen • Wound Care

13-3

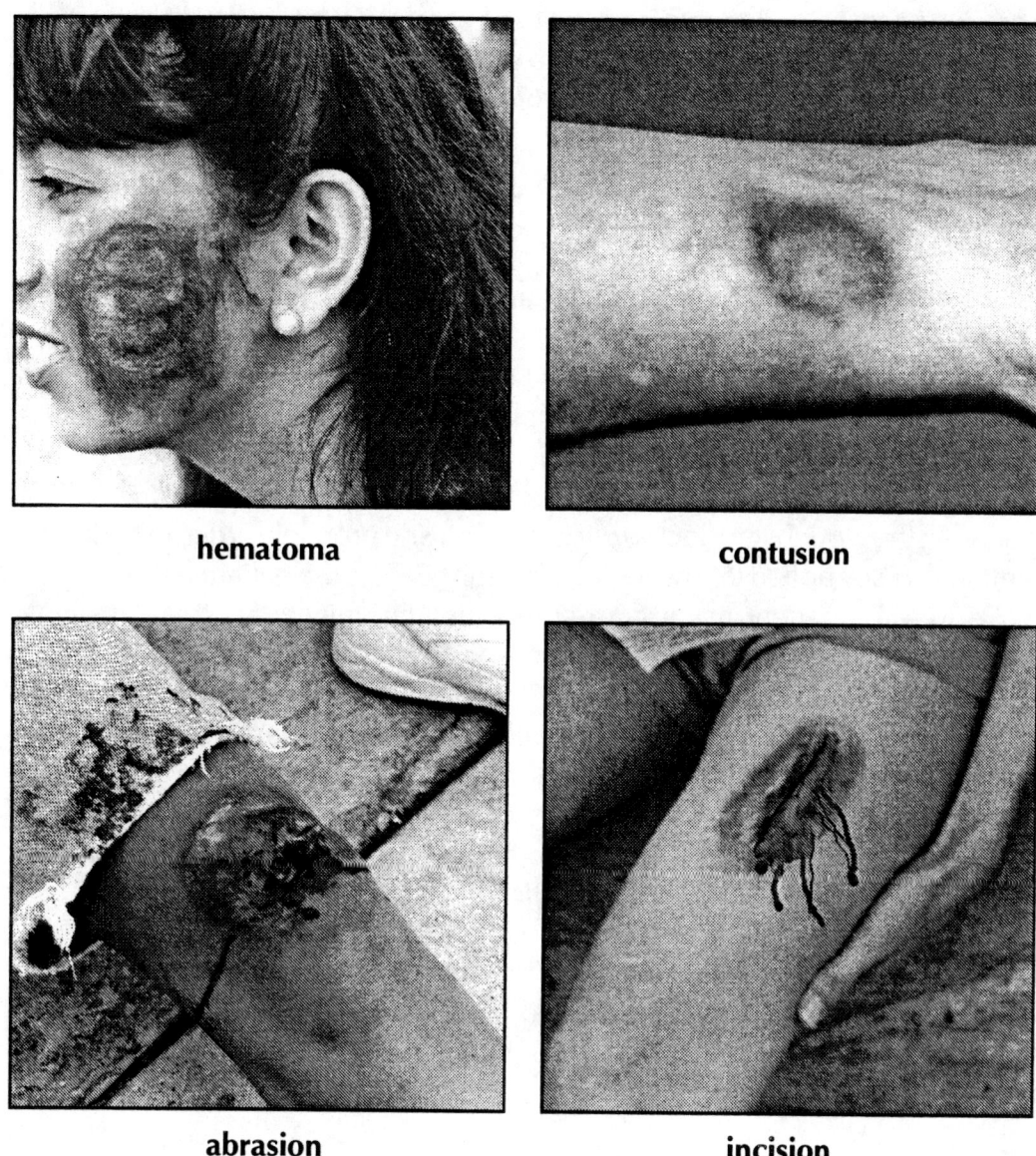

Figure 13-1: Types of Wounds

Open wounds involve a break in the skin or mucous membranes. All open wounds require at least first aid treatment. Even minor cuts and scrapes should be treated to prevent a serious infection. The goals for treating open wounds are to control bleeding and prevent infection. **Abrasions** (road burns) are caused by sliding or skidding on pavement, concrete, dirt, or sand. They result from running, skating, sports, and other activities that cause people to fall.

abrasion: an open wound, road burn, or rug burn in which the outer layer of skin has been scraped off

Abrasions can be quite large and are very painful. Bleeding usually is not a problem in treating these injuries as the wounds are not deep; but because the ground usually is dirty the possibility of infection is great with these injuries. Abrasions should be washed with soap and water. An **iodine** solution is a good solution to use if the person is not allergic to it. Find out which solution your facility prefers for the treatment of abrasions.

All wounds are soaked for ten minutes and cleansed. If the abrasion is painful or deep, or if the victim is a small child, the doctor may order some **anesthetic** jelly to be applied before cleansing it. Dirt may be ground into the wound, so a thorough cleansing is essential. Asphalt that is ground into the skin can cause a permanent tattooing of the skin if it is not removed. A surgical scrub brush or sterile tooth brush can be used to ensure a thorough cleansing. After cleansing the wound, the doctor will evaluate it and probably order an antibiotic ointment to be applied followed by a dressing. Before the patient is discharged, make sure the patient has a current tetanus immunization. If the patient's immunization has lapsed, alert the nurse or physician.

incision: a clean, straight, knife-like cut

Sharp, knife-like objects cause cuts called **incisions**. These wounds are the result of food preparation from kitchen knives, can openers, or broken glass, or they can be caused by razors, paper cuts, or a knife fight. These usually are clean cuts, but they can be very deep and other tissues may be involved. A deep incision can cut muscles, tendons, ligaments, veins, arteries, and nerves. These wounds are soaked if possible, cleansed, and the wound edges pulled together. A **butterfly bandage** or **Steri-Strips** can be used to pull the edges of the wound together, or the wound may require **sutures** (stitches).

butterfly bandage: a type of dressing used to pull the edges of the skin together

suture: a surgical stitch taken to close a wound

laceration: a jagged tear in the skin

Lacerations are wounds that are caused by a tearing motion, resulting in wound edges that are jagged. Like incisions, these wounds can be minor or very deep, and they can involve other tissues. Accidents from power tools will cause lacerations and deep tissue injuries. These serious wounds will have associated nerve, blood vessel, muscle, tendon, ligament, and bone damage and usually will be repaired in the operating room. Some of these wounds will require special attention from a **cosmetic surgeon**. All lacerations are cleansed thoroughly and surgically repaired. If the repair is done in the ER, the physician will need your help in setting up the suture tray and preparing the patient. Your assistance also may be required to help restrain a young patient or maintain a certain patient position while the wound is sutured.

Chapter Thirteen • Wound Care

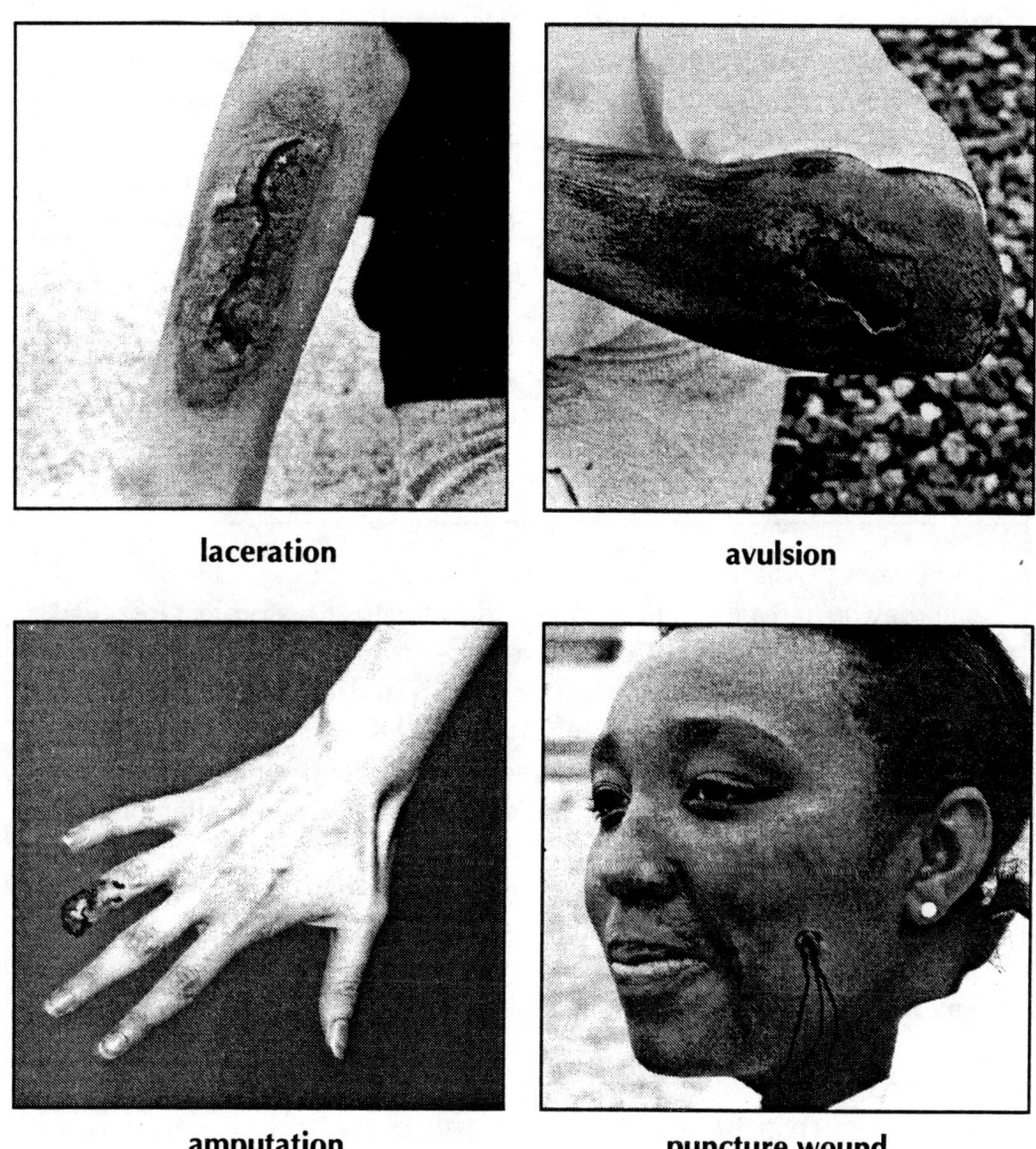

Figure 13-2: More Types of Wounds

An **avulsion** is a loss of tissue. If the tissue is still attached it is called a flap avulsion. These wounds are cleansed, and the flap is replaced and taped or sutured in place. If the tissue has been torn away, efforts are made to locate it, because some tissue can be replaced. The avulsed tissue should be placed in a gauze wrap that has been moistened with **normal saline** and sealed in a plastic bag to prevent destruction of the tissue. The bag should be placed on iced normal saline. The area of avulsion should be protected with a moist saline dressing, and bleeding must be controlled.

avulsion: a painful soft tissue injury in which a flap of tissue is torn loose or pulled off completely

amputate:
to remove a body part

puncture:
to pierce or penetrate

A body part that has been accidentally **amputated** is cared for in the same way as an avulsion. The stump is dressed with a moist dressing, and bleeding is controlled until the surgeon arrives to repair the wound. **Puncture** wounds are the result of penetrating objects and usually occur by stepping on a nail, metal, or glass, or they can result from an assault. Because these wounds are a potential source of infection (particularly **tetanus**), the immunization status of the victim must be determined.

All of these types of wounds are known as *soft tissue injuries*. Soft tissue injuries can involve the skin, muscles, tendons, ligaments, veins, or arteries. These injuries can occur alone or they may accompany a fracture or blunt trauma. Imagine the following scenario.

John Davis enjoys fixing odds and ends around the house. On this typical Saturday he had a list of things to do for his wife. One project involved removing the sliding glass door to replace some bent metal. As he was lifting out the glass door, John lost his balance and fell, breaking the glass. As the glass shattered, one of the arteries in his right arm was seriously cut. He also had glass in his eyes and face, and multiple cuts and scratches over his face, chest, arms, and legs. His wife attempted to control the bleeding by placing a dish towel over the arterial arm wound and applying pressure. She hurriedly guided him to the car and drove him to the ER. On the way to the hospital John passed out, became very pale, and continued to lose blood. As she drove the car into the emergency entrance she honked the horn.

You hear the honking of the horn and respond. Seeing the bleeding, unconscious patient, you immediately call for assistance to get John out of the car. You perform a primary survey and find that John is breathing and has a rapid, weak pulse. Taking the extra pair of gloves out of your pocket, you put them on and apply direct pressure to the arm wound by placing your hand over the towel. The nurse answers your call for help and, together, you lift John out of the car and bring him into the ER. The nurse obtains his blood pressure, administers oxygen, and starts an IV. You continue to hold direct pressure over the bleeding area. With your other hand, you locate the **brachial** artery and apply pressure while elevating the arm above the level of the patient's heart.

Chapter Thirteen • Wound Care

Controlling Bleeding

Since the body does not have an excess supply of blood, all bleeding must be controlled. Profuse bleeding, or a **hemorrhage**, is a serious life-threatening condition that can lead to **shock**. Bleeding can be either internal or external. Internal bleeding often is the result of **blunt trauma** or a catastrophic medical condition (i.e., ulcers, ectopic pregnancy).

blunt trauma: a mechanism of injury describing a sharp blow or driving force to a part of the body, usually resulting in internal injuries

External bleeding can occur from **capillaries**, **veins**, or **arteries**. Capillary bleeding is the most common type of external bleeding, and occurs with most injuries. Applying a sterile pad and ice will usually control the capillary bleeding found in minor cuts, scratches, and abrasions. If a vein is punctured or severed by a cutting instrument, the dark maroon blood will flow steadily. The amount of blood loss depends on the size of the vein.

To control venous bleeding, a sterile compress is placed over the wound and a gloved hand applies **direct pressure** to the site. It takes normal blood 4-6 minutes to **clot**, so pressure should be applied for at least 6 minutes. If a person has a bleeding condition such as **hemophilia** or takes blood thinning medication (i.e., Coumadin, heparin, or aspirin), the pressure will have to be continually applied until the patient is seen by the doctor. If the first compress becomes saturated with blood, apply another over the top of it and reinforce it. Arterial bleeding is caused by a punctured or severed artery. Arterial blood is bright red and pulsates (spurts) because it is under pressure. These are more serious injuries, and the bleeding must be controlled to prevent shock. Direct pressure is the best method for controlling arterial bleeding.

hemophilia: a condition in which the blood does not clot normally, resulting in excessive bleeding

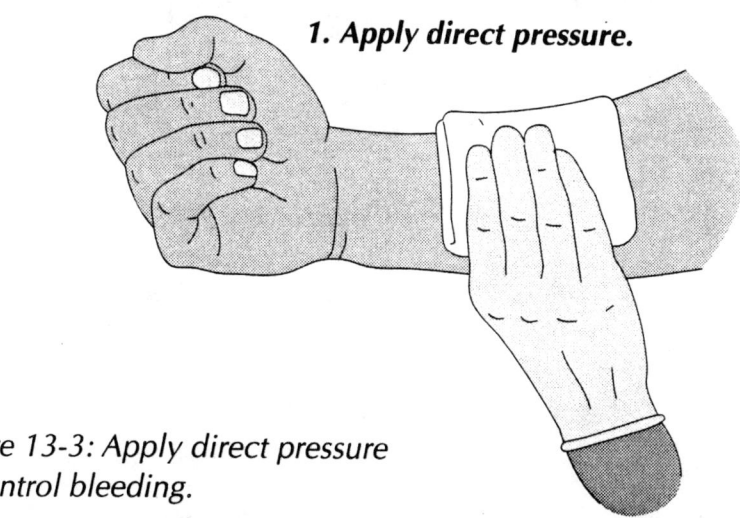

1. Apply direct pressure.

Figure 13-3: Apply direct pressure to control bleeding.

pressure point: a pulse point on the body, located above an injury, to which pressure can be applied to control bleeding

If direct pressure is not successful, the second method is to use indirect pressure, or **pressure points**. To apply indirect pressure, locate the pressure point directly above the injury and apply pressure to that artery until the pulsation in the artery stops, or the bleeding from the wound is controlled. Pressure points exist at the following arteries:

- the temporal artery, located in front of the ear
- the carotid artery, located to the side of the Adam's apple just below the jaw bone
- the subclavian artery, located deep in the hollow near the collarbone
- the brachial artery, located on the inner side of the upper arm, about 3 inches below the armpit
- the ulnar artery, located on the inside of the bend in the elbow
- the radial artery, located in the wrist
- the iliac artery, located in the groin
- the femoral artery, located in the groin between the crotch and the hip
- the popliteal artery, located behind the knee
- the dorsalis pedis artery, located on top of the foot at the bend in the ankle

2. Apply indirect pressure.

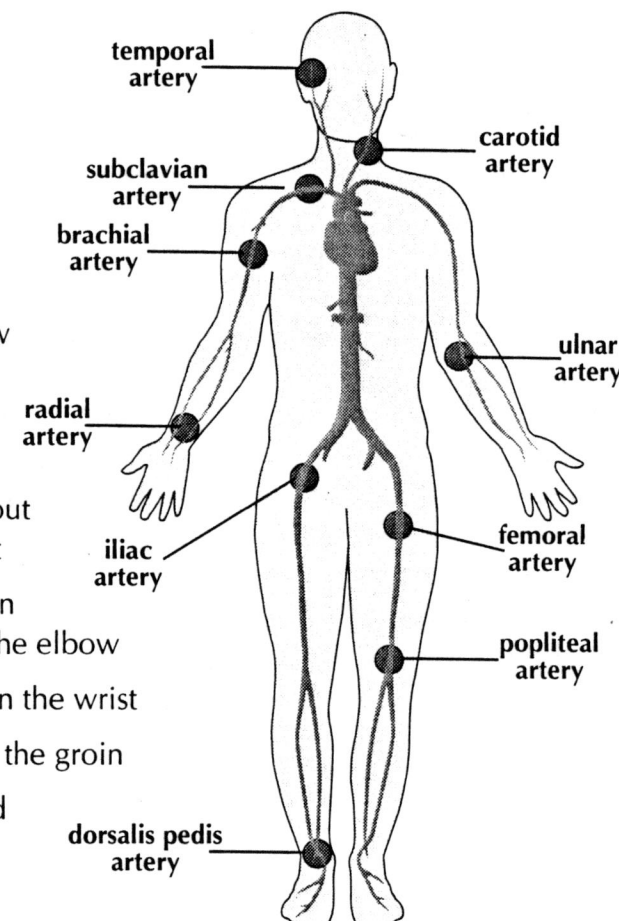

Figure 13-4: If bleeding cannot be controlled through direct pressure, apply indirect pressure.

Ice is the third method of controlling the flow of blood. The ice, because it is cold, causes **vasoconstriction** and slows the flow of blood.

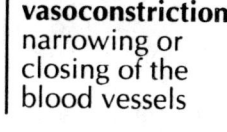

vasoconstriction: narrowing or closing of the blood vessels

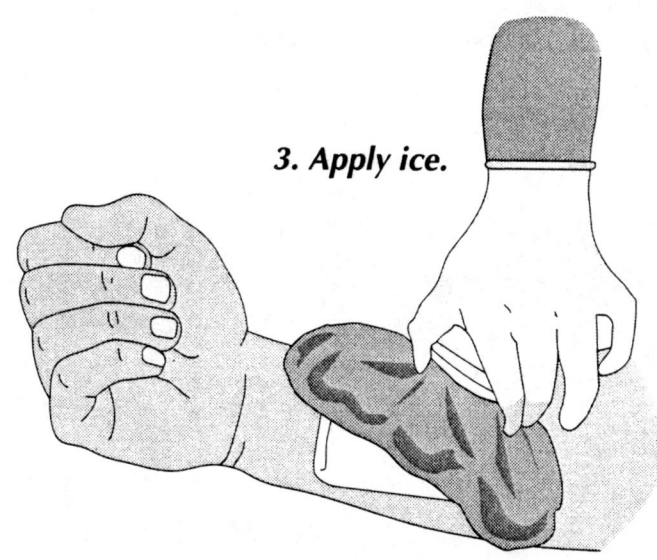

Figure 13-5: Ice can slow the loss of blood if direct and indirect pressure are unsuccessful at controlling the flow.

Elevating the injured part also can help control bleeding. However there are some circumstances in which the extremity should not be moved, such as with a fracture or spinal injury. Therefore, NOT ALL INJURIES WILL BE ELEVATED.

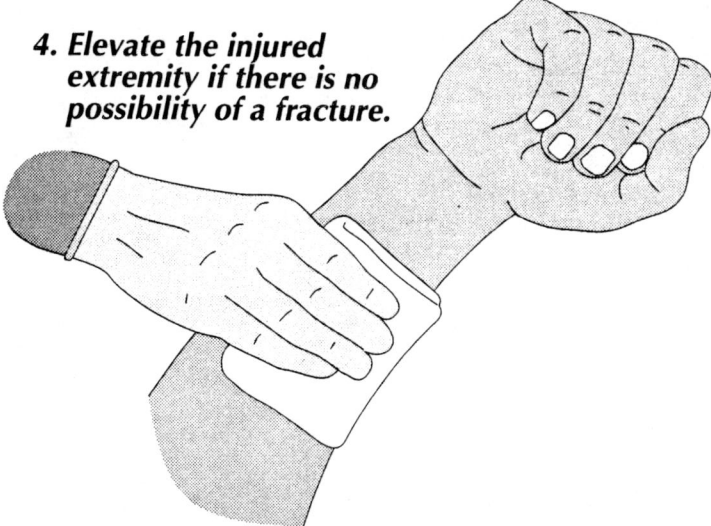

Figure 13-6: Elevating the injury can help control bleeding if there is no possibility of a fracture.

tourniquet:
a constricting band used to apply pressure to an artery above a wound on an extremity to control bleeding

A **tourniquet** is the last resort for controlling bleeding. A patient may arrive with a tourniquet in place. If so, do not take it off, but notify the doctor immediately. This patient must be seen by the physician. The doctor will decide whether to leave it on or remove it. It is essential to find out what time the tourniquet was first applied and how long it has been in place.

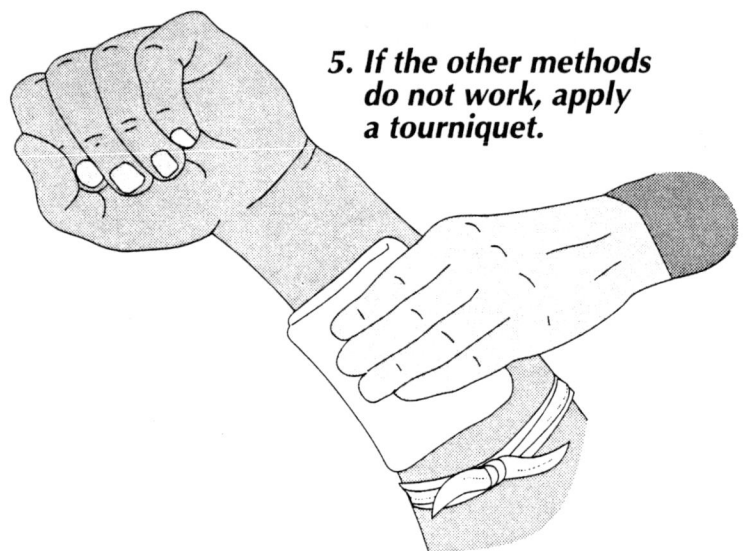

Figure 13-7: Apply a tourniquet only as a last resort.

To recap, the preferred methods for controlling bleeding are as follows:

1. direct pressure

2. indirect pressure

3. ice

4. elevation

5. a tourniquet

Foreign Bodies

Foreign bodies that are embedded in tissue are a challenge to the ER physician. A history of the location, the method of entry, and type of object are helpful items of information. If the person has stepped on a broken needle and feels the object in the foot, an x-ray will be ordered. Some objects, like wood, do not show up on x-ray as well as metal does. If the object lies close to the skin or protrudes, it may be easily removed with **forceps**. If the object is deep in the tissues the physician may have to do a surgical exploration. If the foreign body is recovered, it may be sent to pathology for examination or affixed to the chart with transparent tape as a permanent part of the medical record.

Wood splinters require special attention. Wooden splinter wounds should NOT be soaked, because the water will cause the wood to decompose. Some woods, like cedar and redwood, can cause serious tissue reactions and must be dealt with immediately. Special pointed splinter forceps are used to remove the object, and efforts are made to prevent squeezing and pressure to surrounding tissue. Splinters under the fingernail may require partial removal of the fingernail in order to remove the splinter.

Fish hooks also can become embedded in the skin. These are usually not very deep wounds. Because the hook has a barb on it and more damage would occur from backing out the hook, the doctor will push the barbed end through the skin, cut off the barb, and then remove the fish hook. The amount of blood loss is small in these wounds, but the danger of infection is great. These wounds must be cleansed thoroughly after the hook is removed.

People can become **impaled** by penetrating objects like arrows, darts, ice picks, screw drivers, and numerous other items. When someone is impaled, the object is still in the body and is partially sticking out. The immediate treatment is to stabilize the object in place, and then evaluate the patient for further injuries. To stabilize the object, tape it securely in place with very minimal movement. The patient may be taken to the operating room for removal of the object, but first it may be necessary to obtain x-rays with the object in place to evaluate the extent of damage. Be very careful and move the victim as little as possible. PROTRUDING OBJECTS ARE LEFT IN PLACE AND SHOULD NOT BE REMOVED UNTIL THE PATIENT IS EVALUATED BY THE PHYSICIAN.

impaled: penetrated or pierced by an object that remains in the body

Bites

Bites occur from insects, reptiles, animals, and even humans. They can result in puncture wounds, lacerations, or avulsions. The wound is cared for by controlling any bleeding and preventing infection through thorough cleansing. The wound is soaked in a cleansing solution and then scrubbed with an **antiseptic** solution. Since many types of bacteria live in **saliva**, human bites are serious wounds. Because of this, a human bite may be cultured prior to repair to check for the presence of infectious disease. Some wounds are left open to heal themselves, and some are sutured closed. Bites of the tongue may be deep, and can bleed profusely. To treat this type of wound, make sure the airway is clear, and control the bleeding. Animal bites must be thoroughly cleansed. The physician may decide to let these wounds heal on their own, or he or she may apply sutures.

rabies: a potentially fatal infection of the central nervous system caused by a bite from an infected animal

Animals can be infected with **rabies,** a potentially fatal disease of the nervous system. Therefore, if the bite is from a domestic animal, information about the animal's rabies immunization must be obtained. If the bite is from a wild animal, and the animal can be captured, it will be examined by an animal control officer. If the animal is unavailable, it will be assumed that the animal had rabies, and a rabies **prophylaxis** treatment will be given to the victim. These are injections which increase the patient's **immunity** to the disease and may prevent rabies from developing. Rabies is a very serious disease and almost always is fatal once symptoms develop.

Snakebites can be deadly if the bite is from a poisonous snake. Sometimes the snake is brought in with the patient to help with identification of the snake. The most common types of poisonous snakes in the United States are rattlesnakes, cottonmouths, water moccasins, copperheads, and coral snakes. If the victim has been **envenomated** (injected with **venom** from a poisonous snake) attention is given to the ABCs of emergency care. If the venom is in the person's circulation, a **systemic reaction** will occur and may result in respiratory arrest, cardiac arrest, or both.

venom: a poisonous or toxic substance from an insect or an animal

Chapter Thirteen • Wound Care

Watch for the signs and symptoms of shock, and prepare the patient for rapid treatment by the physician. The patient will require an IV, anti-venom and other medications, and admission to the intensive care unit. If the reaction is a local one, attention is paid to the site of the bite. You may be able to see two fang-type puncture marks and a great deal of swelling or **ecchymosis** (bruising). The area of the bite must be immobilized, and efforts must be made to calm the patient and **localize** the **toxins**. A constricting band may be applied close to the wound. This is done to prevent the venom from entering the circulation. With a constricting band in place, a **distal pulse** should be present. ICE IS NEVER APPLIED TO A SNAKEBITE WOUND. Ice causes **vasoconstriction** and slows down the healing process.

The symptoms of a snake bite are as follows:

- fang marks
- swelling
- **paresthesia** (numbness)
- ecchymosis
- pain

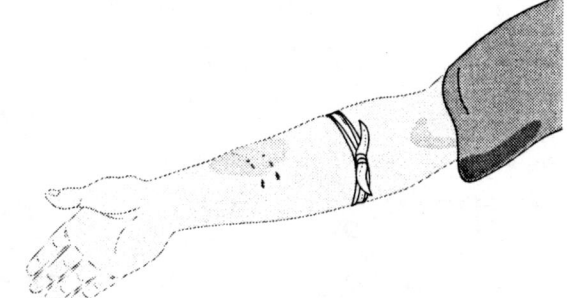

Spiders, scorpions, ticks, chiggers, wasps, bees, and ants are all insects known to bite or sting man. Some spiders, such as the brown recluse and black widow, are poisonous. Bites from these spiders can cause extreme tissue damage that may require skin grafting. Ticks can carry a number of infectious diseases and transmit the infection to man from a bite. Many people are allergic to bees and wasps. For those who are allergic, a sting from one of these insects can cause an immediate **anaphylactic**, reaction that requires resuscitation and IV medications. If the stinger is still attached, remove it with a scraping motion using a wooden tongue depressor. Do not squeeze or apply pressure to the area.

Bites produce all types of wounds. They must be cleansed thoroughly, and any bleeding must be controlled. Watch for signs of allergic reaction to the venom. The patient history is very important in the treatment of poisonous bites. The patient may have seen the snake or spider, or he or she may have awakened with a red, sore, itching, painful, and swollen area and not know what caused it. Bites from animals are reported to the animal control officer. Bites from humans, if they are acts of assault, should be reported to the police.

General Principles of Wound Care

Remember the following principles when treating any type of wound.

- ALWAYS WEAR GLOVES WHEN HANDLING WOUNDS.
- Control any bleeding.
- Prevent infection.
- Cleanse the wound.
- Immobilize the injured part.
- Apply ice (except for snakebite).
- Handle the wound gently.
- Prepare the wound for suturing.

Preparing a Wound for Suturing

A great deal of attention must be paid to the preparation of a wound for suturing. A clean wound will heal quickly; but a dirty wound will become infected and can cause multiple complications; therefore, the wound must be soaked and scrubbed. When sutures are required, the patient must be prepared both emotionally and physically for the process. Try to keep the equipment away from the patient's direct sight and avoid talking about needles, medications, and stitches. These subjects are upsetting to most people (especially children). You can inform the patient of what you are doing to obtain greater cooperation; but at the same time, try to direct the conversation to subjects that will decrease the anxiety level of the patient. It is always best to be honest and prepare the patient for anticipated outcomes.

You may need to remove some of the patient's clothing to gain access to the wound. If the cut is a result of an automobile accident, be careful of the glass fragments that may be in the patient's hair and clothes. Do not cause additional injuries by scraping the glass against the skin. Glass can be washed away with **irrigating saline**.

Chapter Thirteen • Wound Care

Before scrubbing the wound you can tell the patient, "This may hurt a little bit, but it's important to clean the wound thoroughly." The wound should be soaked for ten minutes if possible. Wounds on the extremities are easy to soak; but depending on their size and location, wounds elsewhere on the body can be difficult, if not impossible, to soak.

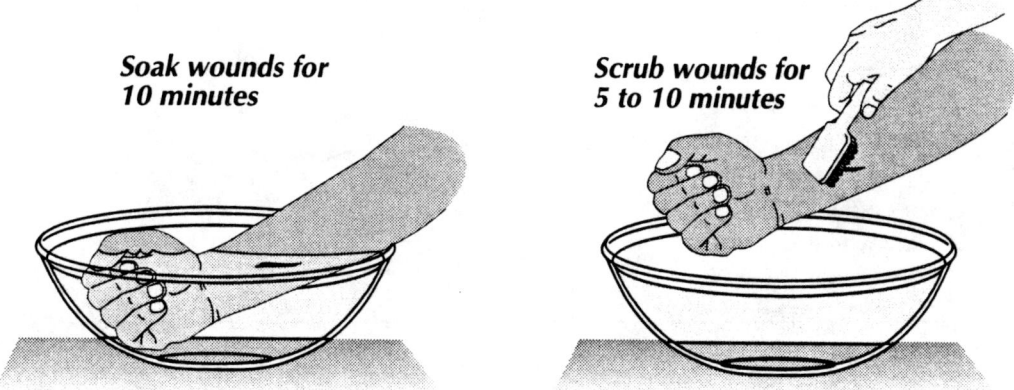

Figure 13-8: Wounds must be soaked and scrubbed before suturing.

Scrub all wounds to be sutured with a brush and shave the surrounding area. Shave as little hair as possible, but make sure it is enough to view the wound clearly. NEVER SHAVE EYEBROWS. Using **sterile technique**, scrub the wound for five to ten minutes. Start from directly over the wound, and scrub the area in a circle working away from the wound. Rinse with sterile water or **saline**. The doctor will **irrigate** (wash out) the wound with sterile saline again later. Dry the area with a dry, sterile towel and cover the wound with additional dry, sterile towels. Remove any wet towels from the surgical area, placing disposable towels in the trash and non-disposable towels in the linen hamper.

The doctor may anesthetize the wound before you scrub it to enable you to do a more thorough cleansing. Even if the wound is not anesthetized prior to cleansing, the physician almost certainly will want to do this prior to suturing. If so, he or she will inject the area around the wound with an **anesthetic** solution.

Preparation for Suturing

Materials needed:
- ✓ sterile gloves (size for physician)
- ✓ sterile gloves for yourself
- ✓ a suture set
- ✓ sterile towels
- ✓ a small sterile basin
- ✓ irrigating solution
- ✓ sutures (size requested by the doctor)
- ✓ a **Mayo stand**
- ✓ a stool for the physician
- ✓ an overhead light
- ✓ **Xylocaine** 1% or 2%

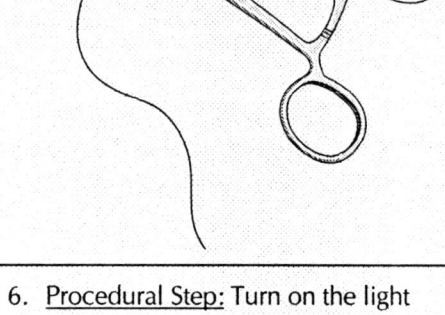

1. <u>Procedural Step:</u> Wash your hands.
   <u>Reason:</u> *Universal precaution*

2. <u>Procedural Step:</u> Identify the patient.
   <u>Reason:</u> *To ensure you are providing care to the correct patient.*

3. <u>Procedural Step:</u> Open the sterile suture set on the Mayo stand.
   <u>Reason:</u> *To prepare for suturing.*

4. <u>Procedural Step:</u> Open the pack of sterile gloves for physician.
   <u>Reason:</u> *To assist the physician.*

5. <u>Procedural Step:</u> Position the patient so that the physician can access the affected area.
   <u>Reason:</u> *To expose the wound for the physician.*

6. <u>Procedural Step:</u> Turn on the light and adjust it to light the area properly.
   <u>Reason:</u> *The physician must be able to clearly see the operative site.*

7. <u>Procedural Step:</u> The doctor will put on sterile gloves and drape the patient.
   <u>Reason:</u> *Suturing is a sterile procedure.*

8. <u>Procedural Step:</u> Assist the physician with necessary supplies.
   <u>Reason:</u> *The physician is wearing sterile gloves, and therefore, does not have access to the supply cupboard.*

9. <u>Procedural Step:</u> If you are assisting with the suturing, put on gloves.
   <u>Reason:</u> *Suturing is a sterile procedure.*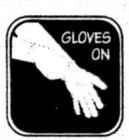

10. <u>Procedural Step:</u> Document the procedure as appropriate.
    <u>Reason:</u> *To provide documentation*

The patient is draped by placing sterile towels around the wound. The doctor will put a needle on a syringe and request the anesthetic solution. There are numerous anesthetic solutions available, but the one that is most commonly requested is Xylocaine. This solution will come in different strengths and it may have **epinephrine** added to it. Pick up the vial of medication and read the label aloud to be sure it is what the doctor requested (i.e., 1% Xylocaine, 2% Xylocaine, etc.). Remove the protective metal top, and wipe the rubber top with an alcohol wipe. Hold the vial upside down with the label visible to the physician. The doctor will insert the needle and syringe into the vial and aspirate the dose he or she desires. (To obtain the proper amount, the physician may request a different size needle.) The physician then will inject the medication into the patient's skin. You will need to talk to the patient and hold the area still.

If the patient is uncooperative, or if he or she is a small child, you will need to restrain the individual to prevent any unwanted movement while the physician injects the medication. Assist the physician by obtaining any extra supplies that are necessary, adjusting the light or height of the stool, or repositioning the patient. If you must touch near the wound area, put on sterile gloves.

There are many different kinds of **suture** available. They vary both in material and needle size. The needle size that will be requested depends on the location, depth, and length of the wound. Smaller needles are used for plastic surgery, and larger needles are used for abdominal surgery. Obtain the correct suture from the storage area and open the package by pulling down on the two top sides of the package. Drop the sterile suture onto the sterile field, being careful not to contaminate the contents by touching the inner wrapper as you do so. If the physician needs extra gauze or other supplies, they should be handled in the same way.

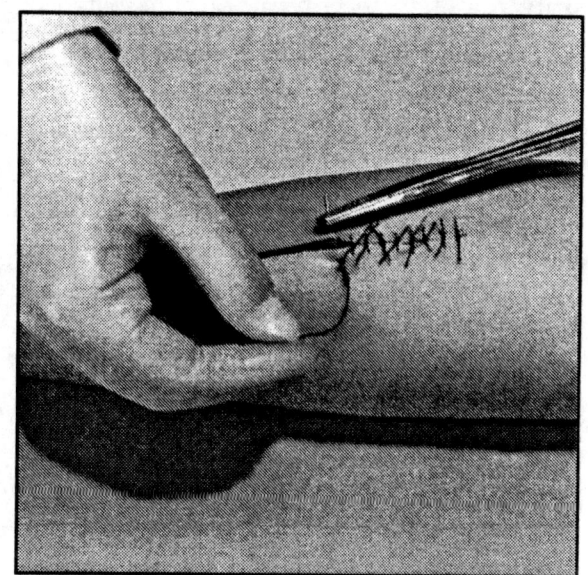

Figure 13-9: The physician will specify which type of suture will be needed.

suture: the material used for surgical stitches

If wounds have severe tissue damage, as in a dog bite, a skin graft may be needed. Some grafts, such as fingertip skin grafts, are done in the ER and some are done in the operating room. The skin to be grafted may be from a tissue bank, a donor, or from another area on the patient. If the patient is to have his own skin grafted, then a surgical scrub is done to the graft site prior to removal of the skin. The doctor may ask you to apply an antibiotic ointment to the wound. Using a cotton-tip applicator, place a small amount of ointment on the applicator and then directly on the suture line. Discard the applicator after touching the suture line. Use a new applicator each time you obtain ointment.

The doctor may wish to apply skin strips, steri-strips, or small tape to reinforce the incision line. If so, the edges of the skin must be prepared with Tincture of Benzoin, which will make the tape stick to the skin. Use a cotton-tip applicator to apply the benzoin to the skin edges, or it may already be packaged as a swab. Be careful not to put it directly on the incision line because it will burn. Steri-strips may be used on minor cuts instead of sutures.

Dressings and Bandages

After the wound has been sutured closed, the physician will order a dressing. Dressings and bandages prevent infection to open wounds, promote healing, and offer comfort to the patient. Use a great deal of care in putting on the dressing and bandage. The dressing must cover the wound and be constructed so that it will stay in place until the dressing is to be changed and the wound is evaluated. A great deal of creativity is allowed in designing a dressing that will fit the area of injury and accommodate the needs of the patient. Dressings applied to children must be foolproof and sturdy enough to stay in place throughout the day's activities. Dressings protect the wound, so padding is needed to cover tender areas. Some dressings apply pressure to help control bleeding. Stretchy roller bandages are designed to be used for pressure dressings such as these. Dressings must be absorbent enough to soak up blood and drainage. Design a dressing that covers the entire wound area and that is both comfortable and neat.

adaptic: a non-stick dressing material

Dressings are materials applied directly on the wound. Bandages are the material used to hold the dressing in place. There is usually drainage from the wound, so the first dressing that is applied should be of sterile, soft, non-stick material and be able to conform to the shape of the wound. Some examples of this type of dressing include Vaseline gauze, telfa, **adaptic**, and **xeroform** gauze.

xeroform: a non-stick, occlusive dressing material

occlusive: airtight

The second layer of dressing should be of absorbent material and large enough to cover the wound. Dressings should not be any bigger than necessary. This layer protects the wound and absorbs the drainage. Examples of material suitable for this layer of dressing include 4x4s, fluffs, ABD pads, 5x9s, tube gauze, sanitary pads, oval eye pads, **occlusive** plastic wrap or foil, and Band-Aids.

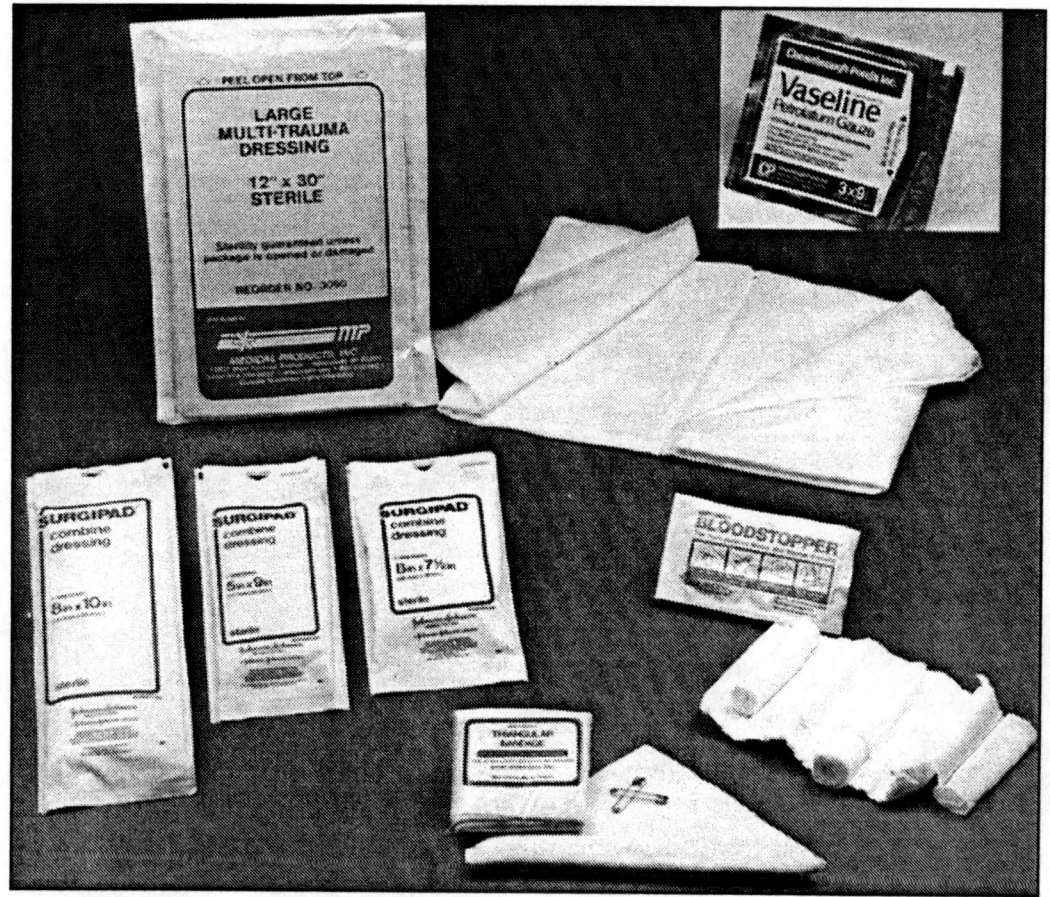

Figure 13-10: (Clockwise) Multi-Trauma Sterile Dressing, Vaseline Gauze, Bloodstopper, Triangular Bandage, Surgipad Combine Dressing

The outer layer is the bandage that holds the dressing in place. It should conform to the wound and be stretchable enough to allow for any swelling to occur. It should be snug enough to hold the dressing in place, but not so tight that it interferes with the circulation. Examples of appropriate bandages include roller gauze, Kerlix, Kling, rolled Stockinette, and Ace bandages.

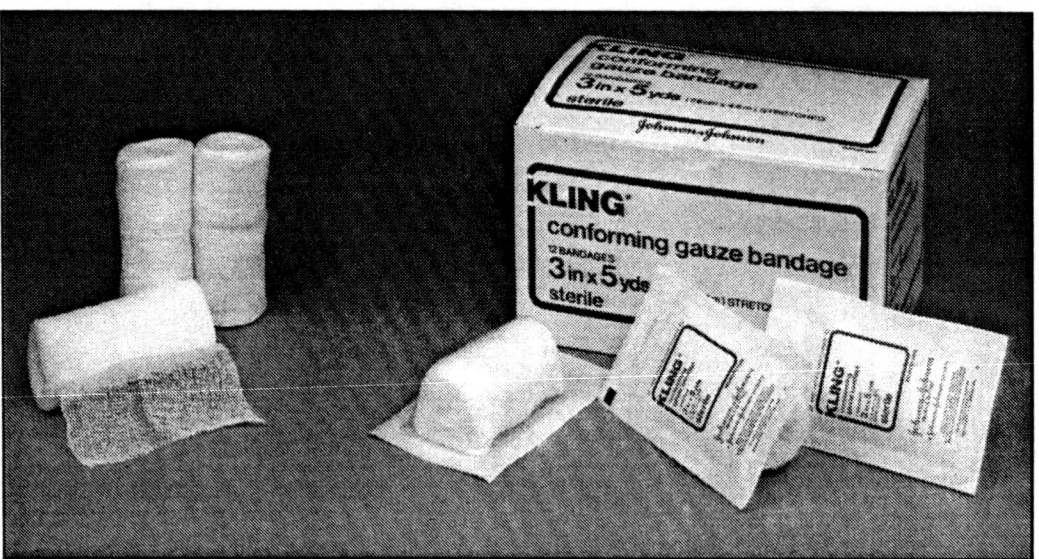

Figure 13-11: Kling® Conforming Gauze Bandages

The bandage is secured to the skin with tape. Choose a tape that is best suited for the patient's skin and the type of dressing you used. Tape can be adhesive, cloth, paper, or **hypoallergenic**. Paper tape is used on the face and other sensitive skin surfaces. It may be necessary to shave hairy skin before applying adhesive tape. Another way to secure the dressing in place is with a stretchy net dressing. This type of dressing, called stockinette, is especially suitable for head dressings, burns, and dressings for children.

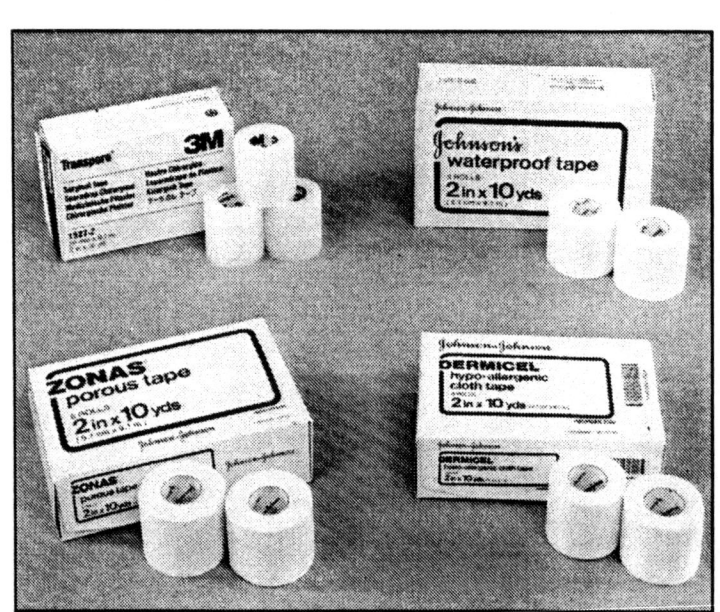

Figure 13-12: (Clockwise from left) Transpore™ Clear Hypoallergenic Tape, Waterproof Cloth Tape, Dermicel® Cloth Tape, Zonas® Cloth Tape

Chapter Thirteen • Wound Care

There are many different ways to apply a bandage and many different kinds of material from which to choose. Some doctors are very specific about how to dress a wound, but others will leave it up to you. Here are some guidelines to remember.

- Always remove rings, watches, or bracelets from the patient if you are dressing a hand or wrist. If the hand swells, these items can interfere with normal circulation. Put the ring on the other hand or give it to the patient or a family member. Be sure to document on the chart what you did with the patient's belongings.
- Try to leave the fingers and toes exposed so the circulation can be checked.
- Use sterile material.
- Control any bleeding.
- Open the dressing package using sterile technique, and touch only the corners, NOT the part that goes directly over the wound.
- Cover the entire wound.
- Apply the bandage snugly, but not too tight.
- The bandage should not be too loose or it may slip.
- Secure all loose ends with tape or tuck them inside the bandage.
- Put the bandage on in the position in which it is to remain. Do not try to bend a bandaged joint.
- Ask the patient how the dressing feels. If it is uncomfortable, rearrange it.

The following are types of bandages on patients.

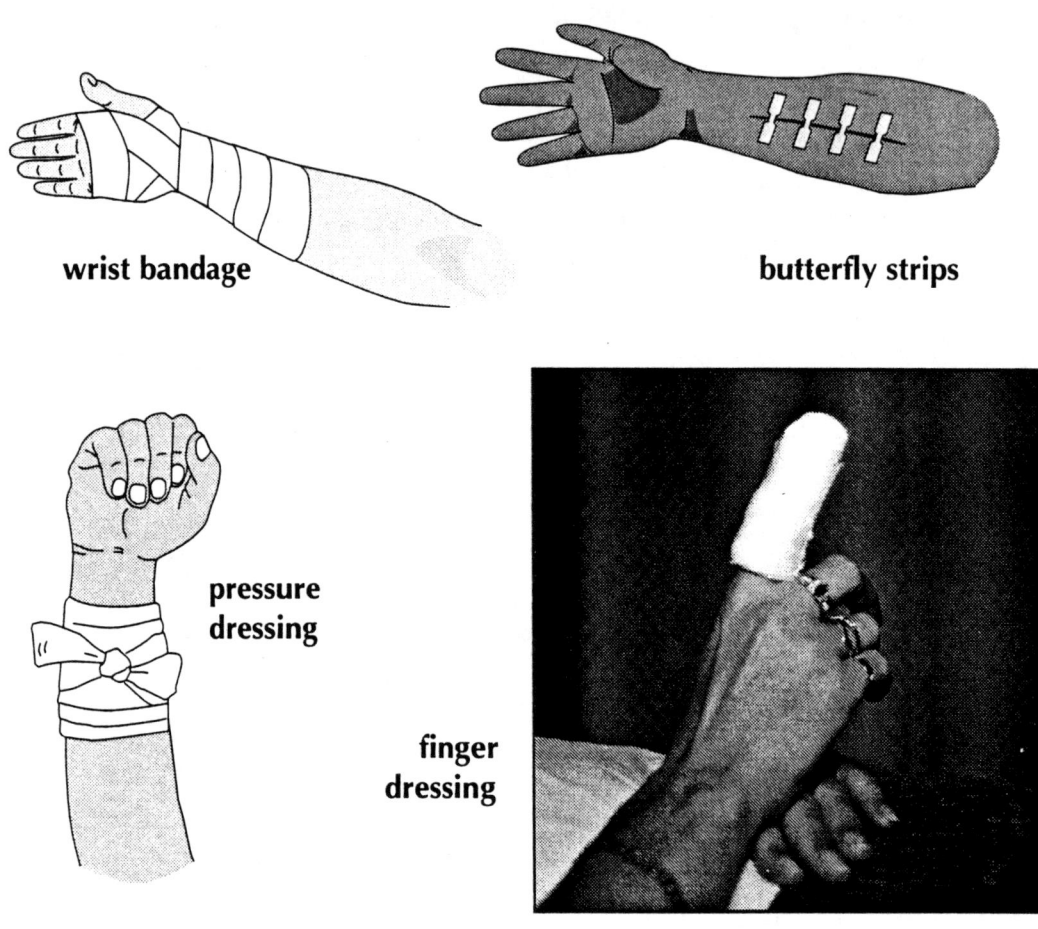

wrist bandage

butterfly strips

pressure dressing

finger dressing

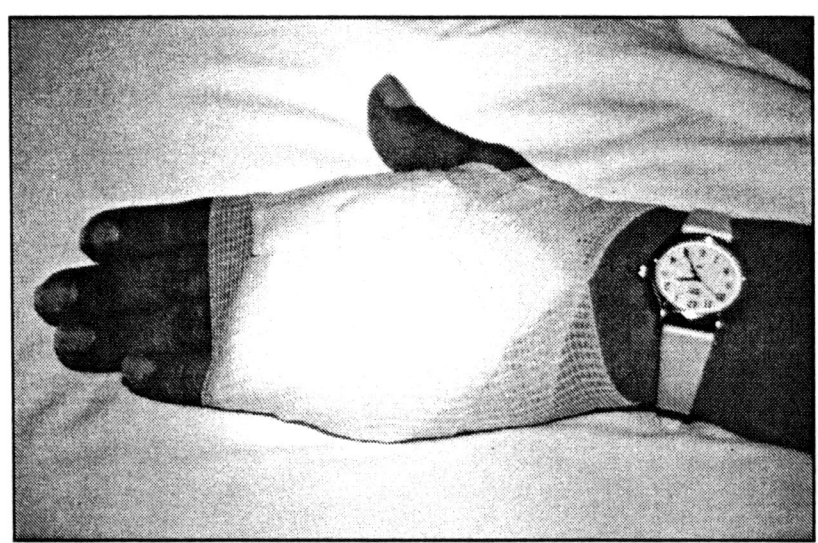

hand dressing

Chapter Thirteen • Wound Care

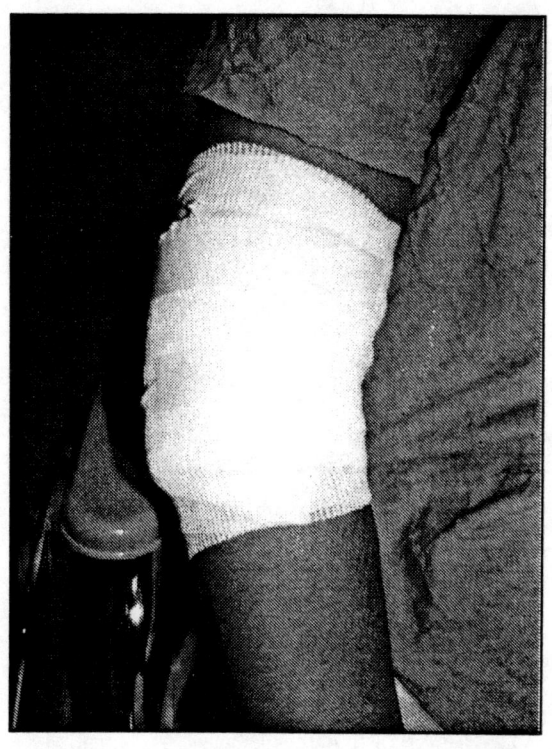

elbow dressing

shoulder and elbow dressing

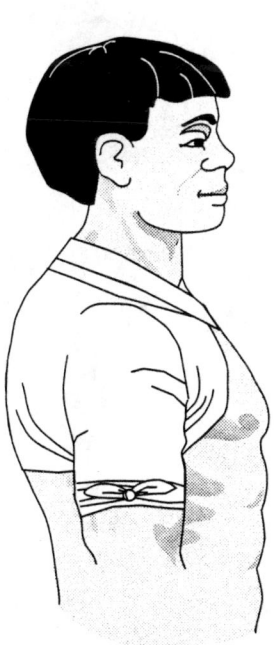

shoulder dressing

sling

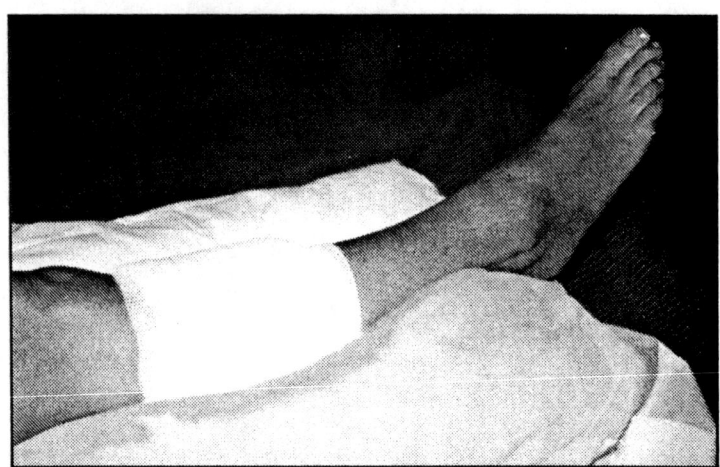
leg bandage

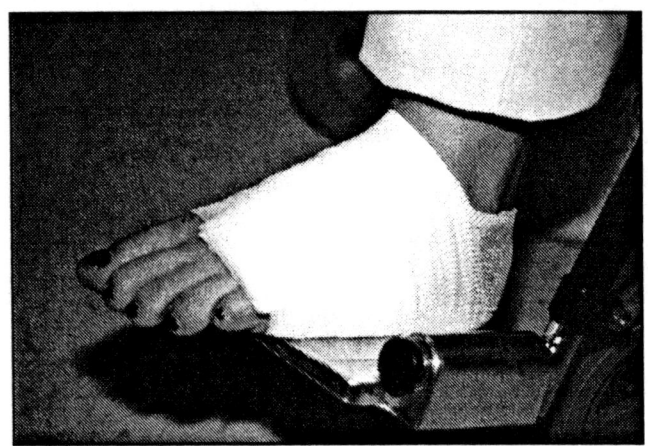

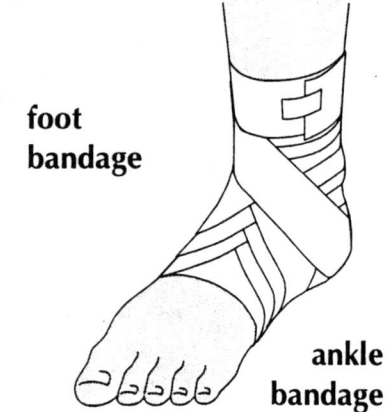
foot bandage

ankle bandage

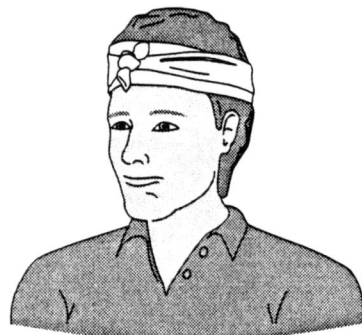
head dressing

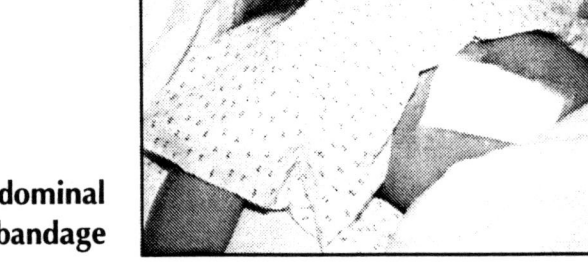
abdominal bandage

Chapter Thirteen • Wound Care

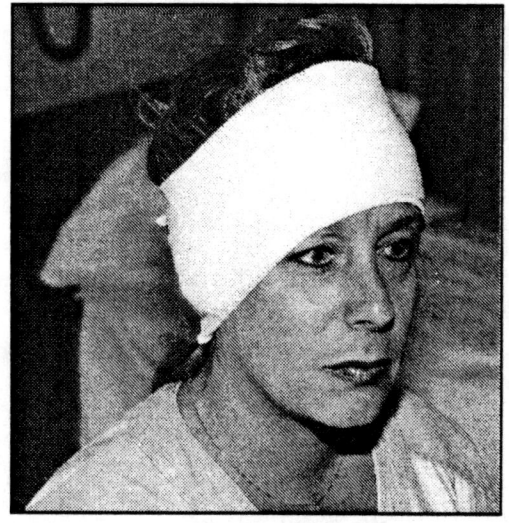
ear dressing

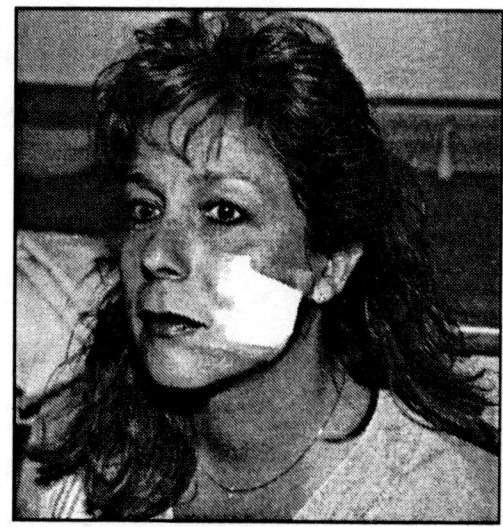
cheek dressing

eye dressings in different stages

1.
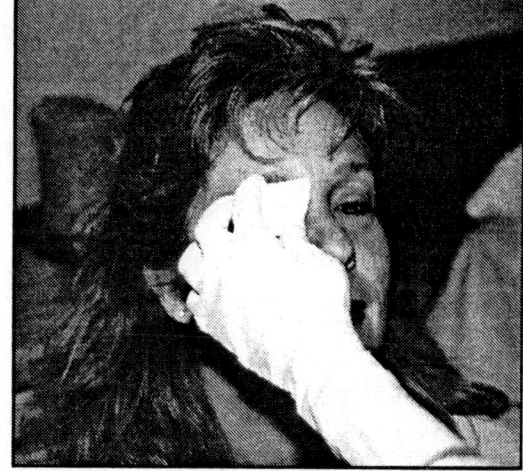

2.
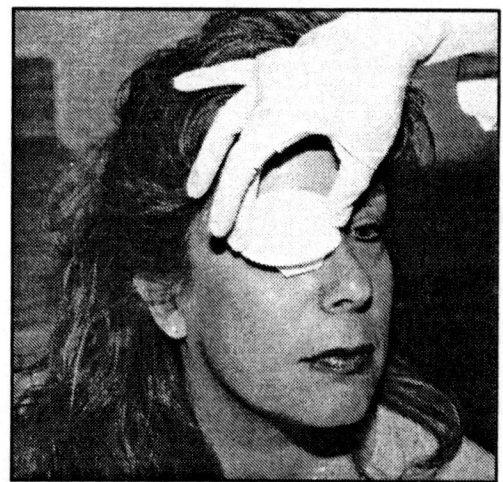

3.
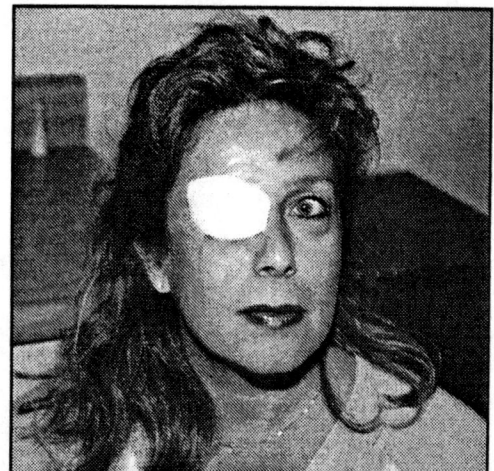

Patients are always given the following discharge instructions for wound care.

1. Keep the dressing clean and dry.

2. If the dressing soaks through, reinforce it with another gauze pad.

3. If it gets wet, remove the dressing and replace it or return to the doctor.

4. Watch the circulation in the injured extremity. Call the doctor if the extremity becomes numb, tingly, pale, blue, or cold.

5. Cleansing of the suture area can be done twice a day using a solution of hydrogen peroxide, followed by an antibiotic ointment.

6. Watch for the following signs of infection.

    - Redness
    - Swelling
    - Increased pain
    - A red streak up the arm or leg
    - Foul-smelling drainage
    - An elevation in temperature

7. Return for suture removal in 5-7 days. (If the injury is to the scalp or joint, it may be 10-14 days.)

Suture Removal

The patient will return to the hospital for suture removal. The doctor must inspect the wound and determine that the sutures are ready to be removed, but you may be asked to remove them. To do this, use the following procedure.

Suture Removal

Materials needed:
- ✓ a suture removal set (forceps and scissors)
- ✓ sterile gloves

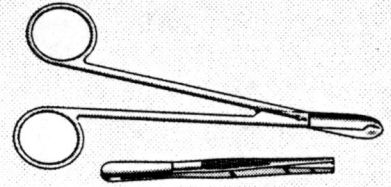

1. Procedural Step: Wash your hands.
   Reason: Universal precaution.

2. Procedural Step: Put on gloves.
   Reason: Universal precaution.

3. Procedural Step: Identify the patient.
   Reason: To ensure you are providing care to the correct patient.

4. Procedural Step: Explain the procedure to the patient using terms he or she can understand.
   Reason: To keep the patient calm and provide the information necessary for the patient to give informed consent.

5. Procedural Step: Remove the soiled dressing and discard it.
   Reason: The dressing is contaminated.

6. Procedural Step: Open the suture removal set.
   Reason: To prepare for the procedure.

7. Procedural Step: Pick up the forceps with your non-dominant hand.
   Reason: The other hand will be used to cut the suture.

8. Procedural Step: Grasp the knot of the suture with the forceps and lift it away from the skin.
   Reason: This gives you room to cut.

9. Procedural Step: Pick up the suture scissors with the dominant hand.
   Reason: You can cut better with your dominant hand.

10. Procedural Step: Place the curved tip of the scissors under the suture next to the knot.
    Reason: This is where you will cut the suture.

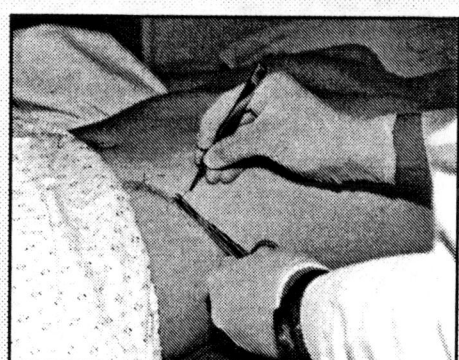

Suture Removal (Cont.)

11. **Procedural Step:** Cut the suture, and place the curved tip of the scissors next to the knot at the other end of the line of sutures.
    Reason: You need to cut both ends of the suture.

12. **Procedural Step:** Cut the suture, and with the forceps, pull the suture through the skin.
    Reason: This is how sutures are removed.

13. **Procedural Step:** Check to see that the entire suture is removed.
    Reason: You don't want to leave any suture in the patient's skin.

14. **Procedural Step:** Discard the suture.
    Reason: The suture is contaminated.

15. **Procedural Step:** Remove any remaining sutures.
    Reason: You don't want to leave any suture in the patient's skin.

16. **Procedural Step:** Inspect the incision line to make sure it is free of sutures and knots.
    Reason: Retained sutures can cause infection.

17. **Procedural Step:** Cleanse the wound site with antiseptic solution.
    Reason: To prevent infection.

18. **Procedural Step:** Reapply the dressing, skin tapes, or butterfly dressing if ordered.
    Reason: To keep the area clean and dry.

19. **Procedural Step:** Dispose of the equipment properly.
    Reason: The equipment is contaminated.

20. **Procedural Step:** Remove your gloves.
    Reason: Universal precaution.

21. **Procedural Step:** Wash your hands.
    Reason: Universal precaution.

22. **Procedural Step:** Document the procedure as appropriate.
    Reason: To provide documentation

Chapter Thirteen • Wound Care

Staple Removal

If patients return to the ER for post-operative staple removal, it will be your responsibility to remove the staples. After the doctor has viewed the wound, you will need to gather the necessary equipment and proceed as follows:

Staple Removal

Materials needed:
- ✓ staple remover
- ✓ clean gloves
- ✓ dressing

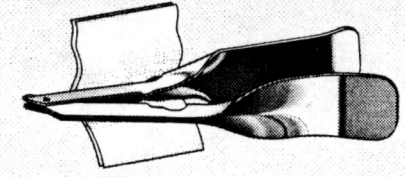

1. Procedural Step: Wash your hands.
   Reason: Universal precaution.

2. Procedural Step: Put on sterile gloves.
   Reason: Universal precaution.

3. Procedural Step: Identify the patient.
   Reason: To ensure you are providing care to the correct patient.

4. Procedural Step: Explain the procedure to the patient using terms he or she can understand.
   Reason: To keep the patient calm and provide the information necessary for the patient to give informed consent.

5. Procedural Step: Remove the soiled dressing and discard it.
   Reason: The dressing is contaminated.

6. Procedural Step: Place the lower tip of the staple remover under the staple.
   Reason: To prepare for staple removal.

7. Procedural Step: Press the handles together to depress the center of the staple.
   Reason: This allows the staple to be removed.

8. Procedural Step: Lift the staple remover upward to remove the staple.
   Reason: The staple should come out easily.

9. Procedural Step: Release the staple over the disposal area.
   Reason: To prepare for the next staple.

10. Procedural Step: Remove all staples.
    Reason: Staples left in the skin for a prolonged period can cause infection.

11. Procedural Step: Clean the incision area with antiseptic solution.
    Reason: To prevent infection.

Staple Removal (Cont.)

12. **Procedural Step:** Place a sterile dressing or butterfly over the wound.
    Reason: To keep it clean and dry.

13. **Procedural Step:** Dispose of sharps in the sharps container.
    Reason: To prevent injuries.

14. **Procedural Step:** Remove your gloves.
    Reason: The procedure is complete.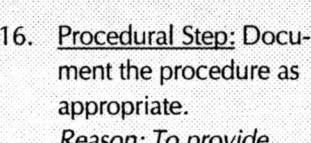

15. **Procedural Step:** Wash your hands.
    Reason: Universal precaution.

16. **Procedural Step:** Document the procedure as appropriate.
    Reason: To provide documentation

Chapter Summary

The control of bleeding is essential in wound management. The best methods to control bleeding are: direct pressure, indirect pressure, elevation, ice, and as a last resort, a tourniquet. Any type of open wound has the potential for developing an infection, but cleansing the wound will decrease this potential. Tetanus can be prevented by administering tetanus toxoid immunizations in patients whose tetanus immunizations are not current. Taking universal precautions is another means of preventing the spread of infections and communicable diseases. The precautions are used by all healthcare workers, and are effective measures in controlling disease. Sterile technique, used for wound closure, is another means of preventing infections. Follow-up wound care is necessary for inspection of the wound as well as for the removal of sutures and staples.

Chapter Thirteen • Wound Care 13-31

Name _____
Date _____

Student Enrichment Activities

1. Describe the following types of wounds.
   laceration: _____
   incision: _____
   avulsion: _____
   puncture: _____
   amputation: _____

2. List the methods of controlling bleeding in order of importance.
   A. _____   D. _____
   B. _____   E. _____
   C. _____

3. Describe how you would cleanse a four-inch laceration to the right lower leg obtained from a barbed wire fence.
   _____
   _____
   _____
   _____

4. Apply bandages and dressings on a fellow classmate for the following wounds. Have your instructor initial the appropriate place when you have done them correctly.

   Instructor's Initials
   A. fingertip avulsion   _____
   B. incision to wrist   _____
   C. large laceration to lower leg _____
   D. head wound   _____
   E. puncture to bottom of foot   _____

5. To whom do you report animal bites? _____

6. List the equipment needed to remove sutures.
   A. _____
   B. _____

7. How do you open a sterile package without contaminating it?
   _____

8. Describe the treatment for a foreign body.
   _____
   _____
   _____
   _____

9. List the supplies needed to assist with suturing.
   A. _____   G. _____
   B. _____   H. _____
   C. _____   I. _____
   D. _____   J. _____
   E. _____   K. _____
   F. _____

10. A 6-year-old boy has a 4-inch laceration to his left knee from a bicycle accident. Describe how you would prepare the wound for suturing and what type of dressing you would apply after the sutures are in place.
    _____
    _____
    _____
    _____

Chapter Fourteen
Traumatic Emergencies

Objectives

After completing this chapter you should be able to do the following:

1. Define and correctly spell all key terms.
2. Establish priorities of care in severely traumatized patients.
3. Recognize the signs and symptoms of shock.
4. Care for a comatose patient.
5. Care for a patient who has been admitted with an antishock suit in place.
6. Care for a patient with a head injury.
7. Care for a patient with a spinal cord injury.
8. Care for a patient with a chest injury.
9. Assist with the care of a multisystem trauma patient.

Key Terms

- aspiration
- bag-valve mask
- Glasgow Coma Scale
- golden hour
- hemorrhagic shock
- mastoid process
- multisystem
- neurostructures
- oxygenation
- palpate
- perfusion
- pleura vac
- pocket mask
- stylet
- rehabilitation
- traumatized

Injuries Resulting From Trauma

The word **trauma** refers to a physical injury caused by some type of external force. Traumatic injuries, therefore, refer to physical injuries. Traumatic injuries involve patients of all ages. An older person might fall and break a hip, a construction worker might injure himself with a power tool, a teenage driver might be involved in a traffic collision, or a small child might fall off of a swing set. All of these are examples of injuries that are treated in the Emergency Department.

Trauma can occur at any time and in any place. Traumatic injuries can be the result of an accident, or they might result from violence. A person can have a single traumatic injury, such as a broken arm, or he might sustain multisystem trauma from an accident involving a head injury, broken bones, and internal injuries.

Obviously, some traumatic injuries are more serious than others, but all must be treated as quickly as possible. Traumatic injuries can lead to additional complications, so whenever a trauma patient arrives in the Emergency Department, the emergency care team must work quickly to evaluate and treat the patient for life-threatening conditions.

Chapter Fourteen • Traumatic Emergencies

Imagine the following scenario:

You have just been notified by the emergency dispatcher that the paramedics are bringing in a severely **traumatized** patient with **multisystem** injuries. They are enroute to the hospital **code 3**. You know from your experience in the clinical area that a code 3 means the ambulance will arrive with lights and sirens. The victim, a 23-year-old motorcycle rider, is in critical condition. The report given to the nurse includes the following information.

- This patient was riding too fast on a motorcycle and lost control of the vehicle.
- He was wearing a motorcycle helmet.
- His estimated speed was 50 mph.
- He hit a stopped car and was thrown about 20 feet from the motorcycle.
- The patient is unconscious.
- His breathing is labored, and the respiratory rate is 8 per minute.
- The pulse rate is rapid and weak.
- The paramedics have not been able to hear a blood pressure, but have **palpated** one of about 90 mm/Hg (millimeters of mercury).
- There is a deformity over the middle of the left thigh.
- The abdomen is **rigid** (board-like).
- There are multiple abrasions and lacerations over the head, face, and chest and the bleeding has been controlled.

traumatized:
affected by trauma; suffering from a wound or injury

multisystem:
involving more than one body system

palpate:
to examine by feeling with the hands

This is a seriously injured, **multisystem** trauma victim who will require rapid assessment and emergency treatment. Depending on the emergency care that was rendered at the scene, many things will need to be done as soon as the victim arrives in the ER.

- An airway must be established and maintained.
- **Ventilation** must be assisted, and **oxygen** must be given.
- The pulse must be checked. If none is present, **CPR** must be started or continued.
- **Stabilization** of the cervical spine (rigid neck collar, log roll, backboard, head bed) must be maintained.
- Bleeding must be controlled.
- Vital signs must be measured.
- The level of consciousness and pupils must be checked.
- Movement, sensation, and response to pain must be checked.
- Obvious injuries must be affirmed.
- Preparations must be made for X-rays and lab work.
- Necessary **IVs**, **catheters**, **airways**, and tubes must be inserted.
- The victim must be placed on a cardiac monitor.
- Vital signs must be checked every 5 minutes. (More often if necessary.)
- The victim must be prepared for transport to the operating room.
- All life-threatening injuries must be treated.

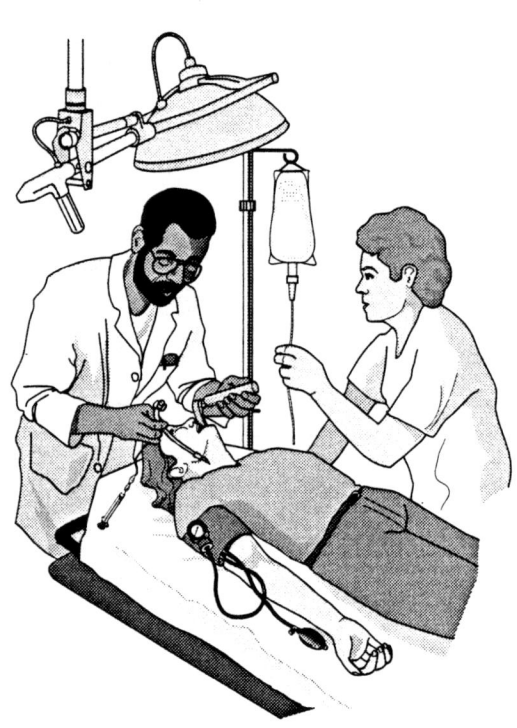

Trauma Centers

A trauma system has four primary components:

- access to care
- pre-hospital care
- hospital care
- **rehabilitation**

All of these components are necessary if the trauma victim is to survive the initial injury and return to society as a functioning person. Access to care is provided by the 911 system in most communities; but in order for it to be beneficial, it must be operational and the public must know how to use it. Pre-hospital care providers at the EMT and paramedic level, as well as air and ground transportation units, also are essential. Without them, many trauma victims would not make it to the hospital alive. Furthermore, the hospitals must be staffed with surgeons and physicians who are ready to provide emergency care. They also must have the equipment necessary to make a rapid assessment of the patient.

In trauma cases much is said about the **golden hour**. Each minute that elapses is critical; vital seconds can be saved by having things ready. The sooner the patient is evaluated and treated for **shock,** the greater the patient's chances of survival will be. The first sixty minutes after the accident count. To avoid wasting time, everything must be organized to meet the needs of the critically injured patient. If your hospital is a designated trauma center, a trauma surgeon always will be available to do immediate surgery. An **anesthesiologist** and an anesthesia team also will be on standby to begin lifesaving measures. If your hospital is not a trauma center and a trauma system exists in your community, this patient will be transported either by air or by ground to that facility. If there are no trauma centers in your community, critically ill patients will be transported to the nearest appropriate receiving center.

Once the patient is stabilized and treated, surgery will be performed, and then the patient's recovery will be monitored in the Intensive Care Unit. Rehabilitation, including physical therapy, also may be necessary. Sometimes rehabilitation is quite extensive.

---

rehabilitation: the restoration of a patient or a part of the body to normal or near normal following an illness or injury

golden hour: the sixty minutes that immediately follow an accident or injury in which lifesaving treatment must begin

Airways and Breathing

If the patient is not breathing, open the airway using the **jaw-thrust maneuver**. Assume that there is a neck injury in each trauma patient until the physician rules that out by performing a physical examination and looking at x-rays or a **CT scan**. Begin rescue breathing using a pocket mask.

pocket mask: a folding face mask for use in artificial ventilation that is designed to be carried in the pocket

The **pocket mask** has an air-filled cushion that fits snugly over the patient's nose and mouth. There are two ports: one for oxygen and one into which you, the rescuer, can blow into the bag-valve mask. The mask is held snugly on the victim's face by your thumbs. If you are unable to ventilate the patient, attempt to remove the obstruction by suctioning the patient and repositioning the airway. If you are unsuccessful in your attempts, try using the Heimlich maneuver. (See Chapter Eight.)

The **oropharyngeal airway** is a rigid tube that conforms to the mouth and **pharynx**. It is used to maintain the airway position, but only in an unconscious patient without a **gag reflex**. If you attempt to use this type of airway on a conscious patient, he or she will gag and spit it out. An oropharyngeal airway is intolerable to a conscious patient.

The **nasopharyngeal airway** is placed in the nostril and advanced to the pharynx. It is used to hold the tongue forward and maintain an open airway. This airway is used in an unconscious person, a partially conscious person, or someone with mouth and jaw trauma. This is a good airway to use if the person is breathing on his or her own. If the person is not breathing on their own, an **endotracheal tube** will be inserted by the paramedic, respiratory therapist, or physician.

Chapter Fourteen • Traumatic Emergencies

The **bag-valve mask**, or **Ambu bag**, is a resuscitation mask attached to a manually squeezed bag. The bag is connected to a 100% oxygen source. As it fills with oxygen, it is squeezed by the rescuer into the patient's lungs every five seconds. The mask fits snugly over the patient's face and, because it is portable, can be used while transporting the patient.

Since the lungs are inflated by the pressure in the bag, it is important to obtain an airtight seal over the victim's nose and mouth. Watch for the rise and fall of the patient's chest. If a deeper inspiration is necessary, increase the pressure in the bag. If the patient has an **endotracheal tube** in place, the bag-valve device can still be used. Just remove the face mask. The universal adapter on the end of the bag will fit directly onto the end of the endotracheal tube. If the patient vomits, immediately remove the face mask, suction the patient, and continue with ventilation using the bag-valve mask.

bag-valve mask: a manual resuscitator

The endotracheal tube is a tube that the physician or paramedic will place directly into the **trachea**. This is the most effective airway because it is inserted directly into the windpipe. This is the airway that is used on patients in the operating room to control their breathing while they are under the effects of **anesthesia**. Ventilation is assisted or controlled either by the Ambu bag or by a **positive pressure demand valve**. You may need to assist the physician with endotracheal intubation. Endotracheal tubes have a cuff on them that is inflated with 5 to 10 ml of air. Placed in an unconscious patient, this tube will prevent **aspiration** if the patient vomits. The inflated cuff in the windpipe will prevent the gastric contents from entering the lungs. Emergency intubation is a lifesaving procedure. Therefore, the emergency tray should always be checked routinely to make sure that all contents are in working order.

aspiration: inhalation of vomit or other fluid into the lungs

To assist with endotracheal intubation, use the following procedure.

Assisting With Endotracheal Intubation

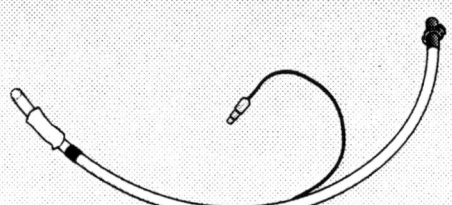

Materials needed:
- ✓ a stylet
- ✓ several endotracheal tubes (in various sizes)
- ✓ a laryngoscope
- ✓ lubricating jelly
- ✓ gloves for the physician
- ✓ gloves for yourself (If blood or other body fluids are present.)

1. <u>Procedural Step:</u> Wash your hands.
   <u>Reason:</u> Universal precaution.

2. <u>Procedural Step:</u> Put on gloves if blood or other body fluids are present.
   <u>Reason:</u> Universal precaution.

3. <u>Procedural Step:</u> Identify the patient.
   <u>Reason:</u> To ensure you are working with the correct patient.

4. <u>Procedural Step:</u> Set up the suction equipment and check to make sure it is in working order.
   <u>Reason:</u> The equipment must function properly.

5. <u>Procedural Step:</u> Prepare both a flexible **suction catheter** and a hard-tipped tonsil suction attachment.
   <u>Reason:</u> To be prepared for whatever is needed.

6. <u>Procedural Step:</u> Make sure the Ambu bag is nearby.
   <u>Reason:</u> To assist with respirations.

7. <u>Procedural Step:</u> Select the endotracheal tube in the size requested by the physician from the **crash cart**.
   <u>Reason:</u> An airway will not work properly if it is the wrong size.

8. <u>Procedural Step:</u> Check the cuff for leaks by inserting 5 ml of air into the side port.
   <u>Reason:</u> If the airway leaks, the patient will not get enough oxygen.

9. <u>Procedural Step:</u> Insert a **stylet** into the endotracheal tube, making sure it does not extend beyond the length of the tube.
   <u>Reason:</u> The stylet makes the tube easier to insert.

10. <u>Procedural Step:</u> Connect the laryngoscope blade to the laryngoscope handle and check to make sure the light is working.
    <u>Reason:</u> The batteries may need to be replaced.

---

stylet: a rigid wire guide used for tube placement

Assisting With Endotracheal Intubation (Cont.)

11. **Procedural Step:** The physician will insert the tube into the nose or the mouth and pass it into the trachea.
    Reason: This is the correct position for the endotracheal tube.

12. **Procedural Step:** The cuff will be inflated and the tube taped securely in place.
    Reason: To maintain tube placement.

13. **Procedural Step:** The tube will be connected to a **ventilator** by the respiratory therapist.
    Reason: To assist the patient's breathing.

14. **Procedural Step:** Listen for lung sounds on both sides of the chest.
    Reason: To make sure the tube is still in place.

15. **Procedural Step:** Remove your gloves if you are wearing them.
    Reason: Universal precaution.

16. **Procedural Step:** Wash your hands.
    Reason: Universal precaution.

17. **Procedural Step:** Document the procedure as appropriate.
    Reason: To provide documentation.

The airway must be maintained in the proper place. When moving the patient from a bed to a gurney always make sure the tube does not become dislodged accidentally. Check the tube frequently to make sure it is taped securely in place.

Controlling Arterial Bleeding

Obvious arterial bleeding is controlled by placing a sterile compress over the bleeding wound with a gloved hand. Indirect pressure (pressure on a pulse directly above the wound) can be used to stop the bleeding. The paramedics may bring a trauma patient into the emergency room wearing antishock trousers. The **MAST** (military anti-shock trousers), **PASG** (pneumatic anti-shock garment), or air trousers aid in the treatment of **hemorrhagic shock**. (Figure 14-1) The trousers consist of three pieces that encase the abdomen and each leg. By inflating each section, you can squeeze blood out of the legs and back into the circulation. If there is bleeding into the abdomen, the pressure of the inflated suit will slow down the bleeding. These trousers are very effective in the prevention of shock and are an important part of emergency care.

hemorrhagic shock: shock that is brought on by blood loss

If the patient is brought to the emergency room wearing these trousers, do not remove them. X-rays can be taken while the MAST suit is in place, and in some cases, surgery can be performed while the patient is wearing it. A spare suit can be given to the paramedic unit as a loaner until theirs is returned. When this patient no longer needs the MAST suit, it is cleaned with a 10% chlorine bleach solution and returned to the supply cart or the paramedic unit.

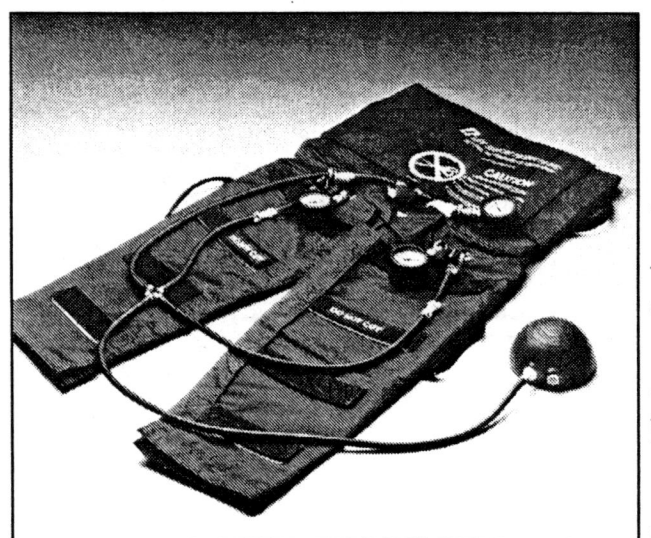

Figure 14-1: A MAST Suit

perfusion: the process of supplying the tissues with oxygen and other nutrients by the passage of blood through the arteries

Shock

Shock is a life-threatening condition in which there is inadequate tissue **perfusion**. This means that the organs are not receiving enough oxygen. In trauma victims this is the result of blood loss. Therefore, vital signs are very important to monitor in severely traumatized patients. Sometimes vital signs must be taken every minute or two. A drop in blood pressure and a rise in pulse is an indication of shock. Shock is treated by controlling obvious hemorrhages, restoring the circulating blood volume with IVs and blood **transfusions**, maintaining adequate **oxygenation**, and preparing the patient for surgery.

oxygenation: the state in which the blood is saturated with oxygen

Chapter Fourteen • Traumatic Emergencies

Using a MAST Suit

Materials needed:
- ✓ a MAST suit
- ✓ gloves (If blood or other body fluids are present.)

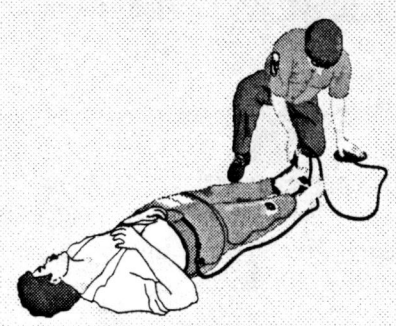

1. Procedural Step: Wash your hands if in the hospital setting.
   Reason: Universal precaution.

2. Procedural Step: Put on gloves if blood or other body fluids are present.
   Reason: Universal precaution

3. Procedural Step: Identify the patient if in the hospital setting.
   Reason: To ensure you are working with the correct patient.

4. Procedural Step: Unfold the MAST suit and lay it out flat.
   Reason: This makes it easier to put on the patient.

5. Procedural Step: Slide the suit under the patient's raised feet to the buttocks.
   Reason: To position the suit properly.

6. Procedural Step: Enclose the patient's legs in the suit and secure it with Velcro.
   Reason: The straps prevent overinflation.

7. Procedural Step: Enclose the patient's abdomen with the suit and secure the velcro strap.
   Reason: For proper fit.

8. Procedural Step: Open the stopcocks.
   Reason: Air will flow in the direction of the open valve and fill that section of the suit.

9. Procedural Step: Connect the foot pump.
   Reason: The pump is used to inflate the suit.

10. Procedural Step: Check the patient's blood pressure.
    Reason: A baseline blood pressure is needed. You must monitor the blood pressure closely while the MAST suit is in place.

11. Procedural Step: Inflate the suit with the foot pump.
    Reason: The suit is inflated when the Velcro makes a cracking sound.

12. Procedural Step: Close the stopcocks.
    Reason: This will prevent air leaks.

Using a MAST Suit (Cont.)

13. **Procedural Step:** Check the patient's blood pressure.
    Reason: Stop inflating the suit at 100 mm/Hg systolic pressure.

14. **Procedural Step:** Maintain the blood pressure between 90-100 mm Hg.
    Reason: This is an adequate blood pressure for a shock victim.

15. **Procedural Step:** IV lines are established, fluid is replaced, and the blood pressure increases.
    Reason: The suit is not removed until the blood pressure rises to the appropriate level as determined by the physician.

16. **Procedural Step:** Check the patient's blood pressure.
    Reason: If the blood pressure has dropped, do not remove the suit.

17. **Procedural Step:** To remove the suit, gradually deflate it at the physician's request.
    Reason: Rapid deflation can return the patient to shock.

18. **Procedural Step:** Open the stopcocks.
    Reason: To deflate each section.

19. **Procedural Step:** Release the pressure slowly in each section and take the blood pressure every 5 minutes.
    Reason: To ensure the patient is stable.

20. **Procedural Step:** Remove your gloves if it was necessary to put them on.
    Reason: Universal precaution.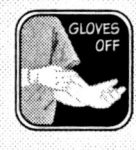

21. **Procedural Step:** Wash your hands.
    Reason: Universal precaution.

22. **Procedural Step:** Document the procedure as appropriate.
    Reason: Universal precaution.

Head Injuries

Trauma frequently involves head injuries. A victim with a head injury may be alert and oriented at the scene of the accident, and then lose consciousness later. This is due to the fact that as swelling in the brain increases, the level of consciousness decreases. This condition can progress to a coma. Therefore, the emergency care staff have a tremendous responsibility in evaluating patients with head injuries.

Chapter Fourteen • Traumatic Emergencies

Continuous observation of a head injury patient means that you must do the following neuro check.

1. Check the blood pressure.

2. Count the pulse rate, and monitor the rhythm and the quality (i.e., faint, weak, bounding, etc.).

3. Observe the number and depth of respirations.

4. Monitor the skin temperature and moisture.

5. Observe the color of the skin.

6. Look at the pupils with a light for equality and reaction.

7. Talk to the patient and determine if they are oriented to time, day, place and person.

8. See that the patient has feeling and motion in all extremities.

A **concussion** is a temporary loss of consciousness due to a blow or a fall. If the patient has been "knocked-out" it is important to determine the length of time the patient was unconscious. It may have been for just a few minutes, or it could have been for several hours. A patient with a concussion may be dizzy, confused, nauseated, drowsy, or irritable. He or she also may vomit or exhibit an altered level of consciousness. These patients must be watched very carefully, and any change in the level of consciousness, pupil reaction, or vital signs must be reported to the nurse immediately. While this patient is in the emergency room, vital signs are taken every 5, 10, or 15 minutes. The doctor may order skull x-rays or a CT scan to rule out the possibility of a fracture.

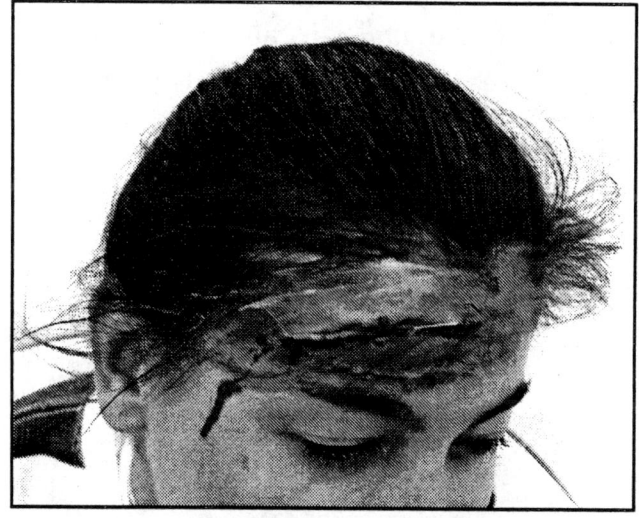

Figure 14-2: Head trauma can lead to concussion, brain hemorrhage, or a skull fracture.

Brain hemorrhages are very serious injuries. A patient with this type of injury will be in critical condition, and will be admitted either to the operating room or to the intensive care unit. The symptoms seen in these patients are a direct result of the pressure caused by the bleeding in the brain. A patient experiencing a brain hemorrhage may exhibit any of the following symptoms.

- **paresthesia** (tingling or numbness)
- **seizures**
- **paralysis**
- **coma**
- confusion
- speech difficulties
- lack of coordination
- drowsiness
- irritability

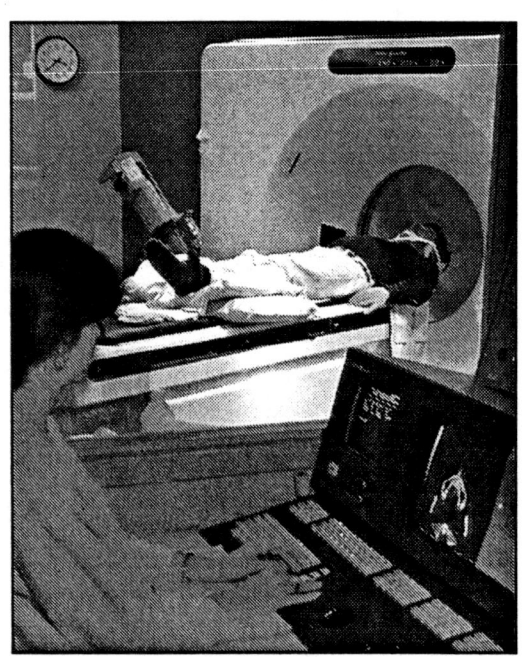

Figure 14-3: CT Scan in Progress

Skull fractures are another possible result of trauma. Patients who have suspected skull fractures must have x-rays or a CT scan taken. Sometimes both tests are necessary to determine the extent of the injury.

Fractures of the skull can cause both of the eyes to blacken. This condition is called "raccoon's eyes." There also may be clear drainage from the nose or mouth. The drainage is known as **cerebrospinal fluid (CSF)**. If there is a large amount of facial bleeding, the blood can mix with CSF and appear as a pink or red, watery liquid. If this occurs, tape a sterile dressing over the nose and ear to stop the bleeding. Bruising also can occur behind the ear on the **mastoid process**. This bruising behind the ear, known as a **Battle sign**, may be caused by bleeding in the brain and can indicate a skull fracture. The bruise may take 24 hours to appear, and is monitored on a person who is admitted in a coma or who has an altered mental status when there is no history available.

mastoid process: the portion of the temporal bone that protrudes from the side of the skull and to which various muscles are attached

Increased Intracranial Pressure

The brain is protected by the rigid skull. There is very little room for expansion within the skull cavity. In a traumatic head injury, the brain immediately begins to swell. **Cerebral edema** (swelling in the brain) is a serious condition that must be treated immediately. Patients who experience cerebral edema are in critical condition and require a specialist, or **neurosurgeon** for evaluation and treatment. All head injury patients are continuously observed and monitored for the signs and symptoms of increased intracranial pressure. Any changes in the patient's condition may indicate an increase in intracranial pressure and must be reported immediately to the nurse. The following observations must be made frequently on head injury patients:

- What is the patient's level of consciousness?
- Does the patient have the ability to move extremities?
- How do the pupils respond to light?
- What are the vital signs?
- Is there any pain or headache?
- Is there any projectile vomiting?
- Does the patient experience any seizure activity?

Frequent and quick neurological assessments can help to determine the patient's progress and determine which direction the patient's condition is heading. The nurse may check the patient using the **Glasgow Coma Scale**. This scale involves three responses: eye opening, verbal response, and muscle response. These responses are measured using a scoring system that ranges from *mild* to *severe loss of response*.

Glasgow Coma Scale: a measure of the degree of a coma patient is experiencing, in which motor responses are converted to a standard set of numbers

Glasgow Coma Scale		
Eye Openings	Spontaneous	4
	To voice	3
	To pain	2
	None	1
Verbal Response	Oriented	5
	Confused	4
	Inappropriate words	3
	Incomprehensible words	2
	None	1
Motor Response	Obeys command	6
	Localized pain	5
	Withdraw (pain)	4
	Flexion (pain)	3
	Extension (pain)	2
	None	1
Total		15

A patient scoring 7 or less is comatose and critically ill.

Spinal Injuries

Any patient who is admitted with a head injury also is suspected of having a neck injury, and is treated as such until the doctor determines differently. Spinal injuries damage **neurostructures**, and can interfere with normal breathing patterns. This interference can be mild and **transient**, or it can be severe and permanent. The patient's breathing must be closely monitored and may need to be assisted. The use of the modified jaw-thrust is recommended to maintain an adequate airway as this avoids hyperextending the neck. The patient may already have an airway in place when he or she arrives in the ER. If so, breathing will be assisted with a bag-valve mask or positive pressure breathing.

neurostructures: structures within the nervous system

Chapter Fourteen • Traumatic Emergencies

Spinal injuries can cause **paralysis** (the inability to move either the arms or legs or both). A patient with suspected spinal injuries who is brought in by paramedics will have a rigid neck collar in place, and will be stabilized on a backboard. (Figure 14-4) The backboard and neck collar prevent additional spinal injuries during transport. The patient will be transferred to the gurney while still on the backboard. After the x-rays are taken and the doctor orders the backboard removed, the patient is log rolled from side to side as the backboard is removed.

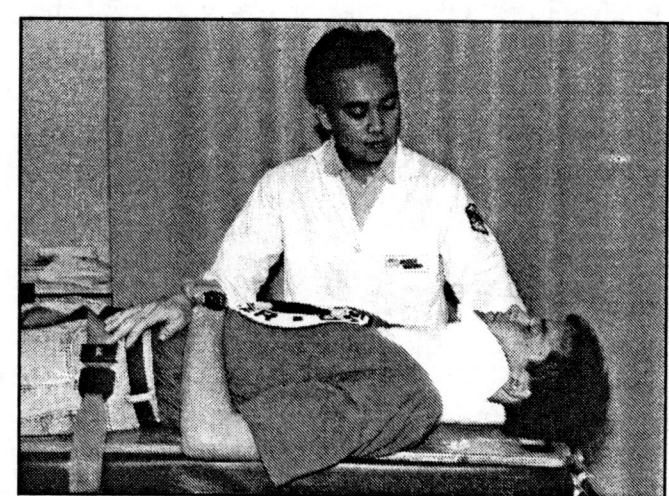

Figure 14-4: Stabilization of a Spinal Injury

To log roll a patient with a neck injury, one person stands at the head of the bed and holds the patient's head and neck. Two additional people stand at the side of the patient; one person supporting the upper body, and the other person supporting the lower body. On the count of "THREE," all assisting persons turn the patient to the side, keeping the body straight (like a log), rolling the patient to the side. (See Chapter Six.) The backboard is removed, the patient's back is examined for other injuries, and the patient is placed on the back or side as ordered by the physician. If more treatments are needed the patient is positioned on his or her back.

Spinal injuries can be caused by the following:

- automobile accidents
- diving accidents
- falls
- sports-related injuries

A patient with a history of any of these mechanisms of injury must be evaluated by the physician. If a patient complains of pain in the neck, numbness and tingling in either the arms or legs, a loss of feeling, or the ability to move, he or she should be stabilized immediately with a rigid neck collar, positioned flat in the bed, and advised not to move his or her head or neck until x-rays have been taken. Every effort must be made to avoid rough handling of this patient, and movement should be kept to a minimum to avoid additional injuries.

Chest Trauma

A traumatic injury to the chest is one of the most urgent problems that is seen in the Emergency Department. This injury is associated with respiratory distress and can be the result of a gunshot wound, stabbing, motor vehicle accident, fall, fire, or other trauma. (Figure 14-5) The patient will require immediate attention by the physician. Watch the patient's breathing pattern and prepare to assist with **ventilation**. The physician may wish to insert an airway or endotracheal tube, and if the lung is collapsed, the physician will insert a chest tube. If a chest tube is necessary, you will need the following supplies:

pleura vac: a piece of equipment used for closed-seal underwater chest drainage

- ✓ a thoracotomy tray
- ✓ a chest tube
- ✓ a **pleura vac**
- ✓ skin prep solution (iodine)
- ✓ sterile gloves
- ✓ suture
- ✓ petroleum gauze
- ✓ 4 x 4 gauze
- ✓ tape

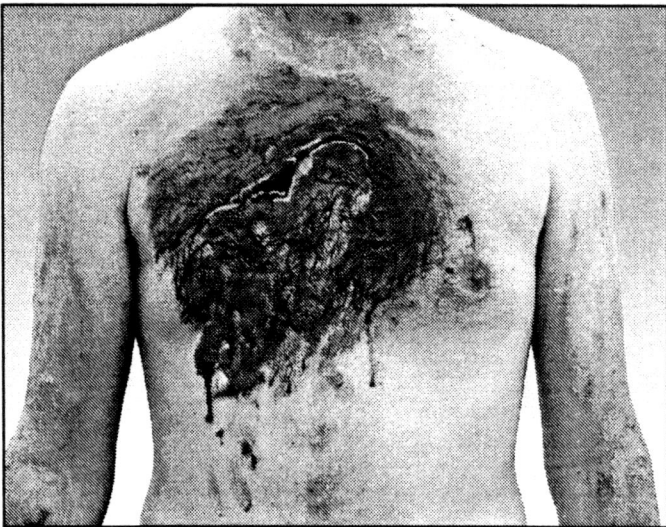

Figure 14-5: Chest Trauma

Chapter Summary

As an ER technician, you will care for trauma victims whether you work in a rural or an urban area. Assessment of the patient's injuries is a critical factor, and a patient history can help you do this. Knowledge of the mechanism of injury is very important in determining the extent of injury a patient may have received. Timing of emergency care is crucial. A well-organized EMS that includes trauma centers and rapid transportation methods can dramatically decrease the time it takes to treat trauma cases. As an ER technician, YOU are part of this system. By cooperating with all members of the healthcare team, the patient can be guaranteed rapid, lifesaving care.

14-20

Chapter Fourteen • Traumatic Emergencies   14-21

Name _____
Date _____

Student Enrichment Activities

1. A 22-year-old female was involved in a traffic accident. She is unconscious, has a large bump on her left forehead, and is groaning with each breath. Her blood pressure is 80/40; her pulse is 120, weak, and irregular; and her respirations are 8 and shallow. Her left arm is swollen and the fingers on the left hand are cold.

    A. What do you do first?
    _____
    _____

    B. How often should you take the BP, P, and R? _____

2. List five signs and symptoms of shock.
    A. _____   D. _____
    B. _____   E. _____
    C. _____

3. How would you care for a patient in an antishock suit?
    _____
    _____
    _____
    _____

4. What are some mechanisms of injury for head and spinal injuries?
    A. _____   C. _____
    B. _____   D. _____

5. Explain the three things that are measured on the Glasgow Coma Scale.

   A. _____

   B. _____

   C. _____

6. Ben Green has arrived in the Emergency Care Unit after falling from a rooftop. Using the Glasgow Coma Scale assign a score for the following:

   Responds to pain _____

   Confused _____

   Obeys commands _____

   Total GCS _____

7. How do you perform a neuro exam?

   _____
   _____
   _____
   _____

8. Define the term *log roll*.

   _____
   _____

9. List the steps that must be taken to care for a patient with a chest injury.

   _____
   _____

Chapter Fifteen
Bone and Joint Injuries

Objectives

After completing this chapter you should be able to do the following:

1. Define and correctly spell all key terms.
2. Care for a patient with a fracture.
3. Assist the physician with cast application.
4. Apply an elastic bandage to a sprained ankle.
5. Measure and fit a patient for crutches.
6. Instruct the patient in the proper technique for walking with crutches.

Key Terms

- carpals
- compound fracture
- crepitus
- dislocation
- fracture
- grating
- hyperextend
- metacarpals
- metatarsals
- neurovascular
- pallor
- phalanges
- splint
- sprain
- stockinette
- strain
- tarsals
- traction

Injuries to the Bones and Joints

There are 206 bones in the human body, all of which can be damaged in some way or another. The most common injuries occur to the arms, hands, legs, and feet. These injuries to the extremities can be soft tissue injuries involving the supportive structures such as tendons, ligaments, and muscles, or they can be **fractures**.

fracture: a crack or break in a bone

Though most injuries to the extremities are not life-threatening, many of them can be disabling. Proper handling of injuries to the arms and legs can do much to preserve the function of the arm or leg, prevent disability, and promote the healing of wounds. Therefore, it is vitally important for emergency care workers to be properly trained in the treatment of both life and limb.

Figure 15-1 shows some of the more commonly injured bones.

Chapter Fifteen • Bone and Joint Injuries

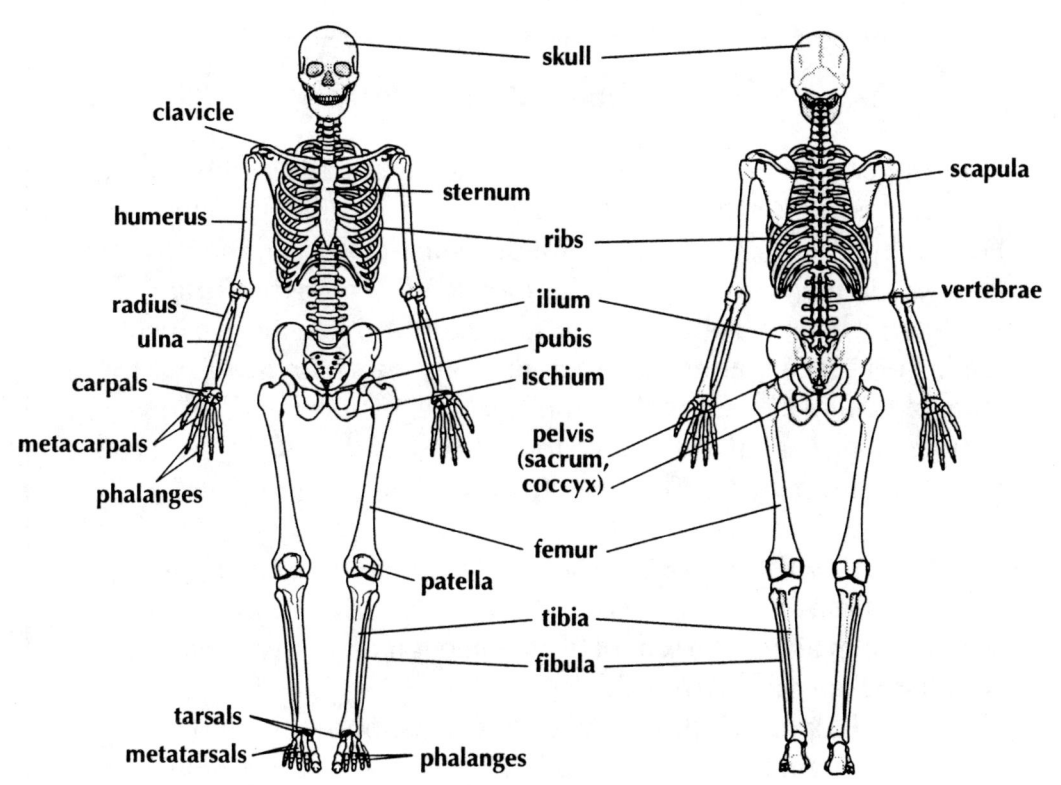

Figure 15-1: Commonly Injured Bones

carpals: small bones in the wrist

metacarpals: the bones of the hand

tarsals: the bones of the foot

metatarsals: the bones of the foot between the tarsals and the phalanges

phalanges: the bones of the fingers and toes

Fractures

Anyone can break a bone, but some injuries occur more frequently in specific age groups. For example, as people get older their bones become more brittle. This is part of the aging process, and as a result, the elderly often suffer broken hips after relatively minor falls. Fractures also can result from sports-related accidents: skiers break legs; wrestlers break wrists; and skateboarders break arms. Fractures often are complicated by injury to the supportive tissue surrounding the area of the break. A fracture can occur as the only injury, or it may be associated with a multisystem trauma. For example, a seriously injured accident victim might have internal bleeding, a head injury, and a fractured **femur** or thigh.

Case Study

Christopher, a very active fourth grader, waits anxiously in the classroom for the recess bell. At the sound of the bell he heads directly for the soccer field. While at play, Christopher collides with a classmate and falls to the ground. He attempts to break his fall by extending his right arm and lands with his full body weight on the outstretched arm, causing it to **hyperextend**. He hears a **grating** noise and instantly feels pain in his wrist. He is unable to move his arm or hand and tears begin to stream from his eyes. Besides being in pain, he is afraid that if his injury is serious it will cause trouble for his parents. This anxiety makes him breathe faster.

hyperextend: to move beyond the normal range of motion

grating: the sound of two bones rubbing together

Christopher's wrist begins to swell from the injury. One of his fellow classmates runs for the teacher. The teacher arrives and calls for the school health aide. The school health aide is a person with office skills who has taken the emergency department technician class. The aide checks Christopher's injured arm, paying attention to the temperature of the skin, the color of the skin, and the presence of a pulse below the fracture. She also checks Christopher's ability to move his fingertips and puts a cardboard splint on him that extends from his elbow to his fingers.

Courtesy St. Jude Medical Center, Fullerton, California

The health aide makes sure there is enough padding under the elbow and around the wrist and fingers. After the splint is in position, she elevates Christopher's arm on a pillow, and applies ice over the swollen area. He is taken to the health office and his father is notified at work. His father drives to the school, reassures Christopher that he will feel better soon, and takes him to the Emergency Department for care.

Chapter Fifteen • Bone and Joint Injuries

The Signs and Symptoms of a Fracture

The preceding case study emphasized several common findings in a fracture.

- pain at the site of the injury
- deformity (the extremity is not in a normal anatomical position)
- **grating** or **crepitus**
- **edema** (swelling) over the injury site
- **ecchymosis** (bruising or changes in skin color)
- **pallor**
- **immobility** (stabilized so as not to move)
- anxiety
- **paresthesia** (numbness or tingling)
- **paralysis** (inability to move)
- cold skin due to impaired circulation

crepitus: the sound of air in the tissues

pallor: pale skin due to a decrease in blood supply to the area

There are different types of fractures. A closed fracture is one in which there is no open wound. An open fracture, or **compound fracture**, occurs when the bone protrudes through the skin and, sometimes, becomes visible. The wound that exists may be a **laceration**, **avulsion**, or **amputation**. If the break is a compound fracture, a sterile dressing is applied over the wound and bleeding is controlled using a **pressure point**.

compound fracture: a break in a bone that causes the bone to penetrate the skin

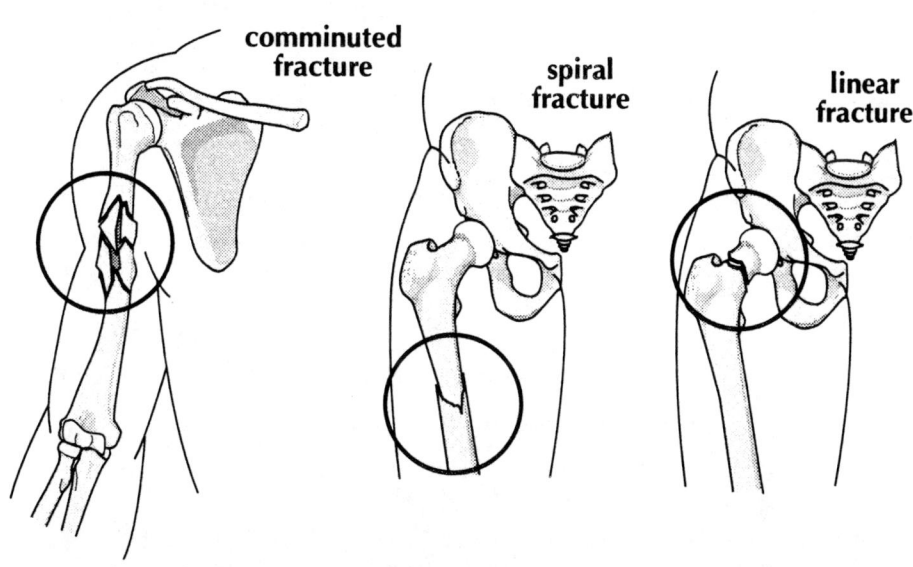

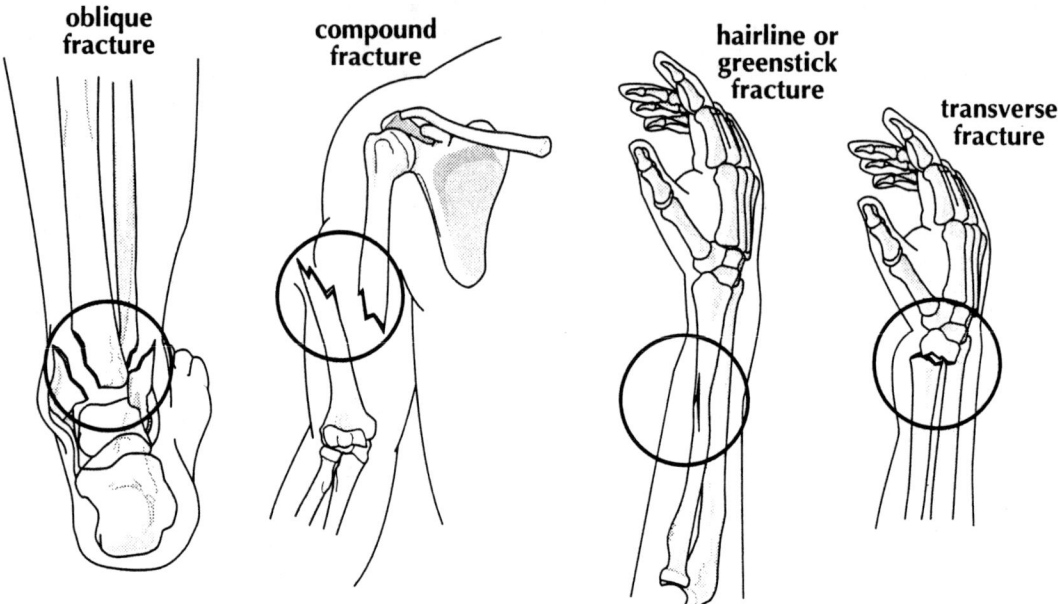

Sometimes a compound fracture exists, but it is not obvious because the bone ends have slipped back under the skin. For this reason, determining the mechanism of injury is essential when treating open wounds. If the mechanism of injury is suspicious, the injury should be treated as if it were a compound fracture. Certain types of injuries can increase the possibility of a fracture.

- direct trauma: some injuries occur at the point of impact (i.e., a broken leg from a car bumper, or a broken nose from someone's fist).

- indirect trauma: injuries can occur away from the point of impact (i.e., a broken wrist from an outstretched hand to prevent a fall).

- disease process: some illnesses, such as cancer, can cause the bones to weaken, or a disease can deplete the body's supply of calcium, resulting in **pathological** fractures.

- **compression**: injuries can result from a force that presses bones together. (A fall from a roof can cause the vertebrae in the spine to compress together.)

- muscle contraction: if muscles contract violently, they can cause a fracture. (This sometimes occurs with seizure or electrical shock.)

- stress: factors that cause repeated stress on the bone can cause them to break (i.e., a runner in a marathon, soldiers marching repeatedly).

Splints

Bone and joint injuries often involve pre-hospital care. Paramedics may be summoned to the scene, or someone who has been trained in first aid may already be present. Whenever possible, a **splint** is applied to the site of the injury prior to transport. Splints stabilize the injured extremity, prevent further damage, and reduce the pain of the injury. Splints can be made from any rigid device. Patients may arrive in the emergency room with an arm tied to a board, magazine, or metal object. Commercial splints are available too; patients may arrive with a cardboard splint, air splint, or traction splint that has been applied by a first aider or paramedic at the scene.

splint:
a rigid device that holds parts of the body together and limits motion

A person with a broken arm may automatically splint the arm by supporting it with the uninjured hand until another splint can be applied. This is because a splint usually reduces the pain that is caused by the injury. Reducing the movement of the extremity with a splint will decrease much of the pain associated with a fracture.

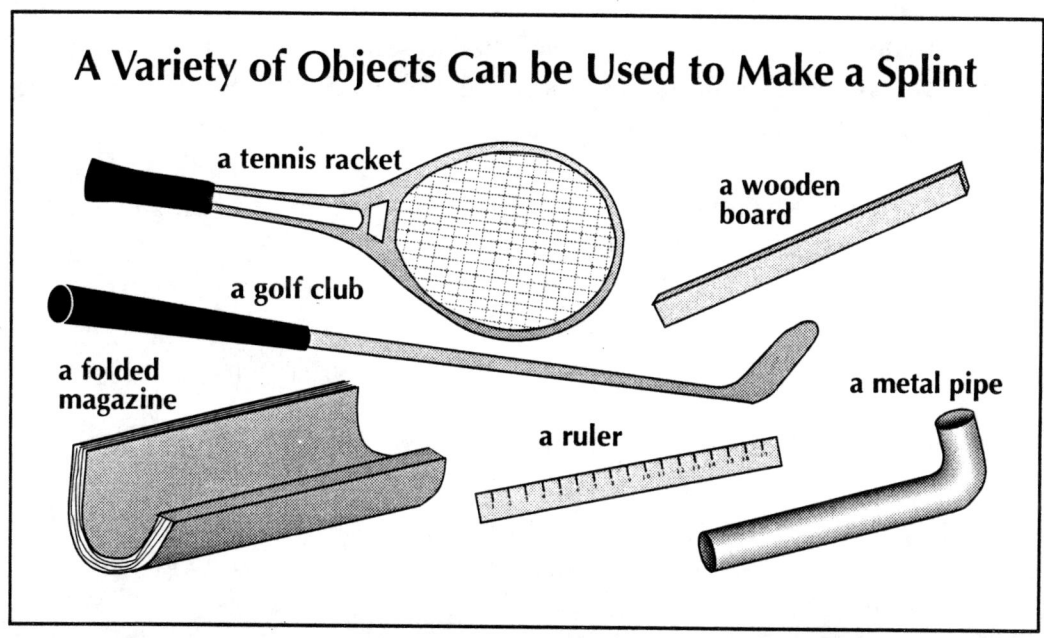

A Variety of Objects Can be Used to Make a Splint

- a tennis racket
- a wooden board
- a golf club
- a folded magazine
- a ruler
- a metal pipe

Cervical Collars

Patients who arrive by ambulance from an accident in which the mechanism of injury suggests involvement of the head or neck will have a rigid neck collar in place. If the patient arrives by private automobile and there is evidence from the history that there may be an injury to the cervical spine or neck, a rigid **cervical collar** is applied immediately to stabilize the neck and spine. (Figure 15-2) Any patients with facial cuts from a motor vehicle accident, or who have been involved in a diving accident, or who have fallen should have a rigid neck collar applied. This collar will stay in place until the patient is evaluated by the physician. DO NOT REMOVE THE COLLAR UNTIL YOU ARE INSTRUCTED TO DO SO BY THE NURSE OR DOCTOR!

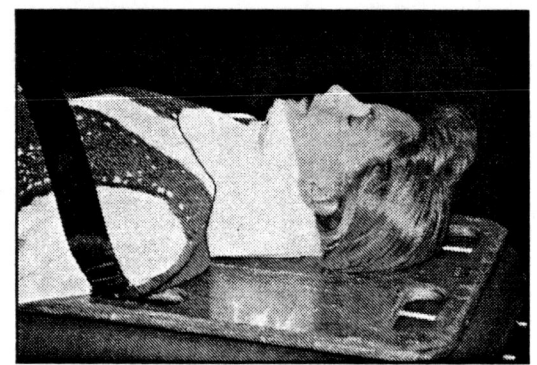

Figure 15-2: All suspected spinal injuries should be stabilized with a cervical collar.

Treating a Fracture

As you become more experienced, it will become evident why it is so important to obtain adequate information from the patient about the injury. Many times the mechanism of injury can alert the ER staff to serious injuries and associated fractures that may not be apparent. Some of the signs and symptoms of a fracture are obvious, and others are not.

If the patient arrives with a splint in place, the doctor will evaluate the patient and may have you leave the splint in place until after the x-ray is taken. Some metal splints must be removed before the x-ray is taken. Metal shows up on x-rays and can prevent visible fractures from being seen. However, a **traction splint**, a metal splint used by the paramedics for the treatment of a closed fracture of the femur, can be left in place for x-rays. (Figure 15-3) THE TRACTION SPLINT IS NOT TO BE REMOVED BY ANYONE EXCEPT THE PHYSICIAN.

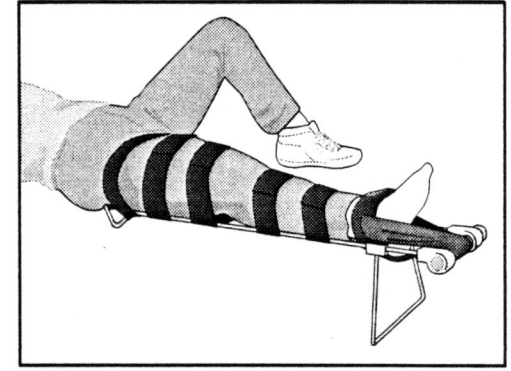

Figure 15-3: A Traction Splint

Chapter Fifteen • Bone and Joint Injuries

A person with a fractured extremity should be placed on the gurney in a comfortable position. Some patients will be comfortable sitting up, but others will want to lie down. The broken extremity should not be moved unnecessarily, and ice is applied to the fracture site to decrease the swelling. To apply ice, put crushed ice in a disposable bag and place a cloth or paper towel between the ice and the patient's skin. Do not apply the ice directly to the skin; this may cause frostbite. (Figure 15-4) Elevate the extremity to decrease the swelling and check the **distal pulse** (the pulse directly below the fracture) frequently. It tells you whether circulation is present below the area of injury. Check the skin for both temperature and color.

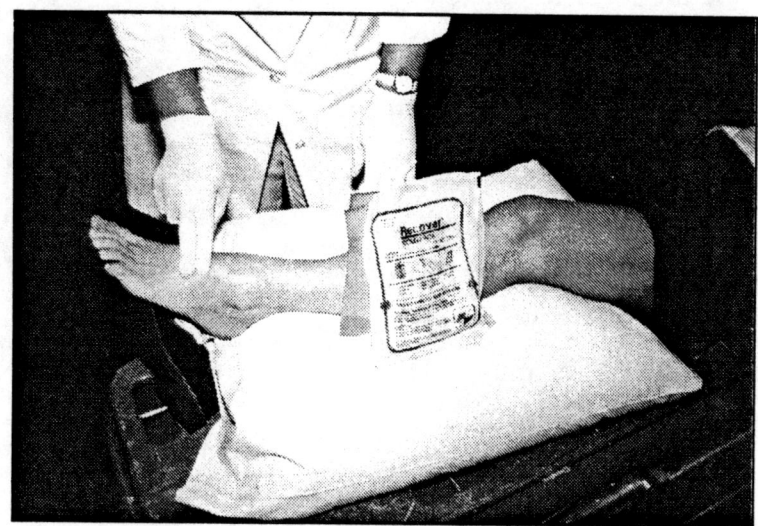

Figure 15-4: Check the patient's circulation by checking the distal pulse.

If the patient is wearing jewelry on the injured arm or leg, remove it before the swelling increases. All valuables must be handled according to hospital policy. Most hospitals have a place on the chart to document the **disposition** of valuables. If you give the valuables to one of the patient's relatives or place them in the safe, be sure to document it on the chart. It is always a good idea to have a fellow employee witness what you do with the valuables. If you are removing a ring and placing it in the safe, you would document your actions and a description of the ring. For example:

> A yellow metal band with a clear stone was removed from the fourth finger of the left hand and placed in the hospital safe.

Determine the **neurovascular** status of the injured extremity:

- Is there a pulse below the injury?
- Is there any movement or sensation in the extremity?
- If the **humerus** is fractured, can the patient wiggle the fingers?

neurovascular: of or relating to the nervous system and circulation

Make sure you do not move the fracture site while trying to determine if there is any sensation or feeling. A fracture is bad enough, but it is even worse to have a fracture and impaired circulation or nerve damage.

The physician will examine the x-ray to locate any fractures. If a fracture exists an **orthopedic** doctor (bone specialist) may be called in to treat the patient. Many orthopedic procedures are done directly in the Emergency Department, but some are done in the operating room.

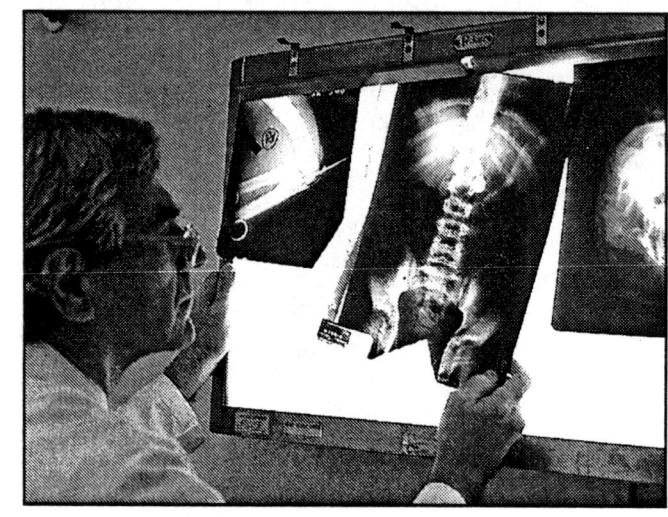

Figure 15-5: X-rays are used to locate fractures.

Other Orthopedic Injuries

sprain: an injury to the soft tissues of a joint, characterized by the inability to move, deformity and pain

dislocation: the separation of a joint and malposition of an extremity

strain: a pulled muscle

Injuries can occur to the joints as well as to the bones. The symptoms of a joint injury are similar to those of a fracture, but no fracture is seen in the x-ray. A **sprain** occurs when a joint is pushed beyond its normal range of motion, stretching and tearing the supporting **ligaments**. A sprained ankle or wrist can be so painful that the patient cannot move the wrist or walk on the foot.

A **dislocation** occurs to a joint when the bones are pushed beyond the normal range of motion and the ends of the bones are no longer in contact. Symptoms of a dislocation include pain, deformity, swelling, loss of movement, and bruising. A **strain** is a stretching or pulling of the muscle. A strain can occur to the back by lifting a heavy object and not using proper **body mechanics**. If this happens, the person will experience immediate pain at the site of the injury. He or she may not be able to stand up straight, and there may be a shooting pain down the leg. Some back strains result in extremely limited mobility.

When caring for bone and joint injuries, remember the following guidelines.

1. Expose the area of injury by gently removing any clothing covering it.

2. Look for obvious signs of injury (i.e., bone, deformity, swelling).

3. Compare one extremity to the other (i.e., the injured and uninjured leg).

4. Control any bleeding.

5. Check the patient's distal pulse.

6. Check for sensation or movement in the injured body part.

7. Support the injured extremity.

8. Apply ice.

9. Remove any constricting clothing or jewelry.

Compression Bandages

An elastic bandage is used to limit the amount of internal bleeding surrounding the injury to a joint. A sprained ankle is wrapped in a figure eight pattern, leaving the toes exposed. This way, the color and temperature of the toes can be checked for circulation. If the bandage is too tight it can be rewrapped.

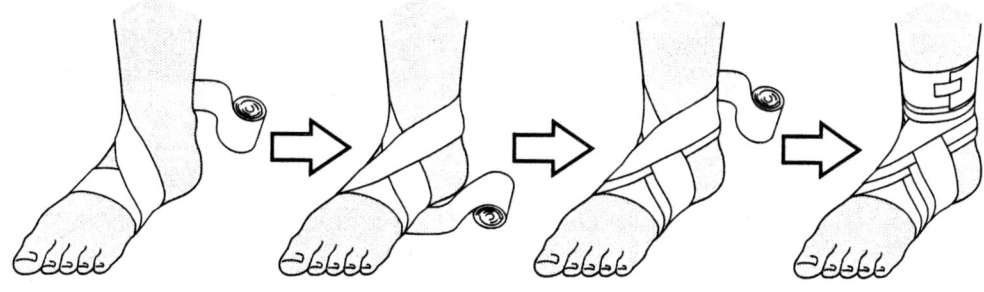

There are also elastic support bandages for knees, elbows, wrists, and ankles.

Immobilizers

Several orthopedic devices are available for the treatment of injuries. If the physician orders one of these devices for the patient, it will be up to you to obtain the correct size and put it on the injured person. The patient will need to know whether he or she must wear it all the time or if it can be taken off periodically. He or she also will need to know how to adjust it and how to clean it. Answer the patient's questions to the best of your knowledge and check with the physician or nurse regarding proper application if you need more information. Some of this information, such as cleaning instructions, can be found on the written material that is included in the product package. Since the patient will purchase this piece of equipment, make sure he or she is given the box it came in as well as the written information it contains. This will be useful information to which the patient may refer after he or she has gone home. Make sure you are familiar with the following orthopedic devices.

shoulder immobilizer (side)

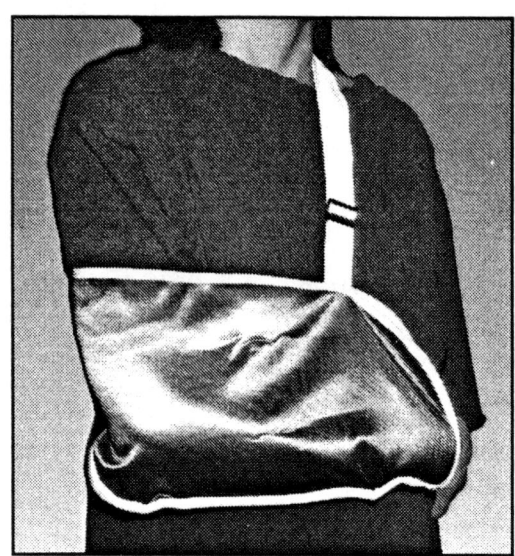
shoulder immobilizer (front)

Figure 15-6: Types of Immobilizers

Chapter Fifteen • Bone and Joint Injuries

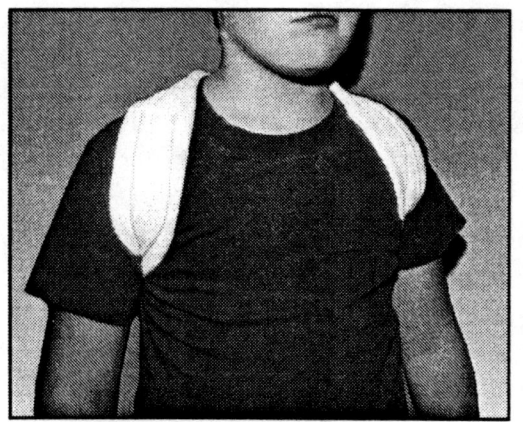
clavicle brace (front)

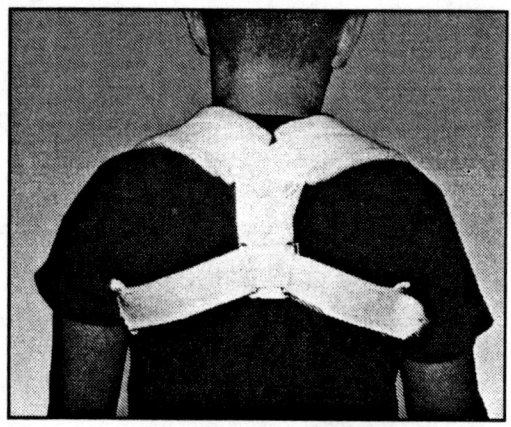
clavicle brace (back)

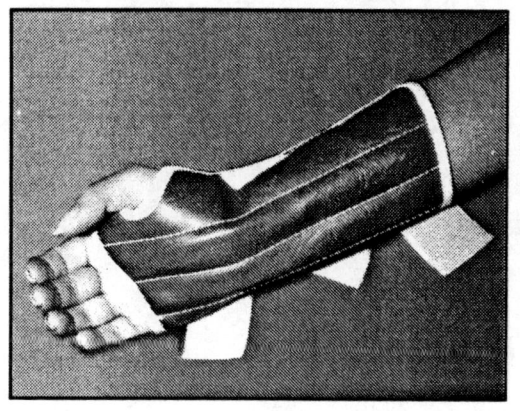
wrist immobilizer (front)

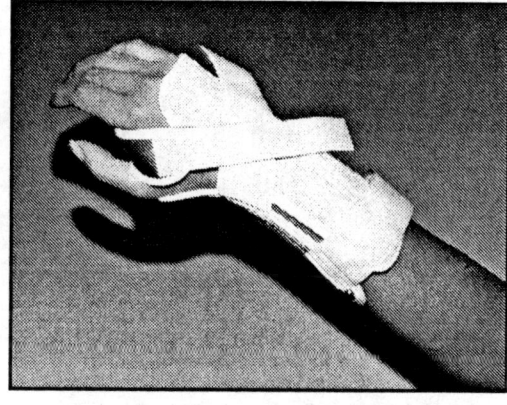
wrist immobilizer (back)

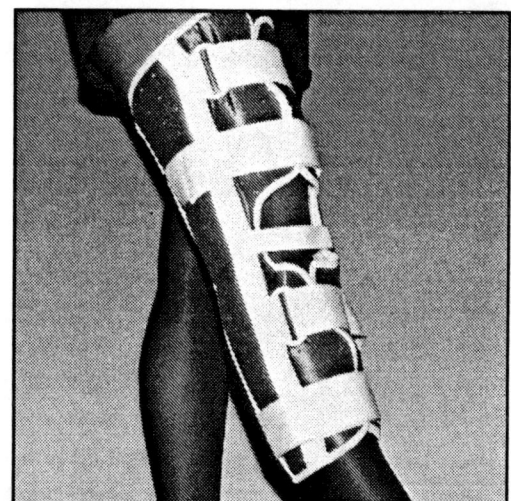
post operative knee splint

Figure 15-7: Types of Immobilizers Cont.

Applying a Sling

A sling is a support for an upper extremity. Commercial slings are available, but a triangular bandage also can be used. Place one end of the triangular bandage over the shoulder of the unaffected arm. Place the cloth against the body and bring it under the affected arm. Place the point of the triangle at the elbow. Bring the opposite ends of the triangle around the affected shoulder and tie them at the side of the patient's neck. Fold the pointed piece over the elbow and adjust it to fit. Pin the point in place.

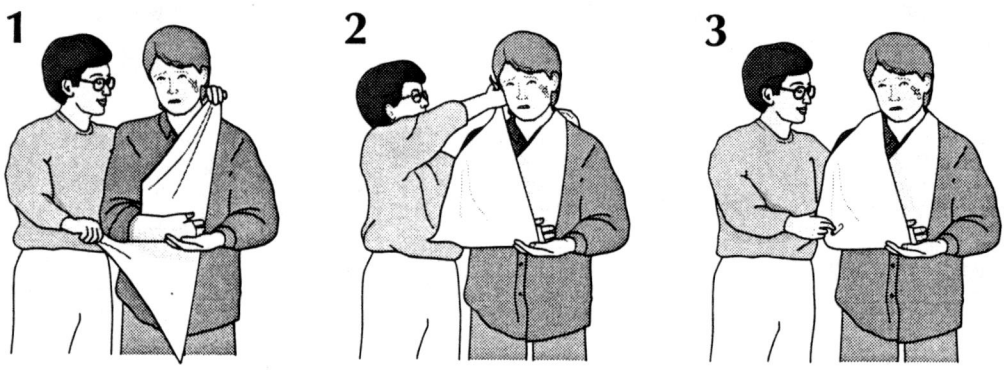

Assisting With a Cast Application

The principles of cast application are universal, but the supplies that are available to you at your hospital may vary tremendously. As you work closely with an orthopedic surgeon you will learn the specific ways in which he or she applies various casts. Your job will be to prepare and obtain the appropriate supplies and equipment, assist the physician, and care for the patient. This involves supporting the injured part or applying manual **traction** to the injured extremity while the physician applies the cast. Following the procedure your job will be to clean the area and restock the supplies.

traction: the process of pulling a part of the body into proper alignment

Some Emergency Departments have a special room designated for cast application. However, if such a room does not exist in your ER, a cast cart will be available to roll to the bedside. As you assist the physician, pay close attention to the patient. Many patients become dizzy, faint, or nauseated during this procedure. The patient may have to sit up, or he or she may have to maintain a strained position while the cast is applied. Make sure you watch to see how the patient tolerates the procedure. If the patient becomes light-headed and moves suddenly, you must support both the patient and the injured extremity. It may be necessary to call for additional help to ensure the safety of the patient.

The extremity is covered first with **stockinette**. This is a stretchable sock-like material that protects the skin from the plaster or fiberglass cast. Then the bony **prominences** are padded with cotton. If plaster is used, it will be available in rolls or in sheets. Obtain the size and quantity requested by the physician. The plaster is soaked in a bucket filled with cool to warm water. The wet strips must be wrung out slightly before they are used, and applied rapidly to prevent them from hardening prematurely. Once the cast has been applied it should be handled carefully with the palms of the hands. It will set quite rapidly, but it will not dry completely for at least 24 hours. If the cast is to be a walking cast, a rubber heel also will be applied to protect the heel of the cast from wearing out. The casted extremity should be elevated on one or two pillows.

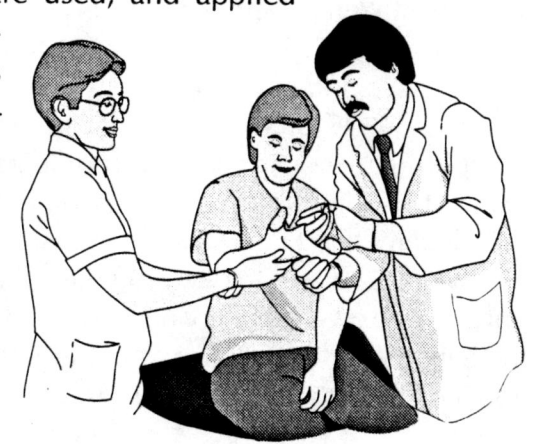

> **stockinette:** a type of tubular dressing or padding used underneath a cast to protect the skin

Patient Instructions for Cast Care

Once a cast is in place, many patients are discharged home. When patients leave the hospital they are given written instructions regarding the care of their injury. However, the patient probably will ask you for information as well. You can give him or her the following instructions:

1. Allow the cast to dry for 24 hours.

2. Do not get the cast wet.

3. Do not place anything inside the cast to scratch the skin.

4. Joints above the cast must be exercised to strengthen the muscles.

5. Keep the extremity elevated on a pillow until cast is dry.

6. Check the color and temperature of the toes or fingers. Call the doctor if they become cold or turn pale or dark.

7. Call the doctor if a foul odor is detected from the cast.

Crutches

Patients with injuries to the lower extremities will need to use crutches to assist with walking. Crutches need to be individually fitted for each patient and the patient must be instructed in how to use them. Measurements for crutches should be taken while the patient is wearing his or her shoes. This measurement can be taken with the patient lying in bed or standing at the bedside. Check with the doctor to find out if the patient is allowed to put any weight on the limb and on which leg. Crutches should fit so that the armpiece is 2 inches from the **axilla** (armpit). The tip of the crutch should be 6 to 8 inches to the side and front of the foot. Adjustable wing nuts or pop-out pins allow the crutches to be individually fitted for each patient. The handpiece should be fitted so that the elbow is flexed at a 30 degree angle. (Figure 15-8) Patients must be told not to put pressure on the axillary nerve by leaning the top of the crutch into the armpit; the hands should provide all the support. Check to make sure the rubber tip is applied correctly and that the handles are padded sufficiently.

Figure 15-8: Proper Crutch Measurement

When using crutches, a supportive shoe with a non-slip sole is needed. Sandals and slip-on slippers are not acceptable. Not all patients are able to use crutches. The patient must have some upper body strength as well as good coordination and balance to use crutches properly. A walker may be more suitable for many elderly patients.

Chapter Fifteen • Bone and Joint Injuries

Gait Training

Before he or she is allowed to go home, the patient must demonstrate proficiency in using the crutches. The patient should know the following:

1. How to walk using crutches.

2. How to get in and out of the chair and bed.

3. How to go up and down stairs.

4. How to get in and out of a car.

The three-point gait is the most common means of **ambulation** for patients with injuries to the lower legs. The three points are maintained by two crutches and the uninjured leg. To do this, the patient must stand and balance. When you are sure the patient is properly balanced, instruct him or her to advance the INJURED leg and both crutches, keeping the uninjured leg on the ground. Then he or she should transfer the weight to both hands, and follow through with the uninjured leg. The patient should maintain a tripod position for stability: two points forward, and one point behind. (Figure 15-9) This is because the balance is lost if both crutches and the uninjured leg are placed in a straight line. Place a safety belt (gait belt) around the patient's waist as he or she practices in case the patient loses his or her balance.

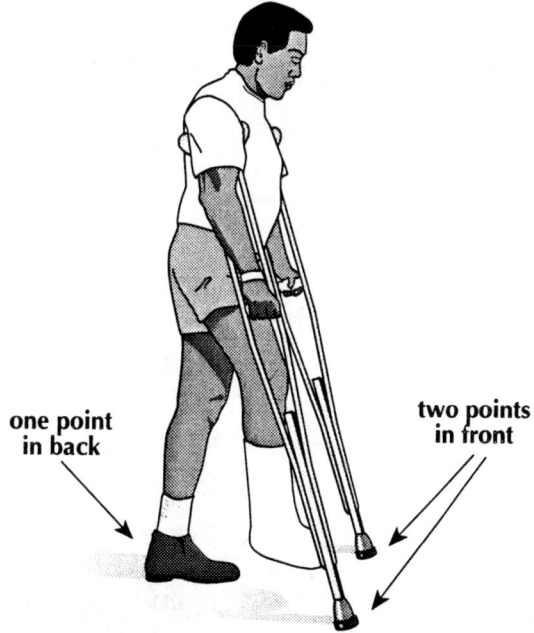

Figure 15-9: The Three Point Gait

To move from a sitting position to a standing position, the patient should follow these steps.

1. The patient should move forward to the edge of the chair.

2. He or she should place both crutches in the hand of the affected leg.

3. The opposite hand should be placed on the arm of the chair.

4. The patient can now rise, placing weight on the unaffected leg. (Figure 15-10)

5. He or she should transfer one of the crutches to the other arm.

6. The patient now can begin walking using the above procedure.

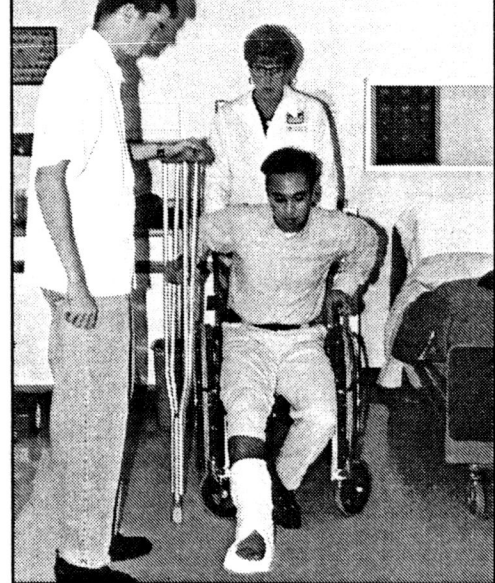

Figure 15-10

To move from a standing position to a sitting position the patient should follow these steps.

1. The patient must back up to the chair.

2. His or her weight should be placed on the stable leg.

3. Both crutches should be transferred to the hand on the injured side.

4. The hand on the uninjured side should locate the chair.

5. Now the patient can sit down.

Note: The same procedure is used to get in and out of an automobile.

Using Crutches on Stairs

To ascend stairs using crutches the patient should follow these steps.

1. Place the crutches and the INJURED leg on the step.

2. Bear weight on the hands with crutches, and step up with the UNINJURED leg. If the stairs have a railing, the patient may switch both crutches to one hand and use the railing. (Figure 15-11)

Figure 15-11

To descend stairs using crutches the patient should follow these steps.

1. Place the crutches and INJURED leg on the step below.

2. The UNINJURED leg steps down, and the weight is placed on the hands through the crutches.

Work with the patient until he or she understands the technique of using crutches. Some patients will be able to use them very quickly, and other patients will take a few extra minutes of instruction.

Canes

Canes are used to assist with balance and provide minimum support. They come in different lengths, and must be adjusted before they can be used to assist with ambulation. To fit a cane to a patient, hold it next to the person's heel. The elbow should be flexed at a 30 degree angle. If both arms are functional and one lower extremity is injured, the cane is used on the side of the injured leg for support. If the patient has had a stroke and has **hemiplegia** (paralysis of half the body), the cane is used on the side of the functional arm.

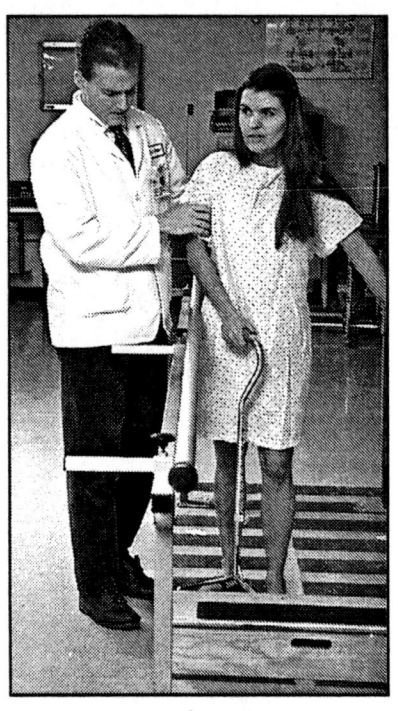

Chapter Summary

Injuries to bones and joints are challenges for the emergency room staff. Injuries such as these require assessment of the circulation and the potential for nerve involvement. Treating bone and joint injuries involves applying splints and casts. As an ER technician, your responsibilities will include listening to and following directions, obtaining necessary supplies, assisting with and cleaning up after procedures, and teaching patients to use ambulation devices. Victims of these types of injuries often experience a great deal of pain. Remember to watch your patients closely for signs of discomfort and question them regarding the mechanism of injury. This can alert you to injuries that otherwise might go undetected.

Chapter Fifteen • Bone and Joint Injuries

Name _____
Date _____

Student Enrichment Activities

1. Look around the classroom. What three items do you see that would make suitable splints?
   A. _____   C. _____
   B. _____

2. Match the correct term in the first column with the letter of the definition from the second column.

   _____ dislocation   A. break in a bone
   _____ sprain   B. pulled muscle
   _____ strain   C. joint separation
   _____ fracture   D. bone ends grating
   _____ crepitus   E. joint injury

3. Label the following diagram of a skeleton.

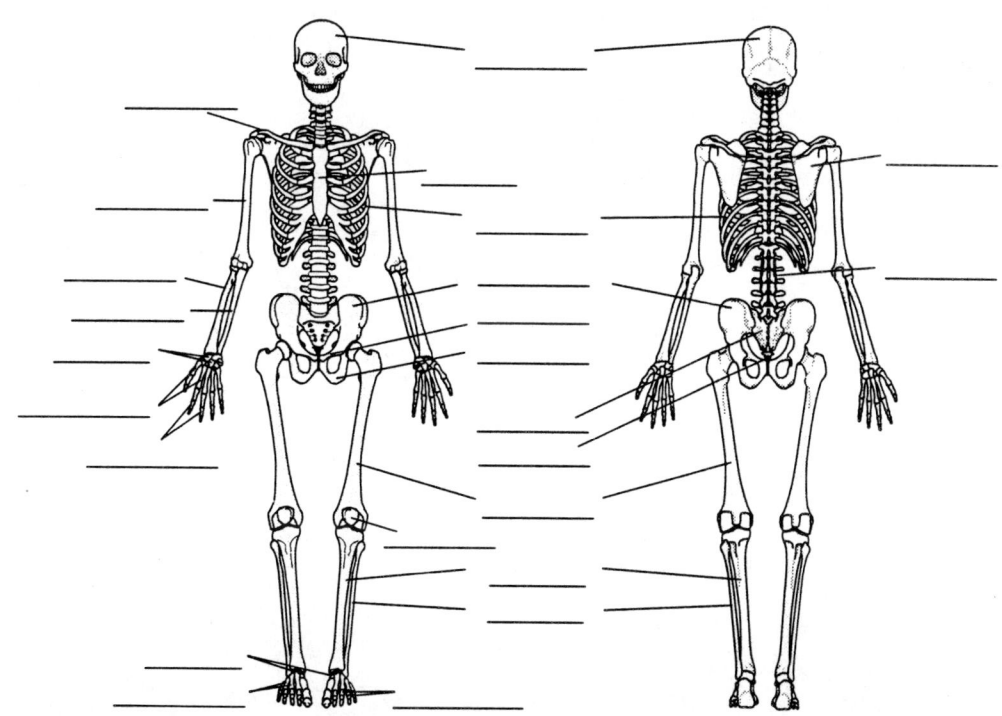

After performing the following tasks and procedures, have your instructor initial each item to indicate that you have done each of them correctly.

                                                      Instructor's Initials

4. Bring something from home that you could use as a splint.   _____

5. Apply an ace bandage in the figure eight style to a fellow classmate's ankle.   _____

6. Using a pair of crutches:
    - A. assume a tripod position   _____
    - B. walk 200 yards   _____
    - C. sit in a chair   _____
    - D. walk up and down the stairs   _____
    - E. get in and out of a car   _____

7. Apply the following to a fellow student:
    - A. arm sling   _____
    - B. shoulder immobilizer   _____
    - C. leg splint for a fracture of the distal tibia and fibula   _____
    - D. arm splint for a fractured wrist   _____
    - E. splint for a broken foot   _____

Chapter Sixteen
Moving and Positioning Patients

Objectives

After completing this chapter you should be able to do the following:

1. Define and correctly spell all key terms.

2. Use proper body mechanics when lifting objects or patients.

3. Assist a patient from a car to a wheelchair.

4. Safely transport patients from the ER to a patient room, the OR, or the ICU using a gurney.

5. Name and describe the positions patients are placed in for treatment.

Key Terms

- alignment
- body mechanics
- debilitated
- dorsal recumbent position
- Fowler's position
- hydraulic
- lithotomy position
- prone
- reverse Trendelenburg position
- right lateral recumbent position
- semi-Fowler's position
- Sims' position
- supine
- Trendelenburg position

Body Mechanisms

As an emergency department technician you will be very active in your daily work. Your body will be in constant motion. Think of your body as a motion machine. Your muscles, bones, and joints all work together to give you the range of motion you need to perform your daily activities. These are the parts of the machine. But, like any other machine, the parts of your motion machine must be maintained to keep it working properly. Every day many people are accidentally injured because they do not care for their machines (their bodies) properly. Some of these injuries can be prevented by using **body mechanics**. Learning the correct way to lift equipment and patients will keep your machine healthy.

body mechanics: the efficient and safe use of the body during activity

The best way to use your body efficiently is to let the strongest muscles do all the work. These long, strong muscles are found in the arms and legs, not in the lower part of the back. When lifting heavy objects, bend your knees and use the strength in the arm and leg muscles to avoid strain on the back.

Chapter Sixteen • Moving and Positioning Patients

Remember these principles when loading and lifting.

- Use slow, smooth movements rather than jerky ones.
- It is easier on your body to pull or push an object than to lift it.
- Less energy is needed to keep an object in motion than to stop and start a move.
- The closer you are to an object, the easier it is to lift.
- Avoid reaching; get close to the object to be moved.
- Place your feet apart to form a wider base of support.
- When lifting an object bend at the knees, not at the waist.
- Move your feet to turn an object you are moving, don't twist your upper body.
- Rocking back and forth on your feet uses the body weight as a force for pulling or pushing.

In the work setting, you must strive to keep your body in **alignment**. If the body is in alignment, all the muscle groups will work together. (See Figure 16-1) To properly align your body you must do the following:

- Stand straight.
- Tuck in your buttocks.
- Pull your lower abdomen in and up.
- Keep your back flat and straight.
- Lift your head up.
- Keep your chin in.
- Place your weight on the outer part of the feet.

This position makes the most efficient use of your body's muscles.

alignment: a physical position in which there is no stress or strain on any part of the body; the positioning of parts in a straight line

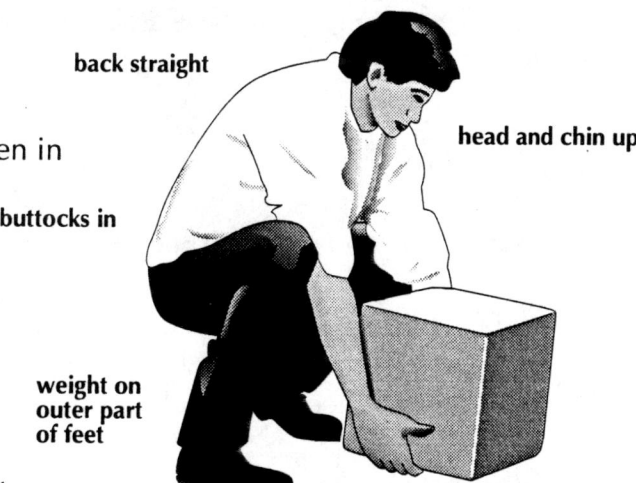

Figure 16-1: When the body is properly aligned, all the muscle groups work together.

When getting ready to move patients from a bed to a gurney, or from a wheelchair to a gurney always assess the situation first. This means taking an overall look at what it is you need to accomplish. Look at the patient you will be moving and determine if he or she can assist you in any way. The job will be much easier if the patient can help. If the patient is not able to assist in the move, then you must determine the type and amount of additional help that will be needed.

No one expects you to be "SUPER EMERGENCY DEPARTMENT TECHNICIAN." Always take the time to determine if additional help is needed and then get it. It is better to wait a few moments for help than to risk injuring the patient or yourself. There are many staff members in the emergency room who can help you lift a patient. The house orderly, security officers, X-ray staff members, and ambulance or paramedic personnel all are available to assist you. All you have to do is ask them.

Helping a Patient Get Out of a Car

Many of the patients who are brought to the ER will arrive by car. Some patients may not be able to walk into the hospital because of an injury to the foot or leg, or due to a medical problem that is causing breathing difficulty, chest pain, or weakness. These patients must be assisted with a wheelchair. Help them get out of the car by following these steps.

1. Open the car door.

2. Remove the patient's seat belt.

3. Slide the front seat as far back as possible.

4. Position the wheelchair as close to the car as possible.

5. Lock the wheelchair brakes.

6. Find out if the patient can stand at all.

Chapter Sixteen • Moving and Positioning Patients

7. Swing the patient's legs to the outside of the car. (Figure 16-2)

8. Help the patient to a standing position.

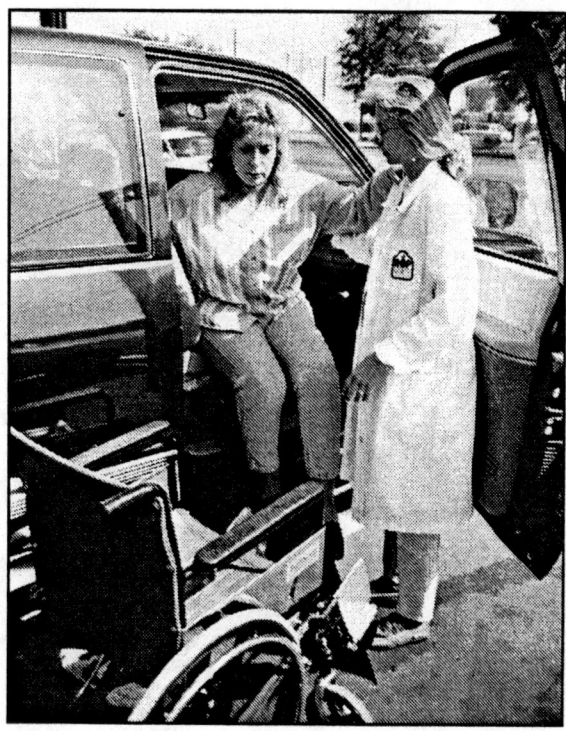

Figure 16-2

9. Support the patient under his or her armpits. (Figure 16-3)

10. Have the patient pivot and sit in the wheelchair.

11. Check to see if the patient is seated properly and comfortably.

12. Fasten the safety strap on the wheelchair.

13. Adjust the footrests.

14. Unlock the brakes.

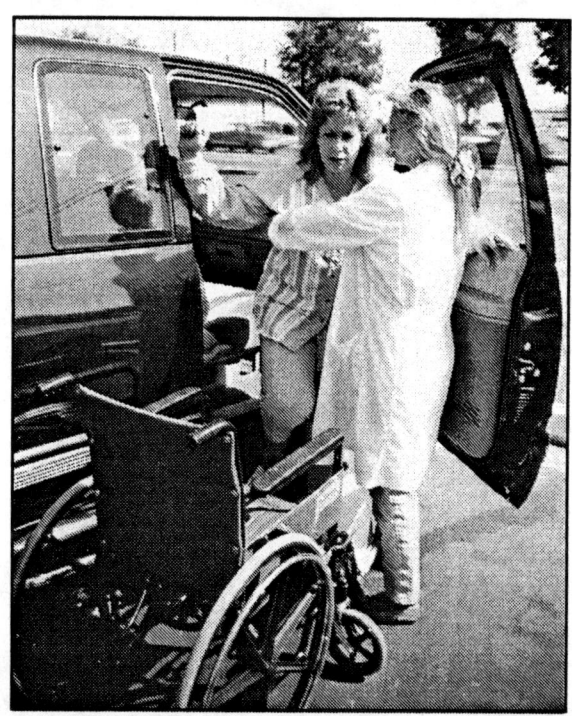

Figure 16-3

15. Push the patient and wheelchair into the emergency treatment area. (Figure 16-4)

Figure 16-4

Once the patient is brought into the treatment area he or she will be placed on the gurney. These stretchers are higher than a normal bed, and are designed for mobility and ease of treatment for the healthcare staff. Some of these gurneys may have high-low settings. If this is the case, place the gurney in the low position. If the gurney is not adjustable, find one of the stools that are located in various parts of the department. Make sure the gurney is in the locked position and the brakes are on before moving the patient. Raise the side rail of the gurney on the opposite side, and raise the head of the gurney to a sitting position. Position the wheelchair by the side of the gurney, face the head of the gurney, and lock the wheelchair brakes. Stand in front of the patient and help him or her to stand, supporting the patient under the armpits. Have the patient pivot (turn) and sit on the edge of the gurney. If a footstool is used, the patient should step up on the stool with both feet, turn, and sit on the edge of the gurney. Rest the patient's head and upper body on the already raised gurney. Lift both legs onto the stretcher. Make sure the patient is comfortable and raise the remaining side rail. Every occupied patient bed in the Emergency Care Unit should have both side rails up at all times.

Unloading Patients Who Arrive in Ambulances

Patients arriving by ambulance may arrive **code 3** (lights and sirens blaring) and in acute distress. Code 3 patients are in critical condition and CPR may be in progress. They must be unloaded quickly and safely, and taken immediately to the ER. Other patients arrive by ambulance for a variety of reasons. They could be **debilitated**, bed ridden, unable to walk, or in some other condition that warrants an ambulance transport. As an emergency department technician, part of your job will be to assist with the unloading of ambulance patients. Listen for the ambulance approach and go outside to meet the ambulance personnel. Stay in a safe place until the ambulance is parked and the motor is turned off. You can open the back door of the ambulance by using the door latch. The ambulance personnel will unload the gurney with the patient on it, and you can assist with the oxygen, IV, or other equipment.

debilitated: weakened; sickly

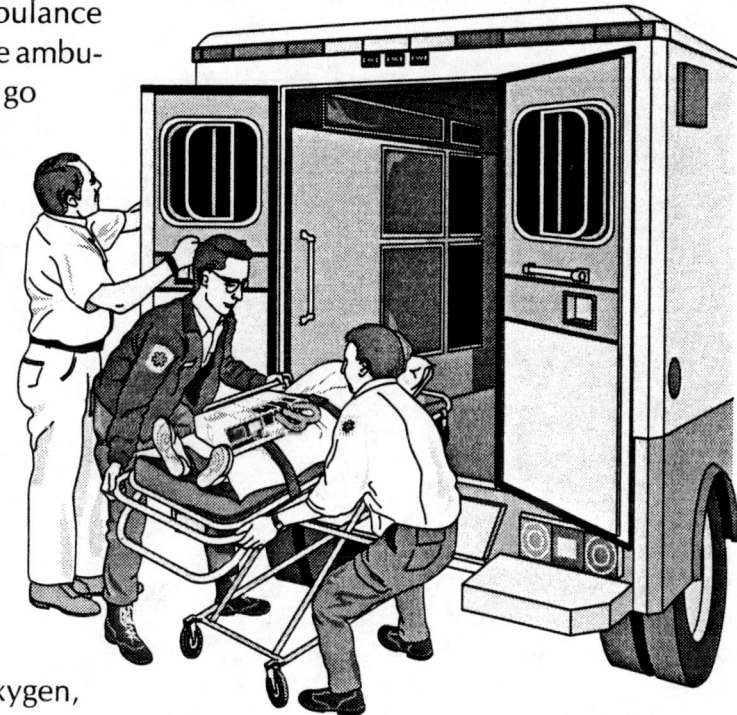

Each person involved with the care of the patient is part of a team effort. It is important to establish a team approach when working with ambulance personnel, police officers, and paramedics. Your duties will vary from patient to patient, but always do what you can to expedite the transfer of the patient. This means clearing the hallways, assisting with patient handling, or caring for the supplies and equipment. Each of these jobs is very important.

Using a Gurney

A gurney is a four-wheeled cart with a mattress that is used to transport patients. Some gurneys have brakes on each wheel, which are used to lock the gurney into position during patient transfers. Others have a single foot pedal that locks all four wheels at once. Some gurneys have both a high and a low position. This makes it possible to adjust the gurney to make patient transfers and procedures easier. The stretcher or gurney position can be changed so that the feet can be elevated to treat for shock, or the head can be elevated for patients who are having difficulty breathing. Some of the gurneys are operated by **hydraulics** or air pressure to make adjustments very easy.

hydraulic: operated or moved by water pressure

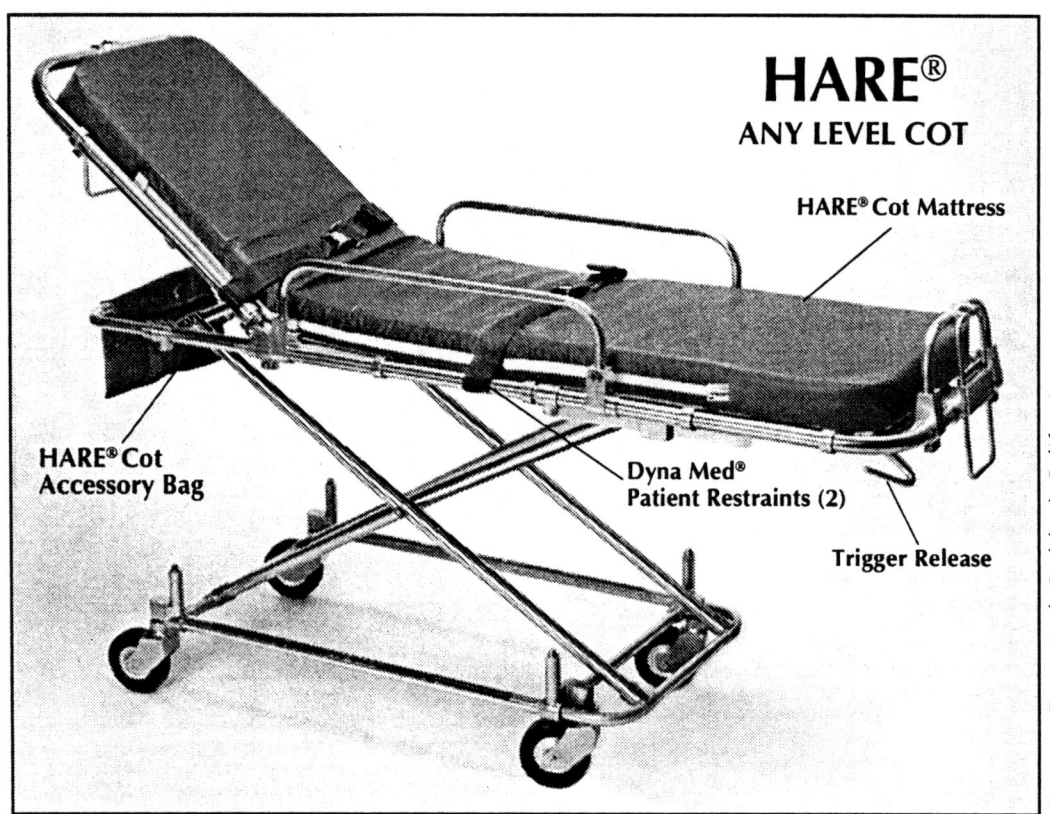

Figure 16-5: A Gurney

Chapter Sixteen • Moving and Positioning Patients

To transport a patient on a gurney, follow these steps.

1. Make sure the side rails are raised.

2. Secure the necessary safety restraints.

3. Secure a portable oxygen tank to the bracket under the gurney.

4. Position an IV pole in the slot provided.

5. Secure all drainage tubes.

6. Gather the patient's chart, his or her belongings, and any equipment that is to be transferred with the patient.

7. Lock the back wheels so they cannot turn from side to side. This will help you steer the gurney.

8. Make sure the patient's arms and legs are not dangling.

9. Push the gurney feet first. (Do not pull it.)

10. Stand at the patient's head as you push the gurney. This allows you to watch where you are going and to observe the patient.

11. When going around corners, check the mirrors on the ceiling for oncoming traffic.

12. Avoid sharp turns that could cause harm to the patient.

13. Do not go fast.

14. Watch for wet or slippery floors.

15. You may be able to push the patient alone. However, if the patient is heavy, needs to sit upright (which would block your vision), or has a lot of added equipment, get help from another person.

16. Provide a smooth, safe ride, avoiding sudden stops and jerky turns.

17. Check the ceiling mirrors when exiting the elevator to avoid collisions.

Assisting Patients From a Gurney to a Bed

When you enter the patient's room press the call light or intercom to let the unit personnel know you have arrived. The nurse from that floor should assist you with the patient transfer to the bed. Make sure all is ready before moving the patient.

- Is the oxygen set-up ready for use?
- Is an IV pole hooked to the bed?
- If a cardiac monitor is needed, is there one available?
- Is the bed linen turned down?
- Are the brakes on the bed in the locked position?
- Is the bed at the proper height?

Once you have confirmed that everything is ready for the move, follow these steps to transfer the patient.

1. Remove the pillow from the bed.
2. Position the gurney next to the bed.
3. If it is an electric bed, raise it to the same height as the gurney.
4. Lock the brakes on the gurney.
5. Lock the brakes on the bed.
6. Lower the side rails of the gurney.
7. Remove all safety restraints from the patient.
8. Check all tubes and equipment.
9. Unhook the Foley catheter drainage bag.
10. Locate the IV bottle and tubing and transfer them to the IV pole on the bed.
11. Locate the ECG monitor cable and connect it to the bedside monitor.

12. Obtain additional help if the patient is immobile.

13. Two persons stand on the gurney side.

14. Two persons stand on the side of bed.

15. Reach over the bed and gurney, and on the count of three, lift the patient into the bed.

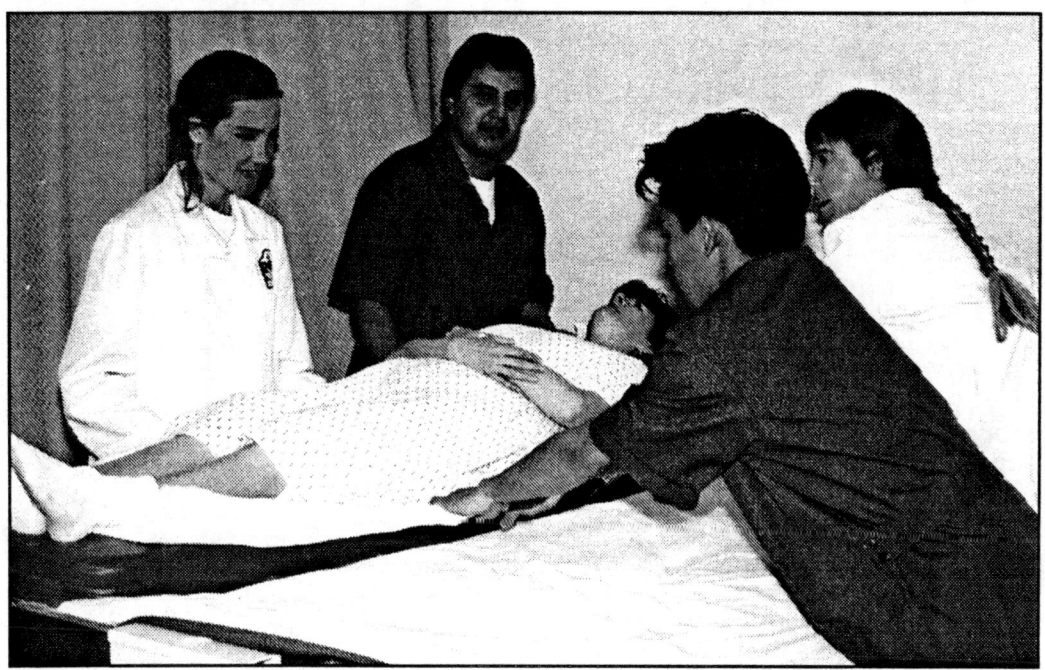

Figure 16-6

16. Secure all tubes in place.

17. Help the patient find a comfortable position.

18. Raise the side rails.

19. Adjust the bed to the low position.

20. Fasten the nurse call light within easy reach of the patient.

21. Put the patient's belongings in the designated area of the closet.

22. Deliver the patient's chart to the nurse.

Patient Positioning

The doctor may direct that the patient be placed in a particular position to make treatment easier, or to protect the patient due to his or her condition. For example, patients who are having difficulty breathing are better positioned in a sitting position. If they are forced to lie flat, their condition will become much worse. Study the following positions.

prone: a position in which a patient is lying face down, with the head to the side

supine: a position in which a patient is lying flat on the back

Fowler's position: a position in which a patient is semi-sitting with the head raised 45-60 degrees

semi-Fowler's position: a position in which a patient is sitting with the head elevated 15-30 degrees

Sims' position: a position in which a patient is lying on the right or left side

lithotomy position: a position in which a patient lies on the back with the legs elevated in stirrups; the position usually used for a pelvic exam

PRONE

SUPINE

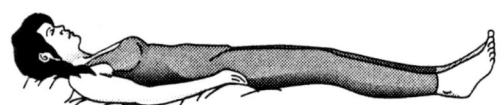

FOWLER'S POSITION

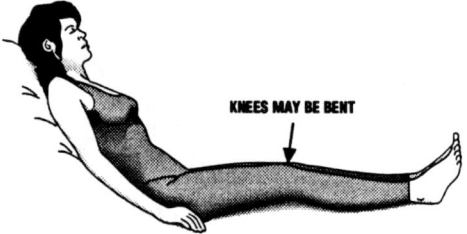

SEMI-FOWLER'S POSITION

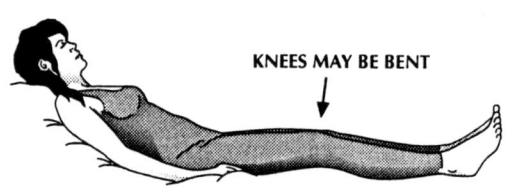

SIMS' POSITION

LITHOTOMY POSITION

Chapter Sixteen • Moving and Positioning Patients

TRENDELENBURG POSITION

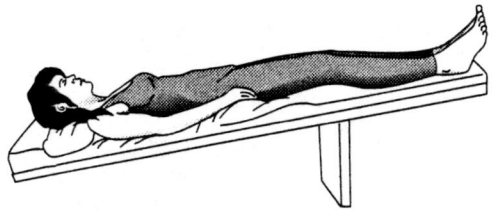

REVERSE TRENDELENBURG POSITION

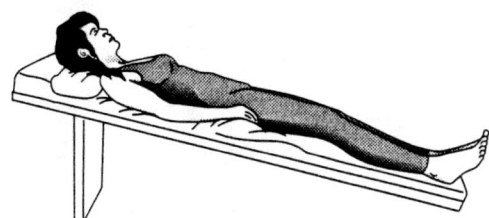

RIGHT LATERAL RECUMBENT POSITION

DORSAL RECUMBENT POSITION

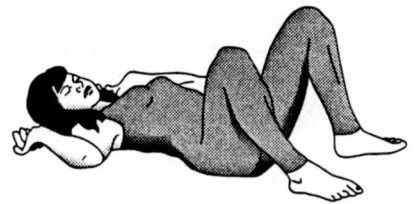

Trendelenburg position: a position in which the patient lies flat on the back with the feet elevated above the level of the heart to promote the flow of blood to the brain

reverse Trendelenburg position: a position in which the patient lies on the back with the feet down and the head elevated

right lateral recumbent position: a position in which the patient is lying on the right side with the knees flexed

dorsal recumbent position: a position in which the patient is lying on the back with the knees flexed

Make sure you know and understand each of these positions so that you will be able to position the patient properly. If the physician orders the patient to be placed in one of these positions, make sure you explain to the patient that the position must be maintained and why.

Chapter Summary

Working in the emergency room is a physically demanding occupation; it requires both strength and coordination. As an ER technician, transporting patients and equipment is part of your responsibility. You must plan the patient move, organizing all equipment and supplies before moving the patient. Using proper body mechanics will make your job easier and safer for both you and the patient. Moving the patient safely is your responsibility.

Chapter Sixteen • Moving and Positioning Patients 16-15

Name _____
Date _____

Student Enrichment Activities

1. Observe four people doing their job. Describe the job that was done and how body mechanics were used properly, or what the person should have done to use good body mechanics.

   _____
   _____
   _____
   _____
   _____

2. Label the following patient positions with the correct terms.

   _____   _____   _____

   _____   _____   _____

   _____   _____

3. Describe the procedure for transporting a patient from department to department on a gurney.

_____
_____
_____
_____
_____

Chapter Seventeen
Environmental Emergencies

Objectives

After completing this chapter you should be able to do the following:

1. Define and correctly spell all key terms.
2. List three types of heat-related emergencies.
3. Care for a burn injury.
4. Apply a burn dressing.

Key Terms

- core temperature
- fatal
- frostbite
- hyperthermia
- hypothermia
- protocol
- respiratory tract burn (RTB)
- rule of nines
- scald
- syncope
- Telfa

How Environmental Emergencies Occur

We live in a continually changing world. As a result, our bodies must constantly adjust to various environmental conditions. For example, if the air temperature is too hot, the human body will attempt to cool itself through evaporation by perspiring. If the air temperature is too cold, the body will attempt to warm itself by shivering to produce heat.

Environmental emergencies result when the normal body temperature is exposed to external temperatures that are either too hot or too cold. If the body is not able to adjust to these differences, serious medical problems result.

Types of Burns

fatal: death-producing

In the United States alone there are more than two million burn accidents each year. Many of these victims are children. Some of these burn injuries can be **fatal**. Furthermore, patients who survive serious burn accidents often suffer from additional complications that can occur from the burn itself. **Infection**, **shock** from the loss of body fluid, internal injuries, changes in physical appearance, and scarring that can affect muscle and joint movement are all complications that can result from a severe burn.

Chapter Seventeen • Environmental Emergencies

Burns are classified according to degree and the depth of the layers of skin that are involved. A first degree burn is the most common type of burn. A sunburn is an example of a first degree burn. It creates red and painful skin, and damages the top layer of skin. This damage leads to the peeling of the outer layer of skin.

A second degree burn is more serious than a first degree burn. Following this type of burn, the skin will become white or red, and blisters will form.

A third degree burn is a serious burn through all layers of the skin. The skin becomes dry and leather-like, and it can be white, waxy, or charred. A third degree burn can cause severe pain, but if the nerves are damaged there will not be any pain at all.

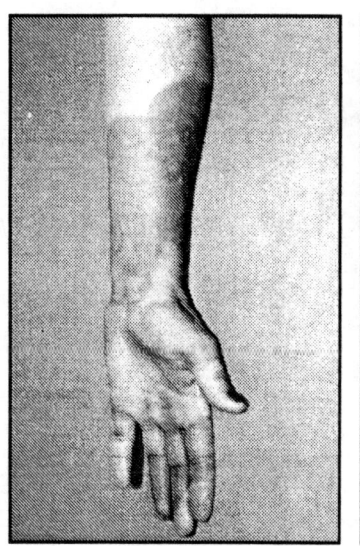 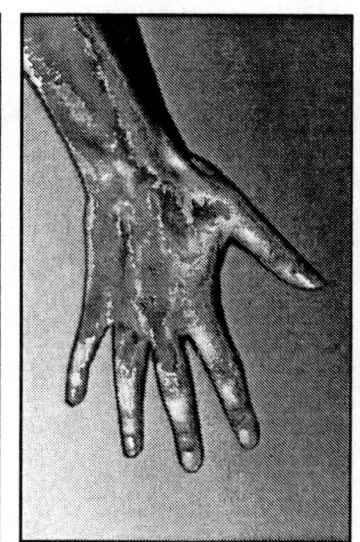 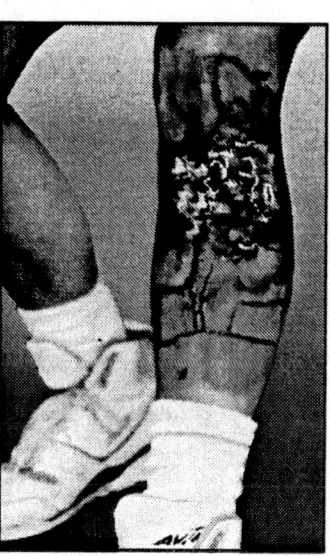

First Degree Burn   **Second Degree Burn**   **Third Degree Burn**

Figure 17-1: Types of Burns

rule of nines: a method used to calculate the extent of burn injury. Each part of the body is assigned a percentage based on a multiple of nine and the total burn area is estimated

The **rule of nines** is used to measure or calculate the severity of the burn. Each section of the body is given a percentage, and the area of burn is calculated accordingly. Figure 17-2 shows the percentage that is given to each section of the body for adults and children.

Rule of Nines

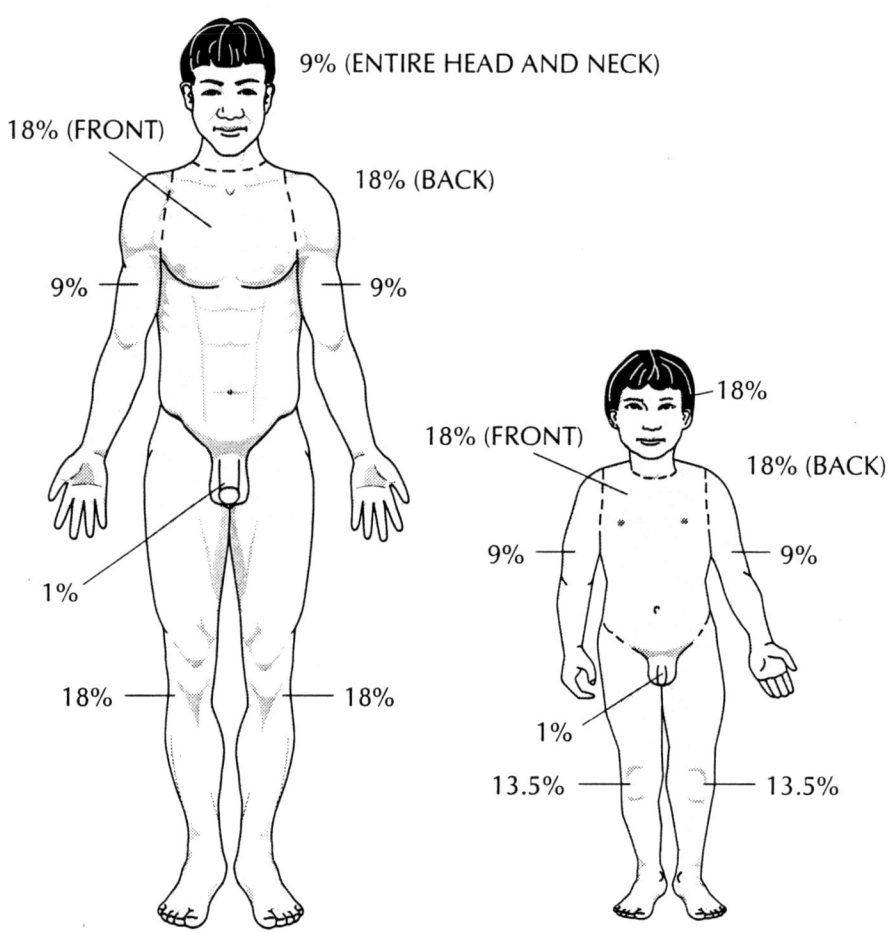

Figure 17-2: The Rule of Nines

Chapter Seventeen • Environmental Emergencies

Causes and Treatment of Burns

Burns can be caused by a variety of things: excessive exposure to the sun can result in a sunburn; a person who is doing housework can be burned by touching a hot iron or stove, or splashing a household chemical on the skin; or a young child can be **scalded** by hot water. The following case study is an example of how easily a scald can occur.

scald: a burn from hot liquid or steam

Case Study

Two-year-old Joey is a very curious child. While his mother is preparing dinner, Joey decides to "help." He reaches for the pot handle of boiling potatoes on the stove, and OOPS...

The pot is pulled off the stove, dumping the scalding water on Joey's chest and arms. He cries out from the pain, and his mother instantly grabs him and places him in a cool shower of water to decrease the pain and stop the skin from burning. Joey has first, second, and third degree burns from the boiling water.

Electrical accidents can cause burns as well as other challenging problems for the ER staff. If an electrical current enters the body, the heart can go into irregular rhythms. These patients must be observed closely on the **cardiac monitor**. Patients with electrical burns will have both an entrance and an exit wound.

Many burns are the result of a fire. If the person was in a burning house, he or she may have burns to the skin as well as smoke inhalation. Smoke inhalation, also known as a **respiratory tract burn (RTB)**, is a very serious emergency. As the hot air and **toxic** chemicals from the smoke are inhaled, the air passages become damaged and swollen, increasing **congestion**. If this happens, the patient will have **dyspnea** (difficulty breathing), the respirations will be noisy, and there may be a productive cough with sooty-colored **sputum**. As the respiratory difficulty increases, the patient will become restless, **cyanotic** (blue) from lack of oxygen, and increasingly confused. This patient must be placed on oxygen immediately, and the doctor must be notified. ALL patients with **respiratory distress** are seen immediately by the physician.

respiratory tract burn (RTB): respiratory distress as a result of exposure to a fire, characterized by smoke inhalation, singed facial hairs, and the coughing up of sooty sputum

When the patient arrives in the ER with a burn, he or she is seen immediately by the doctor. The treatment of burns depends on the location, type, degree, and extent of the burn. For example, if a chemical, like bleach, is splashed in the patient's face, the eyes must immediately be **irrigated** (washed) with **normal saline** for at least twenty minutes. A dressing usually will be applied to a burn, but not always. It may not be possible to put a dressing on the burned area, especially if it involves the nose or the mouth. The doctor will prescribe the treatment for each burn patient who enters the emergency room, so check with him or her before doing anything.

protocol: a standardized treatment procedure approved by an authorized source

There may be a standard procedure for burn care in your hospital, so follow the hospital **protocol**, or approved routine, for burn care. Your hospital may have a burn center to which the patient may be admitted, or the patient may need to be transferred to the community burn center.

Sometimes a person will arrive in the emergency room having already done some "first aid" at home to the burn. Many people will have applied ointment or some other home remedy on the injured skin. This will need to be removed. Unfortunately, this process can be very painful for the patient. It is best to teach people not to put anything on the burn.

The first aid treatment for burns is to cool the burned skin. If it is a first degree burn, immediately place the burned area in cool water. If the burn is a second or third degree burn, cool it immediately with cool water and place a sterile or clean dressing over the burned area. If the burn covers a large area, cover it with a sheet.

Chapter Seventeen • Environmental Emergencies 17-7

The doctor may clean the burned area and ask you to put a dressing over the burn. He or she also may order an antibiotic cream, such as **Silvadene, silver sulfadiazine**, or a spray-type medication to be applied to the wound. Then you can place a dressing and a bandage over the area. When applying a burn dressing, remember the following key points.

- Remove any jewelry as the extremity may swell, affecting circulation.
- Remove any clothing on or near the burn.
- Put on sterile gloves.
- Apply the dressing and bandage so that it will stay in place until the patient's next appointment.
- If you are applying a dressing to a child, make sure he or she can't remove it.
- **Stockinette** is very effective for keeping dressings in place.
- Completely cover the burn area with the ordered medication.
- Use sufficient fluff-type dressing between toes and fingers.
- Make dressings that are well padded.
- Use sterile procedure for all open wounds.
- Use **Telfa** or another non-stick dressing directly over the broken skin.
- Avoid applying any pressure to the burn site.
- The burn dressing must extend well beyond the wound.

Telfa: a non-stick, plastic dressing

Victims of serious burns are given emergency care, wrapped in sterile burn sheets, and then transferred to the burn unit. It also is important to find out when the patient received his or her last **tetanus** injection. Burn victims are susceptible to tetanus and, therefore, should have current tetanus **immunizations**. A tetanus booster is recommended every ten years unless the patient receives an open wound or burn. In that case, a tetanus booster is given every five years. If it has been longer than five years since the last tetanus injection, the injured person will need a tetanus booster immunization.

Emergencies Resulting From Excessive Exposure to Heat

Extremes in temperature affect everyone, but the very young and the very old are more susceptible to both heat and cold related emergencies. Since extreme temperatures can affect the heartbeat, all of these patients are placed on a cardiac monitor. Overexposure to heat can cause **syncope**. Heat exhaustion will occur from being in a hot, stuffy place. Victims of heat exhaustion become dizzy and **nauseated**, and often faint after standing in one place for several minutes in a hot and stuffy room or after extended exposure to intense heat. This person will have a slow, weak pulse, and his or her skin will be warm to the touch and moist with **perspiration**.

syncope: fainting; temporary loss of consciousness; passing out

Victims of heat exhaustion usually regain consciousness after lying down flat for several minutes. Cooling measures must be started as quickly as possible, either at the scene or in the ER. Remove any heavy outer clothing, place a cool cloth on the patient's forehead, and turn on the air conditioner if one is available. Upon arrival in the ER, the patient's vital signs must be taken. It also is essential to do a complete **secondary survey**, because there may be an additional injury that occurred from fainting, or the patient could have another problem like heart disease or diabetes.

hyperthermia: an unusually high body temperature

core temperature: the internal body temperature

Heat stroke, also known as **hyperthermia**, is a true emergency condition. When heat stroke occurs the body's ability to cool itself becomes inadequate, and the **core temperature** rises. The patient's skin will be red, hot, and dry. There will be signs and symptoms of shock, and the person may be **delirious** or unconscious. The patient's rectal temperature will be VERY high, and immediate cooling measures will be needed. Most heat stroke patients arrive by ambulance and are taken into the **Critical Care Unit** immediately. Intravenous lines will be started, an airway inserted, and every effort will be made to cool the patient. You may need to locate and connect fans, or go to Central Supply for the **cooling blanket** or **hyperthermia unit**.

Emergencies Resulting From Excessively Cold Temperatures

Frostbite results from extreme exposure to cold. There is water in all of the body's cells. If this water freezes it can injure the **tissue**. (Figure 17-3) Frostbite most frequently affects skin that is exposed, such as the nose, ears, fingers, and toes. Frostbitten areas burn, tingle, and become numb, and the skin turns white or gray and feels hard to the touch. **Hypothermia** occurs when the body's temperature drops below 95°F. The normal body temperature is 98.6°F. As the body temperature drops, all the organs in the body slow down. The heart rate drops; the respirations become slow; and the thought process is hampered, making the victim confused.

frostbite: the effect of freezing or severe cold on skin or other tissues

hypothermia: an unusually low body temperature capable of causing problems with the central nervous system and cardiac arrest

It is important to note that victims who are found by paramedics may have a heat or cold-related emergency as well as additional problems. Someone who has been outdoors or in an excessively hot or cold environment could fall victim to one of these emergency conditions.

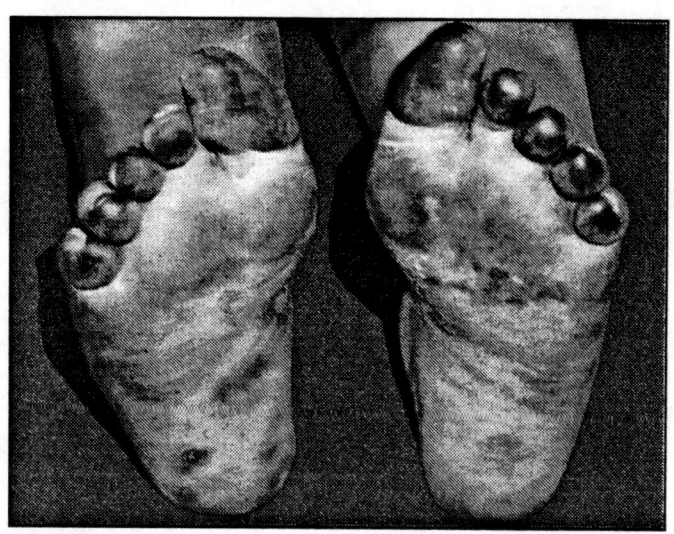

Figure 17-3: Frostbite

For example, near-drowning victims may also suffer from hypothermia if they have fallen into very cold water. In cases such as these, both resuscitative and warming measures must be taken to save the victim. Many near-drowning victims who have fallen into very cold water have been successfully resuscitated even after being submerged for a very long time. This is because the cold temperature slows the body's processes and reduces the organs' need for oxygen. CPR always should be done on these victims, and efforts must be taken to rewarm the person. The Emergency Department has a special thermometer that will accurately measure rectal temperatures in victims of both heat stroke and hypothermia.

Chapter Summary

Extreme temperatures can cause serious medical problems. These are known as environmental emergencies. Treatment for most of these emergencies involves returning the patient's body temperature to the normal 98.6° F.

Burns are another type of environmental emergency. Though mild sunburns rarely cause any additional complications, severe burns can lead to a variety of other problems including diminished movement in the muscles and joints. Burn care is determined by local protocol and is centered on the prevention of shock and infection. Burns are classified as first, second, or third degree according to their severity, and the extent of a burn injury is determining using the Rule of Nines.

Chapter Seventeen • Environmental Emergencies 17-11

Name _____

Date _____

Student Enrichment Activities

1. Using the rule of nines, estimate the percent of burn in the following cases:

   A. A 29-year-old firefighter burned on the . . .

   right arm　　　　　　　_____%

   right upper chest　　　_____%

   right side of face　　　_____%

   　　　　　　　　　　　_____% Total Burn

   B. An 18-month-old child sitting on her mother's lap upsets a cup of hot tea and is burned on the . . .

   lower abdomen　　　　_____%

   both thighs　　　　　　_____%

   　　　　　　　　　　　_____% Total Burn

2. Identify the name and location of the burn unit in your community.
   _____

3. Apply a burn dressing to a fellow student in the class. Have your instructor initial here when you have done this correctly. _____

Match the following terms with the appropriate definition.

4. _____ Hyperthermia   A. Blisters on skin

5. _____ Hypothermia   B. Elevated core temperature

6. _____ Frostbite   C. Red painful skin

7. _____ Heat exhaustion   D. Fainting, wet skin

8. _____ First degree burn   E. Decreased core temperature

9. _____ Second degree burn   F. Frozen tissue

10. _____ Third degree burn   G. Painless, charred skin

11. Cut out a newspaper article about a recent fire emergency and list two things that could have been done to prevent this accident. Paste or tape the article in the space below.

   A. _____
   B. _____

Chapter Eighteen
Poisoning and Overdose

Objectives

After completing this chapter you should be able to do the following:

1. Define and correctly spell all key terms.

2. Understand the importance of knowing the number of your regional Poison Control Center.

3. List the routes in which poison can enter the body.

4. Position an unconscious patient to prevent additional complications.

Key Terms

- absorption
- antidote
- emesis
- Foley catheter
- ingestion
- inhalation
- injection
- intake
- output
- toxicity

How Poisonings and Overdoses Occur

A **poison** is a liquid, solid, or gas that interferes with the body's normal processes. Depending on the type and amount that enters the body, these substances can result in severe illness, permanent brain damage, or even death. Some normally harmless substances can become a poison if they are used incorrectly. For example, taken as directed, aspirin normally is harmless. However, if someone ingests an entire bottle of the medication, the substance can become toxic and may even be fatal! Other normally harmless substances can become poisonous when they are combined with other substances.

Accidental poisoning and overdoses are among the most common of household accidents. Due to their tendency to put all kinds of things in their mouths, children are the most frequent victims of these emergencies. However, adults too, sometimes become victims after misinterpreting dosage instructions. Sometimes poisoning and overdose emergencies are the result of deliberate attempts to end one's life. Although these situations are rare, the possibility of intentional self-abuse must not be overlooked. A patient who has tried once to commit suicide may try it again. Therefore, the patient will be observed carefully while in the ER, and will be referred to psychiatric counseling after being treated.

Poisons enter the body in several ways. They can be **ingested**, **inhaled**, **absorbed**, or **injected**. (Figure 18-1)

ingestion: the act of taking something into the gastrointestinal tract by mouth

inhalation: the act of breathing something into the lungs

absorption: the passing of a substance through the skin or mucous membranes into body fluids or tissues

injection: the act of forcing a liquid under the skin or into a vessel or cavity intramuscularly

Chapter Eighteen • Poisoning and Overdose

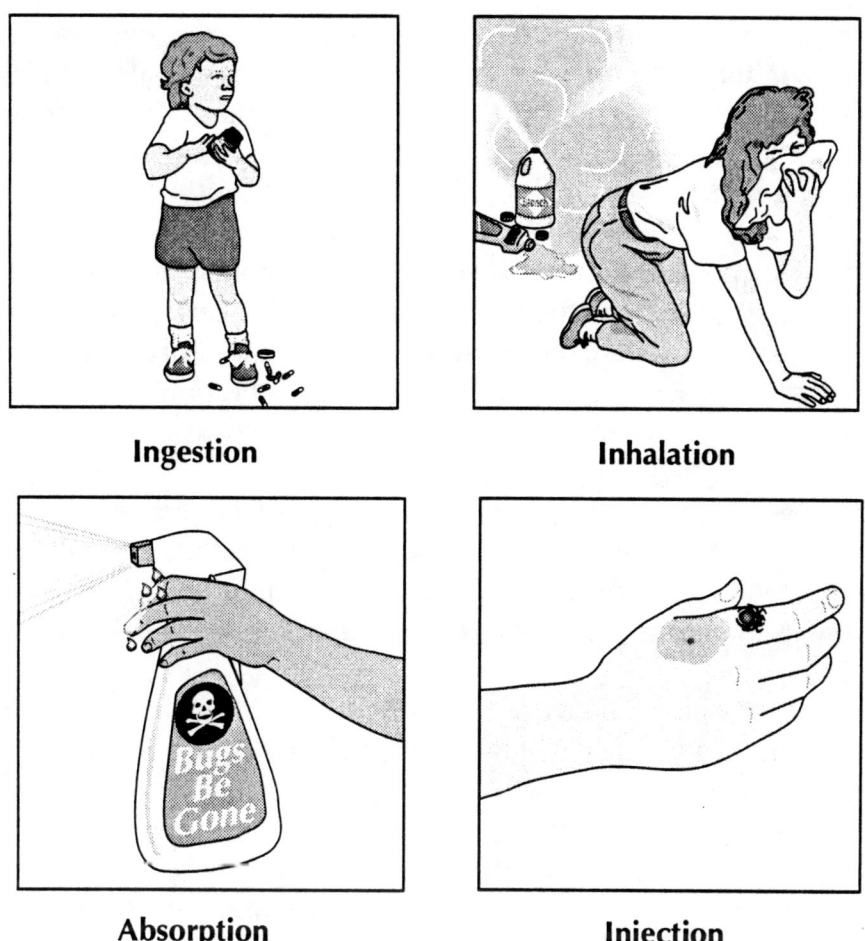

Figure 18-1: How Poisonings Occur

Caring For a Poisoning or Overdose Victim

Anyone who is reported to have taken an overdose or who is suspected of taking one must be seen in the emergency room immediately. This patient should not wait in the lobby, nor should their treatment be postponed. This is because the body processes can deteriorate after an overdose. A patient can be awake and talking one minute, and in **cardiac** and **respiratory arrest** the next minute. Overdose victims should be checked for the ABCs:

- Airway
- Breathing
- Circulation

Many drugs can cause **cardiac** irregularities, so overdose patients are placed on a **cardiac monitor**, and their heart rhythm is observed by the nurse. Many drugs can cause the breathing to slow to a dangerously low rate. When this condition, known as **respiratory depression**, occurs the patient is given oxygen and his or her respirations are observed carefully.

Some drugs or poisons can cause **seizures**. The patient is placed in a safe position on the gurney with the side rails up, and blankets or pillows are used to pad the area. This patient should be placed in an area that is easily observed, and a staff member will stay with the patient during his or her treatment in the emergency room.

Regardless of the type of drug or poison that is involved, the doctor will order an IV to be started by the nurse, and some type of medication will be given. Some medications are **antidotes**, which work to undo the effects of another drug. If a person has taken an overdose, an antidote is given.

antidote: a substance that neutralizes a poison

If the victim is awake, the doctor may order a medication that will make the patient vomit. The stomach will be emptied when the person vomits, and the contents, or **emesis**, may be sent to the laboratory for analysis. The emesis may contain pill fragments or traces of the source of the poison that can be identified in the laboratory. This important information can be used by the doctor to formulate a method of treatment for the patient. Do not discard the emesis until you are certain the physician does not want it sent to the laboratory.

emesis: vomit

If the patient is unconscious, the stomach will be pumped. The nurse will insert a large tube into the stomach and then wash the stomach out with a normal saline solution. It may be necessary to do this stomach washing, or **gastric lavage**, several times to result in a fluid that returns clear. This technique can be used to remove pill fragments as well as other chemicals or poisons.

Getting a History of the Incident

When a poisoned patient arrives in the ER it is very important to get a history of the incident. Paramedics or the patient's family may bring in the empty bottle of pills, the poison container, a plant, or even a dead snake. The sooner the poison is identified, the sooner the antidote can be given. Therefore, knowing the trade name, the chemical compound, or the prescription drug can be vital in beginning treatment. Valuable information can be obtained by calling your regional poison control center.

Chapter Eighteen • Poisoning and Overdose

The Poison Control Center is a central clearinghouse of information about various substances. There is a 24-hour response on the telephone line. The poison can be readily looked up in many different ways. If the label from the container is available, the substance will be researched using the name on the label or the chemical compound. Information is given about emergency treatment, signs and symptoms to observe for **toxicity**, and follow up instructions. Poison Control is a source of information that is available to anyone in the community needing information.

toxicity: the extent to which a substance is poisonous

To obtain the history of the incident, try to get the following information.

- What was taken?
- When was it taken?
- How much was taken?
- How much of the substance was originally in the container?
- How much is in the container now?
- How much was spilled?
- When was it taken?
- Was anything done at home for treatment?
- Are there any other medical or emotional problems with the patient?

Depending on the substance taken, many signs and symptoms can appear during a poisoning emergency. The following is a list of the most common poisoning symptoms.

- slow or rapid breathing
- a slow or rapid pulse
- changes in the pupils
- nausea
- vomiting
- diarrhea
- abdominal pain
- seizures
- an altered mental status

- excessive sweating
- unusual odors
- a low blood pressure
- burns or stains on the mouth or tongue

Poisoning and overdose victims must be watched very carefully. Because of the potential for vomiting, the patient must be positioned on his or her side. You may need to get extra pillows to prop the patient in this position. If vomiting occurs, this important step will allow the emesis to drain out of the mouth instead of down into the lungs. **Aspiration**, or fluid in the lungs, is a complication that can be prevented by keeping suction equipment available and in working order. If the patient is on his or her back and begins to vomit, immediately roll the victim onto his or her side, suction the patient, and call for the nurse.

Caring for an Unconscious Patient

Foley catheter: a catheter for the urinary tract that has a balloon attachment at one end to prevent the catheter from accidentally leaving the bladder

Patients who are unconscious will present a variety of challenges. Remember, the ABCs (airway, breathing, and circulation) are always the first things to check when the patient arrives. CPR may be in progress already. If the patient is breathing and has a pulse, attention must be paid to maintaining the position of the airway. The doctor will evaluate the quality of an unconscious patient's respirations. If the breathing is not adequate, an **endotracheal tube** will be inserted and the patient will be connected to a respirator (or ventilator). As soon as the patient is stabilized he or she will be transferred to the ICU for further care.

intake: the amount of liquid or solid that is put into a body

Unconscious patients will be placed on a cardiac monitor, vital signs will be taken, and the pupils will be checked for response to light. A **nasogastric tube** will be inserted by the nurse and a **Foley catheter** ordered.

output: the measure of the body fluids that are excreted

It is very important to watch the balance of fluid in the comatose overdose patient because some chemicals can cause kidney damage. The **intake** and **output** both are noted. These two numbers should balance. If they do not, it may mean that the patient is experiencing either kidney or heart failure. The nurse may ask you to empty the Foley catheter and measure the urine output. To do this, follow the procedure on the next page.

Chapter Eighteen • Poisoning and Overdose

Measuring Output From a Foley Catheter

Materials needed:
- ✓ graduate
- ✓ gloves

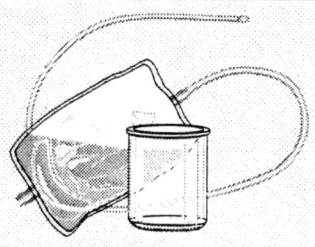

1. **Procedural Step:** Wash your hands.
   Reason: Universal precaution.

2. **Procedural Step:** Identify the patient.
   Reason: To ensure you are dealing with the correct patient.

3. **Procedural Step:** Put on gloves.
   Reason: Universal precaution for handling body fluids.

4. **Procedural Step:** Obtain a **graduate**.
   Reason: This measuring container is marked in ml.

5. **Procedural Step:** Empty the catheter bag into the graduate by opening the valve or clamp on the drainage bag.
   Reason: This allows you to measure the amount of urine in the catheter bag.

6. **Procedural Step:** Measure the amount of urine in the graduate.
   Reason: This is the patient's output.

7. **Procedural Step:** Discard the urine in the toilet.
   Reason: This is the proper place to dispose of urine.

8. **Procedural Step:** Remove your gloves.
   Reason: Universal precaution.
   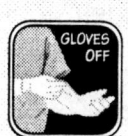

9. **Procedural Step:** Wash your hands.
   Reason: Universal precaution.

10. **Procedural Step:** Record the output on the patient's chart.
    Reason: To provide documentation.

Chart it like this:

500 ml clear yellow urine from Foley catheter.

If this patient is sent for x-rays or other procedures, you will go with the patient to watch the airway, breathing, pulse, and level of consciousness. Vital signs should be taken every five or ten minutes. Immediately report any changes in the level of consciousness to the physician. Check the patient frequently, and be prepared to respond quickly if the patient begins to vomit. If vomiting occurs, immediately turn the patient to the side, begin suctioning, and notify the nurse.

Chapter Summary

Caring for a victim of a poison or overdose can be a challenge. It is very important for you, as the ER technician, to get a detailed history of the incident. This history is very important to the physician in determining the course of treatment for the patient. When the patient arrives in the ER, the airway, breathing, and circulation are the first three things to check. Watch the patient closely for any changes in mental status or level of consciousness. Be alert for signs of nausea, and if the patient begins to vomit, position him or her on the right or left side. Overdoses and poisonings are frightening for both the patient and his or her family, so it is important to treat them compassionately. Remember—treat the patient, not the poison.

Chapter Eighteen • Poisoning and Overdose

Name _____
Date _____

Student Enrichment Activities

1. Look up the phone number for the poison control center in your community and record it in the space below.

    The phone number for the poison control center in my community is: _____

    Place this number near your phone at home.

2. Make a list of the contents of your medicine cabinet at home:

NAME OF MEDICATION	NUMBER OF PILLS IN CONTAINER
_____	_____
_____	_____
_____	_____
_____	_____
_____	_____
_____	_____
_____	_____
_____	_____
_____	_____
_____	_____
_____	_____
_____	_____
_____	_____
_____	_____
_____	_____

3. List the items found under your sink at home and place an **X** next to the ones that are poisonous.

ITEM	X
_____	_____
_____	_____
_____	_____
_____	_____
_____	_____
_____	_____
_____	_____
_____	_____
_____	_____
_____	_____
_____	_____
_____	_____
_____	_____
_____	_____
_____	_____
_____	_____
_____	_____
_____	_____
_____	_____
_____	_____
_____	_____
_____	_____
_____	_____
_____	_____

Chapter Eighteen • Poisoning and Overdose   18-11

Name _____

Date _____

Match the poison in Column A with the route of intake in Column B.

Column A   **Column B**

4. _____ chlorine bleach   A. ingestion

5. _____ poinsettia plant   B. injection

6. _____ carbon monoxide   C. absorption

7. _____ Valium tablets   D. inhalation

8. _____ cocaine

9. _____ heroin

10. _____ gasoline

11. _____ aspirin

12. _____ insect killer

13. _____ rattlesnake bite

14. _____ furniture polish

15. _____ cough syrup

16. _____ vitamins with iron

17. _____ spray paint

18. _____ bee sting

19. Draw a picture of the best way to position an unconscious overdose patient on the back of this page.

Chapter Nineteen
Emotional and Behavioral Emergencies

Objectives

After completing this chapter you should be able to do the following:

1. Define and correctly spell all key terms.

2. Recognize normal reactions to stress brought on by illness or injury.

3. Recognize abnormal behavior.

4. Use therapeutic communication to deal with emotionally disturbed patients.

Key Terms

- denial
- depression
- hallucination
- hostility
- paranoid
- regression
- stress
- therapeutic communication
- withdrawal

Stress

stress: a psychological or physical force that is experienced by a person and that requires a response or change on the part of that person

There is no **stress** greater than that associated with a sudden illness, injury, or death. Everyone involved is affected: the patient, family members, bystanders, paramedics, EMTs, and other people at the scene. The emergency department technician is also under a great deal of stress on the job. In life-threatening situations certain behavior patterns emerge that help individuals deal with these stressful events. Understanding these behaviors and levels of stress can help you deal with your personal reactions and those of your patients and coworkers.

Doctor Elisabeth Kubler-Ross is a well-known **thanatologist** and author who has worked extensively with dying patients. In doing so, she has identified several methods these patients use to deal with this stressful situation. These same methods of coping surface when a person is faced with the possibility of a life-threatening injury.

Confusion and Emotional Shock

Some patients, upon arrival in the ER, do not know what happened to them or where they are. This confusion and disorientation can be the result of an injury to the head, or it can be related to the shock of a sudden injury or illness. People at the scene of an emergency also have a tendency to be disoriented or confused. Bystanders typically try to do something to help, but in doing so they may overreact and race from one treatment to another. Emotional shock can affect family members by making them forget well known items, such as addresses, telephone numbers, etc. This can make getting information from them very frustrating. You must be patient and understanding. Recognizing that this state of confusion and emotional shock is a result of the stressful situation is a critical step in developing this compassion.

Fear

Fear causes **anxiety** and results in many symptoms: sweating, shaking, weakness, rapid heart rate, nausea, and nervousness. An emergency patient experiences fear of the unknown. He or she does not know what to expect for the future. The patient may want to know if he or she will be able to walk again or if surgery will be required. The family members also are afraid and may ask if the patient is going to die. The person may be so afraid that he is unable to ask these questions; but whether he or she voices these questions or not, chances are that the person is thinking about them. It is important for healthcare workers to maintain a calm, reassuring atmosphere and to assure the patient and family members that everything possible is being done. Fear and anxiety can lead to a loss of self-control and can cause a feeling of helplessness.

Denial

Many patients admitted to the emergency room will try to minimize or completely deny the problem. They might claim that a heart attack is only indigestion. A patient may say he is all right, or even deny that there is any pain. Therefore, it is important to watch the patient's behavior along with what he is saying. If the patient says that he is not having chest pain, but at the same time is frowning and clutching his chest, this person is in **denial**. Another example of denial occurs when a patient attempts to walk on a broken leg or insists on being discharged from the hospital without treatment.

denial: refusing to believe that which is true or real

Regression

regression: acting in a childlike manner

When there is a great deal of stress in a person's life, he or she may find comfort in **regression**. An adult may return to a previous behavior pattern in a crisis. For instance, he or she might react to a stressful situation with a temper tantrum, by crying uncontrollably, or by withdrawing completely and refusing to talk about it.

Depression

depression: extreme feelings of sadness or hopelessness

withdraw: to retreat into oneself, often ceasing or reducing communication with others

Whenever a person experiences a loss or a threat of a loss, he or she becomes depressed. If an accident results in the loss of a person's health or ability to work, **depression** typically follows. If a person loses a family member to an accidental death there will be immediate shock and disbelief, followed by depression. Depression can cause the patient or family member to **withdraw** partially or completely. In some cases, the person may stop communicating with others completely.

Anger

hostility: aggression, animosity or antagonism

Some people react with anger and **hostility** to stressful situations. This anger may be directed at you, or you may see it aimed at another person. For example, a mother may shout at you if she feels that nothing is being done to help her sick son. This anger is a result of frustration and helplessness. People get angry when they cannot change a difficult situation.

Dealing With Behavioral Problems

Your ability to deal with behavioral problems in a stressful situation is very important. You must be able to take care of the physical needs of the patient as well as the emotional needs of the patient, his or her family, and other healthcare team members. Remember the behaviors that occur in stressful situations, and understand why a doctor may be angry that supplies are not immediately available. Show compassion for the wife of the patient when she has difficulty giving you the needed information for the admission record, and understand why parents are impatient with delays in treatment for their injured child.

You can do much to reduce the anxiety level of your patient by having a calm and reassuring attitude. Knowing your job and doing it well will reassure the patient and relieve his or her feeling of helplessness. You can bring a sense of well-being to the patient by caring for both the patient and family members in a calm and efficient manner. Speak in a calm, strong voice, show compassion, and do your job. Any directions that are given to the patient or family member must be very clear and simple. This will reduce the panic and confusion. You may find that you need to repeat even simple directions several times.

Do not lie to patients. If a procedure is painful, gently explain what is going to be done. Maintain hope. Let the person and the family members know that you are doing all that is possible. Communicate with the patient, family members, and staff. Allow family members to visit the patient as soon as possible.

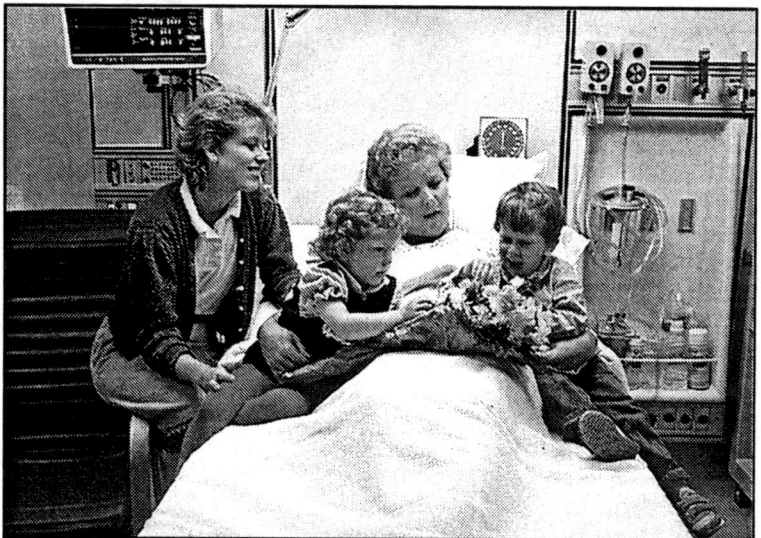

Figure 19-1: Visits from family members are an important part of a patient's healing process.

Remember to be aware of sources of embarrassment for the patient, and do what you can to minimize them. If the patient's clothes must be removed, explain why this must be done and reassure the patient that you will provide him or her with a hospital gown. Provide privacy for the patient whenever possible.

Let the person express his or her feelings. If the patient wants to cry or express anger, he or she should be allowed to do so. Give the patient permission to express himself. Tell the patient, "It's OK to cry, I know you must hurt a great deal." Don't take what is said personally. Remember that you are not the cause of the patient's pain. If the patient seems to be full of hostility, you might try saying, "You must be very angry about this situation." This opening will give the patient permission to talk about what is bothering him or her.

Psychiatric Emergencies

A psychiatric emergency exists when a person's behavior seems abnormal or bizarre and presents a danger to himself or to another person. The patient may have a history of psychiatric problems, nervous breakdowns, mood disorders, alcohol or drug related problems, emotional disorders, or an attempted suicide. The patient already may be under the care of a mental health professional, or this may be the first experience. Some disturbances in behavior can be related to physical problems as well. For example, lack of oxygen to the brain, **diabetes**, and head injuries can cause personality and behavioral changes as well as psychiatric problems.

A psychiatric patient may have an emotional outburst. If so, it is important to have a quiet area or room where this patient can be taken. This patient will be removed from the main lobby and placed in a treatment area. He or she must be supervised at all times, so you may be asked to sit with this person until the doctor can evaluate him. Watch the patient constantly, and never leave him or her alone. If there is an increase in activity, attempt to calm and reassure the patient. Never argue with a psychiatric patient as this will increase his or her agitation. If you feel that this person poses any kind of a threat to your safety, summon hospital security immediately.

Chapter Nineteen • Emotional and Behavioral Emergencies

Abnormal Behavior

Abnormal behavior can be a symptom of psychiatric problems. Assess the following characteristics in your patient to determine the likelihood of an emotional or behavioral emergency.

Appearance:

- Is the patient's clothing appropriate for the situation and temperature?
- Does he or she seem ill-kept?
- Is the patient displaying any anxiety-related mannerisms (i.e., pacing, wringing hands, can't sit still)?
- Is his or her speech rapid or very slow?
- Does the patient appear to be under the influence of drugs or alcohol?

Personality:

- What is the patient's mood (i.e., excited, depressed, agitated)?
- Does he or she seem angry?
- Is the patient unable to control his or her feelings?
- Does he or she appear to be afraid?

Mental Status:

- Does the patient seem disoriented?
- Is the patient unable to explain his or her actions?
- Is he or she unable to recognize the hospital?
- Does he or she appear confused?
- Is the patient oriented to reality?
- Does he or she seem to be suspicious of you or others?

Orientation:

- Are the patient's thoughts disconnected or confused?
- Does he or she seem to hear imaginary voices?
- Does he or she see things that aren't there?
- Is the patient talking to him or herself?
- Is he or she suicidal?
- Does the person seem depressed?
- Is he or she **paranoid**?

paranoid: experiencing abnormal or unfounded fear

Approaches to Therapeutic Communication

therapeutic communication: communication that is designed to relieve stress or obtain information that can be used to aid in healing emotional or psychological wounds

Therapeutic communication requires the ability to listen and obtain vital information. It involves a non-judgemental attitude and acceptance of patient responses. Communication is encouraged by asking open-ended questions. Open-ended questions require more than a "yes" or "no" response from the patient. For example, "Tell me about how you got here," is an open-ended question, whereas, "Did you come by car?" is a closed-ended question which merely requires a "yes" or "no" response. Observance of the following guidelines will promote therapeutic communication with your patients.

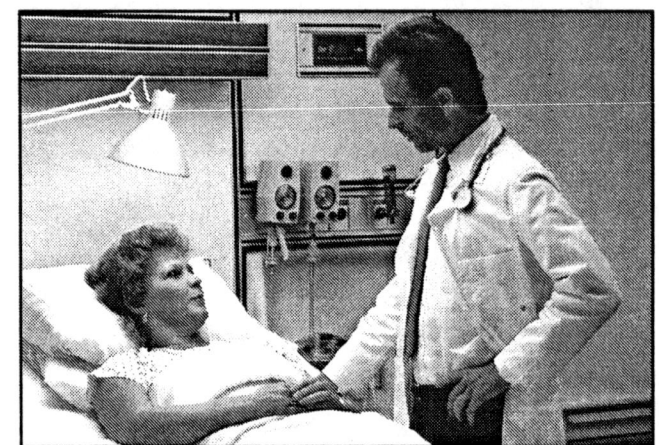

1. Observe the patient. Look at the patient's appearance, behavior, and mannerisms.

2. Introduce yourself. Tell the patient your name and what you do.

3. Call the patient by name to promote better communication.

4. Talk with the patient. Get at the same physical level; do not stand over the patient. Try to have the patient sit down with you and talk. Maintain eye contact as you talk. Encourage the patient to talk and avoid making any judgments.

5. Be calm.

6. Let the patient know that you are listening. Ask open ended questions such as, "You seem pretty sad. What has made you feel that way?" Try to get the patient to tell you what happened.

7. Take your time. Don't look at your watch or give the patient any signs that you are not interested.

8. Stay non judgemental. Do not criticize, or blame the patient, and don't argue with him or her.

9. Be honest. Tell the patient what the rules are and what is expected of him or her.

10. Develop trust. Show the patient you care and that you are concerned.

11. Do not leave the patient alone. This person is unpredictable.

12. Avoid making sudden movements. These can be interpreted as threats.

13. If the patient is having **hallucinations**, acknowledge that the patient sees or hears things, but let him know that you do not see or hear them.

14. Try to orient the person to what is going on at the moment.

hallucination: seeing or hearing something that is not there

The doctor may order medications for the patient. If the patient is **sedated**, he or she will need to be in a gurney with the rails up. Patients who are combative or confused may need to be **restrained** as well. The doctor must order the restraints, but you will assist in placing them on the patient. Soft restraints are placed over the wrists or ankles and tied to the bed frame with a square knot. Do not tie them to the side rail because moving the rail will make the restraint too tight. A jacket restraint, or **posey**, is used on patients who are in danger of falling out of bed or from the gurney. The jacket is placed on the patient and secured in the back. The side ties are secured to the bed frame. Strong leather restraints are used for severely combative, confused, and hostile patients. These restraints are placed on the wrists and ankles. The rules for using restraints on a patient are very strict. The doctor must order the restraints before they can be put on, and frequent and accurate documentation on the medical record is essential. Frequent notations are made about the patient's behavior, the reason for the restraint, and the method of restraint that is used.

Patients who are in custody will be wearing handcuffs or plastic wrist ties. A peace officer will be in attendance with these patients. After emergency care is rendered, the person in custody will either be admitted to the jail ward or released to be booked into the city or county jail.

Disposition of Psychiatric Patients

Always check the vital signs on psychiatric patients. If your hospital has a psychiatric facility, the patient will be admitted for treatment. The type of psychiatric care that will be provided will depend on whether the patient needs an inpatient or an outpatient facility. A patient who is a danger to himself or to others, or who is gravely disabled may be put on a 72-hour psychiatric hold and admitted without his or her permission for a psychiatric evaluation. It is sometimes very time-consuming to find a resource for care of this patient, so he or she may be in your facility for several hours while efforts are made to find a suitable facility.

If your hospital has an inpatient psychiatric facility a crisis intervention team will be available to assist with difficult situations. However, many psychiatric hospitals in the community have a crisis intervention team on call that is able to respond to your facility for patient evaluation if your hospital does not have a psychiatric service.

Suicidal Patients

A person who threatens to commit suicide must be taken seriously. These patients must never be left alone, and will be given a psychiatric evaluation. If a person calls on the telephone and threatens suicide, attempts must be made to locate the source of the telephone call and dispatch emergency personnel to the scene.

Personal Stress Management

Working in the Emergency Care Unit can cause a great deal of tension and stress. It is an exciting job; but it also is stressful. In order to care for others you must first take care of yourself. It is expected that you will be anxious when dealing with a cardiac arrest situation. This is a stress-producing situation. You and the rest of the ER staff will be under stress. However, certain situations can cause **distress** or a feeling of loss of control. Too much work, not enough help, the inability to save someone's life, and caring for the victim of child abuse all can result in a feeling of helplessness and lack of control.

Talking about these situations with the staff nurses and doctors will help reduce some of this anxiety, as will expressing your feelings about some work experiences to your supervisor. Some hospitals provide in-house counseling to staff members. These facilities may review the care and treatment of patients in case study presentations as a method of helping staff members deal with the pressures of the job. Patient confidentiality always is maintained in this learning environment.

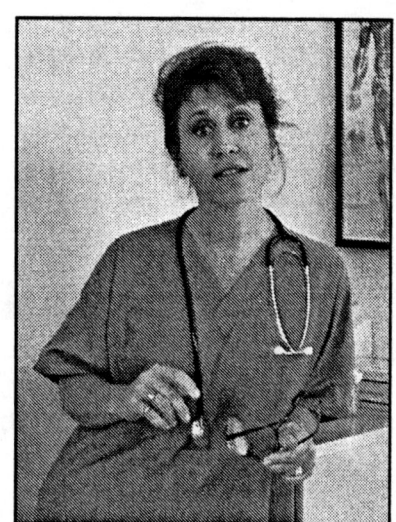

You must take care of yourself and learn to enjoy your free time for rest and recreation. Keep physically fit, and find a person with whom you can talk. Try to find a person to talk to on the job, as well as a person to talk to off the job. Try to leave your work at work, and your personal life at home; and remember—if you feel that the stress of the job is affecting your work and your home life it is time to seek professional help.

Chapter Summary

Emotional and physical well being go hand-in-hand. A crisis can trigger various coping mechanisms in one's behavior. Therefore, it is important to recognize the stress that individuals are under in emergency settings. All efforts must be made to improve communication between the staff, patients, and family members. Therapeutic communication plays an important role in reducing stress for psychiatric patients, whereas understanding and honesty can reduce the levels of stress for other patients and their families. Finally, don't forget to monitor your own stress levels. As an emergency department technician you will be exposed to all kinds of stressful situations. By keeping yourself physically fit and finding someone to talk to about these events you can reduce the effects that stress will have on you.

19-12

Chapter Nineteen • Emotional and Behavioral Emergencies   19-13

Name _____
Date _____

Student Enrichment Activities

Match the words with the appropriate definition.

1. _____ Angry   A. childlike behavior

2. _____ Regression   B. to threaten harm to another

3. _____ Depression   C. mad

4. _____ Withdrawal   D. failure to accept that something is true

5. _____ Denial   E. sadness

6. _____ Hostile   F. failure to communicate

7. _____ Paranoia   G. unsubstantiated fear

8. List ten behaviors that are abnormal.
   A. _____   F. _____
   B. _____   G. _____
   C. _____   H. _____
   D. _____   I. _____
   E. _____   J. _____

9. List four things that you should do to stay healthy and reduce stress.

   A. _____
   B. _____
   C. _____
   D. _____

10. Write a paragraph about a personal reaction you had to an illness or injury.

    _____
    _____
    _____
    _____
    _____

11. Using the approaches to therapeutic communication, tape a ten minute conversation with a friend and evaluate the conversation by answering the following questions.

	YES	NO
Did you introduce yourself?		
Did you state what you do?		
Did you call the person by name?		
Did you avoid making judgements?		
Did you stay calm?		
Did you ask open-ended questions?		
Did you let the person know you were listening?		
Did you take your time?		
Were you critical of the person?		
Were you argumentative?		
Were you honest?		
Did you show concern?		
Did you show you care?		
Did you acknowledge the person?		

Chapter Twenty
Caring for Children

Objectives

After completing this chapter you should be able to do the following:

1. Define and correctly spell all key terms.
2. Recognize normal vital signs for children.
3. Measure the height and weight of an infant and a child.
4. Assist with procedures that are performed on children.
5. Demonstrate the proper way to hold an infant.
6. Use the papoose board or mummy restraint on a toddler.

Key Terms

- cleft lip
- cleft palate
- clubfoot
- croup
- Down syndrome
- febrile seizure
- hydrocephalus

Emergencies Involving Children

Caring for children involves caring for the entire family. Not only will the child need care, his or her parents and other family members will need compassion too. The hospital setting is unfamiliar to children and may frighten them. If a child is afraid, it will be harder to examine the patient, obtain vital signs, and perform any treatments or tests than it would be on an adult who understands what is happening. Furthermore, the parents usually are anxious, and may demand that you help their child first. This is a situation that requires compassion, patience, and good judgment. One of your responsibilities will be to **triage** the patients. Children with life-threatening conditions must be identified immediately. The following signs and conditions require immediate attention.

- breathing problems
- unconsciousness
- near drowning
- bleeding
- shock
- seizures
- trauma
- burns
- child abuse
- **dehydration**
- rash
- eye injuries
- fever
- poisoning
- neck pain

Chapter Twenty • Caring for Children

The Patient History

It is important to obtain a history on all patients. The child may be too young to give you any information, so the parents are the ones who will provide the history for emergencies involving a child. When gathering information about children it is very important to use all the observation skills that were discussed in Chapter Five. Because the child cannot always tell you what is wrong, you must be able to make observations about his or her condition. Children and infants who are ill can deteriorate rapidly, so it is essential that those who are at high risk (those with the problems listed on the previous page) are seen by the doctor right away.

The following information should be obtained on all children who are admitted to the ER.

- age
- weight
- chief complaint
- vital signs
- known allergies
- medications the child is taking
- immunization history

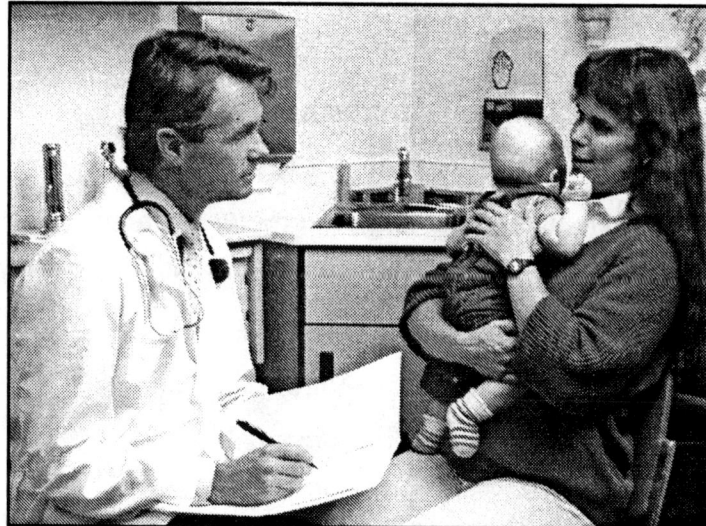

Figure 20-1: Observation skills are just as important as patient histories when caring for children.

Safety Measures

Accidents are the major cause of death in infants and children. As an emergency department technician you must monitor the safety of the infant or child at all times. Your hospital will have policies to ensure the safety of patients, but the following rules apply when caring for all children.

- Keep a crib available for infants and children to be placed in while they are waiting for treatment.
- Keep the side rails up at all times when not providing direct care.
- Wash your hands before and after caring for each patient.
- Keep all sharp needles, instruments, and small objects out of the child's reach.
- Identify the child by the identification bracelet—not by calling his or her name.
- Apply restraints correctly.
- Keep all medication out of the child's reach.
- Use the tympanic thermometer if there is one available.
- If you must use a rectal thermometer, hold it in place.
- Do not use oral thermometers on children under the age of 5.
- Keep hot liquids away from the patient.
- Do not allow children to share toys.
- Handle infants and children with care.
- Use elevators, not stairs.
- Always keep one hand on the child when working with him or her.
- Support the child when you hold him or her.
- Always use safety straps with wheelchairs or gurneys.

Figure 20-2 shows the proper ways to handle an infant or small child.

Chapter Twenty • Caring for Children

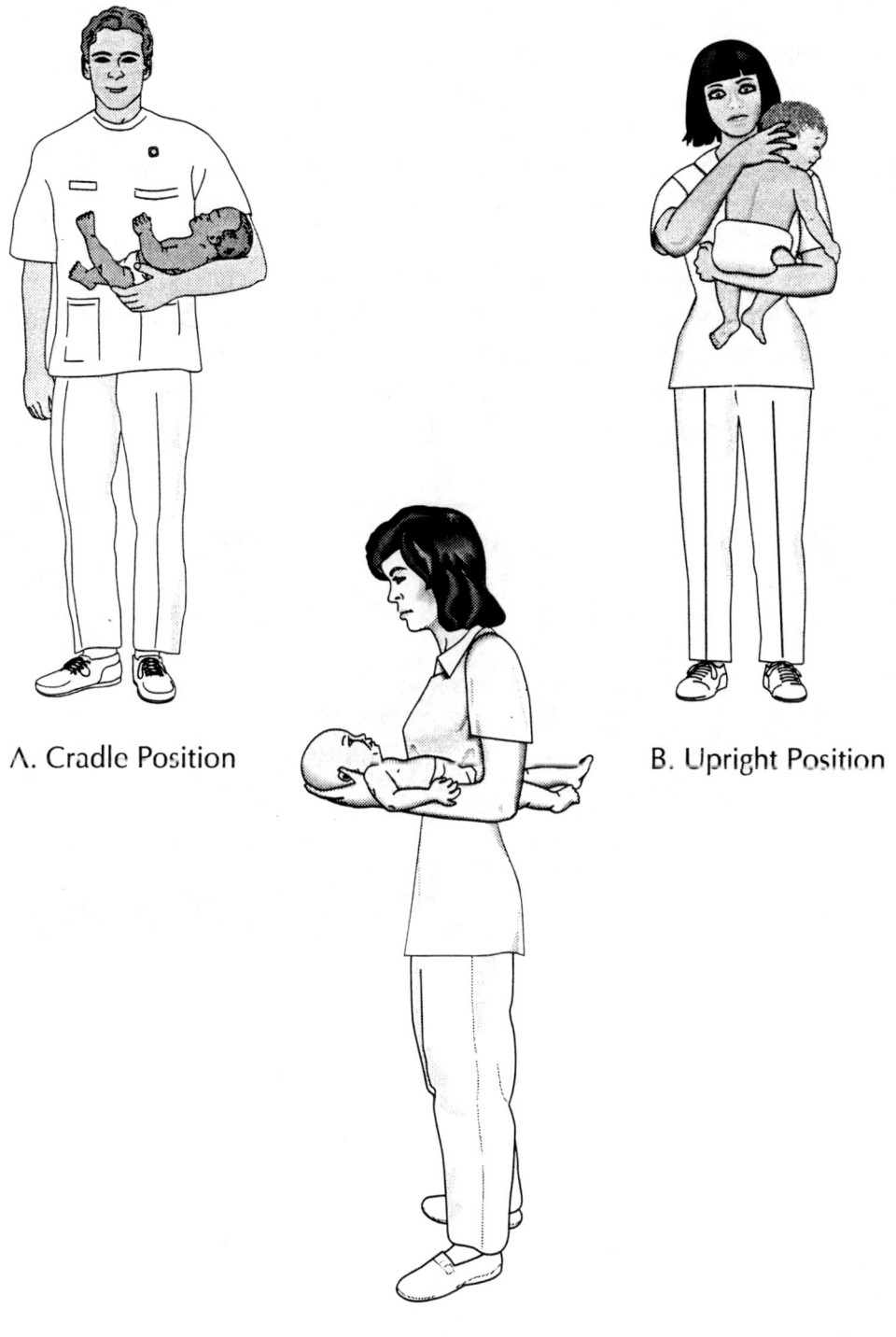

A. Cradle Position

B. Upright Position

C. Football Position

Figure 20-2: Proper Ways to Hold or Carry an Infant or Child

Restraints

The physician may order restraints for a child or infant during a procedure to prevent the child from moving about, dislodging an IV line or a tube, or causing further injury. For example, a child who needs **sutures** will need to be restrained during the procedure to prevent further injury, or a child may need to be restrained to prevent him or her from falling out of a crib or a bed.

A **mummy restraint** is used to restrict movement in infants. You can create this type of restraint by wrapping a blanket around each of the child's shoulders and arms. A **papoose restraint** is a board with cloth and Velcro straps that is used to immobilize infants and small children for procedures. (Figure 20-3) Do not place the restraints on too tight—it will interfere with circulation.

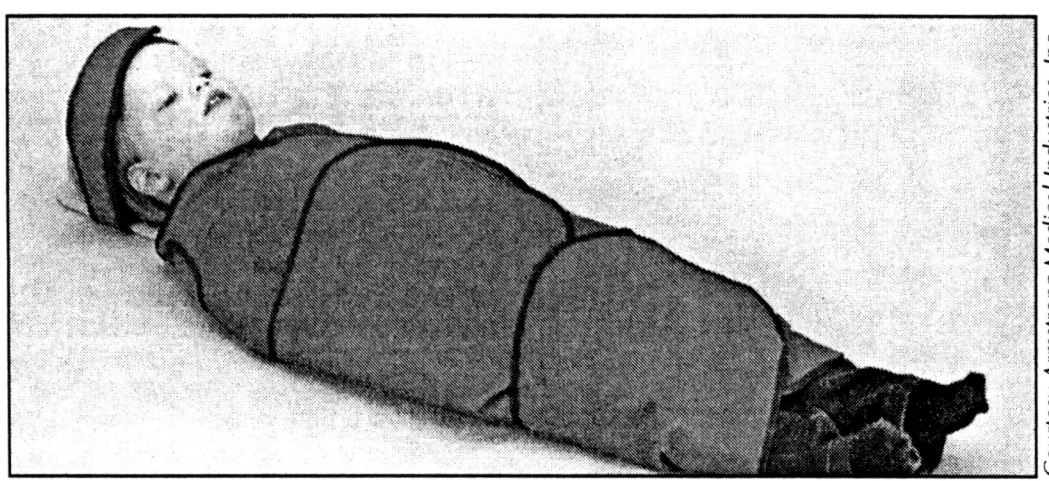

Figure 20-3: A Papoose Board

Chapter Twenty • Caring for Children

Vital Signs

Vital signs must be taken on children when they are admitted to the ER and as often as necessary after that. On children under the age of 5, the temperature will be taken either rectally or using a tympanal thermometer. Children's vital signs will vary with age.

The pulse may be difficult to obtain on a crying, wiggling child. If this is the case, ask the mother to hold the infant to quiet him. If you cannot feel a pulse, use your stethoscope to obtain an **apical** pulse. The blood pressure is taken the same way on an infant or child that it is taken on an adult. Make sure you use the proper size blood pressure cuff for this procedure.

When caring for infants it is important to remember to keep one hand on the child at all times. (Figure 20-4) Babies move suddenly and forcefully at times, but with little control. By maintaining contact with the child, you can keep the baby from falling and prevent other injuries.

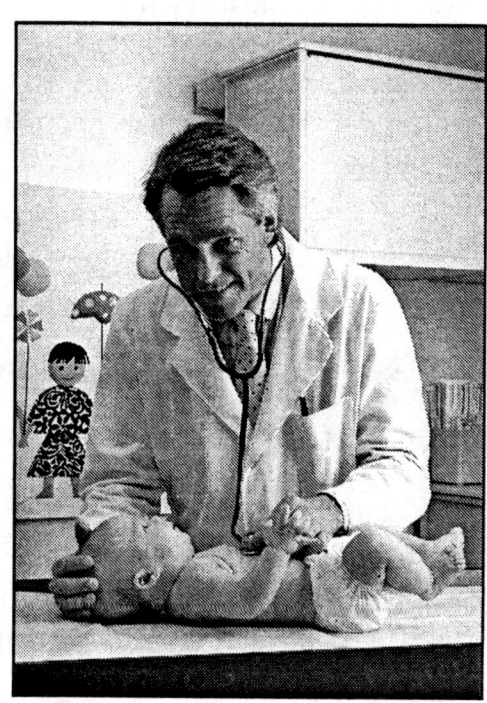

Figure 20-4: Keep one hand on the infant at all times.

AGE	PULSE	RESPIRATIONS	BLOOD PRESSURE (systolic/diastolic)
newborn	125/min	35	64-96/30-62
1-12 months	120	32	60-118/42-80
2 years	110	25	74-124/39-89
4 years	100	25	79-119/45-85
6 years	100	20	85-115/48-64
8 years	90	18	89-121/48-66
10 years	70	18	93-125/48-68

Measuring Height and Weight

When an infant is admitted to the Emergency Department the baby's clothes and diapers are removed. The infant is measured and weighed and then examined by the physician. The height of an older child can be measured on the stand up scale using the height ruler. To measure an infant, place the baby on the examination table and a make a mark on the disposable sheet at the top of the head. (Figure 20-5) Straighten one leg and make a mark at the heel. Now you can measure the distance between the two marks with a tape measure. Record the child's height in centimeters.

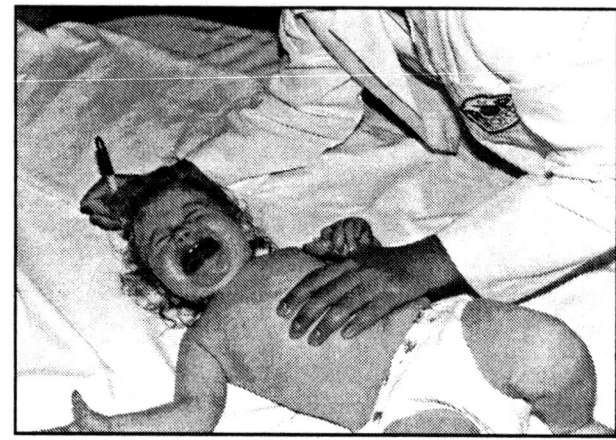

Figure 20-5: Measure the height of a baby by marking the disposable sheet.

To weigh a baby, remove all of the infant's clothes. Place a paper towel or a diaper on the baby scale and balance the scale with the paper or diaper in place. Next, place the baby on the scale. Keep your hand above the baby at all times, but do not touch him. This way, you will be able to steady him if he or she jumps up or rolls. Record the infant's weight in pounds and ounces or in grams on the chart.

When you have finished, remove the baby from the scale, and diaper and dress him or wrap him in a blanket, according to the physician's instructions. You may need to wait until after the infant has been examined by the physician to put a new diaper on the baby. Use gloves when changing a diaper. There are disposable diapers located in the pediatric supply cabinet. Place the diaper under the infant's buttocks with the sticky side of the tapes toward the front of the diaper. Bring the front of the diaper between the infant's legs and fasten the tapes securely.

If the child is old enough to stand still and well enough to stand, use the stand up scale to weigh him or her. The patient should be in a gown and have bare feet. Before he or she steps on the scale you must balance it. Then place a disposable towel on the platform and ask the patient to stand on the scale. Record the weight on the patient's chart. Remember that while the patient is undressed it is an excellent time to make observations about skin condition, general health, cleanliness, rashes, or abnormal marks.

Chapter Twenty • Caring for Children

Collecting Specimens

If the child is old enough to understand directions explain the specimen collection procedure to him or her using very clear directions and defining any terms that may be new to the child. For example, the child may not know the words **urinate**, **defecate**, or **bowel movement**. The parent may be able to assist you with this. It is important to obtain a specimen that is not contaminated, so make sure the child cleanses the perineum with a mild soap before voiding.

A pediatric urine collecting bag is used on infants and children who are not toilet trained. Again, the perineal area should be cleansed first with a mild soap and dried. Remove the protective cover from the collection bag and apply the adhesive patch over the perineum. Secure the patch in place.

Infection

A child who is admitted with fever, cough, rash, drainage, irritability, or changes in the level of consciousness, may be suffering from an infectious process. This child should be removed from the main lobby as soon as possible and placed in a room away from other patients. This is because many childhood diseases are **contagious** and are spread rapidly from one child to the next. Infections can occur anywhere in the body; the child may have a sore throat, headache, earache, cough, stomach ache, or wound infection.

Injuries

As children become older, they also become more active. For this reason, toddlers and older children are more apt to have accidents that can cause a **laceration**, **fracture**, poisoning, or burn. These injuries and the treatment for them have been discussed in the previous chapters. Remember, when emergency treatment is given in a timely manner, healthy children recover speedily.

Illness

A child with a sudden illness can have symptoms that become very serious in a short time. **Appendicitis** is the most common reason for abdominal surgery in children. A child with an inflamed appendix will have a fever and pain in the lower right **quadrant** of the abdomen. Children also can have **diabetic** emergencies. This is a very serious disease in children and must be treated immediately. It can be complicated by the fact that the parents may not yet know that the child has this condition.

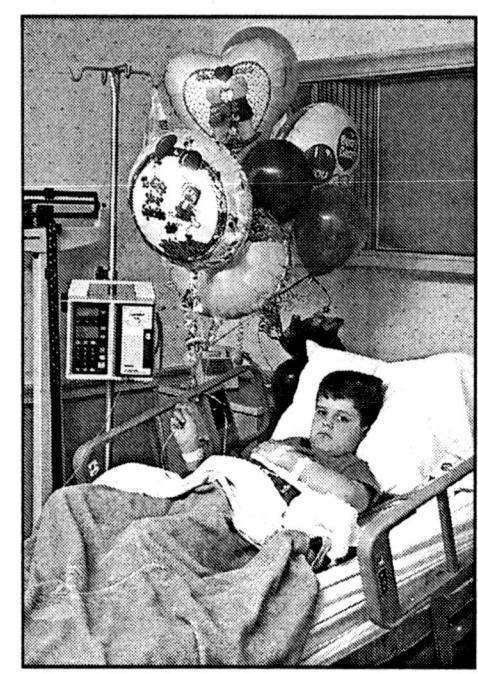

croup:
a viral infection of the respiratory tract that mostly affects children below the age of three; characterized by a barking cough, hoarseness, fever, and difficult breathing

Laryngotracheobronchitis, also known as **croup**, can occur between the ages of 3 months and 3 years of age. A virus causes inflammation in the upper airway, and the swelling leads to the respiratory distress and a "croupy" cough. **Epiglottitis** is another type of inflammation that involves swelling of the airway. It can lead to respiratory distress, or it can cause the breathing to stop completely. This child will be very ill, drooling, unable to swallow, and the voice will be muffled. Since the child will have trouble breathing, the physician must see this patient immediately. **Asthma** is a respiratory disease that can occur in children and adults. Treatment for asthma requires medication and breathing assistance.

febrile seizure:
a convulsion or seizure associated with a fever

Infections can cause the temperature to rise. In some children between the ages of three months and five years a temperature increase can cause a **seizure**. If this generalized seizure is caused by a fever it is called a **febrile seizure**. As an ER technician, you will protect the child from any further injury and maintain the airway. The doctor may order cooling measures that include removing the child's clothing and gently reducing his or her temperature with a sponge bath using **tepid** water.

Chapter Twenty • Caring for Children

20-11

Congenital Conditions

Some babies are born with conditions that require special care and treatment. These are called **congenital** problems or defects. The child may be brought to the emergency room for a complication of the congenital problem, or the child may have an illness or an injury along with the congenital problem. **Down syndrome**, **hydrocephalus**, heart disease, a **cleft lip**, a **cleft palate**, **clubfoot**, hip dislocation, and blood diseases are examples of birth defects.

Child Abuse

Dealing with child abuse is very sad and extremely traumatic for everyone involved. Children can be abused physically, sexually, emotionally, or by neglect. Abuse is a non-accidental injury. When child abuse is suspected it must be reported by the physician or charge nurse to the local authority of child protective services. Healthcare professionals are part of the team in the detection and prevention of child abuse because the life and safety of the child are at stake. Certain injuries which may indicate child abuse include the following:

- stocking mark burn (scald burns of feet and ankles from being held in hot water)
- definable burn shapes (i.e., the shape of an iron, stove, or heating grate)
- multiple bruises in various stages of healing
- hair that has been pulled out
- cigarette burns
- strap marks
- bites
- pinch marks
- slap marks
- eye injuries
- fractures
- **venereal disease**
- **welts**
- poisoning

Down syndrome: a congenital defect resulting in moderate to severe mental retardation and a variety of physical defects

hydrocephalus: an abnormal amount of spinal fluid within the ventricles of the brain

cleft lip: a birth defect which manifests as a cleft or separation of the upper lip; a harelip

cleft palate: a congenital abnormality resulting in a hole in the roof of the mouth, forming a passageway between the mouth and nasal cavities

clubfoot: a congenital foot deformity in which the bones in the front part of the foot are misaligned

If you see any of the above injuries, or perceive that the child has been neglected by being deprived of food, clothing, protection, or medical care, you should remember that these could be signs of abuse. Make sure the doctor or nurse is aware of the situation too. They also are aware of the signs of abuse, but they may not have all of the patient history that you do, particularly in cases of neglect. Be sure to document all information on the patient's chart. If you notice strange behavior from a parent, feel that a story does not match the injury, or sense extreme fear in the child, you should report this to the doctor immediately.

Sudden Infant Death Syndrome

Sudden infant death syndrome (SIDS) is the sudden, unexpected death of an apparently healthy baby. The cause of SIDS is unknown, and scientists continue to study why it occurs. If CPR has been started in the pre-hospital setting, it may be continued in the emergency room with no response. The physician will pronounce the infant dead and will face the difficult task of informing the parents. This is a very emotional situation. It is a time when parents, family, and staff need a great deal of emotional support to deal with their grief. Most hospitals have a **chaplain** or religious person available to help the survivors cope with this sudden death, or the family may ask you to call a close family member or **clergy** for support. Make time to locate these important people. They will be greatly needed.

Chapter Summary

Most children are born healthy and strong, but illness and injury can make it necessary to bring a child to the Emergency Care Unit for treatment. These conditions can develop quickly in children and lead to life-threatening situations. When a child becomes a patient the whole family becomes involved in the care of that child. Learning about the care of children can help you establish priorities and develop methods for dealing with children.

Chapter Twenty • Caring for Children   20-13

Name _____

Date _____

Student Enrichment Activities

1. Write the normal range of vital signs for the following:

	Pulse	Respirations	Blood Pressure
Infant			
2 year old			
4 year old			
6 year old			
8 year old			
10 year old			

2. Using a doll or a manikin do the following tasks and have your instructor initial in the appropriate space when you have done them correctly.

   A. Demonstrate the way to hold a baby. _____

   B. Put a diaper on the baby. _____

   C. Use a blanket to demonstrate the mummy restraint. _____

   D. Using a child manikin or doll, secure it to a papoose board. _____

3. Take vital signs on ten children and record the results below.

Patient Initials	Pulse	Respirations	Blood Pressure
1.			
2.			
3.			
4.			
5.			
6.			
7.			
8.			
9.			
10.			

Chapter Twenty • Caring for Children

Name _____

Date _____

4. Measure the height and weight of ten children and record the results below.

Patient Initials	Height	Weight	Age
1.			
2.			
3.			
4.			
5.			
6.			
7.			
8.			
9.			
10.			

20-16

Chapter Twenty One
Care of the Elderly

Objectives

After completing this chapter you should be able to do the following:

1. Define and correctly spell all key terms.
2. Recognize the potential for injury when caring for the elderly.
3. Describe how aging affects the human body.

Key Terms

- geriatrics
- osteoporosis

How Age Affects the Human Body

People are affected by the aging process in different ways. Some people never seem to age, and some seem to grow old very quickly. Some of these characteristics may be genetic, but many of these physical and emotional changes can be greatly influenced by one's attitude about aging. For example, a person's interest in life and his or her degree of activity often can influence the effects of his or her age. People who are active and who are interested in life seem to age much slower than those who simply sit and watch life pass them by. Likewise, those who interact with other people on a regular basis seem to be less affected by age than people who spend all of their time alone.

Although attitude can influence some of the affects of the aging process, some changes are inevitable as the body grows older. It is important to understand these changes so that we can better communicate and care for the increasing number of older patients. The hair and the skin undergo obvious changes. The skin becomes dry and wrinkled and turns darker, sometimes in spots, due to an increase in pigment. The hair becomes drier, thinner, and turns white or gray. Women may grow facial hair and some men become bald. The physical size and shape of the body also change. This is due to the fact that aging depletes both bone and muscle tissue, causing the elderly to become smaller and shorter than they were in their youth.

A less obvious change that occurs is that the digestive system becomes less effective. This leads to a loss of appetite, weight loss, and problems with bowel and bladder elimination. **Osteoporosis** can cause the bones to become shorter and easier to break. Muscle tone is lost, and joints become stiff. All of the senses diminish too, especially vision and hearing.

osteoporosis: a condition in which a decreasing calcium level in the bones causes them to become brittle

There are emotional changes as well. Older people may want to be physically active, but are unable to do so because of health reasons. Because they have seen so many years come and go, the elderly frequently experience many losses as family members and friends die. Then too, they must deal with the reality that their own death is inevitable.

As their ability to care for themselves diminishes, they may need to move in with family members, or they may have to move to a nursing home. It often is difficult to face all of these changes. Sometimes these changes in lifestyle become overwhelming and lead to depression.

Consider the following typical scenario:

Case Study

Hazel Whitehead is 88 years old and lives alone. This morning she fell down the stairs and hurt her hip. Fortunately, a neighbor heard her calling for help and called the paramedics. Due to the mechanism of injury, the paramedics determined that she may have fractured her hip and summoned an ambulance to take her to the hospital.

As she is wheeled into the ER you ask her how the injury occurred. She gives you the following explanation:

"I don't know why I fell. I guess they just don't make lights like they used to. I can barely see the stairs these days. Maybe I'm just getting too old. I can't even climb my stairs any more without getting out of breath."

When you ask her if she felt dizzy before she fell, Hazel asks you to repeat the question several times before she understands what you are asking her. She also complains that everyone mumbles these days. "No one seems to speak clearly anymore," she says. She also has difficulty reading the "small" type on the admission form you ask her to sign, and cannot remember her daughter's phone number. In pain, Hazel sighs heavily and concludes that she must be getting "old and crabby" like so many of her friends.

Caring for Elderly Patients

As an allied healthcare worker, you must remember that elderly patients may need help in taking care of their basic needs. You will need to treat each patient on an individual basis. No two patients are going to be exactly alike; you cannot simply lump all elderly patients into a category and label it "old and helpless."

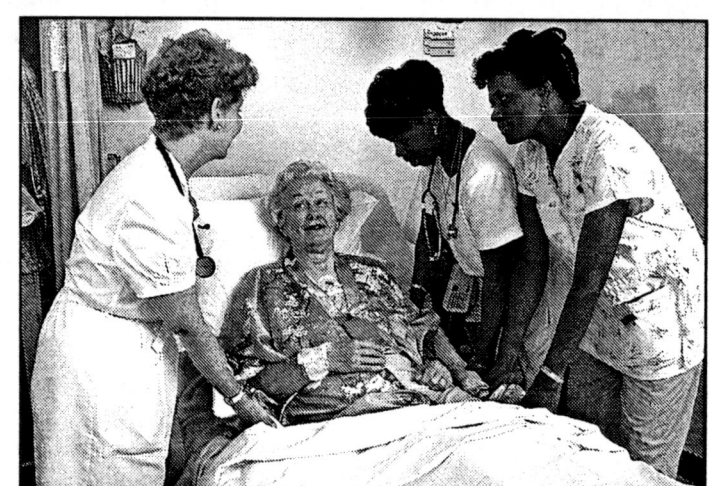

These patients, like all others, must be treated with sensitivity and respect. Do everything you can to preserve their dignity; but keep in mind that they may THINK they are capable of doing more than they actually can. You also will find that some people will surprise you. Many elderly people are sharper and more agile than others think.

Dealing with older people requires good judgement on your part. Remember the following guidelines.

- **Geriatric** patients sometimes are unsteady on their feet, and they may need assistance when walking or standing up.
- Speak slowly and clearly when you are talking to an elderly patient.
- You may need to speak louder to an older person than you would to another patient. However, don't assume that just because a person is old he or she is hard of hearing. This can be insulting.
- Face the patient when you talk to him or her. Some patients will read your lips if they have trouble hearing you.
- If hearing seems to be a problem, hand gestures can be helpful in communicating what you need.
- Provide adequate lighting and steady the elderly patient's hand when he or she must write something.
- Orient the patient to the surroundings and show him or her how to call for assistance.
- Assist elderly patients whenever they rise from a sitting position. Be available to support the person if he or she becomes unsteady and begins to fall.
- Treat the elderly with respect and call them by name, not "grandma" or "pop."

geriatrics: the branch of medicine that deals with the problems of aging

Chapter Summary

The result of aging is the deterioration of body tissues and organs. Therefore, elderly people sometimes are less able to heal following an illness or an injury. Although older people suffer the same injuries and illnesses as younger people do, multiple health problems can make some of these conditions much more serious in the elderly. As an emergency department technician, you must be aware of the effects of aging on the human body and the special circumstances that can be brought about by age. Aging triggers a variety of physical, mental, and emotional changes. You can help your patient deal with some of these changes better if you treat him or her with sensitivity and respect. This applies to any patient!

Chapter Twenty One • Care of the Elderly

Name_____
Date_____

Student Enrichment Activities

1. Observe a person aged 65 or older and note the changes they have made in order to perform the activities of daily living.

   _____
   _____
   _____
   _____
   _____

2. Survey your community and count the number of the following:

   A. Senior citizen centers   _____
   B. Retirement communities   _____
   C. Senior housing facilities _____
   D. Skilled nursing facilities _____

3. Circle the following injuries and illnesses that can occur in the elderly.

burns	poisoning	heart attack	appendicitis
heat stroke	fractured hip	laceration	dislocated shoulder
head injury	diabetes	arthritis	emphysema
infection	pneumonia	kidney stones	stroke
seizures	overdose	high blood pressure	

Glossary

A

ABCs: an abbreviation used to refer to airway, breathing, and circulation.

abdominal distension: enlargement of the abdominal body cavity caused by air or fluid.

abdominal trauma: injury to the abdomen that can cause the internal organs to tear and bleed, or lose fluids and other contents.

abortion: the ending of a pregnancy before the fetus is viable, before the twenty-fourth week; miscarriage.

abrasion: an open wound, road burn, or rug burn in which the outer layer of skin has been scraped off.

abscess: an infected, pus-filled sac that is swollen, red, and painful.

absorption: the passing of a substance through the skin or mucous membranes into body fluids or tissues.

acquired immune deficiency syndrome: AIDS; a viral disease caused by the human immunodeficiency virus (HIV), which destroys the immune system and renders the patient susceptible to other infections. It is contracted through blood and other body fluids, and is incurable.

acuity: the clearness or sharpness of the senses.

acute abdomen: signs and symptoms of a traumatic or medical emergency including pain, distention, shock, nausea, vomiting, or diarrhea; may require immediate surgery.

acute: sudden onset.

adaptic: a non-stick dressing material.

adolescent: a teenager; someone who is 13 to 19 years of age.

AIDS: the abbreviation for acquired immune deficiency syndrome; a viral disease caused by the human immunodeficiency virus (HIV), which destroys the immune system and renders the patient susceptible to other infections. It is contracted through blood and other body fluids, and is incurable.

air hunger: a lack of oxygen; shortness of breath characterized by rapid, difficult breathing.

airway: a tube (either natural or man-made) that provides a passageway for air to and from the lungs.

alert: awake, conscious, and aware of one's surroundings.

alignment: a physical position in which there is no stress or strain on any part of the body; the positioning of parts in a straight line.

allergic: of or relating to an allergy.

allergy: a reaction to a substance.

alveoli: microscopic air sacs in the lungs responsible for the exchange of oxygen and carbon dioxide.

Ambu bag: a type of bag-valve mask used for assisting respirations and increasing oxygenation.

ambulate: to walk.

ambulation: the process of walking.

ambulatory care: a type of healthcare in which patients are treated and released, such as in a walk-in clinic; outpatient services.

American Red Cross: a national organization for the community assistance of disaster victims; a center for the collection and distribution of blood.

amniotic fluid: the liquid contained in the amnion that protects the fetus from injury.

amputate: to remove a body part.

amputation: the removal of a body part.

anaphylactic shock: a life-threatening allergic reaction that causes the blood pressure to drop, the pulse to increase, and respirations to become labored and difficult; can lead to cardiac and respiratory arrest.

ancillary personnel: non-licensed staff; support personnel, clerical aides, and technicians.

anesthesia: the blocking of sensation or consciousness through the administration of certain drugs (usually done through inhalation or injection).

anesthesiologist: a medical doctor who specializes in surgical anesthesia.

anesthetic: an agent that induces a loss of feeling or consciousness.

anesthetize: to take away feeling; to put to sleep.

aneurysm: a weak section in the wall of a blood vessel that could rupture and cause a hemorrhage.

antibiotic: a drug with the ability to kill or prevent the growth of living organisms; medication used to treat infections.

antidote: a substance that neutralizes a poison.

antiseptic: an agent capable of inhibiting the growth of microorganisms. Used when referring to living tissue.

anus: the rectal opening that lies in the fold of the buttocks.

anxiety: a feeling of dread, worry, or nervousness.

apex: the pointed tip of a conical structure; the location where the heartbeat is the loudest.

Apgar score: a test to measure the health of a newborn based on appearance, pulse, grimace, airway, and reflex.

apical: refers to the apex of heart, located at the left fifth intracostal space, mid-clavicular line.

apical pulse: the pulse that is obtained by listening to the heart rhythm at the apex of the heart.

appendicitis: inflammation of the appendix.

apprehension: anxiety; fear; nervousness.

arterial blood gas: any of the gases that normally occur in the blood such as oxygen and carbon dioxide, when analyzed from the artery rather than from a vein.

arterial: pertaining to the large vessels that carry oxygenated blood.

arteries: blood vessels that carry oxygenated blood from the heart to the tissues.

asepsis: a condition in which no pathogens are present.

aseptic: sterile; preventing infection.

ashen: a gray skin color seen in shock patients.

asphyxiation: lack of oxygen.

aspirate: to take foreign material or vomit into the lungs; to remove fluid using suction.

aspiration: the inhalation of vomit or other fluid into the lungs.

assessment: an evaluation of a patient's condition.

asthma: a lung disorder that causes breathing difficulty, wheezing, and coughing, and that can lead to airway obstruction.

astride: straddled; sitting or standing on something with one leg on each side.

asystole: cardiac arrest.

aura: a subjective sensation of warmth or light that may precede a seizure or a migraine.

aural: relating to the ear.

auscultate: to listen.

authorized radio nurse: a registered nurse with specialized training, certified to communicate with paramedics over a radio.

autoclave: a device that is used to sterilize items by steam under pressure.

avulsion: a painful soft tissue injury in which a flap of tissue is torn loose or pulled off completely.

axilla: the armpit.

axillary: under the arm.

B

bacteria: more than one bacterium; plural of bacterium.

bacterial: of or relating to the small, one-celled microorganisms in the class Schizomycetes.

bacteriology: the study of bacteria.

bacterium: any of the small, one-celled microorganisms in the class Schizomycetes.

bag-valve mask: a manual resuscitator.

Battle sign: a bogginess or area of bleeding under the skin behind the ear or near the temple that indicates a skull fracture.

belligerent: argumentative.

bimanual pelvic exam: an examination of the pelvis in which the physician uses both hands to palpate the area.

biological death: brain and other cell death caused by a lack of oxygen to the tissues; occurs within 4 to 6 minutes of respiratory arrest.

biopsy: the removal of a small piece of living tissue for examination under a microscope.

blood sugar: sugar, in the form of glucose, that exists in the blood and which is necessary to process food.

blunt trauma: a mechanism of injury describing a sharp blow or driving force to a part of the body, usually resulting in internal injuries.

body mechanics: the efficient and safe use of the body during activity.

bowel movement: the evacuation of feces from the rectum.

brachial pulse: the pulse that can be heard or felt at the brachial artery.

brachial: refers to the large artery in the arm on the anterior inner aspect of the elbow.

bradycardia: a pulse rate below 60 beats a minute.

brain hemorrhage: bleeding of the brain tissue.

breathing: the process of taking air into the lungs and releasing it.

bronchitis: a lung condition with a productive cough and difficulty breathing; inflammation of the air passages.

bulb syringe: a portable hand-held suction device for clearing the air passages of a newborn.

butterfly bandage: a type of dressing used to pull two edges of skin together.

C

cannula: a tube that delivers oxygen through the nose.

capillaries: tiny blood vessels in the circulatory system that link arteries and veins.

carbon dioxide a clear, odorless gas; exhaled air.

cardiac: pertaining to the heart and its structures.

cardiac arrest: asystole; the absence of a heartbeat.

cardiac compressions: controlled and repeated application of pressure to the sternum of a cardiac arrest victim to keep the oxygen supply moving throughout the body.

cardiac monitor: an electronic device that provides a visual and auditory record of the heartbeat.

cardiopulmonary resuscitation: CPR; a basic lifesaving procedure of artificial ventilation and chest compressions that is done for cardiac arrest.

cardiovascular: of or relating to the heart and blood vessels.

carotid: the large artery in the neck that carries oxygenated blood to the brain.

carotid pulse: the pulse that can be heard or felt at the carotid artery.

carpals: small bones in the wrist.

carrier: a human or animal who is infected with a pathogen, and who can spread the disease to others, but who does not show any outward signs or symptoms of the disease.

catheter: a tube that is passed through the body to transport fluids in or out of a body cavity.

catheterization: the process of inserting a catheter into a patient.

cauterize: to burn or destroy tissue using heat, cold, electricity, or chemicals.

CCU: an abbreviation for critical care unit.

census: the number of patients in the facility.

central nervous system: the body system composed of the brain, the spinal cord, and their nerves.

central supply: the area of a hospital designated for the distribution of supplies and equipment, and the sterilization of used supplies.

central venous pressure tray: a tray containing all the sterile equipment that is necessary to insert a catheter into a central vein.

central venous pressure: CVP; the measure of the circulating volume of the blood.

cerebral edema: swelling of the cerebrum.

cerebrospinal fluid: CSF; the fluid that flows through and protects the brain and the spinal cord.

cerebrospinal: relating to the brain and spinal cord.

cerebrovascular accident: a stroke; the blockage, hemorrhage, or compression of a blood vessel in the brain.

certified emergency nurse: a registered nurse who has passed a national exam in emergency nursing.

cerumen: ear wax.

cervical collar: a rigid device placed around the neck to limit motion.

cervical spine: the bones of the neck.

chaplain: a clergyman affiliated with an institution such as a hospital.

chart: a form used by the hospital staff to record the progression of a patient's illness or injury, and which becomes a part of the patient's medical record (includes vital signs, treatments, output, and physicians and nurses notes).

chicken pox: an acute viral infection that often occurs in the childhood years, characterized by headache, fever, and malaise followed by the eruption of macules, papules, and vesicles, and crusting.

chief complaint: the main reason a patient is to be seen by the doctor.

chlamydia: a microorganism that causes a sexually transmitted disease.

cholecystitis: inflammation of the gall bladder.

chronic obstructive pulmonary disease: COPD; an incurable condition in which the lungs' ability to provide ventilation is decreased over time.

chronic: slow to develop; persisting for a long time.

circulation: the movement of blood through the blood vessels.

circulatory: refers to the system responsible for transporting blood throughout the body.

circumflex artery: the artery that supplies blood to the back side of the heart.

clammy: moist.

clavicle: the collar bone.

cleft lip: a birth defect which manifests as a cleft or separation of the upper lip; a harelip.

cleft palate: a congenital abnormality resulting in a hole in the roof of the mouth, forming a passageway between the mouth and nasal cavities.

clergy: a group of people who are ordained to perform pastoral duties in a Christian church.

clinical death: the lack of a pulse, respiration, and blood pressure.

clot: a fibrous network of platelets that forms and helps stop bleeding.

clubfoot: a congenital foot deformity in which the bones in the front part of the foot are misaligned.

clutch: grasp.

cobalt lamp: a light used to examine the eye for injuries.

code 3: emergency transport with lights and sirens.

code blue: the emergency call signal in the hospital for a full arrest situation, which alerts all emergency resuscitation team members to respond to a specific location.

code red: the verbal alarm for a fire.

coherent: a logical pattern of speech and behavior.

cold pack: an ice bag or chemical cold application.

colitis: inflammation of the colon.

coma: a state of unconsciousness or deep stupor.

comatose: unconscious.

combative: wishing to fight.

comminuted fracture: a break in a bone in which the bone is splintered into pieces.

compound fracture: a break in the bone that causes the bone to penetrate the skin.

compression: the condition of being squeezed or pressed together; the application of pressure.

computer: an electronic device that is used to receive, store, process and retrieve data.

concussion: an injury or loss of function resulting from a blow to the head or a fall.

confidentiality: privacy; refers to the limiting of access to information to authorized personnel only.

congenital: to be born with; from birth.

congestion: the abnormal buildup of fluid (blood, bile, or mucous) in an organ or in tissue.

conjunctiva: a membrane in the eye.

conjunctivitis: inflammation of the white of the eye, characterized by redness and a sticky discharge; pink eye.

conscious: able to respond; awake, alert, and aware.

constipation: a condition in which bowel movements are infrequent and the stools are hard and dry.

constrict: to become smaller.

contagious: capable of being transferred from one person to another, either directly or indirectly.

contaminated: not sterile; unclean; exposed to harmful bacteria or radiation.

contusion: a soft tissue injury caused by the seepage of blood into tissue; a bruise.

cooling blanket: a blanket filled with cool circulating water that is used to control a patient's temperature.

core temperature: the internal body temperature.

cornea: the transparent front part of the eye; the lens of the eye.

corneal abrasion: a scrape to the cornea of the eye.

coronary care unit: an area in the hospital that is specially equipped to treat patients with sudden, dangerous heart conditions.

cosmetic surgeon: a surgeon who specializes in the repair of skin or tissues, often around the face or the neck, to preserve a patient's appearance.

CPR: the abbreviation for cardiopulmonary resuscitation.

crackles: fine noises caused by moisture in lungs.

crash cart: a portable supply cabinet that contains all of the emergency equipment necessary to treat a full arrest or code blue.

crepitus: the sound of air in the tissues.

critical care unit: a specialized nursing unit that is staffed and equipped to care for the most seriously ill patients.

critical: life-threatening.

cross infection: the spread of contagious disease from one person in a hospital to another.

croup: a viral infection of the respiratory tract that mostly affects children below the age of three, characterized by a barking cough, hoarseness, fever, and difficult breathing.

crowning: the presence of the baby's head in the birth canal indicated by the bulging of the perineum; a signal that delivery is imminent.

crutches: supports that fit under the armpits, and that are used to assist with walking.

CT scan: an abbreviation for computerized tomography scan; a technique for examining the internal structures of the body in which a precise image of a given area is constructed.

culture: a laboratory test for bacterial growth that involves instilling microorganisms in a special media and monitoring it for the growth of pathogens.

Culturette: a test tube with a cotton tip applicator used for obtaining a culture.

cyanosis: a bluish discoloration of the skin and mucous membranes caused by a decrease in oxygen.

cyanotic: affected by cyanosis.

D

data: information; facts.

debilitated: weakened; sickly.

defecate: to evacuate the bowels from the rectum.

defibrillate: to stop rapid fibrillations (contractions) of the heart by applying electric shock to the chest.

defibrillation: the stopping of fibrillation (fluttering) of the heart with the use of drugs or by physical means.

defibrillator: an electronic device used to shock the heart into a normal rhythm.

dehydrated: dry, lacking fluid.

dehydration: the loss of water from a body or substance.

delayed: able to wait for emergency treatment.

delirious: disorientation regarding time and place along with hallucinations, a wandering mind, and incoherent speech.

denial: refusing to believe that which is true or real.

depression: extreme feelings of sadness or hopelessness.

diabetes: a metabolic disease that causes an increase in blood sugar and prevents the body from producing insulin.

diabetic: pertaining to diabetes; a person with diabetes.

diagnose: to identify a disease or condition.

diaphoretic: profuse perspiration.

diaphragm: the dome-shaped muscle separating the thoracic cavity from the abdominal cavity; the portion of the stethoscope used for picking up sound.

diarrhea: abnormally frequent, watery bowel movements.

diastolic: refers to the period of time between heart contractions; the bottom number in a blood pressure reading.

dilate: to enlarge or make bigger.

diphtheria: an acute infectious disease that produces a poison in the body as well as a false membrane in the throat and other mucous surfaces.

direct pressure: a method of controlling bleeding in which pressure is applied directly over the wound.

direct transmission: the transfer of an infection by immediate contact with infected body fluid or tissue.

disaster: an event that causes great damage and depletes or exhausts currently available resources.

disease: an illness causing symptoms; a condition causing abnormal stress to an organ or body system.

disinfect: to remove infectious material from an item.

disinfection: the removal of infectious material from an item.

dislocation: the separation of a joint and malposition of an extremity.

dispatcher: an emergency communication system worker who receives incoming calls, prioritizes them, gives emergency directions to the caller, and sends appropriate personnel to the location.

disposition: the outcome of a patient's visit (ie, admitted, discharged, or expired).

distal pulse: the circulation point below the level of injury.

distend: to expand or swell.

distention: the enlargement of a body cavity caused by air or fluid.

distress: physical or mental suffering.

diverticulitis: inflammation in the wall of the intestine.

DOA: the abbreviation for dead on arrival.

dorsal recumbent position: a position in which the patient is lying on the back with the knees flexed.

dorsalis pedis: the artery on top of the foot.

Down syndrome: a congenital defect resulting in moderate to severe mental retardation and a variety of physical defects.

drape: a sheet or covering that is used to cover an undressed patient during a physical examination or a procedure.

duct: a tube connecting one body organ to another.

duration: the time throughout which something lasts.

dyspnea: difficult or painful breathing.

dysrhythmia: abnormal heart rhythm.

E

ear canal: the tube that leads from the outside of the head to the eardrum, also known as the external auditory canal.

ecchymosis: the black and blue color caused by the seepage of blood into tissue as in a contusion.

ECG: an abbreviation for electrocardiogram.

ectopic pregnancy: a fertilized egg implanted outside the uterus, usually in the fallopian tube.

edema: swelling due to fluid in the tissues.

EENT: an abbreviation for eye, ear, nose, and throat.

EKG: an abbreviation for electrocardiogram.

electrocardiogram: a diagnostic test for heart disease that measures the electrical activity of the heart.

electrocautery: a device used to burn or destroy tissue, and which causes the blood to clot.

electrode: a conductor used to establish contact for recording electrical activity within the body.

elevate: to raise; a method for controlling bleeding.

emergency care unit: ECU; a specific area of an acute care facility staffed and equipped to handle patients with life-threatening illnesses or injuries; also known as the Emergency Department or ER.

emergency department: a specific area of an acute care facility staffed and equipped to handle patients with life-threatening illnesses or injuries.

Emergency Medical Services: EMS; a national network of emergency care providers, from the first responder to basic life support and advanced support providers, coordinated by a central communication system (911).

Emergency Medical Technician: a person with specialized training in prehospital emergency care who works under the direction of a physician, nurse, or county health officer.

emergent: life-threatening condition; urgent; sudden or unforeseen.

emesis: vomit.

empathy: to understand and relate to the emotional state of another; to show concern.

emphysema: a chronic lung disease that destructs the alveoli.

endotracheal tube: a large tube inserted into the trachea through the mouth or nose to assist in administering oxygen.

envenomate: to inject poison from an insect, reptile, or animal into a person or animal (usually from a bite).

epiglottis: tissue in the throat that allows air to enter the trachea and food to enter the esophagus.

epiglottitis: inflammation of the epiglottis; can be fatal if untreated.

epilepsy: a term that describes a group of nervous system disorders that involve disturbed rhythms of the electrical impulses that fire throughout the cerebrum, resulting in seizure activity or abnormal behavior.

epinephrine: a hormone secreted primarily from the adrenal gland that narrows the blood vessels and causes some of the physiological expressions of fear and anxiety.

epistaxis: a nosebleed.

equilibrium: a person's sense of balance.

ER: an abbreviation for emergency room or department; a specific area of an acute care facility staffed and equipped to handle patients with life-threatening illnesses or injuries.

esophageal airway: a special breathing tube that is inserted into the esophagus to allow the trachea to be ventilated.

expiration: to exhale; the act of breathing out.

expired: died.

exposure: the state of being subject to the effects or influence of something such as radiation, heat, cold, etc.

F

fallopian tube: the part of the female reproductive system through which the egg travels on the way to the uterus.

false imprisonment: restraining a person against his or her will, either physically or with verbal threats.

fatal: death-producing.

febrile seizure: a convulsion or seizure associated with a fever.

femoral: the area in the groin near the femur.

femur: the thigh bone.

fibrillate: to rapidly flutter; the failure of the heart to completely contract.

fibula: the smaller of the two bones in the lower leg.

finger sweep: a method of removing a foreign object from a choking patient's mouth.

flammable: capable of producing fire.

fluorescein sodium: a red powder used primarily for detecting injuries to the cornea of the eye.

Foley catheter: a catheter for the urinary tract that has a balloon attachment at one end to prevent the catheter from accidentally leaving the bladder.

forceps: any of a large number of instruments used to hold, seize, or extract.

Fowler's position: a position in which the patient is semi-sitting with the head raised 45 to 60 degrees.

fracture: a crack or break in a bone.

frostbite: the effect of freezing or severe cold on skin or other tissues.

full arrest: respiratory and cardiac arrest.

fungal: of or relating to a fungus.

fungi: a group of plant-like parasitic organisms that includes molds, yeasts, mildews, and mushrooms.

G

gag reflex: a normal reflex of gagging and/or vomiting as a result of irritation to the throat or pharynx.

gall stones: calcium deposits in the gall bladder that may block the bile duct.

gastric lavage: the irrigation or washing of the stomach.

gastrointestinal: of or relating to the stomach and the intestine.

genitalia: the reproductive organs.

geriatrics: the branch of medicine that deals with the problems of aging.

Glasgow coma scale: a measure of the degree of coma a patient is experiencing in which motor responses are converted to a standard set of numbers.

glaucoma: an eye disorder caused by an increase in intraocular pressure.

globe: the eyeball.

glottis: the voice apparatus of the larynx consisting of the two vocal cords and the slit between them.

glucose: a simple sugar; used in the human body to produce energy.

golden hour: the sixty minutes that immediately follow an accident or injury, in which lifesaving treatment must begin.

gonorrhea: a sexually transmitted disease, characterized by a foul-smelling, white, thick discharge, burning on urination, and abdominal pain.

graduate: a container used to measure liquids in milliliters.

grating: the sound of two bones rubbing together.

grimace: a facial expression that reflects discomfort; a frown.

groin: the area where the abdomen joins the thighs.

grounding pad: a safety device used with an electrocautery to prevent electrical shock.

guarding: protecting a painful area; pulling the knees up in reaction to abdominal pain.

gurgling: an abnormal, course sound produced by the movement of air through fluid in cavities; can be heard through a stethoscope.

gurney: a stretcher with wheels used for transporting patients.

H

Haemophilus influenza: an organism that causes meningitis.

hairline fracture: a minor break in a bone in which the pieces of the bone remain in perfect alignment.

hallucination: seeing or hearing something that is not there.

hazardous: dangerous.

head bed: a stabilizing device that limits the motion of the head.

head-tilt/chin-lift maneuver: a procedure for opening a blocked airway in which the head is tilted back and the chin is lifted; the most effective method for opening the airway of an unconscious person without a neck or back injury.

heart attack: a myocardial infarction; a condition caused by the blockage of one or more coronary arteries.

heart block: a condition in which the conductive tissue of the heart fails to send signals from the atrium to the ventricles, resulting in dysrhythmia.

heat stroke: a rising body temperature that causes central nervous system symptoms.

Heimlich maneuver: an obstructed airway maneuver in which sudden, upward pressure is applied to the abdomen with a fist to remove a foreign body in the trachea.

hematoma: a blood-filled swollen area; a goose egg caused by bleeding under the tissues.

hematuria: the presence of blood in the urine.

hemiplegia: paralysis of half of the body.

hemophilia: a congenital condition in which the blood does not clot normally, resulting in excessive bleeding.

hemorrhage: profuse bleeding that can lead to shock.

hemorrhagic shock: shock that is brought on by blood loss.

hepatitis: inflammation of the liver.

herpes: a viral infection, a form of which can be a sexually transmitted disease.

hormone: a chemical produced in one part of the body that stimulates the activity of another part of the body.

hospital disaster plan: a pre-defined set of procedures for the care and evacuation of hospital patients and personnel during and after a natural disaster.

host: an organism that is invaded by a parasite, and from which the parasite obtains its nutrition.

hostile: to be aggressively angry; antagonistic.

hostility: aggression, animosity, or antagonism.

humerus: a bone in the upper arm.

humidifier: a device used to deliver moisture to the air a patient breathes.

hydraulic: operated or moved by water pressure.

hydrocephalus: an abnormal amount of spinal fluid within the ventricles of the brain.

hygiene: cleanliness.

hyperextend: to move beyond the normal range of motion.

hyperglycemia: an elevated blood sugar level.

hypertension: high blood pressure that has been diagnosed on the basis of several random readings of 140/90 or higher; known as the silent killer.

hyperthermia: an unusually high body temperature.

hypoallergenic: reduced potential for causing an allergic reaction.

hypoglycemia: a low blood sugar level.

hypotension: an abnormally low blood pressure that impairs normal functioning.

hypothermia: an unusually low body temperature capable of causing problems with the central nervous system and cardiac arrest.

hypothermia unit: a machine that helps control a patient's temperature.

hysterical: a temporary loss of emotional control that leads to confusion and loss of reason.

I

identiband: an identification bracelet that is placed on all patients, and which includes the patient's name, doctor, room number, patient number, and any allergies the patient has.

immediate: in need of care right away.

imminent: immediate.

immobility: the inability to move.

immunity: protection from a disease; a person's insusceptibility to a disease.

immunization: a vaccination against a disease.

impaled: penetrated or pierced by an object that remains in the body.

incident: a happening, event, or occurrence.

incision: a clean, straight, knife-like cut.

incoherent: an illogical pattern of speech and behavior.

incontinence: loss of bladder or bowel control.

incubator: a temperature-controlled, isolated baby bed.

indigestion: gastric distress; stomach pain.

indirect transmission: the transfer of an infection by the touching of a contaminated object.

infection: the invasion of the body or a part of the body by a pathogen.

inflammation: the response of tissue to injury or irritation, characterized by redness, swelling, pain, heat, and possible loss of function.

ingestion: the act of taking something into the gastrointestinal tract by mouth.

inhalation: the act of breathing something into the lungs; inspiration.

injection: the act of forcing a liquid under the skin or into a vessel or cavity intramuscularly.

inspiration: inhalation; the act of breathing something into the lungs.

insulin: a hormone secreted by the pancreas that causes glucose, or sugar, to leave the bloodstream and enter the cell.

intake: the amount of solid or liquid that is put into a body.

intensity: severity.

intensive care unit: ICU; a specialized unit staffed and equipped to care for the most acutely ill patients.

internal: within the body.

intoxicated: in a drunken state.

intravenous: IV; directly into the vein.

intubate: to insert a tube, such as placing an airway into the trachea of a patient.

iodine: a nonmetallic element that aids in the development and function of the thyroid gland.

iris: the part of the eye that gives the eye its color.

irrigate: to wash out with a steady stream of fluid.

irrigating saline: a sterile solution of sodium chloride that is used to cleanse wounds and wash chemicals from the eye.

isolation: an area that is able to be closed off to contain contaminated patients and equipment.

Isolette: a trademark name for an incubator that is used in the care of premature infants and low-weight newborns.

IV: the abbreviation for intravenous.

J

jaw-thrust maneuver: a method used to open the airway in a neck-injured patient in which the jaw is lifted up and the neck is not moved.

K

kidney stones: a mineral build-up in the kidney that may block the passage of urine.

KY jelly: a brand of lubricating jelly.

L

labia: the two folds of skin that lie on either side of the vaginal opening.

laceration: a jagged tear in the skin.

laryngeal edema: swelling of the larynx.

laryngectomy: the surgical removal of the larynx, which leaves a permanent opening in the neck for breathing and causes the loss of speech.

laryngoscope: a lighted instrument used to view the voice box.

larynx: the upper end of the trachea; the voice box.

latex: rubber.

lavage: to wash or irrigate.

lethargic: sleepy.

level of consciousness: a patient's state of alertness and orientation to time, person, place, and situation.

Levine tube: a nasogastric tube.

licensed vocational nurse: a licensed nurse trained in patient care procedures, treatments, and medication administration who must practice under the supervision of a registered nurse.

life skills: skills that involve the ability to perform critical duties.

ligament: a band of white, fibrous, connective tissue, formed from adipose tissue, that helps hold bones together.

linear fracture: a break in a bone that runs along the length of the bone.

lithotomy position: a position in which the patient lies on the back with the legs in stirrups; the position usually used for a pelvic exam.

litter: a stretcher.

localize: to occur in one special area.

lockjaw: a contraction or spasm of the muscles in the jaw.

log roll: the method used to turn a victim with a spinal injury in which the patient is moved to the side in one motion.

Lubifax: a brand of lubricating jelly.

lubricating jelly: a gel that is applied to catheters or tubes for ease of insertion.

lumbar: of or relating to the lower back between the thorax and the pelvis.

LVN: an abbreviation for licensed vocational nurse.

M

mannikin: a doll used to practice lifesaving procedures.

manual dexterity: physical coordination; the ability to perform specialized tasks requiring fine motor movements.

MAST: an abbreviation for military anti-shock trousers; a garment, which when inflated, will apply even pressure to the lower extremities to keep the blood circulating through the vital organs of an accident victim.

mastoid process: the portion of the temporal bone that protrudes from the side of the skull and to which various muscles are attached.

Mayo stand: a stainless steel tray on wheels that is used as a small table.

measles: an acute, highly communicable viral infection characterized by fever, discomfort, sneezing, nasal congestion, eye irritation, sensitivity to light, spots on the buccal mucosa, and a maculopapular eruption all over the body.

meatus: the anatomical opening where urine is expelled from the body.

mechanism of injury: the cause of an injury.

Medic-Alert: a symbol that indicates important medical information.

medical asepsis: the removal or destruction of infected material or organisms.

medical record: a legal document that is a record of patient care.

meningitis: the inflammation or infection of the membranes covering the spinal cord and the brain marked by severe headache, vomiting, and a stiff neck.

mental status: state of mental ability and wellness.

metabolize: to produce energy within living cells through chemical changes for life processes and activities.

metacarpals: the bones of the hand.

metatarsals: the bones of the foot between the tarsals and the phalanges.

mid position: in the middle.

mild: low in intensity.

miscarriage: the ending of a pregnancy before the twenty-fourth week; expelling the products of conception; abortion.

mobile intensive care nurse: a registered nurse with specialized training who is certified to communicate with paramedics over a radio.

moderate: serious.

modified jaw-thrust maneuver: a procedure for clearing the airway in an unconscious victim in whom a spinal injury is possible or suspected. The jaw is pulled forward to move the tongue away from the hypopharynx, without moving the head or neck.

monitor: an electronic device used to observe the electrical activity of heart.

mucous membranes: the linings of the mouth, digestive, reproductive, urinary, and breathing passages.

mucous: sticky material released by glands.

multisystem: involving more than one body system.

mummy restraint: a safe method of restraining children.

mumps: an acute infectious disease marked by swelling of the parotid glands and other salivary glands. Usually affects children between the ages of 5 and 15.

mutual aid: refers to agreement among local agencies to provide emergency services without geographical boundaries.

MVA: abbreviation for motor vehicle accident.

myocardial infarction: a heart attack; a condition caused by the blockage of one or more coronary arteries.

N

nasal speculum: a device used to spread the nostrils and look into them.

nasogastric tube: a catheter placed in the stomach through the nose for removal or insertion of fluids.

nasopharyngeal airway: a flexible tube that is inserted into the nose of an unconscious patient to maintain the patient's airway.

nasopharyngeal: of or relating to the nose and throat.

nasopharynx: part of the pharynx, located behind the nose, reaching from the back of the nasal opening to just above the soft palate.

nausea: a sensation leading to the urge to vomit.

nauseated: to feel the urge to vomit.

neonatal: a term used to describe an infant from the moment of birth to one month in age.

nephritis: inflammation of the kidney.

neuro check: a quick assessment of a patient's neurological condition, usually done upon the patient's entry to the ER.

neurological check: a neuro check; a quick assessment of a patient's neurological condition, usually done upon the patient's entry to the ER.

neurological: of or relating to the nervous system.

neurostructures: structures within the nervous system.

neurosurgeon: a brain surgeon.

neurovascular: of or relating to the nervous system and circulation.

non-urgent: able to wait for care.

normal saline: a saltwater solution.

nosocomial infection: an infection that is acquired during a stay at a hospital.

NPO: nothing by mouth (from the Latin, *non per os*).

O

OB kit: a kit that contains the necessary equipment and supplies for an emergency childbirth.

obesity: a condition characterized by excessive body fat.

objective data: observable information such as vital signs, color of skin, and orientation level.

oblique fracture: a break in a bone in which the break is at a slanting angle.

obstetrical: of or relating to the branch of medicine dealing with pregnancy, childbirth, and the time immediately following childbirth.

obstructed airway maneuver: a procedure used to clear a foreign body from the trachea; the Heimlich maneuver.

occlusion: a blockage.

occlusive: airtight.

OD: right eye; an abbreviation for overdose.

onset: the point at which symptoms first appear.

ophthalmologist: a doctor who specializes in the treatment of eye diseases.

ophthalmoscope: an instrument with a light that is used to view the eye.

oral-fecal: of or relating to the mouth and the rectum; a potential route for the transfer of disease.

oral: by way of the mouth.

orbit: the eye socket.

orientation: the ability to comprehend one's environment regarding time, place, situation, and identity of persons.

oriented: understanding where one is with regard to time and place, and the ability to recognize one's self and others.

oropharyngeal airway: a tube that is inserted through the oropharynx to maintain a patient's airway.

oropharyngeal: of or relating to the mouth and throat.

orthopedics: the branch of medicine that deals with the prevention or correction of disorders relating to the skeleton, and its joints, muscles, and other related structures.

orthopnea: difficulty in breathing, requiring the victim to sit up or stand to breathe.

OS: left eye.

oscilloscope: a device with which variations in electrical activity can be detected.

osteoporosis: a condition in which a decreasing calcium level in the bones causes them to become brittle.

otitis media: an inner ear infection.

otoscope: an instrument with a light that is used to see inside the ear.

OU: both eyes.

output: the measure of the body fluids that are excreted by a patient.

overdose: the ingestion of too much of a particular drug, so as to cause an acute, and sometimes fatal reaction.

ovum: a female reproductive cell; an egg.

oxygen: a colorless, odorless gas essential for human life.

oxygenation: the state in which the blood is saturated with oxygen.

P

pacemaker: a device that electrically stimulates the heart to cause it to beat.

pallor: pale skin due to a decrease in blood supply to the area.

palpate: to examine by feeling with the hands.

palpation: an examination using the hands.

palpitation: fluttering, pounding, or racing of the heart.

pancreas: the organ in the abdominal cavity that produces insulin and aids in digestion.

pancreatitis: inflammation of the pancreas.

papoose restraint: a safe method of restraining children.

paralysis: the inability to move.

paramedic: a certified or licensed prehospital care provider trained in advanced life support procedures.

paranoid: experiencing abnormal or unfounded fear.

paraplegia: the paralysis of both legs.

paresis: a partial inability to move.

paresthesia: numbness or tingling.

PASG: an abbreviation for pneumatic anti-shock garment; a garment that, when inflated, will apply even pressure to the lower extremities to keep the blood circulating through the vital organs of an accident victim.

pasteurize: to apply heat to kill or slow the growth of harmful bacteria.

patella: the kneecap.

pathogen: a disease-causing microorganism.

pathological: of or relating to disease.

patient history: a form that is filled out by the patient or close family member that describes the patient's medical history and chief medical complaint.

patient log: a patient roster; a roster kept by the nurses that documents the status of every patient in that department, including information about admissions, diagnoses, and discharges.

patient roster: a patient log; a log kept by the nurses that documents the status of every patient in that department, including information about admissions, diagnoses, and discharges.

pediatrics: the branch of medicine that cares for infants from 6 weeks in age, children, and adolescents to 18 years of age.

pelvic inflammatory disease: PID; an infection that ascends from the vagina or cervix to the uterus.

pelvis: the lower part of the trunk of the body; the hip bone, tail bone, and back bone.

penicillin: an antibiotic.

peptic ulcer: an area of inflammation and/or bleeding in the stomach.

perfusion: the process of supplying the tissues with oxygen and other nutrients by the passage of blood through the arteries.

perineum: the part of the body between the inner thighs from the anus in the rear to the vulva in the front of the female, and between the anus and the scrotum in the male.

peripad: an absorbent dressing to place on the perineum.

peritonitis: inflammation of the lining of the intestines.

PERL: the abbreviation for pupils equal and react to light.

perspiration: sweat; fluid that is secreted by the sweat glands and released through the pores of the skin to cool the body; the process of sweating.

pertussis: whooping cough; an acute, infectious disease characterized by inflammation of the mucous membranes and sudden bouts of coughing that end in a whooping inspiration.

phalanges: the bones of the fingers and toes.

pharynx: the throat; the passageway for both air and food that extends from the base of the skull to the esophagus.

PID: the abbreviation for pelvic inflammatory disease; an infection that ascends from the vagina or cervix to the uterus.

pinpoint: very small; dot-like.

placenta: a structure in the uterus from which a fetus obtains its nourishment.

pleura vac: a piece of equipment used for closed-seal underwater chest drainage.

PMI: abbreviation for point of maximal impulse; the point on the chest over the heart where it is easiest to see or hear the contraction of the heart.

pneumonia: inflammation of the lung tissues due to bacteria, viruses, and other irritants.

pneumothorax: the presence of air in the thoracic cavity resulting from the perforation of the chest wall or the visceral pleura.

pocket mask: a folding face mask for use in artificial ventilation that is designed to be carried in the pocket.

poison: a toxin; a substance that interferes with normal physiological functions when it is introduced to the body.

poisoning: the taking in of a poisonous substance into the body.

popliteal artery: the large blood vessel located behind the knee.

popliteal: of or relating to the large blood vessel located behind the knee.

posey: a jacket restraint used on patients who are in danger of falling out of bed or off of a gurney.

positive pressure demand valve: an automatic regulator used to assist with ventilation and provide oxygen.

post-partum: after childbirth.

premature ventricular contraction: an early electrical beat in the heart that can lead to serious cardiac dysrhythmias.

pressure point: a pulse point on the body, located above an injury, to which pressure can be applied to control bleeding.

priapism: a penile erection caused by a central nervous system disorder.

primary survey: an examination of the patient to determine the presence of any life-threatening emergencies; the initial assessment of airway, breathing, and circulation.

prominences: objects or parts of objects that project or protrude.

prone: a position in which a patient is lying face down, with the head to the side.

prophylaxis: protection against disease; any of a variety of methods of killing germs or preventing them from entering the body.

prosthesis: an artificial device such as for an extremity (ie, an artificial arm or leg).

protocol: a standard treatment procedure approved by an authorized source.

psychiatric emergency service: a facility that deals with mental, emotional or behavioral problems on a 24 hour basis.

psychiatric: of or relating to the mind, emotions, and behavior.

pulmonary edema: the swelling of the lung tissues with fluid.

pulmonary: of or relating to the lungs.

pulse oximeter: a device that uses a sensor attached to the fingers or toes to measure oxygen levels in the blood.

puncture: to pierce or penetrate.

purulent: pus-like.

Q

quadrant: a fourth.

quadriplegia: the paralysis of the body from the neck down.

R

rabies: a potentially fatal infection of the central nervous system caused by a bite from an infected animal.

radial: of or relating to the area of the radius in the wrist.

radial pulse: the pulse located in the wrist near the radial bone.

radiate: to release rays or move in different directions from a common point.

radius: the larger bone in the lower arm on the thumb side.

rapport: a relationship with others.

reality: the present state of affairs.

rectal: the part of the large intestine near the anus.

referred pain: pain at a location other than the injured organ or site.

registered nurse: a nurse who has completed a course of study at a state-approved nursing school and who has passed the state licensing exam for nursing; this nurse is granted the right to practice for hire.

regression: acting in a childlike manner.

rehabilitation: the restoration of a patient or a part of the body to normal or near normal following an illness or injury.

reoxygenate: to replace or replenish with oxygen.

residual: that which is left over; the portion that remains after the majority of it has been removed.

respiratory: of or relating to breathing.

respiratory arrest: the absence of breathing.

respiratory depression: a decrease in the rate of breathing.

respiratory distress: severe impairment of the ability to breathe.

respiratory tract burn: RTB; respiratory distress as a result of exposure to a fire, characterized by smoke inhalation, singed facial hairs, and the coughing up of sooty sputum.

restrain: to prevent movement.

resuscitation: the process of applying artificial respiration and/or chest compressions to keep a patient experiencing heart and/or lung failure alive.

retinal artery occlusion: the blockage of a blood vessel in the eye.

retinal detachment: the separation of the retina of the eye from the choroid in the back of the eye, leading to the loss of retinal function.

reverse Trendelenburg position: a position in which the patient lies on the back with the feet down and the head elevated.

rickettsia: small, round, or rod-shaped parasitic bacteria capable of causing a wide variety of dangerous diseases.

right lateral recumbent position: a position in which the patient is lying on the right side with the knees flexed.

rigid: firm and board-like.

rigidity: firmness.

RN: an abbreviation for registered nurse; a nurse who is licensed by the state to practice nursing and who has completed a state-approved nursing program and passed the State Board Test Pool Examination.

rubella: an acute, infectious disease characterized by a slight fever, mild upper respiratory infection, swollen lymph nodes, joint pain, and a red rash.

rule of nines: a method used to calculate the extent of burn injury. Each part of the body is assigned a percentage based on a multiple of nine and the total burn area is estimated.

rupture: to break, separate, or lose contents.

ruptured ectopic pregnancy: a break in a structure outside of the uterus (most commonly the fallopian tube) due to the implantation and growth of a fertilized egg in that structure.

ruptured spleen: a break or tear in the spleen.

S

sacral: of or relating to the lower portion of the vertebrae of the back.

saline: a saltwater solution.

saliva: a clear fluid secreted by the mouth that moistens and partially digests food.

sanitization: the act of making something free from dirt.

scald: a burn from hot liquid or steam.

scapula: the shoulder blade.

sclera: the tough, fibrous membrane that covers the white of the eye, and to which the muscles of the eye are attached.

secondary survey: a head-to-toe physical assessment; an additional assessment of a patient to determine the existence of any injuries other than those found in the primary survey.

sedated: calmed, usually by means of medication.

sedation: the calming of a patient through the use of medication.

seizure: a neurological dysfunction characterized by loss of consciousness and involuntary, spasmodic muscle twitching; a sudden attack of pain or symptoms.

semi-Fowler's position: a position in which the patient is sitting with the head elevated 15-30 degrees.

sensation: a feeling.

septic shock: a form of shock that occurs when pathogenic bacteria are present in the blood.

shallow: restricted; not deep.

shock: a condition that occurs when an inadequate amount of blood flows through the body, causing extremely low blood pressure, a lack of urine, and other disorders; a potentially fatal condition.

Silvadene: a trade name for silver sulfadiazine, a topical drug that kills bacteria.

silver nitrate: a chemical used on the skin to treat infection.

silver sulfadiazine: a topical drug used in the treatment of burns to kill bacteria.

Sims' position: a position in which the patient is lying on the right or left side.

sling: a bandage or device used to hold or support a part of the body.

slit lamp: a microscope used to view the eye.

sluggish: slow to respond.

Snellen eye chart: an alphabet chart used for testing visual acuity.

snow blindness: irritation and strain of the conjunctiva due to the reflection of the sun on snow.

spasm: an involuntary and abnormal muscle contraction.

speculum: an instrument, often disposable, used for inspecting canals.

sphygmomanometer: a blood pressure cuff.

spiral fracture: a break in a bone in which the break follows a corkscrew pattern down the long axis of the bone.

splint: a rigid device that holds parts of the body together and limits motion.

sprain: an injury to the soft tissues of a joint, characterized by the inability to move, deformity, and pain.

sputum: mucous coughed up from the lung.

stabilization: the act of making something stable; the prevention of movement, shifting, or change.

stabilize: to hold still, limit motion, or equalize.

STD: the abbreviation for sexually transmitted disease.

Steri-strips: a type of tape used to close wounds.

sterile: aseptic; free from all contamination.

sterile field: the area considered to be free of contamination during a surgical procedure.

sterile technique: the procedure used by healthcare workers when performing or assisting with sterile procedures.

sterilization: the complete destruction of all forms of microbial life.

sternum: the breast bone.

stethoscope: an instrument used to amplify sounds from within the body; the device used to listen for a pulse, blood pressure, and bowel or lung sounds.

stiff-neck collar: a rigid device placed around the neck of a patient with a spinal injury to limit motion in the neck.

stimulant: an agent that temporarily increases activity.

stirrups: a pair of metal rings attached to either side of an examining table that are designed to hold a female patient's legs apart for a pelvic examination or childbirth.

stockinette: a type of tubular dressing or padding used underneath a cast to protect the skin.

stoma: a small opening; such as that which is created during a tracheostomy.

stool: waste discharged by the bowels.

strain: a pulled muscle.

stress: the result produced when a person perceives that events or circumstances have challenged or exceeded his or her coping mechanisms, and the person's mental, spiritual, and physical state of balance becomes disturbed.

stretcher: a litter used for transporting a sick, disabled, or dead person.

stridor: a harsh, high-pitched sound created by breathing through obstructed nasal passages.

strip: an electrocardiogram; a record of the electrical activity of the heart that is generated by an electrocardiograph.

stroke: a cerebrovascular accident.

stump: the remaining portion of an amputated part.

sty: an infection of a gland in the eyelid.

stylet: a rigid wire guide used for tube placement.

subclavian: under the clavicle.

subclavian tray: a tray containing all the sterile equipment that is necessary to insert a catheter into the subclavian vein.

subjective data: information the patient tells you about his or her physical or mental condition.

suction catheter: a narrow tube used to suction gas or fluid.

suction: to remove gas or fluid by sucking it up, usually by mechanical means; involves lowering the air pressure over the surface.

suffocation: the inability to inhale sufficient oxygen to maintain life.

supine: a position in which a patient is lying flat on the back.

surgical asepsis: the prevention of infection before, during, and after surgery through the use of sterile technique.

suture: to close a wound or incision with surgical stitches; a surgical stitch taken to close a wound; the material used for surgical stitches.

suturing: the process of making one or more stitches to close a wound.

symmetry: equal or similar sides.

symptoms: a group of complaints about an illness; characteristics of disease.

syncope: fainting; temporary loss of consciousness; passing out.

syphilis: a chronic, sexually transmitted disease characterized by lesions on an organ or on the skin; may be present without symptoms for years.

syringe: a device used to inject fluids or medications into the body or withdraw them from the body.

systemic reaction: a reaction that involves the whole body rather than just a part of it.

systole: the contraction of the heart; the part of the heart cycle that occurs between the first and second heart sound.

systolic: the top number in a blood pressure reading; refers to the time between the first and second heart sound.

T

tachycardia: a rapid heartbeat, more than 100 beats a minute.

tarsals: the bones of the foot.

telemetry: the monitoring of a patient's condition via a central nurses station.

Telfa: a non-stick, plastic dressing.

temporal: of or relating to the temples.

tendon: fibrous, connective tissue around a joint that connects muscle to bone.

tepid: lukewarm.

tetanus: a deadly bacterial infection of the central nervous system that results from a contaminated wound.

thanatologist: one who studies the psychological coping mechanisms for dealing with death and its processes.

therapeutic communication: communication that is designed to relieve stress or obtain information that can be used to aid in healing emotional or psychological wounds.

thermometer: an instrument used to measure an oral, rectal, or axillary temperature.

thoracic: pertaining to the area of the body between the base of the neck and the diaphragm.

tibia: the inner and larger of the two bones in the lower leg.

tinnitus: ringing in the ears.

tissue: a collection of similar cells and their intercellular substances that work together to perform a particular function.

tolerance: a fair and objective attitude toward others of different race, creed, color, or opinion; the ability to withstand the introduction of a substance without adverse effect.

tongue blade: a wooden or metal tongue depressor.

tongue-jaw lift: a method of opening the mouth of a choking victim to help ensure that the tongue is not part of the obstruction.

tonometer: an instrument used to measure intraocular pressure.

tonsillitis: inflammation of the tonsils.

torsion: twisting.

tourniquet: a constricting band used to apply pressure to an artery above a wound on an extremity to control bleeding.

toxic: poisonous.

toxicity: the extent to which a substance is poisonous.

toxin: a poison.

trachea: the windpipe; a tube of cartilage that extends from the larynx to the bronchial tubes and which leads air into the lungs.

tracheostomy: a surgical incision into the trachea for the insertion of a breathing tube.

track marks: puncture marks left from repeated IV drug use.

traction splint: a splint that applies traction to the extremity by pulling the limb back into proper alignment.

traction: the process of pulling a part of the body into proper alignment.

transfusion: the placing of blood or a blood component into the bloodstream.

transient: brief; not lasting.

transverse fracture: a break in a bone in which the break line is at right angles to the long axis of the bone involved.

trauma: physical or psychological injury caused by an accident, violence, or a poisonous substance.

trauma center: a medical facility or department in a medical facility that is capable of providing care to critically injured patients 24 hours a day.

traumatized: affected by trauma; suffering from a wound or injury.

Trendelenburg position: a position in which the patient lies flat on the back with the feet elevated above the level of the heart to promote the flow of blood to the brain; the position for shock victims.

triage: to sort or prioritize care for a group of patients.

tubegauze: a dressing material used for a finger or toe.

tuberculosis: a long-term, tumorous, infectious disease characterized by listlessness, vague chest pain, pleurisy, loss of appetite, fever, night sweats, bleeding in the lungs, dyspnea, and coughing up pus with sputum.

tuning fork: an instrument used to check for hearing loss.

tympanic membrane: the ear drum; the thin membrane in the middle ear that carries sound vibrations to the inner ear via the ossicles.

U

ulceration: a skin lesion.

ulna: the smaller of the two bones in the lower arm.

ultrasound: a diagnostic tool that uses inaudible sound frequencies to create an image of various tissues and organs in the body.

umbilicus: the belly button.

unit secretary: a member of the clerical staff who is responsible for answering the phone and ordering lab work, x-rays, and other tests.

universal adapter: a mechanical device that fits all equipment.

universal precautions: a concept that stresses that all patients should "be assumed to be infectious for HIV, Hepatitis B, and other blood-borne pathogens." This theory, developed by the Centers for Disease Control sets forth guidelines to prevent the spread of infection. Guidelines include washing hands and wearing gloves, masks, gowns, and protective eyewear whenever exposure to body secretions exists.

upper respiratory infection: (URI) a general term used to describe an infectious disease process involving the nasal passages, pharynx, and bronchi.

urgent care center: a walk-in, free-standing emergency care clinic.

urgent care: needing immediate medical attention.

urgent: to be seen as soon as possible.

URI: an abbreviation for upper respiratory infection; a general term used to describe an infectious disease process involving the nasal passages, pharynx, and bronchi.

urinary retention: the inability to void the bladder.

urinate: to expel urine from the bladder.

urine: the liquid waste produced by the body.

uterus: the organ in the female reproductive system responsible for holding the embryo and fetus from conception until birth.

V

vagina: the muscular tube in females that forms the passageway between the cervix and the vulva.

vaginal speculum: an instrument used in a pelvic exam to view the female reproductive system.

vasoconstriction: the narrowing or closing of the blood vessels.

vasodilation: the widening of the blood vessels.

vein: a vessel that carries deoxygenated blood to the heart.

venereal disease: a disease that is transmitted through sexual intercourse.

venom: a poisonous or toxic substance from an insect or animal.

venous: of or relating to a vein.

ventilate: to assist a patient's breathing.

ventilation: breathing; respiration.

ventilator: a machine that mechanically breathes for a patient who is unable to breathe on his or her own; a respirator.

ventricular fibrillation: a rapid, irregular or chaotic, deadly heart rhythm.

vertebrae: the thirty-three individual bones of the spine that are separated by discs.

vertigo: dizziness.

virus: a microscopic parasitic organism capable of causing an infectious disease; can only be seen with an electron microscope.

visual acuity: the degree to which a person can see objects clearly.

vital signs: assessments of blood pressure, pulse, temperature and respirations; body functions essential to life.

void: to urinate.

vomiting: emesis.

vomitus: the contents of the stomach that are ejected during vomiting.

W

welt: a raised portion of the skin resulting from a lash, blow, or allergy.

wheelchair: a special chair that is equipped with wheels for transporting patients.

wheeze: a high-pitched, whistling sound produced by the flow of air through a narrowed airway.

withdraw: to retreat into oneself, often ceasing or reducing communication with others.

X

xeroform: a non-stick, occlusive dressing.

xiphoid process: the bone tip of the sternum.

Xylocaine: a type of anesthetic.

NOTE: Adapted from *Taber's Cyclopedic Medical Dictionary, 17th Edition*, F.A. Davis Company, Philadelphia, Pennsylvania, 1993, and *The Mosby Medical Encyclopedia, Revised Edition*, C.V. Mosby Company, New York, New York, 1992.

Abbreviations

ABC	airway, breathing, and circulation.
ABD	abdomen.
AD LIB	as desired.
AIDS	acquired immune deficiency syndrome
AMA	against medical advice; American Medical Association.
APGAR	a test for newborns based on appearance, pulse, grimace, airway, and reflex.
ARN	authorized radio nurse.
BID	twice a day.
BP	blood pressure.
CAT scan	computerized axial tomography scan.
CC	cubic centimeter.
CCU	coronary care unit.
CEN	certified emergency nurse.
CODE III	lights and sirens.
COPD	chronic obstructive pulmonary disease.
CPR	cardiopulmonary resuscitation.
CSF	cerebrospinal fluid.
CT scan	computerized tomography scan.
CVA	cerebrovascular accident.
DOA	dead on arrival.
DTs	delirium tremens.
ECG	electrocardiogram.
ECU	emergency care unit.
EEG	electroencephalogram.
EENT	eye, ear, nose, and throat.
EKG	electrocardiogram.
EMS	Emergency Medical Services.
EMT	emergency medical technician.

ER	emergency room.
ETOH	ethanol.
FX	fracture.
GYN	gynecological.
HIV	human immunodeficiency virus.
HX	history.
ICU	intensive care unit.
IM	intramuscular.
IV	intravenous.
KO'd	knocked out.
KY	lubricating jelly.
LOC	level of consciousness; loss of consciousness.
LVN	licensed vocational nurse.
MAST	military antishock trousers.
MD	medical doctor.
MI	myocardial infarction.
MICN	mobile intensive care nurse.
ML	milliliter.
MVA	motor vehicle accident.
NPO	nothing by mouth.
OB	obstetrics.
OD	overdose; right eye.
OS	left eye.
OU	both eyes.
P	pulse.
PAST	pneumatic anti-shock trousers.
PEDS	pediatrics.
PERL	pupils equal and react to light.
PERLA	pupils equal and react to light and accommodation.
PI	present illness.
PMD	primary medical doctor.

PO	by mouth.
PRN	when necessary.
PVC	premature ventricular contraction.
QD	daily.
QID	four times a day.
R	respirations.
RN	registered nurse.
RTB	respiratory tract burn.
RX	treatment, prescription.
SIDS	sudden infant death syndrome.
SOB	shortness of breath.
STAT	at once.
STD	sexually transmitted disease.
TC	traffic collision.
TEMP	temperature.
TIB-FIB	tibia-fibula.
TID	three times a day.
TPR	temperature, pulse, respiration.
URI	upper respiratory infection.
UTI	urinary tract infection.
VD	venereal disease.
VS	vital signs.

Appendix B • Community Resources   Appendix B-1

Community Resources

Referrals for continuing services are very important for patients seen in the emergency room. Follow-up care is vital; therefore the patient may be referred to a private physician or community agency for additional services.

It is important to be aware of the various community resources available for the care and treatment of emergency patients. Look up these numbers in your community.

AGENCY   **PHONE NUMBER**

Emergency Services
Poison Control   _____
Hazardous Materials Team   _____
City Fire Department   _____
County Fire Department   _____
City Police Department   _____
County Sheriff   _____
Federal Bureau of Investigation   _____
Organ Transplant Team   _____
Ambulance Companies   _____

_____   _____
_____   _____
_____   _____

Community Agencies
Crisis Intervention Team   _____
County Health Officer   _____
Animal Control   _____
Elder Abuse Hotline   _____
Child Abuse Hotline   _____
Coroner   _____

Appendix B-2   The Emergency Department Technician

AGENCY	PHONE NUMBERS
Healthcare Facilities	
Area Hospitals	
_____	_____
_____	_____
_____	_____
_____	_____
_____	_____
_____	_____
_____	_____
_____	_____
Burn Center	_____
Children's Hospital	_____
Cancer Center	_____
Dialysis Centers	_____
	_____
	_____
Chemical Dependency Centers	_____
	_____
	_____
Psychiatric Facilities	_____
	_____
	_____

AGENCY	PHONE NUMBERS
Religious Clergy	
Catholic Priest	_____
Jewish Rabbi	_____
Baptist Minister	_____
Lutheran Minister	_____
Episcopalian Minister	_____
Methodist Minister	_____
Seventh Day Adventist Minister	_____
Mormon Elder	_____
Others	_____
Transportation Services	
Dial-A-Ride	_____
Taxi	_____
Societies for the Prevention of Disease	
American Red Cross	_____
American Cancer Society	_____
American Heart Association	_____
Multiple Sclerosis Society	_____
American Diabetic Association	_____
Cerebral Palsy Association	_____
Crippled Children Society	_____

Appendix B-4

Appendix C • The Manual Alphabet

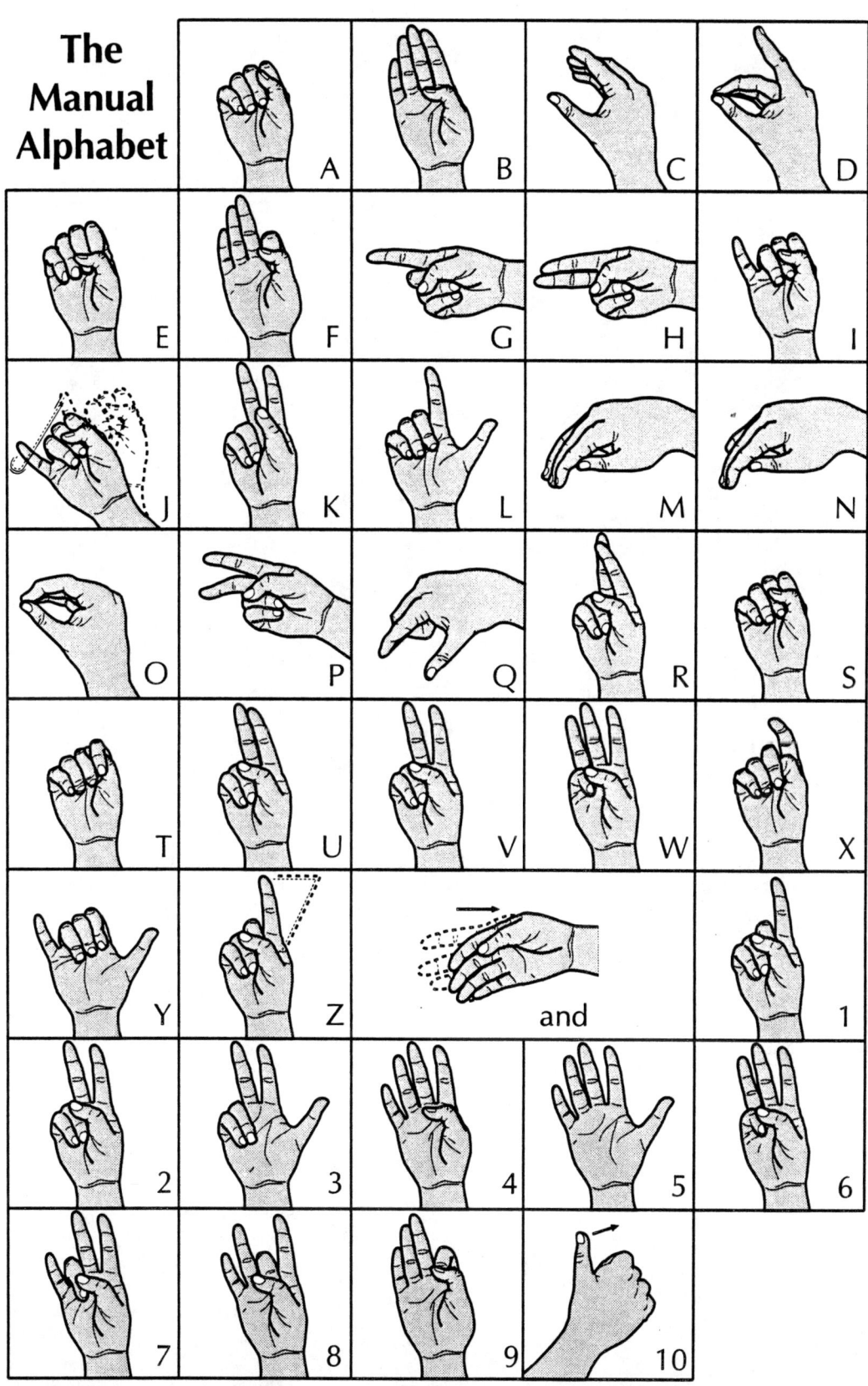

Appendix C-2

Bibliography

Badasch, RN, MA, Shirley, and Doreen S. Chesebro LVN. *The Health Care Worker: An Introduction to Health Occupations.* Bowie, MD: Brady Communications Company, Inc., 1985.

Badasch, RN, MA, Shirley, and Doreen S. Chesebro, LVN. *Workbook for the Health Care Worker: An Introduction to Health Occupations.* Bowie: Brady Communications Company, Inc., 1985.

Budassi, RN, MSN, MICN, CEN, Susan A., and Janet M. Barber, RN, MS. *Emergency Nursing, Principles and Practice.* St. Louis: The C.V. Mosby Company, 1981.

Cox, RN, MA, Kay. *Being a Health Unit Coordinator, Third Edition.* Bowie: Robert J. Brady Co., 1991.

Fong, BS, MS, Elizabeth, Elvira B. Ferris, BSS, MMS, and Esther G. Skelley RN, MS. *Body Structure and Function.* New York: Delmar Publishers, Inc., 1984.

Ford, Regina Daley. *Handbook of Emergency Care.* Springhouse, PA: Springhouse Corporation, 1985.

Humphrey, PhD, Doris, and Kathie Sigler EdD. *The Modern Medical Office.* Cincinnati: South-Western Publishing Co., 1986.

Keir, CMA-A, Lucille, Barbara A. Wise, BSN, RN, MA, and Connie Krebs-Shannon, CMA-C. *Medical Assisting: Administrative and Clinical Competencies.* New York: Delmar Publishers, Inc., 1989.

Kelly, Relda Timmeney. *Workbook for Nursing Assistants.* Washington D.C.: C.V. Mosby Company, 1987.

Kinn, CPS, CMA-A, Mary E., and Eleanor F. Derge, RN, MS, CMA. *The Medical Assistant Administrative and Clinical.* Philadelphia: W.B. Saunders Company, 1988.

Lewis, RN, MA, LuVerne Wolff. *Fundamental Skills in Patient Care.* Philadelphia: J.B. Lippincott Company, 1984.

Lodge, Dwight W., and Harvey D. Grant. *Handbook of Emergency Care Procedures.* Englewood Cliffs, NJ: Prentice Hall, Inc., 1988.

Memmler, MD, Ruth Lundeen, and Dena Lin Wood, RN, BS, PHN. *The Human Body in Health and Disease.* Philadelphia: J.B. Lippincott, 1987.

Milliken, BSN, MS, EdD, Mary Elizabeth, and Gene Campbell BSN, MEd. *Essential Competencies for Patient Care.* Princeton: The C.V. Mosby Company, 1985.

Newkirk, MD, William L., and Richard P. Linden, MBA. *Managing Emergency Medical Services: Principles and Practices.* Reston, VA: Reston Publishing Company, Inc., 1984.

New York State Department of Emergency Medical Services. *Critical Trauma Care.* New York: New York State Department of Emergency Medical Services, 1989.

Programmed Instruction in Asepsis, Surgikos. Arlington, TX: Johnson and Johnson, 1989.

Shea, RN, BA, MBA, Margaret A., and Sharron M. Zakus, RN, BA, MS, CMA. *Fundamentals of Medical Assisting.* Princeton: The C.V. Mosby Company, 1984.

Sormunen, Carolee. *Terminology for Allied Health Professionals.* Cincinnati, OH: South-Western Publishing Company, 1985.

Sorrentino, Shelia A. *Textbook for Nursing Assistants.* Washington D.C.: C.V. Mosby Company, 1987.

Thompson, RN, MS, Eleanor Dumont. *Pediatric Nursing.* Philadelphia: W.B. Saunders Company, 1987.

Thompson, BSN, MSN, Sharon W. *Emergency Care of Children.* Boston: Jones and Bartlett Publishers, 1990.

Timby, Barbara K. *Clinical Nursing Procedures.* Philadelphia: J.B. Lippincott, 1989.

Index

A

ABCs 5-5, 8-10, 10-4
   airway 6-4, 8-10
   assessment of 6-6
   breathing 6-5, 8-10
   circulation 6-6, 8-10
abdominal
   distention 11-6, 11-8
   emergencies 11-1
   pain 11-5
   thrusts 8-17, 8-21
   trauma 11-4, 11-9
abnormal behavior 19-7
abortion 12-5
abrasion
   defined 13-3
   photograph 13-3
absorption 18-2
abuse 20-11
acquired immune deficiency syndrome
   (AIDS) 4-2
acute
   abdomen 11-2, 11-6, 11-20
      symptoms 11-2, 11-3
   defined 5-4
adaptic 13-18
admissions
   procedures 3-3, 5-1, 5-6
   triage 5-4
   using computers in 5-3
adult
   airway obstruction
      conscious 8-28
      unconscious 8-28
   CPR
      one-rescuer 8-11 thru 8-15, 8-27
      two-rescuer 8-11 thru 8-15, 8-27
   recue breathing 8-23
   respiration 6-28
advanced life support (ALS) 2-8
Against Medical Advice form 5-18
age 21-1 thru 21-5
   affects on the human body 21-2
airways 6-4, 8-10, 8-12, 8-18, 8-20,
   9-17, 14-6, 14-9
   nasopharyngeal 14-6
   obstruction 8-16, 8-21, 8-23
      obese victim 8-17
      pregnant victim 8-17
      in adults 8-28
      in infants and children 8-21, 8-23
   oropharyngeal 14-6

alignment 16-3
allergic reactions 8-5, 9-17, 10-9
alveoli 6-30
Ambu bag 8-14
amputation 13-5, 13-6
anaphylactic shock 8-9
aneurysm 11-4
anger 19-4
antidote 18-4
Apgar score 12-8
apical pulse 6-22
   charting 6-22
   defined 6-21
   measuring 6-21, 6-22
   procedure for measuring 6-21
appendicitis 11-4
arterial 6-15
arterial blood gases 10-12
asepsis 4-8
   defined 4-8
   medical 4-9, 12-7
   surgical 4-10
ashen 5-5, 6-10
aspirate 10-5
aspiration 14-7
assessment 6-3, 6-6
asthma 10-8
aura 10-3
aural temperature
   charting 6-38
   measuring 6-38
auscultate 6-11
auscultating a blood pressure 6-49,
   6-50, 6-51
auto accidents 9-18
autoclave 4-16
avulsion
   defined 13-5
   photograph 13-5
axillary temperature 6-44, 6-45
   charting 6-45

B

back blows 8-22
bacteria 4-6
   defined 4-3
bag-valve mask 14-7
bandages 13-18, 13-21
   compression 15-11
   types 13-18 thru 13-25
basic life support (BLS) 8-1 thru 8-34
   adult victim 8-27
   child victim 8-29
   infant victim 8-31
   pediatric 8-17
Battle sign 14-14
behavioral emergencies 19-1 thru 19-11
behavioral problems 19-5
biological death 8-5, 8-6
   defined 8-6
biopsy 4-10
bites 13-12
   treating 13-12
bleeding
   controlling 13-8, 13-9, 13-10, 14-10
   vaginal 12-5
blood pressure 6-17, 6-46 thru 6-49, 6-54
   auscultating 6-50, 6-51
   charting 6-49, 6-51, 6-54
   continuous monitoring 6-52
      automatic 6-52
   measuring 6-46
   palpating systolic 6-47, 6-48, 6-49
blood sugar 10-6
blood transfusions 11-8
BLS (see also basic life support) 8-1 thru 8-34
body mechanics 7-9, 16-3
   defined 16-2
bone and joint injuries 15-1 thru 15-20
      treating 15-11
bradycardia 6-18
brain hemorrhages 14-14
breathing 6-5, 8-10, 8-12, 8-22, 14-6
   equipment 10-10 thru 10-12
   rescue 8-12, 8-13
breathlessness 8-18
bruise 13-2
burns 17-4
   causes 17-5, 17-6, 17-7
   eye 9-8
   rule of nines 17-4
   treatment 17-5 thru 17-7
   types of 17-2, 17-3, 17-5
butterfly bandage 13-4

C

canes 15-20
cannula 10-10
cardiac arrest 8-4, 8-5, 18-3
Cardiac Care Unit 10-16
cardiac compressions 8-14, 8-15
cardiac emergencies 10-14
   symptoms 10-14
cardiac monitor 2-11, 18-4
cardiopulmonary resuscitation (CPR)
   1-5, 7-10, 8-2, 8-5, 8-6, 8-8, 8-9,
     8-11, 8-14, 8-15, 8-17, 8-19, 8-24
   defined 1-5
caring for patients
   children 20-1 thru 20-12
   elderly 21-1 thru 21-5
carotid pulse 6-23
   charting 6-24
   measuring 6-23, 6-24
carpals 15-3
cast care 15-15
catheters 11-10 thru 11-17
catheterization 11-10, 11-12
   female patient 11-13 thru 11-15
      charting 11-15
   male patient 11-16, 11-17
      charting 11-17
Central Supply 3-6, 4-16
cerebrovascular accident (CVA) 10-3
cerumen 9-13
cervical collars 15-8
chain of infection 4-7
Chapter Summary 1-6, 2-15, 3-8, 4-29,
   5-19, 6-62, 7-11, 8-26, 9-18, 10-17,
   11-20, 12-12, 13-30, 14-19, 15-20,
   16-13, 17-10, 18-8, 19-11, 20-12, 21-5
charting 3-3
   aural temperature 6-38
   axillary temperature 6-45
   blood pressure 6-49, 6-51, 6-54
   carotid pulse 6-24
   catheterization 11-15, 11-17
   height
      adult 6-61
      infant or child 20-8
   lung sounds 6-30
   neuro check 6-57
   oral temperature 6-33, 6-36
   output from a Foley catheter 18-7
   radial pulse 6-20
   rectal temperature 6-40, 6-43
   respiration 6-28
   weight
      adult 6-60
      infant or child 20-8

chest compressions   8-19, 8-20
   for infants   8-19
   on a child   8-20
chest trauma   14-18
child abuse   20-11
childbirth
   emergency   12-7 thru 12-10
children
   abuse   20-11
   airway obstruction   8-21 thru 8-23
   basic life support   8-29, 8-30
   caring for   20-1 thru 20-12
     emergencies   20-2
     restraints   20-6
     safety measures   20-4
     vital signs   20-7
   collecting specimens   20-9
   congenital conditions   20-11
   CPR   8-18 thru 8-20
   gathering information   20-3
   handling   20-4, 20-5
   illnesses   20-10
   infections   20-9
   injuries   20-9
   measuring height and weight   20-8
   rescue breathing   8-23
   sudden infant death syndrome   20-12
choking   8-4, 8-16, 8-17
cholecystitis   11-4
chronic obstructive pulmonary disease (COPD)   10-8
circulation   6-6, 8-10
circulatory   6-17
clammy   6-10
clamps   4-18
Clara Barton   2-3
cleaning   4-29, 7-3
   following a procedure   7-7
cleft lip   20-11
cleft palate   20-11
clinical death   8-5, 8-6
   defined   8-5
clubfoot
   defined   20-11
code blue   8-10, 8-24, 10-14
   defined   7-10, 8-8
code red   7-2
cold temperatures
   emergencies resulting from   17-9
colitis   11-4
coma   6-6, 10-7, 10-9, 14-14
   defined   10-7
communicable diseases
   controlling   4-26
communication systems   2-6

compound fracture   15-5
compression bandages   15-11
computers   5-3
concussion   14-13
confidentiality   5-17, 12-2, 12-12
   defined   5-17
confusion   19-2
congenital conditions   20-11
conjunctiva   9-9
conjunctivitis   9-2
consumer
   education   2-8
   information   2-8
contaminated   3-7
   defined   3-7, 4-2
   gloves
     removal   4-14
contaminated infectious waste   7-7
continuous monitoring of blood pressure
     automatically   6-52 thru 6-54
controlling arterial bleeding   14-10
contusion
   defined   13-2
   photograph   13-3
   treatment   13-2
core temperature   17-8
cornea   9-9
Coronary Care Unit   10-17
CPR (cardiopulmonary rresuscitation)
   1-5, 7-10, 8-2, 8-5, 8-6, 8-8, 8-9,
   8-11, 8-14, 8-15, 8-17, 8-19, 8-24
   ABCs   8-10
   adult one-rescuer   8-27
   adult two-rescuer   8-27
   child one-rescuer   8-29
   defined   1-5
   for children and infants   8-18
   in transport   8-24
   one-person   8-11, 8-15
   two-person   8-11, 8-15
crackles   6-28
   defined   6-28
crash cart   8-11, 8-25
   defined   3-5, 8-11
crepitus   15-5
Critical Care Unit (CCU)   2-7, 3-5
   defined   2-7
cross infection   4-9
croup   20-10
crowning   12-7
crutches   15-16
   measurement   15-16
   using on stairs   15-19
curette   4-18
cyanosis   6-9

D

data collection 5-10, 5-14
dealing with behavioral problems 19-5
debilitated 16-7
defibrillation 7-10
   and safety 7-10
defibrillator 7-9, 8-24
dehydration 6-9
denial 19-3
dental emergencies 9-16
Department of Transportation 2-5
depression 19-4
diabetes 10-6
diabetic emergencies 10-6
diaphragm 6-22, 6-26
diastolic 6-46
direct transmission 4-3
disaster plans 2-9
disasters 7-5, 7-6
diseases
   communicable 4-26, 4-28
      controlling 4-26
   prevention 4-7
   spread of 4-7
   transmission 4-2
disease-causing agents 4-2
disinfection 4-15
dislocation 15-10
disorders
   female reproductive system 12-3
   male reproductive system 12-11
dispatcher 2-10
disposition 5-14
distended 6-7
distention 11-2
diverticulitis 11-4
Division of Emergency Medical Services (DEMS) 2-5
DOA 5-14
documentation 6-62
   patient chart 6-62
dorsal recumbent position 16-13
Down syndrome 20-11
dressings 13-18, 13-19, 13-20, 13-21, 13-22, 13-23, 13-24, 13-25
   adaptic 13-18
   eye 9-7
   occlusive 13-18
   types 13-18
   xeroform 13-18
dyspnea 6-28, 17-5
dysrhythmias 10-16

E

ear
   cleaning 9-13
   emergencies 9-12
edema 6-13
EENT 9-2
   disorders 9-2
elderly patients
   caring for 21-1 thru 21-5
electrocardiogram (ECG) 10-16
   defined 10-16
electrocautery 9-14
emergencies
   911 8-10
      and the EMS system 2-10
   abdominal 11-1 thru 11-20
   behavioral 19-1 thru 19-11
   call 2-10
   cardiac 10-14
   care 2-9
      history of 2-2
   childbirth 12-7, 12-8, 12-9, 12-10
   dental 9-16
   diabetic 10-6
   ear 9-12
   emotional 19-1 thru 19-11
   environmental 17-1
   eye 9-3, 9-12
   eye, ear, nose, and throat 9-1 thru 9-24
   healthcare team 2-12
   involving children 20-2
   medical 10-1
   medical situations 10-2
   medical technicians 2-13
   nasal 9-14
   overdose 18-2
   poisoning 18-2
   procedures 1-3
   psychiatric 19-6
   record 5-14, 5-15
   reproductive system 12-1
      female 12-3
      male 12-11
   respiratory 10-8
      asthma 10-8
      chronic bronchitis 10-8, 10-9
      emphysema 10-8
   resulting from exposure to heat 17-8
   resulting from exposure to cold 17-9
   resuscitation 8-8
   rooms
      history of 2-3, 2-4
   signals 7-6
   throat 9-16
   traumatic 14-1 thru 14-19

Emergency Care Units (ECU) 2-4, 3-8
  layout 3-8
Emergency Department 2-4, 3-7
  documentation 5-2
  layout 3-4, 3-6, 3-7
    illustration 3-5
  location of 3-2
  technician 2-14, 4-29
    characteristics of 1-4
Emergency Medical Services (EMS) 2-5
  components of 2-5, 2-8, 2-9
  history of 2-2
Emergency Medical Services Systems (EMSS)
    Act 2-5
emergent 5-4
emesis 18-4
emotional emergencies 19-1 thru 19-11
emotional shock 19-2
empathy 1-4
emphysema 10-8
EMS system 2-8, 2-9, 8-10
endotracheal intubation 14-8
endotracheal tube 8-14, 14-6, 14-7
environmental emergencies 17-1 thru 17-10
epiglottis 8-12
epistaxis 9-14
equilibrium 9-2
equipment 4-15
  contaminated 4-29
  transporting 7-9
ER record 5-7
esophageal airway 8-14
evaluations 6-2
  patient 6-1 thru 6-62
examinations
  eye 9-4
  pelvic 11-6, 12-3, 12-4
  rectal 11-6
expiration 5-7, 6-11
exposure 7-7
eye
  burns 9-8
  dressings 9-6
    applying 9-7
  emergencies 9-3, 9-12
  examinations 9-4
  foreign bodies 9-6
  infections 9-9, 9-11
  trauma 9-9

F

facilities 2-7
fallopian tube 12-6
fatal 17-2
fear 19-3

febrile seizure 20-10
female reproductive system 12-3
finger sweep 8-17, 8-21
fire 7-2, 7-4
flammable 7-2
Florence Nightingale 2-2
fluorescein
  sodium 9-9
  staining
    assisting with 9-10
Foley catheter 18-6, 18-7
  defined 18-6
football position 8-19
forceps 4-18, 4-24, 4-25, 9-15, 13-11
foreign bodies 13-11
  affecting the reproductive system 12-12
  in the eye 9-6
foreign body airway obstructions 8-16
  conscious victim
    adult 8-28
    child 8-29
    infant 8-31
  unconscious victim
    adult 8-28
    child 8-30
    infant 8-32
Fowler's position 16-12
fracture 15-3
  defined 15-2
  signs and symptoms 15-5, 15-6
  treating 15-8, 15-9
frostbite 17-9
full arrest 8-6, 10-14

G

gait training 15-17
gall stones 11-4
geriatrics 21-5
Glasgow Coma Scale 14-15, 14-16
  defined 14-15
glaucoma 9-2
gloves 4-11, 4-13, 7-7
  donning 4-11, 4-12
  safety 7-7
  technique 4-10, 4-29
  using 4-11
goggles 7-7
golden hour 14-5
gonorrhea 12-6
gowns
  safety 7-7
grating 15-4
guarding 11-3
gurney 3-2
  defined 1-3, 3-2

H

hallucination 19-9
handwashing 4-3, 4-5, 6-17
   technique 4-4, 4-5
hazards 7-2
head injuries 14-12, 14-13
   brain hemorrhages 14-14
   concussion 14-13
   increased intracranial pressure 14-15
head-tilt/chin-lift maneuver 6-4, 8-12, 8-18
   defined 8-12
health careers 1-2, 1-3
healthcare professionals
   characteristics of 1-4
heart 8-6
heart attack 8-4, 8-7, 10-16
heart block 10-16
   defined 10-16
heat
   emergencies resulting from 17-8
   exhaustion 17-8
   stroke 17-8
height 6-58
   adult 6-58, 6-61
   child 20-8
   infant 20-8
Heimlich maneuver 8-16, 8-17, 8-21
   adult 8-16, 8-17
   child 8-21 thru 8-23
   infant 8-21 thru 8-23
hematoma 13-2, 13-3
hematuria 12-11
hemorrhage
   defined 12-5
   examination 12-5
hemorrhagic shock 14-10
hemostats 4-18
Henri Dunant 2-2
hepatitis 11-4
herpes 12-6
history
   of incident 18-4, 18-5
   patient 20-3
hospital disaster plan 7-5
host 4-7
hostility 19-4
hydraulic 16-8
hydrocephalus 20-11
hyperextend 15-4
hyperglycemia 10-7
hypertension 10-14
hyperthermia 17-8
hypoglycemia 10-7
hypotension 10-14
hypothermia 6-10, 17-9

I

immobilizers 15-12, 15-13
immunizations 4-7, 4-8, 7-8, 13-4
impaled 13-11
incision 13-3, 13-4
increased intracranial pressure 14-15
incubator 12-8
indirect transmission 4-2
infants
   airway obstruction 8-21 thru 8-23
   basic life support 8-17, 8-31 thru 8-32
   caring for 20-1 thru 20-12
   CPR 8-18 thru 8-20
   rescue breathing 8-23
infections 12-6
   chain of 4-7
   eye 9-9
   prevention 4-5, 4-8
   respiratory 10-9
   spread of 4-5, 4-26
   symptoms of 4-6
infectious diseases
   transmission of 7-8
inflammation 11-4
information
   documenting 5-14
   obtaining 5-9 thru 5-13, 5-17, 6-2
   patient 5-9 thru 5-15, 6-2
   vital 5-15
ingestion 18-2
inhalation 18-2
injection 18-2
injuries
   bone 15-2
   head 14-12 thru 14-15
   joints 15-2
   neck 9-18
   orthopedic 15-10
   spinal 14-16, 14-17
   traumatic 14-2 thru 14-4
inspiration 6-11
instruments 4-9, 4-17 thru 4-26
   cleaning 4-16
   contaminated 4-9
   handling 4-26
   parts 4-17
   types 4-18 thru 4-25
insulin 10-6
intake 18-6
intoxicated 5-6
intravenous 2-11
intubate 8-8
isolation 3-5, 4-28, 4-29, 7-8, 9-11
   defined 3-5
Isolette 12-8

Index

J

jacket restraint 19-9
jaw-thrust maneuver 6-4, 8-12, 8-18, 14-6
  defined 8-12
joints
  injuries 15-1 thru 15-20

K

Key Terms 1-2, 2-2, 3-2, 4-2, 5-2, 6-2, 7-2, 8-2, 9-2, 10-2, 11-2, 12-2, 13-2, 14-2, 15-2, 16-2, 17-2, 18-2, 19-2, 20-2, 21-2

L

laboratory forms 11-10
laceration 13-4, 13-5
lavage 9-8
licensed vocational nurse (LVN) 2-13
life skills 1-6
lifting 16-3
listening
  for lung sounds 6-29
  therapeutic communication 19-8, 19-9
lithotomy position 12-4, 16-12
localized 11-2
lockjaw 4-7
  defined 4-7
log roll 6-14, 8-11, 14-17
lung sounds 6-29, 6-30
  charting 6-30
  listening for 6-30

M

male reproductive system
  emergencies 12-11
manual dexterity 1-4
masks
  safety 7-8
MAST suit 11-9, 11-10, 14-10, 14-11, 14-12
  cleaning 11-9
mastoid process 14-14
  defined 14-14
measuring
  apical pulse 6-21, 6-22
  carotid pulse 6-23, 6-24
  output from a Foley catheter 18-7
  radial pulse 6-19, 6-20
  respiration 6-27, 6-28
  height of an adult 6-61
  weight of an adult 6-59, 6-60
meatus 11-11

mechanisms of injury 14-18
Medic-Alert 6-3, 10-8
medical
  asepsis 4-9, 12-7
    defined 4-9
  emergencies 10-1 thru 10-17
  records 5-2, 5-7 thru 5-19
    keeping 2-8
    computers 5-3
metacarpals 15-3
metatarsals 15-3
mid-stream urine specimen 11-11, 11-12
military anti-shock trousers 11-9, 14-10
  cleaning 11-9
mobile intensive care nurse (MICN) 2-13
modified jaw-thrust maneuver 6-4
monitor
  automatic blood pressure 6-52 thru 6-54
  cardiac 10-15
motor vehicle accident 11-9
moving
  patients 14-9, 16-1 thru 16-13
    from a bed to a gurney 16-4
    from a gurney to a bed 16-10, 16-11
    out of a car 16-4, 16-5
    using a gurney 16-8, 16-9
    who arrive in ambulances 16-7
multisystem 14-3
mummy restraint 20-6
mutual aid agreements 2-9
myocardial infarction 8-7, 10-16

N

nasal emergencies 9-14
nasal speculum 9-14
nasogastric tube 11-8
nasopharyngeal airway 14-6
National Highway Safety Act 2-5
neck injuries 9-18
neonatal 12-9
nephritis 11-4
neuro check 6-6, 6-55, 6-56
  charting 6-57
  performing 6-56
neurostructures 14-16
neurovascular 15-9
non-urgent 5-4
nosebleeds 9-14, 9-15
nosocomial infections 4-10
NPO 12-5
  defined 11-6

O

Objectives
  chapter   1-1, 2-1, 3-1, 4-1, 5-1, 6-1,
    7-1, 8-1, 9-1, 10-1, 11-1, 12-1, 13-1,
    14-1, 15-1, 16-1, 17-1, 18-1, 19-1,
    20-1, 21-1
observational skills   6-3
obstructed airway maneuver   8-13
  defined   8-13
obstructions   8-17
  airway   8-16, 8-23, 8-28 thru 8-32, 9-17
  nasal   9-15
occlusive   13-18
one-rescuer CPR
  adult   8-11, 8-15, 8-27
  child   8-29
  infant   8-31
ophthalmoscope   9-3
oral temperature
  glass thermometer   6-34 thru 6-36
  electronic thermometer   6-32, 6-33
orientation   6-55
oropharyngeal airway   14-6
orthopedic injuries   15-10
osteoporosis   21-2
otoscope   9-3
output   18-6
overdose   8-3, 18-1 thru 18-8
  victim   18-3, 18-6
  unconscious   18-6
oxygenation   14-10

P

pallor   15-5
palpated   14-3
palpitation   10-14
pancreatitis   11-4
papoose restraint   20-6
paralysis   14-14, 14-17
paramedic   1-3, 2-14
paranoid   19-7
paresthesia   14-14
PASG suit   11-9, 14-10
  cleaning   11-9
pathogen   4-2, 4-6, 4-9
patient(s)
  admission form   5-15
  chart   6-62
  confidentiality   12-2
  evaluation   6-1 thru 6-62
  history   3-3, 5-12, 20-3
  log   3-4
  moving and positioning   16-1 thru 16-13
  positioning   16-1, 16-12

patient(s) (cont.)
  psychiatric   19-10
  suicidal   19-10
  unconscious   10-5
  who are in custody   19-9
patient's
  record   1-3
  right to privacy   12-2
pediatric basic life support   8-17
pelvic
  examination   11-6, 12-3, 12-4
  inflammatory disease (PID)   12-6
peptic ulcers   11-4
performing a neuro check   6-56, 6-57
perfusion   14-10
perineum   12-4
peripad   12-5
peritonitis   11-4
PERL   6-9
personal
  safety   7-7
  stress management   19-10
pertussis   4-28
phalanges   15-3
placenta   12-9
pleura vac   14-18
pneumatic anti-shock garment (PASG)
  2-13, 11-9, 14-10
  cleaning   11-9
pocket mask   14-6
  defined   14-6
Poison Control Center   18-5
poisoning   8-5, 18-1
  causes   18-2
  symptoms   18-5, 18-6
  victim
    caring for   18-3, 18-6
    unconscious   18-6
popliteal artery   6-25
positioning patients   16-1 thru 16-13
pre-surgical checklist   11-18, 11-19
pregnancy
  ruptured ectopic   12-6
premature ventricular contractions
  (PVCs)   10-16
pressure point   13-8
priapism   6-12
primary survey   6-4, 6-6
privacy
  patient's rights   12-2
probe   4-18
procedures
  aural temperature   6-37, 6-38
  auscultating a blood pressure   6-50, 6-51
  axillary temperature   6-44, 6-45

procedures (cont.)
   blood pressure   6-47 thru 6-49
      continuous monitoring   6-53, 6-54
   catheterizing
      female patient   11-13 thru 11-15
      male patient   11-16, 11-17
   continuous monitoring of blood pressure
      automatically   6-53, 6-54
   endotracheal intubation   14-8, 14-9
   glove removal   6-17
   handwashing   6-17
   height
      adult   6-61
      child   20-8
      infant   20-8
   listening for lung sounds   6-29, 6-30
   measuring
      apical pulse   6-21, 6-22
      carotid pulse   6-23, 6-24
      output from a Foley catheter   18-7
      radial pulse   6-19, 6-20
      respiration   6-27, 6-28
      height of an adult   6-61
      weight of an adult   6-59, 6-60
   neuro check   6-56, 6-57
   obtaining a mid-stream urine
      specimen   11-11, 11-12
   oral temperature   6-32 thru 6-36
   performing a neuro check   6-56, 6-57
   rectal temperature   6-39 thru 6-43
      glass thermometer   6-40
   secondary survey   6-7 thru 6-14
   staple removal   13-29, 13-30
   suture removal   13-27, 13-28
   using a MAST suit   14-11, 14-12
   weight
      adult   6-59, 6-60
      child   20-8
      infant   20-8
prone   8-11, 16-12
protocol   17-6
psychiatric
   emergencies   19-6
   patients   19-10
public safety agencies   2-7
pulse   6-17, 6-18, 8-18
   rates   6-18
   rhythm   6-18
   sites   6-25
pulselessness   8-14
puncture wound   13-5, 13-6
purulent   4-6, 7-8

Q
quadrants
   abdominal   11-2, 11-5

R
rabies   13-12
radial pulse   6-18, 6-20
   charting   6-20
   defined   6-6
   measuring   6-19
   procedure for measuring   6-19, 6-20
rates
   respiratory   6-28
reassessment   8-15
rectal
   examination   11-6
   temperature   6-42, 6-43
      charting   6-40, 6-43
      measuring   6-39, 6-40, 6-41
Red Cross   2-2, 2-3
   American   2-3
   disasters   2-3
referred pain   11-2
registered nurse (RN   2-13
regression   19-4
rehabilitation   14-5
reoxygenate   8-14
reproductive system
   emergencies   12-1 thru 12-12
   foreign bodies   12-12
rescue breathing   8-12, 8-13, 8-18, 8-23
   adults, children, and infants   8-23
respiration   6-17, 6-26
   charting   6-28
   measuring   6-27, 6-28
respiratory
   arrest   8-4, 18-3
      defined   8-5
   defined   6-17
   depression   18-4
   distress   17-5
   emergencies   10-8
      asthma   10-8
      chronic bronchitis   10-8, 10-9
      chronic obstructive pulmonary
         diseases   10-8
      emphysema   10-8
   failure   10-9, 10-10
      symptoms   10-9
   infection   10-9
   rates   6-28
   tract burn (RTB)   17-5
restrain   19-9
resuscitation   8-8

reverse Trendelenburg position 16-13
review and evaluation 2-9
right lateral recumbent position 16-13
roster 3-4
rule of nines 17-4
ruptured ectopic pregnancy 11-4, 12-6
ruptured spleen 11-4

S

safety 5-7
   in the emergency department 7-1 thru 7-11
   procedures in the ER 7-3
   responsibilities 7-2
scald 17-5
scalpel 4-18
scissors 4-18, 4-23
sclera 9-6
secondary survey 6-2, 6-6 thru 6-14
   procedure for 6-7
seizure(s) 10-3, 10-4, 14-14, 18-4, 20-10
   defined 10-3
   febrile 20-10
   your responsibilities 10-4
Self-Assessment Test 1-5
semi-Fowler's position 16-12
septic shock 4-6
serious injury
   symptoms of 5-5
sexual assault victims 12-6
sharps
   disposal of 7-7
shock 14-10
   signs 11-6
   symptoms 11-6
Sims' position 16-12
skills
   observational 6-3
sling
   applying 15-14
Snellen eye chart 9-3
snow blindness 9-8
specimens 1-3
   collecting 20-9
   mid-stream urine 11-11, 11-12
   sputum 10-13
   stool 11-6, 11-7
   urine 11-10
speculum 4-18, 4-22
   defined 9-12
spinal injuries 14-16, 14-17, 15-8
splint 15-7
sprain 15-10
spread of disease 4-7

sputum
   obtaining a specimen 10-13
stab wounds 9-18
staple
   removal 13-29, 13-30
STD 12-6
sterile 4-10
   field 4-10
   gloves 4-11, 4-13, 7-7
      donning 4-11, 4-12
      safety 7-7
      technique 4-10, 4-29
      using 4-11
sterilization 4-15, 4-16
   defined 4-7
sternum 8-15, 8-19, 8-20
stirrups 12-4
stool sample 11-6, 11-7
   checking for blood 11-7
strain 15-10
stress 19-2
   management 19-10
Student Enrichment Activities 1-7, 2-17, 3-9, 4-31, 5-21, 6-63, 7-13, 8-33, 9-19, 10-19, 11-21, 12-13, 13-31, 14-21, 15-21, 16-15, 17-11, 18-9, 19-13, 20-13, 21-7
stylet 14-8
substance abuse 6-13
suction 11-8
sudden death 8-3 thru 8-5
sudden infant death syndrome 20-12
suffocation 8-4
suicidal patients 19-10
supine 8-11
   defined 8-11, 16-12
supplies 3-6
surgery
   preparing a patient for 11-18
surgical asepsis 4-10
suture
   defined 13-4, 13-17
   removal 13-26 thru 13-28
suturing 13-14, 13-16, 13-17
   defined 1-3
syncope 17-8
syphilis 12-6
systolic 6-46

T

tachycardia 6-18, 10-9
  defined 6-18
tarsals 15-3
Telemetry Unit 10-17
Telfa 17-7
temperature 6-17, 6-31
  aural
    measuring 6-37, 6-38
    tympanic thermometer 6-37, 6-38
  axillary
    measuring 6-44, 6-45
  oral
    charting 6-33, 6-36
    electronic thermometer 6-33
    glass thermometer 6-34 thru 6-36
    measuring 6-32 thru 6-36
  rectal
    electronic thermometer 6-41 thru 6-43
    glass thermometer 6-39, 6-40
    measuring 6-39 thru 6-43
tetanus 4-6
therapeutic communication 19-8, 19-9
  defined 19-8
thermometer
  aural
    tympanic 6-38
  electronic 6-32, 6-33
  oral
    electronic 6-33
    glass 6-34
  rectal 6-41
    electronic 6-40 thru 6-43
    glass 6-39, 6-40
throat emergencies 9-16
tolerance 1-4
tongue-jaw lift 8-17
torsion 12-11
tourniquet 13-10
toxicity 18-5
trachea 8-14
traction 15-14
training 2-6
transfer of patients 2-8
transportation 2-6
  patient 2-11, 7-9, 8-24, 14-9
trauma 8-4, 14-2
  abdominal 11-9
  center 2-11, 14-5
    defined 2-4
  chest 14-18
  defined 1-4
  eye 9-9
traumatic emergencies 14-1
traumatized 14-3

treatment
  refused 5-18
Trendelenburg position 16-13
triage 2-14, 3-3, 5-4, 9-4
  defined 2-14
two-rescuer CPR 8-11, 8-15
types of burns 17-2
types of wounds 13-2

U

ulceration 7-8
ultrasound 12-5
unconscious patients 10-5
  caring for 18-6
universal precautions 4-26 thru 4-28, 6-3, 7-7, 12-4
  defined 4-26
unloading patients who arrive in ambulances 16-7
upper respiratory infection (URI) 9-12
urgent 5-4
urgent care centers 1-2, 1-3
urinary retention 11-3
urine 11-2
  specimens 11-10
using a gurney 16-8

V

vaginal bleeding 12-5
valuables
  handling of 15-9
vasoconstriction 13-9
vasodilation 13-2
venereal disease 20-11
venom 13-12
ventilate 7-9
ventilation 8-13, 8-15, 8-24, 10-10, 14-7, 14-18
  to compression ratio 8-15, 8-19, 8-20
ventricular
  fibrillation 8-3, 10-16
    defined 7-10
  tachycardia 10-16
vertigo 9-13
visual acuity 9-4
  defined 9-4
  testing 9-5
vital information 5-15
vital signs 1-3, 6-2, 6-17 thru 6-54, 6-62, 20-7
  defined 1-3
void 11-10

W

weight 6-58
  adult 6-59, 6-60
    charting 6-60
  child 20-8
  infant 20-8
withdraw 19-4
wounds 13-2
  bites 13-12
  care 13-1 thru 13-30
  cleaning 13-15
  stab 9-18
  suturing 13-14, 13-16, 13-17
  treating 13-2, 13-4, 13-5, 13-11, 13-14, 13-15, 13-26
  types 13-2

X

xeroform 13-18
xiphoid process 8-21
  defined 8-16